A Biblical History of Israel

A Biblical History of Israel

Iain Provan
V. Philips Long
Tremper Longman III

WESTMINSTER
JOHN KNOX PRESS
LOUISVILLE · KENTUCKY

© 2003 Iain Provan, V. Philips Long, and Tremper Longman III

Scripture quotations, unless otherwise indicated, are from the New Revised Standard Version of the Bible, copyright © 1989 by the Division of Christian Education of the National Council of the Churches of Christ in the U.S.A., and used by permission.

Scripture quotations from the Revised Standard Version of the Bible are copyright © 1946, 1952, 1971, and 1973 by the Division of Christian Education of the National Council of the Churches of Christ in the U.S.A. and are used by permission.

Scripture quotations marked NIV are from *The Holy Bible, New International Version.* Copyright © 1973, 1978, 1984 International Bible Society. Used by permission of Zondervon Bible Publishers.

Scripture quotations marked JPS are from *The Tanakh: The New JPS Translation According to the Traditional Hebrew Text.* Copyright 1985 by the Jewish Publication Society. Used by permission

Book design by Sharon Adams
Cover design © 2003 Eric Handel/LMNOP
Cover art: *Rachel's Tomb at Ramah,* by Joseph Mallord William Turner courtesy of Blackburn Museum and Art Gallery, Lancashire, UK/Bridgeman Art Library.

First edition
Published by Westminster John Knox Press
Louisville, Kentucky

This book is printed on acid-free paper that meets the American National Standards Institute Z39.48 standard. ∞

PRINTED IN THE UNITED STATES OF AMERICA

05 06 07 08 09 10 11 12 — 10 9 8 7 6 5 4 3

Library of Congress Cataloging-in-Publication Data is on file at the Library of Congress, Washington, D.C.

ISBN 0-664-22090-8

Contents

Preface

Just when you think everything in history has happened, it hasn't.
(Duncan Provan, age eleven)

Among the many useful roles filled by the utterances of babes and sucklings and their older brothers is that of removing the need for authors to write long justifications of their work for the benefit of people who would like to read them. We restrict our comments here, therefore, to expressions of thanks to all those who have helped us bring this project to a conclusion, most especially to Jason McKinney and Carrie Giddings, who did so much of the legwork and the proofreading. We add only the following information in order to spoil the fun of those who enjoy redaction criticism of multiauthor volumes and who therefore need to get outdoors more: chapters 1–3, 5, and 9–10 are largely Provan's; chapters 4 and 7–8 are mainly Long's; and chapters 6 and 11 are predominantly Longman's. Provan pulled the whole thing together as overall editor, and Long shepherded the book through the publication process.

Iain Provan
Phil Long
Tremper Longman III

Simplified Chronology
of Archaeological Periods in Canaan

Middle Bronze Age (MB)	2100–1550
MB I	2100–1900
MB II	1900–1550
Late Bronze Age (LB)	1550–1200
LB I	1550–1400
LB II	1400–1200
Iron Age (Iron)	1200–332
Iron I	1200–1000
Iron II	1000–586
Iron III	586–332

Abbreviations

AB	Anchor Bible
ABD	D. N. Freedman et al. (eds.), *The Anchor Bible Dictionary*
AJSL	*American Journal of Semitic Languages and Literatures*
ANEP	J. B. Pritchard (ed.), *The Ancient Near East in Pictures*
ANET	J. B. Pritchard (ed.), *Ancient Near Eastern Texts*
AOAT	Alter Orient und Altes Testament
ASOR	American Schools of Oriental Research
ATDan	Acta theologica danica
AUSDDS	Andrews University Seminary Doctoral Dissertation Series
AUSS	*Andrews University Seminary Studies*
BA	*Biblical Archaeologist*
BARev	*Biblical Archaeology Review*
BASOR	*Bulletin of the American Schools of Oriental Research*
Bib	*Biblica*
BibOr	*Biblica et Orientalia*
BibS(N)	Biblische Studien (Neukirchen, 1951–)
BJS	Brown Judaic Studies
BKAT	Biblischer Kommentar: Altes Testament
BN	*Biblische Notizen*
BR	*Biblical Research*
BSem	The Biblical Seminar
BTB	*Biblical Theology Bulletin*
BZAW	Beiheft zur Zeitschrift für die alttestamentliche Wissenschaft
CAH	*Cambridge Ancient History*
CBQ	*Catholic Biblical Quarterly*
ConB	Coniectanea biblica
ConBOT	Coniectanea biblica, Old Testament

EA	Tell el-Amarna tablets
ESHM	European Seminar in Historical Methodology
ETL	Ephemerides theologicae lovanienses
FB	Forschung zur Bibel
FCI	Foundations of Contemporary Interpretation
FOTL	Forms of the Old Testament Literature
HSM	Harvard Semitic Monographs
HTh	*History and Theory*
HTIBS	Historic Texts and Interpreters in Biblical Scholarship
HUCA	*Hebrew Union College Annual*
IEJ	*Israel Exploration Journal*
JANES	*Journal of the Ancient Near Eastern Society*
JAOS	*Journal of the American Oriental Society*
JBL	*Journal of Biblical Literature*
JCS	*Journal of Cuneiform Studies*
JETS	*Journal of the Evangelical Theological Society*
JJS	*Journal of Jewish Studies*
JNES	*Journal of Near Eastern Studies*
JNSL	*Journal of Northwest Semitic Languages*
JSOT	*Journal for the Study of the Old Testament*
JSOTS	Journal for the Study of the Old Testament, Supplement Series
JSS	*Journal of Semitic Studies*
JTS	*Journal of Theological Studies*
JTT	*Journal of Text and Translation*
LAI	Library of Ancient Israel
LBI	Library of Biblical Interpretation
NAC	New American Commentary
NBD	I. H. Marshall et al. (eds.), *New Bible Dictionary*
NCB	New Century Bible
NIBC	New International Biblical Commentary
NIDOTTE	W. VanGemeren (ed.), *New International Dictionary of Old Testament Theology and Exegesis*
OBO	Orbis biblicus et orientalis
OBS	Oxford Bible Series
OTG	Old Testament Guides
OTL	Old Testament Library
OTS	*Oudtestamentische Studiën*
PEQ	*Palestine Exploration Quarterly*
RA	*Revue d'assyriologie et d'archéologie orientale*
SBET	*Scottish Bulletin of Evangelical Theology*
SBib	Subsidia Biblica
SBLDS	Society of Biblical Literature Dissertation Series
SBLWAW	SBL Writings from the Ancient World

SBT	Studies in Biblical Theology
SBTS	Sources for Biblical and Theological Study
ScrB	*Scripture Bulletin*
ScrHier	Scripta Hierosolymitana
SEÅ	*Svensk exegetisk årsbok*
SHANE	Studies in the History of the Ancient Near East
SHCANE	Studies in the History and Culture of the Ancient Near East
SHJPLI	Studies in the History of the Jewish People and the Land of Israel Monograph Series
SJOT	*Scandinavian Journal of the Old Testament*
SMNIA	Tel Aviv University Sonia and Marco Nadler Institute of Archaeology Monograph Series
ST	*Studia Theologica*
StudP	Studia Phoenicia
SWBA	The Social World of Biblical Antiquity
TOTC	Tyndale Old Testament Commentaries
TRu	*Theologische Rundschau*
TSTT	Toronto Semitic Texts and Studies
TynBul	*Tyndale Bulletin*
TZ	*Theologische Zeitschrift*
UCOIP	The University of Chicago Oriental Institute Publications
VT	*Vetus Testamentum*
VTS	Supplements to *Vetus Testamentum*
WTJ	*Westminster Theological Journal*
ZAW	*Zeitschrift für die alttestamentliche Wissenschaft*
ZDMG	*Zeitschrift der deutschen morgenländischen Gesellschaft*

PART I
HISTORY, HISTORIOGRAPHY, AND THE BIBLE

Chapter 1

The Death of Biblical History?

It is now time for Palestinian history to come of age and formally reject the agenda and constraints of "biblical history." . . . It is the historian who must set the agenda and not the theologian.

. . . the death of "biblical history" . . .

The obituary is penned by K. W. Whitelam.[1] By "biblical history," he means a history of Palestine defined and dominated by the concerns and presentation of the biblical texts, where these form the basis of, or set the agenda for, historical research.[2] The result can be described as ". . . little more than paraphrases of the biblical text stemming from theological motivations."[3] It is this kind of biblical history that is dead. It remains only to proclaim the funeral oration and move on.

The pronouncement of death is an appropriate point at which to begin our own book, which deliberately includes the phrase "biblical history" in its title, and which certainly wishes to place the biblical texts at the heart of its enterprise. The obituary compels us to address some important questions before we can properly begin. How have we arrived at the funereal place that Whitelam's comments represent? Was our arrival inevitable? Has a death in fact occurred, or (to borrow from Oscar Wilde) have reports of the demise of biblical history been greatly exaggerated? What chances exist for a rescue or (failing that) a resurrection? In pursuit of answers to these questions, we require some understanding of how the history of Israel as a discipline has developed into its present shape. Our first chapter is devoted to this task; we begin at the end, with a discussion and analysis of Whitelam's arguments.[4]

3

ANALYSIS OF AN OBITUARY

Whitelam's central contention is that the ancient Israel that biblical scholarship has constructed on the basis primarily of the biblical texts is nothing more or less than an invention that has contributed to the silencing of real Palestinian history. All texts from the past, he argues, are "partial," both in the sense that they do not represent the whole story and that they express only one point of view about that story (they are "ideologically loaded"). Particular accounts of the past are, in fact, invariably the products of a small elite in any society, and they stand in competition with other possible accounts of the same past, of which we presently may happen to have no evidence. All modern historians are also "partial," possessing beliefs and commitments that influence how they write their histories and even the words they use in their descriptions and analyses (e.g., "Palestine," "Israel"). All too often in previous history-writing on Palestine, claims Whitelam, writers who were for their own theological or ideological reasons predisposed to take their lead from the biblical texts in deciding how to write their history have in the process simply passed on the texts' very partial view of events as if it represented simply "the ways things were." In so doing, these historians have both distorted the past and contributed to the present situation in Palestine. They have contributed to the present situation because the current plight of Palestinians is intrinsically linked to the dispossession of a Palestinian land and past at the hands of a biblical scholarship obsessed with "ancient Israel." Historians have distorted the past because their presentation has had little to do with what really happened. The "ancient Israel" that they have constructed out of the biblical texts is an imaginary entity whose existence outside the minds of biblical historians cannot be demonstrated and whose creation, indeed, is itself not unconnected with the present political situation.

The "fact" of a large, powerful, sovereign, and autonomous Iron Age state founded by David, for example, has dominated the discourse of biblical studies throughout the past century, and happens to coincide with and help to enhance the vision and aspirations of many of Israel's modern leaders. In Whitelam's view, however, the archaeological data do not suggest the existence of the Iron Age Israelite state that scholars have created on the basis of biblical descriptions of it. At the same time, recent scholarship that has helped us to appreciate more fully the literary qualities of the biblical texts has in the process undermined our confidence that they can or should be used for historical reconstruction at all. The people of Israel in the Bible are now seen more clearly as the people of an artistically constructed and theologically motivated book. According to Whitelam, little evidence exists that this "Israel" is anything other than a literary fiction.[5]

We have arrived at a point in biblical scholarship, then, where using the biblical texts in constructing Israelite history is possible only with great caution. Their value for the historian lies not in what they have to say about the past in itself, but ". . . in what they reveal of the ideological concerns of their authors, if, and only if, they can be located in time and place."[6] The biblical texts should not be allowed, therefore, to define and dominate the agenda. "Biblical history" should be allowed to rest quietly in its grave, as we move on to a different sort of history altogether.

We can better contextualize Whitelam and assess his work if we briefly note two recent trends in biblical scholarship that underlie the book and that have led to the present debate about the history of Israel in general.[7] First of all, recent work on Hebrew narrative that has tended to emphasize the creative art of the biblical authors and the late dates of their texts has undermined the confidence of some scholars that the narrative world portrayed in the biblical texts has very much to do with the "real" world of the past. There has been an increasing tendency, therefore, to marginalize the biblical texts in asking questions about Israel's past, and a corresponding tendency to place greater reliance upon archaeological evidence (which is itself said to show that the texts do not have much to do with the "real" past) and anthropological or sociological theory. Over against the artistically formed and "ideologically slanted" texts, these alternative kinds of data have often been represented as providing a much more secure base upon which to build a more "objective" picture of ancient Israel than has hitherto been produced.

A second trend in recent publications has been the tendency to imply or to claim outright that ideology has compromised previous scholarship on the matter of Israel's history. A contrast has been drawn between people in the past who, motivated by theology and religious sentiment rather than by critical scholarship, have been overly dependent upon the biblical texts in their construal of the history of Israel, and people in the present who, setting aside the biblical texts, seek to write history in a relatively objective and descriptive manner. T. L. Thompson, for example, finds among previous scholars ". . . an ideologically saturated indifference to any history of *Palestine* that does not directly involve the history of Israel in biblical exegesis . . ."; he opines that a critically acceptable history of Israel cannot emerge from writers who are captivated by the story line of ancient biblical historiography.[8] These two trends—the increasing marginalization of the biblical texts and the characterization of previous scholarship as ideologically compromised—are perhaps the main distinguishing features of the newer writing on the history of Israel[9] over against the older, which tended to view biblical narrative texts as essential source material for historiography (albeit that these texts were not *simply* historical) and was not so much inclined to introduce into scholarly discussion questions of ideology and motivations.

In this context, Whitelam's book may certainly be characterized as an exemplar of the newer historiography rather than of the older. The kind of argument we have just described, however, is now pushed much further than ever before. Following (or perhaps only consistent with) some lines of thought found in P. R. Davies,[10] Whitelam now argues that not only is the information that the biblical texts provide *about* ancient Israel problematic, but the very *idea* of ancient Israel itself, which these texts have put in our minds, is also problematic. Even the newer historians are still writing histories of "Israel," which Whitelam argues is a mistake. Indeed, this approach is worse than a mistake, for in inventing ancient Israel, Western scholarship has contributed to the silencing of Palestinian history. If among other newer historians the ideological commitments of scholars are considered relatively harmless and without noticeably important implications outside the discipline of biblical studies, Whitelam certainly disagrees. He sets ideology quite deliberately in the sphere of contemporary politics. Biblical studies as a discipline, he claims, has collaborated in a process that has dispossessed Palestinians of a land and a past.

IS THE CORPSE REALLY DEAD?

Is biblical history really dead, or only sleeping? At first sight, the arguments of Whitelam and other similar thinkers may seem compelling, yet some important questions still need to be asked.

Biblical Texts and the Past

First, reflect on Whitelam's attitude toward the biblical texts. Even though accounts of the past are invariably the products of a small elite who possess a particular point of view, can these accounts not inform us about the past they describe *as well as* the ideological concerns of their authors? One presumes that Whitelam himself wishes us to believe that what he (as part of an intellectual elite) writes about the past can inform us about that past as well as about his own ideology—although we shall return to this point below. All accounts of the past may be partial (in every sense), but partiality of itself does not necessarily create a problem. Then again, changes in perspective in reading biblical narrative have indeed raised questions in many minds about the way in which biblical traditions can or should be used in writing a history of Israel. Certainly much can be criticized with respect to past method and results when the biblical texts have been utilized in the course of historical inquiry. Whether the texts ought not now be regarded as essential data in such historical inquiry—as witnesses to the past they describe, rather than simply witnesses to the ideology of their authors—is another matter. The assertion or implication that scholarship has more or less been compelled to this conclusion partly as a result of what we now know about our texts is commonplace in recent writing about Israel and history. In the midst of all this assertion and implication, however, the question remains: given that Hebrew narrative is artistically constructed and ideologically shaped, is it somehow less worthy of consideration as source material for modern historiographers than other sorts of data from the past? Why exactly, for example, would the fact that the biblical traditions about the premonarchic period in their current forms were late (if this were established) mean that they would not be useful for understanding the emergence or origins of Israel?[11] The answers to such questions remain to be clarified.

Archaeology and the Past

Second, what about the attitude to archaeology that is evidenced in Whitelam's book? Like others among the "newer historians," Whitelam sets considerable store by archaeological evidence over against the evidence of texts. In fact, one of the linchpins of his argument is that archaeology has *demonstrated* that certain things are factually true, which in turn *demonstrates* that the ancient Israel of text and scholar alike is an imagined past. For example, primarily archaeological data, in combination with newer ways of looking at Hebrew narrative, have "shown" various modern models or theories about the emergence of ancient Israel ". . . to be inventions of an imagined ancient past."[12] The puzzling thing about this kind of assertion, however, is that Whitelam himself tells us elsewhere that archaeology, like literature, provides us with only partial texts—a partiality governed (in part) by political and theological assumptions that determine the design or interpretation of the archaeological projects. The historian is always faced with partial texts—however extensively archaeological work might be carried out—and the ideology of the investigator itself influences archaeology.[13] These points are important ones for Whitelam to make, for he goes on to question much of the existing interpretation of the excavation and survey data from Israel, particularly as provided by Israeli scholars. He claims that this research itself has played its part in creating Israel's "imagined past," and he resolutely resists interpretations of the archaeological data that conflict with the thesis developed in his book: that ancient Israel is an "imagined" entity.[14]

Whitelam's book thus offers a rather ambivalent attitude to archaeological data. Where such data appear to conflict with the claims of the biblical text, these data are said to "show," or help to show, that something is true. They represent solid evidence that historical reality looked like "this," rather than like "that." Where archaeological data appear to be consistent with the claims of the biblical text, however, all the emphasis falls on how little these data can actually tell us. We are reminded of the ideological dimension either of the data or of the interpretation. Yet Whitelam cannot have it both ways. Either archaeological data do or do not give us the kind of relatively objective picture of the Palestinian past that can be held up beside our ideologically compromised biblical texts to "show" that the ancient Israel of the Bible and its scholars is an imagined entity. If Whitelam wishes to say that they do *not*—that "the historian is faced with partial texts in every sense of the term"[15]—then he must explain why archaeology is in a better position than texts to inform us about a "real" past over against an imagined past. He must explain why these particular "partial texts" are preferred over others. As things stand, Whitelam might be taken to be working with a methodology that invests a fairly simple faith in interpretations of data that happen to coincide with the story that he himself wishes to tell, while invoking a maximal degree of skepticism and suspicion in respect of interpretations of data that conflict with the story that he himself wishes to tell.

Ideology and the Past

A third area where some reflection is required concerns the ideology of the historian. Whitelam repeatedly asserts that the ancient Israel of biblical studies is an "invented" or "imagined" entity, and his discussion proceeds in such a way as to suggest that modern histories of Israel tell us more about the context and the beliefs of their *authors* than about the *past* they claim to describe. The picture he presents is of a biblical scholarship with a will to believe in ancient Israel—a will that overrides evidence. In responding to these assertions, we should acknowledge that modern histories of Israel no doubt do tell us *something* about the context and the beliefs of their authors. It is a simple fact of life that in all our thinking and doing, human beings are inextricably bound up with the world in which they think and do. We cannot help but be shaped at least partially by our context, regardless of whether we consciously strive to be aware of that context and its influence upon us. Our thinking is shaped in terms of the categories available to us. It is, however, not demonstrably the case that the authors of Israelite history have generally been influenced by ideology *rather than* by evidence—by a will to believe that has not *taken account* of evidence. Whitelam himself concedes that it is ". . . not easy to make these connections between biblical scholarship and the political context in which it is conducted and by which it is inevitably shaped. For the most part, they are implicit rather than explicit."[16] A reading of his book should indeed convince the reader that making these connections is not easy. One is left wondering by the book's end, in fact, how precisely Whitelam's position on the ideology of historians coheres. Do other scholars possess an ideology that compromises their scholarship because it leads them inevitably to abandon reason and ignore evidence, whereas Whitelam, unencumbered by ideology, is able to see people and events more clearly? Sometimes this conclusion appears clear, yet elsewhere he equally clearly suggests that *everyone* brings ideology to scholarship. Is Whitelam's position, then, that reason and evidence always and inevitably function in the service of an ideology and a set of commitments; is his objection that other scholars simply do not share his *particular* set of commitments—that they do not support him in the story about Palestine that he wishes to tell? Again, sometimes this does appear to be his view. If so, it seems that we are no longer speaking about history at all, but merely about scholarly stories. This outcome is somewhat ironic in view of Whitelam's critique of the biblical narratives in terms of their nature as story rather than history.

In truth, the discussion about scholarly ideology obscures the real issue, which has to do with evidence. There is ample documentation that past scholarship, while acknowledging that historiography is more than simply the listing of evidence, has nevertheless accepted that all historiography must attempt to take *account* of evidence. The real disagreement in this whole debate is, in fact, about what *counts* as evidence. Whitelam happens to believe that bringing the biblical texts into conjunction with other evidence in our examination of Israel's ancient past is not right. Scholars (and not just *biblical* scholars) have hitherto generally believed otherwise, at least in the case of many of the biblical texts. To portray this scholarship as not dealing seriously with evidence because of ideological commitments of one kind or another ("imagining the past"), when in fact the real issue is *which* evidence is to be taken seriously, significantly misrepresents reality.

A Premature Obituary?

We can see from the above discussion that Whitelam's case for the death of biblical history is neither convincing nor coherent. In these circumstances, for his readers to make themselves ready too hastily for attendance at a funeral would be a mistake. First we need to do some further thinking about the important issues that have been raised. Before beginning, however, we should explore further the background to the current debate about Israel's history—the background that lies in the older modern histories of Israel. It is here that our sense of the questions that need to be further pursued, in advance of a death certificate being issued, will be sharpened and refined.

A LONG-TERM ILLNESS: TWO INITIAL CASE STUDIES

Although we have thus far characterized Whitelam as an exemplar of the newer historiography rather than of the older, in that he gives virtually no place to the biblical texts in his quest for the history of Palestine, this distinction is not intended to give the impression that a gulf always or in general separates older modern historians of Israel from the newer ones. On the contrary, much of the ground upon which the newer historians take their stand was prepared for them long ago, in the sense that the governing assumptions and methods of much earlier historiography lead on directly to the place in which we now find ourselves. Earlier historians, as it happens, may often have depended upon biblical texts more than many of their recent successors. Their general approach, however, often leads naturally to the postures that many scholars now strike. If a death is to be reported with regard to biblical history, a long illness has preceded the demise.

Whitelam himself draws attention to two histories from the 1980s that to his mind already illustrate a crisis of confidence in the discipline of biblical history.[17] Because of what they characterize as problems with the biblical texts, both J. A. Soggin, on the one hand, and J. M. Miller and J. Hayes, on the other,[18] while depending to a great extent on the biblical narratives for their construal of Israel's history in the monarchic period, venture into historical reconstructions for the earlier periods either minimally or with a high degree of self-doubt. Even with regard to the monarchic period, some of what they write is noticeably tentative. For Whitelam, this approach illustrates clearly the problem of ancient Israelite history as a "history of the gaps," continually forced to abandon firm ground from which the enterprise can be said securely to begin. The patriarchal narratives are abandoned, then the exodus and conquest narratives, as sources from which history can be meaningfully reconstructed; a farewell to the Judges and the Saul narratives follows shortly thereafter. With Soggin and Miller/Hayes, we find the texts about the Israelite *monarchy* now under differing degrees of suspicious scrutiny. From this starting point, Whitelam moves on to suggest a wholesale and principled abandonment of biblical texts as primary sources for Israel's history. As the following analysis of both books reveals, the move is a natural one. The governing assumptions and methods of both books invite it.

Soggin and the History of Israel

After an introduction, Soggin's volume opens with a lengthy and revealing chapter on methodology, bibliography, and sources.[19] He begins with the claim that, after more than a century of scientific studies in historical criticism, writing a history of Israel at all, especially from its beginnings, is increasingly difficult. Oral and written traditions from the past, he claims, are subject to "contamination" of various kinds, whether through accident or because of the interests of people who have handed them down. These traditions also often contain stories of heroes and heroines, designed to inspire later generations of readers but of little importance to the modern historian. Our biblical traditions about the origins of Israel are precisely like this, according to Soggin. They are traditions about exemplary figures that were collected, edited, and transmitted (successively so)[20] by redactors living many centuries after the events. The horizon of the final redactors is chiefly the exilic and postexilic period, and the problems with which they are concerned chiefly reflect the consequences of the exile in Babylon and the end of both political independence and the Davidic dynasty in Israel. The picture that we have of earliest Israel is thus the one presented to us by the preexilic monarchic period (because with the formation of the Israelite state, Israel for the first time faced the problem of its own national identity and legitimacy, and began to reflect on its own past). The portrait is profoundly influenced, if not determined, by the exilic and postexilic rereading and redaction of the texts. It is people interested in exile and return from exile who have passed down to us the stories of the migration of the family of Abraham from Ur in Babylonia to Haran, the exodus from Egypt, the journey through the desert, the conquest of the land, and the period of the judges.

All this being so, it is always a difficult undertaking to establish the antiquity of individual biblical traditions, although Soggin thinks it improbable that the later redactors should generally have created texts out of nothing to meet their needs. Nevertheless, even where traditions do seem to be early, they clearly have generally been separated from their original context and inserted into a new context, which inevitably has had a marked effect on their interpretation and modified their content. The redactors exercised their creative bent freely and sometimes capriciously, suggests Soggin, in choosing and restructuring the material that came down to them, so as to make it support their own theories. For example, he claims that the arrangement of the persons of the patriarchs in a genealogical sequence is generally accepted to reflect the work of redactors. On the historical level, the patriarchs may in fact have existed contemporaneously, or not at all. The sequence of patriarchs-exodus-conquest seems, moreover, to be a simplification that the redactors introduced to cope with the problems raised by more complex features of the traditions. The conquest in the book of Joshua is pictured in terms drawn from the liturgy of public worship, its first part comprising a ritual procession and celebration rather than being warlike and political. This characteristic fits well into the context of a postexilic rereading of the material. In the context of the monarchy's failure on the political (as well as the theological and ethical) level, the people of God are recalled to their origins, in which they accepted humbly and passively what God offered in his mercy. The book of Judges, likewise, with its description of a tribal league and its stress on common worship as a factor of political and religious unity, also fits this late context (although Soggin concedes in this instance that the description could also correspond to premonarchic reality). The monarchy had been replaced in the postexilic period by a hierocratic order centered on the temple of Jerusalem. Finally, the narratives about the reign of Saul have turned someone who must have been a skillful and rough warrior—without blemish or fear, who ended his career in glory—into a hero of Greek tragedy, consumed by insecurity and jealousy, as well as prey to attacks of hypochondria and homicidal moods. Here the redactor has become an artist. The consequence is that any history of Israel seeking to deal with the period before the monarchy simply by paraphrasing the biblical texts and supplementing them with alleged parallels from the ancient Near East is not only using inadequate method, but offers a distorted picture of those events that certainly took place. This portrayal accepts uncritically the picture that Israel had of its own origins.

Such, then, is the "proto-history" of Israel for Soggin. Where does a true *history* of Israel begin? Is there a time after which the material in the tradition begins to offer credible accounts—information about people who existed and events that happened or are at least probable, about important events in the economic and political sphere and their consequences? Soggin chooses the period of the united monarchy under David and Solomon as his starting point. He acknowledges that the sources for knowledge of this period also contain many episodes (especially in relation to David) which concern more the private than the public sphere, and that these sources were themselves, like those for the proto-history, edited at a late date. He recognizes that no trace of the empire of David and Solomon appears in other ancient Near Eastern texts, that external verification is for this period, as for earlier periods, lacking. He considers the possibility, therefore, that the biblical tradition at this point also is pseudo-historical and artificial, aimed at glorifying a past that never actually existed. He thinks it improbable, however. There are in the David and Solomon narratives too many details of a political, economic, administrative, and commercial kind—too many features bound up with the culture of the time. From the information that these narratives provide us about politics, economics, and administration (e.g., military expeditions with territorial conquests, local rebellions, building works, foreign trade), we can create a picture of a nation ultimately close to economic collapse and driven to emergency measures to cope with this situation. Behind the facade of family life, we begin to find here important information that a historian can use, in Soggin's opinion, to construct a plausible picture of the united Israelite kingdom that is consistent with what our sources tell us occurred later: various forms of protest, then open rebellion and the secession of the northern kingdom at the death of Solomon. If admittedly romanticized elements reside in the tradition, the overall view of the past is not one of romanticized glorification. We may safely take the period of the united monarchy, therefore, as a point of reference from which to begin a historical study of ancient Israel.

In considering Soggin's argument, the first and (in the present context) most important point to note is the weakness of his distinction between the patriarchs-Saul material, on the one hand, and the David-Solomon material on the other. What essentially distinguishes these two groups of traditions from each other? Not that archaeological evidence lends more support to the latter than to the former, nor that the latter are, any less than the former, traditions about exemplary figures from the past that were collected, edited, and transmitted by redactors living many centuries after the events. Nevertheless, Soggin argues, a distinction is possible between them. That we have pseudo-history in the case of the David and Solomon narratives is "improbable" because, first, they contain "negative elements" which make them, overall, anything but a romanticized glorification of the past; second, sufficient important information is detectable behind the "facade" of the story for the historian to be able to form a plausible picture of the united Israelite kingdom. To these assertions, however, the following responses are appropriate.

First, it is far from clear that the present form of the traditions earlier in the Bible are any less mixed when it comes to "romantic" and "negative" elements (to use Soggin's categories) than the present form of the traditions about the united monarchy. Soggin's attempts to describe the earlier traditions according only to the former category are, in fact, far from convincing. He explains the book of Judges, for example, as a book designed to legitimate the postexilic hierocracy, in that Judges presents the tribal league as an early and authentic alternative to the monarchy. Taking such a hypothesis seriously is difficult; the most casual reader of Judges can see that, for the most part, it presents an Israelite society that is far from ideal, and that the book ends with a portrait of societal chaos that results from the lack of a king. The narrative of the book of Judges certainly does not offer the reader a romanticized glorification of the past. Only a very poor reading of the text can possibly lead to such a conclusion; and what is true of Soggin's reading of Judges is also true of his reading of Genesis-Joshua.[21] To make his kind of distinction between Genesis-Judges and Samuel-Kings requires one to read Genesis-Judges highly selectively.

Second, and following from the previous point, finding information of the kind that Soggin seeks (e.g., information on military expeditions with territorial conquests) behind the "facade" of the story in Genesis-Judges as well as in Samuel-

Kings is clearly possible. Therefore, how does the presence of such information in Samuel-Kings lead us to think of these texts in terms different from the texts that precede them? Soggin appears to put the weight of his argument here partly on the *number* of such political, economic, administrative, and commercial details; however, he fails to demonstrate that the fact that we have now moved from "proto-history" to "history," rather than simply the dynamic of the story, has multiplied them. After all, we are now reading a story about a state with international contacts, rather than a story about a tribal confederation. Why is the presence of such detail in the story of David and Solomon not simply evidence, then, of the kind of narrative art that Soggin finds in the story of Saul? In part, too, Soggin lays weight on the claim that the historian has used such detail in Samuel-Kings to build up a plausible picture of the united Israelite kingdom, consistent with what our biblical sources tell us later occurred. On the one hand, however, the reason that we are to view the intention of the authors of our earlier stories, in including this kind of detail, as being other than likewise telling us about the past is not entirely clear, even if it is a not a past that Soggin imagines "plausible"; equally unclear, on the other hand, is what exactly is proved by the fact that Soggin's reconstruction is consistent with what our biblical sources tell us later occurred. Soggin himself, at one point in his discussion, compliments the collectors and redactors of our biblical traditions as possessing "remarkable artistic skills, creating out of the small units substantial major works which at first sight are a coherent unity . . . a work of art" (28). Presumably one aspect of such artistic skill is that writers tell stories consistent with other stories that come later. One wonders, then, why Soggin believes it especially significant that the story of the united kingdom which he tells on the basis of some of the biblical texts is consistent with the story the biblical authors tell about the later kingdoms of Israel and Judah. If consistency of one story with the next is evidence in Samuel-Kings that we are dealing with history rather than with proto-history, then such consistency is also evidence of the same at earlier points in the tradition. If, on the other hand, coherence in the *earlier* parts of the Bible is evidence *only* of narrative art and *not* of history, for Soggin to argue that in *Samuel-Kings* coherence is evidence of history and *not* narrative art is inconsistent. In either case, the distinction that he attempts to make between the biblical traditions about the united monarchy and the biblical traditions about earlier period of Israelite history is poorly grounded.

This discussion shows how well a writer like Soggin prepares the way for later writers like Whitelam. Whitelam speaks of the history of the history of Israel as one in which historians are continually forced to abandon firm ground upon which the enterprise can be built securely. Soggin's "firm ground" is located in the united monarchy. The problem is that the governing assumptions and method with which Soggin operates make his own position ultimately untenable. The very perspectives that have caused him, before he has even begun, to abandon ground in Genesis-Judges and early in 1 Samuel can all too easily be brought to bear on and used to undermine the ground of his own choosing in the remainder of Samuel-Kings. If traditions earlier in the Bible are not "firm ground" because they contain stories of heroes and heroines that redactors living many centuries after the events have transmitted, then why are later traditions regarded so highly? If the earlier traditions are problematic because redactors exercised their creative bent freely or capriciously in the choice and restructuring of the material that came down to them, then why exactly are the later traditions not equally problematic, or do we just "know" in some undefined way that they are not? If the narrative art of redactors is a serious problem for historians with regard to the earlier traditions, then why is that art not a problem in regard to the later traditions as well? Finally, in consequence of everything that is true about the biblical traditions, if any history of Israel that seeks to deal with the period before the monarchy simply by paraphrasing the biblical texts is using inadequate method and ends up offering the reader a distorted picture of the past, then why is the same not true of a history of Israel that adopts such an approach for the monarchic period and afterwards?

The truth is that Soggin's choice of starting point for the writing of Israel's history is quite arbitrary. It is not a matter of reason; it is simply a matter of choice, buttressed by assertions about the "naiveté" of people who think otherwise. We have more to say below about the use of this kind of assertion as a substitute for argument. Under these circumstances, Whitelam—reminding us of the very lack of external evidence for the Davidic-Solomonic empire of which Soggin is himself aware—can all too simply undermine Soggin's "firm ground" and suggest that the Bible can no more be trusted in Samuel-Kings to tell us about Israel's real history than in Genesis-Judges. This is especially the case when work on biblical narrative in the period between the publication of Soggin's and Whitelam's books has only increased our awareness of its literary artistry. Under such circumstances Whitelam sounds entirely plausible, when he suggests that modern scholars' attachment to the David-Solomon narratives as valuable historical sources has more to do with their context in the period of European colonialism, and also with their need to believe in a powerful, sovereign, and autonomous Iron Age state of Israel, than with anything else. The judgment of Soggin (who seems to believe that the only "real" history is the history of states operating in the public economic and political sphere rather than, for example, individuals operating in the private, family sphere) on *other* scholars who are overreliant on the biblical traditions for the earlier period of Israel's history thus comes back upon his head. For Whitelam, overreliance on biblical traditions by scholars like Soggin is precisely what has led *them* to impose an inappropriate model on the past with regard to Israel's "monarchic period," distorting the past in the search for the nation-state in the guise of Israel. In truth, from Soggin's view (that the picture of Israel's *origins* that we find in the Bible is a literary fiction) to Whitelam's still more radical view (that the picture of Israel's past as presented *in much of the Hebrew Bible* is a literary fiction) is no great step. In precisely such a way has the general retreat from "firm ground" in the biblical text progressively taken place, as each historian of Israel demonstrates in turn how what previous scholars have written applies equally clearly and devastatingly to texts that those scholars themselves accept as starting points. Each scholar in turn can thus be accused of arbitrariness, for there is no logical stopping place on the slippery textual slope; and by degrees this leads to the death of biblical history entirely.

Miller and Hayes and the History of Israel

Leading elements in the approach adopted by Miller and Hayes to the biblical texts and to history are already open to view in their comments on the narrative in Genesis-Joshua.[22] Here they note the reflection of ". . . certain historical perspectives that were popular in ancient times but are no longer in vogue and that raise questions about the material's credibility" so far as history is concerned.[23] Miller and Hayes refer to the concept of a golden age as evidenced by the following items:

- the early chapters of Genesis
- the schematic chronology of the whole
- the idea that divine activity and purpose are throughout considered to be the primary forces determining the shape and course of the historical process
- the assumption that the origins of the various peoples of the world are to be understood in terms of simple lineal descent from a single ancestor or ancestral line
- the presence in the narratives of traditional story motifs that had widespread currency in the ancient world

Other aspects of the Genesis-Joshua narrative also cause difficulty: the implausibility of many of the numbers, the contradictory character of much of the information, the fact that much of the material is folkloric in origin, and that all of it owes its present shape to compilers who were not primarily concerned with objective reporting but with theological import. The narrative thus faces the modern historian with real difficulties, claim Miller and Hayes. Yet they concede at the same time that if any specific conclusions are to be reached about the origins and earliest history of Israel and Judah, they must be based primarily on this narrative, given the paucity and nature of our extrabiblical sources of information. Extrabiblical documents and artifactual evidence recovered from archaeological excavations in Palestine are useful for understanding the general background against which Israel and Judah emerged, but they are not helpful for tracing specific origins.

What is a "reasonably cautious historian"[24] to do under these circumstances? Miller and Hayes consider and reject both the option of presuming the historicity of the Genesis-Joshua account as it stands—ignoring the credibility problems and the lack of specific nonbiblical control evidence—and the option of rejecting the account out of hand as totally useless for purposes of historical reconstruction. They favor a compromise approach: the development of a hypothesis for the origins of Israel and Judah that is based to some degree on the biblical material yet that does not follow the biblical account exactly, perhaps not even closely. They find themselves nevertheless unwilling actually to produce such a hypothesis for the *earliest* history of the Israelites. Miller and Hayes consider the view of Israel's origins as advanced in Genesis-Joshua to be idealistic and in conflict with the historical implications of the older traditions that the compilers incorporated into their account. The main storyline is in fact "an artificial and theologically influenced literary construct."[25] Little can thus be said about Israel before its emergence in Palestine. Miller and Hayes content themselves, therefore, with a few generalized statements about various places whence Israelites may possibly have come, and pass on quickly from Genesis-Joshua to Judges, beginning their history proper with a description of the circumstances that appear to have obtained among the tribes in Palestine on the eve of establishing the monarchy.[26] The authors have greater confidence in using Judges for historical reconstruction, not because the book is any less marked than Genesis-Joshua by the editorial overlay of its compilers, but because earlier traditions beneath this overlay can be isolated with less difficulty; because these traditions are not so dominated by miraculous events and extraordinary occurrences; because the general sociocultural conditions that these narratives presuppose are in keeping with what is known about conditions existing in Palestine at the beginning of the Iron Age; and finally, because the situation reflected in these narratives provides a believable and understandable background for the rise of the Israelite monarchy depicted in 1–2 Samuel. Thus the component narratives of Judges can serve as a tentative starting point for a treatment of Israelite and Judean history—not because they provide the basis for reconstructing a detailed historical sequence of people and events, but because they provide accurate information about the general sociological, political, and religious circumstances that existed among the early Israelite tribes.

We may pause at this point to reflect on the logic of the argument so far. How solid is the ground upon which Miller and Hayes stand in beginning their history of Israel where they do? They acknowledge that both Genesis-Joshua and Judges share the same manner of overarching editorial scheme, which they characterize as artificial, unconvincing, and of little use to the historian. They further agree that the individual stories in each case are problematic for the historian. What basis exists, then, for the greater confidence displayed in the Judges material over against the Genesis-Joshua material? Miller and Hayes maintain that the earlier traditions beneath the "editorial overlay" can be isolated with less difficulty in the former than in the latter, but they have apparently already isolated earlier traditions that the compilers incorporated into the Genesis-Joshua account. Moreover, Miller and Hayes have done this sufficiently ably as to use the traditions as evidence that the view of Israel's origins advanced in Genesis-Joshua is idealistic (how else would they *know* that it is idealistic?). They maintain, too, that the component Judges narratives are not so dominated as the Genesis-Joshua narratives by miraculous events and extraordinary occurrences, but they argue at the same time that these Judges narratives are folk legends ". . .

not unlike the patriarchal narratives in Genesis . . ."—that the detail in the individual stories strains credulity.[27] Miller and Hayes opine that the general sociocultural conditions that the Judges narratives presuppose are in keeping with what is known about conditions existing in Palestine at the beginning of the Iron Age; they have not at any point, however, demonstrated that this is untrue of the general sociocultural conditions presupposed by the Genesis-Joshua narratives. In fact, they have cited some evidence consistent with the contrary view.[28] They maintain, finally, that the situation reflected in the Judges narratives provides a believable and understandable background for the rise of the Israelite monarchy as depicted in 1–2 Samuel. Miller and Hayes do not demonstrate, however, how the fact that the *literature* in Judges prepares us for the *literature* in 1–2 Samuel tells us anything about *history* (an important point in view of their skepticism about "literary constructs"). Nor do they demonstrate in any case how Judges provides a believable and understandable background for the rise of the Israelite monarchy in ways that Genesis-Joshua *does not* for the period of the emergence of Israel in Palestine. If Miller and Hayes truly believe, then, that the nature of the literature in Genesis-Joshua forbids the "reasonably cautious historian" from saying anything about Israel before its emergence in Palestine, seeing why they believe they can say anything about the later premonarchic period either is difficult. They are entirely vulnerable to the charge that their starting point in using biblical traditions for writing history is arbitrary, which is in fact the charge laid at their door by the "newer historians."

The situation does not improve very much when still later periods of Israelite history come under consideration. First and Second Samuel are said to reflect many of the same literary characteristics as Genesis-Judges. Thus, none of the materials in 1 Samuel can be taken at face value for the purposes of historical reconstruction. Now, however, we find Miller and Hayes "inclined to suppose that many, perhaps even most, of these stories contain at least a kernel of historical truth."[29] No justification is offered for this position, which is immediately hedged with qualifications concerning the nonverifiability of this "kernel" and the difficulty involved in identifying it. The fact that under such circumstances "any attempt to explain the historical circumstances of Saul's rise to power and his kingdom must be highly speculative" nevertheless does not prevent the authors from proceeding to speculate.[30] Nor does this prevent them, indeed, from telling a Saul story that happens to correspond in various respects to what the biblical text has to say. Why this approach is taken with 1 Samuel when it could not be taken with Genesis-Joshua is never made clear.

When we come to David, this dependence on the Genesis-Kings account is still more marked. Even though they regard most of the traditions here as folk legends from pro-Davidic Judean circles, Miller and Hayes presuppose that "many, perhaps most, of these traditions are based ultimately on actual historical persons and events."[31] Unclear again is why these "folk legends" can divulge historical content, and indeed why they produce a Miller/Hayes storyline remarkably similar to the biblical storyline, when earlier "folk legends" cannot. How can

Miller and Hayes compose their history of David's time largely on the basis of the biblical account in 1–2 Samuel—*clearly* ignoring in the process any perceived credibility problems and the lack of specific nonbiblical control evidence[32]— while at the same time dismissing such an approach to Genesis through Joshua *because of* perceived credibility problems and a lack of specific nonbiblical control evidence there? To do so is inconsistent; that later historians should have pressed the point, demanding to know why the David stories should be treated differently from the Abraham stories, is unsurprising. Responding that one has a "presupposition" in the case of David that the traditions are based on actual historical persons and events is simply insufficient—unless one wishes to be accused of arbitrariness and inconsistent method.

What we find in Miller and Hayes, then, is that the authors happen to use biblical texts in various ways in constructing their history of Israel. They happen to use such texts more than some recent historians. Between Miller and Hayes and Whitelam, however, no great gulf is fixed in terms of governing assumptions and method. All that Whitelam does is push Miller and Hayes to be more consistent in following through to their conclusion their governing assumptions and method. If the latter argue that the nature of the biblical literature is such in the case of Genesis-Judges as to forbid the historian, completely or virtually, from writing history based on this literature, they cannot argue that the case is different in Samuel, or indeed in Kings. Miller and Hayes go on in the case of Solomon, after all, to say that the "Genesis–II Kings presentation of Solomon is characterized throughout by editorial exaggeration. A cautious historian might be inclined to ignore it altogether if there were any other more convincing sources of information available."[33] The cautious historian has reemerged. But whereas caution, when confronted with the literature of Genesis-Joshua, declined to proceed, in the case of the Solomon narrative in Kings, caution is (by comparison) thrown to the wind. An account of the history of Solomon follows, largely utilizing the biblical narrative in its construction. We (and Whitelam) are entitled to ask why. Is the fact that the Bible is the only source of information we possess a sufficient ground for using it? If so in the case of Solomon, why not also in the case of Abraham? Conversely, if we can say nothing about Abraham, should we say anything about Solomon? Whitelam thinks not; indeed a very short step takes one from Miller and Hayes's "A cautious historian might be inclined to ignore . . ." to the suggestion that the responsible historian *ought* to ignore the biblical text, because it presents an imagined past rather than a real one.[34]

A BRIEF HISTORY OF HISTORIOGRAPHY

Miller and Hayes and Soggin lead on naturally, then, to Whitelam. The illness that preceded the "death" of biblical history was not contracted in the 1980s, however. Symptoms of the disease can be seen in still earlier histories of Israel stretching all the way back to the origins of the modern discipline of history in the post-Enlightenment period. If the patient has only now entered a critical phase in the illness, perusal of the case notes indicates that the problems began long ago. Because an exhaustive account of all such previous histories, and indeed of all the ways in which these histories foreshadow our more recent exemplars, would consume an entire volume, we content ourselves with a discussion of arguably the main underlying trend that has produced the current crisis. We refer here to the general suspicion of tradition that has been such a feature of post-Enlightenment thought generally and which has in differing degrees marked out the history of the history of Israel in the same period.

The immediate background to be sketched briefly here[35] is the overall shift in the modern age from philosophy to science as the foundational method for human endeavor: the institution under the influence of thinkers like Bacon and Descartes of an empirical and critical approach to all knowledge (not merely knowledge of the natural world), which tended to eschew prior authority in its pursuit of truth and to hold all tradition accountable to reason. The consequences for historiography of the popularity of this general approach to reality were ultimately profound. It is not that questions had never been asked in earlier times about the plausibility of tradition—whether individual traditions or parts of traditions could in fact be regarded as reflecting historical truth. In relation specifically to the history of Israel, for example, the early Jewish historian Josephus, although his work depends heavily upon biblical tradition as contained in the Hebrew Scriptures, nevertheless elucidated these Scriptures in relation to the science and philosophy of his day, harmonizing where necessary and sometimes rationalizing events that struck him as extraordinary. More generally, features of Renaissance scholarship were an acute awareness of the difference between past and present—a sense that the world described in tradition was not the same as the one inhabited by its receivers—and both a critical stance towards the literary evidence of the past and an openness to archaeological evidence as a way of reconstructing the past. Yet broadly speaking, tradition can be said to have provided the accepted framework within which discussion of the past took place, even where elements of tradition might be criticized or considered problematic. This situation generally obtained throughout the succeeding period until the late eighteenth century—a period during which history was not in any case widely regarded as a source of reliable truth. The idea that a "scientific method" could discover such truth in history had not yet arisen. History was the story of the merely contingent and particular—a view that Aristotle himself enunciated and which a great variety of thinkers throughout the sixteenth to the eighteenth centuries also held. The Jesuits who produced the *Ratio Studiorum* (1559), for example, assigned no significant role in their curriculum to history (in contrast to logic and dialectic, which were regarded as approaches to truth). The seventeenth-century philosopher Descartes, who rooted his thinking in self-evident axioms, moving on to trustworthy knowledge and certainty by way of deductive reasoning and mathematical method, likewise did not think highly of history, because historians employed observation and interpretation rather than logic and mathematics.

Writing in the eighteenth century, Lessing famously opined (succinctly summing up the general belief of the age), "Accidental truths of history can never become the proof of necessary truths of reason." Where history writing was valued in the rapidly emerging scientific age, it was in general so valued as an art with close links to the ancient art of rhetoric. History's purpose was to delight the reader and to teach morals through examples. The ancient words of Dionysius of Halicarnassus encapsulate the position on history that was thus commonly adopted: "History is philosophy teaching by examples."

Only in the late eighteenth and nineteenth centuries do we find a pronounced shift in how history and history writing was conceived, as the idea emerged that the past itself might, if subject to the appropriate sort of inductive scientific analysis, reveal truths about human existence. The factors involved in this general change in perspective are many and complex. On the one hand, tradition about the past, including tradition rooted in the Bible, had been progressively undermined for many people. It had been undermined by the work of humanist text critics since the Renaissance, with all their work's potential for destroying claims to authority for a document that had been accepted as authoritative for centuries; by geographical exploration, which subverted long-held perspectives on the nature of the world; by philosophical perspectives that were either new or were new versions of older pre-Christian ideas with which scholars had become reacquainted during the Renaissance revival in classical learning; and by the Reformation assault on church authority and medieval faith. On the other hand, the scientific approach to reality was already beginning to enjoy prestige as a way in which certain and timeless truth might be appropriated and human existence understood. It remained only for the suggestion to be widely adopted, that perhaps a scientific approach to *historical* reality might shed further light on this human existence—an idea already found in earlier thinkers like Machiavelli.

The catalyst for this change of general viewpoint was undoubtedly some of the intellectual activity that preceded and surrounded the French Revolution, as represented by the thought of many of the French *philosophes*, who argued that history revealed the transformation of a *potentially* rational humanity into an *actually* rational humanity—a story of inevitable progress. Tradition should no longer guide actions in the present and hope for the future, especially given that tradition was seen as deriving from earlier stages of human history characterized as periods of folly and superstition. Institutional religion was itself perceived as embodying such superstition. Rather, expectations for the *future* should govern both the life of the present and the evaluation of the past. God had created the universe, setting an orderly system of causes and effects in motion, and from there the universe proceeded of itself (in the realm of human affairs as well as the realm of nature) in Newtonian orderliness. The increase in rationality that would inevitably occur over time would in due course lead to an increase in happiness, as everyone was drawn to live in accordance with principles enshrined in nature. Newtonian science thus provided the model for understanding not only present and future human existence, but past human existence as well.

The particular viewpoint that these French *philosophes* advanced was by no means generally adopted elsewhere by people reflecting on the nature of history. For example, the German historiography of the late eighteenth and early to mid-nineteenth centuries that responded to this French worldview was far less inclined to see the past in terms of the simple cause-and-effect relationships envisaged in Newtonian physics. The Germans were more inclined to believe that reason itself had to be seen within its total human context; that Nature did not encompass everything; and that religion was not just the convenient tool of a not-yet-rational mankind, but a basic element of human life. This perspective preferred to view history not as the story of rationality ascending through time to ever-greater perfection, but rather as a series of discontinuities. The aim of the historian was the intuitive grasping of complex, intertwining forces inaccessible to simple explanations. German historiography in this mode is often referred to as "historicism." Yet for all that this German response to French developments was in many ways antagonistic, it was itself framed as a response that was scientific in nature, illustrating the way in which the scientific model had now come to dominate the discussion— at least in continental Europe. One of the main German criticisms of the *philosophes* was that they speculated about the past without properly consulting the sources. The Germans, in turn, sought to ground their historiographical work in "the facts," building on a long, erudite tradition that itself inherited elements from Italian humanist historiography (in its critical attitude toward texts and undocumented traditions); from work on French legal history, which stressed the importance of primary sources; and from antiquarianism (with its concern, for example, with the physical remains of the past). Vigorous study of the sources (utilizing proper empirical scientific method) would reveal, in Leopold von Ranke's famous words, *wie es eigentlich gewesen*—"the way it really was." For most of the nineteenth century, Ranke himself presided over the vast scholarly enterprise of searching out the facts and presenting them in an objectively scientific form, allegedly free from bias and presupposition. The historian's task was conceived, indeed, precisely as that of the natural scientist, at least insofar as it was conceived as letting the facts (envisaged as simply "out there") speak for themselves, and as allowing people to form judgments about the facts at a later stage. Historiography was now to be firmly understood, at least in the first instance, as an endeavor with the purely theoretical interest of reconstructing the past without any practical interest in the purposes for which such a reconstruction might be used (whether in terms of moral instruction, religious devotion, entertainment, or propaganda). By the end of the 1880s, this history-as-science had replaced philosophy as the discipline to which many educated people in Europe and elsewhere in the Western world turned as the key that would unlock the mysteries of human life. The move away from the limits set by tradition, towards an unlimited freedom of explanation after the model of the natural sciences, had become ever more decisive. The value and authority of all older historiographical models and all histories based on them had, indeed, come into serious question. Because histories written prior to the nineteenth century had not been produced using proper scientific methods, everything now had to be done again in the proper manner by people who employed such proper methods.

Ranke himself stopped well short of a full-blown scientific positivism in the narrower sense of the term, in that he did not believe that the finding of facts through critical research was to be followed by induction leading to more and more general and hence abstract concepts—that is, scientific "laws." Ranke was a Christian and an idealist, believing that a divine plan and will stood behind all the phenomena of the past, and that the ideas that shape phenomena and events were not only the keys to *understanding* the past, but also provided an absolute moral structure and a yardstick for *assessing* the past. He did not, then, believe with Auguste Comte (the original proponent of positivism as a philosophical system) that science provides us with the only valid knowledge that we can possess, superseding theology and metaphysics—that only positive facts and observable phenomena count as knowledge. Soon, however, Ranke's manner of scientific approach to the past, which we may rightly refer to as a kind of "quasi-positivism" (insofar as it at least advocates establishing or verifying positive "facts" through empirical inquiry and the construction thereby of an objective, scientific picture of "the way things were"),[36] gave way to a more thoroughgoing version of positivism, in an era in which many had long since ceased to share his Christian faith and now came to doubt also his idealism. Having used science so well to debunk the uncritically presented past, nineteenth-century historiography in the German tradition in the end found that such science was a sharp and dangerous two-edged sword; it could be brought to bear no less decisively on the broadly shared nineteenth-century idealist philosophical framework that dominated much of the historiography of that century. Idealism itself could be seen only as a traditional view or prejudice—one of those philosophical explanations of the world's order that could not be inductively demonstrated and that the truly scientific person should therefore reject as a component of historiography. By the end of the nineteenth century, precisely this suggestion had been made and adopted, as many historians began to adopt a fully positivist stance on the past—in common with scholars in other fields who noted the immense prestige that the sciences enjoyed and felt impelled to emulate their success by transferring their views and methods from the inquiry into nature to the inquiry into human phenomena. Positivism thus strictly defined holds not only that all knowledge should be based on directly observed phenomena (i.e., it is not simply committed to empiricism and verification in the Rankean sense), but further that all scientific endeavors should aim at finding general laws governing phenomena. Observing, searching for regularities, generalizing from research results, and forming laws must be the tasks of all scientific disciplines, and only this positivist approach can yield knowledge sufficiently reliable to function as a guide for the reshaping of human life. On this view only sensory experience counts, so the whole structure of idealist philosophy collapses (because gods, ideas, and the like cannot be "known" in this positivistic manner); the structure of idealist *historiography*, with its emphasis upon the unique individual or nation in their idiosyncratic context falls also. Positivist historiography is, by contrast, resolutely deterministic, focusing on general (and hence predictable) phenomena or forces in history *rather than* on the unique and idiosyncratic.

With this kind of historiography, the marginalization of tradition in pursuit of the past becomes more complete. Tradition becomes, at best, only a mine out of which may be quarried such "facts" as can be ascertained empirically. The task of the historian is then to establish the true, scientific relationship between the "facts" (as opposed to the traditional interpretation of them) and to progress then towards broad generalizations and laws arising from them (the approach, e.g., of Hippolyte Taine, who believed that the past could be wholly explained through this process). It was not even clear to some intellectuals at the turn of the twentieth century that it was any longer the *historian's* task to relate these "facts" or to generalize from them. Emile Durkheim argued, on the contrary, that historians should only find, cleanse, and present the "facts" to the sociologist for generalization. In such a generalizing process, causal analysis was to be given priority over description and narration, the general given priority over the unique and the individual, and the directly observable present given priority over the unobservable past.

Whether in Durkheim's precise formulation or not, historiography on the positivist model clearly ceases to be a story about the past in which human individuals and groups play the central and crucial roles. Instead historiography becomes a narrative about the impersonal forces that shape both the past and the present. The early positivist history of H. Buckle foreshadowed many later works in the same spirit, emphasizing climate, food, soil, and nature more generally—rather than *people*—as the shapers of civilization, and argued that historians, if they did not wish to be ignored, must abandon the historiography of description and moral lessons for a historiography modeled on the successful natural sciences. In general, the twentieth century indeed saw an increasing preference for such social and economic interpretations of history, with the emphasis on collective forces, quantifiable aspects, and repeatable developments over against political, event-oriented interpretations that stress the unique and human (especially the individualistic) dimensions of history. Perhaps most influential among the more recent proponents of such interpretations are the French *Annales* group, with their interest in "total history" and their emphasis on the larger structures that provide the context in which particular events take place and human beings think and act. Most important for understanding the past, on this view, are the relatively stable geographical and demographic forces of history. These forces are followed in order by economic and social developments involving the masses of the people, the culture of the common people, and last the political phenomena. Such an approach, in practice if not entirely in intention, has tended to neglect the importance of the individual, as well as radically diminishing the importance of the political, in the past.

The history of historiography since the Enlightenment, at least as we have told it to this point (and we have more to say in chapter 2), can thus be seen as the story of a discipline progressively seeking to escape from a dependence upon tradition, under pressure as a result of the perceived success of the natural sciences to justify itself as a proper academic discipline by becoming more "scientific" (whether interpreted in a Rankean-empirical or a positivist-empirical way). The new empirical and critical approach to knowledge in general was increasingly brought to bear in a thoroughgoing way on historical knowledge in particular, the aim of historians in general becoming, certainly by the end of the nineteenth century, to reconstruct past history "as it had actually happened," over against traditional claims about what had happened. History and tradition were no longer assumed to be closely related to each other. Rather, history was to be assumed to lie *behind* tradition and to be more or less *distorted* by it. The point, then, was not to listen to tradition and to be guided by it in what it said about the past, but if possible, to see through tradition to the history that might (or indeed might not) exist behind it. The onus now fell on tradition to verify itself, rather than on the historian to falsify it. The "science" of historiography had been born. Its character is well exemplified in the following quotation from J. Huizinga:

> History adequate for our culture can only be scientific history. In the modern Western culture the form of knowledge about occurrences in this world is critical-scientific. We cannot surrender the demand for the scientifically certain without damaging the conscience of our culture.[37]

THE HISTORY OF THE HISTORY OF ISRAEL

Within the matrix just described, the development of the discipline of the history of Israel in the nineteenth and on into the twentieth and twenty-first centuries has taken place. Not surprisingly, therefore, already early in the nineteenth century, some people in pursuit of the "scientifically certain" were prepared to argue in a Whitelamesque manner that if the history of Israel should be the subject of scholarly interest, then the traditions found in the Old Testament were of no help in discovering anything about it. W. M. L. de Wette, for example, asserted that the Old Testament, produced by authors intent on creating myth rather than recounting history, was entirely inadequate as a historical source. Practitioners of the historical sciences should accept that the nature of the tradition absolutely disallowed the reconstruction of Israelite history from it. Other scholars were generally reluctant to adopt this radical stance, and even de Wette himself did not maintain it consistently. The significant point, however, is that the search had now begun in earnest for "firm ground" upon which to initiate the construction of a modern history of Israel. In this environment, any use of the biblical tradition had to be justified in terms of the adopted scientific model. The tradition in itself could not necessarily function as a starting point. Thus, another famous German scholar, H. G. A. Ewald, could write in typically Rankean fashion in the middle of the nineteenth century that his ultimate aim as a historian of Israel was "the knowledge of what really happened—not what was only related and handed down by tradition, but what was actual fact."[38] If it was generally agreed that the biblical traditions in their current form date from an era well after most of the events they claim to describe, then it was incumbent on those people who accepted this new model, with its emphasis on primary sources—and especially eyewitness accounts, "objective facts," and external corroboration—to demonstrate how these traditions could function, at least in part, as reliable sources for the historian. The ultimately unconvincing nature of the arguments for such partial use of biblical tradition have led directly from de Wette to Whitelam. The search for firm ground, as Whitelam correctly points out, has failed. The history of the history of Israel from the nineteenth century until the present is in fact largely—and not just in the case of Soggin and Miller and Hayes—a history of indefensible starting points and not entirely coherent argument. Judged in terms of the criteria that have driven the enterprise or at least heavily influenced it, it stands condemned.

The Patriarchal Traditions

How is use of the patriarchal traditions, for example, to be defended on such criteria? Even when the literary forms of these traditions were generally dated as early as the tenth to the eighth centuries B.C.—that is, particularly in the era of biblical scholarship when the Graf-Wellhausen "Documentary Hypothesis" about the composition of the Pentateuch was widely granted the status of self-evident truth—many scholars felt that the traditions were too far distant from any patriarchal era to tell us very much of value. Ewald himself, whose multivolume history of Israel predated Wellhausen's influential work, and who generally displayed a high regard for the relationship of Pentateuchal tradition to historical facts, thought the patriarchal traditions of questionable reliability. Tradition in general, he maintained—though rooted in facts—preserves only an image of what happened. Fact is mixed with imagination and distorted by memory. Tradition is a pliable entity that can be molded, as time passes, by religious interests, etiological concerns, and mythological perspectives. It has great inherent power, so that even the substitution of writing for memory only checks the process rather than stopping it. In the oral phase of transmission, before a historiographical tradition arises, no effective constraints exist, so that not even serious effort on behalf of the tradents to pass their stories on uncorrupted can prevent the molding. Thus the patriarchal traditions in particular, now contained in Ewald's "Great Book of Origins" (Genesis-Joshua)—which he dated to the period of the early monarchy—must come under suspicion, for they arose before the beginnings of historiography in Israel (in the Mosaic era and just afterwards). Ewald even considered (but rejected) the view that we can know *nothing* of the patriarchs' historical existence and residence in Canaan. He preferred rather to extract such history from the tradition as he felt he could.[39]

W. F. Albright's solution to the problem that tradition thus understood presents to the historian was to appeal to archaeological evidence for verification. For Albright, archaeological remains, both literary and artifactual, provided a source of material external to the Bible that could be used as a scientific control in relation to the tradition, since archaeology gives us concrete facts rather than interpretation or theory.[40] This kind of argumentation has, however, proved particularly vulnerable to critique. If we are truly to appeal to archaeology as a means of verifying the patriarchal tradition, then as Thompson and others have shown, archaeology offers little support of the kind that is necessary. As Thompson asserts, "Not only has archaeology not proven a single event of the patriarchal traditions to be historical, it has not shown any of the traditions to be likely."[41] If proof or even an increase in likelihood is sought from the archaeological data, then this conclusion is indeed true. We are left, then, with relatively late traditions that cannot be corroborated; some people even conclude that the datings of the Pentateuchal material known as JE produced by scholars like Wellhausen are now indefensible. The later the tradition as a whole is placed and the more it is questioned whether we can really get behind it to earlier material—and this claim is often questioned in the current climate, where interest in the artistry of Hebrew narratives as whole compositions is intense—the less plausibly one can take the tradition seriously as reflecting historical actuality.[42]

To argue the case, one would have to subject the whole "scientific" approach to historiography to critique. One would have to question whether the general attitude expressed towards tradition is intellectually well founded—for example, whether one must believe that religious interests or etiological concerns inevitably distort the past, or that "mythological perspectives" are incompatible with historiography.[43] One would need to move on then to ask whether we should expect archaeology to "prove" events of the patriarchal traditions to be historical, what exactly using such language means, and what is signified when such "proof" fails to materialize.[44] This kind of critique has been thin on the ground in the history of the history of Israel since the nineteenth century, because of the broad agreement among Old Testament scholars about how the discipline should proceed methodologically.[45] Given this agreement, it was inevitable that the patriarchal era would certainly not function as the starting point for most histories of Israel that wished to be credited with the label "critical."[46]

The Moses/Joshua Traditions

If we abandon the patriarchal era as our starting point, where next should the attempt be made to lay foundations? The biblical narratives concerning the eras of Moses and Joshua are just as problematic with regard to external verification as those concerning the patriarchal era;[47] and unless one is prepared to argue along with Ewald that the biblical tradition is rooted in written sources that reach back to the Mosaic era, one is unlikely (on the presuppositions generally shared by the scholarship under discussion here) to think that that tradition has a great deal to tell us about those periods in any case.

Wellhausen is quite inconsistent at just this point, which is intriguing considering how much his influence can be detected on the history of the history of

Israel in the last century or so.[48] Wellhausen goes considerably further than Ewald in his views of the patriarchs, arguing that the Genesis narratives cannot be used for historical purposes *at all*. We attain to *no* historical knowledge of the patriarchs from these stories, he asserts, but only of the period when the stories about the patriarchs arose—the period of the monarchy before the Assyrian conquest of the northern kingdom of Israel in the eighth century B.C. (in the case of the J source), and indeed, later, the period of the exile (in the case of the P source).[49] One might think that the corollary of this argument should be that we attain to *no* historical knowledge of the eras of Moses and Joshua either, but only of the time when the stories about *them* arose, for we read of these eras in the same Hexateuchal sources. Wellhausen's general view of Hebrew literature, moreover, is that the period before the late ninth century B.C. may largely be characterized as a nonliterary age, albeit that some literature (including prose history) had existed prior to that time.[50] How is it, then, that he does not in fact advocate the agnosticism in respect of the *postpatriarchal* era upon which he insists in the case of the *patriarchal* era? One searches in vain for a convincing argument.

Wellhausen himself evidently feared the charge of inconsistency, for he sought to preempt it by asserting that the "epic" tradition of Moses and Joshua, unlike the "legend" of the patriarchs, contains elements that cannot be explained unless historical facts are underlying it. Its source must be in the period with which it deals, while the patriarchal legend has no connection whatever with the times of the patriarchs.[51] Assertion is not argument, however, and labeling traditions with different genre descriptors does not of itself make them different. It is difficult to avoid the impression, in fact, that the distinction in view here has much more to do with Wellhausen's need to have an historical J with which he can contrast a less historical or fictional P (the focus of his preceding pages), than with anything else. Wellhausen himself thus supplies a good early example of the way in which arbitrary choices about starting points in the tradition, ungrounded in convincing argument, have marked out the history of the history of Israel.[52] If justification is required for finding in patriarchal narratives contained in a monarchic source anything other than reference to the present time *of the monarchic source*, then such justification is also required in the case of postpatriarchal narratives found in the same source. To that extent Whitelam again appears as the more consistent *alter ego* of an earlier scholar; for Whitelam is the one who presses the point about the primacy of the period in which stories arose to its logical (if in our view ultimately self-defeating) conclusion.

The Judges Traditions

Another arbitrary starting point for histories of Israel that seek "firm ground" in the tradition is the book of Judges. M. Noth, for example, although he did not (like Wellhausen) deny that the patriarchs had existed as historical persons, took the view that the nature of the biblical tradition about them precludes us from writing any history of them as such.[53] The same can be said of the traditions concerning everything else that happened before the appearance of Israel as a tribal confederation in Palestine. The problem for the historian is that, although there can be no doubt that the Pentateuch sets out to relate events that have happened—and contains a good deal of material relating to historical traditions—the Pentateuch certainly did not (in Noth's view) originate and was not planned from the outset as a historical work. It was not designed and drafted as a coherent historical narrative. Rather, the Pentateuch is the product of the successive coalescence of sacred oral traditions. The various tribal traditions that it contains were first given their definitive unified form within an Israel that was already united in Palestine. This league of twelve Israelite tribes first imposed the "all Israel" concept on what were originally independent traditions. The whole people of Israel now read various independent pasts as their unified past. Thus, the earlier traditions in their present form simply personify in Jacob/Israel and his twelve sons, for example, the historical situation as it existed after the occupation of the land; they are based on presuppositions that did not exist until the tribes had already settled. As a careful reading of the book of Joshua reveals, Noth claimed, no such unified Israel existed before the time of the Israelite league. The various tribes of Israel did not, in fact, all settle in the land at the same time. Since the association together of the earlier independent traditions is only a secondary phenomenon, then—reflecting the perspective of a later time—the historical outline that the material presents must be considered historically unreliable. Only with the occupation of Palestine do we have a fully united "Israel" at all, and therefore only from this point can the real history of Israel take its departure.

The question must be asked, however: How does Noth know that the "all Israel" perspective of the book of Judges is any less an anachronism than the "all Israel" perspective of Genesis or Exodus? How can he justify a starting point in the tradition here, if he is not prepared to adopt one earlier? He is aware of the problem.[54] He acknowledges the impossibility of conceiving of any period in which the actual situation of Israel corresponded exactly to the twelve-tribe system described in the tradition, and he accepts that the number twelve is itself "suspicious" and "apparently artificial."[55] He considers the possibility, therefore, that we have in the notion of a twelve-tribe entity an arbitrarily constructed picture of ancient Israel dating from a later time. Noth is, however, swift to reject this possibility. We find other twelve-tribe entities in the Old Testament and in Greece and Italy, which means that the Israelite tribal system is not an isolated phenomenon in the ancient world. For that reason it cannot be an aspect of a secondarily constructed picture of Israel, in which a larger whole is schematically divided. The Greek parallel in particular demonstrates to Noth that we are concerned in the Old Testament twelve-tribe Israel with a historical association of the Israelite tribes rather than a fiction. It indicates the nature of this association as an ancient Israelite "amphictyony" (a sacred society centered around a particular shrine): "The number twelve was part of the institution which had to be maintained even when changes took place in the system: it proves therefore to have been neither the mere result of the natural ramification of a human group nor the invention of a later period, but rather an essential element in the historical organization of such a tribal confederation."[56] Thus does Noth find his firm ground in the tradition upon which to build his historical edifice.

Noth's position is now well-enough known that this summary of it will perhaps occasion little surprise; yet that he adopted the position is perhaps surprising, when we remember that in general he did not adopt a positivistic attitude at all when it came to the question of the relationship between external data and literary (including biblical) tradition. He was, for example, insistent that archaeology must in principle be subservient to literature in the composition of historiography, since he was somewhat skeptical about what archaeology could achieve of itself and he was convinced of the need, in any event, to give primacy to the study of tradition.[57] Such opinions inform his critique of those who followed Albright in attempting to use archaeology to prove the historicity of the patriarchal period. His arguing in such a positivistic manner with regard to the Greek amphictyony is thus ironic. He might have done better to reflect upon and extrapolate from his own comment on archaeology and what it can be said to demonstrate: "The fact that an event can be shown to have been possible is no proof that it actually occurred."[58] Even if the parallel with the Greek amphictyony were more convincing than in fact it has turned out to be, it would not be sufficient for the purpose to which Noth puts it. The fact that such a Greek confederation existed would certainly not demonstrate that the particular tribal association described in Judges was a historical reality rather than a literary one, nor that its nature was that of an amphictyony. The claim simply has no logic, nor would there be logic in it, even if the claimed parallel were Semitic rather than Indo-European and were closer to the time period under consideration in relation to the book of Judges.[59] If verifying the tradition is required, then sociological parallels are as inadequate to the task as archaeology.[60] Parallels do not of themselves prove that what is claimed in literature was actually the case in historical reality—in this case, that the "all Israel" of the book of Judges is any less the creation of hypothetical redactors, secondarily linking originally independent tribal traditions, than the "all Israel" of the Pentateuch or Joshua. In reality, however, the parallel is less than perfect in any case. The extrabiblical confederations that Noth mentions did in fact belong to the Indo-European rather than to the Semitic world (a point that he himself recognized as a weakness).[61] Moreover, they date from a much later time than their hypothetical Israelite counterpart— a fact devastating to Noth's claim that, because the Israelite tribal system is not an isolated phenomenon in the ancient world, it cannot be an aspect of a secondarily constructed picture of Israel; too, these confederations largely form part of an urban rather than a rural culture.[62] The number twelve was not in fact a primary characteristic of the extrabiblical amphictyony, as Noth asserted. The number of its members could vary. He was correct, on the other hand, in identifying a central shrine as "the essential feature of the institutions of these tribal associations";[63] unfortunately, the central shrine is a feature that he finds great difficulty in identifying in the book of Judges.[64] Even among scholars who think that verification through sociological parallel is something to be sought, therefore, Noth's attempt at such verification is generally considered a failure.

If Noth's position as a positivist in respect of sociology where he refuses to be so in respect of archaeology is ironic, there is nevertheless a certain inevitability about it. Given his general stance in regard to tradition, which he shares with the majority who have written on the history of Israel in the past 150 years, he must demonstrate in some way that he has grounds outside the tradition for adopting a starting point within it. Without the amphictyony parallel, he cannot demonstrate that what he says of Genesis–Joshua does not apply also to Judges—in which case Judges poses all the problems for the historian that are posed by the Hexateuch, and Noth's starting point in Judges is indefensible. If he is correct in what he says about earlier biblical tradition in general, then he cannot suddenly invest faith in tradition when he reaches the book of Judges. If, on the other hand, he were to begin to question his view of tradition in general, because of a desire to take his stand on Judges, his case for beginning his history in Judges rather than at some earlier point would also collapse. It is already clear from the rather muddled argumentation in the *History* how few internal grounds there are for any generalized distinction between Genesis–Joshua and Judges.

If, for example, as Noth asserts, the traditions in the Pentateuch are based on historical events and, indeed, the Pentateuch sets out to relate events that have happened, in what sense is the Pentateuch not a historical work, while the Deuteronomistic History is?[65] The answer cannot lie in *intention* to speak about the past (both works possess this). The answer must lie in the fact that the Deuteronomistic History was allegedly designed and drafted as a coherent historical narrative, whereas the Pentateuch allegedly was not. Yet how such design and drafting would imply that the Deuteronomistic History is *in fact* more reliable as a source for history than the Pentateuch is not clear, especially considering that its existing form (like that of the Pentateuch) dates from well after most of the period it describes. Nor is it clear how we *know* that the Pentateuch was not designed and drafted as a coherent historical narrative, nor (if it was not) how we *know* that the coalescing process during oral transmission necessarily distorted the traditions in bringing them together. Much depends here on Noth's contention that the biblical tradition itself reveals, in various statements, that the tribes of Israel did not all settle in the land at the same time and thus that "all Israel" is a misleading construct imposed on earlier traditions by a later generation. These revelations are above all how *he* "knows" that the historical outline presented by the earlier material is unreliable. Yet he only "knows" this because he already "knows" that the later material is to be interpreted, like the earlier, in terms of original diversity and an editorial overlay that, as he puts it, takes "too simple a view of the events" of the settlement in Canaan.[66] We might well ask how this knowledge is itself obtained, and what sense it makes to characterize the tradition as taking too simple a view of events when that very tradition furnishes evidence of allegedly underlying complexity. Are the biblical authors really offering an overly simplistic reading of Israel's occupation of the land, or, rather, is Noth himself offering an overly simplistic reading of the *biblical tradition*? Might not the same apply to his reading of the Pentateuch? If he *is* misreading the Pentateuchal tradition, however, then the arguments that follow on from this misreading—arguments against the use of the tradition in writing a history of Israel—lack any basis. For example, the mere fact (if this could somehow be established) that the original purpose of an ancient tradition was to explain the origin of things (that is, it was an etiology—a favored explanation of texts in Noth's writings) does not of itself lead logically to the conclusion that the explanation thus offered of the origin is unreliable. Nor does the secondary combination of traditions (if that is what the authors of the Hexateuch achieved) of itself imply that in the process of combination historical reality has been distorted.[67] In sum, one can see why historians who share Noth's overall suspicion of tradition have found themselves unable to join him in standing on the "firm ground" upon which he seeks to build his history of Israel, and why they have progressively abandoned it for a better place.

Conclusion

So we might go on in our description of scholarly migration. We have already seen another set of foundations in the biblical texts about David and Solomon crumble under our critique of Soggin and Miller and Hayes that is offered above. As the presumed dates of the biblical traditions have been pushed in recent scholarship into the postexilic era, and their nature as artful narrative has been underlined (lessening the plausibility of excavating underneath the tradition so as to "dig out" pieces of history), so also the capacity of *any* of these traditions to speak about the past has come to be widely questioned. Thus even the fairly radical stance (for its time) that A. Kuenen adopted in 1869[68]—that getting back beyond the eighth century B.C. in writing a history of Israel is impossible because only in this era do we possess the kind of written external evidence that allows us to check the biblical tradition against it—has now been left well behind. As P. R. Davies argues, the mere fact that we find in the books of Kings a story that happens to correlate in some small ways with extrabiblical texts does not mean that the particular story which Kings narrates is necessarily true—that *here* the tradition can be trusted, whereas *beforehand* it cannot.[69] Davies himself advocates a thoroughly nonbiblical approach to Israel's history, more in the manner of de Wette than Kuenen.

Yet even in Davies we find a lingering nostalgia for the tradition, when he surprisingly gives the books of Ezra and Nehemiah the central place in his historical reconstruction of the postexilic period.[70] His justification is that, unlike the case with Iron Age Israel, the nonbiblical data in the case of Ezra-Nehemiah do "to a degree" afford confirmation of "some" of the basic processes described in the biblical narrative at this point; and second, processes of the kind described in Ezra-Nehemiah are "necessitated" by the subsequent developments in the emergence of Judean society and its religion.[71] The language is somewhat imprecise;

but Davies seems to be trying to maintain here (and only here) that once we have taken the biblical tradition seriously as literature, we can still take it, along with the nonbiblical data, as reflecting history. However, this precise argument is what some scholars would wish to frame in respect of other biblical texts as well—those very scholars who, when they proceed in this way, Davies accuses of producing a sanitized version of the biblical story, rather than doing "proper history."

If Davies thus falls on his own sword, and his own "firm ground" in the tradition turns out to be no such thing, then the path is clear for Whitelam. If Davies is reluctant to follow the logic of the positivist attitude to tradition through to its logical conclusion—perhaps because, without the biblical texts, we can no more write a worthwhile account of Israel in the Persian and Hellenistic periods than we can in the earlier period, and without such a history Davies has no foundation for the thesis argued in his book—Whitelam is not so reluctant. Davies, rather than say nothing, is quite prepared to engage in the kind of arbitrariness that we have seen is endemic to the history of the history of Israel. He starts from tradition where it suits him to do so. Whitelam is prepared to say nothing at all, at least nothing that has anything to do with the Israel of biblical tradition.

CAN THE PATIENT BE SAVED?

Now that we have a fuller understanding of the context in which the death of biblical history has been pronounced, we can perhaps more easily see how this pronouncement has come about. We have found ample evidence of a malaise in the "History of Israel" discipline that goes back some distance and has deep intellectual roots. Inconsistency and arbitrary starting points mark out this discipline. In one moment, biblical testimony about Israel's past is embraced as reflective in reality of that past. In the next, such testimony is rejected for the most unconvincing of reasons, which in some cases comes down to little more than prejudice. In one moment, extrabiblical evidence is apparently to be regarded as providing "knowledge" about the ancient past that is the solid rock upon which biblical claims founder. In the next, such evidence is marginalized and relativized, and the biblical version of events retained regardless of what other sources of evidence have to tell us. General agreement exists that, for critical scholarship, suspicion of tradition should be the starting point; that tradition cannot be given the benefit of the doubt where history is concerned. Yet, having adopted this principled stance of suspicion towards the tradition, none can agree with the other as to where suspicion should then be suspended and faith in the tradition reinvested. The stance is adopted in the first instance in the name of critical inquiry: the pursuit of "the facts." Yet critical inquiry itself raises questions about whether the suspension of suspicion that characteristically has followed shortly after its initiation has any rationally defensible grounds.

It is no doubt a deep-seated unease on this point that has led so many writers who take up a particular critical position on Israel's history to adopt not a defensive posture, but an aggressive one, the point of which appears to be to deflect questions about the critical credentials of the writer by suggesting that it is, in fact, others who are being uncritical. In criticizing Ewald, for example, J. H. Hayes (who himself accepts that "the Hebrew scriptures have been and remain the primary sources for reconstructing the history of Israel and Judah")[72] characterizes the nineteenth-century scholar's work as more of a historical commentary on the historical books than a history of Israel, since Ewald "basically adhered to the theological perspective of the biblical text while modifying the miraculous element."[73] Quite what is wrong with Ewald's approach is never made clear. Apparently he is simply rather more dependent upon biblical tradition than suits Hayes's taste. Soggin provides an even more striking example of the same approach. In objecting to W. W. Hallo's view that the history of Israel begins at the time of the exodus, he asserts that Hallo's attitude "can be understood in the context of a naive Sunday-school-like conception of the history of Israel by a writer who is not a biblical scholar."[74] Hallo's naïveté is apparent, Soggin claims, if we look at his proposal in the light of what he (Soggin) has said beforehand. One looks in vain on the preceding pages, however, for anything that truly demonstrates by way of argument that the sort of position Hallo adopts must be considered naïve. Hallo simply chooses a different starting point in the tradition from Soggin, and rather than taking the trouble to argue with him about this, Soggin adopts the easier course of insulting him.

Examples of this kind of discourse abound in histories of Israel that covet the label "critical." The entire modern history of the history of Israel can, in fact, be characterized as one in which scholars seeking to qualify as critics—as members of what has been called "the post-Enlightenment club of historical scholarship"[75]—have applied "scientific" methodology partially to the subject matter at hand, hoping to demonstrate in their jettisoning of this or that aspect of the tradition that they are worthy of inclusion. Denouncing others in a given group for not being true believers has always been an effective way of suggesting one's own commitment to the cause. Like the decisive moves that lie behind modern historiography itself, this tactic can be traced back at least as far as the French Revolution. As those who live by denunciation tend also to die by it, however, so scholars who have won their critical spurs in this way have in due course found themselves accused by still others of not being sufficiently critical—of naïveté (or, worse still, devotion) in respect of some aspects of the tradition. For one could always say that their arguments against the traditional material they chose *not* to use in composing their history applied equally to the material they *did* utilize, and thus, one could always claim that factors other than criticism were exercising undue influence upon them. Thus, by degrees, dependence on tradition has been purged from the collective, not so much through argument as through intellectual intimidation. Scholars have been denounced as naïve, or even as fundamentalist, not because they depend on the tradition *in the face of* other evidence, but simply because they depend on parts of the tradition disliked by the denouncer.[76] Coherent argument vanishes in the process; all that remains is ideological warfare.

That some who have accurately perceived aspects of the illness that has thus so long afflicted the discipline of biblical history, having last seen the invalid in a parlous state, should have prematurely pronounced it dead is unsurprising. The unedifying spectacle of scholars scrambling to outdo each other in pursuit of the critical holy grail—yet each, in the end, taking up positions indefensible from the point of view of the agreed rules of the critical game—is one from which many gentle souls might wish to turn their heads, assuming that death would quickly follow.

How Whitelam has arrived at his deadly conclusion is, then, easy to see. Equally clearly, any move toward a different conclusion cannot simply involve the kind of disputation with Whitelam that opened this chapter. Whitelam's own claim concerning the death of biblical history is made in the context of argumentation that appears to be just as problematic as that of the predecessors we have just described, yet showing that biblical history is alive and well requires more than simply establishing that fact. It must involve, rather, a discussion of all the fundamental issues of epistemology and of procedure that we have raised throughout this chapter in relation to what is commonly referred to as "critical method." Which conclusions may truly be drawn from the fact that our biblical traditions are artistically constructed and ideologically shaped entities that are perhaps distanced in time from the past they apparently seek to describe? What in reality is the role that extrabiblical data, including archaeological data, can or should have in the reconstruction of the history of Israel? How should the relationship between biblical and extrabiblical testimony be regarded? What role does or should the ideology of the historian play in such reconstruction, and what should be the relationship between ideology and evidence? Is historiography a science or an art? Questions such as these must be addressed if we are to form any judgment on whether biblical history is alive or dead. They are basic questions, tied up in large measure with the fundamental question of how we know things about the past at all. However, if our discussion to this point has shown anything, it is that, if any rescue of the patient is to be attempted, mere bandages of the sort sometimes applied in the past will not do. We must engage in extensive surgery to move right to the roots of the problem. We attempt in the succeeding chapters, therefore, something for which "critical scholars," who have shown themselves generally well able to criticize the tradition and each other, have often not demonstrated a great capacity: criticism of their own governing assumptions. We shall in the process reflect on what critical thinking really is, and what it is not.

We begin in chapters 2 and 3 with some fresh reflection on epistemology, focusing on the centrality to knowledge of trust in the testimony of others. A fundamental justification of the use of biblical texts as primary sources for the history of Israel is offered here, in the context of a discussion of the nature of our extrabiblical sources of information. Chapter 4 offers a more detailed exploration of the nature of our biblical texts as narrative (as art, history, and theology) and the implications of this for their use as sources for Israel's history. We are then in a position in chapter 5 to offer a more precise description of the kind of history that we are (and are not) attempting in this book, in comparison and contrast to previous histories of Israel. We are in a position to justify a renewed attempt to write a "biblical history of Israel"—a project that we undertake in the hope, not only of saving the patient, but of restoring her to a more vibrant state of health than she has known for some time.

Chapter 2

Knowing and Believing:
Faith in the Past

There is no more "ancient Israel." History no longer has room for it. This we do know. And now, as one of the first conclusions of this new knowledge, "biblical Israel" was in its origin a Jewish concept.[1]

T. L. Thompson's strong and confident assertion of knowledge represents a helpful starting point for our discussion of the issues of epistemology that must be addressed in this chapter and chapter 3. The claim is that we "know" a considerable amount about something rather solid called "history," and that this knowledge of history means that we cannot any longer believe in "ancient Israel." There are no "gaps" left in the historical record into which we can fit the ancient Israel about which scholars (in considerable dependence on the Old Testament) have hitherto been writing. This claim is fundamental to some recent historiography on Israel, and any renewed attempt to write a biblical history of Israel must address it directly. How has Thompson arrived at the "knowledge" of "history" that allows him to make his bold claim? What sort of entity is this "knowledge"? How do we know what we claim to know about the reality of the past at all?

As we have already seen in chapter 1, a general tendency in modern times when answering this question has been to downplay the importance of *testimony* about the past which has come down to us via a chain of human carriers of tradition, and in contrast, to emphasize the importance of empirical research in leading us into knowledge. We proceed from the "facts" that we can establish to some larger hypothesis about the past that can be constructed upon this empirical foundation. Thompson himself exemplifies this approach to historical reality. Now, however, is the place to advance an alternative view of this matter of "knowing" about the past, which we spend the remainder of the chapter and all of the next exploring and defending, particularly in relation to the history of Israel. Our view can be expressed as follows.

We know about the past, to the extent that we know about it at all, *primarily* through the testimony of others. Testimony lies at the very heart of our access to the past. We have the testimony of people(s) from the past about their own past, communicated in oral and written forms. There is the testimony of people(s) from the past about the past of other peoples, also communicated in oral and written forms. Then, too, figures from the *present* offer testimony about the past, whether the past of their own peoples or of others. In this last group are contemporary figures like archaeologists, who make certain claims about what they have found and what it means in respect of what has previously taken place. *Testimony* gives us access to the past, to the extent that anything does. All historiography involves such testimony. Even if I am the person who digs up an artifact from the Palestinian soil, I am still entirely dependent upon the testimony of others who have gone before me when I try to make sense of its significance—when I try to decide how I shall add my testimony to theirs.

Testimony—we might also refer to it as "storytelling"—is central to our quest to know the past; therefore, *interpretation* is unavoidable as well. All testimony about the past is also interpretation of the past. Testimony has its ideology or theology; it has its presuppositions and its point of view; it has its narrative structure; and (if at all interesting to read or listen to) it has its narrative art, its rhetoric. We cannot avoid testimony, and we cannot avoid interpretation. We also cannot avoid faith. We began this section by using the language of "knowledge": how do we know what we claim to know about the past? In truth, however, this question is a concession to the view of what historians are doing from which this chapter wishes to distance itself. What is commonly referred to as "*knowledge of the past*" is more accurately described as "*faith in the testimony*," in the interpretations of the past, offered by other people. We consider the gathered testimonies at our disposal; we reflect on the various interpretations offered; and we decide in various ways and to various extents to invest faith in these—to make these testimonies and interpretations our own, because we consider them trustworthy. If our level of trust is very strong, or we are simply not conscious of what we are in fact doing, then we tend to call our faith "knowledge"; but this term is dangerous to use, since it too easily leads us into self-delusion, or deludes others who listen to us or read what we write, as to the truth of the matter. This delusion seems to lie at the heart of the problem with much of our modern writing on the history of Israel. In particular, it is this delusion (among other things) that has led many historians of Israel, in common with many of their colleagues elsewhere in the discipline of history, to make the false move of sharply differentiating in principle between dependence upon tradition and dependence upon "scientifically established" facts.

In essence, then, we dispute the accuracy of the description of reality that modern historians (including historians of Israel) commonly advance when they claim to describe how we "know" what we claim to know about the past. The implications of what we claim as our own more accurate description of reality, which asserts that we "know" by listening to testimony and interpretation, and by making choices about whom to believe, shall become clear.

"SCIENTIFIC HISTORY" REVISITED

Beginning our exploration of epistemology (the technical term for the study of the grounds of knowledge) and history with some reflection on science itself is only appropriate, given that the scientific model has so influenced the development of historiography since the Enlightenment. This reflection will then lead on naturally to a critical review of the idea of "scientific history."

Science and the Philosophy of Science

We described in chapter 1 the way in which the developing Newtonian science of the Enlightenment and post-Enlightenment eras came to provide the common model for understanding not only present and future human existence, but past human existence as well. Historiography came to be widely understood, on the analogy of the natural sciences in relation to the natural world, as the attempt to discover exactly what historical reality was like. Science itself has continued, however, to develop. The firm hope of previous generations of thinkers that science would soon reveal "the true order of things" has been disappointed. As it turns out, the deeper scientists have penetrated into reality, the less understandable it has become; and doubts have arisen about our ability ever to find out "what exactly reality is like." These doubts arise in part because of the inevitable involvement of the observer of the natural world in the very act of observing.

We understand more clearly than many of our predecessors how what is perceived in the so-called "real" world is inevitably connected with the knowledge, prejudices, and ideologies that the perceiving person brings with him or her. We understand also how the myth of "the neutral, uninvolved observer" has functioned and continues to function as an ideological tool in the hands of those whose political and economic interests it has served. The "objective" spectator of classical Newtonian physics has thus become the "impossible" spectator of the newer physics, and scientists are becoming much more aware (as a result of the work of philosophers of science)[2] of the ways in which the great broad theories of science are underdetermined by the facts. They have become aware, too, of how experiments themselves are, from the moment of their conception, shaped by the theories of the people conducting them. Scientific theories come and go, argue the philosophers and sociologists of knowledge, partly on the basis of their success in prediction and control of the environment, but partly also on the basis of the interests which they serve in a particular culture, whether theological and metaphysical, sociological or simply aesthetic. Scientists cannot, any more than other human beings, escape from this matter of "interests." Value-free academic endeavor does not exist.

The Newtonian scientific model, then, is an inadequate account of reality even in terms of the natural world and of human inquiry into that world. As twentieth-century science itself suggested, we live in a much less rigid and more complex world than was previously suspected: multistructured, far from any simple materialism, and mysterious. What the "facts" are about this world, as a totality, is impossible for science (as science) to say. Science can, at a practical level, tell us much about how things normally work in the natural world, insofar as the world does demonstrably possess predictable, mechanistic aspects that can be revealed through experimentation leading to reproducible results. Even in so far as science succeeds in this demonstration, however, it must of necessity operate within the larger context of what is taken to be valid human knowledge—albeit that this knowledge itself cannot be established "scientifically." The grounding belief of modern science itself falls into this category; that the universe as a whole is rational and intelligible is a presupposition, not a scientific finding. Clearly, too, science of itself cannot properly tell us what to do with its findings. The ends to which science provides the means must be (and always are) chosen according to what is believed and valued by the people doing the choosing, which is a matter of religion, ethics, and politics, not a matter of science as such. Science does not and cannot fill the realm of valid knowledge. On the contrary, the very way in which people do science, and what they do with it, depends on ideas or beliefs derived from a larger reality than science embraces.

If the Newtonian scientific model is an inadequate account of reality even in terms of the *natural* world and human inquiry into it, however, then we must clearly return to consider whether this model can helpfully be applied to inquiry into the world of the *human past.* Here we pick up the threads of the history of historiography that we began in the previous chapter; for as we explore that history further, we find that not every historian in the nineteenth and twentieth centuries embraced the "scientific" view of history that is described there. Some of those who have resisted the temptation will help us to gain clarity on the matter for ourselves.

History as Science: A Brief History of Dissent

In the previous chapter, we identified the period of the French Revolution as a decisive one for the development of modern historiography. This particular period of radical social and political change in France, with its lasting repercussions throughout Europe, can be considered in some measure responsible in the nineteenth century for the triumph of historiography over philosophy as the crucial interpretative discipline in respect of human reality. Philosophy as it had been, with its emphasis on static and eternal essences, did not appear capable of the explanatory task in a period of notable change and development. It is important to note, however, that it was also the French Revolution itself, and its aftermath, which confirmed in some minds the folly of abandoning tradition entirely in favor of reason. F. R. de Chateaubriand argued that all attempts to change conditions radically and quickly, as in the French Revolution, must fail because they are based on the illusion of human control over unknown forces that are subject only to divine providence. "The French past illustrated how the true, the gradually changing, and the lawful always prevailed over all sudden and violent changes . . . the cultivation of rationality in isolation from emotion and imagination . . . destroyed a civilization by eroding age-old tradition."[3] E. Burke argued similarly that a good society was shaped by tradition and attempts to employ weak reason and will in place of this traditional wisdom could only result in anarchy, which could not be put right once tradition has been destroyed. These two thinkers represent a more positive view of tradition than some of the others we have encountered to this point. Burke and de Chateaubriand hold a less affirming view of a scientific approach to reality that remakes reality *de novo* by means of appropriate scientific method. They form a suitable starting-point, therefore, for our analysis here, in that they remind us that, even in an age of science, nothing was historically or intellectually inevitable about the adoption of an all-embracing scientific approach to human reality in general. Keeping this point in mind is important, since the rhetoric of modern scientific historians is often designed to make us forget it. However, we pick up the threads of our story at the turn not of the eighteenth and nineteenth centuries, but of the nineteenth and twentieth centuries. In particular we are interested in three German thinkers: J. G. Droysen, W. Dilthey, and W. Windelband.

Droysen, well aware of the increasing prestige of the natural sciences and of the challenge that positivism represented to the Rankean historiographical tradition, was driven as a result to fresh reflection on the methodology of the discipline of history. The result was not only a rejection of positivism, but also a critique of Ranke's historical school. He denied the Rankean idea of what historians do—that is, that they retrieve the remains of the past, mostly documents; critically assess them; and synthesize the parts through empathetic intuition into a whole that reflects a transcendent reality. On this view historians stood apart from ongoing life, re-creating in methodological purity what was taken to be objective past reality. Droysen, conversely, understood all historical work as resulting from the encounters of the historian, whose own life was shaped by elements of the past, with that past. "From such encounters came a creative and critically controlled recreation of the past, clearly from the standpoint of the present."[4] A reconstruction that assumed a static past, testified to by its remains, was possible neither by Rankean nor positivistic method. Indeed, the positivists compounded the error of objectivism with the error of transforming all aspects of reality, including intellect and morality, into natural phenomena. Such things could not be submerged in nature, according to Droysen, as if all belonged in one sphere of life.

Dilthey also "rejected the attempts to see the world of human phenomena as an analogue to the world of atoms and mechanical forces and to separate strictly the subject and object in all research"[5] along Cartesian lines. He found elements in the human realm—intentions, purposes, and ends, and the actions guided by them—that were absent in nature and that rendered human reality too complex to grasp by a counting and measuring which resulted in the finding of regularities and the formulation of laws. Historians could only grasp this complexity through *Verstehen* (entering empathetically into the motives and intentions of actors in the past).

Windelband similarly distinguished between two kinds of analysis of reality: nomothetic analysis, which aims at general insights (and is typical for the natural sciences) and idiographic analysis, which attempts to understand the unique, individual event (typical for the humanities). He argued that the idiographic could make use of the nomothetic as a helpful tool without surrendering to its generalizing aim.

In these three thinkers, we find in different ways an unhappiness with the notion of scientific history, connected in part with the false objectivism of such an approach to the past and in part with the implausible reductionism that seeks to explain all reality in terms of a mechanistic model of the universe, and which especially gives no place to the individual and the unique. They have not been lone voices as the decades of the twentieth century have passed. B. Croce, for example, saw human life as an ever-creative process in which the historian fully participates, striving for impartiality while never able to be objective. The historian's task is not the collection and critical assessment of sources, as facts on which to build an interpretation (as in Ranke) or general laws (as in positivism). It is the incorporation of a living past into the present. C. Becker expressed skepticism about the possibility of capturing the real past, noting that historians can only deal with statements about events, not with the events themselves, which they do not observe. Early philosophical neopositivists were themselves apt to draw attention to the pseudo-empiricism of scientific historians in these terms, since these philosophers recognized only statements based upon direct observation as having the status of hypotheses. Statements that were not accessible to proper verification were declared meaningless, leading some to wonder "whether we have sufficient ground for accepting any statement at all about the past, whether we are even justified in our belief that there has been a past."[6] C. Beard affirmed more optimistically (having abandoned an earlier conviction that history should be a science in the positivist manner) that the past could be "grasped" as an external object, yet that "the subject matter of history is so charged with values that historians themselves cannot avoid making judgments when they select and arrange facts for their accounts."[7] He wrote of the historian's "act of faith" in determining the meaning of history, since every historian has to choose nonobjectively and nonscientifically whether history is simply chaotic, moves in a cycle, or moves in some linear direction. Finally in this brief list of examples, the philosopher H.-G. Gadamer distinguished the conventional approach to the past through sources, with objective knowledge as its goal, from *Verstehen*, involving a sympathetic acceptance of tradition by the historian.

We could extend much further this list of thinkers who, while certainly not all agreeing with each other in their overall perspective, have at least qualified the idea that history is a science in the old sense of that term—even if we were to grant that the older model of science is an adequate one for the study of the natural world. The fact is that an ongoing debate among philosophers and historians has taken place since the turn of the twentieth century about the nature of history as a discipline. Widespread unease exists with regard to the positivist-empiricist model, as does resistance, in particular, to the assimilation of history into the social sciences. The focus for the defense of history as an autonomous discipline has been a rejection of the generalizing tendencies of science and a historicist insistence upon the importance of grasping the separate eras and moments of the past in all their nonreducible uniqueness. At the same time, awareness has increased that even to think of history as a science in the more limited Rankean sense is far from unproblematic, precisely because of doubts about the historian's ability to see things "as they really were." Widely accepted is the notion that in history, if not in science, the subject does not observe a clearly defined object (i.e., historical reality), but rather an object that is at least partially constructed in the process of observing. As the twentieth century came towards its end, indeed, and as we have moved into what many refer to as the postmodern era, the emphasis upon the historian's *construction* of the past has increased. Scholars now abound who deny that the one object, the past, exists for the historian to discover. Historians (it is said) *construct*, rather than *discover*, the past. They narrate a story about it. Indeed, whereas older philosophers of history who favored the scientific model worried about the narrative form of much historiography because narrative statement remains art and not science, more recent contributors to the debate have moved in the opposite direction, questioning any strict distinction between history and story.

We may with confidence say, then, that the whole movement of the last century was in general a movement away from the notion that history is a science and back towards the notion that history is an art. To be entirely accurate, in fact—and drawing in our comments above on science itself—we should say that the idea that history is a science in the nineteenth-century sense, already questioned by some in the nineteenth and early twentieth centuries for reasons unrelated to what was happening in the philosophy of science, has come under increasing pressure as the nature of science itself has further been clarified. As one set of authors recently put the matter, "In the nineteenth-century sense, there is no scientific history, nor is there even scientific science."[8] Moreover, an earlier author had already written, "Even the most casual reader of the *American Historical Review* . . . realizes that the scientific historian with his definitive picture of what really happened is an extinct breed."[9]

The hope of notable nineteenth-century historians and their successors—that by embracing an empirical and critical approach to historical knowledge they might achieve a purely objective reconstruction of the past, whether in the Rankean or the positivist manner—has thus turned out to be an impossible dream. To the extent that historians have believed that they have achieved this result, with the benefit of hindsight we can now see that they have been sadly self-deluded. Even while embracing science in place of philosophy as the foundational method for human endeavor, and setting their hearts on discovering "the way it really was" rather than accepting traditional accounts of the way things were, they have been entirely unable to escape the influence of philosophy and tradition when articulating their own vision of the past. They have each possessed their own pre-suppositions about the nature of reality in general and of historical reality in par-ticular—their own story about the world of the past, present, and future. Although not deriving this story from historical research itself, they have nevertheless brought it to bear on the "facts" of the past in an attempt to explain them coher-ently. In establishing what these "facts" are, moreover, these historians have been dependent to a greater or lesser extent upon the stories of other people about the past, since they have themselves lacked any independent access to the events of the past and have been unable to "reproduce" them in experiments. That is, they have been unable to proceed as natural scientists are often able to do when attempting to verify for themselves the truth of certain claims about reality. Philosophy and tradition in fact underlie all historiography of the nineteenth-century scientific kind, no matter what may be the rhetoric to the contrary. It is important to grasp that this is not simply because of some deficiency in practice rather than in the-ory. It is, rather, *inevitably* the case. Philosophy and tradition necessarily set the parameters for all thinking about the world with which human beings engage.

TESTIMONY, TRADITION, AND THE PAST

To this collapse of the nineteenth-century historiographical model, three possible responses can be made. The first is the response of the intellectual ostrich: to place one's head firmly in the sand and to deny reality. One is tempted to describe much recent writing on the history of Israel as ostrichlike in this way, in that it stead-fastly continues, on the whole, to regard scientific history in either the Rankean manner, or more recently the positivist manner, as the only proper kind of acad-emic history. Ostriches are at least aware of the reality that they deny, however; as we shall see, many historians of Israel may have simply been unaware of the wider developments in science and history that we have been describing to this point. These kinds of developments have not in fact impinged *generally* on the world that is inhabited intellectually by scholars in *various* disciplines, who continue to cling to the popular mechanistic and reductionist outlook on the world that the suc-cesses of early modern science engendered. Perhaps only when the blessings of modern science, and its offspring modern technology, are more widely perceived as mixed will attachment to this worldview diminish. Be that as it may, the ostrich approach is not one that will appeal to those genuinely interested in what is true.

The second response we may characterize as postmodern. Convinced that sci-entific history is impossible—and, further, that the great stories about reality that have been depended upon to make sense of historical reality[10] are simply creations of the human mind—postmodernists are apt simply to deny either the *existence* of a given past or at least any *access* on our part to it. History writing as such is, therefore, impossible. This postmodern response to "modernist" scientific history represents an extreme reaction to it, overemphasizing the subjectivity of historiography just as much as modernism overemphasized its objectivity.[11] This response flies in the face of common sense just as much as did the theses of logical positivists about external reality, whether historical or present reality, in the earlier part of the twentieth century. We cannot but believe that a past did take place, even if we cannot (in their terms) justify our belief and even if we now know that speaking about it is a somewhat more complex business than hitherto suspected. We know that we may partially *construct* reality that is external to us, whether present or past; we also know that reality is "out there" and independent of us. Indeed, speaking about the past as a reality that is external to us is a human necessity. A postmodernist view of history is thus a view that cannot ultimately be held with intellectual and moral integrity. It is the last, desperate refuge of those who have come to see the impossibility of modernist scientific history, but cannot bring themselves to accept the true implications of their discovery.

The third possible response to the collapse of the nineteenth-century scientific historiographical model, our response in this volume, embraces these same implications in preference to avoiding them. The respondents in this case interpret the crisis with regard to the scientific model of historiography—and indeed the self-defeating postmodernist response to this crisis—as an invitation to revisit some fundamental questions about epistemology. We agree with postmodern analyses which claim that the nineteenth-century perception of progress in historiography was, to a large extent, self-delusion. The modernist suggestion that all previous historiography was fatally flawed because it had not been produced by those who possessed proper scientific methods but was produced, rather, by those who were in thrall to philosophy and tradition—made by historians who were and are themselves just as bound by philosophy and tradition—cannot be taken seriously. Such a claim is merely rhetoric in pursuit of the validation of one's own particular view of the past.

Yet the proper response to this fact is not subjectivism. It is no rational rejoinder to the failure of modern historiography to construct a past that is independent of philosophy and tradition, to claim that *nothing that is not already in our heads can be known about the past*. A more coherent response—rather than offering facile statements that simplistically oppose philosophy and tradition to "scientific method" as routes to historical knowledge—is to seek to articulate a view of the historiographical task that gives a proper place to philosophy and tradition. This inevitably involves questioning the rationality of the principled suspicion of tradition, and ultimately (if not initially) of philosophy, that lies at the heart of Enlightenment thought about the past. Thus, having cleared some ground with regard to questions of science and history, we return to our opening description of the nature of our "knowledge" of the past.

Testimony and Knowledge

The wise author of nature hath planted in the human mind a propensity to rely upon human testimony before we can give a reason for doing so. This, indeed, puts our judgment almost entirely in the power of those who are about us in the first period of life; but this is necessary both to our preservation and to our improvement. If children were so framed as to pay no regard to testimony or authority, they must, in the literal sense, perish for lack of knowledge. I believed by instinct whatever they [my "parents and tutors"] told me, long before I had the idea of a lie, or a thought of the possibility of their deceiving me. Afterwards, upon reflection, I found they had acted like fair and honest people, who wished me well. I found that, if I had not believed what they told me, before I could give a reason for my belief, I had to this day been little better than a changeling. And although this natural credulity hath sometimes occasioned my being imposed upon by deceivers, yet it hath been of infinite advantage to me upon the whole; therefore, I consider it as another good gift of Nature.[12]

In seeking to capture more accurately than "scientific historians" the reality of the process by which we gain knowledge of the past, we set testimony at the heart of the enterprise. In doing so, we consciously take our stand against an intellectual tradition, reaching at least as far back as Plato and certainly underlying the scientific view of the world that we have been discussing, which marginalizes testimony as a source of knowledge about reality in favor of such things as perception. We propose, rather, that reliance on testimony is fundamental to knowing about reality in general—*as fundamental* as perception, memory, inference, and so on. We depend upon it extensively, not only in everyday life (for example, when as tourists we rely on a map to guide us around a foreign city), but also in areas like legal process or scientific endeavor (as when psychologists rely on the testimony of subjects about their perception of reality, or scientists more generally rely on the testimony of colleagues about their research results). We are, in short, intellectually reliant upon what others tell us when it comes to what we call knowledge. This statement simply represents the fact of the matter, whether we like it or not and however much we are aware that the testimony of others may sometimes be untrustworthy. Admittedly the facts of the matter have not been readily *perceived* as such since the Enlightenment, which requires some explanation. An explanation lies readily at hand, however, in the dominance of individualist ideology in the modern period—an ideology articulated by Descartes himself, with his emphasis on the centrality of the individual as the knowing subject, dependent upon reason alone rather than upon the knowledge provided by such things as education. This individualist ideology has often prevented modern thinkers from describing accurately how they acquire knowledge, even as they are plainly doing so in dependence upon others (including their educators).

In the same way that reliance on testimony is fundamental to knowing about reality in general, so it is also fundamental to knowing about historical reality in particular. We depend here primarily on the testimony of people who lived in the past. As R. G. Collingwood once put it (albeit only to take issue with the statement), "history is . . . the believing of someone else when he says that he remembers something. The believer is the historian; the person believed is called his authority."[13] Collingwood himself stands firmly in the tradition of scientific (though not positivist) history, setting his face against both ancient/medieval and seventeenth- and eighteenth-century historiography precisely because the earlier historians were so thoroughly dependent on testimony—even if they exercised some judgment in selecting, editing, and sometimes rejecting material—and thus were not properly scientific historians. On this view, proper (i.e., scientific) history does not depend on testimony at all. In fact, to depend on testimony is to give up one's intellectual autonomy as a scientist—to give up "the condition of being one's own authority, making statements or taking action on one's own initiative and not because those statements or actions are authorized or prescribed by anyone else."

One could hardly ask for a better example of individualist ideology. Collingwood clearly thinks, at least in one part of his mind, that history "as a science" requires that the historian as an individual must somehow do everything for himself. The consequence of this must inevitably be (if his position is taken entirely seriously) that the "scientific" historian will not write history, but rather a fantasy spun out of his own theorizing imagination. Because Collingwood aspires to write history, however, he is constantly to be found retreating from what is apparently his theoretical position on testimony and depending upon testimony (that is, an "authority") to provide the basic material for his own imaginative reenactments of the past. The situation could not be otherwise, even in the case of a historian who seems to wish that it could be. History, it turns out, is indeed, *fundamentally*, "the believing of someone else when that person says that he remembers something"; or to put it more accurately, history is the openness to acceptance of accounts from the past that enshrine such people's memories.

Of course, the past has left traces of itself besides such testimony, most notably materials that an archaeologist can examine: coins, pots, the remains of dwellings, and the like. In the modern period of historiography, some observers (those bewitched by the prestige of the sciences and anxious to ground historical statements in something more solid than testimony) have assumed that such archaeological remains offer us the prospect of independent access to the past. Here, after all, are data that are directly observable and upon which scientific testing can be carried out, akin to the data available to the natural scientists.

Yet we maintain, in our description of the acquisition of historical knowledge, that the assumption is false. Archaeological remains (when this phrase is taken to exclude written testimony from the past) are of themselves mute. They do not speak for themselves, they have no story to tell and no truth to communicate. It is archaeologists who speak about them, testifying to what that they have found and placing the finds within an interpretive framework that bestows upon them meaning and significance. This interpretative framework is certainly not entirely, or even mainly, derived from the finds themselves, which are mere fragments of the past that must somehow be organized into a coherent whole. The framework is, in fact, derived largely from testimony, whether the testimony of people from the distant past who have written about the past, or the testimony of other, more recent inquirers into that past who have gone before and were themselves dependent upon testimony from the distant past. It is this testimony that enables the archaeologist even to begin to *think* about intelligent excavation. It is this testimony that helps in the choice of where to survey or dig, imparts the sense of the general shape of the history one might expect to find in any given place, enables a tentative allocation of destruction levels related to specific, already-known events, and permits material finds to be correlated with certain named peoples of the past. The "filling out" of the picture of the world that is thus produced is itself much more general than specific. The reason is that literary remains are much more useful where specific historical issues are to the fore; nonliterary artifactual remains are most useful to the person interested in general material culture and everyday life.

The whole business of correlating archaeological finds with the specifics of the past as described by texts is, in fact, fraught with difficulty. Interpretation inevitably abounds as to what has in fact been found. Is this destruction layer to be associated with this or that military campaign?[14] Is this site in fact the site of the city mentioned in that particular text?[15] Leaving aside specific sites, the data collected even in large-scale regional surveys represent a highly selective sampling at best, and these data are open to a range of interpretations. Interpretation also abounds as to what has *not* been found, because the absence of evidence on the ground for events described by a text cannot necessarily be interpreted as evidence of the absence of those events, even if a site has been correctly identified.[16] The archaeologist interprets data in the context of testimony, adding his or her own suggestions to the mix about what has been discovered—one's own nuance to the story of the past that is history. As one author has put this so well:

> Data derived from archaeological artifacts exist only in linguistic form. Being elements of a linguistic structure, however, they are subject to an interpretation as well. The description of archaeological findings is already interpretation and it is subject, like any other literary form of expression, to the singular choice of the narrative procedure, to the concept of explanation, as well as to the value-orientation of the descriptive archaeologist.[17]

No "objective knowledge" is available here, independent of testimony about the past. As Wright has correctly said, "archaeology, dealing with the wreckage of antiquity, proves nothing in itself."[18] Making sense of the fragmentary traces of the past is only possible, rather, when testimony about the past has already been embraced; in fact, suggestions about this "sense" only confront the majority of us, who did not witness the archaeological discoveries and were not involved in the process of interpretation, as testimony. Whatever the value of archaeology, then, in filling out our picture of the past, history is *fundamentally* openness to acceptance of accounts from the past that enshrine other people's memories.

As we have noted (and as the quote from the philosopher Thomas Reid at the head of this section underlines), as a matter of fact the testimony of others naturally may sometimes be untrustworthy. Maps may mislead; subjects may fail to tell the truth to psychologists; scientists (including archaeologists) may fake their research results or simply produce poor interpretations of the data; witnesses at a trial may commit perjury; and the bearers of tradition may distort the past, whether by accident or design. Clearly, among the tools that individuals bring to the task of comprehending reality, critical thinking must be among the foremost. We are by no means advocating, in insisting on the inevitability of our reliance on testimony, a *blind faith* in testimony, whether it concerns present or past reality. Given the mixed nature of testimony, this approach would be far from rational. Some *kind* of autonomy in respect of testimony, of the sort after which Collingwood is grasping, is clearly necessary if the individual is to have any possibility of differentiating falsehood from truth. Yet just as autonomous agency in normal adult life does not necessitate the renunciation of dependence on others, so autonomous *thinking* is entirely compatible with fundamental reliance on the word of others as a path to knowledge. We need only conceive of critical thought, not as the enterprise of working everything out for ourselves from first principles, but as the open-minded but deliberate exercise of controlling intelligence over the testimony that we receive, so that such judgments as we feel able to make about its truth or falsehood are indeed made. Neither blind faith in testimony, nor radical suspicion in response to it, is necessary. We require merely what we would characterize as "epistemological openness."

Most of us characteristically adopt this approach to testimony in regard to everyday reality. We do not characteristically and as a matter of principle bring suspicion to bear on the testimony of others, demanding of each and every person that they validate their testimony to us before we accept its veracity. In fact, we generally regard it as a sign of emotional or mental imbalance if people ordinarily inhabit a culture of distrust in testimony at the level of principle, and most of us outside mental institutions do not inhabit such a universe. Suspicion, we know, may sometimes be justified. Yet we recognize that healthy people generally place trust in the testimony of others, reserving suspicion for those who have given grounds for it. In everyday life, then, the exercise of a thoroughgoing "hermeneutic of suspicion" with regard to testimony is considered no more sensible than the exercise of blind faith in terms of our apprehension of reality in general. Nor should either approach be considered sensible in terms of our apprehension of *past* reality in particular.

In making judgments about testimony in respect of present reality, moreover, we do not characteristically view the adoption of a "method" as a rational course of action. For example, we do not always (as a matter of "method")—if we are intelligent, critical people—invest faith in eyewitnesses as opposed to those people who testify to us secondarily, nor vice versa. More generally, if we characteristically believe the testimony of one sort of person rather than another—for example, if we are Caucasians and consistently accept "insider" accounts of reality offered by Caucasians over against "outsider" accounts such as those offered by Asians—then we are considered prejudiced, not intelligent. Reality, we recognize, is more complex than method allows. We do not, therefore—if we are intelligent, critical people—allow method overly to influence us in seeking to apprehend reality; or rather, we try to ensure that whatever method we might embrace is sufficiently nuanced and complex that it allows for nuance and complexity in the world outside our heads.

Why, then, should it be commonly believed that "scientific method" can in some way help us to distinguish between testimonies about the past in terms of their likely truthfulness? The idea goes at least as far back as Ranke himself, who proposed that texts produced in the course of events as they were happening are more worthy of the historian's attention than texts produced afterwards. Priority is thus to be given in scientific historiography to what are called primary over against secondary and later sources. However, we have no good reason to assume in advance that so-called "primary" sources are going to be more reliable than any others. The assumption has quite a bit to do with the naïve belief that eyewitnesses "tell it like it is," while others inevitably filter reality through various distorting screens. As in art, however, so it is in history: close proximity to subject and canvas by no means guarantees a more "accurate" portrait (since the painter sometimes gets lost among the proverbial trees, and loses sight of the overall shape of the forest). On the one hand, eyewitnesses, like everyone else, have a point of view, and in the process of testifying they must inevitably simplify, select, and interpret. On the other hand, people who secondarily pass testimony along, whether oral or written, may do this not only accurately but also intelligently and with a better sense than the eyewitness of the way in which a particular testimony fits the larger picture.[19] We must exercise our judgment on a case-by-case basis. Method will not help us, whether in the Rankean mold or—more absurdly—the mold of those who have brought mathematical probability theory to bear on testimony in an attempt to attain greater scientific certainty as to its truthfulness.[20]

The History of Historiography Reconsidered

Testimony—"storytelling"—is central to our quest to know the past. In fact, all historiography is story, whether ancient, medieval, or modern. Historiography is ideological narrative about the past that involves, among other things, the selection of material and its interpretation by authors who are intent on persuading themselves or their readership of certain truths about the past. This selection and interpretation is always made by people with a particular perspective on the world—a particular set of presuppositions and beliefs that do not derive from the facts of history with which they are working, but are already in existence before the narration begins. All historiography is like this, whether we are thinking of the ancient Greek Thucydides or the mediaeval English Bede; or of the modern Gibbon, Macaulay, Michelet, or Marx;[21] or indeed of T. L. Thompson, with whom we began this chapter. All knowledge of the past is in fact more accurately described as faith in the interpretations of the past offered by others, through which we make these interpretations (in part or as a whole) our own. "Acts of faith" do not simply have to be made at the level of our presuppositions about history—whether history is chaotic, cyclical, or moving in a linear way towards a designated end; whether history can be explained in terms of simple cause-and-effect relationships or not; and so on. They are intrinsic to the very process of coming to "know" *particular* things about the past as well.

This situation is just the way things are, we claim, as a matter of fact and regardless of the attempts of rhetoricians to persuade us otherwise, and this claim brings us to the conclusion of this section and to the end of our review of the history of historiography in general. The rhetoricians whom we mainly have in mind are those same scientific historians of the nineteenth and twentieth centuries with whom we take issue in these opening chapters, and who have sought to persuade the rest of us to adopt a view of reality that is, upon inspection, deeply implausible. In their world, the history of historiography is one of progress from darkness into light: The Greeks laid the foundations of science and history and kindled the torch of intellectual freedom, but the onward march of humankind towards truth was halted in medieval times by barbarism and religion. The Renaissance rekindled the torch, which became a blazing beacon in the nineteenth century when scientific historiography was born, providing us with "the method" that for the first time enabled us to speak the truth about the past.

The narrative, while stirring, has little relationship to the truth. No generalized distinction of this kind between the historiography that precedes the nineteenth century and the historiography since that time can plausibly be defended. Modern historians, like their precursors, in fact depend on testimony, interpret the past, and possess just as much faith as their precursors, whether religious or not. But also, ancient, medieval, and post-Reformation historians as a group were no less concerned than their modern counterparts with differentiating historical truth from falsehood, as even a passing acquaintance with their work demonstrates.[22] Critical thought did not begin in the nineteenth century, but was to be found throughout the preceding centuries happily coexisting with faith about the nature of the world (religious and otherwise) and in the midst of much that was truly barbaric. Critical thought has continued to coexist since the nineteenth century and down to the present with all kinds of faith about the nature of the world (religious and otherwise) and in the midst of even greater barbarism. Such critical thinking was not always found in the earlier periods of historiography, certainly; but then, it has not always been found in the modern period either, even (and perhaps especially) among many of those who have claimed to employ it. The claim to be a critical thinker is easy to make; the reality that lurks beneath it has all too often proved to be only a mixture of blind faith in relation to the writer's own intellectual tradition and arbitrary, selective skepticism in relation to everything else.

Chapter 3

Knowing about the History of Israel

In essence, what we commonly refer to as historical knowledge is only a more fragile form of our knowledge of friends, family, institutions, and so on in the present. We are easily led, and so easily mistaken. On the other hand, more often than not, about friends and family, we are right (if we are not insane). Most of us live complacently with uncertainty as to how friends and even drivers of automobiles will behave or react at this or that time, because we have to. A similar level of uncertainty attaches to how we reconstruct history. Why some scholars expect to be as certain about the human past as about the human present, when in both instances we are concerned with humans, is puzzling at best.[1]

As we now return to reflect, in the broader historical and philosophical context provided by chapter 2, on the history of the history of Israel as we began to outline it in chapter 1, we should understand just what kind of history of Israel has increasingly dominated the scene in the past two hundred years: scientific history. Historians of Israel, no less than other historians, have felt the pressure to conform their work to the scientific model. They have progressively done so, abandoning biblical testimony in favor of the "knowledge" that scientific inquiry produces, until we have arrived at claims like Thompson's: "There is no more 'ancient Israel' . . . This we do know"[2]—an affirmation of "certainty" if ever there was one. It is clear that many scholars who work with the Old Testament and are interested in the history of Israel are deeply uneasy about this kind of radical claim and would like to avoid having to agree with it. That they can do so with any logical consistency, however, is not so clear. They have often and in large measure already embraced a Thompson-like approach to the relative worth of testimony and empirical inquiry *in general*. They therefore already feel the need to justify the acceptance, rather than justify the rejection, of biblical testimony *in particular*. Modern biblical study was indeed forged in the fires of the nineteenth-century scientific worldview, which is why the Enlightenment myth of "progress ever-onwards-and-upwards until truth and goodness are attained" so often finds expression in its writings. Not surprisingly, therefore, we find among modern historians of Israel—just as much as among modern historians generally—both the tendency to exalt the modern period as that blissful time in which we discovered, in Rankean terms, "how it really was," and the concomitant disparagement of the "precritical" era (that is, all of human history before the nineteenth century) as that benighted time in which the whole truth about the past could not be, and was not, told.

What is perhaps at first sight a little more surprising, and requires some explanation, is the fact that such a nineteenth-century view of the historiographical task should still, at the beginning of the twenty-first century, be so widely held among biblical scholars in general and among historians of Israel in particular. Indeed, we must face the remarkable fact that for most of the twentieth century, the discipline "history of Israel" proceeded in apparent ignorance of the furious debate about the nature of history that was raging among historians more generally, so that the nineteenth-century scientific model should still be widely seen at present as the only viable scholarly model that exists and, as such, to require no justification. Only in such a closeted environment could most of the recent debate about the history of Israel have taken the shape that it has, as a rerun of already decades-old disputes between Rankean and positivist empiricists in which the participants have appeared generally unaware both of these earlier disputes and of the wider issues they raise. Only in such an environment could T. L. Thompson, without any evident embarrassment or need to justify his position with respect to epistemology, claim knowledge of the past such that we "know" that Israel's testimony about its own past is fiction.

Only a lack of interdisciplinary and integrative thinking could have produced such a state of affairs. Since the origins of modern biblical studies lie not just in the nineteenth century generally, however, but specifically in a reaction against integrative thought of a philosophical or theological kind in favor of attention to the biblical text in itself, that this closeted environment should have arisen is perhaps not unexpected. Narrow specialist training, and the need to demonstrate specialism and love of detail in order to advance in the profession, leave many modern biblical scholars ill-prepared for anything other than occasional raids on the territory of other disciplines in order to find some new "angle" on biblical studies that will enable them to make a distinctive contribution to their field. The intellectual booty that is brought back from such raids is sometimes not well understood in relation to the intellectual context from which it was stolen. The consequence is a discipline that is sometimes (inaccurately) derivative of other disciplines, and more often than not is dependent on ideas taken from these other disciplines that are already at least several decades out of date in terms of their popularity and general plausibility. Perhaps for these general reasons the history of the history of Israel in the past twenty years has seen the widespread and enthusiastic adoption of a positivist approach to history without any great awareness of the problems to which this approach gives rise or of the debate that it has previously engendered among historians, philosophers, and theologians alike. In what can sometimes seem like the Lost Valley of biblical studies, cut off from the wider intellectual world around it, the scientific historian with his definitive picture of "what really happened" is apparently far from an extinct breed.

Be that as it may, our own philosophical and historical reflections to this point allow us to take a very different view from Thompson's as to what is "known" about the history of Israel. The knowledge that he professes is, in fact, merely faith in disguise. What Thompson "knows," he "knows" because he has decided to invest faith in certain testimonies about the past rather than others, the most notable of the "others" being the testimony of the Old Testament. He has, in essence, privileged nonbiblical testimony epistemologically. He is open to receive testimony about Israel's past predominantly or entirely from nonbiblical sources, and he generally exercises a high level of trust in these sources. He is predominantly or entirely closed to testimony from the Bible itself about Israel's past, generally exercising a high level of distrust in these sources. The question arises as to which defensible grounds could possibly be advanced for such a stance. This question is to be answered by historians of Israel other than Thompson, for he only makes explicit the kind of position that others have commonly and implicitly adopted. In fact a *common* feature of the discourse of biblical studies is that knowledge of Israel's past has been assumed to have been accumulated in various ways that can then be used as a yardstick against which to measure biblical testimony and come to some judgment upon it—or indeed as a basis upon which to build a "scientific" history in complete *independence* of biblical testimony. Further inquiry into this matter will not only consolidate our grasp of the general issues of science and history already reviewed, but will help us form a clear idea of how an alternative, biblical history of Israel should proceed.

We return, then, to some of the issues already discussed, now with the particular focus upon the history of the history of Israel itself and upon the way in which some of the issues have presented themselves in this specific context.

We "know" what we claim to know about the history of Israel, we assert here, by listening to testimony, to interpretation, and by making choices about whom to believe. In the biblical literature, we evidently have, among other sorts of texts, testimonies about (and interpretations of) Israel's past in narrative form. Indeed, the literature is unique in the ancient world in its interest in the past:

> Alone among Orientals and Greeks, it addresses a people defined in terms of their past and commanded to keep its memory alive . . . a people "more obsessed with history than any other nation that has ever existed" . . . [who] "stand alone among the people of the ancient world in having the story of their beginnings and their primitive state as clear as this in their folk-memory." . . . Recall how often customs are elucidated, ancient names and current sayings traced back to their origins, monuments and fiats assigned a concrete reason as well as a slot in history, persons and places and pedigrees specified beyond immediate needs, written records like the Book of Yashar or the royal annals explicitly invoked.[3]

To tell us about Israel's past is certainly not the only purpose of these narratives; it is arguably not even their main purpose. Yet so far as can be deduced from the texts themselves, telling about the past is clearly one of their purposes. Whether it were one of their purposes or not, they might still succeed in doing it. What sense does it make in our pursuit of knowledge of Israel's past, therefore, to adopt the kind of principled distrust of major sections of, or even the totality of, the Old Testament that is so often evident in the histories of Israel of the past two hundred years? What defensible grounds exist for such a position?

VERIFICATION AND FALSIFICATION

A review of the literature indicates that one of the reasons scholars have for their doubts about the Old Testament is the difficulty, if not the impossibility, of verifying so much of biblical tradition; without verification, the implication or assertion is that we cannot have great confidence in the material as source material for the doing of historiography. Thus Miller and Hayes, to take one example, are concerned about the general lack of what they call "non-biblical control evidence" throughout Genesis–Samuel and into 1 Kings. They do not think that one can presume the historical reliability of the Genesis–Joshua narrative in the absence of such evidence; they are extremely hesitant about using the Samuel narrative in writing about Saul because the truth of the kernel of the stories there cannot be externally verified; they would clearly prefer to have the same kind of verification in the case of David.[4] In the absence of such verification, which they regard as essential to the task of properly writing a critical historiography, they are to be found either not attempting to say anything (in the case of Genesis–Joshua) or offering virtual apologies for what they *do* attempt to say.[5] The author of the other watershed history of Israel dating from the 1980s, Soggin, is just as unwilling in general to presume historical reference in biblical accounts without external verification.[6] Both histories are indeed regarded as *watershed* histories in part precisely because they apply the verification principle to the extent that they do.

If some more recent scholarship has found Miller and Hayes and Soggin deficient, it is not because they are thought to have gone too far in this direction, but because they are considered not to have gone far enough. External verification for the Davidic and Solomonic periods, it is claimed, is just as lacking, and is also far more sparse than hitherto suspected for the period of the later monarchy. Since we are struggling for verification in the postexilic period as well, it is not surprising that a number of scholars are calling for what they see as simple consistency in the approach adopted to the Old Testament and history. If Genesis through to sections of 1 Samuel is not to be considered primary source material at least partly for the reason that verification is not available, why treat any differently the remainder of 1 Samuel through to 2 Kings and into Ezra-Nehemiah? Thus it is made to seem inevitable that any truly critical scholar will adopt a principled suspicion of the whole Old Testament in respect of historical work; conversely, those historians who partially or generally adopt the biblical story line in writing their histories of Israel are, to the extent that they do this, religiously motivated obscurantists rather than critical scholars.

Our view, on the other hand, is that this headlong rush to skepticism is a result not of being more purely critical, but rather of being insufficiently critical. Criticism is indeed widely employed, but not in respect of the sacred cow at the heart of the matter: the verification principle itself. Why should verification be a prerequisite for our acceptance of a tradition as valuable in respect of historical reality? Why should not ancient historical texts rather be given the benefit of the doubt in regard to their statements about the past unless good reasons exist to consider them unreliable in these statements and with due regard (of course) to their literary and ideological features? In short, why should we adopt a verification rather than a falsification principle? Why should the onus be on the texts to "prove" themselves valuable in respect of history, rather than on those who question their value to "prove" them false? It cannot be, as many seem to assume, that verification is necessary because of the merely general *possibility* that any given biblical text is not in fact reliable as historiography.[7] We must grant the possibility in any given case, but the individual case still must be examined in order to come to an individual decision about it. How the general possibility leads on logically to the methodological stance just described is not clear.

Neither is it clear that the notion of verification or "proof" under consideration here is at all coherent. How exactly is verification thought to be possible? Suppose that we have an archaeological datum that is consistent with the claims of a biblical text about the past. Does this "verify" that the text is historically accurate? Certainly such a connection has often been argued or assumed. Yet the archaeological datum, even if it is a written text, is still only another testimony to the past; the datum does not "prove" that the event to which the text refers happened. Nonwritten data are even less precise and more ambiguous.[8] How many testimonies are needed, then, before verification happens? And for whom does it happen—for everyone, or only for some? Recent discussion on the history of Israel clearly suggests that the answer is indeed "only for some." One person's sufficiency of data is another's insufficiency, or even another's forgery.[9]

This point raises the question as to how far verification lies in the eye of the beholder, and whether one's primary attitude to the texts in the first instance is far more decisive in terms of one's approach to the history of Israel than the discovery of this or that piece of external data.[10] This question then thrusts us back to, and indeed sharpens, our opening queries on the point of method. Why, exactly, is verification commonly regarded as so central to the historiographical task, especially when even agreement on what counts as verification is so elusive? To this question we may add another, which sharpens the point still further. How much history, ancient or otherwise, would we "know" about if the verification principle were consistently applied to all testimony about it—for example, to the testimony of Julius Caesar about his invasion of Britain in 55–54 B.C., which we know about only because Caesar himself tells us of it? The answer is clearly "very little"—which is precisely why people who employ the verification principle, whether historians in general or historians of Israel in particular, only do so selectively, choosing their targets for rigorous skepticism very carefully. That delusion already mentioned earlier—the delusion that we possess knowledge unmediated by faith—is indeed only possible if skepticism is directed at *some* testimonies about, and interpretations of, the past, and not at *others*. Nothing solidly "known" otherwise remains to be appealed to in respect of verification of the data being "tested."

Method that holds verification to be centrally important can therefore only ever be method that is partially (in every sense) applied. The more consistently the method is applied, the more it collapses in upon itself, until the point is reached where it is realized that nothing can truly be known at all. It is one of the remarkable (if also tragi-comic) aspects of recent writing on the history of Israel that a number of its practitioners seem to imagine that it is an advance in knowledge as a result of empirical research that has led to the end of "ancient Israel," when in fact it is only an advance in ignorance as a result of the quasi-consistent application of the verification principle.[11]

In sum, there is in fact no reason why any text offering testimony about the past, including the Old Testament, should be bracketed out of our historical discussions until it has passed some obscure "verification test." We agree with Wright:

> [T]he solid *proofs*, which so many assume possible at the end of either scientific or historical work, cannot be attained by finite beings. We are historical organisms by intrinsic nature, and ambiguity is always a central component of history, whether of the humanities, of social science, or of natural science. [12]

It is indeed intriguing that biblical scholars are still working with the verification principle in mind over thirty years after Richardson could say that "no-one believes that historical judgments can be 'proved' after the fashion of verification in the natural sciences."[13]

EARLY AND LATER TESTIMONY

There is a second, connected set of reasons, however, why scholars have increasingly expressed doubts about whole sections of the biblical tradition. It is not just that the Bible has "failed" the verification test, but also that so much of the biblical literature is now widely considered intrinsically deficient in its very ability to testify about the past that it claims to reflect. Here we have to deal with an accumulated inheritance of rules about which kinds of testimony really count, so far as the historian of Israel is concerned, and which kinds of testimony do not count as much or at all. These rules have apparently been designed to make life easier for the historian, on the one hand, by absolving him from thought in specific instances, and, on the other hand, to reduce the subjectivity otherwise inevitably involved in deciding between witnesses to the past. We may list the most influential of these rules—as appropriated, comprehended, and used by historians of Israel in particular—as follows.

First, eyewitness or otherwise contemporaneous accounts are to be preferred on principle to later accounts.[14] Second, accounts that are not so ideological, or not ideological at all, in nature are to be preferred to accounts that are ideological in nature.[15] Third and finally, accounts that fit our preconceptions about what is normal, possible, and so on, are to be preferred to accounts that do not fit such preconceptions.[16]

These rules have, of course, been in operation for some time, and as such have been applied for some time to smaller or greater sections of biblical tradition. What has changed in recent times is not the rules, but the extent to which the biblical text is seen as unsatisfactory in respect of them. Scholars have found in the Bible fewer of the kinds of traditions that score highly in respect of their granting of direct access to the past (for example, eyewitness or early sources), and more and more of the kinds that do not score highly. Thus once again there has seemed to be a certain inevitability about the marginalization of the Bible by historians, as the places where "history" might be found therein have been by degrees eliminated. Again, this perceived inevitability has led also to the perception that those who insist on finding history, say, in the books of Samuel are simply committed to being conservative and are not properly critical scholars.

Once again, however, the interesting question is: who is really being critical? The rules just enunciated are by no means self-evidently "true." The claims that are made about them (taken together and labeled as rules of "scientific method") in terms of their capacity to lead us into all truth, or at least to enable us to pronounce upon the probability that something did or did not happen in the past, are inflated. We address them in turn, beginning in the current section with the first: the "rules" about early and later testimony.

We have already touched on this matter briefly and in general terms in chapter 2. Now we articulate our position in more detail, as follows. No good reason at all exists to believe that those claiming to be eyewitnesses are not (like the later reporters of events) interpreters of those events, nor is there any reason to assume on principle that their testimony is going to be more or less trustworthy. There is, indeed, no reason to believe that earlier accounts are generally more reliable than later accounts. No necessary correlation at all, in fact, exists between the sort of interaction that "witnesses" have with events and the quality of access to events provided to others through them. Of course, people who have passed on particular testimony have possibly in the process distorted that testimony, rendering it false. Yet, it is also possible, even as they have contextualized it in a fresh way and have perhaps drawn fresh meaning and significance from it, adding their own testimony about the past to that which they have received from the past, that they have not distorted the original at all.

The common belief in modern times has been to the contrary: that inevitably something about the nature of what we might call "testimonial chains,"[17] stretching back in time, makes our historical beliefs, at least about the distant past, rationally insecure. However, demonstrating inevitability in this area is far from possible, whether generally or in the particular case of Israel.

Much oral tradition in societies lacking writing is strongly institutionalized, with strict controls governing its transmission in terms of the frequency and location of its repetition and in terms of the people who are allowed to be involved in that process of repetition. Variation in the story that is communicated is sometimes allowed within certain prescribed limits, but often it is not (for example, when the story touches upon questions of identity), and sanctions can be brought against the storyteller who makes mistakes in these cases. Possibly some of our Old Testament tradition (e.g., in Gen. 12–50) has its origins in oral transmission, but it could not be deduced from this mere fact that such Old Testament tradition inevitably distorted memories of the past. In any case, the civilization in the Mesopotamian region from which the Old Testament claims that Abraham originated was already a literate one, and had been for some time beforehand. The assumption that our Genesis traditions were only communicated in oral form, then, is only that: an assumption. Just as possibly they were communicated in both written and oral forms from an early stage—thus allowing for the relative fixity of tradition that writing produces even in the midst of the relative flexibility that oral tradition may allow—or that the written form predominated even early on. The point is an important one, not because we wish to concede any inevitable flaw in oral testimonial chains, but simply because of the undeniable fact that written records in general establish still greater security against memory lapses and other mistakes in the transmission of testimony.

The Old Testament itself certainly implies writing among the Israelites from the time of Moses onwards (Exod. 17:14)—another entirely plausible claim in view of the fact that we are also told that Moses was raised in the Egyptian court. A historical Moses who was a product of the royal nursery would have been trained in the Egyptian scribal tradition, and would possibly have been bilingual. Nothing is unlikely in the idea that such a person might have inherited both oral and perhaps written sources from earlier times and have shaped them into the primary Israel tradition that we find reflected in the Pentateuch. Nor are there grounds for assuming that if he did, he must inevitably have done so untruthfully, nor for assuming that those who later passed on the Pentateuchal tradition of early Israel, even as they expanded and nuanced it, distorted it. A clear indication of the reverse, indeed, is the fact that the tradition has as one of its central emphases—and though unflattering, it governs both Israelite religion and ethics—that the nation Israel was in the beginning a slave-people in Egypt. This tradition does not look like the type that a people invents about itself, nor that a people passes on in such a blunt manner, if they are in the business of distortion.

Certainly by the end of the second millennium B.C. and the beginning of the first—the period by which Israel had emerged as a recognizable entity in Palestine and the Israelite monarchy had been founded—we find that literacy was widespread in the region in and around Palestine, and writing was being employed in legal, business, literary, and religious texts. Writing was already widespread in the pre-Israelite period, "even in relatively small and isolated towns"—a simple fact that undermines popular recent arguments against literacy in Palestine based on low population.[18] The extant extrabiblical materials suggest in fact that writing was practiced from north to south in Canaan and that, furthermore, a shift occurred following the Amarna period from Akkadian as the "lingua franca" to the local scripts and languages of Palestine. In Iron Age Israel itself from 1200 all the way through to 587/586 B.C., writing was also a pervasive phenomenon, and not just in the larger population centers.[19] Nor does the evidence justify recent attempts to limit literacy to specific classes of people (such as priests, scribes, or administrators); rather, apparently "many individuals . . . could write the simpler alphabetic script and . . . did so for a variety of reasons and purposes."[20] It is entirely plausible, then, that written historical tradition as well as oral tradition was produced in this period, and was (either near the time or later) available to the biblical authors as they claim (e.g., in 1 Kgs. 11:41; 14:19, 29; etc.)—in the same way that tradition was likewise available, for example, to Assyrian royal scribes as early as the twelfth to tenth centuries B.C. Israelite royal scribes are mentioned in 2 Samuel 8:17 and 20:25 and 1 Kings 4:3, and scribelike material is extensively found throughout Samuel and Kings, no doubt deriving at least in part from the kind of palace archives that were a well-known feature of ancient Near Eastern life.

These scribes, and their successors as recorders of the past, may well have had access also to temple libraries like those found in Egypt in the second half of the first millennium, which were used for the education and training of scribes and contained a wide range of material. The function of holy places, and specifically temples, as repositories of texts is well attested throughout the ancient world. The Egyptians used holy places in this way as early as the third millennium B.C., for example, as the Greeks and Romans did in later times. The Old Testament itself reflects such practice when it describes, for example, the laying up of the Ten Commandments in the Tabernacle (Exod. 40:16–33; Deut. 10:1–5); Josephus later tells us that a copy of the Jewish Law was taken away to Rome from the Jerusalem Temple in A.D. 70.[21] Temple library resources like these, reflecting traditions stretching back for generations, enabled Berossus to write his *Babyloniaca* (280–270 B.C.), which sought to persuade his Greek masters of the venerable age and achievements of the Mesopotamian peoples, and enabled Manetho to write his *Aegyptiaca* (c. 280 B.C.), a history of ancient Egypt. Aside from palace archives and temple libraries or archives, through which transmitters of the past could have had access to earlier Israelite tradition and law, it is possible that individuals or groups of individuals also had library resources of their own. Other likely sources of information would have included foreign annals and inscriptions of various kinds, recording personal information (note, for example, 2 Sam. 18:18; burial inscriptions would also have been useful) or Israelite and foreign victories (such as the Mesha stela or the Tel Dan inscription—see further in part 2 of this volume, where the monarchic period of Israel's history is described).

There is no reason to think, then, that biblical historians of the monarchic period could not have had access to written as well as oral sources of information about that period as well as the earlier period. They often specifically claim otherwise; and there are many indications in the texts of the post-Pentateuchal corpus in Joshua–Kings that we should take these claims seriously. Both the account of Solomon's reign in 1 Kings 2–11 and the account of the Israelite conquest of Canaan in Joshua 1–12 are, for example, similar in structure to ancient

"display inscriptions."[22] Other internal evidence also points to the early monarchical or even premonarchical composition of at least some of the source material behind the books of Joshua[23] and Judges.[24] First and Second Samuel overall,
with their emphasis on the legitimation of the new constitution for Israel, the
continuity of political leadership, and the Davidic succession, make much better
sense as a narrative composed in a contemporary rather than a later context—as
an account of and apology for Davidic kingship deriving from that early time.
The account of Saul may indeed be partially patterned upon an old ritual ceremony for the installation of the king.[25] The Solomon of the Kings account,
finally, matches the Assyrian royal ideals of the eleventh to ninth centuries but
not thereafter, suggesting that the account was first formulated during that time
period in conscious interaction with those ideals.

Many incidental features of our texts, and especially of Samuel–Kings, also
imply the antiquity of these texts. Among these features are the scattered references to diverse and unorthodox deities, the foreign names that often reflect a
phonology not present in later materials, the many toponyms associated with
David's heroes that do not appear in the later material either, the presupposition
in 2 Samuel of a distribution of Negev settlements that conforms to the archaeology of the tenth century but not of later centuries, and the extraordinarily high
number of defective Hebrew spellings in 1–2 Samuel, in contrast not only to the
remainder of Joshua–Kings but (more starkly and significantly) to postexilic
works.[26] Just how accurately the sequence of Assyrian kings presented in the
books of Kings matches the sequence as we know it from the Assyrian records
themselves is particularly noticeable.

We find in all these facts abundant evidence, not only that the accurate passage
of tradition in Israel from the preexilic period to the postexilic period in which the
tradition received its final shape was *possible*, but that it *happened*. Our biblical texts
simply do not have the appearance of being produced, as some have maintained,
out of the vivid imaginations of late postexilic authors. There is every indication that
these authors, rather, had access to already relatively fixed and (to them) authoritative written tradition as represented by Genesis–Kings, as well as to their own
resources. The books of Chronicles support this assertion very clearly, displaying as
they do a marked dependence on the books of Samuel–Kings—a source that they
often reproduce word for word, while evidently drawing into their account of Israel's
past a whole range of other materials designed to fill out the account. Some ongoing shaping of Genesis–Kings no doubt took place throughout the postexilic period,
but that is not to say that Genesis–Kings is essentially and substantially itself late.
On the contrary, many good reasons exist for thinking that it is not.

Nothing about the nature of an Israelite "testimonial chain" conceived in this
way inevitably makes historical beliefs based upon it rationally insecure. It may
be objected that we cannot in fact "prove" that such a chain existed, because we
lack access to all the resources upon which the tradents are alleged to have drawn
in producing their testimony. However, that is to suppose that proof is necessary
as the foundation of faith in testimony, which is precisely what we are disputing
in this chapter. We are much more interested not in the question of "proof," but

in the question of what constitutes "reasonable belief"; and the contention that, in order reasonably to exercise faith in testimony, we ourselves must actually be acquainted individually with a testimonial chain stretching back to past events and situations, is patently absurd.[27] All that needs to be shown for the purposes of this section of the chapter is that we may reasonably believe that conditions existed in the ancient Near East, particularly Palestine, such that we cannot assume disjunction between the early testimony about Israel's past and the later forms of tradition in which this testimony has come down to us. We are not required to produce all the intervening texts.

This production of intervening texts would not be a reasonable expectation even in the case of mediaeval and modern history. Such production is certainly not a reasonable expectation in the case of ancient Israel. In all likelihood, many of these texts would have been written on papyrus, as suggested by the Wadi Murabbat fragment (c. 600 B.C.) and by the many clay bullae, once used to secure papyrus writings, that have been found in preexilic Israelite sites. The numerous Israelite ostraca that have been found were themselves probably administrative notes whose information would have been quickly transferred to papyrus—a practice attested in Babylonia, Assyria, and Egypt. This fact is important, for papyrus only survives in dry, hot conditions. The Wadi Murabbat fragment was itself preserved only because of unusual dehydration. We are not surprised, then, that epigraphic finds from preexilic Israel are meager; they are meager also in such cases as pre-sixth-century Athens and Sparta. Monumental inscriptions, likewise, are not easy to find, whether in rural locations in which no one knows where to look, or in settled areas where much building and renovation has occurred over the centuries and the inhabitants often do not share modern scholars' concerns about preservation. The history of Israel itself—overrun constantly by armies, absorbed successively into great empires and greatly resettled over the course of time—does not help the historian in this regard. Even in the other parts of the ancient world we do not find such surviving inscriptions, although we may well think that they likely existed. We possess no Aramean stelae from the territory of the contemporary kingdom of Damascus to Israel's north. Nor do we possess monumental inscriptions of any kind from seventh-century Athens or Sparta; the later eras of Herod, the greatest builder Palestine has ever seen, and the Hasmonean rulers; or the much later Carolingian empire of the eighth century A.D. This lack demonstrates, among other things, the folly of interpreting an absence of a particular sort of evidence as evidence of the absence of a particular people known from written sources. The fact is that the data available to us apart from these written sources, so far as the ancient world is concerned, are far too fragmentary and insecure a base from which to make deductions of that kind.[28]

We conclude this section, then, by asserting again that any facile and general distinction between earlier and later testimony in terms of the reliability of the testimony cannot be defended. The contention is false that testimony about Israel's past which comes towards or at the end of a chain of testimony is in principle more suspect than that which comes at or towards the beginning of the chain. There is no reason to assume that a particular rendering of earlier tradition at a later date cannot be a truthful rendering, any more than there is reason to assume that an early rendering cannot be false. That any modern historian should argue otherwise is perhaps surprising, since many modern historians have typically wished to argue that *their* very late renderings of earlier tradition are truthful—and indeed, more truthful than earlier attempts. Presumably because these historians have typically regarded their contributions as "scientific truth" rather than as fresh renderings of tradition, this inconsistency has not occurred to them. Be that as it may, we possess no "rule" or "method" with regard to the chronology of testimony that can truly help us in deciding, in advance, in which testimonies about the past to invest our faith. Each testimony, including all biblical testimony, must be considered on its own terms.

IDEOLOGY AND ISRAEL'S PAST

A priori suspicion or doubt, then, on the ground of the distance that is supposed to exist between the beginning and the end of the testimonial chain, cannot be defended in respect of biblical testimony. Nor can it be justified on the grounds that the biblical testimony is ideologically loaded—that is, that it carries a particular perspective on Israel's past and has an intention to persuade others of the truth of that perspective. No account of the past anywhere is free of ideology, and thus in principle is to be trusted more than other accounts; nor should one presume that an ideological account cannot also be historically accurate.

Prejudice against biblical testimony because of its ideological or theological orientation is, of course, commonly found throughout modern writing on the history of Israel. As one author has rightly noted, a basic presupposition of critical historical study at least since the Enlightenment has been that skepticism is the appropriate stance to adopt in relation to texts whose primary aim is to deliver a religious message.[29] The stance is well expressed in the following chain of quotations from G. W. Ahlström:[30]

> Because the authors of the Bible were historiographers and used stylistic patterns to create a "dogmatic" and, as such, tendentious literature, one may question the reliability of their product.
>
> Biblical historiography is not a product built on facts. It reflects the narrator's outlook and ideology rather than known facts.
>
> [T]he biblical narrators were not really concerned about historical truth. Their goal was not that of a modern historian—the ideal of "objectivity" had not yet been invented.

Previously many historians of Israel thought that "facts" were nonetheless *embedded* in the Old Testament narrative, allowing us partially to redeem the narrative testimony for the purposes of modern historiography. The general tendency was to view material within the narrative that *appears* less ideological than the remainder (e.g., material that has a form suggesting dependence on royal annals) as if it *were* less ideological in reality. This tendency is still found in more recent writing, although a more common approach now is simply to characterize all Old Testament narrative as ideologically compromised, whether it "appears" so or not,[31] and to look elsewhere for historical truth—truth that is not compromised in the same way. Having decided that the Bible as religious literature cannot be regarded as primary source material, attention is given to nonwritten archaeological data and to extrabiblical textual data instead. We shall consider each of these kinds of data in turn, indicating why this move is a false one. We then conclude this section with some general comments on ideology and critical thought.

Archaeology and the Past

We noted in chapter 2 that in the modern period of historiography it has sometimes been assumed that archaeological remains offer us the prospect of grounding historical statements in something more solid than testimony. This assumption has certainly been prevalent in much writing on the history of Israel. From the late nineteenth century onwards, archaeology in Palestine has in fact been governed by a desire to "show" objectively that certain things are true and others are not true— successively, that chosen races are superior to others; that German higher criticism was not right in its denigration of Israelite religion and society, nor in its undermining of the earlier history of Israel; and most recently, that the emergence of Israel in Palestine can be explained in terms of "normal" secular cultural evolution. Not surprisingly, for example, we find G. W. Ahlström (with his strong convictions about the deficiencies of the Old Testament as testimony about Israel's past) insisting that, if we wish to get as close as possible to the "actual events" in Palestine's past, the *archaeology* of Palestine must become the main source for historiography.[32] He is clear about the distinction between the two kinds of data (textual and archaeological): "If the meaning of the archaeological evidence is clear, one might say that it gives a more 'neutral' history than the textual material. It is free from the *Tendenz* or evaluation that easily creeps into an author's writings."[33]

This kind of view of the nature of archaeological evidence has been common among historians of Israel, even where they have sometimes recognized that it cannot be entirely correct and have found space in one part of their minds for the contrary idea, developed earlier in this chapter, that archaeological data are no more "objective" or "neutral" than other sorts.[34] We saw in chapter 1 how K. W. Whitelam's recent contribution to the debate about the history of Israel manifested this kind of double-think: the objectivity of archaeological data is firmly accepted insofar as this data is thought to *conflict* with biblical testimony, while the nonobjectivity of archaeological data is suggested when the claim is made by others that this data and biblical testimony correspond. The latter instinct about the data is in fact far nearer the mark than the former. In fact, *all* archaeologists tell us stories about the past that are just as ideologically loaded as any other historical narrative and are certainly not simply a neutral recounting of the facts. Archaeologists could not possibly *add* their testimony to other testimonies about the past in a nonideological manner. We need not labor the point, which we have already discussed. Simply consider the following two perceptive comments on the reality of archaeological nonobjectivity, which stand in stark contrast to many of the statements about archaeology from modern scientific historians. The first relates in its original context to the limited usefulness of archaeology for the historian of tenth-century Israel in particular, but it is of wider application:

> [I]t is not up to archaeology to decide an essentially theoretic debate, whose course until now has demonstrated only that the so-called hard facts are determined by the discussants' perspectives.[35]

The second is more general:

> Good scholars, honest scholars, will continue to differ about the interpretation of archaeological remains simply because archaeology is not a science. It is an art. And sometimes it is not even a very good art.[36]

Extrabiblical Texts and Israel's Past

If archaeology has commonly been thought to provide us with a way in which to escape ideology in our attempts to understand Israel's past, so too have extrabiblical texts. Aside from archaeology, these data are thought to provide the "knowledge" that we possess about that solid entity called "history"—the "knowledge" that means that we cannot any longer believe in "ancient Israel." Egyptian, Assyrian, and Babylonian texts, in particular, are often regarded as providing us with not only a reliable, overarching chronological framework for ancient Near Eastern history, but also with a basic narrative about that past in relation to which any testimony from the Old Testament must be assessed. These texts are some of the main resources to which we can turn if we wish to "verify" particular Old Testament claims because (it is claimed or implied) they do not share the deficiencies of Old Testament narrative when it comes to the ideological, and particularly the religious, aspect. They grant us access to "how it really was."

Two examples of this kind of thinking will suffice. In the course of recent reflections on history writing, L. L. Grabbe compares the Old Testament and other ancient Near Eastern (largely Assyrian) texts with regard to their testimony about the later Israelite monarchy.[37] Grabbe clearly assumes that the ancient Near Eastern texts simply describe for us the facts of the matter. He is therefore able to use these texts to assess the Old Testament material, and he proceeds to conclude that the Bible is "reasonably accurate about the framework" of events, but that the details are at times "demonstrably misleading or wholly inaccurate and perhaps even completely invented."[38] In the same volume, H. Niehr insists that a clear distinction between primary and secondary sources for the history of Israel must be upheld, on the ground that the primary sources "did not undergo the censorship exercised by, for example, the Deuteronomistic theologians nor were they submitted to the process of canonization." The Assyrian sources are among the primary sources. Their historical reliability, Niehr asserts, has recently been shown to be very high.[39]

However, the truly defensible grounds for such an epistemological privileging of extrabiblical texts are entirely unclear; these texts certainly do *not* provide us with immediate access to "the way it was"—not even to "the way it was" for the peoples who produced them, much less for the Israelites. The reality is that we possess only limited insight into the history of these other peoples, and not simply because of historical accident. On the contrary, their literature is no less selective and ideologically loaded than the Old Testament in the way that it presents the past. We may take the Assyrian texts as our primary example.[40]

The various inscriptions and chronicles deriving from Assyria from the ninth century B.C. onwards—specifically from the reign of Shalmaneser III (858–824 B.C.) onwards—are undeniably important external sources for any history of Israel. Shalmaneser and many of his successors campaigned in, and eventually in the eighth century B.C. came to dominate, the entire region between the Euphrates and Egypt. Writings originating during their reigns are therefore often important in setting a broader context within which the biblical narratives can be read.[41]

The first thing to be noted about these records, however, is that they are uneven, particularly where they touch upon the activities of Assyrian kings on their western border—and Israel was situated, of course, to Assyria's west. The written sources for the reign of Shalmaneser III himself are abundant; but the same cannot be said for his successors Shamshi-Adad V (823–811 B.C.), Adad-nirari III (810–783 B.C.), Shalmaneser IV (782–773 B.C.), Ashur-dan III (772–755 B.C.), and Ashur-nirari V (754–745 B.C.). The situation markedly improves when we reach the reign of Tiglath-pileser III (744–727 B.C.) and on through the succeeding reigns down to Ashurbanipal (668–c. 630 B.C.). Here the sources are in general numerous and helpful, although there are notable exceptions: we know virtually nothing, for example, about the reign of Shalmaneser V (726–722 B.C.). Some of these sources, however—even where they are extant—are not in wonderful condition; substantial portions of the annals of Tiglath-pileser III, for example, have come down to us in poor condition, while for Esarhaddon (680–669 B.C.) we possess only fragments of the annals. All this presents certain challenges even to those who are intent on writing a history of *Assyria*. Clearly though, simply on the ground of *coverage*, the extent to which Assyrian sources can be of help in writing a history of *Israel* should not be overstated. As A. Kuhrt says of the whole Levant: "[I]t is the Assyrian royal sources which provide the richest and, chronologically and historically, most useful information for the states with which they came into contact. But, admittedly, it makes for a very partial picture only."[42] However, the problem that exists in reconstructing Assyrian history, as it provides a context for Israelite history, lies not just in the unevenness of our sources as a matter of historical accident but also in their very nature, which brings us to the main point of our section regarding ideology.

The sources that provide the backbone for reconstructing the history of Assyria and adjacent territories from the tenth century onwards derive from the Assyrian royal court; chief among them are the "royal annals" just mentioned—personal memorials of individual kings that provide accounts of royal achievements, especially military campaigns. What is their character?[43]

They are, first of all, clearly selective in what they say; the situation could not be otherwise, since all history writing is selective.[44] For example, although the annals of Sargon II (721–705 B.C.) mention a campaign against Ashdod around 713 B.C., they do not mention in this context the involvement (or possible involvement) of Judah, about which we know from a different source. In this case we are probably to explain the selectivity simply in terms of a lack of Assyrian interest in tiny Judah. More significantly, though, Sargon II's annals claim as his own the conquest of the Israelite capital of Samaria around 722 B.C.; yet both the Old Testament (2 Kgs. 17:1–6) and the Babylonian Chronicle[45] suggest that the conqueror was Shalmaneser V. This fact raises at least the possibility that Sargon's scribes were intent on embellishing Sargon's record by giving him a victory as king that was not strictly his. Likewise, Sennacherib's Que and Til-Garimmu campaigns of the first decade of the seventh century B.C. appear to have been edited out of later versions of that king's annals, perhaps because the king did not himself lead them or perhaps because their outcomes were less than fortunate (the former was a costly victory, and the latter a victory with no apparent long-term gains).[46]

These latter examples in fact fit a much larger pattern which helps us to see that the Assyrian royal annals are selective not merely because their authors were faced with too much material, but because these authors had particular ends in view. That is, the annals are ideologically loaded. Perhaps the word "annals" itself has helped to obscure this fact from some of the Old Testament scholars who have interacted with this material in recent years, for "annals" carries with it the connotation (for the modern reader) of "objective chronicle." "Objective chronicles" do not in reality exist, of course, but if they did, one still could not regard these so-called "annals" as being of this nature.[47] They are, in fact, primarily commemorative texts, dedicatory building inscriptions, originally written as pious reports by the ruler to a god and with an eye to inspiring the admiration of the future peoples who would read them. This purpose must always be taken into account in assessing what they have to say. Assyrian kings regarded themselves as viceroys of the gods on earth. The tasks of the kings (that is, those tasks worth recording) were to rule their subjects, to extend their sway to the furthest ends of the earth, and in return for the power and victories given to them by the gods, to build temples and maintain their worship practices. Assyrians recorded such things on memorial tablets, prisms, and cylinders of clay or alabaster; on obelisks and stelae; and on the walls of palaces and temples. The annals in particular were commonly reedited many times during a reign; most texts now extant are the products of considerable redaction, selecting and conflating of various sources by scribes intent on finding the best way to laud their ruler. Each fresh edition could involve not only the updating of the king's record, but a significant reshaping of the whole account.

Under these circumstances, an accurate portrayal of events was not always necessarily the main or guiding motive of the royal scribes. Moreover, we certainly cannot expect these inscriptions to be "objective," even where we may be reasonably sure that they were intended to be accurate. On the contrary, they are works of literary art with a political and religious focus. As such, their detailed accounts of the

conquests of states are stylized and repetitive, and their claims about royal dominion are often hyperbolic and biased. The point is not that they lack factual content, nor that they necessarily engage in outright falsehood as a matter of habit.
Nevertheless, in pursuit of the glorification of the king, failures are omitted, successes emphasized, and the whole account artistically slanted to the point that a
careless reader who did not understand their genre and style could be seriously misled about the historical reality to which they seek to refer.[48] As A. Kuhrt puts it:

> [C]onsiderations such as factual truthfulness, balanced assessments, histor-
> ical precision and objectivity were bound to play a less important role in
> inscriptions of this nature than an emphasis on spectacular exploits, success
> rather than failure, and the king's personal role in these achievements: the
> king as centre of all action. What was presented was the truth according to
> Assyrian ideology. . . .[49]

Assyrian royal scribes were, in fact, more concerned about the *image* of the king
and his activity as a warrior than about merely recording the facts of his reign,
which was the case whether they were composing "annals" or "display inscriptions" for the palace walls. The artists who produced the narrative reliefs with
which Assyrian kings decorated their royal palaces shared the same objectives.
They too focused on war, victory, and building, presenting their monarch as mas-
ter of all aspects of life (albeit with direct help from the gods).

Obviously, then, our Assyrian sources are not granting us all but unmediated
access to the naked facts of history, in the light of which we may then make judgments on the accuracy or otherwise of our "selective and ideologically loaded" Old
Testament texts. In fact no grounds exist for granting the Assyrian sources any epistemological primacy in principle in our striving for knowledge about Israel's past.
The shaky ground upon which we stand when we do this is evidenced by well-
known examples from the past, such as the case of Sargon II's claim to have conquered Samaria. In earlier times, when scholars only possessed Sargon's annals and
the Bible, the common thought was that Sargon was simply "telling us how it was,"
and that 2 Kings 17 was simply wrong. The Babylonian Chronicle has now provided further food for thought on this point. Ancient history is vast and complex,
and all of our meager testimony about it is only capable of providing us with glimpses
into this vastness and complexity. To absolutize *some* of this testimony as the standard against which everything *else* should be measured makes no sense at all. That
such extrabiblical testimony is sometimes said to be preferable to biblical testimony
on the grounds of the *religious* nature of the latter is particularly strange. Religion
clearly permeates the former as well, not least in the common references within it to
divine involvement or intervention in military affairs. Theological intent is just as
clear in Sennacherib's inscriptions, for example, as in the literature of the Bible.

Having focused on the Assyrian texts, we should make it clear more briefly
that the situation is no different with any other of our nonbiblical sources. Egyptian pharaohs, for example, also regarded themselves as viceroys of the gods on
earth, and their texts unsurprisingly present precisely the same kinds of challenges

that we find in the Assyrian texts. Additionally, the chronology of ancient history before the tenth century—the period in which historians of Israel are most interested in Egypt, given the centrality of Egypt in Israel's story before the settlement in the land—is far less secure than for the period that follows the tenth century. Chronological issues continue, therefore, to be debated and to cause difficulty in reading Israel's history against the background of the Egyptian texts that are thought relevant to this history.[50] The main point, however, is that whether we are dealing with Mesopotamian, Egyptian, or Hittite texts, or indeed with a more local inscription from one of Israel's near neighbors, such as the Moabite Stone— itself written in stereotypical language and with some degree of hyperbole, at least in its claim that "Israel has perished forever" (see further the chapter dealing with the Israelite monarchy)—we are only and ever dealing with selective and ideologically focused texts. All historiography is, in fact, like this: written by people possessing both a general *world*-view and a particular *point* of view that they bring to bear on reality, seeking selectively to organize the facts of the past into some coherent pattern and in respect of some particular end.

Ideology and Historiography

In summary of the whole section thus far: there is no account of the past anywhere that is not ideological in nature, and therefore in principle to be trusted more than other accounts.

Still, true access to the past is not unavailable. Our discussion in this section has aimed only at dispelling the myth that extrabiblical testimony represents an order of evidence available to the historian of Israel that is different from the evidence that the Bible presents—the myth that extrabiblical texts can be used to produce a solid entity called "factual history" that can then be deployed to arrive at definitive judgments on the Old Testament testimony about Israel's past. Since *all* texts that speak of the past are ideological, certain of them cannot be prioritized in respect of the remainder on the ground that they are somehow "neutral." However, our purpose has not been to suggest that ideological texts cannot speak truly about the past. On the contrary: we should not assume *in advance* that *any* testimony about the past, whatever its ideological shaping and partiality, does not speak about the past truthfully. This assertion holds whether we think of the testimony of the archaeologist, the Assyrian scribe, or biblical author. We may find it necessary to believe on particular occasions that a particular testimony is false, especially when we are faced with what appears to be, after careful consideration, straightforward conflict in testimony. The mere *presence* of ideology itself, however, should never lead us to this conclusion. We should not assume in advance, for example, that the "censorship" exercised by the Deuteronomistic theologians (as Niehr puts it) has necessarily prevented a true (albeit a partial) picture of the past emerging in those texts for which the Deuteronomists are believed responsible. Nor should we assume in advance, just because the narrative of David's rise to power in 1 Samuel is pro-Davidic in the sense of seeking to acquit David of guilt—and indeed follows a literary pattern found elsewhere in the ancient Near East when attempts are being made to exonerate individuals in this way—that "the traditional materials about David cannot be regarded as an attempt to write *history* as such" and do not grant us access to the real past.[51] The fact that we are dealing with apologetic material, in form and content, does not of itself demonstrate that what the text claims is untrue (for example, and centrally, that David was indeed innocent). All historical writing must inevitably use the literary forms and conventions available to the author and known to his audience, if the author is to communicate to that audience anything meaningful about the past. However, the presence of these forms and conventions themselves in a text does not preclude the intention to speak about the real past, nor does it mean that no possibility exists of speaking about this past accurately. A fuller discussion of this point must await chapter 4. For the moment, we can note that few students of ancient history would doubt that a particular campaign report from Assyria or Babylonia does correlate accurately to a real historical campaign *just because* the account is written in stereotypical, stylized language and with literary flair, and claims divine intervention on the side of the winners. That biblical scholars so often seem tempted to make just such a facile connection between form and substance in the case of ancient Israelite literature is therefore astonishing. Ideological literature can also, in whole or in part, be historically accurate literature.

Ideology and Critical Thought

A final comment on ideology and critical thought: As we have already seen in chapter 2, a common modern view is that critical thought was not a marked feature of premodern historiography—albeit that the early Greeks allegedly approximated towards what was desirable. This prejudice reemerges in relation to the history of Israel in particular when the claim is made, as it commonly has been, that our biblical authors are not *critical* historians (like some of the Greeks), thus making access to the past for us through their (ideological) texts problematic. To "deduce" from the *claims* of certain ancient Greeks about their critical intentions and the *absence of such claims* in ancient Hebrew texts (as in other ancient Near Eastern literary traditions) that inevitably a substantive difference *in reality* exists between (some) Greeks and (all) Hebrews is questionable enough. As we have seen, one cannot defend any generalized distinction between the historiography that precedes the nineteenth century and the historiography since that time, in terms of authorial concern about historical truth and falsehood. To this point may now be added the further one that Greek historians like Thucydides and Herodotus were certainly not without a worldview, and certainly did not describe the ancient world "as it really was," free from ideology. Critical thought coexisted with faith in their cases too. Beyond this, however, what is entirely curious about the claim we are currently addressing is the assumption that any necessary correlation exists between the *stated intentions* of a historian and the usefulness to us of the historian's account. One can as well imagine an author whose intentions to be critical caused him to *fail* to pass on important testimony about the real past, as one can imagine an author who uncritically but *successfully* passed on such important testimony. Perhaps the imagination of some modern contributors to the debate on the history of Israel is limited at this point, however, as a result of an incapacity to believe that any gulf is possible between *their* intention to be critical, on the one hand, and *their* grasping of and transmission of historical truth, on the other.

ANALOGY AND ISRAEL'S PAST

Our final claim in respect of the "rules" of scientific historiography is this: that there is no good reason to believe that just because a testimony fails to violate our sense of what is normal and possible, it is on this account more likely to be true than another; and there is no good reason to believe, either, that an account which describes the unique or unusual is for that reason to be suspected of unreliability.

When scholars assert otherwise, they have in the back of their minds the principle of analogy, as famously articulated by E. Troeltsch. Troeltsch's argument was that harmony with the normal, customary, or at least frequently attested events and conditions as we have experienced them is the distinguishing mark of reality for the events that criticism can recognize as really having happened in the past. We sift the testimony of the past in terms of our experience of the present, coming to judgments on what is historical by reflecting on "normal experience." The principle of analogy thus articulated has been central to much historical endeavor since the nineteenth century, for it is evidently consonant with the scientific approach to history in general and with the positivist approach, with its generalizing tendencies, in particular.

Yet some critical thinking is in order here too. Who are the Troeltschian "we"? Whose "normal experience" is to be employed in making judgments about "what really happened" in history? It cannot be the normal experience of the individual historian himself—the Cartesian individual, working outwards from individual certainties to grand theories about the world he or she inhabits. Historians regularly accept the reality of events and practices that lie outside the realm of their own immediate experience, and they are wise to do so, since their time-conditioned and culture-bound experience is drastically limited. Perhaps, then, we should widen the notion of normal experience, and refer instead to "common human experience"—that great pool of wisdom that the human race in general possesses. This has in fact been a popular move in modern approaches to the past, reaching back at least as far as D. Hume. Hume himself rejected reports of miracles on this basis. He also rejected reports of things like human acts and dispositions that run counter to the uniformity in human motives and actions that, he supposed, the study of both history and contemporary society had revealed.

A moment's reflection should persuade us, however, of the weakness of such a move. How do we ascertain what is in fact normal, usual, or frequently attested, so far as humanity-at-large is concerned? Presumably we must do so by listening to the testimony of other people—the vast majority of the world's population, in fact—if we are to be truly "scientific" in our approach to the matter. We note in passing the irony of invoking this "common human experience" as the ground for history-writing while at the same time claiming steadfastly to eschew dependence upon testimony in principle! Irony aside, however, we must draw attention to the obvious problem: that listening to the testimony of the vast majority of the world's population is, of course, impossible, and always has been. What do people mean, then, when they refer to "common human experience"? Further inquiry reveals that they have only ever been referring *in fact*, whatever they have *believed* to be the case, to a construct dependent at best upon the testimony of *some* other people. Indeed, these "others" are themselves only those people who are believed to be speaking *truly* about what they claim to be their experience. Such a sifting process with regard to testimony would also be necessary if it were in actuality possible to talk to the entirety of the world's population about their experience. Real human experience (as opposed to the artificial construct of "common human experience") is, of course, vast, differentiated, and complex. Testimonies about it, and interpretations of it, are diverse; faith is required of those who seek to give any account of it, as they interact with the various testimonies and interpretations and choose which ones to integrate with their own beliefs. It is no less, and indeed vastly more, complex a matter to narrate the human present than to narrate the human past. How then can "common human experience" be appealed to as a solid reality against which testimony about the past can be measured? This "experience" is by no means the kind of objective entity that would be required for the procedure to have any kind of plausibility.

Moreover, even if we were somehow able to ascertain in the midst of this complexity what is normal, usual, or frequently attested, why should we think that a claim is untrue that something happened in the past simply because it does not *conform* to this "common human experience"? For example, at the point at which it happened in history (if we are sufficiently "unscientific" to believe that it did), the first human landing on the moon was an event beyond *any* human being's experience. The event had no analogy, and indeed was a "miracle" of the technological age. Even *common* human experience, then—insofar as we can speak of such a phenomenon—clearly cannot be the arbiter of what is possible in history. Common human experience is time-conditioned human experience—a snapshot of reality as experienced by many people at one point only in the historical continuum. In fact, analogy properly and consistently applied to the past leads us into evident absurdities, for we would be compelled by its tenets to reject otherwise compelling testimony about unique or unusual events that we find there simply on the basis that they are unique or unusual. Hume himself suspected the veracity of Quintus Curtius, for example, when the latter describes the supernatural courage of Alexander the Great, merely on the ground that the courage was "supernatural"; yet his skeptical principles could just as easily be applied to available testimony (for example) about the life and deeds of Napoleon Bonaparte—leading to serious doubts, one assumes, about the history even of the early nineteenth century—not to mention the history of an ancient world in which Hannibal uniquely (and indeed miraculously) crossed the Alps with his elephants. This kind of argument proves too much—unless, of course, one wishes to move by degrees into the kind of neopositivist position that we described earlier, in which all history is suspect just because it is history. This tack, however, is simply to move by degrees into still greater absurdity.

The fact of the matter is that it is impossible to say what "common human experience" is; even if one *could* say what it is, why it should be accepted as the touchstone of historical reality is not clear. Appeal to "common human experience" is in truth nothing other than a rhetorical device of great use to those who favor a "scientific" view of the universe—a device whose deployment is intended only to make us lose the individual historian in the midst of the crowd, as it were, and to disguise the fact that what is being appealed to is actually the writer's own *individual* experience (and perhaps the experience of a few other people besides, with whom the historian happens to share a particular worldview). The principle of analogy in fact never operates in a vacuum. There is always ". . . an intimate relation between analogy and its context or network of background beliefs."[52] We see the truth of the matter clearly when we move, for example, from Hume's own theoretical philosophy to his practical historiography. His claim in the *History of England* (1756–1764) was that he had written an impartial history, influenced neither by tradition nor by enthusiasm. He had provided the interpretation of England's past that "all reasonable men" would give, as they surveyed it with rational minds that contained truths already universally acknowledged—in particular the truth that uniformity exists in human nature and action throughout history. In retrospect, however, Hume's history was clearly very far from impartial. It promotes a very specific worldview, namely that of the eighteenth-century rationalist; the appeal to what "all reasonable men" think is, in fact, an appeal only to others of rationalist persuasion who already share Hume's philosophical outlook in whole or in part. Troeltsch too, in postulating the basic homogeneity of all reality, simply turned historical theory into an explicit metaphysic of a positivistic kind—a metaphysic smuggled in under the guise of being a "modern" understanding of history, as Pannenberg has rightly asserted.[53] *Why* this metaphysic should be embraced is never made clear.

No good reason, then, exists to believe that just because one testimony does not violate our sense of what is normal and possible, it is more likely to be true than another, nor to believe that an account that describes the unique or unusual is for that reason to be suspected of unreliability. As the philosopher C. A. J. Coady tells us:

> [T]he lack of a suitable explanation of reports, other than their truth, is a consideration against rejecting them, but it is only one consideration and it is defeasible in various ways. The explanatory requirement is an ingredient in the overall verdict, along with the internal and external circumstances mentioned earlier [in his chapter on "astonishing reports"]. I think it very

unlikely that any hard and fast rule can be laid down for determining the outcome of such assessments of so diverse factors—what is required, as Locke saw, is not a criterion but a judgement.[54]

It is, indeed, *judgment* that is required: the judgment of the epistemologically open person, and indeed the truly empirical person, who does not approach the past, any more than the present, with an already closed mind that inhabits an equally closed universe. Somewhat ironically, although Hume is widely remembered as an empiricist, his historical writing clearly shows that he was not particularly interested in discovering anything about human nature from records of the past. Like his successors who depend so greatly on analogy, he already knew that what the past had to say would conform to what "reasonable people" already believed in the present.

We may happily conclude this section of the chapter on analogy with a general summary that applies both to it and to the preceding sections on early and later testimony and on ideology. "Rules" of evidence cannot prejudge whether particular testimonies are worthy of faith or not. To think that they can is an illusion. No intellectually defensible way is available to avoid, in the particular case, the inevitable consideration of all testimonies together, weighing them up on their own terms and in comparison with each other and asking how far they are each likely (or not) to be in actual relationship to the events to which they refer. All that the so-called "rules" of evidence do is to provide a helpful background in terms of generalities—an accumulated wisdom that may or may not help in the resolution of any particular case. In the final analysis, no substitute exists for the judgment of the individual reader of the testimonies—judgment that moves towards resolution in each particular case, and comes to a settled view on the testimonies in which faith might reasonably and intelligently be invested.

CONCLUSION

[H]istory cannot base itself on predictability. . . . Lacking universal axioms and theorems, it can be based on testimony only.[55]

We have been arguing essentially this case in this chapter—albeit that we disallow any such sharp distinction between inquiry into the *natural* world and inquiry into the world of the *past* as this statement may imply. Our knowledge of the past is dependent on testimony. This being the case, and biblical testimony being the major testimony about Israel's past that we possess, to marginalize biblical testimony in any modern attempt to recount the history of Israel must be folly. Considering that testimony along with other testimonies should be considered perfectly rational. It should be considered irrational, however, to give epistemological privilege to these other testimonies, even to the extent of ignoring biblical testimony altogether. Perhaps we shall find good reason in considering what the Bible has to say—as in considering what other sources have to say—to question in one way or another the extent to which statements are reflective of history at any given point. We should make our judgments on a case-by-case basis, however, rather than prejudging the matter by utilizing faulty methodological criteria that allegedly lead us to "firm ground" for historiography within or outside of biblical testimony. We juxtapose the above quotation, therefore, with the following, with which we profoundly disagree:

> If we have no positive grounds for thinking that a biblical account is historically useful, we cannot really adopt it as history. True, the result will be that we have less history than we might. But what little we have we can at least claim we know (in whatever sense we "know" the distant past); this, in my opinion, is better than having more history than we might, much of which we do not know at all, since it consists merely of unverifiable stories.[56]

We disagree, because history *is* the telling and retelling of unverifiable stories. Knowing any history aside from the history in which we are personally involved requires trust in unverified and unverifiable testimony. The kind of historical knowledge beyond tradition and testimony that this author seeks is a mirage. We do not require "positive grounds" for taking the biblical testimony about Israel's past seriously. We require positive grounds, rather, for *not* doing so. Only by embracing such epistemological openness to testimony, biblical and otherwise, can we avoid remaking the past entirely in our own image—can we avoid submitting to the delusion that we already "know" about reality and to the consequent mistake of trying to impose that "knowledge" on everything that questions it. Only thus can the history of the history of Israel hope in the future to be different from what it has been in the past—a slow capitulation to those who have asserted, without good grounds, that the principled suspicion of tradition should be considered the *sine qua non* of the intellectual life. "Critical history" has all too often meant, in the debate that has surrounded this capitulation, "history that does not criticize the tradition as much as I, a truly critical historian, would prefer it to." "Critical history" has not sufficiently often meant simply "thoughtful, intelligent history"—history that involves the exercise of critical thought *both* about tradition *and* about modern presuppositions about reality. The fact is that we either respect and appropriate the testimony of the past, allowing it to challenge us even while thinking hard about it, or we are doomed—even while thinking that we alone have "objectivity" and can start afresh on the historical quest—to create individualistic fantasies about the past out of the desperate poverty of our own very limited experience and imagination. To conclude:

> [T]he objectivity of modern historiography consists precisely in one's openness for the encounter, one's willingness to place one's intentions and views of existence in question, i.e., to learn something basically new about existence and thus to have one's own existence modified or radically altered.[57]

Chapter 4

Narrative and History: Stories about the Past

The essence of our argument in the preceding three chapters has been that the pronouncement of the "death of biblical history" is premature (chap. 1) and that, on the contrary, since we are dependent upon *testimony* for most of what we claim to know about the past or otherwise, to marginalize the biblical text in writing a history of Israel (chaps. 2–3) is folly. Attempts to find firmer ground in the supposedly more scientific fields of archaeology and/or social theory overlook the fact that these means of access to Israel's past are no more "objective" in any meaningful sense than the biblical testimony, given that each involves a significant measure of interpretation the moment results are reported or an attempt is made to integrate them into anything approaching a "history."

In this chapter, our aim is to explore further and more positively just *how* the Bible testifies to the past—how it reflects history. Because the bulk of the biblical material that purports to recount Israel's history is narrative in genre, our discussion focuses predominantly on the narrative mode of historical explanation.[1] Inasmuch as we tend to share our own "personal histories" by telling stories about them (that is, by constructing narratives), one might suppose that "narrative" as a legitimate mode of historical reportage would require no defense. Analytical philosophers of history, however, have raised concerns about narrative historiography. They have argued that narratives involve art, not science; are thus by nature interpretive; and are therefore insufficiently objective. Because of these concerns, we need to look further into the debate over "narrative history," taking as our starting point the state of the question among secular historians.

In this chapter, we first consider the status of "narrative history" within the field of historical studies in general. Here we observe that after a period of decline during which more statistical, quantifying histories were preferred, narrative history has made a strong comeback among historians (though without jettisoning the gains achieved by quantifying approaches). We argue that this renewed acceptance of narrative histories should call into question the tendency of some biblical scholars to discount the historical value of biblical narratives simply because they are storylike in form.

Of course, to be appropriately used in historical reconstruction, biblical narratives must be rightly understood, which means that they must be read well, with as much literary competence as can be achieved with the available evidence. Thus, we next consider the recent burgeoning of literary studies of biblical texts and the potential effects of this trend on historical studies. We believe that as we read biblical narratives better as narratives, in keeping with ancient conventions and techniques, better historical reconstructions become possible. But this approach raises further questions. What kind of information can we hope to glean from (biblical) narratives? Isolated facts only? Or does their narrative structure itself convey something of past reality? What are we to make of the fact that biblical narratives have, for example, discernible plots and careful characterizations? Are these not the stuff of fiction, not history?

In the light of these questions, we then explore whether "narrativity" is in some sense a property of reality itself or is merely imposed by narrators on isolated historical "facts." In particular, we consider the "constructionism" debate that continues apace among historians. This discussion leads naturally to a consideration of the kinds of creative contributions historians make in writing their histories and to a discussion of history writing as both an art and a science. We will argue that historians, though constrained by such "facts" as can be discovered, do exercise judgment and creativity in several respects. First, they exercise judgment in weighing the available evidence and in catching a "vision of the past." They then must make creative choices in seeking to present this vision to their target audiences. This means, of course, that historians themselves are central to the historiographical enterprise, which, in turn, means that the character and competence of historians are not inconsequential concerns; the greater their skill and goodwill, the more deserving of credence will be their reconstructions.

Having viewed narrative historiography from these several angles, we then take up the question of how best to become good readers of the biblical narratives, and so to use them responsibly in historical reconstruction. The chapter then closes with a specific case study.

THE NEAR-DEATH AND REVIVAL OF NARRATIVE HISTORY

It may seem curious to some readers that "narrative history" should ever have come under fire. Surely, through most of the history of history writing, the dominant mode of recalling (or recounting, or representing) the past has been *narrative*, with all that this implies about literary crafting and persuasive intent. History writing itself was formerly regarded as a branch of literature, or rhetoric.[2] But all that began to change in the nineteenth century.

Hoping to set historical study on a more scientific foundation, many historians in the nineteenth century abandoned the narrative mode of historiography, with its predominant focus on great individuals and events, in order to pursue more quantifying approaches that focused not on particulars but on large-scale environmental and societal trends. The shift, to use technical terminology, was from *idiographic* ("describing the separate, distinct, individual") to *nomothetic* ("lawgiving") historical research and writing.[3] Motivating the shift, as Lawrence Stone explains,[4] was a sense that narratives, with their descriptions of events in sequence and their focus on significant personal agents, were capable of answering *what* and *how* questions, but were unable to offer satisfying answers to the fundamental *why* question. They could trace an unfolding story, but they could not explain why the story unfolded as it did. The sense that narratives were inadequate to answer why questions stemmed from the fact that many "historians were at that time strongly under the influence of both Marxist ideology and social science methodology" and thus "were interested in societies not individuals."[5] Put simply, many historians believed that the true explanation of historical process had less to do with individual actions and events than with larger-scale environmental and societal forces. Optimistic attempts to develop "scientific" history took various forms,[6] but common to each was

> the belief that material conditions such as changes in the relationship between population and food supply, changes in the means of production and class conflict, were the driving forces in history. Many, but not all, regarded intellectual, cultural, religious, psychological, legal, even political, developments as mere epiphenomena.[7]

Historians of the French *Annales* school, which flourished from the 1950s to mid-1970s (and is still influential in biblical studies), believed that forces driving historical change could be hierarchically arranged. As Stone explains:

> [F]irst, both in place and in order of importance, came the economic and demographic facts; then the social structure; and lastly, intellectual, religious, cultural and political developments. These three tiers were thought of like the storeys of a house: each rests on the foundation of the one below, but those above can have little or no reciprocal effect on those underneath.[8]

In essence, "only the first tier really mattered," so that the subject matter of history became "the material conditions of the masses, not the culture of the élite." The result was "historical revisionism with a vengeance."[9]

As in so many areas within the field-encompassing field of biblical studies, the above trends in general historical study are paralleled (albeit with a significant time lag) in current scholarship on the history of ancient Israel. "Historical revisionism with a vengeance" is apparent in the writings of various scholars—preeminently at the Universities of Sheffield and Copenhagen, but elsewhere as well. Skeptical of narrative histories in general, these scholars find little use for the biblical narratives in particular, at least when it comes to historical reconstruction.[10] Representative of this approach is N. P. Lemche of Copenhagen, who in one of his more recent volumes declares that little relation can exist between "biblical Israel" and "the Israel of the Iron Age,"[11] a viewpoint that P. R. Davies already articulated in 1992.[12] "Biblical Israel," in Lemche's view, is little more than a literary entity, while "the Israel of the Iron Age" is a historical entity about which little if anything can be learned from what the biblical texts have to say. Preferring first- and second-tier data (that is, material evidences and sociological analyses) to the third-tier textual data of the OT, Lemche ultimately finds himself in "a situation where Israel is not Israel, Jerusalem not Jerusalem, and David not David."[13]

Revisionist assertions notwithstanding, however, it is a very open question whether the evidence of the first and second tiers (such as is available) so radically undermines the biblical narratives, with their largely third-tier focus on particular people and events. To keep matters in proper perspective, one must first remember that archaeological artifacts do not simply present themselves as *facts*, nor do objects out of the ground constitute *objective* evidence. Rather, these very objects, or artifacts, must be interpreted, which is precisely what scholars do, wittingly or unwittingly, the minute they begin to describe and discuss them.[14] Further, one must bear in mind that scholarly interpretations are seldom if ever devoid of broader concerns. The laudable notion of scholarly objectivity does not and cannot mean that a scholar approaches each new problem with a freshly erased mental hard drive. All scholars approach their work as whole persons, with beliefs and convictions of various sorts in place. Objectivity is never absolute. The inevitable presence of deep-seated convictions and commitments—background beliefs—need not, however, vitiate scholarly practice, provided that these background beliefs are acknowledged and made discussible.[15] Where a scholar's core commitments are not explicitly stated, inferring them may still be possible. Consider, for instance, the following passage from Lemche's *The Israelites in History and Tradition*:

> It is traditionally believed to be a respectable enterprise to try to show that a certain event narrated by the Old Testament really happened and that the narrative is for that reason a valuable source. It is at least as respectable, however, to try to show that the text does not carry any information about the period worth speaking about.[16]

While Lemche does not, to our knowledge, discuss his background beliefs in the volume just cited,[17] the last sentence above does approximate an agenda statement, and Lemche's sometimes startling assessments of the evidence[18] confirm his commitment to demonstrating the negligible value of the OT, except where unambiguously verified by external evidence (in which case the OT texts would be superfluous at any rate). In the preceding chapter, we discussed the issue of verification and falsification and noted serious problems in the former, both in terms of logic and application. Our own preference is for the falsification principle, by which ancient texts are given the benefit of the doubt unless compelling reasons to distrust them are apparent.

Ironically, revisionist studies such as Lemche's are discounting the historical import of biblical narratives just at a time when interest in narrative has experienced a major resurgence among historians in general. In the 1979 essay already cited, Stone highlights several reasons for this renewed interest. Not only is there a general "disillusionment with the determinist model of historical explanation and [the] three-tiered hierarchical arrangement to which it gave rise," but the recognition is also emerging from actual research that there is an "extraordinarily complex two-way flow of interactions between" environmental, material conditions, on the one hand, and "values, ideas and customs on the other." Add to these a decline in ideological commitment, Marxism, for example, and a renewed conviction that individuals "are potentially at least as important causal agents of change as the impersonal forces of material output and demographic growth," and little remains to commend any longer an antinarrative stance.[19] In short, as Stone explains:

> Disillusionment with economic or demographic monocausal determinism and with quantification has led historians to start asking a quite new set of questions, many of which were previously blocked from view by the preoccupation with a specific methodology, structural, collective and statistical. More and more of the "new historians" are now trying to discover what was going on inside people's heads in the past, and what it was like to live in the past, questions which inevitably lead back to the use of narrative.[20]

Given the now decades-old revival of interest in narrative history among historians, that some biblical scholars simply dismiss the OT as "essentially useless for the historian's purposes," nothing more than "a holy book that tells stories" is remarkable.[21] More encouragingly, the majority of historically minded biblical scholars continue to take the biblical narratives seriously.[22] For these scholars, as for historians more generally, the resurgence of interest in narrative history raises afresh the question of the relationship between history and literature, to which we now turn.

LITERARY READING AND HISTORICAL STUDY: HAPPY MARRIAGE OR OVERDUE DIVORCE?

The burgeoning of interest in the literary study of the Bible during the last quarter of the twentieth century is perhaps as dramatic as any other trend during the same period. The long-term effects of the enthusiasm for literary approaches on the *historical* study of the Bible, however, remain to be seen. Will literary approaches devolve into dehistoricized, purely literary readings that treat the Bible—despite considerable internal and external evidences to the contrary—as little more than an elaborate novel?[23] Or will improved literary sensitivities lead to sharpened perceptions of the full range of the Bible's testimony, including its historical testimony? It is too early to tell which path, if either, a majority of biblical scholars will take, but it is already abundantly clear that there are *some* who would drive a wedge between literary and historical study.[24] Philip Davies voiced the opinion in 1987 that, so far as the history of Israel is concerned, "the way forward—if it exists—would seem to lie" not with literary study but "with the (combined) methods of the social sciences: sociology, anthropology and archaeology": in other words, with the first- and second-tier concerns discussed above. In Davies's view, "*literary* study is turning its face away from history, concentrating on what is *in*, not *behind*, the text." There "remains a legitimate task for the *historian*," but "this task will be increasingly divorced from literary criticism."[25]

Examples of literary biblical studies that follow the ahistorical path—that exhibit what John Barton calls "counter-intuitive" tendencies such as an "unreasonable hatred of authorial intention, referential meaning, and the possibility of paraphrase or restatement"[26]—could easily be multiplied. It is by no means clear, however, that the ahistorical turn in literary studies is inevitable, or justified. It represents yet another instance of biblical scholars embracing trends now outmoded in the corresponding nonbiblical fields. Writing in 1990, Peter Barry observed that just when "literary criticism is . . . taking on board . . . some of the historical concerns which scriptural exegesis has perhaps been overburdened with, Biblical studies are sampling the many radical approaches to criticism and theory which brought about the 'crisis' in literary studies of the early and mid 1980s." At the time of his writing, Barry opined that it remained to be seen "whether a similar crisis [would] enliven the exegetical scene in the 1990s."[27] From our present perspective, we can see that biblical studies at the turn of the millennium indeed finds itself in what some have described as a crisis.

Central questions that must be faced include: Is a divorce between literature and history inevitable and overdue, or is a happy marriage still possible? Could it be that Davies's comments, cited above, simply illustrate the kinds of misunderstandings to which literary approaches can (but need not) give rise?[28] As Gale Yee notes, literary (i.e., "text-centered") approaches can indeed give rise to problems: "severing the text from its author and history could result in an ahistorical inquiry that regards the text primarily as an aesthetic object unto itself rather than a social practice intimately bound to a particular history." In the face of the often sophisticated *literary workings* of biblical texts, one can lose sight of the fact that "the biblical texts were not written [merely] to be objects of aesthetic beauty or contemplation, but as persuasive forces that during their own time formed opinion, made judgments, and exerted change."[29] Most biblical texts were not composed as "pure" literature (i.e., art for art's sake), but as "applied" literature ("history, liturgy, laws, preaching, and the like").[30] They are not "autotelic"—to use T. S. Eliot's coinage for a literary work that has "no end or purpose beyond its own existence."[31] On the contrary, they often instruct, recount, exhort, or some combination of these and more.

What this means is that literature and history cannot be regarded as unrelated, or mutually exclusive, categories.[32] "History may well dream of escaping from ordinary or natural language to the highly formal language of the sciences,"[33] but the fact of the matter, as Hayden White remarks, is that "history as a discipline is in bad shape today because it has lost sight of its origins in the literary imagination."[34] In a classic essay first published in 1951, Umberto Cassuto argued that both Israelite and Greek historiography developed from earlier epic-lyrical poems, the Israelites preceding Greeks and thus being the first true historians.[35] Though the specifics of Cassuto's proposal seem rather uncertain in the light of subsequent studies, the basic notion that narrative historiography is related to literature and is itself a type of literature is sound.[36]

It becomes obvious, then, that *literary understanding is a necessary condition of historical understanding, and both literary and historical understanding are necessary conditions of competent biblical interpretation.* As Robert Alter aptly puts it, "In all biblical narrative and in a good deal of biblical poetry as well, the domain in which literary invention and religious imagination are joined is history, for all these narratives, with the exception of Job and possibly Jonah, purport to be true accounts of things that have occurred in historical time."[37] Simply put, much of the Bible makes *historical truth claims*, and these claims will never be rightly understood unless the *literary* mode of their representation is itself understood. Again, Alter is helpful: "For a reader to attend to these elements of literary art is not merely an exercise in 'appreciation' but a discipline of understanding: the literary vehicle is so much the necessary medium through which the Hebrew writers realized their meanings that we will grasp the meanings at best imperfectly if we ignore their fine articulations as literature."[38] Later in this chapter, we note some of the "elements of literary art" that Israel's narrators and poets employed in their representations of history. Our aim in this section has been simply to establish that a happy marriage between literary and historical concerns is possible, desirable, and necessary. The ahistorical path is a dead end. Where biblical texts make historical truth claims, ahistorical readings are perforce misreadings—which remains the case, whatever one's opinions may be regarding the truth value of those claims.

So then, if biblical *narratives* make *historical* truth claims, this condition brings us to a further fundamental question, one much debated among current historians and philosophers of history: Does life itself have narrative shape, or is this merely an illusion created by historians as they construct their "(hi)stories" from essentially random, isolated events of the past? At its core, the question is whether the past has any inherent meaning or only appears to have meaning by virtue of the historian's narrative shaping of events.

NARRATIVITY: REALITY OR ILLUSION?

Not all history writing is narrative, of course, and certainly not all narrative is historiography. Rolf Gruner may well be correct that "there are two principally different ways of conceiving and portraying an individual stretch of reality, a static-descriptive or non-narrative and a kinetic-descriptive or narrative way."[39] In any case, one must certainly allow for non-narrative modes of reportage that could fairly be called history writing of a sort, or at least historical source material (genealogies, cross-sectional analyses of particular societies at particular points in time, etc.). Nevertheless, as William Dray insists, "[T]here remains the *fact* that a good deal of what historians produce is narrative history."[40] The question, then, is whether narrative structure is an inherent feature of the past reality or merely an artificial construct imposed by the historian.

Precisely this question has loomed large in recent debates over narrative historiography. In a review essay of Hayden White's *The Content of Form: Narrative Discourse and Historical Representation*,[41] William Dray criticizes what he describes as White's "extreme constructionist view of narrative in historical writing."[42] According to Dray, White comes "very close indeed to claiming that everything in an historical narrative that goes beyond sheer chronicle (or even, perhaps, beyond the mere statement of discrete facts) is somehow 'invented' (ix) by the historian." By stressing "the supposedly poetic rather than factual nature of narrative emplotment in history, White seems to want to represent the historical imagination as free—as having 'the facts' very much at its disposal." In our view, White may not, in fact, be as guilty of *constructionism*—the notion that "historians can emplot the past pretty much as they like"—as Dray contends, for Dray himself notes that White seems aware "that it may not be possible to emplot a given series of events in just any way at all."[43] But whatever White's own position, the extreme constructionist (or, as some prefer, constructivist) view—that narrativity is simply imposed by the historian and is not inherent in the events themselves—must be questioned.

Perhaps we can benefit by drawing an analogy between portrait painting, a kind of *visual representational art*, and historiography, which may fairly be described as *verbal representational art*.[44] Portrait artists are in a sense "constructionists"; they make creative choices in composing and rendering their historical subject. But they are far from simply *imposing* structure on an amorphous body of isolated "facts" (an eye here, a nose there). Their task is to observe the contours and the character of their subject, the relationships between the various features, and to capture in a visual representational medium these essentials of their subject. No two portraits are exactly alike, of course, because no two portrait artists see the subject in just the same way or make the same creative choices in rendering it. But neither are competent portraits of the same subject utterly unlike, for they are constrained by the facts—the contours and structures of the subject. In their representational craft, portrait artists *compose* (i.e., construct) their painting, but they do not simply *impose* structure on their subject. Might it not be the same with narrative historians? In principle, of course, the answer is yes. But again the question is whether the past itself has discernible, meaningful contours—a narrative quality, if you will—or whether it consists simply of meaningless, isolated events.

The Narrativity of Life

Tellingly, even those, like Frank Kermode, who are sometimes charged with constructionist leanings[45] find it hard to deny that life has a narrative quality about it. Kermode writes that "it is impossible to imagine a totally nonnarrative Christianity or a nonnarrative Judaism or indeed a *nonnarrative life*" (our italics).[46] Paul Ricoeur, who has written extensively on narrative,[47] notes simply that "a life *examined* . . . is a life *narrated*."[48] One of the more prominent recent proponents of the "narrativity of life" is David Carr,[49] who contends that "narrative is not merely a possibly successful way of describing events; its structure inheres in the events themselves."[50]

Before we pursue this question further, we should perhaps sharpen just what we mean by "narrative," "narrativity," and "narrative history." In an insightful review essay entitled "Narrativity and Historical Representation,"[51] Ann Rigney notes that historians conceive of "narrativity" in a variety of ways, depending on whom one consults. Here is a sampling:

1. Narratives may be distinguished from "annals" or "chronicles."
2. Narratives are concerned with "short- or long-term diachronic processes or transformations."
3. "Narrative (history) involves the figurative representation of unique actors and events and, as such, is distinguished from quantitative, statistical accounts of the world."
4. "Narrative (history) is concerned with (the experiences of) individuals, rather than with groups or social trends."
5. Narrative history "treats political matters rather than social and cultural ones," since it is in the political sphere that "changes initiated by 'free' individuals are most frequent."
6. The function of narrative history, as distinct from analytical discourse, is "to tell *how* and not *why* things happened."
7. "Narrative (history) involves a particular mode of cognition or type of explanation which is distinct from nomothetic explanation and which is proper to the historical sciences."
8. "Narrative (history) is characterized by its rhetorical appeal and aesthetic qualities."
9. "The 'narrativity' of history . . . is the promise of a meaningful pattern in history; the guarantee that what is represented will 'contain' meaning."
10. "Narrativism" involves a recognition of "the mediating role of language in producing historical meaning."[52]

Some of these attempts to capture the essence of narrativity appear incompatible; Rigney notes, for instance, the conflict between the notion that narrative history is a particular mode of explanation (no. 7) and the assertion that it does not tell "*why* things happened" (no. 6).[53] Some appear unjustifiably limited—for example, that narrative history is restricted to the treatment of *political* events (no. 5), or the implication that narrative history must exhibit "rhetorical appeal and aesthetic qualities" (no. 8). Most, however, are compatible observations and taken together can lead to a working definition of narrative and of narrative history. If a minimal definition of "narrative" is "*a representation of a sequence of non-randomly connected events,*"[54] then a minimal definition of "narrative history" would be "a representation of a sequence of non-randomly connected, actual events of the past."

A more expansive definition, drawing on Rigney's ten descriptors, might run as follows: "narrative history" involves an attempt to express through language (nos. 3, 10) the meaning (no. 9)—that is, a particular understanding/explanation (no. 1)—of the relationship of a selected sequence of actual events from the past (nos. 2, 7) and to convince others through various means, including the rhetorical force and aesthetic appeal of the rendering (nos. 3, 8), that the sequence under review has meaning and that this meaning has been rightly perceived. Thus we arrive at a definition for "narrative history" not unlike Ferdinand Deist's more succinct definition of "historiography" as "an explanation of the meaningful connectedness of a sequence of past events in the form of an interested and focussed narrative."[55]

To sum up thus far, and to push the argument a bit further: The crucial question for our current discussion is whether the "meaningful connectedness of a sequence of past events" inheres in the events themselves or is merely imposed on them by the historian. Our position is that, just as the physical world has structure, so life itself has contours, structure, meaningfully connected features. And just as the task of a representational artist is to perceive the subject's contours and represent them in a visual medium, so the task of the historian is to recognize the past's contours and meaningfully connected features and to represent them in a verbal medium. This conclusion does not mean that the historian makes no creative, artistic (literary) choices, nor that all historical representations will look alike (any more than all portraits of a given subject look alike). It does mean, however, that the historian's creativity is constrained by the actualities of the subject, and that legitimate histories, insofar as they focus on the same or similar features of the past, will bear some resemblance to one another.

The Narrativity of (Biblical) Historiography and the Question of Fiction

If life itself is not just a chaotic jumble of isolated events but has a kind of narrative structure and meaning, then one of the chief impediments to taking the OT seriously as a historical source is removed. One cannot simply cite the largely narrative form of the grand sweep of the biblical story as telling against its historicity. Admittedly, as Hans Barstad observes, "biblical historiography is narrative, event oriented and pre-analytical," and thus "does not provide us with the kind of empirical data the anti event-oriented and anti-narrative analytical scientist Braudel could use."[56] But this does not mean that the Bible is disqualified as a historical source. Barstad puts the matter plainly:

> That narratives about the past and narratives from the past may represent past reality is something which has now become more and more clear not only to historical theorists, but also to classical scholars. It is now time that historians of ancient Israel/Palestine start to think along the same lines.[57]

So far so good, and we can only hope that those "historians of ancient Israel/Palestine" who tend to be dismissive of narrative texts in general, and biblical texts in particular, will catch up to the broader field.

As helpful as Barstad's corrective comments generally are, his discussion of *fictionality* in historical narrative is puzzling. Near the end of his essay, he concludes, "Narrative history is not pure fiction, but contains a mixture of history and fiction."[58] He seems to have in mind that some parts of a narrative may be historical in the traditional sense (corresponding to, or at least cohering with, some past reality), while other parts are simply fictional (invented for effect). Should this be the case, then one could, in principle at least, divide between the two. Corresponding to the history/fiction mixture, Barstad also asserts the existence of distinct kinds of truth. He writes, "Since 'truths' may be of different kinds, it is important to realize that we today can no longer make the claim that traditional historical truth is more 'valuable' or more 'correct' than narrative truth."[59]

If our understanding of Barstad's points here is correct, then we have some reservations, based again on our portrait analogy. One would not exactly say of a portrait that it is a *mixture* of history and fiction. In one sense, a portrait is all history, since its essential purpose is to represent a historical subject. Ideally, every brushstroke in the portrait serves that purpose. In another sense, however, a portrait is all fiction—that is, it is all "fabrication," just paint on canvas. No brushstroke or combination of brushstrokes exactly *duplicates* the historical subject. Taken together, however, the brushstrokes *depict*, or represent, the historical subject. Because a portrait depicts but does not duplicate its subject, certain kinds of tests cannot be legitimately run on it and some questions would be nonsense to ask. For instance, one cannot analyze the DNA of a bit of "skin" scraped from the face of a portrait, nor would it make sense to fault a nonsmiling portrait for revealing nothing about the general dental hygiene of the period. The fact that portraits are ill-suited to certain kinds of scientific tests and inquiries does not, however, jeopardize their standing as accurate historical representations—as testimonies to the past.

Applying the analogy to the subject at hand, our argument is that a biblical narrative, as verbal representation, also does not duplicate but, rather, depicts the past. Like a portrait, a biblical narrative is in one sense a fabrication, because it consists of words on paper and not the actual past. Nevertheless, these words on paper, like paint on canvas, can accurately represent the historical past. Also like a portrait, a biblical narrative should not be faulted if it is ill-suited to certain kinds of scientific tests and inquiries. All this discussion would almost seem inane were it not for the fact that some biblical scholars and even historians appear to miss the distinction between fictionality in the sense of artistry, or craft, and fiction in the sense of genre.[60] The former is about *how* a representation is achieved, the latter is about *what* is represented. Both portraiture and narrative historiography involve "fabrication" (better "artistry"), but neither is art for art's sake, which leads to another question: Is historiography best understood as an art or a science?

HISTORIOGRAPHY: ART OR SCIENCE?

When we hear the term "art," we tend to think of something that is aesthetically pleasing: a work of literature, a painting, a sculpture, a piece of music. When we hear the word "science," we tend to think of exacting methods designed to discover information and hard facts. Which is the better descriptor for historiography? Is historiography chiefly interested in aesthetics or in information? It is surely an interest in imparting information (about the past) that distinguishes a history from a novel (even a historical novel, which, though it may contain historical information, is not chiefly designed to impart such information). But does historiography's emphasis on imparting information about the past disqualify it as art? Reflecting on how little we know about "how and when most biblical historical texts were actually read," Marc Brettler observes that "it is likely that authors who feel that their stories are important will have the good sense to offer them in a pleasing form, so that they will be listened to, remembered and transmitted further."[61] In other words, as we have argued, narrative historians—which would include biblical narrators—show concern not only for what information their accounts contain but also for how their accounts are crafted rhetorically. Our view is that, for example, narratives describing Saul's rejection or Solomon's apostasy cannot be fully understood historically unless we give attention to the artistic/rhetorical aspects of their literary depiction.

In stressing the artistic characteristics of biblical narratives, which nevertheless remain firmly representational in purpose, we are not out of step with what historians in general do. Indeed, professional historians frequently adduce the "art analogy." Notice, for instance, the way in which Lawrence Stone describes what he regards as a "most brilliant reconstruction of a vanished mind-set, Peter Brown's evocation of the world of late antiquity":

> It ignores the usual clear analytical categories—population, economics, social structure, political system, culture, and so on. Instead Brown builds up a portrait of an age rather in the manner of a post-Impressionist artist, daubing in rough blotches of colour here and there which, if one stands far enough back, create a stunning vision of reality, but which, if examined up

close, dissolve into a meaningless blur. The deliberate vagueness, the pictorial approach, the intimate juxtaposition of history, literature, religion and
art, the concern for what was going on inside people's heads, are all characteristic of a fresh way of looking at history.[62]

This example may be rather extreme,[63] but the comparison of historiography to
art is by no means unique. Among philosophers of history, advocates of a "pictorial" approach to historical representation[64] include Hayden White (already
mentioned)[65] and Frank Ankersmit.[66] As summarized by Hans Kellner,
Ankersmit presents

> a philosophical challenge to the literary model of historical discourse. In
> contrast to the prevailing textualization of all aspects of representation,
> Ankersmit offers a "preference for the pictural" which makes of the text, and
> especially the historical text, a primarily imagistic form. . . . Ankersmit
> maintains that histories have the "density" and "repleteness" characteristic
> of pictures as opposed to sentences.[67]

Ankersmit has no desire to belittle historians' renewed interest in the relationship
between history and literature. Indeed, he applauds the value and logic of exploring the literary aspects of historical texts. He simply believes that the picture analogy offers a further conceptual advance. He writes:

> In view of the common textual character of literature and history, this [lit-
> erary approach to history] is an obvious step. And if the inquiry is into the
> textual and rhetorical forms of the historical argument . . . this literary
> approach to the historical text is certainly valuable and has enriched our
> understanding of the nature of historical research.
> But the ascertained equivalence of text and picture suggests a "renverse-
> ment des alliances," in which not literature but the visual arts function as a
> model or metaphor of the study of history.[68]

From our own characterization of historiography as portraiture, we obviously see
value in Ankersmit's "picture emphasis," but we remain aware of certain dan-
gers—chief among them the kind of rank *constructionism* discussed earlier.[69]
Rightly or wrongly, both White and Ankersmit have been faulted for allowing
narrative historians "unfettered 'artistic' freedom" in the *construction* of their histories.[70] Contrary to the extreme constructionist position, Chris Lorenz insists
that "historians don't claim to present just a story but a *true* story, and this truth-
claim is its distinguishing hallmark."[71] As we have already argued, historians do
not have the freedom to impose just any plot structure on a given set of individual "facts," any more than portrait artists have the freedom to impose any facial
structure they please on the facial features ("facts") of their subject. Indeed, the
ability to place the features in *right relationship* to one another distinguishes a
good portrait artist from a bad one. Similarly, the ability to place the individual
historical "facts" in right relationship to one another distinguishes a good historian from a bad one. Individual brushstrokes must be "accurate"—which is to

say, they must achieve their representational objective (a single stroke may suffice to represent, say, an eyebrow quite accurately). But even more importantly, the total effect of the brushstrokes in combination must "accurately" achieve its representational objective. The difference between individual brushstrokes and the full portrait of which they are a part is one of degree and not of kind. By the same token, as Lorenz states, "the difference between individual statements and complete [historical] narratives is . . . a difference in *degree* and not in *kind*."[72] To insist in this way that not just individual strokes or facts, but also complete portraits and narratives, must be true to their historical subject is not at all to imply that only one portrait or only one narrative can truthfully represent a historical subject. Not only does much depend on the angle of approach, the chosen emphases, and the light under which the subject is viewed, but the personal style of the artist/narrator also plays its part in the finished product.

All this focus on creative, yet constrained construction underscores the role of the historian in first gaining a vision of the past and then communicating it. It underscores, in other words, the historian's "voice"—an emphasis resisted in some quarters. As Kellner observes:

> The historian's voice has traditionally been an embarrassment to those who envision an unmediated view of the past as the utopia of historical discourse. The ideal for these historical realists would be a composite history of the world in which every particular history would blend seamlessly with the rest in a vast whole consisting of many authors but one transparent voice.[73]

Kellner links embarrassment with the historian's voice with the "de-rhetorization of historical study" and muses whether renewed interest in the literary aspects of historiography may herald "a revival of the personal voice."[74] The fact is, as Ankersmit notes, "When asking a historical question we want an *account*, a *comment* on the past, and not a *simulacrum* of the past itself."[75] That is, we want some explanation of the significance of the past, not simply a mirror image of it. If one accepts a definition of history as "a discourse that is fundamentally rhetorical,"[76] involving "formalized aesthetic objects which make certain claims about the world and our relation to it,"[77] then recognition of the centrality of the historian's vision and voice is unavoidable. History truly exists as the historian's subject; but it may be truthfully represented by more than one portrait-narrative from more than one historian. History is one, but historiographies may be many.

ON READING NARRATIVE HISTORIOGRAPHY

"We have not talked seriously enough about the art of history," writes David Levin.[78] In the present chapter, we have sought to talk seriously about biblical historiographical narrative as both art and history, not in terms of some fifty-fifty, fiction-fact mixture but in terms of true history artfully presented. Like Levin, we disagree with the quite common "assumption that a natural law decrees hostility between good literature and serious history, between literary effects and factual accuracy."[79] Our own position is that this assumption is no more sensible than the assumption that a natural law decrees hostility between good art and serious portraiture.

In what follows we shall seek to enhance our ability to interpret ancient texts, especially the biblical narratives, and in so doing to grasp their historical import. This quest requires that we take the texts seriously in their integrity as texts. We again agree with Levin that the responsible critic's "ultimate concern will be the value of the entire work rather than merely the validity of its paraphrasable content, its argument. [The responsible critic] will devote himself to the relationship between that argument and the form and language in which it is presented."[80] Just as critics of portraiture must concern themselves with the ways in which artistic means serve referential ends, so readers of the biblical narratives must concern themselves with the ways in which literary art serves historical representation. Therefore, as Levin goes on to argue, "One of the first contributions that the critic of history can make is to serve as an intelligent reader who is willing to understand and discuss the rhetoric in which history is written."[81] Attention to literary artistry is especially important when dealing with the idiographically oriented narratives of the Bible.[82] Again, Levin's comments on the work of historians in general are helpful:

> Especially when describing individual characters or groups of men and their actions, historians have to make a number of extremely important literary decisions. Whether or not these decisions are made intentionally, they need to be examined by any criticism that aspires to understand the art of history. . . .[83]

Levin offers a listing of what some of the "literary decisions" that historians must make should be:

> What principle of order does the historian find in his materials that can allow him to relate one episode, one time, with another?
>
> What principles of form does he adopt to express that perception?
>
> How does he define, and by what technique does he portray, 'the People,' or large groups of people?
>
> How, in both quotation and paraphrase, does he use the language of his sources?
>
> How does he select details for the portrayal of character?
>
> From what point of view—that is, technically from what position—does he describe events?
>
> How does he introduce conjecture, and how does he distinguish between conjecture and what he considers documented fact?

How does he manage to arrange the events so that those he considers most important appear actually to be the most important events?

How does he move from individual evidence to general judgment, and what relationship does he establish between the typical character or incident and the larger reality that it represents?[84]

It is worth noting that this listing of questions *historians* should ask is quite similar to listings of questions that *literary readers* of the Bible should ask. In his recent book on the Bible's narrative art,[85] Jan Fokkelman presents the following list of ten (groups of) questions designed to facilitate careful and competent reading of biblical narratives.[86]

1. Who is the *hero*? What are the grounds for your decision (think about criteria such as presence, initiative, who undertakes the quest)?

2. What constitutes the *quest*? What is the hero after, that is to say, what is the desired objective? Does the hero succeed, and if not, why not?

3. Who are *the helpers and the antagonists*? Persons as well as factors, situations or characteristics should be considered. And are there *attributes* (objects) present? What is their contribution? Do they have a symbolic value?

4. Do you sense the presence of *the narrator* anywhere in the text? This applies above all where he offers information, commentary, explanation or evaluation from his perspective. Can you indicate the writer's form of speech? Where is the writer less directly detectable (for example through his structuring or composition)? Does he allow himself to speak at strategic points in the text?

5. Does the narrator hold to the *chronology* of the events and processes themselves? If not, where does he diverge, and why do you think he does so? Develop an impression of the relationship between narrative time and narrated time.

6. Where are there gaps in estimated *narrated time*; are there instances of speeding up, retarding, retrospectives or prospectives? Assuming that they are introduced by the writer at just the right moment, why do they stand where they do? What is their relation to their context?

7. Is the *plot* clear, or is the unit you are reading more or less without its own plot in that it is a part of the larger narrative? What is then the macroplot that controls the larger narrative?

8. Where are the *dialogues*? Are they many? Are dialogues omitted where you could expect them? What factors guide the speaker of a discourse, what self-interests, what background, what desires, what expectations? Are the words of the character well agreed with his deeds? If not, why not? Are there elements in the text that emphasize or suggest that the *writer* supports or applauds his character?

9. What word-choices strike you? What other characteristics of *style or structure*? Take them seriously, ponder them, asking a question such as: what does this contribute to the plot, or to the typing of the characters?

10. What means were used to mark out a unit? (Consider the aspects of time, space, beginning/ending of action, appearance or disappearance of characters.) Can you *partition* the text (divide into smaller units)? On the basis of what signals do you do that? Try to find still other signals or indicators in behalf of another division. To what extent does the division you see illuminate theme or content?[87]

That questions such as these should appear in a book on reading the Bible as literature comes as little surprise. More surprising is the degree of commonality between these and the questions that Levin insists historians must ask. Questions of point of view, characterization, use of dialogue, sequence and arrangement of events, and even plot (i.e., Levin's first question above) are the common fare of literary readers, but may seem more foreign to those wishing to draw historical information from texts. When one considers the character of biblical narratives, however, it becomes apparent just how vital these kinds of questions actually are for the historian. In what follows, therefore, we shall briefly introduce some resources and some guidelines pertaining to biblical poetics, or narrative criticism.[88]

THE POETICS OF BIBLICAL NARRATIVE

Recent decades have witnessed a sharp increase in publications treating the poetics of biblical narrative. A number of book-length treatments offer guidance for beginning and intermediate students, the most influential perhaps being by R. Alter;[89] and there exists at least one quite advanced treatise, written by M. Sternberg.[90] A variety of essays also offer convenient and stimulating introductions to the workings of OT narrative.[91] The intent of each of these works is to push the reader towards greater understanding of OT narrative discourse[92] and thus toward a firmer grasp of sense and significance of the biblical narratives. While there are, as Alter notes, "elements of continuity or at least close analogy in the literary modes of disparate ages," we shall become much better readers of biblical narratives if we adopt a "self conscious sense of historical perspective" towards the "stubborn and interesting differences" between our narrative modes and the Bible's.[93]

To attempt a full-blown poetics of biblical narrative here would serve little purpose, since such treatments are readily available in the works just cited and elsewhere. But at least a few lines of orientation are necessary if we are to read the biblical narratives responsibly with a view toward their historical import. Biblical narratives may be characterized under three rubrics: scenic, subtle, succinct.

OT narratives are scenic—not in the sense of detailed descriptions of the physical setting or scene, but, rather, scenic in the way that a stage play involves scenes. Like a stage play, the OT narratives do more showing than telling. The reader is seldom explicitly *told* by the narrator how this or that character, or this or that action, is to be evaluated (though this does occasionally occur). Instead, the reader is *shown* the characters acting and speaking and is thereby drawn into the story and challenged to reach evaluative judgments on his or her own. In other words, the reader comes to know and understand the characters in the narrative in much the same way as in real life, by watching what they do and by listening to what they say. The scenic character of OT narrative leads quite naturally to a second dominant trait.

OT narratives are subtle. As implied already, OT narrators are generally reticent to make their points directly, preferring to do so more subtly. To this end, they employ an array of more indirect means in developing the narrative's characterizations and in focusing reader attention on those aspects of the narrative that contain its persuasive power. Mention of physical details, for instance, is seldom if ever random. If we read that Esau was hairy, Ehud left-handed, Eglon fat, and Eli portly and dim-sighted, we should anticipate (though not insist) that such details in some way serve the characterizations or the action of the story. Sometimes the words or deeds of one character serve as indirect commentary on those of another character. When Jonathan, for instance, remarks that "nothing can hinder the LORD from saving by many or by few" (1 Sam. 14:6), this casts Saul's excuse in the preceding chapter—"the people were slipping away" (13:11)—into a different light than a first reading might have done. Even small changes in the narrator's commentary on events may have far-reaching implications, not just literarily but historically as well. Immediately following King David's charge to his successor, Solomon, in 1 Kings 2:1–10, the narrator registers David's death (v. 11) and remarks (v. 12) that Solomon's "kingdom was firmly established" (made emphatic by Hebrew $m^{e\bar{o}}d$), and this without Solomon having yet done anything. There follows an account of Solomon's eradication of Joab and Shimei (vv. 13–46), persons deemed dangerous by his father, and the account concludes with another narratorial comment (similar but not identical to v. 12): "So the kingdom was established in the hand of Solomon" (v. 46). Gone is the adverb $m^{e\bar{o}}d$, rendered "firmly" in v. 12. Added is the phrase "in the hand of Solomon," which is better rendered in this context as "by the hand of Solomon." Without coming right out and saying it, the narrator hints that Solomon's initial efforts to secure his kingdom by his own hand have accomplished little or nothing. His early days tell "a fairly sordid story of power-politics."[94] No wonder, then, that Solomon confesses, in the next chapter, to feeling like a "little child" who does not "know how to go out or come in" (3:7).[95] Ironically, it will be news of the death not only of David but especially of Joab that will trigger the return of Hadad the Edomite (1 Kgs. 11:21), the first adversary raised up by Yahweh (1 Kgs. 11:14) when it becomes necessary to "chasten" the apostate Solomon with "floggings inflicted by men" (2 Sam. 7:14; NIV).[96] If such subtleties often go unnoticed by modern literary readers, how much more so do they escape historians, but they can prove essential to proper reading and reconstruction.

OT narratives are succinct. Perhaps in part because of the constraints of writing in a scenic, or episodic, mode, biblical narrators tend to be economical in their craft. They accomplish the greatest degree of definition and color with the fewest brushstrokes. Biblical stories, although written, are "geared toward the ear, and meant to be listened to at a sitting. In a 'live' setting the storyteller negotiates each phrase with his audience. A nuance, an allusion hangs on nearly every word."[97] The very succinctness of the biblical narratives invites close attention to detail, and all the more so because the biblical narrators were masters in drawing special attention to key elements in their texts. They use all manner of repetitions to great advantage—words and word stems (i.e., *Leitworte*), motifs, similar situations (sometimes called "type-scenes" or "stock situations"), and the like. The

effect of repetition is often to underscore a central theme or concern in a narrative, as, for instance, in the repetition of the phrase "listen to the voice/sound" in
1 Samuel 15. As the chapter opens, Saul is exhorted to "listen" to the Lord's
"voice" (v. 1) and destroy all the Amalekites (man and beast); later he claims to
have done so (v. 13); Samuel responds by asking about the "voice" of the sheep
and cattle to which he is "listening" (v. 14); Samuel and Saul debate whether Saul
has or has not "listened to the voice" of the Lord (vv. 19–20); when Saul seeks to
excuse his failure to listen by claiming to have spared livestock only in order to
sacrifice to the Lord, Samuel responds that "listening to the voice" of the Lord is
vastly more important than sacrifice (v. 22); and Saul begrudgingly concedes that
he has "listened to the voice" of the people (v. 24). While the attentive reader can
surely judge from the general flow of the passage that Saul's (dis)obedience is a
central theme, attention to the literary fabric of the passage underscores and
enriches this insight.[98]

Our brief description of the scenic, subtle, and succinct character of biblical
narratives only begins to scratch the surface. Beyond these basics, readers—even
those (or perhaps especially those) whose interests are in historical questions—will
profit greatly from immersing themselves in the works mentioned above, especially those by Alter, Longman, and Sternberg. The key point is that *biblical
accounts must be appreciated first as narratives before they can be used as historical
sources*—just as they cannot be dismissed as historical sources simply because of
their narrative form. Indeed, it is not just biblical narratives but ancient Near Eastern texts in general that show literary patterns and shaping. Nor is it just biblical
narratives that speak, for instance, of divine involvement or intervention in military affairs. Such references are common in ancient Near Eastern battle reports.[99]
And this has not prompted scholars to conclude that these reports are devoid of
historical value. Why should it be otherwise with the biblical narratives?[100]

EXAMPLE: SOLOMON IN TEXT AND IN TIME

We have had much to say above on the importance of paying careful attention
to the literary and depictive aspects of historiography generally and of biblical
narratives in particular. As we bring this chapter towards its close, a specific example may help—the discussion of which addresses not only this matter of "care in
reading," but also some of the other issues that have arisen in earlier chapters.
This example thus provides a convenient conclusion to the whole of chapters
1–4, and prepares us to begin to look ahead in chapter 5.

In their 1986 *History of Ancient Israel and Judah*,[101] Miller and Hayes offer an
extended discussion of King Solomon in history and tradition. In their view, the
Solomon that we find in Kings is largely the idealized Solomon of legend, not
the Solomon of history. The editors responsible for 1 Kings 1–11 present his
reign, indeed, in a way that is artificial and schematic—unconvincing as a historical account. These editors depict Solomon in the first and main part of his

reign as a ruler faithful to God who achieved a "golden age," and they depict his latter years as years of apostasy, during which time Solomon suffered reverses. The chronology of his reign is itself not to be taken literally, since the numbers involved are clearly symbolic. If history is to be found in 1 Kings 1–11, then it must be looked for (suggest Miller and Hayes) not in the sweeping claims and generalizations of the text, but in aspects of the accounts of Solomon's accession to the throne and his cultic activities. History is particularly to be found in those details in the text that conflict with the picture of Solomon that the editors of Kings wished to convey (e.g., the episode involving Jeroboam of Ephraim in 1 Kgs. 11:26–40). The Chronicles account of Solomon's reign is even further removed from history. Chronicles depends heavily on and largely reproduces Kings, yet neutralizes all the negative aspects of Solomon's reign found there and elaborates on his role as Temple builder and cofounder with David of the Jerusalem cult. That account is of no significant help in reconstructing a historical Solomonic age.

For Miller and Hayes, then, neither the books of Chronicles nor the books of Kings are of much help (except accidentally and in small measure) to the historian interested in the historical Solomon. The Solomon of the text is largely unrelated to the Solomon of time. Their argument is, however, open to question on a number of fronts. Right at its heart lies an indefensible distinction between those texts within 1 Kings 1–11 that are said to inform us about what the editors of Kings *really* wanted to say about Solomon and those texts that are said *not* to inform us about this (and which may therefore be of more use to the historian than the bulk of the material). How exactly one is supposed to tell the difference between the two kinds of texts remains something of a mystery, about whose solution Miller and Hayes themselves fail to offer even the slightest hint. Why, in any case, would the editors of Kings include texts in their account that conflicted with the overall picture of Solomon that they desired to paint? In the Miller and Hayes view, the authors of Chronicles had no such scruples; they simply *omitted* any offending material. Were the editors of Kings, then, "better historians" than the authors of Chronicles—quite deliberately including material that they recognized was not consistent with their overall perspective? But then, if their choice of material was deliberate, should we not try to take all their material with equal seriousness in forming our view of the portrait of Solomon they wanted us to see?

Miller and Hayes themselves think that the editors of Kings were *conscious* of the conflict between ". . . the sweeping claims about Solomon's wisdom, wealth and power, on the one hand, and bits of information that seem to undercut these claims, on the other . . ." (196). The editors dealt with this conflict precisely by employing an artificial and schematic presentation of Solomon's reign as comprising two quite different parts. Yet this explanation does not account for the reality that material already exists in 1 Kings 1–10 (before we arrive at the downfall of Solomon in chapter 11) that, as Miller and Hayes acknowledge, suggests a Solomonic reign of more modest and realistic proportions than the one *they* say the editors of Kings wished to convey. Why should all *this* material be regarded as not truly intended to inform us about the views of the biblical writers on Solomon? Yet if it *is* regarded as truly informing us about this, what happens then to the simplistic and schematic presentation of Solomon's reign with which the editors of Kings have allegedly provided us? The argument does not appear to make a great deal of sense; in fact, the move that lies at its heart—the common partition of the reign of Solomon into two distinct periods (good Solomon/bad Solomon)—has been shown by recent exegetical work on 1 Kings 1–11 to be poorly grounded in the textual data. This "partition" has turned out to be more the construction of modern readers' imaginations than the structure the texts' authors actually put in place. The partition has turned out to be, in fact, the result of a lack of care in reading. The authors of Kings—a careful reading suggests—are very far from seeking to idealize Solomon, even in the early period of his reign. Suggestions appear already right back in 1 Kings 1–4 of ambiguity and way-wardness in Solomon's life—a darkness to which Solomon is portrayed as pro-gressively succumbing as his reign moves on.[102] It is difficult to see how such a portrayal could be described as "artificial," although much depends in judgments like these, of course, upon one's general view of reality.

If, then, the portrayal of Solomon by the authors of Kings is rather more com-plex than has often been allowed, what remains of Miller and Hayes's objections to the portrayal as a historical account? One problem that seems to loom large in their thinking is that of literary parallels. If something said of Solomon can be paralleled in another ancient text (e.g., that the king married Pharaoh's daugh-ter), then it must be considered historically doubtful (195). This conclusion seems quite ungrounded in logic. Can events that are similar to each other not occur? Can events that appear in fictional literature not also happen in historical reality and be recorded in texts that seek to speak about that reality?

Again, writing of the passages that focus on Solomon's cultic activities (193–94), Miller and Hayes seem concerned that these passages were formulated long after Solomon's day and address theological concerns of the exilic commu-nity. The implication appears to be that a text from a later time and/or a text shaped to take account of later community interests should be considered innately suspect in its statements about the past. There seems little reason why one should accept this proposition (even if one were to accept that a particular text were late). All statements about the past, near or far from the events they describe, address some interests in the present of their composition. Although it is always possible that they distort the past in addressing these interests, it is not inevitable that they should do so, and one certainly cannot assume distortion *sim-ply on the basis of* their date of composition and the presence in them of an autho-rial "agenda."

Valuable in this connection is a brief return to Chronicles—virtually dis-missed by Miller and Hayes as a source for writing a history of Solomon's age because it both depends on Kings and modifies it "in a notably tendentious fash-ion" (197). Why Chronicles should be dismissed in this way is not entirely clear. Chronicles has a "tendency," certainly, but one cannot move from "tendency" to straightforward dismissal of the book as a historical source. If this were the rule, then all historiography, past and present, would also have to be dismissed—for as we have argued throughout these opening chapters, no account of the past has ever been written free of a philosophy or theology and without seeking to convince its audience of the truth of its message. Perhaps Miller and Hayes think that the authors of Chronicles allowed their "tendency" to distort their account of the past, rendering it essentially untrustworthy. This claim, however, would have to be demonstrated in the individual case, rather than assumed in advance. Certainly Chronicles sometimes takes a very different *view* of aspects of Israel's history than the view expressed by the authors of Kings. "Distortion" would be a strange word to use in such cases, however, when it is reasonably clear that, even where it offers its own interpretation of the past, Chronicles presupposes its audience's familiarity with Kings. That is, Chronicles clearly seeks to provide a *reading* of its base text rather than a *replacement* for it.[103]

What we find at the heart of Miller and Hayes's treatment of Solomon, then, are a number of questionable assumptions and statements about the nature of the biblical texts and about the nature of history. Their treatment of Solomon is in this respect very similar to their treatment of earlier periods of Israel's history. Just the same emphasis is found elsewhere in their writing on the artificial, schematic, and ideologically tendentious nature of the overarching biblical narrative, and just the same deduction is drawn about the lack of historical value that should be attached to such presentation. Just the same confidence is displayed (in some places, at least) in the ability of the scholar, both to differentiate between texts that inform us about what the compilers of the texts really wished to say and texts that do not, and then to extract real history from the latter. It is an approach to literature and to history that does not withstand serious scrutiny well—not least because of its grounding in a lack of exegetical care and attention. It is not the approach that will be adopted in this present volume.

SUMMARY AND PROSPECT

In this chapter, we have sought to place the debate over the historical value of the biblical narratives in the broader context of debates about narrative histories in general. Given the renewed acceptance of narrative histories among historians in general, we have argued that biblical scholars are unjustified in dismissing biblical narratives as "essentially useless for the historian's purposes" and the Bible as nothing more than "a holy book that tells stories."[104] But if biblical narratives are to be used in historical reconstruction, they must be properly read. Thus, in our second section we reflected on the potential effects, for good or ill, of the recent growth of interest in literary readings of biblical texts. The focus of such studies on "narrativity" led us in our third section to consider whether narrativity is in some sense an aspect of real life, or is simply a construct imposed on life's amorphous details by storytellers and narrative artists. Concluding that there is indeed a kind of narrativity inherent in life itself that must be discerned and then depicted by narrative historians, we turned in our fourth section to an exploration of the character of history writing as both an art and a science. Here we emphasized the central role played by historians themselves in *depicting* history; it is historians who must first catch a vision of the past and then devise ways of presenting their vision so as to persuade others that their reconstructions fairly represent some aspect of past reality. In our fifth section, we stressed the importance—even (or especially) for historians—of reading biblical texts with as high a degree of literary competence as possible. We drew attention to recent significant writings that can contribute to the development of such competence. We briefly described the general character of biblical narratives and suggested appropriate questions that any reader should ask. This section was meant to be suggestive only, and to point readers in the direction of further help.

We concluded the chapter with a specific case study (Solomon), which illustrated the kind of approach to matters of text and history that we shall *not* be adopting in this volume. This begs the question, of course: What kind of approach *shall* we adopt? In the next chapter, therefore, we seek to draw together all the threads of our discussion so far in a description of our own working method, which will serve as an introduction to part 2 of this volume: an account of the history of Israel from Abraham down to the Persian period.

Chapter 5

A Biblical History of Israel

Our first chapter opened with some reflections on an attack on the kind of history of Palestine that has been defined and dominated by the concerns and presentation of the biblical texts—a "biblical history" that has allegedly produced ". . . little more than paraphrases of the biblical text stemming from theological motivations."[1] The succeeding chapters have sought to respond to these sentiments and to lay the groundwork for the second part of the present volume, which certainly sets the biblical texts at the heart of its historical enterprise. The time has now come for us to look ahead to these chapters that follow, and to explain their character in the light of the preceding discussion.

We do indeed offer a *biblical* history of Israel in the following pages. That is, we depend heavily upon the Bible in our presentation of the history of Israel, but not because we have "theological motivations" (although we return to that question shortly). It is rather because we consider it irrational not to do so. Here we find literature that is unique in the ancient world in its interest in the past—literature that, in particular, provides us with the only continuous account of ancient Israel's past that we possess. We see every reason to take its testimony about that past seriously, and, as we have argued to this point, no reason to set its testimony aside in advance of the consideration of its claims. In principle no *better* avenue of access to ancient Israel's past is available. Indeed, people who have set aside biblical testimony in favor of some other means of access to ancient Israel's past have inevitably found themselves with little to say about it, and the little they have had to say has had more connection with their own worldview and agenda than with any past about which others have actually testified. Even a "paraphrase of the biblical text" would likely be a surer guide to the real past, in our view, than the replacement story offered by those who systematically avoid the biblical text in seeking to speak about that past—although, of course, not all "paraphrasing" in the past has been of exactly the same kind and of equal merit. We do not view our procedure in the following pages, however, as any kind of mere paraphrasing of the text. We view it as an attempt only to take the text deeply seriously in terms of its guidance to us about the past of which it speaks.

Second, we offer a biblical history of *Israel* in the following pages. Every book must choose its topic; this book is no exception. We have not chosen to write a history of the ancient Near East, nor even a history of the ancient eastern Mediterranean. Nor have we chosen to write a history of Israel in those periods beyond the explicit scope of the biblical testimony. These tasks are all worthy, but none is the task we have chosen. Instead, we present an account of the history of Israel in those periods that biblical texts explicitly reflect—largely because our concern is to demonstrate how history writing with respect to Israel may, with intelligence and integrity, make use of the biblical materials. We begin with the Patriarchs, therefore (Abraham and his descendants), because that is where the Bible begins to speak of Israel as such, rather than of the world in general. We end in the period when the Persian Empire held sway over the ancient Near East, because that is where explicit testimony about Israel as a people comes to its end.[2] Some detractors will dismiss this stance as "conservative," but that assessment proceeds by labeling rather than by argument, and should not be taken seriously. The real question is not whether the stance is conservative, but whether it is intellectually justifiable. We certainly consider it a more sensible approach to the matter in hand than arbitrarily choosing a starting point within the biblical tradition on the basis that it allegedly represents "firm ground," or ignoring biblical testimony altogether (see chap. 1).

We offer, third, a biblical history of Israel that *takes seriously the nature of its primary sources*. If biblical narratives are to be used in historical reconstruction, they must be properly read; much that has been problematic in past efforts at "biblical history," whichever label might have been attached to it (e.g., "conservative," "critical"), has been bound up with poor reading. Historians must read biblical texts, and indeed all texts, with as high a degree of literary competence as possible (chap. 4). This competence we strive to display in the succeeding chapters, endeavoring to appreciate the nature, purpose, and scope of our texts in the process of suggesting how, precisely, they testify to the past in which they are so interested.

This third point leads on naturally to a fourth: we offer a biblical history of Israel that *takes seriously the testimony of nonbiblical texts about Israel and about the ancient world in which ancient Israel lived*. We do not take these texts *more* seriously than the biblical texts, for reasons that we have discussed in the preceding chapters (especially chap. 3). Neither do we take them *less* seriously than the biblical texts, however. For one thing, they provide the context within which we can develop precisely the literary competence mentioned above, as we form judgments about matters of literary convention in the ancient world. For another, the nonbiblical texts provide helpful information about the peoples with whom ancient Israel came into contact, and sometimes about their specific interactions with Israelites. They do not do this in a way that is free of art and ideology on the part of their authors, and so they cannot be regarded as providing *more solid* information than our biblical texts about ancient Israel. Yet hearing their testimony is appropriate and important, as is exploring how it converges or fails to do so with Israel's, in forming our view of the shape of the past.

Fifth, we offer a biblical history of Israel that *takes seriously such nontextual archaeological data as exist and might help us in forming our view of the history of ancient Israel.* Again, we do not take these data and their interpretations *more* seriously than the biblical texts, for reasons discussed in the preceding chapters (especially chaps. 2 and 3). We do take them *seriously*, however, in the expectation that if we have understood our archaeological data properly, and if we have understood our biblical texts properly, and if they are testifying truly about the past, then we should expect convergence between the biblical testimony and the interpretations of the archaeological data.[3] We anticipate above all that the archaeological data can help us to fill out our general picture of the world in which ancient Israel lived, much more than helping us with specific questions; nonliterary artifactual remains are more useful to the person interested in general material culture and everyday life than to the person interested in specific historical issues. For the latter person, ancient *literary* remains are much more helpful.

This fifth point is not unconnected to our sixth: that we offer a biblical history of Israel that *is attentive to what disciplines like anthropology and sociology have to suggest about the possible nature of the past.* We choose the word "attentive" deliberately, to suggest an openness to these disciplines as complementary to the direct testimony of peoples from the past, but also a lack of willingness to allow the agendas of many of their practitioners to dominate our own agenda. Our caution derives from a conviction that, methodologically, we should be careful to distinguish nomothetic analysis, which aims at general insights about reality (including past reality), from idiographic analysis, which attempts to understand the unique and the individual aspects of reality (including past reality). Nomothetic analysis is typical for the natural sciences and for the social sciences that seek to approximate to their method. Yet it is simply a matter of logic that what is generally the case about human reality (to the extent that this can be established) need not always be the case, whether in the present or past, and that whichever models one may build to account for reality in general will always fail to include all the specific data.[4] Nomothetic analysis may be helpful to the historian in illuminating the general background against which specific events unfold.[5] Such analysis cannot be regarded as predicting what *must* happen in particular cases, as individuals and groups of people respond to their circumstances in their own particular and distinctive ways. Where we employ nomothetic analysis in this volume, then, we use it only as an auxiliary tool without surrendering to its generalizing aim.[6] We certainly do not regard human beings of the past, any more than those of the present, as being simply fated or determined to live and act in certain ways by impersonal forces beyond their control (albeit that we recognize larger forces such as climate and geography as playing their part in the shaping of the history of any people). Among the consequences of this decision to refuse to allow nomothetic analysis to dominate over idiographic analysis is this: that the reader will find some emphasis in this volume on the suggestive nature of certain aspects of non-Israelite culture and society in the ancient world in terms of understanding what was happening in ancient Israel. We do not claim, however, that this or that aspect of non-Israelite culture and society *proves* or *disproves* that aspects of biblical testimony about the past are true. This kind of simplistic move we regard as one of the more unhelpful features of the history of the history of Israel in modern times.[7]

Finally, we offer a biblical history of Israel that is written by us, and not by others. That is, this biblical history of Israel is written by people who are themselves caught up in the flow of history and have a particular sense of where that history is heading and what it means, who possess a particular worldview, who hold a particular set of beliefs and values, and indeed possess particular motivations in writing as they do. Our presentation could not be otherwise, but it is as well to be quite candid about it, and indeed to explore the implications of it, especially since so much is made nowadays of the agendas of authors and how these affect what they have to say—especially in respect of the history of Israel.

Who are we? The question is a large one, and we assume that not all the possible answers would be of interest to readers of this volume. In view of how recent debate about the history of Israel has unfolded, however, we hazard a guess that the following facts will be of interest. First, we are students of the Old Testament, interested in these texts at a whole variety of levels of which history is only one—albeit an important one. We are indeed students of the Old Testament who also make our living out of thinking about it, writing about it, and teaching it to others. Second, we are students of history. We are not professional historians, but each of us has studied history both formally and informally to an extent that is not necessarily common within the diverse guild of academic biblical studies, with all its many intersecting interests. History is a passion of ours, and we are particularly interested in dealing with it well in the context of our genuinely professional area of concern, Old Testament studies.

Third, we share some core convictions about the nature of reality, including past reality, which affect the way that we read both the Old Testament and the past. Some of these are already clear from the discussion thus far. We do not believe, for example, that *a priori* suspicion of testimony about reality is a rational starting point for engagement with reality, nor that empirical enquiry into the nature of reality can by itself take one very far in acquiring knowledge. Nor do we believe that the thinking and living of human beings in the world is determined by larger forces of nature that lie beyond their control, and that these forces rather than individual and corporate human beliefs and actions are the driving forces of history. We do not believe, either, that the universe is a closed system in which new and surprising things do not happen, or that the best measure of the factuality of an event is whether something like it has previously occurred. Many people say that they do believe these things (or that their method requires that they be assumed), but our conviction is that such things are, after careful reflection, unbelievable.[8] To these kinds of shared core convictions about the nature of reality we must now add convictions of a definitely theistic and indeed Christian and Protestant kind, for this is also who are. Holding the convictions about reality already described is perfectly possible *without* also subscribing to theism, whether of the Christian and Protestant kind or not; people have done so. Yet in our case these convictions are bound up with a theistic and Christian worldview that has a Protestant dimension to it.

We are Old Testament scholars, then, who are interested in the history of Israel and operate out of the context of Christian theism; and it is we who are writing this book, not some other people possessing a different set of core beliefs and convictions. Do we have "theological motivations" in what we do? Absolutely. Our interest in the history of Israel is bound up with our interest in the Old Testament not only as literature, but also as part of Christian Scripture, and in writing about the history of Israel we hope to produce a volume that is not only interesting to those who do not share our religious convictions but also useful to those who do. Our intended audience is large, and it certainly includes Christians.

What difference do these theistic convictions and the "theological motivations" bound up with them make to the way in which the book is written? They do make some difference, for we have not striven to disguise them. We have no interest in simultaneously being metaphysical theists and methodological nontheists. Some scholars do embrace such a dichotomy. They believe that God exists (and they may even worship God in some way), but they embrace a view of historical science that excludes "God-talk."[9] We are not content with this kind of posture. We think it is far better to strive for the kind of consistency sought by P. R. Davies, whose metaphysical and methodological nontheism leads him to claim "that there is no 'objective' history," understanding that "a certain kind of religious belief *might* well dictate a certain definition of 'history'"[10]—that a connection always exists between the kind of world one believes in and the kind of history that one writes. Since as an atheist Davies does not share the view expressed by the Bible itself—that there exists "a single transcendental being who can comprehend, indeed controls, all history"[11]—he can find no ground for believing in any objective history at all. This striving for consistency we applaud. Our position, however, is that of the metaphysical and methodological theist: one who believes that there is a God, a "sacral being endowed with the authority and power of the Lord," whose story history is and through whose metanarrative human beings can come to understand themselves in relation to their world.[12]

Such a person cannot be content with the a- or antitheological approaches to history that have evolved since the Enlightenment,[13] because he will tend to share the biblical prophets' view of history as God's conversation with his people. Indeed, he will believe that God is central to history, and that it is impossible rightly to understand the *meaning* of history if God is marginalized or denied. And such beliefs are bound to inform the writing of a history of Israel in all sorts of ways—although it should not be assumed that they will always do so in exactly the *same* way (we come back to this point shortly).

Our theistic convictions and theological motivations do make *some* difference in the way in which the book is written. They do not make so much difference, however, that it cannot be read with profit or interest by those who flatly reject or dislike them. At least, so we believe. One reason is that what we have to say about the history of Israel is not *determined by* these beliefs, even though it is *bound up* with them. That is, we are not writing religious propaganda, in which the content of the writing is entirely determined by the prior beliefs and desired outcomes of the exercise, with little attention given to evidence or the kind of argument that counts as public discourse. On the contrary, we are writing *history*; all genuine history, while it no doubt does tell us *something* about the context and the beliefs of its author, is nonetheless interested in evidence and argument and can be read with profit by open-minded people who do not necessarily share the author's presuppositions. Indeed, if we were never able to read books with profit unless we shared the presuppositions of their authors, we should read very few books with profit at all. A second reason is that in the interests of communicating to a wide audience, we have not in any case allowed our core convictions and motivations, whether theistic and theological or not, entirely to surface in the way in which the volume is written. Explicit theistic discussion is, for example, often temporarily set aside in the interest of friendly conversation—even though we recognize that permanent exclusion of "God-talk" is irrational for theists and should not become or remain the *sine qua non* of historical study, lest even theists become *practical* or *methodological* nontheists and find themselves in danger of sliding eventually into *metaphysical* nontheism—or of unwittingly drawing others in that direction.[14]

A good example of our partial suppression of core conviction lies in our common refusal in this volume to draw explicit lessons from the history that we are writing. The reasons for not doing so are twofold. First, the volume is already long enough without further additions. Second, we recognize that it has become unfashionable in modern times to include within historiographical works, along with "facts," moral exhortations and warnings; this book will be read (or not read) in modern times, by readers whom we want to engage rather than irritate. Yet our conviction is certainly not that historiography *should* avoid matters of present existence and morals in articulating a vision of the past. Indeed, it is very far from being our conviction that any work of historiography *has* ever avoided matters of present existence and morals in articulating a vision of the past—even where it has claimed otherwise. Visions of the past are always bound up with visions of the present and the future. It is just that premodern historiography was typically more honest and straightforward than much modern historiography has been in making the connections—in embracing a pedagogic purpose for historiography.[15] History *does* teach us things, we believe. History *should* teach us things. We are with Voltaire at this point: "If you have nothing to tell us other than that one Barbarian succeeded another Barbarian on the banks of Oxus or Iaxartes, of what use are you to the public?"[16]

The reader will understand that for those who believe the Old Testament to be *Scripture* as well as testimony to Israel's past, there is an even greater imperative to attend to the lessons of history in this case than in others. For if the center of history—understood as both event and interpretive word—is God's conversation with Israel and the world as testified to in these and the New Testament writings, then the stakes in this case are particularly high. Nevertheless, we leave the task of drawing lessons from Israel's history largely to those who write other books dedicated to this purpose, like commentaries on the biblical text. We do not engage in that enterprise here. Our task is only to offer an interpretation of the biblical testimony about Israel's past, set within the broader context of the past as it may be established from other sources of information, such that the reader will better understand both the testimony and the past. Our role is that of the art historian, who seeks through interpretation of a portrait to help the audience understand both the past and the portrait better than before.

Should our core convictions and theological motivations, then—thus stated—cause any reader of this volume insuperable difficulty in reading and enjoying it? We think not. At least, they should not cause any greater difficulty than the core convictions and motivations of any author cause. The concerned reader may at least take heart in this, however, that in any case, our shared convictions and motivations do not come to expression in exactly the same way in the various parts of the volume that we have each composed. We are three, and not one; and none of us would have written what the others have written in precisely the same way. This variety should be of some help to the person irritated by a particular.

With this introduction, then, we are ready to turn to part 2 of our volume: a biblical history of Israel from Abraham to the Persian period.

PART II
A HISTORY OF ISRAEL
FROM ABRAHAM
TO THE PERSIAN PERIOD

Chapter 6

Before the Land

At some point during the last quarter of the thirteenth century B.C., the Egyptian pharaoh Merneptah set up a stela celebrating various military victories accomplished during his reign. We shall have more to say about this "Merneptah Stela" in due course. Its main significance for our purposes is that it contains the earliest mention of "Israel" outside the pages of the Bible.

Israel arrived on the international scene, in the late thirteenth century, as an entity of sufficient importance in Palestine to merit mention by a foreign ruler. Prior to the thirteenth century, this status was not the case, however, at least on the basis of the evidence at hand. Throughout the preceding part of the second millennium B.C., in fact, Israelites attract no explicit attention from, and Israel's ancestors pass unnoticed by, those responsible for our surviving sources, which is hardly surprising, for the sources are focused on what is important to their authors and to those who commissioned or governed those authors. They provide us, for example, with glimpses of the shifting centers of power within Mesopotamia in the Old Babylonian and Old Assyrian periods (c. 2000–1600 B.C.), tell us of great kings like Hammurapi of Babylon, and provide significant insight into the nature of everyday life in city-states of this time (especially in the case of the Mari archives).[1] They do not, however, make possible even a coherent political history of this period in this region, much less provide further details of the migration of an obscure family from the Mesopotamian city-state of Ur to Haran and then into Palestine (Gen. 11:31–12:9). They tell us of the glories of the Egyptian Old and New Kingdoms (c. 2686–1069 B.C.), the latter being the Egypt of famous pharaohs like Thutmose III, Akhenaten, and Tutankhamun[2]—but so far as we can tell, they are not interested in singling out one family of Semitic immigrants to Egypt from the many that arrived there during these centuries, nor even one Semite (Joseph) who, like other Semites, rose to a position of power in Egypt (Gen. 37–50). The history of this one family is of little note. The second millennium B.C. was an era of renowned city-states and then great powers—Egypt to the south, Babylonia and then Assyria to the east, the Hittites and the Hurrians to the north.[3] The ancient Near East of this era was their stage, and across this stage the Israelites and their ancestors only flit as shadows, as they move from place to place and interact from time to time with this or that people known to us from other ancient sources. The Israelites are not yet worthy of mention. Consequently, we are almost entirely dependent upon the Bible itself for our information about the Israelites "before the land"—most especially, to the books of Genesis to Deuteronomy, also known as "the Pentateuch."

[handwritten margin note: Except Merneptah]

SOURCES FOR THE PATRIARCHAL PERIOD: THE GENESIS ACCOUNT

Later Israel looked back to Abraham as the father of their nation and their faith. For this reason, Israel remembered him as their "patriarch." He was the one who received God's promises, which anticipated the granting of the land as well as the offspring who would people that land (Gen. 12:1–3). Indeed, the whole period of Israel's history involving Abraham and his immediate descendants is commonly referred to as "the patriarchal period." With this era our biblical history of Israel begins.

The only direct source of information about the period in which the patriarchs of Israel lived is the biblical book of Genesis, which offers episodic and terse patriarchal narratives about Abraham, Isaac, and Jacob (Gen. 11:10–36:43), before giving way to the more novella-like Joseph story of Genesis 37–50[4]—the "bridge" between the time of the patriarchs and the time of Israel's sojourn in Egypt, which leads on to the exodus. These narratives are incorporated into the book by means of the "toledoth formulae," a recurring feature of sentences beginning with the Hebrew phrase 'ēlleh tôlᵉdôt, which has been translated in a number of different ways, including "these are the generations," "this is the family history," and "this is the account." The phrase is always followed by a personal name (with the exception of the first occurrence, which names instead the "heavens and the earth" [Gen. 2:4]), although the person named is not necessarily the main character but only the beginning point of the section of the book that also closes with his death. These formulae structure the book of Genesis and serve to define it as a prologue (1:1–2:3) followed by various episodes: the "generations of" Adam (5:1), Noah (6:9), Noah's sons (10:1), Shem (11:10), Terah (11:27), Ishmael (25:12), Isaac (25:19), Esau (36:1, 9), and Jacob (37:2). The patriarchal narratives themselves are best understood as beginning either with Genesis 11:10, the "account" of Shem, or with Genesis 11:27, the "account" of Terah, Abraham's father.

THE STORY OF THE PATRIARCHS

The story thus begun goes on to tell of a family on the move in pursuit of God's promise to Abraham, which is the main theological interest of Genesis 11:10–36:43 and the theme that binds the various narratives together:[5]

> I will make of you a great nation, and I will bless you, and make your name great, so that you will be a blessing. I will bless those who bless you, and the one who curses you I will curse; and in you all the families of the earth shall be blessed. (Gen. 12:2–3)

The historical movements of the patriarchs link closely to their reaction to the divine promise. The literary structure and selection of stories intend more than simple report of past actions, in fact. They become paradigmatic for the behavior of later generations of God's people as they respond to the promises of God.

The promises are conditional first upon Abraham's departure from Ur in Mesopotamia and his arrival in Canaan, the promised land. He sets out on this lengthy journey with an intermediate stop in Haran, located in the north of the promised land (Gen. 11:31–32; 12:5); upon the death of his father, Terah, he leaves Haran and enters Canaan. At first, the narrative informs us that Abraham, Sarah, and his nephew Lot moved from Shechem to Bethel to Ai to the Negev, a movement from the north to the south of Canaan. Each time he sets up an altar, almost as if he is claiming the land for the Lord who sent him there.

The patriarchal stories that follow often have the purpose of illustrating Abraham's faith or lack thereof in response to some threat or crisis to the fulfillment of the promise. Soon after he reaches the land, a severe famine overtakes it, which threatens Abraham's faith. He has journeyed from Mesopotamia to the land promised by God, but now that land cannot sustain life. He and his family descend to Egypt, but Abraham's confidence in the protection of God seems shaken, and he induces his wife to lie about her relationship with him (Gen. 12:10–20). Nonetheless, God delivers him and even makes him grow richer in Egypt, and when he returns to the Negev his prosperity results in a need to divide his possessions with his nephew Lot. Here we see Abraham as a paradigm of trust in God (Gen. 13). He does not grasp the promise, but rather permits Lot to choose the land he wants. Lot chooses the lush land around Sodom and Gomorrah, the reader knowing of the ultimate fate of those cities (Gen. 18, 19). Abraham avoids catastrophe by his calm faith in God's ability to fulfill the promise.

The next chapter of the patriarchal narrative, Genesis 14, on the surface has the greatest potential for associating Abraham with the broader history (see below). A coalition of four kings under the leadership of Kedorlaomer of Elam engages five kings, including the kings of Sodom and Gomorrah. The former coalition wins and in the process kidnaps Lot. Abraham sets out after the abductors and defeats them, rescuing Lot. In a scene with significant later theological ramifications (see Heb. 7), Abraham encounters Melchizedek, the enigmatic king of Salem.

The narrative continues with two accounts of Abraham's grasping at the promises. The key promise in the patriarchal narratives is the birth of a son. After all, no great nation or land can exist without the first descendent. Abraham grows weary of waiting for God to act, and he first adopts his household servant and then later takes Hagar as a concubine to produce an heir by means of contemporary cultural conventions. In both cases (Gen. 15 and 17), God graciously intervenes and reassures Abraham of his intention to follow through on his promise of a son. The fulfillment of the promise takes place in Genesis 21. Isaac, the child of Abraham and Sarah's old age (demonstrating that God is responsible for this birth), replaces Ishmael, the result of Abraham's attempt to gain offspring by concubinage, as the main heir. Isaac thus becomes the recipient of the promises. However, before the focus of the narrative moves from Abraham, he faces one more threat, perhaps the largest of all. God tells him to take Isaac, this child of promise, and to sacrifice him on Mount Moriah (Gen. 22). In the culminating moment of Abraham's life, he shows his utter trust in God. Without a recorded word, he responds immediately to the request, only to have God substitute at the last minute an animal sacrifice for the child.

The Isaac narrative is the thinnest of the three patriarchal narratives. He is indeed the recipient of the promises, signaled by the repeated expression that God was with him and blessed him (Gen. 25:11, for example). Isaac too faces threats to the fulfillment of the promise and he too responds with doubt (Gen. 26), but the narrative presentation of Isaac leaves us with a flat character, a pale reflection of his father.

Even within the Isaac narrative itself, Jacob, his son, lends it dynamism. Jacob is a crafty character, but again, he is the one who carries the promise to the next generation. Perhaps this narrative indicates that God will work through the most unexpected people.[6] Jacob too must travel from place to place. He has no settled position in Canaan and indeed he ends his life in Egypt with his twelve sons. The fulfillment of the promises is still a future event.

The Patriarchal Narratives as Theology and as History

Without question, the main purpose of the patriarchal narratives is theological: they present a revelation of the nature of God and of his relationship to his human creatures. At the same time, however, they just as clearly intend us to think of this revelation as taking place within history. Theology is inextricably intertwined with actual events in the patriarchal materials. To state this concept in a different way, the genre we are dealing with here is theological history, but it is history nonetheless. The adjective does not undermine the noun. One cannot conceive of the original audience as thinking of Abraham as other than a real person, or of his movement from Ur to Haran to Palestine as other than a real journey. It is inconceivable that the author(s) of Genesis intended the audience to think these persons and events were other than "real." Scholars who use terms like "saga," "fiction," or "folklore"[7] to describe the genre of the patriarchal narratives are therefore not so much telling us about the actual genre of the text as they are expressing their own lack of confidence (for whatever reasons) in the historical reliability of the materials. That is to say, they are making what they consider to be an objective assessment of the text's historicity. They are not seriously dealing with the question of genre—with the question of how the text was intended to be read. As Halpern reminds us: ". . . whether a text is history . . . depends on what its author *meant* [our emphasis] to do,"[8] not on whether modern readers believe this author to have been competent or successful in what he or she meant to do. Van Seters is therefore surely correct when he states "the book of Genesis is a work of ancient history." Van Seters points specifically, in fact, to the genealogies and itineraries that outline the book and give it a chronological and cause-and-effect structure, as evidence of historiographical intentionality.[9] Whatever the reader may think of the success of the project, the "Genesis project" is a project in history writing and should be taken seriously as such. We are dealing with the genre of history.

THE HISTORY OF THE PATRIARCHS AND THE HISTORY OF THE TEXT

The question of the historical value of the patriarchal narratives is itself an important question, of course. This concern has been closely associated, in the modern period, with questions of their authorship and compositional history in particular; many people have come to believe that a direct correlation exists between a text's historical reliability and its proximity to the narrated events.[10] That opinion engenders a strong interest in the dynamics of the composition of texts like the patriarchal narratives. The common belief has been that if one can demonstrate that the patriarchal tradition comes from the patriarchal period or soon thereafter, then a higher probability of its historical reliability exists. Such an opinion leads conservative scholars, on the one hand, to expend great effort to demonstrate the antiquity of the textual material, not least by insisting on its Mosaic authorship.[11] This opinion also leads to skepticism, on the other hand, among scholars who conclude that the material comes from a late period and was certainly not authored by Moses or anyone else close to his time.[12]

We have already explored, in part 1, the difficulties associated with this notion of the "sanctity of proximity," and we do not need to rehearse in detail the arguments here, in the specific case of the patriarchs. We have no reason to believe that a text written centuries after the event that it describes is, for that reason, less likely to describe that event "truly" than a text composed nearer to its time.[13]

This conclusion is just as well, since on the one hand demonstrating that Moses did indeed write the patriarchal narratives is impossible, and therefore using Mosaic authorship as an argument for their early date is unwise. Indeed, the presence of so-called postmosaica[14] is clear evidence that the text either was updated at one or more points in the history of transmission or, perhaps, that the essential authorship of the Pentateuch reflects a later time period. In any case, whether the final form of the account of the patriarchs comes from the time of Moses, David,[15] or later,[16] a considerable gap of time appears to have passed between it and the patriarchs themselves.

The history of modern research has clearly revealed, on the other hand, that the dynamics of the composition of the patriarchal narratives are virtually impossible to unravel. This book is not the place to engage in a full discussion of these issues,[17] but the chaos of perspectives represented in scholarship today boggles the mind.[18] Even if the Genesis text originated from sources that have been brought together over time, the heady confidence of an earlier age—that it would be possible through the reconstruction of these sources to delineate the earliest and therefore "most historical" traditions—has been shattered forever. Scholarly claims about the successful and precise delineation of the sources behind the stories in Genesis ring hollow today. The situation is not that contemporary readers no longer feel the gaps and abrupt transitions in these stories that first led source-critics to think that sources were present. These phenomena are certainly there. But the questions are: What is the right explanation of their presence? Are they signs of ancient literary art?[19] Are they indications of the rough hand of a later redactor on earlier separate sources? Are they the result of the slippage of sign and referent (an "aporia," in the language of deconstruction)?[20] The possible explanations are many, and the multiplication of possible explanations has played its part in undermining confidence in particular source-reconstructions. That statement is not meant to dispute, of course, that sources, either oral or written, were likely used in the composition of the Pentateuch; except in obvious places (cf. Num. 21:14; Exod. 24:7), though, these cannot be seen in the present form of the literature.

THE PATRIARCHS IN THEIR ANCIENT
NEAR EASTERN SETTING

The stories do not suggest a period. !!!

An attentive reading of the patriarchal narratives reveals that no information is given within the accounts themselves that would allow us to assign an absolute date to the period of time from Abraham to Jacob. Genesis 14 at first raises our hopes, but unfortunately we cannot with confidence associate the characters of that story with anyone known from extrabiblical sources (see below). Passages outside the book of Genesis, however, appear to allow us to situate the patriarchs in real time—at least if we believe that the whole Bible gives accurate, though perhaps at times approximate, chronological indicators—and suggest that Abraham was born in the middle of the twenty-second century B.C. The evidence is as follows: 1 Kings 6:1 states that Solomon began temple construction 480 years after the Israelites left Egypt. This year is Solomon's fourth year as king, and if we follow Thiele, that date would be 966 B.C.[21] A straight reading of this passage places the exodus in the middle of the fifteenth century. Furthermore, Exodus 12:40 asserts that the children of God sojourned in Egypt for 430 years.[22] Finally, we may arrive at the length of time from Abraham's birth to Jacob's descent into Egypt by adding the 100 years of Genesis 21:5 (the age of Abraham when Isaac was born) to the 60 years of Genesis 25:26 (the age of Isaac when Jacob was born) to the 130 years of Genesis 47:9 (the age of Jacob when he first arrived in Egypt) to reach a period of 290 years. So beginning with 966 B.C, a number of scholars[23] add the 480 of 1 Kings 6:1 to the 430 years of the Egyptian sojourn to the 290 years of the patriarchal period to end up with a birth date for Abraham in 2166 B.C., which then leads to a date of 2091 B.C. for his arrival in Palestine (cf. Gen. 12:4).

This nice, neat date is not unambiguous even on biblical grounds. For one thing, all the numbers sound like round numbers; but of course this fact would only adjust the date by decades. Second, textual variation is present with some of the dates; for instance, the Septuagint understands the 430 years of Exodus 12:40 to cover not only the time in Egypt but the patriarchal period as well.[24] Nonetheless, even with these uncertainties, the Bible itself appears to situate the patriarchs in Palestine sometime between ca. 2100 and 1500 B.C.—the first half of the second millennium B.C.

A major part of the modern discussion concerning both the dating and the historical portrait of the patriarchs has centered on whether materials from the broader ancient Near East establish their existence or at least support their setting within this time frame. Everyone agrees that no explicit extrabiblical attestation is given to the patriarchs or the events mentioned in the biblical text. The discussion has, rather, centered over whether evidence affirms the biblical picture of the patriarchs in the time period ascribed to them.

This debate over supporting evidence has been intense and has occupied decades of scholarly endeavor.[25] At its center for much of that time stand the Nuzi (and nearby Arrapha) tablets. The Nuzi tablets were discovered beginning in the 1920s, and C. J. Gadd published the first group of tablets.[26] They were from both an official archive and the private archives of rich individuals. While specialists dated the tablets to the second half of the fifteenth century, some biblical scholars argued that they reflected customs earlier in the millennium as well (see the comment on Mari below). The documents, especially the ones from the private archives, reflected social customs relating to real estate, adoption, and marriage. Almost immediately connections were drawn between Nuzi customs (reflecting Hurrian society in the fifteenth century) and the customs of the patriarchs as reported in Genesis. Eichler lists the following examples:

the contractual stipulation that a barren woman give a slave girl to her husband as wife, the ranking of heirs and the preferential treatment of the designated eldest, the association of the house gods with the disposition of family property, the conditional sale into slavery of freeborn daughters, and the institution of *habiru*-servitude.[27]

Soon after the recovery of the Nuzi material came the discovery of the Mari material (from Tell Hariri, a site on the northern Euphrates in the periphery of Mesopotamia)—about twenty thousand tablets dated to the eighteenth century B.C. The Mari texts did not describe social and family customs as did the Nuzi material, but they did reveal some contacts between the two areas. That the Mari material was dated to the first half of the second millennium encouraged the idea that the practices attested in the Nuzi material and allegedly similar to patriarchal customs could legitimately reflect the earlier time period.

For the first couple of decades after their discovery, a consensus of sorts emerged that the Nuzi documents firmly established the patriarchal period as a historical fact of the first half of the second millennium B.C. Scholars asserted parallels between the Nuzi and Mari materials and the patriarchal narratives in order to pinpoint the time period of the latter. The arguments were founded on two presuppositions, often unspoken: (1) the Hurrian customs were unique to their time period and before, and did not endure long afterwards, and (2) the Hurrian texts reflect customs shared with peoples like the patriarchs living in Syria-Palestine. Advocates of this view included the very influential names of W. F. Albright,[28] C. Gordon,[29] and E. A. Speiser.[30]

Space only permits one example of the type of argument presented by this group of scholars. One classic instance is Speiser's argument that the Nuzi material explained Sarah's relationship to Abraham as that of a wife/sister.[31] Speiser pointed to one contract where a brother sold his sister to another person as a sister for the price of forty shekels, and to a second (a marriage contract) where the identical original brother sold the same sister as a wife to the same person who had adopted her as his sister, again for forty shekels. So at Nuzi, according to Speiser, this same woman was both sister and wife to the same third person. He felt that this clear evidence received support from other, less clear sisterhood contracts. Speiser used these texts to understand the relationship between Abraham and Sarah. Twice Abraham protects himself from anticipated harm by calling Sarah his sister and not his wife (Gen. 12:10–20; 20:1–18). According to Speiser, Sarah's presentation as Abraham's wife/sister is an indication that patriarchal society operated by the same customs as that attested at Nuzi and therefore situates the narrative in the first half of the second millennium. Prominent scholars initially supported this view, and this early optimism is well illustrated by an often-quoted statement by J. Bright: "[O]ne is forced to the conclusion that the patriarchal narratives authentically reflect social customs at home in the second millennium rather than those of later Israel."[32] Not too long afterward, however, the weakness of the argument was exposed.

Beginning in the 1960s, criticisms of the comparisons surfaced,[33] and J. M. Weir, in particular, treated the wife/sister custom in a devastating article.[34] Eichler reports that we have a much clearer view of this situation today since there are now eleven relevant Nuzi texts that may be taken into consideration:[35] We now understand that the motivation behind the adoption of a woman as a sister was financial on the part of both seller and buyer. The original brother's family presumably needed money right away, so for a price he sold the rights to a future marriage price to the brother, an investor who would later arrange the woman's marriage and collect the (presumably higher) marriage fee. Therefore, no connection to the biblical text exists. Indeed, the interpretation of the relevant biblical text had to be distorted in order to make the comparison work. When Abraham said that Sarah was his sister, he was suppressing the truth about her status as wife to protect himself. Nonetheless, as Abraham himself points out, Sarah really is in a sense his sister, not by purchase or contract but by virtue of the fact that they have the same father, though different mothers (Gen. 20:12). Speiser, indeed, felt that the later biblical editors did not understand the customs, which is why dissonance occurs between the text and the custom—but this stance is, of course, special pleading in favor of the weak argument.

The criticism of the comparisons between the patriarchal behavior and Nuzi social customs comes to its climax in the work of Thompson and Van Seters.[36] Their arguments run along two lines: (1) the parallels are not real, but forced by distorting the interpretation of the Nuzi texts and the biblical texts, and (2) in many cases the customs are not restricted in any case to the second millennium but continue into the first millennium.[37] These scholars contribute importantly to disabusing readers of false comparisons, but they go further by saying that, as a result, the patriarchal material is a fictional retrojection from a much later period.[38]

This surprising assertion is, of course, explicable only in terms of inattention to logic, for the assertion does not follow, logically, from the fact that certain arguments in favor of the historicity of the patriarchs have turned out to be weak, that nothing whatever can be said in favor of the historicity of the patriarchs. Allied to this, however, is also an apparent inattention to the text, for the text certainly cannot plausibly be taken as a fictional retrojection from a much later period. Indeed, we can point to customs, beliefs, and actions of the patriarchs that are not only anachronistic to a later period, but occasionally downright objectionable. G. Wenham[39] lists the following examples:

1. The patriarchs engaged in sexual/marital relations that were condemned in the later period. While Abraham married his half sister (20:12) and Jacob married two sisters (29:21–30), Leviticus (18:9, 11, 18; 20:7) condemns both practices. Furthermore, Judah and Simeon married Canaanite women and Joseph married an Egyptian woman, a practice condemned by Exodus 34:16 and Deuteronomy 7:3.
2. The patriarchs flout, under divine guidance to be sure, later customs of inheritance. Both Isaac and Jacob give the lion's share of their inheritance to junior sons, a practice contra Deuteronomy 21:15–17.
3. The patriarchs engage in religious practices that later biblical writers condemn. As Wenham puts it, ". . . the patriarchs do indulge in worship

practices that later generations regarded as improper. They erect pillars, pour libations over them, and plant trees (28:18, 22; 35:14; 21:33), whereas Deut 12:2–3 condemns worship 'upon the hills under every green tree' and commends the uprooting of pillars and Asherim."[40] Furthermore, they worship not at Jerusalem, but at places like Shechem, Hebron, Beersheba, and Bethel, the latter of which is particularly interesting because, after Jeroboam II, it is a religious site of infamy.

This list presents just a sample of serious incongruities between the picture of the patriarchs in Genesis and later beliefs, and we must ask: how likely is it that much later writers, writing purely out of their imagination, would paint a picture of their founding fathers that included such things?[41] It is far more likely that this picture is as it is because the authors of Genesis had already inherited a firm patriarchal tradition that they had to accommodate, whatever their larger religious and social aims in telling their story.

Returning now to the matter of comparisons between our biblical and extrabiblical texts themselves, however, even after the critique of parallels has done its necessary and salutary work—disabusing readers of false comparisons—extrabiblical evidence still remains that coheres with the biblical picture of the patriarchs.[42] With regard to the Nuzi documents themselves, for example, Selman refers to a period of mature reflection on the comparison between them and the biblical texts as a "third stage" of the intellectual discussion, following on from the earlier stages of embrace and critique. The defensible comparisons that are made as a result of this mature reflection still do not "prove" the historical reality (or indeed the early dating) of the patriarchal narrative, and they too may be criticized effectively in the future. However, on the basis of our present knowledge, they certainly lend support to the biblical view of the period. As Eichler concludes, "in conjunction with other cuneiform documents, the Nuzi texts will continue to help illuminate biblical law, institutions, and practices."[43] Other evidence also exists that is consistent with the location of a patriarchal period in the first half of the second millennium. Kitchen, for instance, suggests that the slave price for Joseph, cited in Genesis 37:28, is twenty shekels (NRSV: "pieces of silver"), and he presents evidence from other ancient Near Eastern texts that this was the going rate for a slave in the Old Babylonian period (early second millennium). He points out that slave prices in later biblical texts are higher and therefore offers this as a line of evidence that the Joseph narrative reflects the conditions of the time period in which the Bible places it. Kitchen offers this argument among others in an interesting essay.[44]

We do not want to imply a total absence of anachronisms in the patriarchal narratives, which provide evidence either that the texts as we have them now derive from a considerably later time than the period they describe, or at least that they were updated as time passed. We may note, for example, the reference to "Ur of the Chaldeans" (Gen. 11:28, 31) and the mention of the city of Dan (Gen. 14:14). While Ur was an ancient city, the Chaldeans were a tribe from the first millennium B.C. Most likely this tag would be added to the city name after the rise of the Chaldean dynasty after 626 B.C. As for Dan, the biblical tradition itself indicates that the city of Laish was renamed Dan only after the tribe of Dan moved north during the period of the Judges (Judg. 18:29). These simple updatings of biblical references have been long recognized even by conservative scholars as an indication of later glosses to the text.

Harder to explain in the light of present knowledge of the history of the ancient Near East are various references to the Philistines in our narratives. Historical sources indicate that the Philistines moved into Palestine in the twelfth century B.C. during the movement of the Sea Peoples of which they were a part.[45] This information renders suspect, for some, the biblical description of Abraham's encounter with Abimelech and Philcol, described as coming from the land of the Philistines (Gen. 21:22–34). But perhaps this, too, is a sign of editorial updating. Hoffmeier[46] points out, in a discussion of the mention of Philistines in connection with the Song of the Sea in Exodus 15, that Numbers 13:29 indicates that the Israelites knew that the Canaanites occupied the coast in the southern Levant, though Exodus 13:17 refers to the inhabitants as Philistines, the later inhabitants. Another possibility, of course, is that we are not dealing here with an anachronism at all, and that in fact an earlier, smaller wave of Philistine immigrants to the Levant took place before the larger one in the twelfth century.[47] Admittedly no extrabiblical evidence yet supports such a view. However, the history of the study of the patriarchal narratives demonstrates that not every apparent anachronism is indeed a real one, and we should hesitate, given the very partial state of our knowledge about the ancient world, before using the term "anachronism" too dogmatically. It is still commonly asserted, for example, that camels were not domesticated until the twelfth century B.C., and that the presence of camels in the patriarchal narratives is an anachronism (e.g., Gen. 24:9–14, where Abraham's servant traveled to Aram-naharaim by camel). However, we now possess indications of an earlier use of camels in the ancient Near East that render this assertion of anachronism dubious.[48]

In sum, many earlier arguments trying to show that patriarchal customs were peculiarly related to the time period of the early second millennium have been effectively disputed. This notion, however, far from demonstrates that the patriarchal narratives overall are at odds with the picture of the period as we know it from ancient Near Eastern sources, even if we must take account of a certain degree of anachronism in the presentation.

THE SOCIOLOGICAL SETTING OF THE PATRIARCHS

How do the biblical narratives invite us to picture Abraham and his immediate descendants? Of course, the text does not provide a full account of the patriarchs' status within their society, but we do have glimpses that allow us to conjecture about their lifestyle. Many clues point to a nomadic lifestyle. The patriarchs lived

[handwritten margin note: The name chaldeans would be added to provide a recognition point for the audience & whatever does not fit is an editorial addition! Or – A setting familiar to the audience]

in tents (e.g., Gen. 12:8; 13:3; 31:33) and traveled from place to place. Abraham's first trip is a long one, from Ur to the land of Canaan. The reference to the temporary stop in Haran confirms our assumption that Abraham took the traditional route between these two locations by traveling up the Euphrates and then descending into Canaan from the north. However, this long trip was a unique occurrence and does not really inform us about the patriarch's habitual lifestyle.

Once he arrived in Canaan, he did not settle down for long periods of time. When he first arrived, he settled in Shechem. After Shechem, he journeyed to Bethel where he "pitched his tent" (Gen. 12:8) and then on to Ai and finally to the Negev. From the Negev he descended into Egypt to escape a famine. As we read on in the narrative, Abraham keeps traveling, never settling in one place for very long. Isaac and Jacob continue this pattern. The patriarchs sound like tent-dwelling nomads. They lead their flocks from place to place to secure the best pasturage and water supply.

To describe the patriarchs as nomads and then drop the discussion, however, is too simplistic. The text also attests to their relationship with settled areas. The patriarchs do not just move from location to location, but they are often associated with the settled areas of the land. The cities listed above, Shechem, Bethel, and Ai, indicate that they pitched their tent in the vicinity of settled areas. They also have interaction with settled people who treat them with great respect. In his negotiations with Ephron the Hittite, the latter calls Abraham "a mighty prince [nᵉśîʾ] among us" (Gen. 23:6).[49] Elsewhere he has direct dealings with the Egyptian pharaoh (Gen. 12:10–20) and the Philistine king (21:22–34). Y. Muffs describes Abraham in Genesis 14 as one who "functions as a military personage allied by treaty to three local grandees, possesses a private army over three hundred men, and is concerned about the rations of his troops and his rightful share of the booty for his allies like a good commander."[50] These references suggest that Abraham was a man of position and wealth in his adopted country, a tribal chieftain of some importance. Of course, during most of his life he did not own any land as such, though he had grazing and water rights. He was a "resident alien" (ger) in the land. According to A. H. Konkel in a recent article, the resident alien "is distinguished from the foreigner in that he has settled in the land for some time and is recognized as having a special status," a description apropos of the picture we have of the patriarchs in the land of Canaan.[51]

The picture that emerges from the biblical text is analogous to a social pattern attested in the Mari tablets. Mari was a major city. In its surrounding areas lived some tribes (Yaminites and Haneans, for instance) whose movements in and out of the settled area remind some scholars of the lifestyle of the patriarchs.[52] These tribes are not unsettled people who invade the settled areas; rather they live in the shadow of the settled area during the dry season and journey out during the wet period when grazing land and water become scarce. The evidence of the Mari texts is that incorporating these wandering tribes in order to tax them was in the interest of the settled areas.

In sum, we are not to envision Abraham and his descendants as wandering aim-lessly through the land, constantly at odds with the settled inhabitants. Rather, maintaining good relationships (cf. Gen. 26) with the inhabitants of the land was in their best interest. In the words of Cornelius, "the way of life of the 'nomadic tribe' is seen as a symbiosis of pastoral nomadism and village agriculture."[53]

GENESIS 14 AND THE HISTORY OF THE PATRIARCHAL PERIOD

The 5 Kings v the 4. Lot is Captured

Genesis 14 has attracted much interest and discussion, in large part because it appears at first blush to have the most possibility among the patriarchal narratives of a specific connection to extrabiblical history. Elsewhere Abraham wanders the land, occasionally coming into contact with powerful figures who are either unnamed (Gen. 12:10–20) or not so powerful that we would expect to find col-laboration mentioned in extrabiblical sources (Gen. 26). However, in Genesis 14 Abraham comes into contact with powerful figures from powerful lands.

The chapter begins with the description of an incursion by four kings from outside the land of Canaan against five kings, presumably in the land, headed by the kings of Sodom and Gomorrah. The latter had been subject to the head of the former coalition for a number of years.[54] The four kings were reacting to a rebellion and came to bring their vassals back into line. In the process, they defeated other tribes, some of which have significant reputations as warriors (the Rephaites, the Zuzites, the Emites, the Horites, the whole territory of Amalekites and Amorites). When the five kings met the four kings, the former were scat-tered, and in the process they captured Lot, Abraham's nephew, who had moved to the vicinity of Sodom and Gomorrah (Gen. 13).

Abraham soon was informed of this disaster, and he set out with 318 men and defeated the coalition of foreign kings, recovering not only Lot but also the other plunder that the kings had taken from the Canaanite coalition. On his return, the priest-king of Salem met him and blessed him, and Abraham gave the priest-king a tithe. After this scene, the king of Sodom insists that Abraham keep the plunder, but Abraham refuses, not wanting to be beholden to the king of Sodom. His only exception is to allow his Canaanite allies (Aner, Eshcol, and Mamre) to receive their share.

Commentators have noted problems with this story that have raised questions about its historicity. Some have wondered, first, whether it truly "belongs" between Genesis 13 and 15.[55] A close look at the broader context shows, however, that the chapter fits into a broader pattern. The heart of the Abraham narrative is chapters 15–17, which focus on the covenant promises. These chapters are bracketed by two chapters on either side, which have Lot as a major player (Gen. 13–14; Gen. 18–19).

Some commentators have wondered, second, whether the story "belongs" in the Abraham narrative at all. Elsewhere in that narrative, they claim, Abraham is pictured as a simple nomadic figure, wandering from town to town, while here he is a warrior, winning a victory over a sizeable foreign coalition. However, above we have disputed this picture of Abraham. He is not a simple nomad, but a leader with impressive resources, who also has Canaanite allies supporting him.

Third, some scholars also see tensions within the chapter and allege a contradiction between Genesis 14:10, which describes the kings of Sodom and Gomorrah as falling into tar pits, and later in the chapter where the king of Sodom presses the plunder on Abraham. However, others have countered that the Hebrew idiom can and should be understood as the kings *hiding* in the tar pits.[56] Then again, much discussion surrounds the sudden appearance of Melchizedek, king of Salem (14:18–20), who is priest of El Elyon[57] ("God Most High," identified with Yahweh in the broader context). Who is he? Where is Salem? What is the purpose of this little subnarrative, and does it really fit into the broader chapter?[58] Most people see it as an addition to the text, but one that pinpoints its purpose and date. Perhaps the most frequently argued position is that this account reflects the time of David, when that king was trying to forge a coalition of Canaanite and Israelite political and religious forces particularly in Jerusalem.[59] That such a story would have been of interest to people of David's time is certain. Whether the story truly reflects that time rather than Abraham's is, however, another matter. No solid grounds exist for claiming so.

For our purposes, the discussion of the identity of the kings of the chapter has proven the most salient and, in the final analysis, both the most tantalizing and frustrating.[60] Discussing the kings one by one is the best approach. Chedorlaomer king of Elam is the first, who is said to be the head of the foreign coalition. No doubt attends the fact that this king has an authentic-sounding Elamite name. Chedor stands for a common first element in Elamite royal names, Kudur. However, the second part, which certainly could stand for something authentic in Elamite, does not sound like anything associated with a known Elamite king.[61] Then, Amraphel king of Shinar is clearly meant to indicate Babylon from other references in the Bible. At first Amraphel was thought to be Hammurapi, but the philological differences were too large to be overcome, so that identification has been universally dropped. Arioch of Ellasar has had a similar journey. At first, the geographical location was thought to be the city of Larsa, but more recently identifications include lesser-known areas like Alsi in northern Mesopotamia or Ilansura near Carchemish. Arioch at first was thought to be Arriwuk, the fifth son of Zimri-lim of Mari (from the early Old Babylonian period), but this assertion is now considered unlikely. Tidal, the fourth king, has a name that is attested for four Hittite kings (Tudhaliya). He is identified as king of Goyim, which means "nations." This identification is quite strange, but may be like the well-attested ancient name Umman-manda, which is a general term like "people," used in reference to Scythians and Cimmerians.

The names sound authentic, then,[62] even if we cannot with certainty identify the particular kings with names mentioned outside the Bible. In addition, Kitchen may well be correct that the period before the Old Babylonian period, though not directly attesting this group of kings, may be the only period where such a coalition was even possible.[63] After all, the period before Hammurapi was a time when Mesopotamia was carved up between a number of less powerful leaders. He was the one who subjected many of them, because of his imperial tendencies.[64] Beyond this review, however, not much can be said. Genesis 14 does not, after all, provide us with a specific connection to extrabiblical history—at least, not to extrabiblical history as we currently know it.

THE JOSEPH NARRATIVE (GENESIS 37–50)

Later Old Testament tradition lists only Abraham, Isaac, and Jacob as patriarchs (Exod. 2:24; 3:6, 15; 4:5), and so technically, Joseph is not one of them. Nonetheless, the Joseph narrative has connections with the preceding and the following material and links the patriarchal narratives and the account of the exodus. Joseph is the son of Jacob, the son of Isaac, the son of Abraham, and his story is the story of the continuation of the promise. Like the patriarchal narratives, Genesis 37–50 demonstrates how the fulfillment of the promises can overcome obstacles—in this case the threat of a famine that could destroy the family of promise. The story of Joseph also anticipates the exodus narrative by explaining how the people of God found themselves in Egypt in the first place. The burial of Joseph provides a concrete link between the two. At his death (Gen. 50:22–26), Joseph requested that his bones be carried up from Egypt. When Israel finally left Egypt, the text mentions that Moses took the bones of Joseph (Exod. 13:19). Furthermore, the opening phrase of Exodus (1:1) repeats a phrase in Genesis 46:8, both passages naming those "sons of Israel who came to Egypt with Jacob, each with his household."

Literary Analysis

The beginning and end of the Joseph narrative are clear. Joseph becomes the main focus of narrative attention in 37:1, and this section concludes with the account of his death at the end of the book of Genesis. However, this simple explanation may be too simple. The most notable objection to the unity of Genesis 37–50 is Genesis 38, which does not mention Joseph at all but rather concentrates on his older brother Judah. The structure of the last part of Genesis becomes clearer when we take note of the appearance of the final *tol'dot* formula in the book of Genesis in 37:1. We should really consider this section not the Joseph narrative, but rather the account of Jacob's descendants, which include Judah as well as Joseph. However, because the overwhelming focus of these chapters is on Joseph, we retain the traditional name for this unit and focus on him.

The style of the Joseph narrative marks a radical change from preceding material in the book of Genesis, which also accounts for its separate treatment. The patriarchal narratives are made up largely of short episodes (Gen. 24 is a notable exception), but the Joseph narrative has a novella-like quality to it. Coats notes this, and comments that "like a . . . tale, it narrates a plot from a point of crisis to its conclusion."[65] In spite of the overarching narrative smoothness of these chapters, critics have still attempted to separate different sources in the text, most notably a J and E strand. The presence of double naming of tribes, characters, and so forth plays a leading role in inducing such attempts, but alternative explanations to those of source criticism exist. As Coats points out, "[M]ore recent examination of the story softens the argument for two sources by suggesting that one author can use repetition as a narrative technique for emphasis, perhaps simply for variety."[66] Take, for instance, the important issue of the Midianites and the Ishmaelites in Genesis 37. Source critics separate a source that narrates the Midianites as the group that takes Joseph to Egypt (vv. 28 and 36) and another source that ascribes this role to the Ishmaelites (vv. 25, 27, 28; 39:1). In a recent article, E. Fry has alternatively suggested that "'Ishmaelite' and 'Midianite' were both understood as general terms for nomadic people thought to be descended from Abraham, and the two terms were therefore recognized as referring to the same group." He cites Judges 8:22–24 as confirmation, the text there identifying Midianites as Ishmaelites.[67]

[handwritten margin note: specifically if he is a bard.]

While the literary style has changed from the patriarchal narratives, we do not recognize a change in overall genre or historical intentionality. While some argue that the book of Genesis in general and the Joseph narrative in particular are historylike stories, we hold, rather, that they are storylike histories. *[handwritten margin note: Well ?!]*

The Theological Intention of the Joseph Narrative

Joseph's life appears to be under the control of a force greater than himself. At first, the identity of that force is not clear; it might even be bad luck. Joseph was brash as a young man, and certainly he had little tact. He angered his brothers by sharing with them his dreams that announced his superiority over them (Gen. 37:1–11), which so infuriated his brothers that they decided to rid themselves of this pest. As he approached them at Dothan, they thought they might kill him, but then decided to sell him to some Ishmaelite/Midianite traders who were headed for Egypt (37:12–36). Fate, it seemed, had taken him far from his family home, far from the land of promise. In Egypt, he entered into the service of a powerful figure named Potiphar. The account of Joseph in Potiphar's house, found in chapter 39, well documents the fact that Joseph is bearer of the divine promise. The phrase "the LORD was with him" reverberates through the chapter; the result of the Lord's presence is material blessing on Potiphar's household.

However, from a surface reading of the text, fate would apparently intrude again on Joseph. Potiphar's wife lusted after him and invited him into her bed. He refused; she accused him of rape, whereupon he was thrown into jail. However, again, God was with Joseph (39:21–23), and the prison prospered because of his presence.

In addition, Joseph's prison experience brought him into contact with two high-ranking Egyptian officials, the royal cupbearer and the royal baker, both of whom had displeased Pharaoh and found themselves in prison. Joseph again had a dream, predicting the release of both men, but while the cupbearer would be in Pharaoh's good graces, the baker would be executed. Events transpired exactly as Joseph foretold, but the cupbearer forgot his promise to speak well to Pharaoh concerning Joseph. But again, as fate would have it, Pharaoh himself had a troubling dream, and the cupbearer finally remembered the skilled dream interpreter he had met in prison. Thus, events lead to Joseph coming into the presence of Pharaoh and helping him manage a potential disaster by forewarning and preparing for a severe famine.

The famine brings Joseph's brothers to Egypt seeking food for the family. The family of promise finds its very existence threatened. Joseph is not immediately ready to identify himself to his brothers, who after all had earlier conspired to do away with him. He tests them by putting his younger brother Benjamin at risk, seeing if they will act according to their earlier natures by protecting their own lives. When Judah offers to act as a hostage in the place of Benjamin (44:33–34), Joseph breaks down and reveals himself to his brothers. He then intercedes with Pharaoh and brings his family down to Goshen in the delta region of the Nile. In this way, the family of God comes to Egypt.

The Joseph narrative is a finely crafted piece of literature with a subtle theological theme. The lack of explicit theological language throughout the story has led some to categorize it as wisdom literature. However, the theme becomes explicit at the end of the account when Jacob dies. Here the brothers are worried that, with the death of their father, Joseph will finally exact his revenge on them. In response to their pleas for mercy, Joseph responds with a stirring statement concerning the providence of God: "Even though you intended to do harm to me, God intended it for good, in order to preserve a numerous people, as he is dong today" (50:20). This theme of God's providence protecting the bearers of the promise accounts for the selection of episodes from the life of Joseph.

Joseph in Egypt

The Joseph narrative as just described is not primarily concerned with history. However, separating theology and history in such a story is impossible; the story itself is designed to show the reader how God can work in the historical process to overrule acts of evil to bring about his redemptive purposes. Another aspect of the story's design is to bring encouragement to those whose lives seem to be at the mercy of brutal chance. Although not primarily concerned with history, then, the narrative nonetheless presses this question upon us: does it fit well with what we know about Egypt in the first half of the second millennium B.C.? We might certainly expect that it would at least reflect some contemporary Egyptian customs and characteristics, even if specific connections between Egyptian and patriarchal history could not be found. This question has attracted the attention of biblical scholars and Egyptologists alike. Interestingly, as we shall see, the majority of Egyptian specialists (Vergote,[68] Kitchen,[69] and Hoffmeier[70]) have described a strong Egyptological flavor to the narrative, while many biblical scholars have denied it.[71]

We begin by noting with Hoffmeier that "to date, there is no direct evidence for the Hebrew Joseph being an official in the Egyptian court."[72] Scholars who want to show the authenticity of the narrative are, therefore, content to describe indirect evidence and deal with apparent anomalies. Space precludes a detailed discussion of the indirect evidence, but we concur with Hoffmeier's conclusion that it "tends to demonstrate the authenticity of the story. There is really nothing unbelievable or incredible about the narrative."[73] Consider a few illustrations.

First, as noted above, Kitchen makes the interesting observation that the price (twenty pieces of silver [shekels], cf. Gen. 37:28) for which Joseph was sold as a slave fits in best, according to our present knowledge, with the first half of the second millennium. Evidence shows that by the second half of the second millennium the slave price was thirty shekels, and up to fifty shekels in the first millennium.[74] The point is small, but it speaks in favor of authentic historical memory more than of later fictional or semifictional writing.

Second, the Egyptian names (Potiphar, Potiphera, Asenath, and Zaphenath-Paneah) in the narrative have been thoroughly studied through the years. None of these specific people are attested in Egyptian sources, which is not particularly surprising considering the nature of the surviving archeological record. However, although the fact that we have Hebrew transliterations of Egyptian, rather than the Egyptian itself, creates some difficulty, no one doubts that these names are authentically Egyptian. Their dates and their etymology are debated, but Currid, Hoffmeier, and others[75] have shown how these names certainly could have been used in the second-millennium setting that the Bible gives to the Joseph narrative. Kitchen goes further, concluding that "the best equivalents for Zaphenath-pa'aneah and Asenath belong overwhelmingly to the Middle Kingdom (early 2nd millennium BC), rarely later; Potipher(a) is a modernised form (late 2nd millennium BC onwards) of an early-2nd-millennium form (Didire)."[76]

These observations lead to two further comments. First, the one character in the story that we might expect to find in the original sources is the Pharaoh. As is well known, though, the Egyptian leader is never named in Genesis 37–50. Our knowledge of Egyptian kings is such that we could probably date the setting of the story if we knew the Pharaoh's name, but we do not, so we are left with just a relative dating. Some have suggested that leaving the Pharaoh nameless is in keeping with the Egyptian practice of not naming and thus giving fame to an enemy. Others say that since Pharaoh was considered to be a god, his name was avoided by the biblical author.[77] The best explanation rests on the fact that until about the tenth century, a pharaoh's specific name was typically not mentioned by the Egyptians themselves, who referred to the pharaoh simply as "Pharaoh." As Hoffmeier observes, this is precisely the practice

> found in the Old Testament; in the period covered from Genesis and Exodus to Solomon and Rehoboam, the term "pharaoh" occurs alone, while

after Shishak (ca. 925 B.C.), the title and name appear together (e.g., Pharaoh Neco, Pharaoh Hophra).

Thus, the usage of "pharaoh" in Genesis and Exodus does accord well with the Egyptian practice from the fifteenth through the tenth centuries.[78]

A second matter of discussion is the role of Joseph in the Egyptian hierarchy. How likely is it that a Semite would achieve such prominence in the Egyptian government? This question is probably not one in which the author of the Joseph narrative was very interested; the whole purpose of his story is to show that Joseph's life and career were under God's control, and speculation about "likelihood" is, within that frame of reference, beside the point. The question is not even very coherent within a strictly historical frame of reference, unless one believes that only things that are "likely" have ever happened. Be that as it may, other evidence does exist of high-ranking Semites in Egyptian government in ancient times. Hoffmeier records the instance of Bay, who played an important role after the death of Seti II in 1194 B.C. and bore the title "Great Chancellor of the entire land."[79]

These examples could easily be multiplied. Specialists in Egyptian material such as Hoffmeier and Kitchen add information on the role of the magicians in the narrative, the custom of Pharaoh's birthday, the ritual of Joseph's investiture in his office, and so forth. This background material does not, of course, "prove" the historical accuracy of the Joseph narrative.[80] However, from this information we can say that the Joseph narrative fits well into its putative Egyptian setting in the early second millennium, even though it occasionally betrays through anachronistic comment that—like the patriarchal narratives—it has at the very least been updated from time to time as the tradition has come down through the generations.[81]

Although the Joseph narrative thus fits into an Egyptian context in general terms, being dogmatic about how it fits in specific terms within Egyptian history as we know it is impossible. Part of the problem has to do with the ambiguity surrounding the dating of the exodus, to which we now turn our attention.

THE BIRTH OF MOSES

The account of the exodus begins with the story of Moses' birth, which is set in a time of Egyptian oppression of the Israelites. No longer is Joseph's service to an earlier pharaoh remembered, and his descendants are now forced to work on large state projects, specifically the building of the cities Pithom and Rameses, under the hand of oppressive taskmasters. While no specific evidence exists for the Israelites in Egypt at this time, ample evidence does exist for the presence of Semites in Egypt throughout the second half of the second millennium B.C. Most striking is the scene of laborers making bricks found in the tomb of Rekhmire, a high official of Thutmose III (c. 1479–1425 B.C.).[82] The inscription that accompanies the scene describes the workers as prisoners of war from Nubia and Syria-Palestine.[83]

While the Egyptians apparently found the Israelites a fruitful source of labor, the biblical text suggests that they also feared their increased numbers and worried that if an external enemy attacked, the Israelites might become allied with them (Exod. 1:10). The pharaoh therefore decided to control the Israelite population by demanding that Israelite midwives destroy the male offspring, but the midwives refused to carry out the pharaoh's commands, concocting an excuse for the reason they could not do so. So then the pharaoh issued his horrifying command: "Every boy that is born to the Hebrews you shall throw into the Nile, but you shall let every girl live" (Exod. 1:22).

Into this dangerous context Moses, Israel's future leader, was born, and the context, indeed, explains his strange upbringing. When he was born, his mother placed him in a papyrus basket and placed it in the reeds in the Nile. The consequence was that he was discovered by Pharaoh's daughter, who decided to raise him herself with the help of a Hebrew nurse, who just happened to be Moses' own biological mother. Though not explicit, this birth story is designed to show that God provides and protects this special child, who will be the one who delivers Israel from its oppression. In this, the story functions similarly to the birth stories of Isaac, Jacob, and many others—children who are born only after God opens the wombs of their barren mothers.

Since the last part of the nineteenth century, scholars have pointed out the similarity between the Moses birth story and the Sargon Birth Legend,[84] concerning the birth of Sargon, who was born to a high priestess. She placed him in a basket and floated him on the river, where he was picked up by Aqqi the water-drawer. Aqqi raised Sargon, who became a great Mesopotamian king. Any literary connection between the stories, however, is unlikely; Hoffmeier has shown that the language of the account of Moses' birth reflects an Egyptian, not a Mesopotamian background.[85] Of course, the stories share a common theme: the need to dissociate the child from the birth mother for the child's protection. In the case of the Sargon legend, the high-priestess was apparently not supposed to have children. In both cultures, the idea behind the basket on the water was the commission of the child into the care of the deity who controls the waters (in the case of Exodus, Yahweh himself)—the ancient cultural equivalent to the modern practice of leaving an unwanted child on the threshold of a house or hospital.

Moses' name has caused some discussion because of its ambiguous origin. The name is given a Hebrew etymology associated with the Hebrew verb *mšh* "to draw out." Although the Egyptian princess possibly gave her adopted Semitic child a Hebrew name, more likely she named him using an Egyptian verb meaning "to give birth," which is associated with many well-known Egyptian names, including Thutmose and Rameses. Thus, the play on words in the biblical text indicates a Hebrew folk etymology associated with an Egyptian name.

THE CALL OF MOSES
AND THE PLAGUES OF EGYPT

The next scene in the biblical story involves Moses as a grown man (Exod. 3:11–22). The gaps in the biblical text leave the interested reader with all sorts of unanswerable questions about his upbringing, his education, and his connections with the Egyptian as well as the Hebrew communities. However, the fact that he intervened in a conflict between an Egyptian and a Hebrew in favor of the latter indicates that he certainly knew about his Hebrew origins.

Another matter of speculation is the reason he fled in the direction of Midian. Midian was a nomadic tribe that would have heightened his chance to remain undetected.[86] However, the narrative soon makes clear that the "priest of Midian," whose name is alternatively given as Jethro, Reuel, or Hobab, is a co-religionist with Moses. Of course, this information leaves us with all kinds of further unanswerable questions. All that we are explicitly told is that Moses not only ended up residing with the Midianites, but also marrying the daughter of the priest, whose name was Zipporah.

The flight of Moses from Egypt has often been compared to the Egyptian story of Sinuhe.[87] According to this tale, Sinuhe was a high-ranking attendant of Princess Nefru, the wife of Pharaoh Sesostris I, in the first part of the second millennium B.C. Sinuhe fell out of favor with the pharaoh and fled to Syria through Canaan. In addition, he married the elder daughter of the Syrian leader. Close attention to this text indicates, however, that the similarities are extremely superficial. The scenario of an out-of-favor official fleeing for his life from the power of a king like Pharaoh probably played itself out countless times in the long history of Egypt. That the refugee found a life among Asiatics in Canaan or Syria is also not that startling a similarity. The comparison certainly does not give us insight into the meaning or the origin of the Moses story, as some have claimed.

Moses' flight to Midian also brought him into the region of Mount Sinai, which would later play such an important role in the exodus/wilderness wandering narrative. Here, the authors of Exodus tell us, God called Moses to go to Egypt and hither Moses later led Israel in order to receive the law. On both occasions in the narrative, an appearance of God in the form of fire plays a major role. The commissioning of Moses for his task of rescuing Israel from their bondage involves, specifically, a burning bush—or rather, a bush that does not burn and thus attracts Moses' attention. When he goes to examine this strange phenomenon, God speaks to him and commissions him, in a way that is similar to other significant call narratives in the Bible. God calls Moses to a basic task; he objects, and God reassures him. The same pattern can be found in the Gideon (Judg. 6:11–24), Isaiah (Isa. 6:1–13), and Ezekiel (Ezek. 1:4–3:15) commission narratives.[88]

Moses' resistance to this divine call to leadership continues until God finally angrily agrees to allow Aaron, Moses' brother, to function as his spokesperson. With this decision, we witness the first steps toward the later choice of Aaron and his descendants as high priest. Moses then takes leave of his father-in-law and, along with his immediate family, returns to Egypt in order to confront the pharaoh. The biblical text suggests that at first the Israelites received Moses with hope. When Pharaoh not only rejected their request for a three-day festival in the wilderness (Exod. 5:1–5), however, but also increased their burden by not providing the straw for the manufacture of bricks, they quickly turned against their newly designated leaders.

At this point in the narrative the conflict is set. On one level, the conflict pits Moses and Aaron against Pharaoh and his magicians. But, on a more fundamental level, the conflict is between Yahweh and the gods of Egypt. At the height of the conflict, the last plague, God announces, "On that same night I will pass through Egypt and strike down every firstborn—both men and animals—and I will bring judgment on all the gods of Egypt. I am the LORD." Pharaoh himself is, of course, a god according to Egyptian theology. The "war" between deities that ensues takes the form of signs and plagues.

Attempts have been made to understand the plagues as the result of natural phenomena.[89] For instance, the Nile turning into blood has been attributed either to suspended soil particles in the water or an unusual accumulation of bacteria during the period of its inundation. The result of the pollution of the water was the flight of frogs from the Nile. Gnats/mosquitoes[90] are also not uncommon at a certain time of year in Egypt, but perhaps the plague refers to an unusually heavy population. A suggestion has been made that the boils which affected the men and livestock of Egypt may have been skin anthrax transmitted by the bites of flies that had contact with the dead frogs and cattle of earlier plagues. Such connections of cause-and-effect did likely at least partially exist at the heart of the ecological disaster that is said to have engulfed Egypt at this time. At the same time, however, these effects do not interest the authors of Exodus, even if they ever contemplated their possibility. They view the "cause" of the plagues in directly divine terms; where they mention secondary "causes" that led on to "effects," they focus on the supernatural and not the natural and the "normal," in line with the character of the story as the description of a battle between representatives of deity, all of whom claim access to unusual divine power. For instance, the "cause" of the boils was not fly-bites, according to our biblical authors. The appearance of the boils was connected to the throwing of the soot from a furnace (Exod. 9:10). No reading of the past that takes the testimony of the biblical texts seriously can reduce that testimony to naturalistic terms, any more than it can posit a fixed gulf between the supernatural and the natural that leaves no room for complexity in the way in which divine action in history is to be understood.

Attempts have also been made to associate individual plagues with attacks on specific Egyptian deities, rather than simply seeing the plagues as being, in general terms, attacks on "the gods." Some of the connections made in pursuit of this reading appear plausible, to be sure. The sign of the staff turning into a serpent and eventually consuming the serpent-staffs of the Egyptian magicians may have particular relevance because the snake was an important symbol of Egyptian power, most conspicuously demonstrated by the uraeus (snake symbol) on the headdress of the pharaoh. The Nile turning blood-red can certainly be seen as an attack on the heart of Egypt, since the fertility of the land and the sustenance of the people depended on the annual inundation of that river. A god of fertility, Hapi, was closely identified with the Nile, and often the plague is seen as an attack on that god in particular. Perhaps the most powerful connections have been drawn in the case of the last two plagues. Amon-re, the god of the sun, may be in mind when the sun is darkened; the institution of the pharaoh itself may be under direct attack when God kills all the firstborn, presumably including the heir apparent. However, not all the plagues seem to have such a definite reference, and indeed, some of the connections that are made seem to be of a different order than those just mentioned. For instance, the plague of frogs is often connected with Hekhet and the plague on livestock with Hathor. Hekhet and Hathor, however, were not gods *of* frogs and livestock, but rather gods *with* frog and bovine heads, respectively. The connection in this case is much looser. The plagues overall, though an attack on the Egyptian gods who protect their people, may therefore not be correctly seen as specific attacks against particular deities.

THE EXODUS AND CROSSING OF THE SEA

Finally, the text tells us, the pharaoh allows the Israelites to depart from Egypt. The term "exodus" comes from a Greek term that means "departure," so with Israel's departure we are now concerned with the exodus narrowly conceived. At first, the Israelites cannot seemingly leave Egypt quickly enough (Exod. 12:31–42). The Egyptians want them out so badly that they shower the Israelites with gifts, and the Israelites in their haste do not even add yeast to their bread. As they leave, God directs them away from the usual road to Palestine (Exod. 13:17–18), known to the Egyptians as the Way of Horus. The road followed the coastline of the Mediterranean Sea and was the easiest and quickest route, but also the most heavily defended; according to the text, God was helping the Israelites avoid an early battle. Accordingly, we are told, Moses led Israel from Succoth to Etham, then toward Pi-hahiroth, where they camped along the shoreline opposite a site called Baal-zephon.[91] This body of water is the setting for the climactic event of the exodus, and its name in Hebrew is the *yam sûp*.

What is the *yam sûp* and where is it located? These questions have troubled biblical historians for some time. For one thing, *yam sûp* seems to be used in the Bible to refer to different bodies of water.[92] The traditional translation and identification of the *yam sûp* is "Red Sea," a large body of salt water that today is known, at least in part, as the Gulf of Suez. However, *sûp* does not mean "red," and this identification appears to be based on the Septuagint's translation of the term. Much more likely is that this word is to be understood in the light of an Egyptian cognate (*twfy*), which means "reed." The Israelites crossed a "sea of reeds" in escaping from the Egyptian army. A common assertion is that reeds do not grow in salt water, but only sweet, which has led many to argue that the Israelite crossing of the sea could not have taken place at what we now know as the Red Sea but must have been at one of the marshy lakes between the Mediterranean and the Red Sea (Bitter Lakes, Balah, Timsah, Mensaleh). An either-or decision may not be called for in this instance, for not only has Hoffmeier shown that "salt-tolerating reeds and rushes, called halophytes, do thrive in salt marsh areas," he has also demonstrated that the Red Sea and the southern Bitter Lake may actually have been contiguous in antiquity:

> Geological, oceanographic, and archaeological evidence suggests that the gulf of Suez stretched further north than it does today and that the southern Bitter Lake extended further south to the point where the two could have actually been connected during the second millennium. This linking may have stood behind the Hebrew naming the lake *yām sûp* as well as the Red Sea to which it was connected. . . . In view of these observations, it is possible that the body of water called *yām sûp* in the exodus narratives, Numbers 33:8 through 10, and elsewhere in the Old Testament could refer to the line of lakes (especially the Bitter Lakes) on Egypt's border with Sinai as well as the northern limits of the Red Sea.[93]

We should also take note of the fact that the word *sûp* also means "end."[94] This meaning may have echoed in the minds of the earlier readers and signaled that this crossing signified the end of the exodus. In any case, this remarkable event was of the utmost significance to later generations of Israelites. God's unexpected and sudden deliverance of Israel demonstrated his special care to them, while also giving them confidence as they encountered other difficulties that seemed inescapable (Ps. 77). The later prophets even modeled other acts of divine redemption as a reactualization of the exodus (Jer. 16:14–15; 23:7–8). The Gospels, particularly Matthew, also see Jesus as a fulfillment of the exodus, his life following the general pattern of exodus, wilderness wandering, and conquest.

A puzzling feature of the biblical account is the numbers used in reference to the Israelites who left Egypt in the exodus. Numbers 1:46 calculates the total number of fighting men at 603,550; and on the assumption that many of these men would have had wives and children, this implies that approximately 2 million people were involved in the exodus and wilderness wanderings. Many have questioned the logistics of such a massive movement through the wilderness; some indications within the text itself are that the number is far too high. In a recent article, C. J. Humphreys has pointed out that the number 603,550, understood as a literal number of warriors, is in fact inconsistent with other numbers in the text, most blatantly Numbers 3:46, which suggests that there were "273 firstborn Israelites who exceed the number of the Levites."[95] Humphreys works with that number in its context and shows that it points to a much smaller number for the total population, something like 5,000 males and a total population of 20,000. He then reminds the reader of the established fact that the Hebrew word *'elep* ("thousand") which is used in Numbers 1 has other possible meanings in this context, like "leader" or "troop." Space does not permit a full presentation of this view, and it may not in the final analysis be correct, but this approach serves to point out that alternative understandings of the census accounts[96] can exist rather than the one that posits a total population of 2 million Israelites. Numbers in biblical narrative frequently have purposes other than merely to communicate literal fact.

THE DATE OF THE EXODUS

The name of the pharaoh of the exodus is not given to us in the narrative of the book of Exodus,[97] nor is any other information provided there that helps us to date these events. We are compelled to look outside Exodus for help with dating, therefore; the most relevant biblical passage in this regard appears to be 1 Kings 6:1: "In the four hundred eightieth year after the Israelites came out of the land of Egypt, in the fourth year of Solomon's reign over Israel, in the month of Ziv, which is the second month, he began to build the house of the LORD." Solomon's fourth year is commonly accepted as 966 B.C., although being precise about this date is difficult (see chap. 10). Assuming for the moment, however, that this date is not far wrong (even if it is impossible to be precise about it), then the addition to it of 480 years would bring us to around 1446 B.C. as the date of the exodus. The exodus, on this view, occurred in the mid-fifteenth century B.C.[98] This date seems to be generally supported by the reference in Judg. 11:26 to the 300 years before the time of Jephthah that the Israelites controlled the Transjordan region now (in Jephthah's time) disputed by the Ammonites, and the dating is unproblematic in respect of other details of biblical chronology.

However, even among those who support the idea that the book of Exodus is historically valuable, this date is disputed. Indeed, K. Kitchen calls the argument of the previous paragraph the "lazy man's solution,"[99] insisting that the number 480 should not be taken literally but is in fact a symbolic number of sorts. This number represents twelve generations, with each generation itself symbolically represented by the figure of "forty years." The movement from text to historical chronology must be made carefully, therefore; for "forty years" does not represent, historically, the length of time occupied by a generation, which is really more like twenty-five years. Twelve generations, historically, would occupy around 300 years rather than 480, which would place the exodus in the thirteenth century B.C., not the fifteenth. This thirteenth-century date is commonly thought to fit better the results of the archeological investigations in Palestine, as they have typically been interpreted, with respect to the Israelite settlement in the land that followed the exodus from Egypt. The thirteenth century is also thought to better explain the name of one of the cities that the Hebrews were building for the Egyptian pharaoh: the city of Rameses (Exod. 1:11). This name is clearly the same as a number of pharaohs, none of whom ruled before the fourteenth century. The name almost certainly recalls the powerful Rameses II (c. 1279–1213

B.C.), who is himself the most likely candidate for the pharaoh of the exodus if it took place in the thirteenth century. Most scholars today identify the city of Rameses with modern Qantir (Egyptian Pi-Rameses), which had its heyday in the early thirteenth to late twelfth century B.C., not in the fifteenth century.

We shall return to the archaeology of the Israelite settlement in Palestine. Suffice it to say here that we do not believe that archaeology definitively settles the matter. As to the city of Rameses, what the text signifies is uncertain, for a text can possibly have been updated by a later editor and does not reflect the original name of a city. Kitchen himself appeals to a later editor to explain the fact that Genesis 47:11 refers to Goshen, anachronistically, as "the land of Rameses."[100] We are left in uncertainty, then, and we possess no further extrabiblical evidence that might help us.[101] Although he is discussing the later conquest of Palestine, B. Waltke's conclusion concerning its date therefore applies equally well to the associated date of the exodus: "the verdict *non liquet* must be accepted until more data puts the date of the conquest beyond reasonable doubt. If that be true, either date is an acceptable working hypothesis, and neither date should be held dogmatically."[102]

On either date for the exodus the Amarna letters, sent from various kings of the Canaanite city-states to their Egyptian overlords in the first part of the fourteenth century (Amenhotep III and IV, the latter known more widely as Akhenaten), make interesting reading. We return to these letters in chapter 7. In addition, and if the exodus did take place in the fifteenth century, some further extrabiblical material could also profitably be introduced into our discussion of Israel in Egypt that would help to sketch some of the background against which the biblical account might be read. Egyptian sources inform us of a period of at least one hundred years or so at the end of what is now known as the Second Intermediate Period of Egypt's history (c. 1720–1550 B.C.) during which the larger part of the country was ruled by foreign Semitic rulers referred to as "Hyksos."[103] We might plausibly associate the Egyptian fear of the Semitic Israelites, recorded in the book of Exodus, with their fear of these Hyksos who had dominated them from c. 1648 to 1550 B.C. Perhaps the king who did not know Joseph was Ahmose I (c. 1550–1525 B.C.), the pharaoh who defeated the Hyksos, and perhaps some time later the pharaoh of the exodus was someone like Thutmose III (c. 1479–1425 B.C.). Only further archaeological discoveries will help us to clarify, however, whether these identifications are anything more than plausible guesses.

THE WILDERNESS WANDERING

To reach the *yam sûp* from the city of Rameses, the book of Exodus tells us, the Israelites set up intermediate camps at Succoth,[104] Etham,[105] and Pi-hahiroth between Migdol[106] and the Sea, opposite Baal-zephon (Exod. 12:37; 13:20–22; 14:1–9). After crossing the *yam sûp*, they then entered the wilderness (Exod. 15:22). The rest of the Pentateuch has as its background "wanderings" in this wilderness—important to Israel's story, but difficult to reconstruct with accuracy because (1) the geography of the area, particularly coastlines, lakes, and marshes, has changed so dramatically over the millennia,[107] and (2) our biblical texts do not often provide us with unambiguous information.

From Egypt to Mount Sinai

Theoretically, three potential routes connected Egypt and Palestine. The northern route, mentioned above, was where the presence of Egyptian forts rendered armed conflict likely, and for this reason was best avoided. A middle route headed "straight across Sinai's central limestone shield,"[108] but did not have adequate water supplies. The third route was a southeasterly route, and this is the one the Israelites most probably took.

Their first destination was Mount Sinai. To reach Sinai, the Israelites camped at Marah, Elim, the wilderness of Sin, Dophkah, Alush, and Rephidim—sites gleaned from the biblical narrative itself, as well as from the formal itinerary found in Numbers 33. Much discussion has surrounded the reliability of the itinerary in this chapter, which shows signs of having been shaped by literary interests.[109] For people who hold the curious belief that literary and historical interests are necessarily incompatible, this literary shaping is a problem. To believe that literary shaping undermines historical referentiality is a curious belief, however, for we are largely dependent on literature for such knowledge of history as we possess at all. Certainly the genre of the literature with which we are dealing in Numbers 33 is well known in the ancient world. G. Davies[110] has established that the passage fits well into the broader ancient Near Eastern genre of "itinerary" as described by Hallo and others.[111] C. Krahlmakov further comments that "on the face of it, this passage is an impressive and credible piece of ancient historical writing."[112] This is not to say, however, that we are able with any degree of certainty to sketch the precise route taken by the Israelites to reach Mount Sinai, for we do not know exactly where, on the ground, the settlements were that are mentioned in the text, and archaeology is not able to help us.[113] Indeed, even the location of Sinai itself is uncertain. The earliest traditions[114] located Sinai at Jebel Musa in the southeastern portion of the Sinai peninsula. Others have argued, however, that Sinai is to be found in what is today Saudi Arabia.

Momentous events took place at Sinai, according to our biblical texts (Exod. 19:1–Num. 10:10). This mountain was the very place where God had instructed Moses to bring Israel to him; and once Israel had arrived there, God entered into a covenant with them, gave them a law to live by, and gave instructions to Moses to build a tabernacle. All of these served to bind Israel, now grown larger, into a cohesive community centered on Yahweh. Yet the antiquity of covenant, law, and tabernacle have been questioned through the years.

An ancient metaphor for Israel's relationship with God, the covenant is first mentioned in connection with Noah (Gen. 9) and then with Abraham in Genesis 15 and 17.[115] Indeed, the Mosaic covenant presupposes the deliverance from

Egypt (Exod. 20:2), which is connected to the Abrahamic promises. The Pentateuch contains two large sections devoted to a covenant between God and Israel, mediated through Moses. In Exodus 19–24, we read about the establishment of this covenant at Mount Sinai, and the book of Deuteronomy is a covenant renewal ceremony in which Israel reaffirms its commitment to obey Yahweh just before entering the promised land. Yet in the minds of many scholars, the idea of covenant is a retrojection from late in the history of Israel and, they argue, no such idea existed back in Abrahamic or Mosaic times.

Nonetheless, recent research, while not "proving" that the covenant idea is a feature of early Israelite thinking, certainly indicates that speaking of a covenant at the time of Moses is not anachronistic. The evidence is in the form of Hittite treaties from the second millennium B.C.; these treaties are structurally closely related to biblical covenant documents, particularly the book of Deuteronomy, which are dated by our biblical authors to this early period of Israel's history.[116] Indeed Hittite treaties of this era, rather than later, seventh-century Assyrian treaties, bear this close relationship to the biblical documents, particularly in their possession of a historical prologue that the Assyrian treaties normally lack but which is found in Exodus, Deuteronomy, and Joshua 24. Although the genre is not quite so fixed that we can be adamant that the form of our biblical texts fits *only* the second millennium, the covenant concept is clearly not anachronistic in this time period.

The same can be said of the concept of law. Much discussion has taken place over the past two hundred years about the date of the Israelite law, or at least of some aspects of that law. Proponents of traditional source-critical schemas, for example, have tended to associate much of the law with the Pentateuchal source or editor "P," and have tended to date it to the exilic period or after. Even after acknowledging that earlier collections of law are likely embedded in our Pentateuchal narrative, scholars are reluctant to place such law in the context of the second millennium.[117] Leaving aside the question of the date of the final form of Old Testament law, however, and the question of to what extent the law has been successively updated as generations of Israelites have sought to live by it in changing circumstances, we may certainly say that law, as such, is not a late phenomenon in the ancient Near East. Law was already a feature of life in the late third millennium in Mesopotamia, as we discover from the Sumerian law code from the reign of Ur-Nammu of Ur (c. 2112–2095 B.C.);[118] we find similar law codes associated with Lipit-Ishtar of Isin (c. 1934–1924 B.C.), Hammurapi of Babylon (c. 1792–1749 B.C.), and so on down through the ages. The idea that Moses the Israelite, at his God's direction, should have promulgated a law code for his people at some point during the second half of the second millennium is far from problematic.

As for the tabernacle, "no critical scholar accepts the account in Exodus is a literal account of the desert shrine. . . . [R]ather, the tabernacle account may reflect idealized versions of the later tent shrines at Shiloh or the tent of David."[119] The question is not, of course, whether the narrative to some extent reflects the interests of later times, but whether we have good reason to think that it is misleading us, even while reflecting these interests, in its description of a tabernacle from ancient times. Nothing is essentially problematic about the biblical description of the tabernacle from this point of view. Kitchen argues that the technology used to produce the tabernacle was well known by the time of Moses, and indeed that the tabernacle as described in the biblical text is quite simple compared to near-contemporary worship sites in the ancient Near East. He provides good examples from both Mesopotamia and Egypt for earlier and contemporary tabernacle-like structures.[120]

From Sinai to Kadesh-barnea and to the Plains of Moab

The long account in Exodus 19:1 through Numbers 10:10, set near Mount Sinai, actually reports on a relatively short period of time, ending in the second year after the exodus. By the beginning of Deuteronomy, the Israelites will be on the plains of Moab opposite Jericho, poised to enter the promised land; by contrast, a relatively small number of biblical chapters here cover a far greater number of years of wandering. The transitional event between the two periods of time, the biblical text tells us, occurred in Kadesh-barnea in the Desert of Paran. At this point in the journey, Moses sent twelve spies, one representing each tribe, into the promised land (Num. 13). When they returned, they had good news and bad news. The good news was that the land God had given them was beautiful and productive beyond their imagination. The bad news was that its inhabitants were a formidable people, including the legendary Anakim who made them feel "like grasshoppers" (Num. 13:33). An ensuing lack of confidence in the divine warrior who defeated overwhelming forces at the *yam sûp* led to the long sojourn in the wilderness that followed. Only Joshua and Caleb, two spies who did not waver in their faith, would eventually enter the land, after a whole generation ("forty years," Num. 14:34) had died in this wilderness.[121] As D. Olson has pointed out, the entire book of Numbers is structured around this theme of the death of the original exodus generation and the rise of a second generation, a generation of hope.[122] This generation finds itself addressed by Moses on the plains of Moab.

Numbers 33:37–49 lists a number of camps on the route from Kadesh-barnea to the plains of Moab. First the Israelites stopped at Mount Hor, where Aaron died, then at Zalmonah, Punon, Oboth, Iye Abarim, Dibon Gad, Almon Diblathaim, the mountains of Abarim near Nebo, and, finally, on the plains of Moab. Some scholars believe that this passage, as well as Numbers 21:14–21, describes a route straight along the King's Highway, the major road traversing the Transjordan from south to north along the desert border and ultimately connecting Damascus in the north with the Gulf of Aqabah in the south.[123] However, other passages describe an initial turn southwards back towards the *yam sûp* (cf. Num. 21:4; Deut. 2:1) as part of a swing to the east to avoid the Edomites who had refused Israel passage through their land on this same highway (Num.

20:17). Clarity is difficult to attain here, and part of the problem is uncertainty about the identification of many of the sites mentioned. However, the Israelites appear actually to have traveled north on an alternate route located to the east of the King's Highway, called "the way of the wilderness of Edom" and "the way of the wilderness of Moab," farther out in the desert where there were few settlements and little water.[124]

After avoiding conflict with both the Edomites and the Moabites in this way, the Israelites encountered Sihon, king of the Amorites, and Og, king of Bashan. They soundly defeated these two kings, bringing part of the Transjordan region under Israelite control and providing themselves access to the promised land via a crossing of the Jordan River just above the Dead Sea. One more conflict lay on the horizon, on "the plains of Moab" (which were not actually part of the Moabite kingdom at this time, Num. 21:26). Numbers 22–24 narrates the attempts of the Moabites, fearful of a future attack from the Israelites, to preempt this possibility by hiring a seer named Balaam. The text tells us that Balaam, though paid to curse Israel, could only bless them, but the text also suggests that he was responsible for a different Moabite/Midianite[125] strategy of seeking to undermine Israel by having their women seduce the Israelite men (Num. 25; 31:16). This strategy eventually led to conflict with Moab (Num. 31), after which the land Israel took in the Transjordan was given to the tribes of Reuben and Gad and half the tribe of Manasseh on condition that they cross the Jordan to help fight the bulk of the Canaanites on the other side of that river.

The only piece of extrabiblical evidence of relevance to this last phase of the wilderness wandering, and then only indirectly, is an interesting inscription that mentions this same Balaam, the seer of Numbers 22–24. The text, written in Aramaic, was discovered in 1967 at Tell Deir 'Alla and dates to the eighth century B.C. We should also briefly mention, however, the apparent problems raised by the survey of the Transjordan by the archeologist N. Glueck in the 1930s, at least in respect of the date of the Israelite incursion there. Glueck's survey involved mapping sites and then doing a surface study to determine the dates of occupation. The latter, in essence, involved staff and volunteers simply collecting pot sherds from the surface of the tells, then dating the sherds according to chronologies of changing shapes, color, and treatment of pottery that previous digs had developed where pottery was found in various strata. Glueck's conclusion was that this region was basically uninhabited from the end of the Early Bronze IV period (toward the end of the third millennium B.C.) to the Late Bronze IIb period (1300 B.C.). If so, then a fifteenth-century date for the exodus would be ruled out. However, the kind of survey that Glueck supervised has major methodological problems, not the least of which is that the investigators were allowed to pick up sherds at random. They were naturally attracted to "interesting" sherds with color and/or rims or handles, thus skewing the evidence. Also, such a survey does not take into account the fact that a certain type of pottery may have been current in one part of Canaan at a certain time but that its use in another part of the region may have been significantly later. That more recent surveys have indicated some evidence of occupation in Transjordan during the so-called "gap" between Early Bronze IV and Late Bronze IIb is therefore no surprise. "Glueck's own later work found more LB remains in the N(orth), and subsequent survey and excavation shows no MB-LB gap N(orth) of the Arnon," although in the south "remains are still scanty."[126] The archaeological data in respect of Tranjordan, then, do not settle the date of the exodus any more clearly than other data that we have already mentioned.

CONCLUSION

The Pentateuch ends with Israel on the plains of Moab. The work achieves closure with the report of Moses' death in Deuteronomy 34. However, as D. J. A. Clines points out,[127] the Pentateuch, though clearly a literary unity, anticipates a continuation of the story of Israel. The promise of land given to Abraham (Gen. 12:1–3), in particular, means that Israel will not stay on the plains of Moab forever. We turn in the next chapter to the continuation of the story of the Pentateuch.

Chapter 7

The Settlement in the Land

The origin of ancient Israel, their settlement in the land of Canaan and transformation into an organized kingdom is one of the most stimulating and, at the same time, most controversial chapters in the history of early Israel.[1]

If the patriarchal period and the exodus are "dead issues" in the minds of some scholars[2]—a viewpoint with which we clearly disagree—the debate over Israel's emergence in Canaan remains quite lively. After nearly "a century of intensive research on Israel's origin[,] scholars are still divided over literally every aspect of the subject."[3] As we venture to find a path through this difficult terrain, therefore, we should not expect the going to be easy, nor should we be surprised to discover that some travelers have preferred quite different routes.

We begin in customary fashion with a survey of the scholarly landscape. Various models have been proposed to account for the emergence of Israel in Canaan, and we need to gain a general sense of the lie of the land before beginning our own journey. Once we have a sense of the standard proposals, we begin our exploration of the available evidence—both textual and material. Exhaustive exploration is, of course, impossible within the confines of the current work (or, indeed, within the confines of our lifetimes). So, we need to be selective and suggestive. Despite this limitation, we hope that our journey is fruitful—and fair to the larger landscape, even if some points of interest are glimpsed only from a distance.

SOURCES FOR THE ISRAELITE SETTLEMENT

The textual evidence to be considered includes both biblical and extrabiblical texts. Of the former, the books of Joshua and Judges receive the most attention here. Extrabiblical texts of note include the famous Merneptah Stela and the equally famous Amarna Letters. The material evidence includes the findings of archaeological excavations of significant sites as well as the results of regional surface surveys. In principal, our aim is to explore these different kinds of evidence in relative independence from one another. In practice, however, some interplay is necessary in order to maintain adequate focus and readability. When the various bodies of evidence have been explored, we shall be in a position to look for convergences (or divergences) and to begin to move towards a synthetic understanding of Israel's emergence and early history in Canaan.[4] Methodologically, we find ourselves in sympathy with Z. Kallai's approach, which

> seeks the plausible correlation between the independently analyzed factors, the extant archaeological data, the general historical circumstances that can be ascertained, and the literary representation of biblical historiography, bearing in mind the scribal practices that emerge due to this combined examination. Therefore, even if the historiographical representation is extant in stylized formal configurations, historiography conveys essential historical processes.[5]

ISRAEL'S EMERGENCE IN CANAAN: A SURVEY OF SCHOLARLY MODELS

The competing theories of Israel's emergence in Canaan are well summarized in numerous publications,[6] and so our own treatment can be selective. We note various strengths and weaknesses of each approach along the way, but we delay assessment of the central issues until after we have looked at the full range of evidence, textual and material.

Conquest Model

Traditionally regarded as the most biblical of the various approaches, the conquest model is closely associated with W. F. Albright[7] and his disciples in America and with Y. Yadin[8] and his followers in Israel. As its name implies, this model takes seriously the pervasive biblical notion that Israel's entrance into Canaan involved military conquest (e.g., Num. 32:20–22, 29; Deut. 2:5, 9, 19, 24; Josh. 1:14; 10:40–42; 11:23; 12:7; and *passim*). A key aspect of the conquest model as developed by Albright and others was the attempt to tie the thirteenth-century destructions of such cities as Bethel, Debir, Eglon, Hazor, and Lachish to invading Israelites. G. E. Wright, for instance, concluded his discussion of the archaeology of the conquest by noting that "the manifold evidence for the terrific destruction suffered by [the above-mentioned cities] during the 13th century certainly suggests that a planned campaign such as that depicted in Josh. 10–11 was carried out."[9]

Wright was aware, of course, that this conclusion stood in some tension with a face-value reading of the biblical evidence, which seemed to indicate a fifteenth-century, not a thirteenth-century, date for the exodus, with the conquest forty years later. Among the key passages, 1 Kings 6:1 cites the fourth year of King Solomon's reign as the 480th year after the Israelites came out of Egypt. If Solomon's reign began c. 970 B.C., his fourth year would fall c. 966 B.C., and the biblical date of the exodus would fall c. 1446 B.C. Wright's solution, followed by many since, was to understand the 480 years not literally but as a figure representing twelve generations of 40 years each. If, in fact, a generation is closer to 20 or 25 years, the time between the exodus and Solomon's fourth year would be 300 years or less, placing Israel's entrance into Canaan c. 1270 B.C. or later.

Another key passage is Judges 11:26, in which Jephthah challenges his Ammonite opponent with the claim that Israel has been in possession of territory in Transjordan for 300 years. Best reckoning places Jephthah early in the eleventh century,[10] which would then place the conquest of the Transjordanian territories early in the fourteenth century. In response, Wright argued that the round number 300 is suspicious, if for no other reason than that its proximity to the 319 years that one calculates by tallying the years of oppression and deliverance recorded in the book of Judges *prior to Jephthah*.[11] One should also note that it is a *character* in the story and not the authoritative narrator who asserts Israel's 300-year presence in the land; and characters can, of course, be wrong.

Not all scholars are convinced by such explanations of 1 Kings 6:1 and Judges 11:26, and the thirteenth-century date has other problems. As J. Bimson has shown, many sites mentioned in the biblical account of the conquest do not seem to have been occupied in the thirteenth century. Further, the thirteenth-century destructions of Canaanite cities cannot be so neatly correlated with Israelite invaders as was once thought.[12] They are simply too widely separated in time to have been the result of a single, even protracted campaign.

Today, most scholars regard Albright's conquest model as a failure, which is not surprising since, as L. Younger observes, "the [conquest] model was doomed from the beginning because of its literal, simplistic reading of Joshua."[13] It might be more accurate to speak of a simplistic *mis*reading of Joshua, for the conquest model assumes massive destruction of *property* as well as population, whereas the book of Joshua suggests no such thing. Joshua speaks of cities being taken and kings being killed, but only three cities—Jericho, Ai, and Hazor—are said to have been burned.[14] That only these three are mentioned does not imply the others *might not* have been burned, but it underscores the wrongheadedness of insisting that widespread city destructions should be attested archaeologically. In the case of the three burned cities, of course, it is legitimate to seek some archaeological trace. But to insist on wide-scale destruction in Canaan as evidence of an Israelite conquest is a misguided quest based on misread texts. Moreover, comparative studies suggest that even where violent invasions and conquests are well documented, they may "not always be recognizable from archaeological indications."[15]

Peaceful Infiltration Model

While the conquest model was gaining momentum in America and in Israel, European scholars seemed more attracted to Albrecht Alt's so-called "peaceful infiltration model," first propounded in a seminal essay in 1925.[16] The central thrust of Alt's hypothesis was that Israel's entrance into Canaan was neither sudden nor militant but, rather, quite gradual and largely peaceful—at least at first. The immigrants were nomadic or seminomadic peoples who arrived over an extended (perhaps centuries-long) period of time. Alt's basic theory was taken up by Martin Noth, who added to it the idea that early Israel consisted of a twelve-tribe amphictyony—namely, a federation of tribes bound together by allegiance to a common deity (in this instance Yahweh) and to a common cult center. Noth regarded the book of Joshua's account of "the conquest" as largely etiological in character—an etiology being a story whose chief purpose is to explain the existence of certain features in the land or certain customs, names, or beliefs. The archaeological evidence of thirteenth-century destructions was of little moment for Alt and Noth; Alt predated much of the period of archaeological discovery, and Noth, though he did not deny the destructions, was reticent to assign them to Israelites entering Canaan.[17]

The peaceful infiltration theory has been criticized on a number of grounds, not least with respect to Noth's theory of an Israelite amphictyony. Based as it was on classical Greek models, the amphictyony hypothesis seemed anachronistic and out of accord with the biblical testimony that early Israel was bound together ethnically as well as religiously. The peaceful infiltration view has also been faulted for having a deficient view of how pastoralism actually operates.[18] More recent advocates of the theory have adjusted it to allow for symbiotic relationships between settled and nomadic populations coexisting more or less continuously in the land.[19] Thus the idea of "peaceful" remains, but "infiltration" is called into question, which leads us to the next model.

(Peasant) Revolt Model

While the two models discussed so far see "early Israel" as entering Canaan from outside the land (exogenous models), the next two understand "early Israel" as emerging from existing populations within the land of Canaan (endogenous models). The first of the endogenous models is the peasant revolt hypothesis.

As the name implies, this hypothesis holds that Israel emerged in Canaan not primarily by conquest or peaceful infiltration from without but by sociocultural transformations within. George Mendenhall introduced the theory in a 1962 essay[20] and then expanded on it in a book a decade later.[21] In his writings, Mendenhall does not deny entirely the idea of a conquest, but sees most of the "conquerors" as of indigenous—that is, Canaanite—origin:

> The Hebrew conquest of Palestine took place because a religious movement
> and motivation created a solidarity among a large group of pre-existent
> social units, which was able to challenge and defeat the dysfunctional com-
> plex of cities which dominated the whole of Palestine and Syria at the end
> of the Bronze Age.

As the theory goes, peasant farmers grew tired of the urban overlords from whom
they received "virtually nothing but tax-collectors," and so they revolted. Cat-
alyzing the revolt was "a group of slave-labor captives [who had] succeeded in
escaping an intolerable situation in Egypt" and had "established a relationship
with a deity, Yahweh."[22] Plainly put,

> the appearance of the small religious community of Israel polarized the exist-
> ing population all over the land; some joined, others, primarily the [city-
> state] kings and their supporters, fought. Since the kings were defeated and
> forced out, this became the source of the tradition that all the Canaanites
> and Amorites were either driven out or slain en masse, for the only ones left
> were the predominant majority in each area—now Israelites.[23]

For Mendenhall, the glue that held "Israel" together was not ethnicity (common
blood) but "the religious factor."[24]

Mendenhall recognized that his theory did not derive from "sufficient data,"
which he believed to be lacking, but was, rather, an "'ideal model' of what ought
to have been the case . . . inevitably based upon that which is known to have been
true of other times and other places." He felt justified in constructing an "ideal
model," because he believed that the Bible simply did not provide the kind of
information necessary for historical reconstruction. In particular, he balked at the
theological slant of the biblical texts:

> This biblical emphasis on the "acts of God" seems to modern man the very
> antithesis of history, for it is within the framework of economic, sociologi-
> cal and political organizations that we of today seek understanding of our-
> selves and consequently of ancient man.[25]

Not surprisingly, Mendenhall's approach has been characterized as "sociological," though he himself was vexed by the designation, preferring to locate his
hypothesis "within the framework of social and especially cultural history."[26]
More vexing still to Mendenhall was the Marxist spin placed on the revolt
hypothesis by Norman Gottwald in *The Tribes of Yahweh*.[27] Mendenhall had
anticipated that "political propagandists interested only in 'socio-political
processes'" might seek to exploit his theory, but this assertion did not lessen his
dismay at Gottwald's attempt "to force the ancient historical data into the Pro-
custes' Bed of nineteenth century Marxist sociology." Foremost among Mendenhall's criticisms was the reductionism involved in such a process.[28]

Reductionism, however, is a charge from which Mendenhall himself is not
immune—both in his dismissal of the biblical evidence as virtually devoid of "the
kinds of information which the modern historian looks for" (surely the texts con-

tain much of this kind of information, even if not their chief intent) and in his assumption that human understanding can and must be sought first and foremost in what we have earlier called "middle-range" (second-tier) categories of "economic, sociological, and political organizations."[29]

Further criticisms of the revolt hypothesis—especially as developed by Gottwald—include the following four: the urban/rural antipathy that the theory presupposes is not necessarily born out by anthropological research, where symbiosis is often the rule; nomadism does not necessarily imply or require egalitarianism; sedentarization is not necessarily an advance on nomadism; and the "imperialistic" rhetoric of the book of Joshua, so typical of other ancient Near Eastern conquest accounts, would seem self-contradictory as the literary reflex of an egalitarian, peasant revolution.[30]

On the issue of what held early Israel together, religious commitment or ethnicity, Mendenhall's insistence on the former to the exclusion of the latter seems unfounded and unnecessary. Even should he be correct that "it was not until almost a thousand years after Moses that the religious community finally settled on the idea that ethnicity or race was the foundation of the religious community and the basis of individual identity, when Ezra and Nehemiah forced the divorce of non-Jewish wives,"[31] this would not negate the biblical picture of Israel's ethnic origin. There is nothing inherently improbable in the notion that Israel began as a family, which, as it grew, became the core into which other p●ople were incorporated—at the time of the exodus (Exod. 12:38), possibly before, and certainly after. As R. Hess points out, "the possibility of foreign groups joining in with Israel on its journeys and after its entrance into the land might be remembered in the references to the Midianites (Num. 22–25), the Kenites (Judg. 4:11; 1 Sam. 15:6), the Gibeonites (Josh. 9), and others."[32] Nor should the eventual multiethnic character of Israel blind us to the fact that intermarriage with "foreigners" was repeatedly forbidden; it should simply remind us that the grounds of these prohibitions were not racial, but religious, as passages such as Exodus 34:15–16 make clear:

> You shall not make a covenant with the inhabitants of the land, for when they prostitute themselves to their gods and sacrifice to their gods, someone among them will invite you, and you will eat of the sacrifice. And you will take wives from among their daughters for your sons, and their daughters who prostitute themselves to their gods will make your sons also prostitute themselves to their gods.

Other Endogenous Models

While Mendenhall's is the best known of the endogenous models, the last several decades have seen the rise of a bewildering variety of other endogenous models. Younger provides a convenient summary of these recent theories—highlighting works by Dever, Finkelstein, Lemche, Coote and Whitelam, Thompson, Ahlström, Davies, and Whitelam—in his 1999 essay.[33] We may here be selective, focusing on W. Dever and I. Finkelstein as two accomplished archaeologists who have written extensively on the question before us and have both published major works since Younger's summary was composed.[34] That wide differences exist among the scholars Younger surveyed is obvious to all who have any acquaintance with their works—witness Dever's trenchant critique of most of the other names on the list in his 2001 book entitled *What Did the Biblical Writers Know and When Did They Know It?*—but they all share the view that early Israel, whatever each may mean by that designation, emerged mainly, if not exclusively, from indigenous Canaanite society.

Dever advocates what may be called a "collapse model."[35] According to this model, the origin of "Israel" or "proto-Israel"—whose existence is first tangibly evident in a rapid proliferation of hill-country villages during the Iron I period (c. 1200 B.C. and following)—is to be sought in the collapse of Late Bronze Age Canaanite culture, especially in the lowlands. Prompted by this disintegration, fringe-element Canaanites from sedentary, largely rural populations made use of technologies such as hill-side terracing, plastered cisterns, and stone-lined silos to settle the formerly sparsely populated central hill country. Drawing on surface surveys pioneered by Finkelstein, Dever notes that "in the heartland of ancient Israel about 300 small agricultural villages were founded *de novo* in the late 13th–12th centuries."[36] Dever's commitment to the "'indigenous origins' of most early Israelites"[37] does not prevent him from arguing that early Israel represents an ethnic entity. Not only the aforementioned technological advances but also the virtual absence of pig bones and of "temples, sanctuaries, or shrines of any type in these Iron I hill-country villages"[38] constitute for Dever an archaeological "assemblage" pointing in the direction of an "ethnic group." Noting that "we can recognize the remains of the Phoenicians, Aramaeans, Moabites, Ammonites, and Edomites," Dever asks, "why not the Israelites?"[39] Neither does Dever's indigenous-origins view preclude the possibility that early Israel may have incorporated elements from outside the land of Canaan.[40] While he contends that "the whole 'Exodus-Conquest' cycle of stories must now be set aside as largely mythical"—a tale "told primarily to validate religious beliefs"—he nevertheless allows that

> there may be some actual historical truth here, since among the southern groups whom we know to have written much of the Hebrew Bible there is known a "House (tribe) of Joseph," many of whom may indeed have stemmed originally from Egypt. When they told the story of Israel's origins, they assumed naturally that they spoke for "all Israel" (as the Bible uses the term), even though most of the latter's ancestors had been local Canaanites.[41]

Statements such as these betray an affinity, whether acknowledged or not, with Mendenhall's view of the composition of early Israel—i.e., mainly Canaanites with the addition of a smallish contingent of recent arrivals—irrespective of speculations about the actual process.

Like Dever, Finkelstein is a prolific writer on the archaeology of "early Israel"[42] who believes that "early Israel" emerged for the most part from within Canaan.

Both believe that the way forward in the study of early Israel must lie mainly with archaeology and not with the biblical text, which they regard as compromised by ideology and the study of which they consider largely exhausted. For Finkelstein, "'the great leap forward' in the study of the emergence of Early Israel has been the comprehensive [archaeological] surveys,"[43] which he helped to pioneer.[44] The point of disagreement between Dever and Finkelstein is over *where* the Canaanites who founded and populated the Iron I hill-country villages originated. Finkelstein rejects the notion that their origin may be sought in the lowlands of Canaan, contending that "recent studies have shown beyond doubt that the lowland population had never reached close to a 'carrying capacity' point, and hence there were no land-hungry population surpluses eager to expand into new frontiers."[45] Instead of what we referred to above as the "collapse model," Finkelstein advocates what we might call the "cyclic model," according to which the central hill-country populations subsisted in some centuries as mainly pastoralists (herders) and in others as mainly "plow-agriculturalists" (farmers). For Finkelstein,

> the rise of Early Israel was not a unique event in the history of Palestine. Rather, it was one phase in long-term cyclic socio-economic and demographic processes that started in the 4th millennium BCE. The wave of settlement that took place in the highlands in the late second millennium BCE [i.e., the burgeoning of hill-country villages in Iron I] was no more than a chapter in alternating shifts along the typical Near Eastern socio-economic continuum, between sedentary and pastoral modes of subsistence.[46]

Specifically, Finkelstein cites evidence of "plow-agriculture subsistence (more cattle) in the periods of settlement expansion—Middle Bronze II-III and Iron I—and pastoral oriented society (more sheep/goats) in the crisis years—Intermediate Bronze and Late Bronze Ages."[47] But what caused these fluctuations, and particularly the "crisis years"? Finkelstein speaks of "political, economic and social transformations" and resists the notion that *migration* could have played a significant role. He argues that "the overall character of the material culture of these regions shows clear local features with no clue for large-scale migration of new groups from without."[48] By the same token, he is reticent to speak of the Iron I hill-country settlers as a distinctive ethnic group. One is prompted to ask, however, just what material or other evidence one might expect to find that would mark the arrival of a new people group, particularly if (1) the new arrivals had spent time as mainly pastoralists before settling down and (2) the newcomers were of West-Semitic stock to start. Hess maintains that, generally speaking, "material culture is distinctive to a particular region (i.e. the hill country), not necessarily to a particular ethnic group (e.g. Israelite rather than Canaanite)."[49] Thus, "the assumption that every ethnic group must have a distinct, archaeologically observable culture is not well founded."[50] Early in his essay, Finkelstein himself says much the same thing:

> As far as I can judge, the material culture of a given group of people mirrors the environment in which they live; their socio-economic conditions; the

> influence of neighboring cultures; the influence of previous cultures; in cases of migration, traditions which are brought from the country of origin; and, equally important, their cognitive world.[51]

By these criteria, one would *expect* early Israel to have left little archaeological mark, except perhaps in terms of their "traditions" and "cognitive world." Later in his essay, Finkelstein mentions archaeological evidence of an apparent "taboo on pigs" in the Iron I hill-country villages and allows that this may indeed be an ethnic marker, as Stager had suggested some years earlier.[52] Much more excavation of hill-country sites must be completed before firm conclusions can be drawn,[53] but the apparent pig taboo may well be suggestive of culinary-cultic "traditions" and the "cognitive world" supporting them. We return to this issue later.

When compared to the biblical depiction of early Israel, the pictures painted by Dever and Finkelstein involve significant revisions. But it is in the models presented by Lemche, Coote, Thompson, Ahlström, Davies, and Whitelam that we encounter revisionism with a vengeance. It is necessary to speak of models (plural) because of the striking differences among the theories of these scholars.[54] One thing they all tend to agree on, however, is that the biblical material is of minimal value, at best, in reconstructing the character of "historical Israel." Though more moderate than some, Finkelstein's words are typical of revisionist reasoning:

> Theoretically speaking, scholars can use two tools to decipher these riddles: text and archaeology. The importance of the biblical source, which dominated past research on the rise of Early Israel, has been dramatically diminished in recent years. The relatively late date of the text and/or its compilation—in the 7th century BCE and later—and its theological/ideological/political agenda, make it irrelevant as direct historical testimony. Of course, though it reflects the religious convictions and interests of people who lived centuries after the alleged events took place, some historical germs may be disguised in it.[55]

In keeping with this devaluation of the biblical texts, which he would date even later, P. R. Davies insists that "ancient Israel" is a mere construct of modern scholarship and that "biblical Israel" never existed as anything more than an ideological, literary product of the exilic or postexilic period. Thus neither "ancient Israel" nor "biblical Israel" may have much to do with actual, "historical Israel."[56]

What are we to make of all this? Two observations come to mind. First, as we were at pains to argue in part 1, it should by no means be taken for granted that the biblical materials are of minimal value in reconstructing Israel's history. This would have to be demonstrated, and we are not convinced by the commonly cited reasons for discounting the biblical witness—that is, supposed late datings, theological slant, and archaeological disproof. Our own view is that (1) the late datings of biblical texts, including Joshua and Judges, are anything but assured (and in any case would not necessarily invalidate a text's capacity to carry historical information);[57] (2) theological slant need not vitiate the historical usefulness of the texts, so long as that slant is understood and allowance is made for it (after all, "all history writing [ancient or modern] requires a de-biasing process in our reading"[58]); and (3) the conclusions to be drawn from archaeological findings are often anything but obvious, which is as true of regional surveys as of site excavations.[59] And so we continue to affirm the vital importance of the biblical texts and the necessity of rightly understanding their general character and contents.

Second, that any one of the standard models has done justice to the biblical testimony in the first place is by no means clear—though each may, in fact, capture some aspect of it.[60] For instance, the biblical portrayal of Israel's emergence in Canaan undeniably involves military conquest, yet none but the first of the standard theories finds much (if any) room for this aspect. Even the first, the "conquest model" of Albright and others, assumes a kind of conquest that a careful reading of the biblical texts does not support. Our task, then, is to return to the texts and try to read them well.

The biblical texts most pertinent to the question of Israel's emergence in Canaan are the books of Joshua and Judges. Space limitations do not allow full treatment of either, of course, so our readings will of necessity be selective and suggestive. Once we gain a sense of the picture of Israel's early history in Canaan that the biblical texts paint, we shall turn to potentially relevant extrabiblical texts. Only when we have a fair sense of the picture that the texts present will we turn to the material evidence.

As we noted earlier, much can be said, methodologically, for attempting to treat each kind of evidence independently of the other. Our reading of the texts, for instance, should in principle proceed initially without reference to material evidence, and vice versa. The idea would be to prevent the results of the one area of investigation from prematurely influencing results in the other. As logical and desirable as this stratagem is, carrying it out in practice is virtually impossible, requiring scholars either to compartmentalize their thinking dramatically or simply to have no prior knowledge of the area not being considered at a particular time. About the best one can to do is to try to avoid jumping to conclusions about evidence in one area on the basis of assumed knowledge from another.

So why begin with the textual evidence, biblical and extrabiblical? It would also be possible to begin with the archaeological evidence, provided that we limited ourselves to cataloguing the material evidence (perhaps forming tentative judgments about social context and general modes of living) and vigorously resisted the temptation to begin writing our own "stories" about specific events and persons. As is often observed, material evidence alone is ill suited to tell a story, except perhaps a very general story about the *longue durée*. Study of the material evidence is best suited for establishing general conditions and gauging the plausibility of stories that the available texts tell. If our interest is in *human* history, and not just natural history or general social history, texts prove invaluable. Appropriately then, especially in view of our openness to testimony, we begin with the texts. They provide a story, or stories, the plausibility of which we may then test in the light of whatever material remains are known.

READING THE BIBLICAL TEXTS (JOSHUA AND JUDGES)

Beginning with the last quarter of the twentieth century there has been a blossoming of interest in holistic literary studies of many parts of the Bible, with the interest being perhaps keenest in respect to biblical narratives. This literary turn is yielding fresh insights that are reflected not only in recent commentaries on Joshua and Judges, but also in a number of specialized studies. A sampling of significant studies covering both Joshua and Judges would include, in order of their first appearance, works by Polzin,[61] Gunn,[62] Alonso Schökel,[63] Younger,[64] and Gros Louis and Van Antwerpen.[65] Covering Joshua alone are works by Koorevaar,[66] Winther-Nielson,[67] Younger,[68] and Hawk.[69] Significant literary studies of Judges include those by Gooding,[70] Webb,[71] Klein,[72] Brettler,[73] Block,[74] Bowman,[75] O'Connell,[76] and Amit.[77]

While some advocates of close readings of these texts cite literary interests as an excuse for sidestepping historical questions, the fact is that improved literary readings often provide just the needed stepping stones for moving forward along the path of historical reconstruction.[78] Polzin, one of the early advocates of what is often called modern literary criticism of the Bible, observed in 1980 that "historical criticism of the Bible is, after more than a century, something of a disappointment precisely because 'literary criticism of biblical texts is still in its infancy.'"[79] Polzin was distressed by the disinclination of early modern scholars such as Wellhausen and Noth to give adequate attention to biblical texts as sensible wholes and feared the consequences of this failure: "if the best and most influential representatives of modern biblical scholarship often base their arguments on weak and inadequate diachronic guidelines, what must be the case with works of lesser quality?"[80]

Alonso Schökel, commenting on the books from Joshua to 2 Kings, contends that "we cannot understand the nature or the historical value of such documents if we do not take into account the literary conventions that the narrators worked under or used."[81] Even where our interests may be ultimately in the *historical* import of ancient texts, we cannot hope to discern this import correctly unless we approach them on their own *literary* terms. We must be attuned to such standard features of storytelling as plot development, characterization, the use of key words and motifs to develop themes, the narrator's control of narrative time (story time) and narrated time (real time), and so forth (the kinds of general features of narrative "poetics" discussed already in part 1, chap. 4). In addition, we stand to benefit greatly from learning as much as we can about the specific literary conventions, or transmission codes, used in texts we are studying. A model study in this regard is Younger's *Ancient Conquest Accounts*, in which he seeks to place the conquest account of Joshua 9–12 in the broader context of second- and first-millennium B.C. conquest accounts from Assyria, Hatti, and Egypt.

The result of Younger's careful comparative study is to confirm that "while there are differences [between ancient Near Eastern and biblical history writing] (e.g., the characteristics of the deities in the individual cultures), the Hebrew conquest account of Canaan in Joshua 9–12 is, by and large, typical of any ancient Near Eastern account." The "transmission code" shared by biblical and ancient Near Eastern historiography involves "an intermingling of the texts' figurative and ideological aspects."[82] Failure to recognize this intermingling can give rise to flat, literalistic (mis)readings of biblical texts, with the result that textual "straw men" are created and then found wanting in the light of nontextual (e.g., archaeological) evidence. If, for instance, one were to overlook the hyperbolic character of the summary of Joshua's southern campaign found in Joshua 10:40—Joshua "left no one remaining, but utterly destroyed all that breathed"— then the discovery, whether by archaeological exploration or indeed by reading other biblical texts (including other parts of Joshua!), that many Canaanites survived would appear to constitute a contradiction. The problem, however, would lie not with the text but with the inappropriate construal of the text. It is hard to envisage any serious student of the Bible making this kind of blunder, but on a lesser scale such mistakes are often made. An example would be the oft-repeated claim that Joshua and Judges present contradictory accounts of Israel's emergence in Canaan. We will tackle this issue presently, but first we must explore each book individually, seeking to gain an overview of its central structures and messages.

The Book of Joshua

One of the best ways to gain a sense of what a particular narrative is about is to pay close attention to how the narrative begins and ends and to how it is structured as a whole.

Beginning and Ending

The book of Joshua opens with the words "after the death of Moses"[83] and then proceeds to recount the Lord's charge to Joshua, Moses' assistant, to lead the people across the Jordan and into the land of promise. Both the reference to Moses and to the promised land remind the reader of the Pentateuchal story going back not just to the Exodus from Egypt under Moses but also to the "patriarchal promise" first announced to Abraham in Genesis 12:1–3 (note also the reference to the land in v. 7) and reiterated often thereafter to Abraham and his descendants (to Abraham: Gen. 15:5–21; 17:4–8; 18:18–19; 22:17–18; to Isaac: Gen. 26:2–4; to Jacob: Gen. 28:13–15; 35:11–12; 46:3; and to Moses: Exod. 3:6–8; 6:2–8). A striking feature of the charge to Joshua to assume leadership and take the land is the number of times the book stresses that it is actually the Lord who will *give* Israel the land (Josh. 1:2, 3, 6, 11, 13, 15 [twice]). Joshua must be "strong and courageous" to accept his task, to refuse discouragement, and, most importantly, to heed God's instructions (vv. 5–9), but the emphasis clearly falls on God's initiative in giving his people the land.

Looking to the end of the book, the theme of God's giving the land in fulfillment of his promise continues to dominate. Joshua, now "old and well advanced in years" (23:1), summons "all Israel"—as represented by "their elders and heads, their judges and officers" (23:2)—and reminds them of how faithful God has been in giving them the land: "you know in your hearts and souls, all of you, that not one thing has failed of all the good things that the LORD your God promised concerning you; all have come to pass for you, not one of them has failed" (23:14). Chapter 24 continues in the same vein:

> Then I brought you to the land of the Amorites, who lived on the other side of the Jordan; they fought with you, and I handed them over to you [lit. *gave* them into your hand], and you took possession of their land, and I destroyed them before you. (v. 8)

> When you went over the Jordan and came to Jericho, the citizens of Jericho fought against you, and also the Amorites, the Perizzites, the Canaanites, the Hittites, the Girgashites, the Hivites, and the Jebusites; and I handed them over to you [lit. *gave* them into your hand]. (v. 11)

> I gave you a land on which you had not labored, and towns that you had not built, and you live in them; you eat the fruit of vineyards and oliveyards that you did not plant. (v. 13)

Thus, the book of Joshua, which began with repeated affirmations of God's commitment to *give* his people the land he had promised them so long ago, ends with emphatic pronouncements that he has now succeeded in doing just that.

But this is not all that happens in the final chapters of the book. Beginning with the departure of the two and a half tribes whose allotted territories lie east of the Jordan (chap. 22), another theme begins to gain prominence: the duty of God's people to be true to their relationship to him (the Hebrew keyword is ʿbd, rendered "serve" or "worship"). Just before the men of Reuben, Gad, and the half-tribe of Manasseh leave to return home to Transjordan, Joshua charges them to

> Take good care to observe the commandment and instruction that Moses the servant of the LORD commanded you, to love the Lord your God, to walk in all his ways, to keep his commandments, and to hold fast to him, and to serve (ʿbd) him with all your heart and with all your soul. (22:5)

In clearing up the misunderstanding that arises over the imposing altar they erect at the Jordan (22:10), the two and a half tribes insist that the altar is not meant for sacrifice but as a reminder that they, too, *serve* the God worshiped by their relatives west of the Jordan (22:26–27).

From this point on, the emphasis on who is to be *served* picks up rapidly, climaxing in no fewer than sixteen occurrences of the verb "serve" in chapter 24 (vv. 2, 14 [three times], 15 [four times], 16, 18, 19, 20, 21, 22, 24, 31). Having gathered the people in Shechem to renew the covenant (in much the same way that Moses in the book of Deuteronomy renewed the covenant with the people prior to his death), Joshua puts the issue plainly. The people must choose whom they will serve. He charges them as follows: "revere the LORD, and serve him in sincerity and in faithfulness; put away the gods that your ancestors served beyond the River and in Egypt, and serve the LORD" (v. 14). But he will not force them: "if you are unwilling to serve the LORD, choose this day whom you will serve . . . ; but as for me and my household, we will serve the LORD" (v. 15). The people confidently respond with "We also will serve the LORD, . . . " (v. 18), but Joshua remains concerned, implying that perhaps the people do not fully understand the exclusive loyalty required of those who would serve the LORD ("You cannot serve the LORD, for he is a holy God. He is a jealous God" [v. 19]). When the people nevertheless persist, "No, we will serve the LORD!" (v. 21), Joshua cites them as witnesses against themselves that they have chosen to serve the Lord (v. 22). Finally Joshua charges the people to begin to act in accordance with their profession: "Then put away the foreign gods that are among you, and incline your hearts to the LORD, the God of Israel" (v. 23). The people's response, which seems fine at first glance—"The LORD our God we will serve, and him we will obey" (v. 24)—appears slightly more ominous when we notice that it omits reference to the putting away of "foreign gods."[84] More ominous still is the final occurrence of the verb "serve" in the book of Joshua: "Israel served the LORD all the days of Joshua, and all the days of the elders who outlived Joshua and had known all the work that the LORD did for Israel" (v. 31). Without saying it directly, this verse hints at the possibility that Israel's service of the Lord may have its limits (temporal and otherwise). With this hint, the transition to the book of Judges is complete.

The book of Joshua thus begins and ends with an emphasis on God's fulfilling his promise to give Israel the land and on their consequent responsibility to serve him faithfully. How does this frame fit the overall structure of the book?

Structure

One of the more thorough and insightful analyses of the structure of the book of Joshua is articulated by H. J. Koorevaar in his Dutch dissertation "De Opbouw van het Boek Jozua" (The Structure of the Book of Joshua).[85] Koorevaar divides the book into four main sections, each characterized by a key word. The four sections are as follows: 1:1–5:12; 5:13–12:24; 13:1–21:45; and 22:1–24:33. The key words are, in order, "cross" the Jordan, "take" the land, "divide" the land, and "serve" the Lord. In Hebrew, the two sets of keywords correspond to one another in sound and appearance—ʿābar ("cross") resembling ʿābad ("serve"), and lāqaḥ ("take") resembling ḥālaq ("divide").

Each of the first three main sections begins with a divine initiative. By God's command, Israel crosses the Jordan, takes the land (beginning with Jericho), and divides the conquered territories. The fourth and final section, by contrast, does not begin with a divine initiative. Instead, Joshua takes the initiative, charging the people in each of the three final chapters to serve the Lord.

The four main sections also have distinct closings. The "crossing"-into-the-land section closes in 5:1–12 with the reinstatement of the wandering people of God in the land of promise. Their covenant relationship with Yahweh is reaffirmed by the circumcision of those who had been born in the wilderness. The people's redemption from slavery is marked by the reinstatement of the Passover celebration. And at this point, the manna that had sustained them in their wanderings ceases. Israel has landed! The "taking"-the-land section closes in 11:16–12:24 with summaries of Joshua's successes in carrying out his military mission, listing not only conquered territories but also listing conquered kings. The "dividing"-the-land section closes in 21:43–45 with a ringing confession that God has been as good as his word: "Not one of all the good promises that the LORD had made to the house of Israel had failed; all came to pass" (v. 45). God has done his part. Thus, the focus logically shifts in the fourth, "serving"-the-Lord section to the matter of the people's response to what God has done. This final section closes in 24:29–33 where, as noted above, we learn that "Israel served the LORD all the days of Joshua, and all the days of the elders who outlived Joshua" (v. 31). Then what? Again, Judges tells this story.

The (Hi)storyline

As our brief look at beginning, end, and basic structure indicates, the book of Joshua is deeply theological, but does this mean that the book is without value as a historical source? Some would say so, but by now our own position should be clear. Our task in this section is to trace the storyline as simply and briefly as possible, with an eye particularly to aspects of the story that might be tested "on the ground."

The action begins with Joshua's charge in chapter 1 to take up the mantel of leadership, now that Moses is dead. Upon receiving his commission, Joshua's first act is to send spies across the Jordan to reconnoiter the land, particularly Jericho. The spies' presence in Jericho is immediately discovered, however, and after a narrow escape and some time in the hills, they return to Joshua with only two results: (1) word that "truly the LORD has given all the land into our hands" (2:24; no surprise here, after all the assurances in chap. 1), and (2) the fact that Israel, through the auspices of the spies, has now made a pact with the Canaanite prostitute Rahab (2:8–21; a bit more surprising, in view of Israel's mission). Joshua next leads the entire population across the Jordan (chaps. 3–4), after its "waters flowing from above stood still, rising up in a single heap far off at Adam, the city that is beside Zarethan, while those flowing toward the sea of the Arabah, the Dead Sea, were wholly cut off" (3:16). Once in the land of Canaan, the Israelites' first actions are to memorialize Yahweh's faithfulness in bringing them into the land (4:19–24) and to renew their covenant relationship with Yahweh by reinstituting circumcision and Passover (chap. 5).

The first military engagement results in a dramatic victory over Jericho in the Jordan Valley (chap. 6). The city, having been placed under the ban (6:17), is burned (6:24). This victory is followed by an initially disastrous attack on the city of Ai, which is then rectified after the Israelite camp is cleansed of the sin of Achan (chaps. 7–8). Ai, too, is burned (8:28).

The final section of chapter 8 describes a covenant renewal ceremony at Mounts Ebal and Gerizim, in the vicinity of Shechem. In view of the distance between Ai and Shechem (c. twenty miles) and the apparent ease with which Joshua was able to enter the area without a fight, commentators have wondered whether the literary placement of the ceremony may owe more to theological than to chronological considerations. This conclusion is a possibility, especially in view of the fact that the section is a "floating pericope," appearing in several different places in the manuscript tradition.[86] It should be noted, however, that

> Shechem had an ancient tradition of religious significance and covenant making in Israel that went back to Abraham. For example, Abraham built an altar to the LORD after the LORD had appeared to him there (Gen 12:6–7). Jacob bought land there, and he too erected an altar there (Gen 33:18–20), and the city eventually became the family's home (Gen 35:4; 37:12–14).[87]

That Moses' instructions in Deuteronomy 27:1–8, which form the background to the present account, focused on just this region is, therefore, not surprising. Nor is it necessarily surprising that the book of Joshua makes no mention of Shechem being taken by force; "the Shechemites may have been friendly with the Israelites, perhaps due to the earlier ties between the city and Israel."[88] So in the final section of Joshua 8, Joshua builds on Mount Ebal an altar according to Moses' instructions (v. 30), offers sacrifices on it (v. 31), copies on its (or some other) stones the "law of Moses" (v. 32),[89] and then reads "all the words of the law, blessings and curses, according to all that is written in the book of the law" (v. 34).[90]

News of Israel's initial military victories causes different reactions among the Canaanites. Most begin to band together to offer resistance (9:1–2). But one group of hill-country villagers, the Gibeonites, decides on a different course of action and, by convincing Israel's leaders that they are actually from a far country, manages to dupe them into making a covenant of peace (chap. 9). Rightly concerned about Israel's early victories and Gibeon's defection, the king of Jerusalem bands together with the kings of Hebron, Jarmuth, Lachish, and Eglon to teach the Gibeonites a lesson (chap. 10). Israel is called out in defense of their Canaanite partners (!) and wins a smashing victory against the five kings, who are pursued and eventually killed. Following the defeat and execution of the coalition's five kings, Joshua and "all Israel" sweep southward, defeating at least seven southern cities: Makkedah, Libnah, Lachish, Gezer, Eglon, Hebron, and Debir (10:29–39). In the brief summaries of the taking of these cities, much emphasis is placed on putting the populations to the sword and leaving no survivors, but there is little to suggest that the cities themselves were destroyed.

The results of this "southern campaign" are summarized in 10:40–42 in hyperbolic terms characteristic of ancient Near Eastern conquest accounts.[91] Rhetoric such as "he left no one remaining, but utterly destroyed all that breathed" (v. 40) should not be read in a flat, literalistic way, as if hard statistical information were intended. The earlier juxtaposition in Joshua 10:20 of "a very great slaughter . . . until they were wiped out" with the existence of "survivors" who "entered into the fortified towns" should caution against simplistic, literalistic readings of such summaries. Of particular interest is the opening statement of the summary, which lays stress on Joshua's having "defeated," or "subdued" (Hiphil of *nkh*), the whole region. This emphasis on defeating/subduing the enemy, as distinct from occupying the cities "taken," is reinforced by the closing verse of chapter 10, which has Joshua and all Israel return to their base camp in Gilgal.

Chapter 11 opens with the formation of another coalition, this time in the north and centered around Hazor, described in verse 10 as the "head of all those kingdoms." Though a vast army is mustered, "in number like the sand on the seashore" (v. 4; more hyperbole), Yahweh again *gives* the enemy into Israel's hand (v. 8). All the royal cities are captured, along with their kings, and they are "utterly destroyed." While this language might give English readers the impression that the cities themselves were destroyed, and not just their populations, the text is at pains to clarify that Hazor alone was burned (vv. 11–14). Thus far, then, only three cities are explicitly said to have been burned in the taking of the land: Jericho (6:24), Ai (8:28), and Hazor. Having described the successful execution of the "northern campaign," chapter 11 draws to a close with another summary of Joshua's successes, similar to the summary at the end of chapter 10 but lengthier and drawing together the result of all the campaigns—central, southern, and northern. This more complete summary is worthy of closer inspection, not least for what it indicates about the character of biblical historiography.

The first part of the summary (11:16–20) is an intriguing combination of generalities and specifics, of history and theology, of hyperbole and restraint. In one sense, the claim that "Joshua took all that land" (v. 16) sounds exaggerated, because he clearly did not take every city (some were not taken until David's day)[92] and even some whole regions, such as the coastal plain, are not mentioned in the description that follows. In another sense, however, the statement may be quite accurate, claiming only that Joshua gained the upper hand throughout the land as a whole.[93] Verse 16 continues, naming the major regions over which Joshua was successful. First on the list is the "hill country." In the light of verse 21, which distinguishes between the hill country of Israel and the hill country of Judah, and of the mention of the hill country of Israel at the end of verse 16, the first "hill country" mentioned in verse 16 presumably refers to the southerly hills that would later belong to Judah. In addition to the hill country south and north, Joshua took the Negeb (the southern desert area), the land of Goshen (which lay between the hill country and the Negeb; see Josh. 10:41), the western foothills (Shephelah, which designates the foothills between the hill country and the coastal plain), and the Arabah (the rift valley east of the central hill country). Absent from the list, as noted above, is the coastal plain, which Joshua apparently did not take (cf. Josh. 17:16–18; Judg. 1:19). Thus, verse 16 outlines the regions taken in Cis-Jordan. Next, verse 17 specifies the southern and northern boundaries of the territory taken (cf. 12:7).[94] The earlier, briefer summary in 10:40–42 follows the same pattern, first describing the conquered territories and then their outer boundaries.

Also like the summary in chapter 10, the summary in chapter 11 paints the conquest in bold strokes, but not without restraint, either geographically (as we have just seen) or temporally, as evidenced, for instance, by 11:18's admission that "Joshua made war a long time with all those kings." The Hebrew word order is emphatic, placing "a long time" (*yāmîm rābbîm*) in first position. Clearly the conquest as depicted in the first half of Joshua was no blitzkrieg in the traditional sense.

Verses 19–20 complete the first part of the summary in chapter 11, juxtaposing without embarrassment a political reality (no one, save Gibeon, sought peace with the Israelites) with a theological explanation—"it was the LORD's doing to harden their hearts . . . that they might be utterly destroyed . . . just as the LORD had commanded Moses."

The second part of the summary (vv. 21–23) continues with a broad brush, yet not without including a selection of suggestive details. Significantly, this section begins to look forward as well as backward, anticipating the distribution of the land that begins in chapter 13. Chief among the details is the notice that "at that time Joshua came and wiped out [lit. cut off] the Anakim" (v. 21).[95] The pertinence of this notice, coming just at this point in the flow of Joshua, becomes clear when we recall that it was Israel's fear of the Anakim—before whom the Israelites under Moses had felt like "grasshoppers" (Num. 13:33)—that had first prevented them from entering the promised land (see Num. 13:27–28, 33; 14:1–2 in context). Further details in Josh. 11:21 name the regions (hill country) and cities (Hebron, Debir, Anab) from which the Anakim were eradicated. In the light of later notices that Caleb drove the Anakim from Hebron (Josh. 15:13–14) and that Othniel took Debir (Josh. 15:15–17),[96] some have asserted a historical discrepancy here. It is more likely that in the generalizing, transitional summary of Joshua 11:21–23, Joshua is credited with the ultimate results of processes that he *initiated*. This possibility is confirmed by the bridging function of 11:23, which not only credits Joshua with taking "the whole land" but also with giving it "for an inheritance to Israel according to their tribal allotments"— though the latter is yet to be described in the second half of the book of Joshua.

The chief literary function not just of verse 23 but of the entire summary in 11:16–23 is to provide a bridge between the theme of conquest that dominates the first half of the book[97] and the allocation of conquered territories and towns that dominates the second half. The chief theological point is that God, having promised to give the people under Joshua the land, has kept that promise. "The LORD God of Israel fought for Israel," as the earlier summary at the end of chapter 10 stated (10:42), and "not one of all [his] good promises" has failed, as the later summary in 21:45 underscores. The chief historical point is that the war of *subjugation* has been successful—"the land had rest from war" (11:23)—and the *occupation* can now commence.

Before the occupation can actively begin, however, the land must be subdivided and allotted to the various tribes. This process begins in chapter 13, after the listing of defeated kings in chapter 12. If the first half of the book of Joshua has focused on God's *giving* the land to Israel, the second half will focus on the people's duty to *occupy*, or possess, their tribal allotments. The verb *yrš* (possess, dispossess, occupy, etc.) begins to occur with some frequency for the first time since chapter 1.[98]

Instead of working through the allotments tribe by tribe, we shall content ourselves with several general comments. First, these sections delineating the tribal territories are quite candid about the Israelite tribes' occasional (perhaps even progressive) failures to dislodge their foes and occupy towns within their allotments: the tribes east of the Jordan did not drive out (Hiphil of *yrš*) the people of Geshur and Maacah (13:13), nor did Judah drive out the Jebusites from Jerusalem (15:63), nor Ephraim the Canaanites in Gezer (16:10). Manasseh at first had little success at all in occupying its allotted towns (17:12–13). As for the remaining seven tribes, we learn from chapter 18 that, though "the land lay subdued [Niphal of *kbš*] before them" (v. 1),[99] their inheritance had not yet been apportioned (*ḥlq*) (v. 2), and they had not even begun "taking possession" (Hiphil of *yrš*) of the land their God had given them (v. 3). These notices underscore the distinction between subjugation and occupation, and they foreshadow a trend that continues and increases in the book of Judges, as we shall see.

Second, we must approach the territorial allotments listed in Joshua 13–19 with circumspection. In his helpful discussion of the allotments,[100] Hess points out that the lists, which were originally family allotments, would have soon become administrative documents and, as such, would likely have been subject to updating as new towns emerged.[101] Any late monarchic features found in the lists, therefore, might best be understood not as establishing the origin of the lists but as demonstrating their continued use. Furthermore, and along the same lines, "the origins of the divisions and allotments themselves should not be tied exclusively to the dating of the archaeological remains at the sites that can be identified."[102]

Framing the description of the tribal allotments in Cis-Jordan are notices of personal allocations to the two "faithful spies" of Numbers 13–14 fame. Caleb, the Judahite, receives Hebron (Josh. 14:6–15), and Joshua, the Ephraimite, receives Timnath Serah (19:49–50). Thus, in the description of the allotments, we have *historical* information presented in a carefully structured *literary* form with a clear *theological* motive; the faithful spies receive their reward.

Following the tribal allocations, the cities of refuge are designated (Josh. 20), as are also the cities of the priestly tribe of Levi (chap. 21). All these allocations are then concluded with yet another summary in praise of God's *giving* Israel the land in fulfillment of his "good promises" to the forefathers (21:43–45).

The final section of the book (chaps. 22–24) has already been discussed. Here it suffices simply to reiterate the shift that takes place from a focus on the Lord's faithfulness to Israel's responsibility to *serve* him faithfully. Appropriately, the final assembly (chap. 24) takes place at Shechem, where earlier (chap. 8) the covenant had been renewed, an altar built, and the words of the law written as a public reminder of Israel's covenant benefits and obligations. How Israel fares in keeping these obligations is a story the book of Judges tells.

The Book of Judges

Recent studies have increasingly recognized the book of Judges as "a literary unit in its own right."[103] In his 1987 "integrated reading" of the book of Judges,

B. Webb reviewed earlier historical-critical theories by Noth, Richter, Smend, Dietrich, Veijola, Boling, and Auld and concluded that, while "the redactional unity of the central section of Judges has long been recognized," good reasons exist to extend the notion of a unified composition to the book as a whole. L. R. Klein espoused a similar general view in *The Triumph of Irony in the Book of Judges*, concluding that "the book of Judges is a unity, one in which structure—including those figurative devices which contribute to structure—conveys meaning."[104] As with the book of Joshua, so with Judges, we discover that paying attention to how the book begins and ends, and how it is structured overall, yields insights into its basic sense and significance.

Beginning and Ending

On a first reading, the book of Judges seems chaotic—which is not entirely inappropriate, given the chaotic period the book describes. On closer inspection, however, a coherent literary structure emerges. Webb likens the structure of the book of Judges to a symphony comprising three parts: an overture that introduces the fundamental themes (Judg. 1:1–3:6), variations that develop and move these themes along (3:7–16:31), and a coda that characterizes the whole and brings it to conclusion (chaps. 17–21). In this tripartite division, Webb agrees with virtually all commentators on the book of Judges. In some ways, the heart of the book is the central section, which tells the well-known stories of judge-deliverers such as Ehud, Deborah, Gideon, Jephthah, and Samson. The beginning and ending sections, though, provide vital orientation and summation, so we must consider them first.

Just as the book of Joshua opens with a reference to the death of Moses, the book of Judges begins with a reference to the death of Joshua—two references in fact (1:1 and 2:6–9). That the death of Joshua is recorded a second time in Judges 2:6–9 suggests that chronological sequence is not the overriding concern of the book, an impression confirmed also by what appears to be a "flashback" in 1:8–15.[105] The two death notices suggest a division of the "overture" into two main parts, the first (1:1–2:5) focusing on the *sociopolitical* decline that followed upon Joshua's death, and the second (2:6–3:6) highlighting the *religious* cause and consequence of this decline. The first part "deals with the way in which conquest gave way to co-existence as Israel 'came to terms' with the Canaanites."[106] Judges 1:22–26 recounts the first Canaanite compromise in the book of Judges (and the first, even including the book of Joshua, actually *initiated by Israelites* rather than Canaanites): "Show us the way into the city, and we will deal kindly with you" (v. 24).[107] Following this compromise, which allows a Canaanite family to survive and flourish at a distance, verses 27–36 record the varying successes of other tribes in driving out the Canaanites. As Webb has noted, a subtle decline in Israel's fortunes occurs in this section, moving from Canaanites' being allowed to live amongst the Israelites, to Israelites' being allowed to live amongst the Canaanites, to Israelites' (specifically the Danites) being forced to live at a distance (v. 34).[108] The final verse in chapter 1 traces the southern boundary of the tribe of Judah, and thus the southern boundary of the allotted territories (see Josh.

15:2–3), but calls it the "border of the Amorites" (v. 36)! Clearly Israel's political fortunes are waning as it progressively loses its grasp on the conquered territories.

The final verses of the first part introduce a religious explanation for Israel's political woes. In 2:1–5, the messenger of Yahweh ascends from Gilgal (where the "disgrace of Egypt" had been "rolled away"—an apparent wordplay on the name "Gilgal") to Bochim, where, after hearing what the messenger has to say, the people lift up their voices and weep aloud (playing on the name "Bochim," which sounds like "weeping"). What does the messenger say to elicit such a response? That Israel has disobeyed Yahweh and so, in accordance with the warning already issued in Joshua 23:12–13, Yahweh will no longer drive out the enemy before them. But how did Israel arrive in this sorry position? The second part of the overture explains.

The second part begins again with the death of Joshua or, more precisely, with a reference to his dismissing the people to take possession of their allotted inheritances (Judg. 2:6) and a reference to their initial successes in *serving* the Lord during the lifetime of Joshua and the elders who survived him (v. 7). But after Joshua's death and burial at age 110 (Judg. 2:8–9 = Josh. 24:29–30) and the passing of the whole generation that had known him, the next generation is quick to forget what God had done and to forsake him to serve "the gods of the peoples who were all around them" (Judg. 2:10–12). The anger of Yahweh is aroused, and he gives the people into the hands of their enemies (vv. 13–15). He does not abandon them entirely, however, but raises up "judges" (deliverers) to rescue them (v. 16). Still, the people's tendency toward apostasy reasserts itself at the earliest opportunity (vv. 17–19). Because the people abandon their covenant with God (v. 20; cf. Joshua's warning in Josh. 24:19), God determines no longer to drive out the enemy before them (Judg. 2:21). Instead, he uses the enemy presence to test his people (vv. 22–23) and to train them (3:1–4).

If the first part of the overture focuses on Israel's declining *political* fortunes (introducing Israel's religious failure only at the end in 2:1–5), the second focuses on the contributory *religious* factors, as we have just seen. The final two verses of the overture, 3:5–6, draw the threads together—Israel *lived among* the Canaanites, and so on, intermarried with them, and *served their gods*. In short, Israel ultimately fails the test, politically and religiously. This we are told in the book's "overture." But the details of these twin failures remain to be worked out in the "variations" that follow in 3:7–16:31.[109] Moreover, even while depicting Israel's faithlessness, the text subtly underscores Yahweh's faithfulness (first, e.g., in 2:16: "Then the LORD raised up judges, who delivered them out of the power of those who plundered them"). Yahweh meets repeated failure with repeated rescue, which we see again and again in the central, "variations" section of the book. But how does the book end?

Perhaps the first thing that strikes the reader of Judges 17–21—which forms the epilogue, or "coda," of the book—is the repeated refrain that "In those days there was no king in Israel; all the people did what was right in their own eyes" (17:6 and with some variation also 18:1; 19:1; 21:25). On the surface this refrain begins to pave the way for the establishment of a human monarch in Israel (1 Samuel). Thus, as Webb notes, the refrain "serves both to sum up one distinct phase of Israel's history and to point forward to the next."[110] But in the light of Gideon's affirmation in 8:23 that neither he nor his son would rule over Israel but, rather, "the LORD will rule over you," it is hard to miss the deeper issue of Israel's failure to *serve* God as king during the dark days of the judges.

A second point apparent to the reader of Judges 17–21 is that the same issues introduced in the overture—that is, political compromise and religious corruption—return in the coda, but in reverse order, and in much stronger form. Judges 17 tells the story of Micah's idol and the wandering Levite who comes to serve it. Chapter 18 recounts how the Levite, upon encountering a better employment opportunity, steals the idol and throws in his lot with northward-migrating Danites. The Danites, unable to occupy their allotted territory in the south, attack the "quiet and unsuspecting" people of Laish in the north (v. 27), conquer the city, burn it, and rename it Dan. These events are rife with irony. Israel was to have eradicated debased religion by dispossessing the Canaanites, whose iniquity was full (cf. Gen. 15:16; Deut. 20:16–18), and to have established true Yahwistic religion. Instead, the Danites attack and dispossess "quiet and unsuspecting" people outside their allotted territory and institute their own form of debased religion, replete with idols. The shock of such a decline is only made worse by the fact that for the first time the "free-lance" Levite is named, and he is none other than Jonathan son (or descendant) of Gershom son of Moses (18:30).[111]

Religion has become debased and chaotic during the period of the judges. Of this the first part of the "coda" (chaps. 17–18) leaves no doubt. The same is no less true of society and politics, as the second part of the coda (chaps. 19–21) makes plain. Judges 19 tells a tale of Israel's own "Sodom" (cf. the events of Gen. 19 with those in the village of Gibeah) and of an age out of control; even hospitality seems out of proportion (vv. 5–10). The reader searches in vain to discover the "good guys" in this wrenching chapter. The Israelite tribes' attempts to prosecute the horrendous crimes of chapter 19 accomplish little more than civil war (chap. 20), the massacre of an Israelite town, and further abuse of women (chap. 21).

How can Israel have sunk so low? The "variations" composing the central section of the book and, indeed, the whole structure of the book provide an answer.

Structure

One of the more insightful attempts to discern and describe the overarching structure and internal logic of the book of Judges comes courtesy of D. W. Gooding in a 1982 essay entitled "The Composition of the Book of Judges."[112] Like virtually all commentators on Judges, Gooding recognizes the tripartite division of the book into introduction, main body, and epilogue. Further, he argues that not only do the introduction and epilogue display parallel sections in reverse order, but the entire book forms a meaningful chiasm. The gist of Gooding's analysis can be presented in the following chart.[113]

Introduction (1:1–3:6)
    A Politics: Israel vs. Canaanites (1:1–2:5)
      B Religion: Israel forsakes Yahweh and serves other gods (2:6–3:6)
The Judge-Deliverers (3:7–16:31)
        C *Othniel*: his Israelite wife promotes his success (3:7–11; see earlier 1:11–15)
          D *Ehud*: takes message to a foreign king—slays Moabites at the fords of the Jordan (3:12–31)
            E *Deborah*, Barak: a woman, Jael, slays the Canaanite Sisera and ends the war (4:1–5:31)
              F *Gideon*:
                a. his stand against idolatry (6:1–32)
                b. his fight against the enemy (6:33–7:25)
                b.' his fight against his own nationals (8:1–21)
                a.' his lapse into idolatry (8:22–32)
            E' *Abimelech*: "A certain woman" slays the Israelite Abimelech and ends the war (8:33–10:5)
          D' *Jephthah*: sends messages to a foreign king—slays Ephraimites at the fords of the Jordan (10:6–12:15)
        C' *Samson*: his foreign women promote his downfall (13:1–16:31)
Epilogue (17:1–21:25)
      B' Religion: Idolatry is rampant; Levites service idolatrous shrines; Dan conquers Laish and establishes idolatry (17:1–18:31)
    A' Politics: Israel vs. Benjamin (19:1–25)

Even this modest representation of Gooding's much more detailed discussion suffices to suggest that an organizing mind lies behind the overall shape of the book of Judges. We find that not simply the well-known pattern of sin-subjection-supplication-salvation (introduced with Othniel in Judg. 3:7–11 and repeated often thereafter) but indeed "a dense network of interlocking motifs . . . unifies the material of 3.7–16.31 at a deeper level than that of the repeating surface patterns."[114] The significance of the ordering of elements extends well beyond a mere aesthetic interest in symmetry. As noted earlier, the themes of political compromise and religious corruption introduced in the book's first section return in the epilogue as virtual political and religious chaos. These twin themes of political and religious decline are reinforced at least implicitly in the structuring of the central section, with Gideon, the middle judge, serving as the pivotal figure. Despite a relatively positive beginning (see elements Fa and Fb in the chart above), the second half of the Gideon story finds him not only turning against his own compatriots (Fb') but even creating an ephod that contributed to their decline into idolatry (Fa'). Thus, as Webb notes in his summary of Gooding's position, with Gideon "*the judges themselves* become involved by their own actions in the more general pattern of decline."[115] The downward spiral only gets worse with Abimelech, Jephthah, and Samson.

In his own study, which expands, refines, and in some ways differs from Good-ing's, Webb highlights the story of Samson as "the climactic realization of major themes,"[116] providing a mirror of Israel's own experience: "Samson's awareness of his separation to God, and yet his disregard for it, his fatal attraction to foreign women, his wilfulness and his presumption all hold the mirror up to the behav-iour of Israel itself. So too does his fate."[117]

The whole central section is "hinged together" in such a way that "the reader is invited to read each episode in the light of what has gone before."[118] The way in which many of the episodes, especially those earlier in the book, are organized around the sin-subjection-supplication-salvation scheme has led some readers to assume that the "judges period" is presented as simply *cyclical*. But Webb, like Gooding and others before him, rightly insists that not recurring cycles but a downward spiral best characterizes the age as depicted in the book of Judges:

> In short the editorial framework of these episodes is not a fixed grid into which the narrative material is forced regardless of its content. The frame-work pattern is varied in such a way as to reflect the changing state of Israel as seen in the succession of episodes. The change is one of progressive dete-rioration in Israel's condition, in relation to Yahweh, in relation to its ene-mies, and in relation to its own internal stability.[119]

The (Hi)storyline

Even our brief examination of the way in which the book of Judges opens, closes, and is structured discovers a high level of literary composition and didactic pur-pose. A common response to these features of the book is to assume that they somehow diminish the historical value of the texts. In their discussion of the book of Judges, Finkelstein and Silberman, for instance, state simply that "theology, not history, is central."[120] Similarly, Miller and Hayes conclude that "the Book of Judges can hardly be accepted at face value for purposes of historical recon-struction." Not only are they bothered by "matters of detail in the individual sto-ries which strain credulity," but they are particularly vexed by the "editorial scheme which is artificial and unconvincing."[121]

Our approach is to acknowledge the schematic, patterned character of the depiction of the judges period, but not to set this in opposition to the potential historical import of the picture painted. That *testimony* about the past can com-fortably combine compositional technique, didactic intent, *and* historical infor-mation should come as no surprise. In order rightly to judge the nature of the historical information, one must, of course, take account of the nature of the pre-sentation. The book of Judges presents a *portrait* of an age. When viewing a por-trait painting, we instinctively take account of selectivity of detail, simplification, coloration, patterned composition, some artificiality in arrangement, and so forth—and we do not assume that these features detract from the historical like-ness. Indeed, in the hands of an accomplished artist, they further the referential intent of the piece. Our approach to the book of Judges is similar.

As we have already seen, a dominating theological pattern exists in the book. Miller and Hayes describe it this way:

> The basic assumption behind this theological pattern is that fidelity to Yahweh was the determinative factor in the vicissitudes of ancient Israelite history. While such a view possesses theological consistency and homiletical appeal, most historians would have to agree that the dynamics of history are far more complex than this pattern allows.[122]

Of course the dynamics of history are more complex than this (or for that matter *any*) piece of historiography can convey, just as the dynamics of a person's visage are more complex than any portrait could possibly capture. Indeed, the book of Judges itself gives evidence of this complexity, as Miller and Hayes recognize. While the activities of the judges are related in a generalizing fashion to the fate of "Israel" as a whole, "closer examination reveals . . . that the events narrated in the individual accounts are very localized—usually involving one or two clans or tribes at the most."[123] To cite the complexity *indicated by the texts* as evidence against the historical plausibility of the larger picture painted by the very same texts seems a curious procedure. Could the writers have wished to give a sense of the broad dynamics of the period—theological, political, and historical—while at the same time retaining hints of its complexity? Good portraits focus on basic contours with just enough suggestive detail to prompt the viewer's mind to fill in the rest.[124]

In the end, Miller and Hayes conclude negatively that the narratives of the book of Judges do not "provide a basis for reconstructing any kind of detailed historical sequence of people and events," though they conclude positively that "the general sociocultural conditions presupposed by these narratives are in keeping with what is known about conditions existing in Palestine at the beginning of the Iron Age" and that "the situation reflected in these narratives provides a believable and understandable background for the rise of the Israelite monarchy as it is depicted in I–II Samuel."[125]

With the positive conclusions we may readily agree, but what of the claim that the book of Judges provides little basis for a "detailed sequence of people and events"? Our answer depends on what kind of stress is laid on the terms "detailed" and "sequence." Obviously the book of Judges cannot be assumed to present a simple, straightforward chronological sequence. Both the double mention of Joshua's death in the prologue and the possibility that the epilogue tells of events to be located earlier, rather than later, in the judges period show that chronological ordering is not always a concern. It may still be the case, as Bright observes, that "the order in which they [the judges] are presented seems to be a roughly chronological one,"[126] but to attempt to establish a precise chronology on the basis of current knowledge seems precarious. The basic time references presented by the book of Judges may be summarized as in Table 7.1.

Taking 1 Kings 6:1 at face value for the moment—which states that 480 years elapsed between the exodus from Egypt and the founding of Solomon's Temple in the fourth year of his reign—we clearly have a problem if the judges period

Table 7.1. References to Time in Judges

Text	Event	Years
3:8	*Oppression by Cushan-Rishathaim of Aram-Naharaim (Mesopotamia)*	8
3:9–11	Peace after **Othniel** (of Judah)	40
3:12–14	*Oppression by Eglon of Moab*	18
3:30	Peace after **Ehud** (of Benjamin)	80
3:31	**Shamgar** saves Israel from Philistines	?
4:1–3	*Oppression by Jabin, king of Canaan, who ruled in Hazor*	20
5:31	Peace after **Deborah** (of Ephraim) and **Barak** (of Naphtali)	40
6:1	*Oppression by Midianites*	7
8:28	Peace after **Gideon** (of Manasseh)	40
9:22	*Abimelech's abortive kingship*	3
10:2	Judgeship of **Tola** (of Issachar)	23
10:3	Judgeship of **Jair** (of Gilead)	22
10:6–9	*Oppression by Ammonites (and Philistines, see below)*	18
12:7	Judgeship of **Jephthah** (of Gilead)	6
12:8–10	Judgeship of **Ibzan** (of Bethlehem in Zebulun? or Judah?)	7
12:11	Judgeship of **Elon** (of Zebulun)	10
12:13–15	Judgeship of **Abdon** (of Ephraim?)	8
13:1	*Oppression by Philistines*	40
15:20	Judgeship of **Samson** (of Dan)	20
	Total years if simply added together =	**410***

*The total of 410 years does not include the length of Shamgar's judgeship, which is unspecified in Judges 3:31.

alone lasted 410 years. This calculation would leave only 70 years for all the events that preceded and followed the judges period. Prior events would include 40 years of wandering in the wilderness (Num. 14:33; Deut. 2:7), perhaps 7 years for the initial conquest,[127] and an unspecified number of years (20? 30? more?) until the demise of the elders who outlived Joshua (Josh. 24:31; Judg. 2:7). Subsequent events might include 40 years of Eli's leadership (1 Sam. 4:18), perhaps 12 years of Samuel's rule prior to Saul's anointing,[128] an approximately 20-year reign of Saul, 40 years for David, and 4 for Solomon. All these figures added together would yield some 573 years (plus the unspecified years of the elders who outlived Joshua), a sum far in excess of 1 Kings 6:1's 480 years. Obviously, simply adding figures together wreaks havoc with a fifteenth-century exodus, to say nothing of a thirteenth-century one.

Are we to conclude that the biblical data are simply confused? A closer look at the texts suggests better alternatives. First, the periods of peace after Othniel, Ehud, Deborah, and Gideon are 40, 80, 40, and 40 years, respectively, while the period of the Philistine oppression is 40 years and of Samson's judgeship is 20. Some or all of these may be rounded numbers, symbolic numbers, or representative numbers.[129] Others of the numbers could plausibly be taken as more literal (e.g., 8, 18, 7, 3, 23, 22, and the like). From our present vantage point, to be dogmatic with respect to just how each number is to be understood seems unwise, but plausibly we have a mix of different kinds of numbers. Simply to add them up, therefore, may be the wrong approach.

Second, some events to which years are ascribed may actually have been chronologically concurrent or overlapping. Not only do the specific acts of deliverance effected by the different judges typically focus on regional threats involving only a few tribes (even while their activities are presented as significant to the whole of Israel),[130] there are also specific hints of chronological overlap in the texts. A prime example is Judges 10:6–8, which reads:

> The Israelites again did what was evil in the sight of the LORD, worshiping the Baals and the Astartes, the gods of Aram, the gods of Sidon, the gods of Moab, the gods of the Ammonites, and the gods of the Philistines. Thus they abandoned the LORD, and did not worship him. So the anger of the LORD was kindled against Israel, and he sold them *into the hand of the Philistines and into the hand of the Ammonites*, and they crushed and oppressed the Israelites that year. For eighteen years they oppressed all the Israelites that were beyond the Jordan in the land of the Amorites, which is in Gilead. (Italics added)

The context indicates that the 18 years of verse 8b refers to the Ammonite oppression (as indicated in our chart above). The mention of the Philistines in verse 7 suggests, however, that the 40-year Philistine oppression, not mentioned again until 13:1, may in fact have begun at about the same time as the Ammonite oppression, which would prompt a realignment of the latter portion of our chart along the lines of Table 7.2.

This one instance of chronological overlap could reduce the period of the judges by some 49 years. If Samson's judgeship ran concurrently with the Philistine oppression, which seems entirely plausible, then the reduction would be by some 60 years. Moreover, other chronological overlaps, both within the book of Judges[131] and beyond it, may have occurred. Quite possibly, for instance, Eli's 40-year judgeship, mentioned in 1 Samuel 4:18, may have overlapped to a greater or lesser extent with the Philistine oppression to which Samson responded, which could reduce the calculation of total number of years by as many as 40 more.

Taking all this into account, we can easily see the difficulty (perhaps impossibility) of establishing a precise chronology of the period of the judges; there are simply too many open variables. This conclusion does not mean that the book of Judges is unreliable, only that it must be taken on its own terms. With the high likelihood of some overlaps and the possibility of others, plenty of room is avail-

Table 7.2. Revised Time References in Judges

Text	Event	Years	Text	Event	Years
10:6–9	Oppression by Ammonites	18	13:1	Oppression by Philistines	40
12:7	Judgeship of **Jephthah** (of Gilead)	6	15:20	Judgeship of **Samson** (of Dan)	20
12:8–10	Judgeship of **Ibzan** (of Bethlehem in Zebulun? or Judah?)	7			
12:11	Judgeship of **Elon** (of Zebulun)	10			
12:13–15	Judgeship of **Abdon** (of Ephraim?)	8			
	Total =	**49**		**Total =**	**60**

able for the period of the judges, especially for those who assume a fifteenth-century date for the exodus. A thirteenth-century exodus requires a much greater degree of overlap, but is still possible.

To illustrate the general point: even if we only take into account the overlap of Ammonite and Philistine oppressions indicated by Judges 10:6–8 and at least some overlap between the judgeships of Samson and Eli, we arrive at a hypothetical overall picture such as that in Table 7.3.

Table 3 is not intended as an actual chronology from the exodus to Solomon's Temple; many figures are quite tentative, and alternative scenarios are possible.

Table 7.3. Tentative Chronology from the Exodus to Solomon's Temple

Event	Years
Exodus and wilderness wandering	40
Conquest (see above calculation)	7
Elders who survived Joshua	+?
Judges period and Eli's judgeship	350
Samuel's judgeship between Eli and Saul	12
Saul's reign	20
David's reign	40
Solomon's reign until foundation of the Temple	4
Total years =	**473+**

The point is that the general chronological picture painted by the book of Judges is plausible, even if our interpretations must remain fairly imprecise.[132]

To sum up: the period of the judges, according to the biblical texts, is characterized by declining success in driving out indigenous populations in Canaan and by the gradual "Canaanization" of Israel itself. While the Israelite tribes experienced some periods of relative peace, there were also periods of intense pressure from enemies within the land (e.g., Jabin of Hazor and his general Sisera) and from enemies round about (the Moabites, Ammonites, Philistines, etc.). These varied, regional pressures brought gifted leaders (judges) to the fore who would rally troops from one or more tribes, deliver Israel from its immediate distress, and often bring in a period of peace.

Having considered the books of Joshua and Judges separately, we are now in a position to consider how they may relate to one another.

Considering Joshua and Judges Together

The above discussions of the books of Joshua and Judges only begin to scratch the surface of what might be learned had we time for full literary readings, but these reviews are perhaps adequate to establish the general thematic trajectories of the two books. The book of Joshua focuses primarily on Yahweh's faithfulness in giving Israel the land of promise, thus making good on the one aspect of the patriarchal promise still outstanding at the end of the Pentateuch. The book of Judges focuses on Israel's flawed response to the charge issued at the end of the book of Joshua to *serve* Yahweh faithfully and exclusively. Yahweh proved utterly faithful in fulfilling his promise to *give* Israel the land of Canaan, but after the death of Joshua and of his generation, Israel progressively failed in its responsibility to *occupy* the territories it had been given. When read in such a way, the books seem quite complementary and, broadly speaking, sequential.

Nevertheless, many scholars have viewed the two books as contradictory. Ramsey, for instance, can speak simply of the "conflicting accounts of the Hebrew conquest of Canaan."[133] Dever characterizes the book of Judges as "*another* version, back-to-back with Joshua" and insists that the two books are not to be harmonized, since, in his view, "the obvious contradictions are too great."[134] Along similar lines, Ben-Tor and Rubiato assert that the book of Joshua presents a "rapid conquest of Canaan," while Judges "presents an entirely different picture, in which the settlement of Canaan is a slow, generally peaceful infiltration, in which numerous scattered tribes gradually emerge in the hill country, where they coexist with the Canaanites (Judges 4:1–2, 23–24)."[135]

Such thinking is not new. Bright also was of the opinion that "the Bible does not present us with one single, coherent account of the conquest." In his view, the "main account" (i.e., Josh. 1–12) presents the conquest as "a concerted effort by all Israel, . . . sudden, bloody, and complete" and is followed in chapters 13–21 with the apportionment among the tribes of the land whose inhabitants had all been "butchered." By contrast, the book of Judges paints a "picture of the occupation of Palestine that makes it clear that it was a long process, accomplished by the efforts of individual clans, and but partially completed."[136] To his credit, Bright resists the urge to choose one picture over the other, contending rather that "both views doubtless contain elements of truth" and that "the actual events that established Israel on the soil of Palestine were assuredly vastly more complex than a simplistic presentation of either view would suggest."[137]

But is this the best that we can do? Must we agree with Spencer that "the biblical text is not uniform in its portrayal," making it "difficult to move from that text to a firm understanding of the nature of the conquest"?[138] Or might avoidance of a simplistic approach, closer attention to the distinction between initial conquest and eventual occupation, and a clearer understanding of the nature of historiography as selective verbal representation lead to a more satisfying understanding of how the two books, taken together, can indeed yield a better understanding of the conquest and occupation?

Although the tendency to view Joshua and Judges as presenting conflicting pictures of Israel's emergence in Canaan is widespread, the approach is not universal. Dissenters from this view have not been lacking in the history of scholarship—notably G. E. Wright in 1946,[139] Y. Kaufmann in 1953,[140] and others. More recent scholarship is also not lacking in defenders of the complementary view of the relationship of Joshua and Judges.[141] The basic point is that misreading Joshua's initial campaigns—central, south, and north—as "permanent conquests" and setting these in opposition to the slower "occupations" described in Judges 1 are fundamental errors.[142] As Kitchen insists, "Thirty-one dead kinglets (Joshua 12) were not a conquest in depth, merely a cropping of the leadership."[143] Moreover, as we have seen, the book of Joshua itself makes a clear distinction between first gaining the upper hand and then capitalizing on the situation by occupying conquered territories. Simply put, an important difference exists between subjugation and occupation, which is nowhere more evident than in the early verses of Joshua 18. The narrator tells us that as the Israelites assembled at Shiloh, "The land lay subdued before them" (v. 1), but this characterization does not prevent Joshua from asking the Israelites how long they will "be slack about going in and taking possession of the land that the LORD, the God of your ancestors, has given you" (v. 3). The land has been given, it lies subdued, but Israel must still take possession of it and occupy it. Thus it is not just the book of Judges that understands that fully possessing and occupying the land will take a long time. Joshua 13:1 notes that in Joshua's old age there were still large tracts of land remaining to be possessed. Even east of the Jordan, Israel had not fully dispossessed its foes (13:13). West of the Jordan, neither Judah (15:63), nor Ephraim (16:10), nor Manasseh (17:12) fully succeeded in driving out the Canaanites—and it seems unlikely that the other tribes faired any better. In his farewell address in chapter 23, Joshua juxtaposes without embarrassment assertions of the success of the conquest—Yahweh has "given rest to Israel from all their enemies all around" (v. 1); "not one thing has failed of all the good things that the LORD your God promised concerning you" (v. 14)—with clear admissions that work remains to be done.

Nations "remain" (vv. 4, 7, 12) and must yet be dispossessed (v. 5). As with the initial conquest, so with the eventual occupation of the conquered territories: Success can come only as Israel is careful to "do all that is written in the book of the law of Moses" (v. 6), holding fast to Yahweh (v. 8), and refusing to serve the gods of the nations that remain (vv. 7, 16). To do otherwise will constitute a violation of the "covenant of the LORD your God" (v. 16) and will incur the covenant sanctions (v. 15; cf. v. 13). This eventuality becomes a sad reality in the book of Judges.

All things considered, the oft-cited contradiction between Joshua and Judges is ill-conceived in a number of ways. Younger aptly summarizes the situation as follows:

> If scholars had realized the hyperbolic nature of the account in Joshua, if they had compared it with other ancient Near Eastern accounts of *complete* conquest, if they had differentiated a little more closely in the past between occupation and subjugation, the image of the conquest as represented in Joshua would have emerged in far clearer focus than it has, and as a result there would have been no need to regard the first narratives in Judges as historical at the expense of their counterparts in Joshua.[144]

In broad strokes, then, and taking Joshua and Judges together, the biblical depiction of Israel's emergence in Canaan is internally coherent: Israel entered and gained an initial ascendancy by means involving (though not limited to) military conquest, but was far less successful in consolidating its victories by fully occupying its territories. In fact, Israel is depicted as increasingly *un*successful in the latter regard. Taking account of the three impulses of biblical narratives (literary, theological, historical), we may summarize as follows.

Literarily, the story is coherent. It makes sense. Largely successful initial campaigns under Joshua are followed by rather less successful attempts to consolidate victory by occupying the conquered territories.

Theologically, the story is also coherent. The book of Joshua begins with an emphasis on the faithfulness of Yahweh in "giving" Israel the land and then shifts, in the second half of the book, to focus on Israel's at times faltering response. The latter focus continues in the book of Judges, where the recurrent faithlessness of the Israelite people and even of their judge-deliverers establishes a pattern of progressive decline, leading ultimately to Israel's "Canaanization."[145]

Historically, the general picture seems plausible enough but at this point remains unproven, since internal coherence, while a necessary condition of historicity, is not a sufficient condition.[146] The texts of Joshua and Judges do appear to make historical truth claims, and so for those who assume the truth value of the Bible's truth claims, this appearance may suffice. For people who do not share this assumption, though, or for those wishing to build a case, consideration of extrabiblical evidence may prove useful in corroborating, correcting, or overturning these findings. We turn therefore to extrabiblical evidence, first considering the textual evidence.

READING THE EXTRABIBLICAL TEXTS

The Merneptah Stela

The first extrabiblical text to be considered is the famous Egyptian Merneptah Stela, often referred to as the "Israel Stela" because it contains the earliest mention of "Israel" outside the Bible. W. M. F. Petrie discovered the stela in 1896 in the valley of the pharaohs in Thebes, and it was published in 1897.[147] While the bulk of the inscription is a glorification of Merneptah's Libyan victories in his Year 5 (possibly around 1209/08 B.C.),[148] the closing stanza, which celebrates Merneptah's further victories, is of special interest for Israel's history. The precise significance of the line "Israel is laid waste, his seed is not" is debated, but the reading "Israel" is seldom questioned. Preceding the reference to Israel, three Canaanite city-states are mentioned: Ashkelon, Gezer, and Yanoam. These three names are marked by the Egyptian "determinative" appropriate for a foreign territory or city-state (a determinative is a sign attached to a proper name to indicate the nature of the entity named).[149] By contrast, the determinative attached to "Israel" indicates not a foreign territory/city-state but a *people* or possibly, as Dever insists, an ethnic group.[150] Thus, it can be argued that "Israel" should not be lumped together with the three preceding city-states. Support for this judgment may come from a structural analysis of the closing stanza as a whole.

Ahlström and Edelman have offered an interesting analysis of the coda of the Merneptah Stela as comprising a "ring structure" in which "Israel" is not to be grouped with the preceding city-states in a kind of south-to-north sequence that would place Israel in the area of Galilee but, rather, should be seen as paralleling "Canaan," which is named just before the three city-states. On the basis of the Canaan/Israel parallel, they suggest two possible interpretations: either Canaan represents the "coastal plain and adjacent lowland area" and Israel the "hill country area," or both Canaan and Israel are "roughly equivalent as synonyms for the whole region."[151]

Other scholars, whether or not they concur with Ahlström's and Edelman's structural analysis, tend to agree that Merneptah's Israel should be placed "in the uplands and valleys of Canaan,"[152] or, simply, in "the central hill country" of Palestine.[153] This raises two further questions, as Isserlin observes: "[H]ow long had the Israelites been in the country before they were mentioned, and how had they got there?"[154] With respect to the second question, some have argued on various grounds (including the evidence of wall reliefs in the Karnak temple depicting Merneptah's battles against Libyans, Sea Peoples, Canaanite city-states [Ashkelon is actually mentioned], and "Israel") that Merneptah's Israel must have derived from "pastoral elements from outside Cisjordan."[155] But this cannot be demonstrated conclusively on the basis of the Egyptian evidence alone. With respect to the first question—how long Israel may have been in the land of Canaan before being mentioned by Merneptah—textual archaeological evidence provides no answer. If Finkelstein is correct, however, that the rapid increase of hill-country villages in the Iron Age does not necessarily indicate a massive influx of new population from elsewhere but only the sedentarization of peoples who have been living as pastoralists (and thus leaving little archaeological mark), and if he is also correct in linking the pastoralist phase with "crisis years" (which may extend to centuries; for instance, Finkelstein views the entire Late Bronze Age as crisis years), then Merneptah's "Israel" *may* have been in Canaan for a very long time as a largely pastoralist people.[156]

The one certainty at this juncture is that, already by the last quarter of the thirteenth century B.C., Israel was an entity of sufficient importance in Palestine to merit mention by Merneptah.[157] Not surprisingly, some scholars seek to underplay the significance of this fact; as Halpern notes, "the Merneptah Stela is not persuasive to people bent on denying the existence of a kin-based Israel in the central hills in the late thirteenth century."[158] But such a stance seems based more on inclination than evidence. Plainly stated, "There are no grounds for denying a link between the Israel mentioned by Merneptah and biblical Israel, except that such a link is inconvenient for the 'minimalist' position."[159]

The Amarna Letters

The discovery in 1888–89 of the now-famous Amarna Letters with their mention of the ʿapiru (also referred to as Ḫabiru or Ḫapiru) sparked a lively debate over possible links with the "Hebrews" of the Canaanite conquest. More than 380 tablets were discovered in the royal archives at el-Amarna, the site of ancient Akhetaten, around three hundred kilometers south of Cairo on the eastern bank of the Nile.[160] Most of the letters are written in Akkadian (an East Semitic language group including Babylonian, which in the fourteenth century B.C. was the language of international trade and diplomacy). The letters cover less than a thirty-year period from late in the reign of Amenhotep III to the third year of Tutankhamun, with the majority falling within the reign of the "monotheist" Amenhotep IV (called Akhenaten, c. 1352–1336 B.C.). In content, apart from some 32 lexical/literary texts and 44 letters exchanged between Egypt and other major powers in the period, "over 300 tablets . . . were exchanged between Egypt and vassal kingdoms in Canaan and northern Syria."[161] Of the letters stemming from rulers in city-states in Canaan, some 16 mention the troublesome ʿapiru and appeal to Egypt for assistance.[162] These ʿapiru "appear as marauding mercenaries who at times pose a threat to all the Canaanite states and at other times are to be found on opposing sides of intercity warfare."[163]

For a number of reasons, it is not surprising that in the wake of the discovery of the Amarna Letters attempts were made to link them to biblical Hebrews invading Canaan. As Nadav Na'aman explains in a thorough 1986 study,[164] "the resemblance between the names Ḫabiru and Hebrew, the proximity of their location, as well as the close chronological relationship between the Amarna Ḫabiru and the Israelites aroused the imagination of scholars, bringing about the immediate equation of the two groups."[165] The excitement was to be short-lived, however, for it soon became apparent that ⟨*apiru* were widely attested in ancient Near Eastern texts besides the Amarna Letters.[166] In fact, the ⟨*apiru*, often designated in Akkadian by the Sumerian logogram SA.GAZ,[167] seem to have been more or less ubiquitous in the Fertile Crescent throughout much of the second millennium.[168] It became equally clear that the term ⟨*apiru* does not represent an ethnic group *per se* but, rather, appears to designate landless and often troublesome peoples who have been "uprooted from their original political and social framework and forced to adapt to a new environment."[169] Na'aman makes an etymological and contextual argument, based on evidence from Mari, that Ḥabiru (⟨*apiru*) peoples should be understood as "migrants": "it appears that it is only the act of migration, and not any specific status resulting from conditions in the new environment, which defines the appellative designation 'Ḥabiru' in Western Asiatic societies of the second millennium."[170]

Having too quickly jumped to an unsustainable equation of ⟨*apiru* and Hebrews, many scholars simply abandoned the notion that there could be *any* relationship between the Hebrews of the Bible and the ⟨*apiru* of the Amarna Letters. Others, however, remained more cautious and open. Na'aman notes that after a century of discussion, "a scholarly consensus has still not been reached."[171] Obviously, a straight equation of the two terms is out of the question. Not all ⟨*apiru* could possibly have been Israelites; the geographical and temporal distribution is simply too great. But could the Israelites as they are described in the books of Joshua, Judges, and even Samuel have been *viewed as* ⟨*apiru* by their Canaanite opponents, whatever may have been their own self-perception? Na'aman contends that "[W]ith their status as uprooted people living on the margins of society, the bands described in the books of Judges and Samuel are identical to the Ḥabiru of the ancient Near Eastern texts."[172] Quite conceivably, therefore, threatened Canaanites might have viewed menacing Israelites as ⟨*apiru*—a perception perhaps reinforced by the coincidental similarity of the term to the gentilic ⟨*ibri*, "Hebrew," which may be derived from Abraham's ancestor Eber mentioned in Genesis 10:21.[173] Daniel Fleming has recently suggested that a better etymology for biblical "Hebrews" is provided by Mari's ⟨*ibrum*, a designation for backcountry herders that was particularly popular among the Binu Yamina tribespeople of southwest Syria.[174] While not as widely attested as the ⟨*apiru*, the designation ⟨*ibrum* was nevertheless "the dominant social category for the mobile pastoralist communities that ranged across southwestern Syria during the Mari period, probably the mid-18th century." Fleming contends that his ⟨*ibrum* hypothesis offers a better etymology for biblical ⟨*ibri* ("the *qitl* noun form offers an exact match") and a better social fit for biblical "Hebrews" than either the Eberite derivation or the ⟨*apiru* linkage. Fleming's theory would support the notion that Israel's background was indeed tribal and pastoralist.[175]

Given these various possibilities, perhaps the term "Hebrew" is used in the pages of the Bible in various senses. The term is most often applied to Israelites by those wishing to cast aspersions on them (e.g., Potiphar's spurned wife in reference to Joseph in Gen. 39:14, 17; Pharaoh's daughter in reference to Moses in

Exod. 2:6; and the Philistines in reference to Israelites in general in 1 Sam. 4:6, 9).[176] Even the biblical narrators themselves seem at times to distinguish between Hebrews and Israelites, as in 1 Samuel 14:21: "the Hebrews who previously had been with the Philistines and had gone up with them into the camp turned and joined the Israelites who were with Saul and Jonathan."

To draw an interim conclusion: it appears that just as the attempted simple equation of Hebrews and ʿapiru was misguided, so too is the denial of any possible relationship between the two. Just what the nature of the relationship might be depends, of course, on whether one assumes a fifteenth- or a thirteenth-century arrival of Israel in Canaan. If one assumes the latter, then the ʿapiru can at best be precursors of Israel.[177] If one assumes the earlier date, however, the ʿapiru/Hebrew relationship may be closer. Simply put, not every ʿapiru could possibly be an Israelite, but some Israelites—troublesome "migrants"—during the settlement period might well have been regarded by their Canaanite neighbors as ʿapiru. In other words, as an "inclusive term of opprobrium for social outcasts," the term "can tolerably refer to the Israelites in the Canaanite context, even if not elsewhere."[178] Fleming's new etymological hypothesis may offer a better explanation of the designation "Hebrew," and one that would fit the biblical picture of early Israel as mainly "backcountry pastoralists."

Geographical considerations may lend further support to this notion. According to Finkelstein, "the only highland political entities mentioned in the Amarna letters of the 14th century BCE (a period of severe decline in the highlands) are Shechem and Jerusalem,"[179] and even the identification of Shechem has been challenged.[180] This accords well with the fact that Egyptian presence in Palestine from the fifteenth to the twelfth centuries seems to have been felt more in the "strategically and economically important lowlands than in the less vital hill country."[181] It also accords well with the biblical picture, which places the bulk of Israel's population during the settlement period in the hill country. In short, according to Chavalas and Adamthwaite,

> the picture of Amarna Canaan that emerges is that of kinglets ruling precisely those cities that the Israelites are recorded as *not* having conquered under Joshua. Meanwhile, the Hapiru, whom the other kinglets regard as a common enemy, can in this context be identified with the Israelites. While certain exceptions remain, such as Lachish (*La-ki-su*), we need to note that with the various oppressions and occupations during the judges period some territory and cities were lost to enemies. First Samuel 7:14 states that the Israelites recovered territory they had lost earlier to the Philistines. What was true in regard to the Philistines was likely true in regard to earlier conquerors.[182]

Cumulatively, the evidence is not of such a nature as to encourage dogmatism, one way or the other, with respect to the ʿapiru question, but one possible scenario would see in both Merneptah's Israel and the ʿapiru of the Amarna Letters hints of an Israelite (pastoralist) presence in Canaan well before the burgeoning of hill-country villages in the Iron I period.[183]

READING THE MATERIAL REMAINS

Our focus so far has been on reading texts—biblical and extrabiblical. We turn now to the nontextual material remains brought to light by archaeology. These material remains also require careful "reading." If the procedure in the preceding sections is roughly equivalent to listening to witnesses in court (though with the distinction that these witnesses cannot be directly interrogated and so must be heard for whatever information their testimony may yield in respect to the questions at hand), the procedure in the following sections is similar to a court's attempt to gauge the significance of material evidence. Seldom could one hope to reconstruct the past from nonverbal material evidence alone, but material evidence may be quite helpful in at least three respects: (1) as a check on whether the verbal testimony is possible; (2) as a check on whether a given theoretical reconstruction is plausible; and (3) as a means of adding "flesh" to the "skeletal structure" of a testimony-based historical storyline.

As we noted in our discussion of the conquest model, a careful reading of the book of Joshua discovers that, contrary to popular (and sometimes scholarly) opinion, actual property damage caused by the conquest may have been quite modest, so that Israel's arrival may have left little or no archaeological mark. That Israel did not engage in wanton destruction of property is indicated by the fact that Joshua 24:13 finds the Israelites living in cities they had not built and enjoying vineyards and olive groves they had not planted, a situation anticipated in Deuteronomy 6:10–12:

> When the LORD your God has brought you into the land that he swore to your ancestors, to Abraham, to Isaac, and to Jacob, to give you—a land with fine, large cities that you did not build, houses filled with all sorts of goods that you did not fill, hewn cisterns that you did not hew, vineyards and olive groves that you did not plant—and when you have eaten your fill, take care that you do not forget the LORD, who brought you out of the land of Egypt, out of the house of slavery.

From the perspective of the biblical testimony, then, we have no reason to expect archaeological evidence of widespread city destructions in the wake of an Israelite conquest. The cities' inhabitants were purportedly destroyed or driven away, but the cities and lands themselves were, for the most part, left intact. By now we are well familiar with the fact that only three sites are explicitly said to have been burned in the course of Joshua's campaigns: Jericho (Josh. 6:24); Ai (8:28); and Hazor (11:13). To these three we may add the city of Laish in the far north, which some time later was conquered and burned by northward migrating Danites, who renamed the city Dan (Judg. 18:27; cf. Josh. 19:47). In the case of these four sites, at least, we may be justified in seeking an archaeological mark, but even here we must bear in mind the haphazard nature of archaeological survival and discovery. We look first at these four sites, then consider several other sites of particular relevance to the Joshua-Judges testimony, and finally turn to the results of surface surveys conducted in the last several decades.

Archaeology of Jericho, Ai, Hazor, and Laish

Jericho

Jericho was the first city conquered after Israel's entry into Canaan, according to biblical accounts, and usually is the first to be mentioned in debates over the "conquest."[184] In fact, Jericho is often cited as a "parade example" of how archaeology has shown the Bible to be historically unreliable. The reason given is that the city of Jericho purportedly was not even occupied during the putative time of Joshua, whether one assumes an early or a late conquest. This is not to say that the archaeology of the city does not correlate in many remarkable ways with the biblical account. There is evidence of collapsed city walls. There is evidence of burning. There is evidence even of the time of year that the burning must have taken place; it must have been in the Spring, just after the harvest, since substantial quantities of grain have been recovered from the burned-out city by excavators. The presence of grain also suggests that the city must have fallen quickly, and not as the result of a lengthy siege, because such supplies would surely have been exhausted had the city been besieged. If we assume that the city's destruction resulted not from natural catastrophe but from conquest, then the fact that the grain was left *in situ* and destroyed, rather than being taken by the conquerors, is also a suggestive detail. On the face of it, these archaeological discoveries appear to correlate well with the biblical description of events and conditions surrounding the capture of Jericho.[185] To all this data may be added an interesting piece of unintentional evidence from the Joshua story prior to the taking of Jericho: the notice in Joshua 3:16 that, in order for the Israelites to cross the Jordan River into Canaan,

> the waters flowing from above stood still, rising up in a single heap far off at Adam, the city that is beside Zarethan, while those flowing toward the sea of the Arabah, the Dead Sea, were wholly cut off. Then the people crossed over opposite Jericho.

Given that stoppages of the Jordan in the vicinity of Adam have been attested several times over the centuries of recorded geological history,[186] this incidental remark in the biblical texts attests an accurate geographical/geological knowledge of the area and provides a plausible explanation of how the reported stoppage in the time of Joshua may have been effected.

Taken together, all these factors would seem to encourage confidence in the compatibility of the archaeological and textual evidence relating to the fall of Jericho. The problem of Jericho has to do not so much with the material findings as with the dates assigned to these findings. The dating of Jericho's remains has, however, shifted several times in the history of the site's excavation. The earliest modern excavation of the site, an Austro-German expedition lead by Ernst Sellin and Carl Watzinger between 1907 and 1911, found evidence of impressive wall structures, which they dated to the Middle Bronze Age (MB, which, according to the standard chronologies, ended c. 1550 B.C.). In the 1930s, British archaeologist

John Garstang renewed excavations at the site and found evidence of fallen mud-brick walls that he dated to c. 1400 B.C. and linked to the conquest under Joshua. Not surprisingly, Garstang's claim raised quite a stir. At Garstang's request, British archaeologist Dame Kathleen Kenyon conducted her own excavations at Jericho from 1952 to 1958. She also found "fallen red bricks" apparently from the complex wall structure, as well as other evidence of burning and the like. She returned, however, to the MB dating of the destroyed city, leaving the Late Bronze Age (LB) period (the time of Joshua) with minimal occupation at best, and certainly no walls. Kenyon reported her results in several popular publications, and there the matter remained and, for many, continues to remain today.[187]

Ask most working archaeologists, as well as biblical historians, whether the archaeology of Jericho inspires confidence in the biblical accounts, and the vast majority will answer with a simple "no." But a simple answer may not be apt in this case. B. Wood effectively reopened the question in 1990. Armed with expertise in the pottery of ancient Palestine[188] and with access to the posthumously published final excavation reports of Kenyon,[189] Wood built an impressive case for rethinking the dating of the Jericho evidence. Central to Wood's argument is his observation that Kenyon's MB dating of the final destruction of Jericho (City IV) seems to rest on the fact that she did not find a pottery type associated with the LB period.[190] Arguments built on what one has *not* found are never particularly compelling, especially when one considers that only a very modest percentage of the total area of most sites is actually excavated, Jericho being no exception. Moreover, to expect that the index pottery-type for which Kenyon was looking (i.e., imported Cypriot bichrome ware) should be found in her areas of excavation, which seem to have been poorer districts of the city, hardly seems reasonable. Even the city itself is described by Kenyon as "something of a backwater, away from the contacts with richer areas provided by the coastal route,"[191] so the absence of a particular kind of imported pottery that serves elsewhere as an LB indicator may in this case be unremarkable. Nonetheless, Wood did in fact discover in Garstang's published excavation results some pottery that at first seemed to be of the type for which Kenyon was looking.[192] Subsequent testing of Garstang's examples of bichrome ware determined them to be of local manufacture,[193] but they may still attest an awareness of the "real thing" of which they are an imitation.

Leaving aside the issue of imported bichrome ware, Wood insists that "the primary method of dating should be a thorough analysis of the *local* pottery," which "has never been done."[194] With his training in Canaanite pottery of the LB Age, Wood attempts such an analysis (though his detailed study has not yet appeared). In a rejoinder to an attempted refutation of his thesis by P. Bienkowski,[195] Wood does offer a succinct appraisal of "a selection of Late Bronze I forms from Kenyon's excavation." He highlights eight different types of pottery that can now—though not in Kenyon's day—be shown to be diagnostic of the LB period.[196]

To his argument based on pottery, Wood adds supportive arguments relating to stratigraphy, scarab evidence, and radiocarbon dating.[197] Taken singly, none of the latter three is "sufficient to compel a revision of Kenyon's date. Taken together, however, they form a strong case for lowering Kenyon's date" to bring the final major destruction of Jericho (City IV) more into line with Garstang's original judgment.[198]

After its initial impact, Wood's challenge has not succeeded in gaining a large scholarly following, though many observers recognize the potency of his challenge.[199] The lack of success may be due in part to the fact that the publication of Wood's more detailed scholarly study has been delayed, but scholars typically greet new theories with hesitancy, particularly when acceptance would require major rethinking and revision of prior theories. Some reticence may also exist on the part of some to relinquish one of the "parade examples" of archaeology apparently clashing with the biblical picture.

Firm conclusions are premature at this stage, so the best approach is to remain open and observant. To assume that Wood's arguments for a substantial correspondence between the archaeology of Jericho and the biblical depiction of the city's capture will survive scrutiny on every point would be unwise, but simply ignoring his case is obscurantist. Further, until such time as Wood's arguments are fully aired and fairly assessed,[200] for scholars to continue to cite Jericho as a parade example is irresponsible. Even prior to Wood's reopening the debate over Jericho, many scholars recognized the ambiguity of the evidence. In a book appearing the same year as Wood's study (and thus not taking it into account), Amihai Mazar summarized the Jericho situation as follows:

> At Jericho, no remains of Late Bronze fortifications were found; this was taken as evidence against the historical value of the narrative in the Book of Joshua. The finds at Jericho, however, show that there was a settlement there during the Late Bronze Age, though most of its remains were eroded or removed by human activity. Perhaps, as at other sites, the massive Middle Bronze fortifications were reutilized in the Late Bronze Age. The Late Bronze settlement at Jericho was followed by an occupation gap in Iron Age I. Thus, in the case of Jericho, the archaeological data cannot serve as decisive evidence to deny a historical nucleus in the book of Joshua concerning the conquest of this city.[201]

Ai

Most recent scholars have followed Albright in identifying ancient Ai with modern Khirbet et-Tell—an identification dependent on Albright's correlative assumption that Beitin is the site of biblical Bethel. Assuming for the moment that both biblical cities have been correctly identified, we encounter an occupation gap in the case of Ai even more problematic than that believed by many to bedevil the Jericho question:

> Ai, located by fairly wide consensus on the mound of et-Tell near Beitin (regarded by many as the successor of biblical Bethel) presented another problem, for the site was unoccupied between c. 2400 BC (when the Early Bronze Age city fell) and the foundation of a short-lived village in the twelfth century BC. Attempts to find an alternative location with a more suitable archaeological record have not so far been successful.[202]

As Isserlin thus notes, et-Tell appears not to have been occupied between c. 2400 and 1200 B.C.[203] This certainly puts a severe strain on the biblical account of the capture and destruction of Ai, unless perhaps more is going on in the biblical story than a first reading suggests. We note, for instance, that at one point in the battle report the men of Bethel are mentioned as joining the men of Ai in fighting Israel (Josh. 8:17). Bethel is otherwise not mentioned in the report, though the king of Bethel is included along with the king of Ai in the list of conquered Canaanite kings in Joshua 12 (vv. 9, 16). Albright hypothesized that the fight may have historically been against Bethel, but that the focus of the narrative account shifted to Ai for etiological reasons—namely, to explain a prominent "ruin" (one of several possible meanings of "Ai" and also of "et-Tell").[204] Whether one agrees with Albright's "contorted"[205] etiological theory or not, the story's passing mention of Bethel does perhaps hint at a more complex situation than simply Israel versus Ai. Still, the apparent absence of occupation at Ai during Joshua's conquest, whatever date one gives it, poses a difficulty. Some scholars seek to resolve the problem by assuming that the sought-after evidence of occupation at the site either has been eroded away during the long period in which it remained a ruin (cf. Josh. 8:28, "to this day") or that it simply remains buried in the many acres of the site never excavated.[206] Other scholars assume that the biblical account simply got it wrong. Indeed, Callaway sees the conflict as serious enough to require that we "redirect our thinking about the Bible."[207]

Before such "redirection" is justified, however, we must explore the question of whether or not Ai and Bethel have been correctly located at et-Tell and Beitin, for less than complete confidence exists in these identifications, as Isserlin's earlier, carefully qualified phrases suggest ("fairly wide consensus"; "regarded by many"). Albright's et-Tell is not the only et-Tell in Syria-Palestine,[208] which greatly weakens Albright's argument for the identification of Ai and et-Tell simply on the ground that both names seem to mean something like "ruin." The fact is that confidence in the site identifications of both Ai and Bethel has never been strong. For various reasons and with various alternative suggestions, the locations of Bethel and Ai have been challenged by, for instance, Grintz, Kitchen, Luria, Livingston, Bimson, and others.[209] None of the alternative suggestions for Ai has yet gained a strong following, but Livingston's contention that Bethel should be identified with modern Bireh, not Beitin, cannot be ignored.[210] If Livingston is correct in locating Bethel at modern Bireh, then the search for biblical Ai is reopened and other sites can be considered. Indeed several excavations of possible sites have been or are being conducted.[211]

In view of the evidence at hand, in principle a number of possibilities arise with respect to Ai: the site may not be correctly identified; if et-Tell is the correct identification, the archaeological finds may not be representative of the unexcavated portions of the site; the biblical accounts may not yet have been correctly read; or the biblical accounts may simply be wrong. This uncertain state of affairs, far from commending sweeping conclusions, invites caution and a withholding of judgment until more evidence comes to light. Reflecting on the diversity of current opinion on Ai, J. M. Miller wisely warns against basing too much on meager archaeological results: "The fact that these widely variant views about Israelite origins all claim archaeological support simply illustrates, in my opinion, that the archaeological evidence is ambiguous, or essentially neutral, on the subject."[212] In a more general vein, Miller also reminds us that while archaeology "is a good source for clarifying the material culture of times past, artifactual evidence is a very poor source of information about specific people and events."[213]

Hazor

While the proper site identification of ancient Ai remains an open question, identification of Hazor with Tell el-Qedah, first suggested by J. R. Porter in 1875, is today considered virtually indisputable.[214] With its total area of some 210 acres, comprising an Upper City of c. 30 acres and a Lower City of c. 180 acres, Hazor may well have been the largest city in Syria-Palestine in its day,[215] which comports nicely with the biblical description of Hazor as "the head of all those kingdoms" (Josh. 11:10), as well as with its frequent mention in extrabiblical texts.[216] Estimates of the site's LB population range upward from twenty thousand. A general compatibility thus exists between the archaeological evidence and the biblical description of Hazor's importance. But what about specifics? Hazor joins Ai and Jericho in the list of cities explicitly said to have been burned by Joshua (Josh. 11:11, 13). As controversial as the other two sites remain, Hazor is somewhat less problematic, for there is no dispute that it was violently destroyed by fire in the Late Bronze Age—several times, in fact, and before that in the Middle Bronze Age as well. The final LB destruction of the city appears to have been particularly dramatic. In the words of current excavation director Amnon Ben-Tor:

> A fierce conflagration marked the end of Canaanite Hazor. Across the site, a thick layer of ashes and charred wood—in places 3 feet deep—attests to the intensity of the blaze in the northern Galilee city.
>
> Within the walls of Hazor's palace, the fire was especially fierce: The unusual amount of timber used in the construction of the building, and the large quantity of oil stored in huge *pithoi* (storage jars) throughout the palace, proved a fatal combination—creating an inferno with temperatures exceeding 2350° Fahrenheit. In this intense heat, the palace's mudbrick walls vitrified, basalt slabs cracked, and clay vessels melted.
>
> Whoever burned the city also deliberately destroyed statuary in the palace. Among the ashes, we discovered the largest Canaanite statue of human form ever found in Israel. Carved from a basalt block that must have weighed more than a ton, the 3-foot-tall statue had been smashed into nearly a hundred pieces, which were scattered in a 6-foot-wide circle. The head and hands of this statue, and of several others, were missing, apparently cut off by the city's conquerors.
>
> Who mutilated the statues of Hazor? Who burned the palace? Who destroyed this rich Canaanite city?[217]

Who indeed? Yigael Yadin, who directed the only other major excavation at the site, from 1955 to 1958 and 1968 to 1972, was convinced that the massive destruction that brought LB Hazor to an end must have been the work of Joshua and the invading Israelites, and he dated the destruction to c. 1230 B.C. in keeping with his belief in a thirteenth-century conquest. Current excavation director Ben-Tor regards Yadin's dating as "overly confident" in the light of present evidence and is willing to affirm only that the destruction must have taken place in the fourteenth or thirteenth century B.C.[218] He does anticipate, however, that further study may confirm the thirteenth-century date.

Ben-Tor also leans towards ascribing the destruction to the Israelites, though he expresses himself more cautiously than Yadin. Particularly noteworthy are the mutilated Canaanite and Egyptian statues discovered in Hazor's final destruction debris. Who might have been responsible for these mutilations and for the final destruction of LB Hazor? Ben-Tor reasons as follows:

> Only four groups active at the time could have destroyed Hazor: (1) one of the Sea Peoples, such as the Philistines, (2) a rival Canaanite city, (3) the Egyptians or (4) the early Israelites. As noted above, the mutilated statues were Egyptian and Canaanite. It is extremely unlikely that Egyptian and Canaanite marauders would have destroyed statuary depicting their own kings and gods. In addition, as to another Canaanite city, the Bible tells us Hazor was "the head of all those kingdoms," and archaeology corroborates that the city was simply too wealthy and powerful to have fallen to a minor Canaanite rival city. So the Egyptians and the Canaanites are eliminated.
>
> As far as the Sea Peoples are concerned, Hazor is located too far inland to be of any interest to those maritime traders. Further, among the hundreds of potsherds recovered at Hazor, not a single one can be attributed to the well-known repertory of the Sea Peoples.
>
> This leaves us with the Israelites.[219]

Ben-Tor stops short of naming Joshua, preferring to cite "the 'Israel' of the Merneptah Stele" as "the most likely candidate for the violent destruction of Canaanite Hazor."[220]

If one assumes a thirteenth-century date for Israel's arrival on the scene, then it might be reasonable to associate this destruction with Joshua. But here we encounter a difficulty, though perhaps not an insuperable one. It would appear from excavation results to date that, after the final LBA destruction (13th century?), the site was not substantially rebuilt until the days of Solomon (tenth century). What then are we to make of the claim of Judges 4:2–3 that Israel suffered for twenty years under the hand of "King Jabin of Canaan, who reigned in Hazor" before being delivered by Deborah and Barak? How is such an oppression possible if Hazor was not substantially rebuilt after its destruction by Joshua until the time of Solomon?

Scholarly response to this tension has been varied. Yadin simply dismisses Judges 4–5 as unreliable. Aharoni reverses the order of events, placing Barak's victory before Joshua's. Block speculates that "elements of the Hazor dynasty" may have escaped from Joshua and returned to the ruined site and reestablished some level of control, though of such a short-lived nature as to leave no archaeological mark.[221] Hess notes that after the major LB destruction (stratum 13), the next occupation level (stratum 12), although "without city walls or substantial public buildings," did apparently cover "the entire tell."[222] Thus, while not significantly rebuilt and refortified, the site was to some extent at least reoccupied. Moreover, the biblical texts do not, in fact, make any reference to Hazor being destroyed or burned by Barak and company. We only read that Israel grew stronger and stronger against Jabin, king of Canaan, until *he* was destroyed (Judg. 4:24). As in the list of defeated city-kings in Joshua 12, this may not imply destruction of the city but just of its figurehead. Thus, the archaeology of Hazor seems reasonably compatible with a thirteenth-century conquest.

Would a late fifteenth-century conquest fare as well archaeologically? Some would say so, or even better. Bimson, for instance, offers a nice summary of the archaeology of Hazor as it existed in 1978 and notes that "from the end of MB II C to the end of LBA, Hazor was destroyed no less than four times."[223] The only question is which, if any, of these destructions can be credited to Joshua and the Israelites. While Yadin chose the last one, Bimson suspects that Yadin's assignment may have been "arrived at subjectively from an assumed late date for the Exodus."[224] In keeping with his larger attempt to lower the date of the end of the Middle Bronze Age in Canaan,[225] Bimson prefers to assign a late-fifteenth-century date to the violent conflagration that destroyed MB II C Hazor and to credit this destruction to Joshua.[226] He points out that Yadin himself in 1957 suggested that the destruction of Middle Bronze Age Hazor might have come at the hands of Thutmose III or Amenhotep II, which would place the destruction in the latter half of the fifteenth century.[227] A year later Yadin actually placed the end of the MB city at c. 1400 B.C.[228] He subsequently changed his mind, however, and raised the date to the sixteenth century, for reasons that Bimson deemed inadequate.[229] Bimson summarizes his own view as follows: "The city attacked and destroyed by Joshua's forces was in fact the final phase of the MBA city. Hazor was subsequently rebuilt (perhaps after a period of abandonment; . . .), and continued to flourish, though with less importance than it possessed in the MBA . . . , until the 13th century, when it finally succumbed to the Israelite pressure which followed the defeat of Sisera's troops."[230] In support of this conclusion, Bimson argues that chronological notices in, for instance, Judges 2:10; 3:8–11, 14, 30 would suggest that perhaps five or six generations, or something less than two centuries, elapsed between Joshua's defeat of Hazor and Deborah and Barak's battle. If Joshua's victory took place in the waning decades of the fifteenth century, Deborah and Barak's would be expected to fall in the second half of the thirteenth century, thus equating neatly with the final destruction of the LB city and making good sense of the notice in Judges 4:24 that in the aftermath of Barak's victory, "the hand of the Israelites bore harder and harder on King Jabin of Canaan, until they destroyed King Jabin of Canaan."[231]

Our discussion of Hazor could be extended, but perhaps we have seen enough to conclude that reasonable cases can be made for several scenarios, though none without loose ends.[232] On the face of it, for instance, would not the presence of numerous Canaanite and Egyptian statues at thirteenth-century Hazor and their mutilation apparently by Israelites prove problematic to the view that Israelites under Joshua had earlier conquered and destroyed the city? The simple answer to such a challenge is that political fortunes and allegiances ebb and flow, especially over longer periods of time. For instance, after a period of declining Egyptian control, Seti I (c. 1294–1279 B.C.) may have been able to reassert sovereignty over Hazor[233] (which would have allowed ample opportunity for resupply of Egyptian statuary?).

The pieces of the puzzle can be put together in various ways, and at present none is the obviously correct way. The best approach at this stage is not to be too specific or dogmatic about any given reconstruction. We may hope that further excavation and interpretation will clarify more fully the potential relationship between text and artifact, but at present all we can say is that the archaeology of Hazor neither obviously confirms nor contradicts the biblical picture.

Laish/Dan

According to Judges 18, the "quiet and unsuspecting" citizens of Laish (v. 7) fell into Israelite hands not in the course of the conquest but some time later when a contingent of Danites ventured north in search of an alternative to their allotted territory, which they were finding difficult to occupy. Sandwiched between Ephraim to the north and Judah to the south, and bounded by Benjamin on the east and the Mediterranean on the west (cf. Josh. 19:40–46), the Danites found themselves no match for the Amorites (and perhaps the Philistines) on the plain (Josh. 19:47). After suffering confinement to the hill country (Judg. 1:34), they eventually sent scouts northward in search of greener pastures (Judg. 18:2). The scouts were followed by six hundred warriors who conquered and killed the people of Laish, burned their city to the ground (18:27), then rebuilt it, renamed it Dan, and inhabited it (18:28–29).

This, in brief, is the biblical picture of Laish (Dan) in the period of the judges. How does this picture square with the results of archaeological excavation? As with so many biblical sites, the first modern identification of the site was made by E. Robinson in 1838, and, unlike some of his identifications, there is no reason to question this one. He located Laish at modern Tell el-Qadi, an identification that has been borne out both by the general archaeological findings[234] and, most strikingly, by the discovery of an inscription in Greek and Aramaic (probably from the second century B.C.) that reads, "To the god who is in Dan."[235] Tell el-Qadi, better known today as Tel Dan, is located in the far north of Israel at the foot of Mount Hermon, "N[orth] of the Huleh basin, on a main branch road which passes from the Mediterranean inland to Damascus and Syria,"[236] and near perennial springs that form one of the main sources of the Jordan River. The first biblical mention of the city is in Genesis 14:14, where it is called by its later name, Dan. Outside the Bible, references to Laish (often in association with Hazor some distance to the south) are found in the eighteenth-century Execration Texts, in one of the Mari texts,[237] and in a dominion roster of Thutmose III.[238]

Excavation of Tel Dan began in 1966 under the direction of A. Biran and has continued for well over thirty years since. Remarkable discoveries have been made at the site, one of which, the Tel Dan Inscription, figures in our next chapter. At present our concern is with the Danite migration and the purported burning of Laish. According to Biran, while material culture remained much the same at Laish/Dan during the transition from LB to Iron Age,

> a relatively large number of pits, some stone-lined, in all the areas excavated indicates evidence of a new life-style. The pits or silos are reminiscent of similar constructions in the hill country of Judah and Benjamin, which are termed "settlement pits" and belong to the Israelite period.[239]

Biran notes also that at the beginning of the Iron Age "collar-rim" jars appear for the first time,[240] which would comport well with an Israelite takeover of the city. But is there evidence of burning? While Manor asserts that "no evidence for a widespread destruction by fire on this transitional horizon has been found at the site,"[241] Biran does mention that "here and there evidence of fire is visible, and in some places the pits were built into a sterile layer of pebbles."[242] Having taken Dan as a "case study for the examination of the synthetic approach to biblical, historical, and archaeological research," Biran concludes that with respect to the Danite migration described in Judges 18 "there is no reason to doubt the historicity of the event or the narrative, although the date of this migration is by no means certain."[243] Biran is not alone in his view that there are convergences between the archaeology of Tel Dan and the biblical account of the Danite destruction of Laish (Judg. 18:27). Stager summarizes his concurring opinion as follows:

> Evidence for this destruction [i.e., Judges 18:27] has recently been discovered by Avraham Biran in his excavations of Tel Dan. Over the ruins of a prosperous Late Bronze Age city, a rather impoverished and rustic settlement was discovered. It had storage pits and a variety of collared-rim storage jars, but little or no Philistine painted pottery. The biblical traditions and the archaeological evidence converge so well that there can be no doubt that the Danites belonged to the Israelite, not the Sea Peoples', confederation.[244]

In the case of Tel Dan and the Danite migration of Judges 18, then, we seem to have one of the more unproblematic "fits" between archaeology and the Bible. Even here though we should be cautious not to assume too much, for as Biran wisely notes, "Such is the nature of archaeological research that new discoveries often require considerable revision of earlier conclusions."[245]

Before leaving Dan, we should mention one other correspondence that Biran proposed. According to the biblical account, the Danite warriors en route to Laish expropriated an idol that had been made for a man named Micah and took it with them on their northward trek, along with its attendant priest (Judg. 18:17–20). We learn further, in 18:30–31, that after capturing and renaming Laish, "the Danites set up the idol for themselves. Jonathan son of Gershom, son of Moses, and his sons were priests to the tribe of the Danites until the time the land went into captivity. So they maintained as their own Micah's idol that he had made, as long as the house of God was at Shiloh." Despite a common misconception, the captivity mentioned in verse 30 has nothing to do with the Assyrian captivity of the late eighth century.[246] On the contrary, verse 31 makes plain that the termination of the priesthood at Dan coincided with the cessation of the house of God at Shiloh. If Shiloh was destroyed by the Philistines around the middle of eleventh century, as both the Bible and the archaeology suggest,[247] perhaps a similar fate befell Dan about the same time. What does the archaeology of Tel Dan suggest? Biran reports: "Sometime in the middle of the eleventh century B.C.E., the city (our Stratum V) was destroyed in a fierce conflagration dated by ceramic evidence. Who caused the destruction we cannot say."[248]

Other Important Sites

Gibeon

While not as central in debates over Israel's emergence in Canaan as, for example, Jericho, Ai, or Hazor, the town of Gibeon is not without significance. It is first mentioned in the Bible in Joshua 9, in the story of the Gibeonite ruse that drew Israel into its first recorded covenant with a Canaanite city.[249] Many scholars regard reference to Gibeon in the time of Joshua as problematic, because "archaeologists have found no occupational remains at Gibeon in the LB Age in which the conquest stories are set."[250] Miller and Hayes list Gibeon, along with "Arad (present-day Tell Arad), Heshbon (Tell Hisban), Jericho (Tell es-Sultan), [and] Ai (et-Tell)," among the "conquest cities" that "have produced little or no archaeological indication of even having been occupied during the Late Bronze Age."[251]

Like the city of Ai, discussed above, uncertainties surround the site identifications of biblical Heshbon[252] and Arad.[253] But this uncertainty cannot be claimed for Gibeon's identification with el-Jib. J. B. Pritchard's four seasons of excavation at el-Jib unearthed more than thirty jar handles inscribed with the name "Gibeon" in paleo-Hebrew script.[254]

If the site identification is not in doubt, then a lack of LB occupation at el-Jib is problematic. Not surprisingly, scholars have cited this evidence (or, more precisely, lack of evidence) as undermining the biblical picture. Before going too far in this direction, however, we should return to Pritchard's own description of what he and his team did and did not find. For instance, he did find evidence of what he describes as a "cosmopolitan" occupation in the LB period, including "a wide variety of imported artifacts from such distant points as Egypt in the south and Cyprus in the west" and LB tombs containing, among other things, a "scarab bearing the name of Amen-hotep II in hieroglyphics" and another containing a "scarab of Thut-mose III."[255] Pritchard notes further that a campaign report of Amenhotep (Amenophis) II mentions taking "36,300 Kharu, or Horites, the very term used in Joshua 9:7, according to the Greek version, for the Gibeonites."[256] To Pritchard's observations we may note also that Thutmose III mentions encounters with Hurrians ("Hurru") in a coalition gathered by

Megiddo.[257] Pritchard assumed that Joshua's encounter with the Gibeonites took place late in the thirteenth century, and thus he logically assumed that "since Gibeon is described as 'a great city' at this time, one would expect to find city walls and houses if the tradition preserved in the Book of Joshua is historically trustworthy." He expressed disappointment that "traces of this city of the latter part of the Late Bronze period have not come to light in the four seasons of excavations."[258] But while many scholars latched on to this absence of evidence as disproving the biblical picture, Pritchard took quite a different tack. Noting first of all that "two richly furnished tombs of the period discovered on the west side of the mound in 1960 would seem to indicate that somewhere on the mound itself there was a permanent settlement," and noting, secondly, that "to date we have dug into but a fraction of the total area," Pritchard speculated that "the remains of the 'great city' of Joshua's day" might well lie "in an area not yet excavated."[259]

Shiloh

The biblical history of Shiloh begins in Joshua 18:1, where the site serves as the venue for the completion of the tribal allotments (19:51). Here the cities of refuge are designated and the Levitical cities specified (Josh. 20–21), and from this site the two and a half tribes depart to return to their inheritances in Transjordan (22:9). Here also the Israelites assemble to make war, when they hear that the departed tribes have built an altar at the Jordan (22:12). Shiloh became the site of an annual festival (Judg. 21:19) and the eventual home of the priesthood under Eli (1 Sam. 1:3 and *passim*) and of the Ark of the Covenant (1 Sam. 4:3; 14:3). According to Psalm 78 and Jeremiah 7, Shiloh served as the first central sanctuary ("the tent where he dwelt among mortals" [Ps. 78:60]; "where I made my name dwell at first" [Jer. 7:12]), but was presumably destroyed or at least abandoned (Jer. 7:14; 26:6, 9) after the battle of Ebenezer (1 Sam. 4). This review, very briefly, presents the biblical picture. What does archaeology have to say?

The identification of Shiloh with Khirbet Seilun, which lies in the heart of Ephraimite territory between Shechem to the north and Jerusalem to the south, seems assured, its location having been remembered, according to Finkelstein, "throughout the ages."[260] The site has undergone several excavations since the first soundings in 1922.[261] The most recent excavations were conducted from 1981 to 1984 under the direction of I. Finkelstein. These excavations determined that following the destruction of the rather massively fortified Middle Bronze Age city, "Late Bronze Age activity at Shiloh . . . was limited to a cult site which was visited by people from the neighboring hill country."[262] Finkelstein sees this result as in keeping with a general demographic crisis that marked the highlands of Canaan in the Late Bronze period; he notes that "only ca. 30 sites were inhabited at the time."[263] Judging by the ceramic evidence, most of the cultic activity at the site seems to have taken place in LB I, with such activity trailing off "long before the end of the LB Age."[264] The site was resettled near the beginning of the Iron Age and was, according to Finkelstein, "the outstanding candidate to become the sacred center of the hill-country population, since it was an ancient cult site that now stood deserted in an area with only a sparse Canaanite population and a high concentration of 'Israelite' sites."[265]

In fact, the concentration of Iron I sites surrounding the approximately three-acre site of Shiloh was two to three times denser than in other parts of Ephraim, which attests to the importance of the site; Finkelstein moots the possibility that Shiloh may have been "primarily a sacred *temenos* [sacred enclosure] rather than an ordinary village."[266] Lamentably, the summit of the tell, which would have been the likely site of a shrine, has been "badly eroded and destroyed by later occupation."[267] The Iron Age city was eventually destroyed by a "fierce conflagation," which Finkelstein suggests "was probably the work of the Philistines in the aftermath of the battle of Ebenezer in the mid-11th century B.C.E."[268] With this general conclusion, based both on archaeological and biblical evidence, Stager concurs:

> Recent excavations at Shiloh by Israel Finkelstein have confirmed the results of the earlier Danish expedition, as interpreted by W. F. Albright. Shiloh (Stratum V) flourished as a major Ephraimite center in the first half of the eleventh century BCE. Its temple served as a major annual pilgrimage site for the Israelite tribes in the autumn, during the wine (and New Year's?) festival. The destruction of this sanctuary by the Philistines around 1050 BCE reverberated in the memory of the Israelites for centuries (Ps. 78.60–64; Jer. 7.12).[269]

The biblical testimony and the current archaeological results converge to support Stager's historical judgment that "sanctuaries sprang up during the period of the judges at central locations in the highlands, such as Shechem and Shiloh."[270]

Having in this section considered Shiloh, we turn in the next to an interesting find in the vicinity of Shechem. Excavations at Shechem itself have discovered "a sanctuary, with altar and standing stone (cf. Josh. 24:26–27), preserved through the Late Bronze Age and into the period of the Judges." This site may, as Hess observes, provide "evidence of the sanctuary El-Berith ('El/god of the covenant') mentioned in Judg 9:46."[271] By far the most interesting (and controversial) find, however, is on Mount Ebal, which rises beside Shechem and where, according to biblical tradition, Joshua built "an altar to the LORD, the God of Israel" (Josh. 8:30).

Mount Ebal

While the assumed cult site of Shiloh has apparently not survived the ravages of time, the cult site on Mount Ebal may have fared better, at least according to the site's excavator A. Zertal. In a fascinating story of archaeological exploration and interpretation,[272] Zertal describes how, in the course of a regional surface survey, he and his team happened upon a structure on Mt. Ebal, the identity of which was unclear. Not until the third season of excavation did an answer begin to emerge. Early theories regarding the nature of the main structure, an approximately twenty-three-foot-by-thirty-foot rectangle of uncut stones that reached a height of some ten feet, included the notion that it was a farmhouse or perhaps a watchtower, but these interpretations repeatedly ran into problems. Particularly curious was the fact that the five-foot-thick walls of the structure had no opening or entrance; the installation was simply a rectangle filled with earth, ashes, broken pottery of the Iron I period, and animal bones. Later analysis of the bones would find them to be "from young male bulls, sheep, goats and fallow deer," most of them having been "burnt in open-flame fires of low temperatures (200–600 degrees C.)."[273] Not until a visiting archaeologist suggested that Zertal should consider the "fill" to be the key to interpretation did the idea suddenly emerge that the structure could be an altar. Zertal and his team began checking descriptions of altars in the Bible (e.g., Exod. 27:8) and the Mishnah and were astonished at how well these descriptions matched not only the basic features of the structure but also many of its particular features. These features included what appeared to be a ramp leading up to the main structure and a curious ledge that surrounded three sides of the "altar." Zertal became (and remains) convinced "beyond question, [that] our site is a cultic center."[274]

As one might predict, not everyone shares Zertal's certainty. A. Kempinski, for instance, argues that the structure is not an altar at all but, as had earlier been considered, an Iron Age watchtower.[275] Zertal, however, is quick to counter Kempinski's arguments,[276] and, when the full body of evidence is considered, the conclusion that the site seems more like a cult installation than like anything described by the competing theories is hard to deny. To be sure, as A. Mazar notes, "The case of Mount Ebal illustrates the difficulties in interpreting an archaeological discovery, particularly in relation to biblical sources."[277] But, on balance, Zertal's cultic theory may well prevail. Mazar writes, "Zertal may be wrong in the details of his interpretation, but it is tempting to accept his view concerning the basic cultic nature of the site and its possible relationship to the biblical tradition."[278] Zertal readily admits that "certainty as yet eludes us" and that "as scientists, we must say that the case has not yet been proven," but he certainly believes that a strong case can be made that the site is cultic and, indeed, can possibly be linked to "the Biblical traditions concerning Joshua's building of an altar on Mt. Ebal."[279] (The Ebal altar is prescribed by Moses in Deut. 27:1–8, and its eventual construction is described in Josh. 8:30–31.) Zertal bases his linkage on three correlations: the location, the nature of the site, and the period.

At this juncture, however, an interesting question arises. According to Zertal, the site displays at least two distinct levels, the one we have been describing and an earlier one. The earlier level consists of "a circle made of medium-sized field stones laid on bedrock and located at the exact geometric center of the [later] structure."[280] Thus, the larger, more elaborate installation—which receives the most attention in Zertal's article—sits squarely atop the earlier structure, which seems to suggest that the builders of the later structure must have regarded the earlier as significant. Zertal describes the earlier, circular structure as approximately six and a half feet in diameter and "filled with a thin, yellowish material that we have not yet identified. On top of this yellowish layer was a thin layer of ash and animal bones."[281] Zertal places both levels in the Iron I period. Specifically, he dates the earlier level to the "second half of the 13th century B.C., and the later from the first half of the 12th century B.C."[282] While the dating of the later, larger structure seems reasonably well founded on the basis of distinctive pottery forms and a datable Egyptian-style scarab,[283] the dating of the earlier structure seems less assured. Hess exercises due caution when he writes, "the earlier level extends to *c.* 1200 BC and the later level terminates *c.* 1150 BC."[284] How long the earlier level had been in existence prior to its being overbuilt should perhaps remain an open question.

Hill-Country Sites in Iron I

Individual sites such as we have been discussing have always figured prominently in debates regarding Israel's emergence in Canaan, but only in the last several decades has much attention been given to regional surface surveys. This "great leap forward,"[285] which seeks to establish general demographic trends across a larger area, was discussed above in our description of Finkelstein's theory that "early Israel" arose from indigenous Canaanite populations. The most striking discovery of the surveys conducted by Finkelstein is the rapid proliferation of small hill-country villages beginning in the Iron I period. The key question is, Who is responsible for this proliferation? Who were these Iron I settlers? Finkelstein and others have not hesitated to identify them with early (or proto-) Israelites, although, as Hoffmeier cautions, "the archaeological evidence alone at this point in time cannot demonstrate that the sites in question are Israelite without drawing inferences from the biblical text."[286] There is, of course, the matter of an apparent taboo on pig consumption, noted earlier, and it is worth hearing Finkelstein's analysis of the significance of this finding more fully:

> In the Iron I pig remains appear in great numbers in the Shephelah and the southern coastal plain—Tel Miqne, Tel Batash and Ashkelon—and are quite common at other lowlands sites, but they disappear from the faunal assemblage of the central hill country. The most interesting fact is that contemporaneously pig bones continue to be present in significant numbers at Hesban in Transjordan. The faunal assemblages of the Iron II reflect the same traits. Regardless of the complex factors which may influence pig distribution (Hesse and Wapnish 1997), this seems to mean that the taboo on pigs was already practiced in the hill country in the Iron I: pigs were not present in proto-Israelite Iron I sites in the highlands, while they were quite popular in a proto-Amonite [*sic*] site and numerous in Philistine sites. As predicted by Stager several years ago (1991:9, 19), food taboos, more precisely, pig taboos, are emerging as the sole possible avenue that can shed light on ethnic boundaries in the Iron I. This may be the most valuable tool for the study of ethnicity of a given, single Iron I site.[287]

On "foodways" as indicative of "ethnic consciousness" in Canaan, B. Halpern offers the following succinct summary:

> Prior to and during the Sea-Peoples settlement, Canaanite sites reveal low
> levels—but real levels—of pig consumption. The early Philistine layers con-
> versely indicate a very high level of pig consumption. But the Israelite sites
> of the highlands disclose an almost complete absence of pig, showing in
> addition a general preference for sheep over goat.[288]

In view of the above considerations, as well as the fact that no reason exists to
doubt that later Israel descended from these hill country dwellers, calling our Iron
I settlers early Israelites seems fair enough. But where did they come from? We
have already described Dever's "collapse" model, according to which the early
Israelites derived from fringe-element Canaanites in the lowlands who were displaced by the collapse of Canaanite culture and found "greener pastures" in the
hills. We noted also Finkelstein's rebuttal of Dever's collapse model—lowland
populations never reached "carrying capacity"—and his preference for the
"cyclic" model, whereby the early Israelites were not former lowlanders but were
in fact hill-country dwellers who, during the "crisis years" precipitated by the
widespread destructions that brought the Middle Bronze Age to a close, left their
plows behind and took up the pastoralist life. On one thing, at least, Dever and
Finkelstein agree: early Israel arose from native Canaanite populations and not
from an influx of outsiders. This point of agreement, however, is far from proven.
It leaves unanswered, for instance, the question of why pig consumption ceased.

Isserlin endorses Finkelstein's view that the more than three hundred new Iron
I villages in the central hill country are to be associated with early Israelites, and
he agrees that monarchical Israel later developed from this population, but he
queries Finkelstein's theory of their *origin*. He writes:

> [Finkelstein] argues that these early upland dwellers came there neither as
> conquering invaders, nor as mainly pastoralist immigrants from the east, nor
> as similarly displaced peasants from the west. Instead, they were mostly
> descendants from the local population of the Middle Bronze Age period,
> who, after the destruction of their towns *c.* 1550 BC turned to pastoralism,
> but reverted some three centuries later to a settled mode of life. This part of
> his interpretation remains undemonstrated, and among his Israeli colleagues
> A. Zertal, for instance, would opt for immigration from the Jordan Valley.
> Until such supposed pastoral nomad elements are traced archaeologically
> the question must remain undecided.[289]

Thus, on the basis of the archaeological evidence alone, we know that (1) at
the beginning of the Iron Age hundreds of new villages sprang up in the central
hill country; (2) those who settled these villages apparently eschewed pig consumption, in contradistinction to their Canaanite neighbors on all sides; and (3)
the new settlers may have been new arrivals from elsewhere, or (if we follow
Finkelstein's studies that find evidence of large numbers of pastoralists in the area
throughout the crisis years of the Late Bronze Age) they may have already been
in the area *for several hundred years*. As Hoffmeier succinctly remarks, "the villages do not tell us how long the settlers had been pastoralists in the area before

settling, or whether they had moved about inside or outside of Canaan, or both, before becoming sedentary."[290]

INTEGRATING THE TEXTUAL
AND MATERIAL EVIDENCE

Now that we have taken a look both at pertinent texts, biblical and extrabiblical, and at a representative sampling of archaeological findings, we can address the question of "fit." Are the various bodies of evidence compatible? Are there "convergences," or are there serious conflicts?

The place to begin is with a brief reminder of the basic contours of Israel's emergence in Canaan as depicted in the books of Joshua and Judges. As argued earlier, we do not regard these books as presenting competing versions of Israel's emergence but as focusing on its different stages: (1) the entry and "taking" of the land by means including military conquest (depicted in typical ancient Near Eastern style in the first half of the book of Joshua and in occasional "flashbacks" in the early chapters of Judges); (2) the allocation to the various tribal groups of the land that "lay subdued before them" (described in the second half of the book of Joshua, which includes also proleptic references to the varied successes of the tribes in actually occupying their allotments); and (3) the occupation phase and the gradual "Canaanization" of Israel in the period following Joshua's generation (anticipated in various verses in the second half of the book of Joshua and characterized more fully in the book of Judges). In sum, the biblical picture is of a reasonably successful initial conquest of the land—the invading Israelites gaining the upper hand—followed by increasingly unsuccessful attempts to control and occupy the "conquered" territories. In terms of theological slant, the emphasis in the *conquest* phase is on Yahweh's faithfulness in *giving* Israel the land. The emphasis in the *occupation* phase is on Israel's faithlessness and progressive failure to *serve* Yahweh faithfully, as they had been charged to do at the end of the book of Joshua. Leaving aside the theological perspective and focusing only on the basic historical scenario, we may now test its plausibility against the archaeological evidence that we have surveyed.

The Merneptah Stela indicates that already by the final quarter of the thirteenth century B.C. "Israel" was a force to be reckoned with in Canaan. How long Israel had been in the land is an open question. If Finkelstein's theory of extended periods of pastoralism during crisis years has merit, then Israel could possibly have been leading a pastoralist existence in Canaan for a very long time (even centuries) prior to being mentioned by Merneptah.[291] Should that be the case, then two observations follow: (1) the burgeoning of hill-country villages in the Iron Age would mark Israel's *sedentarization*, not its initial arrival or emergence in the land; (2) the Amarna period would become the backdrop for the biblical depiction of the time following the initial subjugation of the land. We have already noted that the bulk of the Amarna correspondences from Canaan come from precisely those sites that Israel did *not* take. We noted also that while the Israelites ("Hebrews") are not to be equated with the *ʿapiru*, they may well have been confused with them by their Canaanite foes. In broad terms, this scenario represents a plausible synthesis of biblical testimony and archaeological evidences, especially in relation to the *occupation* phase of Israel's emergence in Canaan. But what of the *subjugation* phase, the conquest, of which the Bible has so much to say? On this point, specific site excavations come into play.

We noted that Joshua and Judges explicitly mention four sites as having been burned: Jericho, Ai, Hazor, and Laish. (Other burnings may also have occurred, but if so, we have no way of knowing when and where these may have taken place.) Archaeological excavation at Jericho has discovered evidence of burning, fallen walls, and numerous other features that correspond well with the biblical account. The fly in the ointment, however, is the matter of when these material remains are to be dated; here the jury is still out. The city of Ai, if et-Tell, has yielded little that would converge with the biblical story of its defeat and burning, but this is a fairly large "if." Perhaps Ai's partner city Bethel should be located not at modern Beitin, as is generally held, but at Bireh, which would mean that Ai, too, would have to be relocated (and efforts to that end are currently under way). Hazor yields evidence of several burnings from the end of the Middle Bronze Age to the Late Bronze Age. The final burning of the LB city was particularly fierce, and Canaanite and Egyptian statuary were mutilated, prompting excavation director Ben-Tor to speculate that the likeliest incendiaries were Israelites (the Israelites of the Merneptah Stela, he believes). At Laish (Tel Dan), evidence of burning is spotty, but clear evidence exists that the city was destroyed during the LB/Iron I transition and reoccupied by a people whose material culture was typically "Israelite." Excavation director Biran as well as other prominent archaeologists such as Stager are comfortable in asserting a neat correspondence with the biblical account of the Danite migration in Judges 18.

Other sites considered were Gibeon, Shiloh, and Mount Ebal. While some regard Gibeon as a problem because of a lack of LB remains, Pritchard, the site's excavator, believed that evidence of a cosmopolitan LB city was present, and he was confident that its remains might lie in the great unexcavated bulk of the site. Shiloh yields evidence of having served as a cult center in the hill country of Ephraim during the LB period and of having been destroyed about the middle of the eleventh century B.C., which converges nicely with the general biblical picture. The singular structure that Zertal discovered on Mt. Ebal will doubtless continue to elicit debate for some time to come, but it certainly seems possible that it was an altar, perhaps built in commemoration of an earlier altar constructed on the site by Joshua.

So where are we? Our survey of archaeological evidence has of necessity been selective, and our discussions of site and survey results have not been exhaustive. We have chosen to spend our time with some of the more important sites according to the biblical story, rather than to attempt a superficial survey of all the sites that could be mentioned. What we discover in respect to these sites is likely, however, to be representative of what we would discover were we to attempt a more exhaustive exploration; we have in fact discovered nothing in them that would falsify the biblical portrait of Israel's early history in Canaan. How one weighs the evidence will, of course, vary from person to person. In our opinion, the scales tip in the direction of greater rather than lesser confidence in the biblical testimony as a result of our enquiries.[292]

CONCLUSION

The subject considered in this chapter is of far-reaching importance, for as Finkelstein has recently observed, "Apart from the specific issue of the rise of Early Israel, it has become a debate over the historicity of the biblical text and the value of archaeology in historical research."[293] Our own exploration began with a survey of the standard scholarly models of Israel's emergence in Canaan: conquest, infiltration, revolt, and endogenous origins. We moved then to a reading of the pertinent texts, biblical and extrabiblical. We discovered that none of the standard models does full justice to the biblical picture. Even Albright's conquest model is guilty of quite seriously misreading the biblical testimony, and therefore the widespread recognition that Albright's model has failed to find archaeological validation says nothing about the historical veracity of the biblical texts.

But while none of the standard models does justice to the full range of testimony, each may capture some aspect of what actually happened.[294] Conquests and city destructions certainly occurred in LB Age Canaan, and discerning Israelite involvement in a few of them (Hazor, perhaps Jericho) may be possible, but much uncertainty remains, not least in the matter of assigning dates and parties responsible (e.g., when was the final LB Hazor destroyed and by whom? If by Israelites, was it Joshua, Deborah and Barak, or . . . ?). Quite possibly early Israelites encountered little resistance in some areas (e.g., Shechem, Gibeon) and thus were able to "infiltrate" them without coming to blows. Disfranchised or disaffected Canaanites could have revolted against, or at least betrayed, their neighbors (e.g., the Gibeonite ruse) and joined Israel's "mixed multitude." Those who populated the hundreds of hill-country villages that sprang up in Iron I may not have been newcomers from outside Canaan but may have been pastoralists living in Canaan for some time already. Perhaps they once did live outside the land (absence of pig consumption?), and their arrival may have played some part in precipitating the "crisis" years of the LB Age.

The tentativeness with which these concluding observations are made is reflective of the fact that historical reconstruction is in a very real sense "underdetermined" by the evidence. Proving a particular reconstruction is simply not possible—at least not to everyone's satisfaction—any more than in a legal trial one can put a particular reconstruction of events beyond a *shadow* of a doubt. All that one should aspire to is presenting a reasonable reconstruction that does fullest justice to the greatest body of available evidence. As important as material evidence is—in history as in court—without *testimony* the past remains largely mysterious, except perhaps in respect to generalities about "life-ways" and such. Unless someone tells a story, we are left to our own imaginative devices, which may as easily conjure up fantasies as facts.

In the case of early Israel in Canaan, the books of Joshua and Judges tell the story first and, accepting their perspective, best. Their accounts are the most detailed and, in many respects, the most interesting. Our aim has not been to reduce their story to a rationalistic paraphrase, though we are not against paraphrase per se; we simply believe that watching a play is more interesting than reading a playbill. Our aim, rather, has been to explore the question whether historians, and not just theologians or literary critics, should be interested in these works. We have asked whether the biblical testimony is internally coherent and consistent with external evidence. We recognize, of course, that archaeological evidence is by its very nature partial and constantly changing. We recognize that its significance is not always obvious, and that interpretation is as necessary in "reading" material remains as in reading texts. We recognize that some knotty problems remain: Has Ai been correctly located? Has Jericho's destruction been correctly dated? What's that on Mt. Ebal? Finally, we recognize that how we read the evidence is in some measure related to larger issues of how we see the world. All in all, we believe that such archaeological evidence as is known to us in no way invalidates the biblical testimony (provided that both text and artifact are properly read) and that at least some promising "convergences" exist.

In sum, then, we see little reason that an attempt to write a history of Israel's emergence in Canaan should take a path radically different from the one that the biblical texts already suggest. One may, of course, attend to many factors not addressed by the selective and theologically oriented biblical texts—it is certainly legitimate, for instance, to bring in first- and second-tier factors (insofar as these can be determined) in painting a more multifaceted portrait of the period—but we have found nothing in the evidence considered that would invalidate the basic biblical contours.

Chapter 8

The Early Monarchy

The books of 1 and 2 Samuel are perhaps best known for their intriguing stories—of the young Samuel running to Eli only to discover that the Lord is calling him, of Saul going in search of lost livestock and finding a kingdom, of a young David felling the giant Goliath without spear or sword but in the name of the Lord of Hosts, of Absalom's revolt hitting a hairy snag, and on and on. But for the historian, these books have much more to offer than riveting stories. As R. P. Gordon has noted, "1 and 2 Samuel chronicle a structural change within Israelite society which had the profoundest political and religious consequences."[1] As the book of Samuel[2] opens, the period of the judges is drawing to a close, and Israelite society is moving towards becoming a monarchy. The book of Judges ended with repeated reminders that in those days Israel had no king and everyone was doing as he saw fit. The situation has changed little as 1 Samuel begins—even the priests, Eli's sons, seem to be doing whatever they please (2:12–17)—but kingship is in the air. Hannah's Song, recorded in 1 Samuel 2:1–10, makes explicit reference to a coming king, noting that the Lord "will give strength to his king, and exalt the power of his anointed" (v. 10). Before we can meet Israel's first king, however, we must meet the kingmaker. The early chapters of 1 Samuel focus on the birth of Samuel and on his growth to become "a trustworthy prophet of the LORD" (3:20). Samuel's career soon becomes entwined with that of Saul, Israel's first king, and then both become involved with David, founder of Israel's first and most enduring dynasty (lived out, after the division of the kingdom, in Judah).

Because the book of Samuel organizes its account around the intersecting careers of Samuel, Saul, and David, we shall do the same. As works of literature, the stories of these important individuals have received high praise. "It would be hard to find anywhere a greater narrative," writes H. G. Richardson. The narratives in Samuel are written in "a prose which, for combined simplicity and distinction, has remained unmatched in the literature of the world," adds W. R. Arnold.[3] But what of their historical value? Are the Samuel narratives more than merely stories well told? Are they also histories well told? Can they rightly be regarded as historiography? Do they have value for the historian and not just the literary critic or the theologian?

Not so long ago, certain biblical scholars were proclaiming that David and Solomon probably never lived. They were insisting that these kings (and even the whole notion of an Israelite United Monarchy) should be lumped together with biblical figures like the patriarchs, whose historicity had long been considered a "dead issue" by critical scholarship.[4] But just at the time that the "death notices" of David and Solomon were being published, excavators at the biblical site of Dan made a startling find. The discovery in 1993 of the first and largest fragment of the now famous Tel Dan inscription, with its mention of the "king of the house of David," sent shock waves through the scholarly community. For the first time, apparently, we had an extrabiblical reference to Israel's most famous king. An initial cacophony of voices sought to interpret the inscription in some sense other than the apparent one, but after an initial flurry of publications, most dissenting voices fell silent. Not long after the discovery of this so-called "house of David" inscription, several scholars proffered other possible extrabiblical references to David—in the Mesha Inscription (Moabite Stone) from about the same time as the Tel Dan inscription (mid-ninth century B.C.) and in the topographical list of the Egyptian Shoshenq I (late tenth century B.C.). We shall have more to say on all this below.

As interesting as these discussions are, the biblical texts are not dependent on external verification to establish their historical worth—as we argued in part 1. In any case, what the above references may be taken as establishing falls far short of the full picture of David presented in the biblical texts. Thus, while such discoveries—archaeological and epigraphic—may offer encouragement to those inclined to take the biblical texts seriously as historical sources and offer pause to those inclined to discount them, hope of learning much about Israel's transition to monarchy, its first kings, and their descendants must continue to rest largely on the biblical testimony. Archaeological findings also come into play in debates about the plausibility of a Davidic capital at Jerusalem and, indeed, of a Davidic-Solomonic "empire" in tenth-century Syria-Palestine. We shall take all of these matters up in due course.

Before delving into our history proper, though we must fill out the picture of the sources at our disposal and then say a few words about the chronology of the period.

SOURCES FOR THE EARLY ISRAELITE MONARCHY

First and Second Samuel are not the only biblical texts that portray the period of Israel's United Monarchy. In addition, we have the two books of Chronicles, with 1 Chronicles more or less paralleling the material found in Samuel (i.e., Saul and David) and 2 Chronicles paralleling the material found in Kings (i.e., Solomon to the Babylonian exile) and adding the hopeful note of Cyrus's decree, which anticipates the return from exile. While some people have charged the Chronicler as a plagiarist and suppressor of the Samuel–Kings texts, it is more appropriate to view Samuel–Kings and Chronicles as *synoptic histories*, as they have been called. That is to say, they are two different depictions, "paintings" if you will, of (roughly) the same subject matter, and we are the better off for having two paintings, rather than just one. Each has its own interests, its own slant, its own perspective, and so forth, but the latter (1 and 2 Chronicles) should not be viewed as an intentional overpainting of the former (Samuel–Kings). In fact, as has often been observed, Chronicles seems to assume that its readers are already familiar with Samuel–Kings. R. Dillard puts the matter plainly: "[T]he numerous points at which he [the Chronicler] assumes the reader's familiarity with the account in Samuel/Kings shows [*sic*] that he is using the Deuteronomic history as a 'control' to an audience well familiar with that account."[5] Thus, according to B. Childs,

> it is a basic error of interpretation to infer from this [i.e. the Chronicler's] method of selection that the Chronicler's purpose lies in suppressing or replacing the earlier tradition with his own account. Two reasons speak directly against this assumption. First, the Chronicler often assumes a knowledge of the whole tradition on the part of his readers to such an extent that his account is virtually incomprehensible without the implied relationship with the other accounts (cf. I Chron. 12.19ff.; II Chron. 32.24–33). Secondly, even when he omits a story in his selection he often makes explicit reference to it by his use of sources. For example, the Chronicler omits reference to Jeroboam's divine election (I Kings 11), but his explicit reference to the prophecy of Ahijah (II Chron. 9.29) rules out a theory of conscious suppression.[6]

So we have two different "paintings" of the monarchical period, serving two different purposes. The so-called Deuteronomistic History, of which Samuel–Kings would be a part, must have been completed in the Babylonian exile—whatever may have been the composition-history of its different parts.[7] In its final form, it answers the kinds of questions that those in the Babylonian exile must have been asking: "Why are we here? Have God's promises to our fathers and to David failed?" To the latter question, the Deuteronomistic History (DH) responds with a resounding "no." God's promises have not failed, for his promise of blessing for covenant keeping was, after all, always conjoined to a threat of punishment for covenant breaking. The litany of sin and failure recounted in Samuel–Kings more than adequately explains the fall of the Israelite kingdoms, first of the North (2 Kgs. 17) and then of the South (2 Kgs. 25). Thus, the answer to the first question—"Why are we here?"—is that God is as good as his word, whether it has to do with blessing or curse.

The book of Chronicles focuses on a different set of questions. Its addressees were not exiles still in captivity but exiles who had returned or were returning to the promised land from which they had been taken. The questions animating the Chronicler's addressees must have been of the following sort: "Is God still interested in us? Are the covenants still in force?"[8] To such questions, the Chronicler answers with a resounding "yes." The Chronicler's chief purpose in writing his history appears to be to exhort and encourage the returnees. In view of this purpose, it is not difficult to understand why he should reduce his coverage of King Saul to a single chapter (1 Chr. 10) plus some genealogical material, should say nothing of Saul's opposition to David's rise (an important topic in the latter half of 1 Sam. and the early chapters of 2 Sam.), should make no mention of David's adultery and murder in the Bathsheba affair (2 Sam. 11–12), should feel no need to detail the calamitous domestic and political fallout from these actions (2 Sam. 13–20), and should see no reason to remind his readers of Solomon's apostasy (1 Kgs. 11). All these events must have been amply known to the Chronicler's audience and thus could be safely left aside as not pertinent to his intention to hearten his hearers.

Not only did the Chronicler leave out certain material; he also included much material not found in Samuel–Kings, material that underscored the more universal significance of Israel's experiences (e.g., the extensive genealogies stretching back to Adam, with which the book begins), material that emphasized the Lord's *personal* covenant with David (which would have brought comfort in a time when the throne was no more, but the Davidic line remained), material that stressed the importance of the Temple as the focus of God's presence among his people (at a time when the temple was [being] rebuilt), and material that highlighted the significance for "all Israel" of the return from exile.[9]

In short, the two renditions of Israel's monarchical period, the one in Samuel–Kings and the other in Chronicles, are anything but identical, though they cover much of the same ground. A wooden reading of one or both could easily give the impression that they are mutually contradictory, but a *wooden* reading would be entirely inappropriate. Recognition of the distinct purposes and audiences of the two histories goes a long way towards accounting for many of the differences between the two. As we draw on these synoptic histories in seeking to reconstruct the history of the United Monarchy, we must not lose sight of these fundamental issues.

As regards the dating of our biblical sources, we have so far only considered the likely periods in which the corpora as we have them were *finalized*—DH in the exilic period and Chronicles in the postexilic period. It is also instructive to consider when the constituent elements of the larger compositions may have come into being. For instance, Halpern has recently raised the question of the date of the so-called Apology of David: "Is 2 Samuel early, even roughly contemporary with the events it describes?"[10] Halpern concludes that indeed "2 Samuel is early, and very much in earnest," for he believes it to be "inconceivable that the alibis of Samuel could have been written much after David's day."[11] Similar arguments have been made with respect to other portions of the book of Samuel.[12] Thus, the trend in some quarters to regard biblical texts as quite late and quite removed from the events they purport to describe is not a universal one.

Another issue that arises when one considers the textual evidence for the United Monarchy is the matter of source divisions. Miller and Hayes, for example, regard it as obvious that "any attempt to utilize the I Samuel account for purposes of historical investigation must begin with an attempt to disentangle and evaluate the various independent traditions that have been combined to produce the narrative as it stands now."[13] They recognize the speculative nature of any such undertaking and that "any resulting 'historical' conclusions will be speculative also," but this point does not deter them from dividing 1 Samuel and the first part of 2 Samuel along the following, fairly familiar lines:

The Samuel-Shiloh Stories (1 Sam. 1:1–4:1a)

The Ark Narrative (1 Sam. 4:1b–7:2)

The Saul Stories (1 Sam. 9:1–10:16; 10:26–11:15; 13:2–14:46)

The Samuel Narrative (1 Sam. 7:3–8:22; 10:17–25; 12; 15)

The Stories About David's Rise to Power (1 Sam. 16–2 Sam. 5:5)[14]

The notion that sources have been used in the composition of 1 and 2 Samuel is in principal unobjectionable. R. P. Gordon writes, "That 1 and 2 Samuel comprise a number of sources which have been linked together to form a continuous narrative climaxing in the reign of David is a perfectly reasonable conjecture."[15] Such a conjecture would indeed be in keeping with explicit indications of such compositional and redactional activity in the books of Kings and Chronicles. Thus, the tendency in the studies to identify, for instance, "three originally independent narratives" in the books of Samuel—the Ark Narrative, the History of David's Rise, and the Succession Narrative—need, of itself, raise no objection. A tripartite division such as the one just mentioned at least "provides for a convenient break-down of the greater part of the material in these books,"[16] whatever one may think of the source theories themselves, and however in need of supplementation such a breakdown may be. Gordon is aware, for instance, that the books of Samuel comprise much more than the three "independent narratives" most often cited: "In addition, traditions concerning Shiloh, the beginnings of the monarchy, and the reigns of Saul and David have been interspersed to help make up the colourful literary, theological, and historical montage that is 1 and 2 Samuel."[17]

So far so good. Unfortunately, however, many attempts to divine originally independent sources in the biblical texts have been so intent on dividing things up that they have spent insufficient time discerning whatever narrative coherence may in fact already exist in the extant text. And once divisions and rearrangements have been effected and the original narrative flow disrupted, enthusiasm for close readings of the extant texts diminishes, along with the likelihood that they will ever regain their status as sensible wholes.

Our own contention is that recourse to source theories is helpful—if at all—only when the extant text fails to yield an adequate sense. It is, of course, precisely the belief that the texts we have are in some measure incoherent that has motivated several generations of critical scholars to seek to untangle the "mess" source critically. Beginning in the last quarter or so of the twentieth century, however, significant scholarly advances in the literary reading of biblical texts have been made, particularly in the area of narrative poetics, and it is now widely believed that many stretches of biblical narrative formerly viewed as problematic are in fact admissive of more coherent readings than earlier generations of scholars assumed.[18] This in turn may open the door to more positive assessments of their value as historical sources.[19] We discuss the pertinent issues on a case-by-case basis as we proceed. For now, we simply underscore the importance of approaching the biblical texts alert to their literary character—that is, their scenic mode, their economy of means, their reticence and indirection, their use of a variety of rather sophisticated literary techniques such as wordplay and key words, comparative and contrastive characterization, repetitions (with variations), narrative patterning and analogies, and so forth.[20] Often sensitivity to one or more of these literary features opens the door to enhanced appreciation of the coherence and composite unity of the extant biblical narratives, yielding in turn a clearer sense of their potential historical import.

Turning from biblical to extrabiblical texts, we must bear in mind that these, too, are literary works and as such must be approached in a manner commensurate with their literary and ideological character. It is often assumed, for example, that the Tel Dan stela (mentioned above), while confirming the existence of "David," actually *contradicts* the biblical text on the question of who killed the kings of Israel and Judah mentioned in the stela (was it Hazael or Jehu?). Assuming Hazael to be responsible for the Tel Dan stela, Lemaire writes:

> The claim of Hazael to have killed Joram of Israel and Achazyahu of Judah clearly contradicts the detailed story of Jehu's *coup d'état* in 2 Kgs 9.1–10.28. Who really killed the two kings, Hazael or Jehu's partisans? Without entering into details here, it seems clear enough that the main narrative of 2 Kgs 9.1–10.28 is probably close to the event, while the Dan stela may have been engraved twenty or thirty years later.[21]

Lemaire goes on to cite another instance (this time in an Assyrian royal inscription) of a false claim alongside a true account, and then concludes that "This parallel gives us another hint that Hazael is boasting here and that the Dan stela was probably not engraved immediately after 841 but several years later, at least late enough in Hazael's reign, when he controlled Israel, Judah and most of Transeuphrates."[22] But if Hazael is simply boasting, as ancient Near Eastern potentates were generally wont to do, is "contradiction" the best way of describing the difference between the biblical and the extrabiblical accounts? Appropriate sensitivity to the genres of royal inscriptions should warn us against reading Hazael's boasting as a simple statement of fact. Persons in power commonly claim credit for deeds that others accomplish.

From this brief example, we see the importance of approaching not just the biblical texts but also extrabiblical texts with appropriate literary expectations and genre awareness. That said, extrabiblical texts relevant to the United Monarchy are still few. A probably fair conclusion is that they now confirm at least the existence of a David who apparently founded a dynasty ("House of David"), but beyond this comment, they tell us little. For specific information about the period in question, we remain largely dependent on the biblical texts.

In addition to the textual evidence, archaeology may also make its contribution. The archaeology of Jerusalem, for instance, may provide useful background information to fill out the picture of David's reign, but as we shall see, the interpretation of such material evidence as has been collected is nothing if not controversial.

THE CHRONOLOGY OF THE EARLY ISRAELITE MONARCHY

The chronology of the early Israelite monarchy is not much more certain than that of prior periods. Not until the period of the Divided Monarchy are we able to correlate a few biblical events with fixed dates known from Assyrian and Babylonian king lists, the latter allowing rather exact dating because of their occasional mention of lunar and solar eclipses. Two dates that can be fairly confidently fixed are 853 B.C. for the Battle of Qarqar, in which King Ahab of Israel was involved, and 841 B.C. for Jehu's paying of tribute to Shalmaneser III of Assyria. Working then from these fixed points and from the relative chronological information of regnal formulae in the biblical texts, we can arrive at reasonable approximations for the dates of the kings of Israel and of Judah after the division of the Kingdom.[23] With respect to the kings of the United Monarchy, it is generally agreed that Solomon's reign must have ended c. 930 B.C.[24] If Solomon is accorded a forty-year reign (1 Kgs. 11:42), his accession would have occurred c. 970 B.C. David's forty-year reign (2 Sam. 5:4) would have begun c. 1010 B.C. and so forth. It is often assumed that Saul also reigned for approximately forty years, but this assumption is based not on any specific information in the Old Testament but on a reading of Acts 13:21. As in the period of the judges, numbers like forty may at first blush seem to suggest symbolic or paradigmatic numbers. In the case of David, however, his forty years is achieved by combining his seven-and-a-half-year reign in Hebron with his thirty-three-year reign over all Israel (2 Sam. 5:5;

1 Kgs. 2:11; cf. 2 Sam. 2:11). It seems best, then, to assume forty years for David's reign and probably as many for Solomon's. But what of Saul's reign? Saul's regnal formula appears to be given in 1 Samuel 13:1, but as the following translations indicate, the interpretation of these verses is anything but clear:

> Saul was . . . years old when he began to reign; and he reigned . . . and two years over Israel.—NRSV

> Saul was . . . years old when he became king, and he reigned over Israel two years.—JPS

> Saul was [thirty] years old when he became king, and he reigned over Israel [forty-] two years.—NIV

Few verses in 1 Samuel have spawned as many interpretive theories as this first verse of 1 Samuel 13.[25] Of the three translations above, NRSV sticks closest to the Hebrew text, though the latter contains, of course, no ellipsis points. NRSV also reflects the common assumption that 13:1 must have lost numerals in two places or that the numerals were never entered in the first place. Numerals are not entirely lacking, however, as the Hebrew text includes the numeral "two" for the length of Saul's reign. While some have argued that Saul's reign may have lasted only two years[26] (a view reflected in the JPS rendering above), this seems highly unlikely for a number of reasons.[27] NIV follows certain manuscripts of the LXX in making Saul "thirty" years old at his accession.[28] But taken simply as it stands, the Hebrew text reads, "Saul was a year old [lit. son of a year] when he became king, and he reigned over Israel two years." This yields an impossible sense, of course, unless we assume that the narrator is not speaking of Saul's actual age at accession and actual length of reign, but of something else—for example, perhaps a year passed between Saul's anointing, when he was "turned into a different person" (1 Sam. 10:6), and his confirmation as king (11:15–13:1); and perhaps two years passed from the time of Saul's confirmation to his definitive rejection by God in chapter 15. As we shall see when we come to Saul's reign, after chapter 15 Saul is no longer rightful king in God's eyes, though he clings to the throne for some years.[29]

As to the actual length of Saul's reign, the only biblical statement comes in Acts 13:21 ("Then they asked for a king; and God gave them Saul son of Kish, a man of the tribe of Benjamin, who reigned for forty years"). However, the phrase "who reigned" is not present in the Greek text of Acts 13:21, and it may well be that "forty years" refers to the administrations of both Samuel and Saul (just as the "450 years" in Acts 13:20 seems to refer to the time in Egypt, the wilderness wandering, and at least the start of the conquest of Canaan [vv. 17–19] or, according to the Byzantine textual tradition, to the period of judges up to, but not including, Samuel).[30] On the basis of logic and what indirect biblical evidence is available, a reign of about twenty years would seem to make sense for Saul. We know the following: David was thirty years old when he became king in Hebron and thirty-seven and a half when he became king over all Israel after the death of Ishbosheth (2 Sam. 5:4–5); Ishbosheth was forty when he became king over the northern tribes, and he reigned only two years before he was assassinated (2 Sam. 2:10). Logically, then, Ishbosheth must have been at least five years older than David. Assuming that Jonathan was older than his brother Ishbosheth (cf. 1 Sam. 20:31, where Saul views Jonathan as in line for the throne; and note also that Jonathan is listed first among Saul's sons in 1 Sam. 14:49; 31:2), he may have been about ten years older than David. If we assume the events of 1 Samuel 13 to take place at the beginning of Saul's reign (as the ordering of the text seems to suggest), then Jonathan, who is a commander of troops in 13:2, must have been least twenty when Saul began to reign. Saul would have been at least forty and David about ten. Since David became king at thirty, just after the death of Saul, a simple subtraction leaves Saul a reign of about twenty years. This agrees with the figure for Saul's reign given by Josephus in *Jewish Antiquities* 10.143. In *Jewish Antiquities* 6.378, Josephus states that Saul reigned eighteen years during Samuel's lifetime and "two and twenty" thereafter, but the "twenty" is very doubtful on text-critical as well as logical grounds (making David only eight years old at Samuel's death).[31]

Bearing in mind the multiple uncertainties discussed above, we arrive at a tentative, approximate chronology for the period of the United Monarchy. If Solomon's reign ended c. 930 B.C., and if the forty-year reigns of David and Solomon are more than paradigmatic numbers (which seems certain at least for David), then we may extrapolate that David's reign in Hebron began c. 1010, and David was born c. 1040. Further dates in Table 8.1 are only rough estimates based on such assumptions as an approximately twenty-year reign for Saul, an age of perhaps seventy for Samuel at the beginning of Saul's reign (cf. the description of Samuel as "old" in 1 Sam. 8:1 with the similar description of David in 1 Kgs. 1:1, when he was about seventy), an age of at least twenty for Jonathan at the beginning of Saul's reign, etc. On the basis of such reasoning, the *hypothetical* chronology in Table 8.1 can be proposed, but only to provide a very general frame of reference (question marks indicate the most suppositional dates). All dates should be read as "circa . . . B.C."

Having discussed the nature of our source material and the challenges of establishing a chronology for the period, we move now to a reading of the book of Samuel, section by section, with an eye to what value it may hold for the historian.

PREFACE TO MONARCHY: 1 SAMUEL 1–7

The book of Samuel opens with a homely tale of two rival wives, the one barren but loved by her husband, the other fertile but mean-spirited and irritating. Unless we were to anticipate the "reversal of fortunes" theme that will thread its way through the narratives of this book, we would little suspect that out of the barren woman's misery—which drove her neither to distraction nor aggression

Table 8.1. Hypothetical Chronology
for the Period of the United Monarchy

Date	Event
1100?	Birth of Samuel
1070?	Birth of Saul
1050?	Birth of Jonathan
1040	Birth of David
1030?	Beginning of Saul's reign[32]
1028?	Anointing of David
1012?	Death of Samuel
1010	Death of Saul, beginning of David's reign in Hebron
1003	David becomes king over all Israel
970	Death of David, beginning of Solomon's solo reign[33]
930	Death of Solomon

but to God—would be born a child who would grow to become the most significant individual in Israel's shift from tribal confederacy to monarchy. What begins as Hannah's story becomes Samuel's story, and then Israel's and Saul's and David's. Samuel will grow to become the king-maker, but also the king-breaker. He is a transitional figure—last of the judges, successor of the priest Eli, prophet of the Lord.[34] It is he that anoints Israel's first two kings, albeit reluctantly at first, and it is he that stands at the head of what might be called the "prophetic movement." While prophetic gifts were not absent among Israel's earlier leaders, institutional prophecy in Israel was more or less coextensive with the monarchic period. As F. M. Cross has observed, "the institution of prophecy appeared simultaneously with kingship in Israel and fell with kingship."[35]

Chapters 1–3 of 1 Samuel tell the story of Samuel's birth[36] and progressive advancement to replace the aging Eli, who when we meet him is in a state of decrepitude, both physically and spiritually. Unable to restrain his wayward sons, though they served as priests under his oversight, Eli has apparently been unable to restrain himself as well. He, along with his sons, is charged with gaining weight on the offerings of Israel at the expense of giving weight to ("honoring") Israel's God (1 Sam. 2:29–30).

> Why then look with greedy eye at my sacrifices and my offerings that I commanded, and honor your sons more than me by fattening yourselves on the choicest parts of every offering of my people Israel?' Therefore the LORD the God of Israel declares: 'I promised that your family and the family of your ancestor should go in and out before me forever'; but now the LORD declares: 'Far be it from me; for those who honor me I will honor, and those who despise me shall be treated with contempt.'

Eli's failure to "weight" things properly—that is, to give the Lord the honor that is his due—leads to an imbalance that will ultimately bring about the downfall of Eli and all his house, as is predicted by a "man of God" in the prophetic judgment speech of 1 Samuel 2:27–36. As a sign confirming the veracity of the prophet's words, Eli's two sons, Hophni and Phinehas, will die on the same day (2:34).

The prophetic sign is fulfilled in 1 Samuel 4, but not before Samuel receives his own prophetic call in chapter 3 (vv. 19–21 anticipate Samuel's recognition as a "trustworthy prophet of the LORD" by all Israel, "from Dan to Beersheba"). Samuel's first prophetic assignment (3:11–14) is to reiterate the judgment that had already been pronounced on Eli's house by the man of God in chapter 2, and this he does, though reluctantly and only at Eli's insistence (3:17).

Against this background, it comes as no surprise that the sons of Eli die in battle in chapter 4. More distressing, however, and not least to Eli, is the fact that the ark of God is captured (4:11). When the watchful Eli (4:13) is finally told of the day's catastrophic events, including the deaths of his sons, it is not until the mention of the loss of the ark of God that he falls backward off his seat and dies under his own weight ("for he was an old man, and heavy" [4:18]). If our discussion so far of the opening chapters of 1 Samuel is suggestive of a series of plays on the word "weight," this is in keeping with the Hebrew text, where the key root *kbd* occurs (1) in a number of verbal stems connoting the giving or receiving of "weight, honor, glory"; (2) in adjectival form in the sense of "heavy, severe"; and (3) in noun form in the sense of "honor, glory," etc.[37] After Eli's death under his own weight, the root *kbd* continues to appear. When Eli's pregnant daughter-in-law hears of the day's defeat, its deaths, and the capture of the ark of God, she goes into labor prematurely (4:19–21) and gives birth to a son, whom she names Ichabod (which sounds like "Where is the Glory?" or "Glory gone"— or perhaps "No weight" or "Weightless one"). Meanwhile, the ark, now in Philistine territory, becomes the instrument by which Yahweh's hand begins to make its "weight" felt by the Philistines (5:6, 11). Soon desperate to return the (quite literally) pestilent ark back to its former custodians, the Philistines stress the importance of giving "weight"—that is, "honor"—to Israel's God (6:5), and they fervently warn against "hardening" (lit. "weighing down") their hearts as the Egyptians and Pharaoh had "hardened" theirs (6:6). Thus, ironically, the Philistines appear to be quicker studies, theologically, than their Israelite neighbors.

Before coming to the conclusion that the ark must be returned, however, the Philistines shunt it from city to city, perhaps hoping that the catastrophes that befell each city will prove to be only coincidental (cf. 6:9). Their hope is quickly dashed, however, and all that their efforts accomplish is to provide an opportunity for the ark to move about Philistia in "a veritable parody of a victory tour."[38] In several respects, this story is a reprise of motifs from the story of the Exodus— plagues visited upon the enemies of Israel (5:6 and *passim*), judgment executed against the false gods of Israel's foes (5:1–5; cf. Exod. 12:12).[39] Eventually the ark finds its way, providentially guided (6:10–12), back to Israelite territory. But once there, unwarranted trifling with the ark exacts a heavy toll on the citizens of Beth-Shemesh (6:19)—would that they had heard the Philistine exhortation to give "weight/honor" to Israel's God (6:5)—but eventually the ark is brought to rest in Kiriath-jearim, where it is placed under the care of Eleazar, son of Abinadab (6:21–7:1).

After some twenty years have elapsed and "all the house of Israel" is yearning for Yahweh (7:2), Samuel convenes an assembly in Mizpah to challenge the people (7:3) in terms reminiscent of Joshua's charge in Joshua 24: *put away* foreign gods, and *serve* Yahweh alone.

> Then Samuel said to all the house of Israel, "If you are returning to the LORD with all your heart, then put away the foreign gods and the Astartes from among you. Direct your heart to the LORD, and serve him only, and he will deliver you out of the hand of the Philistines.' So Israel put away the Baals and the Astartes, and they served the LORD only. (1 Sam. 7:3–4)

Conceptually and terminologically, the twin issues of *turning* (to/from) and *serving* link the present episode with earlier ones touching on Israel's occupation of the promised land (Deut. 7:4; 11:16; 28:14; Josh. 24:14; Judg. 10:16; cf. also 1 Sam. 12:12). The people are responsive (7:4–6), the Philistines become aggressive (7:7), Samuel prays and sacrifices (7:9), and Yahweh delivers: "the LORD thundered with a mighty voice that day against the Philistines and threw them into confusion; and they were routed before Israel" (7:10b). In the aftermath of the victory, Samuel sets up a memorial stone and calls it Ebenezer ("stone of help"), explaining that "thus far the LORD has helped us" (7:12b). While a geographical connotation is clearly present—that is, to this piece of turf Yahweh has given us victory—"it is tempting," as Gordon observes "to entertain a temporal significance: until this point in Israel's history Yahweh has been her helper. The question soon to be resolved (ch. 8) is whether Yahweh would be allowed to continue that help within the old theocratic framework, or would be set aside as Israel sought to go it alone."[40] The naming of Samuel's stone may have a further significance, for it was at a different Ebenezer that Israel had suffered defeat at the hand of the Philistines in 1 Samuel 4. Now a second Ebenezer "announces the reversal of these indignities; it is a symbol of reintegration."[41] Presumption at the first Ebenezer had led to disaster; penitence now leads to deliverance and a true "stone of help."

This is the story of 1 Samuel 1–7 in its main lines. According to content, these chapters might be outlined as follows: chapters 1–3, the emergence of God's new man (election of Samuel and rejection of Eli); chapters 4–6, a demonstration of God's power (travels of the ark behind enemy lines); chapter 7, deliverance of Israel by God's power working through God's man. First Samuel 1–7 makes a good story, but is it history? One thing that has given scholars pause in this regard is the tendency of many, ever since the seminal work of Leonard Rost,[42] to separate off the so-called Ark Narrative from its current textual context and to postulate an originally independent narrative, which might also have included the story of David's bringing the ark to Jerusalem (now found in 2 Sam. 6). According to the general theory, whatever may have been the origin of the Ark Narrative,[43] its secondary incorporation into 1 Samuel creates something of an artificial (and hence unhistorical) sequence. Evidence for this theory includes chiefly the fact that Samuel, so prominent in 1 Samuel 1–3, makes no appearance whatsoever in chapters 4–6. This is the basic theory, which has been reiterated and variously developed since Rost by a number of scholars.[44]

The idea of an originally independent, secondarily inserted Ark Narrative has not gone unchallenged. Miller and Roberts, for instance, while accepting the general theory, are unhappy with the standard assumption that the Ark Narrative begins in 4:1b. This placement would leave Eli and his sons without introduction (they simply appear in v. 4)[45] and their judgment without explanation. Therefore, Miller and Roberts suggest viewing 1 Samuel 2:12–17, 22–25, and 27–36 as part of the original Ark Narrative.[46] They explain, "To make the ark narrative a complete, self-contained unit, one must supplement Rost's text with a tradition introducing the main characters and alerting the reader to Yahweh's displeasure toward Israel."[47]

A more thoroughgoing critical assessment of the whole notion of an independent Ark Narrative has been presented by J. Willis in several studies.[48] Willis finds the arguments for discontinuity between the sections 1:1–4:1a; 4:1b–7:1; 7:2–17[49] to be wanting and argues instead that the narrative sequence follows a well-attested Old Testament literary pattern in which

> (a) The writer tells how Yahweh prepares a man to lead Israel through some crisis (I Sam 1:1–4a); (b) he describes this crisis (I Sam 4:1b–7:1); and finally (c) he relates the successful manner in which that man guides Israel through the crisis (I Sam 7:2–17).[50]

He discerns similar patterns in the narrative presentations of Jephthah, Samson, Saul, and David.[51]

Willis is not alone in his belief that 1 Samuel 1–7 constitute a sensible unity.[52] At the very least one must admit that "the lineaments of the 'Ark Narrative', if it ever existed, have yet to be restored with a proper degree of exactitude."[53] Na'aman is more bold: "The ark narrative is inseparable both from the story of Eli and Samuel in chaps. 1–3 and from the episode of Samuel's victory over the Philistines in chap. 7; it was never an independent entity."[54] Na'aman may be correct in this judgment; to the arguments already noted, we might add the aforementioned key word *kbd*, "weight, honor," that is introduced in 2:29–30 and continues to recur throughout chapters 4–6, thus effectively (if subtly) tying the sections together. But whatever may have been the process by which the narrative of 1 Samuel 1–7 came to be,[55] the point is that, because these chapters offer a coherent story, they at least deserve consideration as history—unless, of course, there are other problems.

One frequently cited problem is the portrait of Samuel himself, which is regarded by many as being simply too multifaceted—priest, prophet, judge, all embodied in a single individual—when in reality he may have been little more than a village seer.[56] Is it not likely—so the argument goes—that the portrait of Samuel has simply been embellished by later prophetic circles who wished to enhance their own prestige by coopting this famous individual?[57] While it may be difficult to disprove such speculation, there seems little reason to accept it either. Numerous scholars have no trouble envisaging a Samuel who was, as H. Gressmann put it almost a century ago, "really big" ("wirklich gross").[58] M. J. Buss believes it likely that "the combination of functions is older than their separation since societal development has generally been in the direction of increasing specialization";[59] J. H. Grønbæk cites the national and religious situation in which Israel found herself as doubtless prompting a broadening of Samuel's responsibilities;[60] and J. Blenkinsopp sees no reason to deny Samuel a diversity of roles—prophetic, political, and military.[61] Some even cite "the plurality of offices held by Samuel," which "provides a contrast with what was possible at a late date," as supporting "the basic genuineness of the traditions about him."[62] In short,

> The circumstances of the times and the strength of his own personality will have been two decisive factors in the role-casting of Samuel; at a later stage in Israel's history, in an era of specialization, it would not have been possible for an individual to combine the offices of prophet, priest, and judge-administrator as Samuel appears to have done.[63]

If the portrait of Samuel is not implausible historically, if he was indeed a "multitasking" transitional figure, does this not make his conspicuous absence in 1 Samuel 4–6 all the more remarkable and problematic? Not at all, provided that one recognizes the anticipatory nature of the summary verses at the end of 1 Samuel 3:

> As Samuel grew up, the LORD was with him and let none of his words fall to the ground. And all Israel from Dan to Beer-sheba knew that Samuel was a trustworthy prophet of the LORD. The LORD continued to appear at Shiloh, for the LORD revealed himself to Samuel at Shiloh by the word of the LORD. (1 Sam. 3:19–21)

These verses, though placed at the end of the account of Samuel's boyhood audition, clearly look to the future. What they describe could not have happened overnight. They provide an anticipatory summary of the prophetic ministry into which Samuel must have grown over a period of years.[64] By contrast, the judgment that befell the house of Eli (described in 1 Sam. 4) appears to have come quickly, while Samuel was still only a boy. The absence of Samuel in chapters 4–6 is, therefore, in the end quite unremarkable.[65]

In summary, there are various reasons to take the narrative of 1 Samuel 1–7 seriously as a potential historical source and few, if any, reasons to doubt it. But we must not lose sight of the fact that its interests are more than merely antiquarian. Neither this narrative, nor other narratives in the Old Testament, nor indeed most other historical narratives of any age are simply history for history's sake. In 1 Samuel 1–7, we have history with a purpose—or, it might be better to say, several purposes. As an introduction to the book of Samuel, these chapters provide a conceptual and thematic grid by which later events in the book are to be understood: "It is not by strength that one prevails; those who oppose the LORD will be shattered" (2:9b–10a, NIV); "those who honor me I will honor" (2:30b, NIV); and the like. R. A. Carlson[66] has drawn attention to two "pivotal passages" in these introductory chapters, the first being the Song of Hannah in 1 Samuel 2:1–10 and the second the judgment speech pronounced against the house of Eli in 1 Samuel 2:27–36. The Song of Hannah not only introduces the reversal-of-fortune theme that recurs as the book unfolds, but it also raises the issue of kingship, which will form the book's central subject matter. This song is matched at the end of 2 Samuel by similarly toned poems ascribed to David (22:1–23:7), the king with whose rise and reign the book is most concerned. Following the judgment speech uttered against the house of Eli, the reversal-of-fortune theme surfaces again in chapter 3 as the young Samuel rises to replace Eli. Seldom noted, however, is the way in which the rejection of Eli—and Eli's response to his rejection—functions programmatically to provide a "rationale for rejection" that offers a key for understanding the rest of the book, especially the rejection of King Saul.[67] Finally, Yahweh's unmatched power (1 Sam. 4–6) and his willingness to save his people when they turn to him (1 Sam. 7) provide the background for what happens next.

ISRAEL DEMANDS AND GETS ITS KING: 1 SAMUEL 8–14

With the elders' insistence in 1 Samuel 8 that Israel be given a king "like other nations" (v. 5), a new chapter in Israel's history begins. And yet the division between chapter 8 and what has preceded in 1 Samuel 1–7 should not be drawn too sharply, for the earlier chapters provide the backdrop against which the elders' request for a king is to be judged.[68] Of particular significance is the notice in 7:12 that "thus far the LORD has helped us." That Israel's elders should so quickly—in narrative time at least—demand "a king to govern us, like other nations" (8:5) strikes the attentive reader as a foreboding development. The point is not that Israel was never to have a human monarch. Israel's traditions are replete with anticipations of a time when Israel would have a king (e.g., Gen. 17:6, 16; 35:11; 49:10; Num. 24:7, 17–19). Furthermore, given the fact that kingship was commonly practiced among Israel's neighbors (cf. Josh. 5:1; 9:1–2; 10:5; Judg. 3:12 and *passim*),[69] it is perhaps less surprising that Israel should seek a king than that she resisted doing so for so long. Part of her hesitancy may be related to the fundamental tenet of Israelite faith that Yahweh himself is the Great King (for first and last references in the OT, see Num. 23:21 and Mal. 1:14; cf. also 1 Sam. 12:12). Some such understanding must have underlain Gideon's refusal of power in Judges 8:23: "I will not rule over you, and my son will not rule over you; the LORD will rule over you."

The understanding that God is king lies at the heart of the biblical tradition. Nevertheless, as we have noted, it was from the beginning anticipated that human kingship would be part of Israel's future. In Deuteronomy 17:14–20, Moses foresaw its coming and gave instructions about the form that kingship was to take. Therefore, it cannot simply be the idea of kingship per se that raises objection in 1 Samuel 8. Samuel's own displeasure seems to arise from a sense that he, and his judgeship, are personally under attack: the word rendered "govern" in 8:5 is the same word as "judge." As Yahweh is quick to point out, however, the problem runs much deeper than a desire to replace Samuel: "they have not rejected you, but they have rejected me from being king over them" (8:7). In spite of the objectionable tone and timing of Israel's request, Yahweh is willing (after issuing appropriate warnings in 8:11–17)[70] to grant a king. This king is not to be like the kings of "other nations," however, as the continuing story will make clear.

Given the momentous nature of the change, Israel's transition from tribal confederation to monarchy has been of great interest to historians.[71] This is not to say, however, that historians have had much success in reconstructing the period. The contribution of archaeological investigation has been modest. Writing in 1985, Miller and Hayes remark that "while the archaeological record is useful for understanding the general material circumstances of the Early Iron Age, it is not very helpful for clarifying matters of historical detail."[72] Recent discoveries and fresh readings of the evidence have improved the picture somewhat (as we shall discuss presently), but to a large degree we remain dependent on the biblical testimony for specific information about the period. Here we encounter a difficulty, however, for the biblical account of the rise of Saul to become Israel's first king (1 Sam. 8–12) has struck most commentators as problematic. Specifically, the account is regarded as inconsistent in its attitude towards monarchy (is it favorable or unfavorable?) and confusing in its account(s) of how Saul became king (was it by anointing, lot casting, or military victory?). Even such an astute reader of biblical stories as J. Licht[73] finds the biblical account "rather unconvincing as a statement of fact," comprising "a tangle of textual elements." To be sure, the "three stories telling how Saul was made king" have been combined into a "plausible reconstruction of a political process," but with "plenty of contradictions and loose ends in the story," stemming assumedly from the fact that all three stories were originally variant renditions of "a single event."[74] Faced with such difficulties, most scholars would agree with T. Ishida that "it is futile from the outset to attempt reconstruction of a harmonious history from all the narratives."[75] Even Bright concedes that "in view of these varying accounts, we cannot undertake to reconstruct the sequence of events."[76] For most scholars, then, little has changed since W. W. Cannon pronounced in 1932 that "the events by which [Saul] came to the throne are and will remain a mystery."[77]

Our own view is more optimistic. Based on several recent studies,[78] we believe that the Saul narratives tell a more consistent, coherent story and thus are potentially of greater historical import than has generally been assumed. To make our case, we must first look more closely at the perceived difficulties already mentioned, to which we shall add a third.

The first difficulty we may call the problem of *differing attitudes towards the monarchy*. Reflecting the critical consensus since Wellhausen, Bright describes the problem as follows:

> The account of Saul's election comes to us in two (probably originally three) parallel narratives, one tacitly favorable to the monarchy, the other bitterly hostile. The first (I Sam. 9:1 to 10:16) tells how Saul was privately anointed by Samuel in Ramah; it is continued in ch. 13:3b, 4b–15. Woven with this narrative is the originally separate account (ch. 11) of Saul's victory over Ammon and his subsequent acclamation by the people at Gilgal. The other strand (chs. 8; 10:17–27; 12) has Samuel, having yielded with angry protests to popular demand, presiding over Saul's election at Mizpah.[79]

The last strand is regarded as antimonarchical, while the other two are regarded as pro-monarchical. With respect to the historical question, the argument would run something like this: given the fact that the episodes that contain the narrative of Saul's rise exhibit differing attitudes towards the monarchy, they presumably do not offer a credible historical account, given that historical accounts by competent historians should be self-consistent in perspective. Before accepting such an argument, however, we must consider whether the differences in perspective might be explained on grounds other than narrative inconsistency. L. Eslinger has argued, for instance, that not every attitude expressed in a narrative is that of the narrator.[80] Thus, a diversity of attitudes and perspectives can be present in a narrative, without calling into question the consistency of the narrative itself. As Eslinger points out, one must always ask "the simple question of who says what to whom"[81]—and, we might add, in what context.

With respect to context, Tsevat, McCarthy, Childs, and others have observed that the so-called antimonarchical sentiments tend to come to expression in the context of assemblies, while action reports do not give rise to such sentiments and thus appear more pro-monarchical.[82] Obviously, a political change as momentous as the introduction of kingship would not have taken place without controversy, and, more to the point from the perspective of the narrative, the manner in which the elders demanded a king would not have met with universal approval. Negative reactions to these events would presumably find expression somewhere, most naturally in the context of assemblies, where speeches are given and opinions exchanged. The following chart illustrates the general point (so-called pro-monarchical sections are marked with a plus sign, and antimonarchical sections with a minus sign):

–	8:4–22	Assembly:	elders demand a king
+	9:1–10:16	Action:	secret anointing of Saul
–	10:17–27	Assembly:	lot casting and public presentation of Saul
+	11:1–13	Action:	Saul's first victory in battle
–	11:14–12:25	Assembly:	Renewal of kingship and Samuel's warning

In view of the above considerations, the standard opposition of pro- vs. anti-monarchical attitudes is clearly simplistic and misguided. Characters within the story express a variety of attitudes, and neither Yahweh nor Samuel is depicted as, strictly speaking, antimonarchical. The object of their concern is not monarchy per se but, as Eslinger notes, "the anti-covenantal sentiment they hear in Israel's request" for a king "like the nations."[83] Thus, the purported problem of different attitudes towards the monarchy is actually no problem at all.[84] Therefore, the potential historical import of this narrative sequence should not be dismissed on this basis.

But what about the second difficulty, the problem of *multiple accession accounts?* Put simply, this problem relates to the perception that the narrative provides too many explanations of how Saul became king. Writing in 1941, W. A. Irwin exclaimed that we are "embarrassed by our very wealth!" Even limiting himself to what he regarded as the early source (i.e., the so-called pro-monarchical source delineated above), Irwin felt that the text is overfull, with both a secret anointing (9:1–10:16) and a battle report (chap. 11—in Irwin's opinion the "real circumstances" of Saul's rise). He writes, "Either account would suffice as an explanation of this revolutionary change in Hebrew history, to be given both baffles credence."[85] Until recently, this has been the consensus of critical scholars, a consensus well expressed by H. Donner: "It is well-known that there are at least two narrative accounts of Saul's rise to the throne in Israel in the first book of Samuel. . . . They contradict each other: Saul could not have become king in both these ways."[86] With respect to the historical question, the argument from this difficulty would run something like this: given the fact that the various episodes in the biblical narrative of Saul's rise present multiple and contradictory accounts of how Saul became king, presumably the biblical narrative cannot be regarded as historical in any straightforward sense, inasmuch as reliable historiography should exclude internal contradiction.

Our response to this difficulty begins with the observation—based on groundbreaking work by B. Halpern,[87] followed and enhanced by D. Edelman[88]—that the process by which leaders in early Israel came to power seems to have entailed three stages: designation, demonstration, and confirmation.[89] The process would look something like this. First, an individual would be *designated* by some means for a particular leadership role. Next, the new designee would be expected to *demonstrate* his status and his prowess by engaging in some feat of arms or military action. Finally, having thus distinguished himself and come to public attention, the designee would be *confirmed* in his leadership office.

While agreeing on the basic pattern, Halpern and Edelman develop their interpretations differently. Beginning with the assumption that "the first step in investigating Saul's elections is, as the histories recognize, a division of the sources in 1 Samuel 8ff.,"[90] Halpern divines two complete exemplars of the tripartite accession pattern in 1 Samuel 9–14.[91] Edelman, on the other hand, discerns only one instance of the accession pattern in 1 Samuel 9–11,[92] which may be presented as in Table 8.2.

Table 8.2. The Accession Pattern according to Edelman

Steps in the Process	Text	Content
1. Designation	9:1–10:16	Events leading up to and including Saul's anointing
2. Demonstration	11:1–11	Saul's rescue of Jabesh-gilead from the Ammonites
3. Confirmation	11:14–15	Saul's kingship is "renewed"/confirmed

Edelman's interpretation is helpful as far as it goes, but it does not adequately account for the lot-casting episode in 10:17–27,[93] nor does it do full justice to Samuel's charge to Saul at the time of his anointing to "do what your hand finds to do" (10:7). As we shall see shortly, this charge (in context) suggests a feat of arms. Edelman recognizes this charge but assumes that it must be Saul's Ammonite victory in 11:1–11 that is in view, even though, by her own account, the real focus of 10:7 in context is not the Ammonites but the Philistines, and particularly the Philistine presence in Gibeah (which is to become the object of Jonathan's aggression in chap. 13). To account for these factors, Edelman, like others before her, postulates that the events of chapter 13 must have followed more closely on 10:7 at an earlier stage of textual development.[94]

Our own view is that a better solution is possible, one that makes coherent sense of all the episodes in their present sequence without recourse to hypotheses involving textual dislocation. Ironically, it is consideration of what is often regarded as a further difficulty for the literary coherence of the Saul narratives that, in the end, leads to this better solution.

This further difficulty has to do with Saul's first charge (1 Sam. 10:7–8), issued by Samuel at the time of Saul's anointing, and this charge's eventual fulfillment. The perceived problem is twofold. First, to many readers verses 7 and 8 of 1 Samuel 10 seem contradictory. In verse 7 Samuel charges Saul to "do what your hand finds to do, for God is with you."[95] Then in verse 8, Samuel seems to reverse himself, charging Saul to "go down to Gilgal" and wait seven days for Samuel to arrive, at which time he will offer sacrifices and tell Saul what he is to do. Second, and to make matters worse, 10:8 is unmistakably tied to 1 Samuel 13:8, where Saul "waited seven days, the time appointed by Samuel." What then is one to make of all the intervening episodes (e.g., the lot casting at Mizpah, the deliverance of Jabesh-gilead from Nahash the Ammonite)? And what of the fact that Saul did not immediately repair to Gilgal in the aftermath of his anointing, as Samuel's charge appears to suggest that he should have done? How can this narrative *not* be confused?

To begin, let us assume that verses 7 and 8 of 1 Samuel 10 constitute a two-part charge, with the second part to go into effect only after the first part is fulfilled. The first part (v. 7) is that Saul should do what lies at hand ("what your hand finds to do"). In the context of the anointing episode (10:1–8), this action can be nothing other than to attack the Philistine outpost mentioned by Samuel in verse 5.[96] Of the three signs Samuel predicts that will confirm Saul's anointing (vv. 2–6), the third will take place at Gibeah of God, where—as Samuel explicitly reminds Saul—a Philistine garrison is located.[97] As soon as all three signs are fulfilled, Saul is authorized to do what lies at hand. What else can Samuel have in mind but that Saul should strike this emblem of Philistine presence? The place is right. The time is right.[98] Such an action would constitute an effective *demonstration* of Saul's recent *designation*. Militarily, however, the move would accomplish little other than to provoke the Philistines and start a war, so Samuel's further charge to Saul (v. 8) is that he should then repair to Gilgal and wait for Samuel to come (which might take as many as seven days), in order that Samuel might offer sacrifices and give Saul further instructions.

Understood in this way, verses 7 and 8 are not at all contradictory but constitute the two parts of Saul's first charge: Saul's demonstration (v. 7) is to be followed by a meeting with Samuel in Gilgal for his confirmation and further instructions about how to deal with the Philistines, now that they have been provoked. Unfortunately, in the aftermath of his anointing and the fulfillment of all three signs, Saul simply fails to do what lies at hand. Indeed, it is not until 1 Samuel 13 that the Philistine garrison comes under attack, and it is not Saul but his son Jonathan who launches the attack (13:3). Jonathan's bold action has the desired effect (13:4a), and the Philistines come out in force (v. 5). Meanwhile Saul repairs to Gilgal (v. 4b) to await Samuel's arrival, in keeping with the second part of his first charge (10:8).

If this reading is in the main correct, then the following relationships are established. Saul's first charge, on the occasion of his anointing, envisages two events: a defiant gesture against the Philistines (10:7; cf. v. 5), to be followed by a meeting with Samuel in Gilgal (10:8). Relating this to the tripartite accession process discussed earlier, the anointing (10:1ff.) is Saul's *designation*, the striking of the Philistine garrison (10:7) was to have been Saul's *demonstration*, and presumably then the meeting in Gilgal (10:8) would have led to Saul's *confirmation*. The complication arises from the fact that Saul fails to do what lies at hand—thus failing to accomplish the intended demonstration. (For those troubled by the fact that the narrator does not explicitly condemn Saul's inaction, considering the literary technique of "gapping" may help.)[99] The accession process stalls until eventually a number of other events are set in motion that culminate in the kingship being "renewed" (i.e., the accession process put back on track).[100] These events include a second *designation* (10:17–27), a substitute *demonstration* (11:1–13), and a partial *confirmation* (11:14–15). Not until Jonathan takes initiative in 13:3 is part one of Saul's original charge belatedly accomplished, at which point part two is activated, and Saul goes to Gilgal to meet Samuel. Once these relationships are understood, all the intervening episodes in 1 Samuel 9–13 make sense. The general flow of the narrative can be charted as in Table 8.3.

If the analysis in Table 8.3 is basically on target, then it not only resolves questions related to the literary coherence of the biblical story of Saul's rise (and obvi-

Table 8.3. Saul's Faltering Accession

Steps in the Process	Text	Content
Designation	9:1–10:13	Saul's anointing, first charge, and failure to do what lies at hand.
Interlude	10:14–16	Having faltered, Saul doesn't even mention the kingship to his uncle.
(Second Designation)	10:17–27	Saul is brought to public attention by lot casting and is found hiding behind the baggage; some "worthless fellows" ask, "how can this man save us?"
(Substitute Demonstration)	11:1–13	Saul demonstrates his military ability by rescuing Jabesh-gilead from the Ammonites, thus silencing his critics.
(Partial Confirmation)	11:14–15	Saul's kingship is "renewed"/confirmed(?) to the delight of Saul and the people (Samuel is not mentioned as joining the celebration).
Interlude	12:1–25	Samuel warns that a test remains: king and people must yet prove faithful to Yahweh.
Demonstration (originally intended)	13:1–3	Jonathan strikes the Philistine garrison (cf. 10:7).
Confirmation (withheld)	13:4–15	Saul goes to Gilgal (cf. 10:8), fails to wait for Samuel, and is not confirmed.

ates the necessity, though not the possibility, of a complex textual prehistory) but also sheds light on the controversial issue of Saul's rejection.[101] That Saul should be elected and then quickly rejected by Yahweh, on grounds that to many commentators seem trivial, has always been troubling to interpreters. Recent writers on the subject have begun to cast Saul as a victim and Samuel and Yahweh as villains. W. Brueggemann, for instance, describes Samuel in 1 Samuel 13 as "harsh, unresponsive, and accusatory"—a "posturing," "peevish" prophet, who plays a "daring, brutal game with Saul's faith, Saul's career, and eventually Saul's sanity."[102] Particularly baffling, according to Brueggemann, is Samuel's accusation against Saul in 13:13: "you have not kept the commandment of the LORD your God!" Brueggemann writes, "This is a remarkable statement because Samuel cites no commandment that has been broken, nor can we construe one."[103] Our own view is that we can indeed construe precisely the "commandment" (or "charge")[104] that Saul has failed to keep: his two-part first charge, given him at the time of his anointing. Jonathan eventually fulfills the first part (13:3; cf. 10:7), and it falls to Saul only to fulfill the second (10:8). His failure to do so, his failure to wait until Samuel arrives, even if tardy (13:8–9), is no trifling matter, for Saul's first charge was designed to test his suitability to be a king not like those of "the nations" but one who would rule in submission to the word of the Great King. Whether witting or unwitting, Saul's disregard for the prophetic word, both in chapter 13 and later in chapter 15, is from the perspective of biblical historiography a serious business indeed, showing a fundamental inability or unwillingness to submit to the divine rule, as mediated through the prophet, and thus a fundamental unsuitability to be king in Israel.

This interpretation of Saul's failure and ultimate rejection is in full agreement with the Chronicler's verdict (1 Chr. 10:13–14):

> So Saul died for his unfaithfulness; he was unfaithful to the Lord in that he did not keep the command of the Lord; moreover, he had consulted a medium, seeking guidance, and did not seek guidance from the Lord. Therefore the Lord put him to death and turned the kingdom over to David son of Jesse.

We have chosen to spend some time on the chapters recounting Saul's rise to power for several reasons. First, "they purport to record a most significant transformation in the political and ideological life of ancient Israel, viz. the inception of monarchy." Second, they "are often discussed in the context of early Israelite historiography and are thought to reveal something of its nature." Third, they "display a literary complexity that has posed an almost irresistible challenge to the ingenuity of scholars."[105] Indeed, they have been called "the *locus classicus* of source criticism" in the books of Samuel[106] and a "favourite hunting ground for source critics."[107] Ishida refers to the literary analysis and historical evaluation of the "Samuel-Saul complex" (i.e., 1 Sam. 7–15) as "among the most vexed questions in biblical studies."[108] Our own analysis, developed fully elsewhere and recounted only briefly here, does not deny the possibility (even the likelihood) that sources were used in the composition of "Saul's rise," but it finds the resulting product to be both coherent and compelling. This finding invites a more positive appraisal of the historicity of the narrative than would be warranted if it were internally incoherent, as is generally supposed.

The accomplishments of Saul's reign are summarized at the end of 1 Samuel 14 (vv. 47–52), at the end of an episode detailing his rather mixed success in dealing with the Philistines in chapters 13–14. Indeed, 1 Samuel 14:52 notes that "there was hard fighting against the Philistines all the days of Saul." It will fall to David to subdue the Philistines fully (2 Sam. 8:1), and it is hard not to have the impression that the story has all along been moving in David's direction—the man "after God's own heart," or "of God's own choosing" (1 Sam. 13:14); the "neighbor . . . who is better than you" (15:28). This impression comports well with the plausible thesis that the book of Samuel, whatever other purposes it may serve, functions as a royal apology for David. The thesis does not necessarily entail the assumption, however, that Saul has been depicted unfairly or inaccurately. He may have been, but this point would have to be argued, and not simply assumed.[109]

DAVID'S RISE AND SAUL'S DEMISE:
1 SAMUEL 15–31

While treating 1 Samuel 15–31 as a coherent unit is sensible from the standpoint of content—that is, it begins with Saul's definitive rejection ("The LORD has torn the kingdom of Israel from you this very day, and has given it to a neighbor of yours, who is better than you"; 15:28) and ends with his death ("So Saul took his own sword and fell upon it"; 31:4b; cf. v. 6)—scholarly discussion has tended, since the seminal work of L. Rost, to think in terms of a "History of David's Rise" (HDR) that extends at least to 2 Samuel 5:10.[110] Many have assumed that HDR must have once existed as an independent literary unit, but attempts to establish the boundaries of such a unit have failed to achieve a consensus.[111] In the end, one is struck by how well-integrated HDR is in its current context and is prompted to wonder whether in fact it ever existed independently. "As in the case of the Ark Narrative," writes Gordon, "we have to note that not all those who have discussed the subject of the History of David's Rise are convinced that it ever existed as an independent literary entity."[112]

Not surprisingly, for readers conversant with the Bible, David—though smallest of his brothers when first introduced in 1 Samuel 16:11[113]—comes to stand about as tall, metaphorically speaking, as any other character in the Old Testament—Abraham and Moses being perhaps his chief competitors.[114] The story of his rise is complex and well wrought, and the space available here is not sufficient to give each of its parts the attention it deserves. We must limit ourselves, therefore, to dealing with the big questions and exploring select episodes deemed particularly pertinent to or illustrative of the question at hand. The big questions we have in mind are of the following sort. Was David a historical person? Is his depiction in the Bible a reasonably accurate portrait or a whitewash? Did David do the deeds he is credited with or not—for example, did he kill Goliath? Does the Hebrew text (MT) tell a coherent story, or is the often shorter Greek version, the Septuagint (LXX), more credible? Is the biblical account of David's rise to power plausible historically, or are there insurmountable implausibilities?

The necessity of our remaining focused, selective, and relatively brief is partially compensated for by the fact that David has proved as popular among biblical scholars as he is in the Bible itself, and full-scale treatments abound, two very interesting recent exemplars being S. L. McKenzie's *King David: A Biography* (Oxford: Oxford University Press, 2000) and B. Halpern's *David's Secret Demons: Messiah, Murderer, Traitor, King* (Grand Rapids: Eerdmans, 2001). Much can be learned from these two accomplished works, and we have occasion to interact with them from time to time below; readers should take note at the outset, however, that McKenzie's stated aim is to read the biblical account of David "against the grain,"[115] and Halpern's is to "contemplate David as his enemies saw him,"[116] which of course leaves open the question of which perspective—that of David's friends or of his foes—comes closest to the historical David. We turn now to the first of our big questions.

Was David a Historical Person?

Did David exist? Was he historical? Not so long ago, increasing numbers of scholars, though far from a majority, were voicing the opinion that David did not and was not. Perhaps the most oft-repeated dictum comes from P. R. Davies, who opined in 1994 that "King David is about as historical as King Arthur."[117] In a book published the year before, J. A. Soggin, after noting that neither David nor Solomon find mention in extrabiblical texts of the ancient Near East, mused, "So is it possible that the reference to David and Solomon and to their empire is simply a later, artificial construction, tending to glorify a past which never existed to compensate for a present which is dull and gray?"[118]

In one of the more telling ironies of recent years, at just about this time the now-famous Tel Dan Stela was discovered, the first and largest fragment in 1993 and two further fragments in 1994.[119] What made the find so spectacular was that David (actually the "house of David") was mentioned in an ancient text outside the Bible for the very first time, or so it seemed at the time; since the discovery, two other possible references to David have been proposed, one in the long-known Mesha Stela (Moabite Stone)[120] and another in the topographical list of Shoshenq I of Egypt.[121] The most significant sections of each of the three inscriptions have been read as follows:

> "[I killed Jeho]ram son of [Ahab] king of Israel,
> and [I] killed [Ahaz]iahu son of [Jehoram kin]g
> of the House of David."
> (Tel Dan Inscription, lines 7b–8a)

> "And the house [of Da]vid dwelt in Horonen
> [. . .] and Kamosh said to me: "Go down!
> Fight against Horonen."
> (Mesha Inscription, lines 31b–32a)

> "highlands/heights of David"
> (Shoshenq I Inscription, numbers 105 + 106)

The Mesha Stela and the Tel Dan Stela are probably from the same general time period, the latter half of the ninth century, and thus a century and a half after David. The Egyptian reference to David, if such it is (Kitchen regards his reading "highlands/heights of David" as highly probable, though not certain), would come from only about fifty years after David!

Not surprisingly, interest in the Tel Dan discovery was immediate and intense, both for those who welcomed its apparent mention of the "house of David" and for those who did not. There was an initial flurry of publication seeking to discredit the reading proposed by Biran and Naveh, or even the genuineness of the find itself. But few scholars today would seek to deny that the "house of David" is indeed mentioned. Interest in the inscription continues to run high, and the future is likely to see even more studies dedicated to its interpretation.[122] But lest the significance of the inscription be overplayed, J. Van Seters reminds us that "there may well have been a David, or there may have been a dynasty which had an eponymous ancestor named David, but that does not immediately suggest everything in the Bible is true."[123] Well, of course not; no archaeological find (or for that matter any number of archaeological finds) could possibly suggest that "everything in the Bible is true." Nor should archaeology ever be called upon to do such a thing (which is one reason we are concerned to resist verificationist tendencies and to take testimony seriously). But if the question is simply whether David ever existed as a historical person, then the force of the Tel Dan inscription, and of the proposed readings of Mesha and Shoshenq, should not be gainsaid. As McKenzie cautiously concludes with respect to the Tel Dan and Mesha inscriptions: "They do seem to accord with the Bible's depiction of David as the founder of the nation and dynasty of Judah—'the house of David.' Based on their testimony, combined with the Bible's, the assumption that David was a historical figure seems reasonable."[124] This rather modest conclusion leads us to our next big question:

How Accurately Does the David of Tradition Reflect the Actual, Historical David?

Before we can attempt to answer this question, we must clarify what we mean by "tradition." If by tradition we have in mind the kind of popular, sentimental picture of David in which he is virtually flawless right up to his sudden collapse into adultery (with Bathsheba) and murder (of Uriah) in 2 Samuel 11, then surely this altogether too-good-to-be-true David is, historically speaking, just that.[125] If, however, we mean the David of the *biblical* tradition, then the answer may be much more positive. The David that emerges from a careful reading of the biblical texts is a complex, very human character. According to Halpern,

> 1 and 2 Samuel furnish a circumstantial character history whose complexity makes even the most sophisticated ancient biography seem like a cartoon by comparison. . . . David, in a word, is human, fully, four-dimensionally, recognizably human. He grows, learns, he travails, he triumphs, and he suffers immeasurable tragedy and loss. He is the first human being in world literature.

In short,

> The [biblical] narrative of David's career is one of the great accomplishments of Israel's culture. . . . From youth to dotage, it follows David as a human being, never fearing to underscore shortcomings, nor to stress peculiarities.[126]

One would think that such accolades might encourage a high level of confidence that the David of *biblical* tradition rather accurately captures the historical David, allowing of course for the necessary selectivity and partiality of all historiographical representation. And indeed, Halpern is quite confident that the books of Samuel, contiguous with the books of Kings (whose "political coverage of the 9th century is meticulous"), must provide a "reasonably trustworthy" account of the tenth century. Only with respect to "particular details" and, especially, the "spin the sources place on the events" is Halpern unconvinced.[127] McKenzie is similarly skeptical. Using the metaphor of a peach, he relegates the "spin" to the status of "pulp," in distinction from the historical "seed": "One must dig through it to reach the seed." But the analogy is not to be over-pressed, warns McKenzie, "because unlike the peach, in historical or biographical research it is sometimes hard to tell the pulp from the seed; it is not always easy to decide which elements of the David story to peel away and which to keep as historical."[128]

A question arises at this point: Why, if Halpern and McKenzie generally trust the biblical narrative with respect to basic facts, do they dismiss the "spin"? For one thing, the biblical narrative seems apologetic, intent on defending David against the charge that he wrested the throne from Saul by subversive action and even murder, perhaps many murders. In other words, the biblical account of David's rise and Saul's demise bears the marks of a "royal apology," a genre widely attested in the ancient Near East and designed to defend the right of a new king to rule, particularly one who gained the throne under unusual or suspicious circumstances.[129] By the Bible's own account, David was in need of defense. The resentment and suspicion of Saul's former supporters did not die quickly. Even as late as Absalom's revolt, we hear Shimei shouting,

> "Out! Out! Murderer! Scoundrel! The LORD has avenged on all of you the blood of the house of Saul, in whose place you have reigned; and the LORD has given the kingdom into the hand of your son Absalom. See, disaster has overtaken you; for you are a man of blood." (2 Sam. 16:7b–8)

Shimei was surely not alone in his indictment of David as a "man of blood," which would doubtless have been the common view among David's enemies. Nor can one deny that David's ascent to the throne was facilitated by the deaths of a number of individuals who stood in the way, Saul and Ishbosheth being only the two most obvious. But who was responsible for these deaths? The biblical writers are clearly at pains to clear David of any complicity. In the two signal instances just mentioned (as in lesser cases), David is far from the action when the deaths occur; he visits swift justice on those who are (or claim to be) responsible; and he mourns for even Saul, who in his later years seemed to think of little else than helping David to an early grave. While the biblical narratives are in many respects quite honest about David's flaws ("never fearing to underscore shortcomings," to recall Halpern's words), they are adamant that he did not claw his way to the top leaving a trail of corpses behind him. Obviously, David's enemies "spun" the events quite differently.

How then should the modern historian adjudicate between these disparate perspectives? Increasingly, modern scholars seem to be siding with David's enemies. Both McKenzie and Halpern make it quite clear that they consider the *historical* David a serial killer, someone you would not like to ask to dinner.[130] In this view they are not alone, having been anticipated by Tomoo Ishida and others. Ishida views David as (borrowing from Gordon's summary)

> an opportunist rebel waging a vigorous guerrilla war against Saul, and so compelling him to make repeated efforts to flush him out of the Judaean wilderness (cf. 1 Sam. 23:15, 25f.; 24:1f.; 26:2). Further evidence of David's usurpatory intent is found in his association with a band of several hundred malcontents (cf. 1 Sam. 22:1f.), in what Ishida calls "David's ambush" on the basis of 1 Samuel 22:8, 13, and in David's willingness to fight on the Philistine side at Gilboa. . . . So jealousy alone, claims Ishida, fails to explain Saul's intense hatred of David; it was the latter's plotting which drove the two so far apart. And, finally, the narrator's "vehement advocacy of David's innocence" in the History is interpreted by Ishida as evidence to the contrary.[131]

Gordon offers brief but telling responses to Ishida's general approach.[132] Here we highlight only two. First, in response to the guerrilla warrior charge, Gordon points out that while "aggression on David's part was not lacking, as the Nabal episode well shows (cf. 1 Sam. 25:13, 21f., 33f.), . . . it is the direction in which it was applied that is significant," and David's aggression, according to the biblical narrative, is never directed at Saul (see, e.g., 1 Sam. 24 and 26). Ishida might argue that this simply demonstrates his point about the vehemence with which the biblical narrator defends David's innocence. Second, then, in response to "Ishida's charge that the author of the History 'doth protest too much' in the matter of David's innocence," Gordon justifiably objects that such a charge "defies refutation by its own terms." Are we to understand that any protest of innocence, especially a vigorous one, is actually a tacit admission of guilt? On such a principle, the biblical narrators are placed in an untenable position; whenever they admit David's guilt, he is of course guilty, and whenever they deny David's guilt, he is likewise guilty (and the more vigorous their defense, the more obvious his guilt). In the end, the "doth protest too much" charge counts for nothing in the absence of other arguments. So, are there other reasons that some modern scholars tend to take the word of David's enemies over the word of the biblical narrators? Some, of course, may simply prefer to believe almost anything other than the Bible. But this stance is certainly not the case with Halpern and McKenzie, who find much in the biblical text that merits credence. So why do they find so suspicious the biblical "spin" on David's rise to power? A closer look at McKenzie's lucid discussion may help us to understand.

At various points in his discussion, McKenzie articulates assumptions and principles that guide his analysis. At the outset, he sets himself the task to write a book that is "strictly historical": "We will read the Bible not for its model of David as a religious hero nor for the artistry of its story about him, but for the historical information about him that it may provide."[133]

Fair enough, unless the subtext is that the "religious" factor is somehow not a historical datum itself and/or that the "artistry" of the story can somehow be bypassed in the extraction of historical information. McKenzie continues:

> My purpose is not simply to retell the biblical story but to recount the events and details of David's life to the extent that they can be surmised from the available sources. This includes matters such as his real character and personality, physical appearance, deeds and accomplishments, and true motives and ambitions.[134]

Again fair enough, unless McKenzie's emphasis on "real character" and "true motives and ambitions" implies an *a priori* assumption that these cannot be as the Bible describes them. Of course, if the religious factor is banned from historical consideration, one may indeed have trouble accepting (or even understanding) the biblical depiction of David's character, motives, and ambition. Add to this McKenzie's appeal to the "principle of analogy," as he defines it, and the case against the biblical portrait of David is assured. Beginning with J. M. Miller's definition of "analogy" as the principle that "holds that the past was basically analogous to the present and to what is known of similar societies and circumstances," McKenzie expands the definition to hold that "people of all time have the same basic ambitions and instincts."[135] While perhaps helpful at one level, such a statement, if elevated to the level of guiding principle, can hardly escape the charge of reductionism—a reductionism apparent, for instance, in McKenzie's comment on the biblical story of Jonathan's abdication in favor of David: "it is simply beyond belief that the crown prince would surrender his right to the throne in deference to David."[136] But is it actually "beyond belief" that Jonathan should behave in such a manner, particularly in the light of the broader picture of Jonathan painted in the biblical text and in the light of the flow of narrative to that point (e.g., Jonathan would by now be aware of his father's rejection and might even be on the lookout for the "neighbor" who would replace him)? Perhaps *most* people would not willingly surrender royal prerogatives, but are we really to believe that "people of all time have the same basic ambitions and instincts"?

A further principle adduced by McKenzie is to read "against the grain" with the aid of "the rule of *cui bono* (Latin for 'For whose benefit?' or 'To whose advantage?')." This rule "holds that the person who benefited from a certain occurrence is most likely the one responsible for it." Given that "David benefited from the deaths of key individuals at crucial junctures in his career," he must have been—according to *cui bono*—the one responsible. Quite apart from the serious question whether such a principle assumes a far too mechanistic view of historical occurrence,[137] it is doubtful in any case how often the application of the rule of *cui bono* would isolate David as the prime suspect. After all, the Philistines benefited from Saul's death on Mount Gilboa, Ishbaal's assassins hoped to benefit from his death, Joab benefited from Abner's death as also from Amasa's and Absalom's, and Absalom benefited (emotionally and politically) from Amnon's death. This review leaves only the cases of Nabal and Uriah. The biblical narrators make no attempt to hide David's culpability for the death of Uriah, and why they would go out of their way to provide David with an alibi in the death of the brutish Nabal is difficult to see, when they apparently felt no compunction about recording David's violent excursions into the countryside—"leaving neither man nor woman alive" (1 Sam. 27:9ff.)—while sojourning in Ziklag. One could still claim that the common benefactor in all the deaths was David, but even this claim would be open to challenge with respect to Abner, Amasa, Amnon, and perhaps others. The point is that nothing is innately implausible in the biblical ascription of motive and means with respect to each death. So again the question presses, why dismiss the biblical construal of events in favor of some other?

In the end the question may come down to "the principle of skepticism," which McKenzie places first and describes as follows:

> By this I mean that when some aspect of the biblical story fits a literary or ideological theme we should be skeptical about its historical value. We have seen that the biblical authors and editors were not interested in history for its own sake but used it as an instructional tool. But history is often molded or bent to accommodate the lesson the writer wishes to teach. When some detail of the David story fits a clear theological agenda it does not necessarily mean that history has been revised. But we do well to be skeptical.[138]

It is of course true that historians—and not just biblical historians—typically select and arrange the historical material at their disposal so as to teach a lesson. But there is a danger when the principle of skepticism is carried too far, particularly if one overlooks McKenzie's qualification in the next-to-last sentence above. Principled skepticism is hardly the approach we adopt in everyday communication, and it is hard to see how it is justified in approaching the biblical texts, unless one has already decided that the biblical text is not to be trusted.

So where does this leave us with respect to the big question before us: *How accurately does the David of tradition reflect the actual, historical David?* Our own approach is to adopt a more robust confidence in the power of testimony to convey true information (including "spin") about the past, unless and until sufficient contrary evidence emerges to undercut that confidence. To recognize that the biblical narratives present a defense of David does not entail the assumption that he was historically unworthy of defense.

How Accurately Does the Biblical Narrative Describe David's Specific Actions?

Without waxing philosophical or theological, answering this question definitively and globally is of course impossible. The best approach from the standpoint of the historian is an inductive one, testing each case on its own merits. Since we have neither time nor need to attempt a full review of David's story here, we can perhaps do no better than to choose one of the more difficult cruces as a test case. Few episodes in the biblical account of David's life have proved as controversial as his encounter, while still in his youth, with the fearsome Goliath (1 Sam. 17). The genuineness of this episode has been questioned on a number of grounds. First and foremost is the simple fact that Goliath's death, though credited to David in 1 Samuel 17, appears to be ascribed to one "Elhanan son of

Jaare-oregim, the Bethlehemite," in 2 Samuel 21:19. So blatant is the apparent contradiction that the "who killed Goliath" question is often cited, like the supposed conflict between Joshua and Judges, as a parade example of the historical unreliability of the Bible. But there is more. David appears to be introduced for the first time in 1 Samuel 17:12 and to be unknown both to Saul and to Abner in 17:55–58, despite the fact that he has already entered Saul's service in 16:18–23. To make matters worse, the LXX attests a much shorter version of the David vs. Goliath episode, one with apparently fewer loose ends and difficulties than the Hebrew MT.

These and scores of other issues related to the David and Goliath story are discussed and debated in a fascinating monograph arising out of a joint scholarly venture involving D. Barthélemy, D. W. Gooding, J. Lust, and E. Tov.[139] With respect to the longer MT/shorter LXX issue, the four scholars divide down the middle, Barthélemy and Gooding defending MT, Lust and Tov preferring LXX. The first two are a Hebrew scholar and classicist, respectively, and the last two historical critic and textual critic. Barthélemy, while favoring MT, nevertheless does not regard it as a unity and senses several sources underlying it. Gooding, on the other hand, more sensitive to literary and rhetorical concerns, finds MT to be a well-crafted unity, with LXX representing a pedantically shortened version resulting from a misunderstanding of the longer text. Lust divides MT source-critically, claiming to discern an older, shorter version of the David and Goliath story in 17:12–31. Tov finds LXX to be a rather literal translation and concludes on this basis that the translators would not likely have omitted large sections of MT; thus he postulates a distinct and shorter Hebrew Vorlage behind LXX.

The procedure followed by the joint research venture involved an initial exchange of position papers, followed by discussions, written rejoinders, surrejoinders, and so forth. Gooding, for instance, contributed four written pieces in the course of the project. That unanimity regarding the sense and even the likely original shape of the story of David and Goliath was not achieved, despite the thoroughness of the project, is suggestive of the difficulty of the issues involved. Clearly, fine scholars can differ on this one.[140] Given that exegesis is an art as well as a science, it should come as no surprise that the propensities and training of the various scholars have a bearing on the exegetical conclusions to which they come. While the word "objectivity" surfaced from time to time in the discussion, in the end it was difficult not to admit that subjective judgment played a part in each scholar's analysis. Perhaps due to the propensities and training of the present writer, Gooding's exegesis seems to offer far and away the best and most convincing reading. In an exegetical tour de force, Gooding demonstrates that "the MT's account represents a coherent story with an intelligible, carefully constructed, detailed, thought-flow."[141] The Greek text, by contrast, appears to have been truncated, perhaps by ancient scholars as troubled as their modern contemporaries by the longer Hebrew text.[142]

To attempt to summarize Gooding's arguments here would take us beyond allowable limits, but we may at least sample them with respect to one of the discrepancies noted above—namely, the apparent double introduction of David. The problem, of course, is that if we assume a sequential relationship between 1 Samuel 16 and 17, as verses like 17:15 and 18:2 seem to suggest, then Saul's question in 17:55 (as he watched David go out to face Goliath), "whose son is this young man?" seems perplexing. As Halpern remarks, this question seems to "presume that David and Saul are strangers (when Saul asks, 'Who is that boy?' for example, and Abner does *not* respond, 'I don't know, but he's always around when we need him')."[143] Should not Saul already have known David, given the current sequence of 1 Samuel 16 and 17 and the fact that David had been brought into Saul's service already in 16:18–23? From a much broader discussion, we may highlight two salient points from Gooding's interpretation. First, it is important to note just what Saul's question was. It was not simply "Who is that?" but

> "*Whose son* is this youth?" (17,55); "Inquire *whose son* the stripling is" (17,56); "*Whose son* are you?" (17,58); "I am *the son* of your servant Jesse . . ." (17,58). Any but the slowest of readers would surely get the point: it is David's father, not David, that Saul is wanting to inform himself about. And it is hardly surprising, Saul . . . has promised, that if any man can defeat the champion, he (Saul) will make his father's house free in Israel (17,25). It is only natural, therefore, that as he sees David go out to battle, and even more as he sees him come in, he should be concerned to find out all he can about David's father and family.[144]

Second, the sense of discrepancy is dependent upon reading 16:18–22 and 17:55–58 in a particular way:

> This discrepancy depends on the insistence that 16,18–22 must mean nothing less than that Saul informed himself fully on everything to do with David's father, and on a similar insistence that 17,55–58 must not mean anything more than that Saul was interested to know the *name* of David's father. Neither insistence is necessary, nor, in the light of the narrative thought-flow, reasonable. Having been supplied by his servants with an acceptable harpist, it was natural for Saul to "request" (i.e. command) his father to let the young man stay at the royal house. It is not true to life to imagine that that means that Saul sent the message directly himself—he would have left that to one of the officers who had found and suggested David. It is not even true to life to imagine that Saul thereafter necessarily remembered the name of David's father, or cared twopence about him, let alone investigated his background, family and all about him. Similarly, it is not true to life to imagine that in 17,55–58 Saul is simply concerned to know the name of David's father. Saul has just promised to give his daughter in marriage to the man who kills Goliath, and to make his father's house free in Israel (17,25). Naturally, when Saul sees David actually going out to meet Goliath, and even more so when he sees him returning triumphant, Saul will be concerned to know not just the name of, but everything about, David's father and the family which, if he keeps his promise, is now to be allied by marriage to the royal family. And we as readers must at this point be made aware that David is of the house of Jesse, for it is the house of Jesse that has at this moment eclipsed the house of Saul in military prowess, and is destined eventually to supplant it as the reigning house.[145]

To Gooding's comments above, we may add one further observation. If we take account of events that, according to the biblical story, preceded even David's initial introduction to Saul's court, then perhaps the intensity of Saul's interest in discovering more about David—now that he sees him demonstrating military daring beyond that of any others in Saul's entourage—may reflect his certain knowledge that he is to be replaced by a "neighbor" better than he (15:28; and cf. 18:8).

If all this begins to sound a bit complex, consider that "a full, real-life story is often more complicated and difficult to understand than abridged stories make out."[146] But in the end, are we not still faced with the devastating discrepancy over the central question, "Who killed Goliath"? Ask the man on the street who killed Goliath, and if he knows any answer at all it will be David. But 2 Samuel 21:19 knows of another: "Then there was another battle with the Philistines at Gob; and Elhanan son of Jaare-oregim, the Bethlehemite, killed Goliath the Gittite, the shaft of whose spear was like a weaver's beam."

The corresponding verse in 1 Chronicles 20:5 neatly resolves the difficulty, by having Elhanan kill not Goliath but "Lahmi the brother of Goliath"—and for that reason the verse is held suspect by most commentators. Some have sought to explain 2 Samuel 21:19 by suggesting that Elhanan might simply be another name for David (cf. 12:25, where Solomon bears the additional name Jedidiah). Halpern notes that "the Targum, the translation of the Bible into Aramaic, identifies Elhanan as David, seeing as both are from Bethlehem (Targ. to 2 Sam. 21:19)." But why then, asks Halpern, would Elhanan be listed among David's heroes? "And why, as the medieval commentator David Kimhi asks, do the killings occur in different places? Elhanan kills Goliath at Gob, whereas David in 1 Samuel kills him at Socho in Ephes Dammim."[147] Further, why would David be called "Elhanan" in verse 19 but consistently "David" elsewhere in the immediate context (vv. 15, 16, 17, 21, 22)? The David-Elhanan equation does not seem to be the solution, and in any case would entail the awkward (and in our view unlikely) assumption that the Chronicler's text is little more than a misguided attempt at harmonization. Various other attempts to resolve the difficulty have been made: Josephus (*Ant.* 7.302) "simply omits the name of Goliath in connection with Elhanan"; others postulate two Goliaths, one downed by David and the other by Elhanan.[148] Halpern represents perhaps a majority of current scholars in assuming that the most likely explanation is that "storytellers displaced the deed from the otherwise obscure Elhanan onto the more famous character, David."[149]

While the limitations of our knowledge of ancient literary practices prevent us from ruling out this possibility entirely,[150] the removal of this most famous episode from David's curriculum vitae would certainly do no good to the reputation of the biblical testimony as a source of historical information. But before considering the matter settled, it is worth investigating a bit further whether 1 Chronicles 20:5 might not, in fact, preserve the more original reading, of which the Samuel reading would be a corruption.[151] In favor of the originality of the

Chronicles reading, the following observations can be made: (1) scholars widely recognize that the Hebrew text of 1 and 2 Samuel is not among the better preserved in the Bible,[152] and at least one obvious instance of textual corruption occurs in 2 Samuel 21:19 (i.e., "Oregim" appears to be an inadvertent duplication of the same word, translated "weaver's," at the end of the verse); (2) "Bethlehemite" in Hebrew differs (in sight and sound) only slightly from "Lahmi" preceded by the Hebrew sign of the direct object (i.e., *bt hlḥmy* and *'t lḥmy*), so that the Samuel reading could have arisen when a scribe (perhaps under the influence of "Elhanan son of Dodo from *Bethlehem*" in 2 Sam. 23:24—the only other Elhanan mentioned in the OT) mistook the rarer "Lahmi" for the more common "Bethlehemite"; (3) with the loss of "Lahmi" as the direct object of the sentence, the phrase "brother of Goliath" may have been corrupted to make Goliath the direct object: A comparison of the two texts in Hebrew shows how slight the differences are.

1 Chronicles 20:5b   *wyk 'lḥnn bn-y'r*   *'t lḥmy* *'ḥy glyt ḥgty w'ṣ ḥnytw kmnwr 'rgym*

2 Samuel 21:19b   *wyk 'lḥnn bn-y'ry* ~~'rgym~~ **byt** *hlḥmy* *'t* *glyt ḥgty w'ṣ ḥnytw kmnwr 'rgym*

While certainty is likely to remain elusive, a reasonable argument can be made for 1 Chronicles 20:5 as the more original reading, in which case the Elhanan problem would be resolved. Given the various options and uncertainties, continuing to cite the Elhanan issue as a basis for drawing sweeping negative conclusions regarding the overall reliability of the biblical testimony seems unwise and unwarranted. This conclusion leads naturally to a final big question.

Is the Biblical Account of David's Rise to Power Historically Plausible?

According to the biblical picture, David, though already anointed to succeed Saul, joins the royal court quite innocently. Having received a glowing recommendation (1 Sam. 16:18), David is brought to court first as a musician, to soothe Saul's rapidly fraying nerves. He soon distinguishes himself in single combat against Goliath and becomes not only a favorite among the general populace but even within Saul's household, to Saul's growing dismay. Eventually Saul's fear and jealousy drive him to seek David's life, and so, after some initial hesitation, David finds it necessary to flee the court and adopt the life of a fugitive, ultimately finding asylum with the Philistine Achish, whom he dupes mercilessly.[153] When on occasion David has opportunity to better his own situation by lifting his hand against Saul, he refrains on the ground that Saul is the Lord's anointed.[154] There is nothing inherently implausible in this basic storyline, or is there?

In his discussion of David's career in Saul's army,[155] McKenzie finds that "the general perspective on David in this section of I Samuel is historically credible," apart, that is, "from David's relationships with Saul's family members."[156] To the biblical claim that Jonathan relinquished robe, armor, sword, bow, and belt—and thereby claim to the throne—to David (1 Sam. 18:1–5), McKenzie remarks (as mentioned earlier), "it is hard to believe that Jonathan would give up his future as king to someone he had just met." Again, "it is hard to imagine Jonathan joining with David in a conspiracy against his father. And it is simply beyond belief that the crown prince would surrender his right to the throne in deference to David."[157] McKenzie is equally perplexed by the biblical depiction of the strained relationship between Saul and David. While 1 Samuel depicts Saul as jealous and paranoid, McKenzie is convinced that "Saul's jealousy can hardly have been the whole story." Indeed,

> There are several elements in the story that suggest a different answer to this question. The first is Saul's fear. The narrative mentions more than once that Saul was afraid of David (18:12, 15, 19). Exactly what was it that he feared? The answer is clear from Saul's words to Jonathan, "As long as the son of Jesse is alive upon the earth, you will not establish your kingship" (20:31). Saul fears that David will thwart him from establishing a dynasty by preventing Jonathan from becoming king. The way David would do this is to become king himself. But there is more. The stories make it clear that Saul is not just afraid for his heir but for himself. In other words, his fear is that David will lead a revolt and overthrow him as king.[158]

Reading "against the grain," McKenzie speculates that "the ultimate reason for Saul's pursuit of David was a failed coup attempt. All the ingredients were present."[159]

The biblical narrative offers an entirely different explanation of Saul's fear (i.e., he has been rejected as king and will be replaced by one better than he),[160] so why would McKenzie prefer the failed coup theory? Part of the answer may have to do with his understanding of what the genre "apology" implies: "an apology by definition is not objective but seeks to give a distorted idea of the events of the past and especially of the causes behind them."[161] By this measure, the biblical narrative, since it clearly includes an "apology," or defense, of David, is *by definition* distorted, and one must look elsewhere for the true story. Add to this general orientation McKenzie's principles of historical reconstruction discussed earlier (analogy, *cui bono*, etc.), and his conclusions may follow quite seamlessly and logically. As we argued earlier, however, there is a danger of reductionism in McKenzie's principles. Does not the principle of analogy as defined—"people of all time have the same basic ambitions and instincts"—run the risk of excluding from history all exceptional individuals behaving in exceptional ways? And might not the principle of *cui bono*—who benefits?—run the risk of implying that good fortune never simply happens but, rather, is always the result of the machinations of those who ultimately benefit? (Never mind the fact that the text's own explanation of David's good fortune is that "the LORD was with him" [e.g., 1 Sam. 18:12, 14, 28].) Taken together, might not such principles suggest, for example, that persons in power have always arrived there the same way? Or that if Saul is afraid of David, David (and not some other circumstance) must have given cause? There is a measure of truth and wisdom in McKenzie's principles, of course, and he would probably not want to endorse them presented as baldly as above, but it is hard to avoid the impression that they have tipped the scales against the biblical narrative and in favor of the coup theory. Our own contention is that the biblical narrative, in its current sequence and configuration, offers a perfectly plausible explanation of Saul's and Jonathan's disparate reactions to David. Some key observations are as follows.

As noted earlier, 1 Samuel 15 recounts the definitive rejection of King Saul.[162] After 15:28 Saul is no longer king *de jure*, though he continues to be king *de facto* for some years.[163] Moreover, Saul has been warned that a "neighbor" who is his better will assuredly replace him. Just this fact alone goes a long way towards explaining Saul's jealousy and fear of David, especially as he is of no mind to accept his rejection as meekly as Eli had accepted his. Rather than Eli's "It is the LORD; let him do what seems good to him" (1 Sam. 3:18), Saul's every concern is to hold on to the throne: "what more can he have but the kingdom?" (1 Sam. 18:8); "as long as the son of Jesse lives upon the earth, neither you nor your kingdom shall be established. Now send and bring him to me, for he shall surely die" (20:31). So much for Saul's reaction to David. What about Jonathan's? If, as seems likely, Jonathan knew of Saul's *de jure* forfeiture of the throne to the "neighbor" who was to come, is it not entirely plausible (if we take a true-to-life approach) that he would have been on the lookout for such a one? He may even have begun laying aside the prerogatives of crown prince prior to David's bursting onto the scene in 1 Samuel 17. A remarkable fact—though seldom remarked upon—is that Jonathan is entirely absent in chapter 17. Where is the brave warrior of 1 Samuel 14? Are we really to imagine that he is cowering before the Philistine giant, like Saul and the rest of his men? Might it not be more true to life to suppose that Jonathan is simply standing back, so that the "neighbor" may emerge? Allowing that Jonathan is an exceptional individual, a man of no less faith and character than David, nothing is impossible, nor even implausible, in his willing abdication to David. Most people might not do such a thing, but the biblical narrative, and not least David himself (2 Sam. 1:26), is at pains to say that Jonathan is not like most people.[164]

What then of the big question before us: *Is the biblical account of David's rise to power plausible historically, or are there insurmountable implausibilities?* While we have only been able to consider one issue—how best to explain Saul's fear of David and Jonathan's deference—this approach has allowed us to contrast a modern theory (failed coup) with the narrative's own explanation (Saul's rejection in favor of the "neighbor" who would arise). Both offer viable explanations of what could have happened historically, but in the end we see little reason to prefer the modern theory over the biblical depiction. Our sounding in one stretch of text may encourage confidence in the rest, but it does not guarantee it. Now, as then, there will likely continue to be competing viewpoints on how David came to the throne. In the next section, we consider issues of a different sort: how plausible is the biblical claim that David established his capital in Jerusalem? How plausible is the notion of a Davidic (and later Solomonic) empire?

DAVID'S KINGDOM: 2 SAMUEL 1–10

As 2 Samuel opens, the defense of David continues (specifically with respect to the deaths of Abner and Ishbosheth). But now that Saul is dead, David's momentum towards the throne gains intensity. In 2 Samuel 2 he is anointed king of Judah, over which he reigns for seven and a half years in Hebron. Bitter conflict exists between the "house of Saul" and "house of David" (2 Sam. 2:8–3:1) but by 2 Samuel 5:4 David finds himself king also over Israel. Following his regnal formula in 5:4–5, David's first recorded accomplishment is the capture of the Jebusite city, Jerusalem (5:6–14). David's second recorded accomplishment, not insignificantly, is the defeat of the Philistines (5:17–25). In 2 Samuel 6, David manages, after some costly missteps, to bring the Ark of the Covenant to Jerusalem, where he establishes his capital. Or did he?

The Jerusalem Question

At the heart of the debate over the historical plausibility of a Davidic kingdom as described by the Bible is the archaeology of Jerusalem. If the biblical accounts of the tenth-century kingdoms of David (and Solomon) are accurate, so the argument goes, should one not expect to find considerable material remains from the tenth century in Jerusalem? This question, logical enough on its face, is often posed by revisionist historians who then proceed to argue that, since by their reckoning few if any tenth-century remains have been discovered in Jerusalem, the biblical accounts must be legendary at best, or simply fictional retrojections from a much later age.

For those not already inclined in revisionist directions, however, a first reflex when hearing such an argument is to recall the oft-quoted dictum that "absence of evidence is not evidence of absence." The instances of singular finds, such as the Merneptah Stela and now the Tel Dan Inscription, should be sufficient to caution against drawing sweeping conclusions from what has *not* been found.[165] But more can be said regarding the archaeology of Jerusalem.

The two most significant modern excavations in Jerusalem were conducted by Kathleen Kenyon in the 1960s and Yigal Shiloh in the 1970s and 1980s. Final reports on these excavations are currently being prepared by Margreet Steiner (along with H. J. Franken of the University of Leiden) for Kenyon and by Jane Cahill for Shiloh. Curiously, the conclusions to which Steiner and Cahill come could not be more different. Steiner,[166] citing the paucity of archaeological evidence for a city or even a town at the site of Jerusalem in the Late Bronze Age and Iron Age I, insists that there simply "was no city here for King David to conquer," that "the United Monarchy . . . is not a historical fact," and that "the history of Jerusalem is going to have to be rewritten."[167] Cahill[168] finds Steiner's historical conclusions "startling" and insists that they are simply "not substantiated by the archaeological record." On the basis of preliminary reports by both Kenyon and Shiloh, Cahill shows that at least four separate areas in the City of

David exhibit "stratified remains containing architecture, pottery and other arti-facts attributable to the Late Bronze Age."[169]

Nadav Na'aman joins Cahill in opposing Steiner's conclusions. Noting the "unqualified certainty" with which Steiner insists that archaeologically there is no evidence of a "town, let alone a city" of Jerusalem in the Late Bronze Age, Na'a-man asks how it is that "this gap in occupation escaped the two modern archae-ologists [Kenyon and Shiloh] who directed excavations on the spur south of the Temple Mount known as the City of David."[170] Na'aman adds a helpful perspec-tive in the debate by citing the case of fourteenth-century Jerusalem, for which there is little archaeological evidence but which is clearly attested in the Amarna archives. Six letters are written to one of the pharaohs of Egypt by one ʿAbdi-Ḥeba,[171] who is called "mayor" of Jerusalem (*Urusalim*), who lived in a house in Jerusalem, and who dispatched "exceptionally rich caravans to the pharaoh."[172] From this contemporary documentary evidence alone, it is apparent that Jerusalem was a significant city in the fourteenth-century, even holding sway over other towns; one letter explicitly mentions "a town belonging to Jerusalem."[173] But archaeological excavations at the site have turned up little that would have hinted at Jerusalem's fourteenth-century importance. A similar situation exists, according to Na'aman, with respect to Taanach and Megiddo. The point is that

> apparent discrepancies between documentary evidence and excavation results should caution against too hasty conclusions on the basis of negative archaeological evidence. The survival of archaeological material depends on many variables. The admitted paucity of Late Bronze Age remains recovered from Jerusalem may be explained as the result of an uninterrupted conti-nuity of settlement for thousands of years. . . . The Late Bronze Age build-ings in Jerusalem were utterly destroyed by later building activity and their stones robbed and reused, so that only fragments of the former Canaanite city survived the destruction of later periods.[174]

But surely the pottery evidence should resolve the question. Unlike building stones and timbers, which are often cleared away and/or reused in later con-struction (thus removing evidence of earlier structures), broken bits of pottery usually remain where they fall and are quite durable. Why then is the pottery evi-dence not more conclusive? Several comments are in order. First, more pottery evidence for Late Bronze and Iron Age I occupations in Jerusalem does survive than some scholars have acknowledged.[175] Second, neither Kenyon nor Shiloh considered the tenth-century significance of Jerusalem to be in any doubt, so they made no special effort to note and publish pottery evidence related to that ques-tion.[176] Third, some of the most important areas associated with the reigns of David and Solomon according to the Bible—such as the Temple Mount—are closed to excavation. Thus, they remain *terra incognita*.[177]

In sum, while Jerusalem may well be "the most excavated city in the world,"[178] the excavations themselves and the nature of the site suggest that our expecta-tions of what can and will be found should be modest. Halpern correctly observes that "one cannot judge from the vagaries of material survival and recovery alone," especially "in a site such as Jerusalem, where monumental construction especially in the Persian through Herodian periods was repeatedly carried down to bedrock, and where the overburden of modern settlement and political constraints prohibit extensive soundings."[179] The fact is, as Dever notes, that "few 10th-century archaeological levels have been *exposed* in the deeply stratified and largely inaccessible ruins of ancient Jerusalem, so the paucity of finds means nothing."[180] For many reasons, then, the results of archaeological excavation in Jerusalem may fall short of "verifying" the biblical picture to everyone's satisfaction. But surely, even on the basis of logic alone, the notion that a site as defensible, strategically located, and well supplied with water and arable land as Jerusalem should have remained unoccupied for very long hardly commends itself.[181]

The Empire Question

Broadening our discussion beyond the confines of Jerusalem, we encounter another hotly debated question: Is the notion of a Davidic "empire" historically plausible or, as some revisionist scholars have claimed, an anachronistic retrojection by scribes familiar with the Persian empire?[182] The answer to this question depends, of course, on what we mean by "empire." If we have in mind something analogous to the Egyptian empire, or the Assyrian, or the Persian, or the Roman, then the answer will have to be no. The assertion that David ruled over such an empire is simply not historically credible. But the point to notice here is that the Bible never ascribes an empire of that sort to David in the first place. Only disregard for the actual data of the Bible could ever lead to such a notion. So what kind of Davidic empire does the Bible describe?

In the summary of David's victories in 2 Samuel 8, we read of his "subduing" ("humbling" Hiphil of *knʿ*) the Philistines (v. 1); of his subjecting to tributary status the Moabites (v. 2), Zobahites (vv. 3–4), and Arameans (vv. 5–8); and of his receiving congratulatory greetings from Toi, the king of Hamath, who sent gifts by the agency of his son Joram (vv. 9–10).[183] Verses 11–12 add the Edomites, Ammonites, and Amalekites to the list of peoples "subdued" (Piel of *kbš*) by David—the reference to the Edomites perhaps anticipating verses 13–14, to the Ammonites anticipating 2 Samuel 10–12, and to the Amalekites recalling 2 Samuel 1:1, and so on. A close analysis of this summary section in 2 Samuel 8 suggests some interesting distinctions. While the Philistines are "humbled," no mention is made of their becoming "servants" of David nor of their sending tribute. By contrast, Moab and Aram are explicitly reduced to tributary status, as are also, it appears, Edom and Ammon. Hamath welcomes David's defeat of Aram and apparently allies itself to David without the necessity of conquest. This description suggests a state of affairs in which David's "empire" comprised territories over which he gained political control by various means and exercised dominion in different ways and to varying degrees. How best to describe the different levels of political control is open to discussion,[184] but the general concept of a multitiered empire seems appropriate to the time of David, as contrasted with anachronistic notions imported from the Persian or any other later period. Reflecting on what counted as "political control" in the Levant of the late second millennium, M. Liverani writes:

> The physical presence of the king in a remote country is sufficient (although necessary) to demonstrate his political control thereon. A victorious raid, even a pacific one, an expedition aiming at knowledge more than at conquest, is the [only] required symbolic achievement—not an effective administrative organization.[185]

When we compare the specific biblical claims with what, according to Liverani, constituted political control in the late second millennium, it is difficult not to agree with Na'aman that "there is nothing impossible about the Biblical description of the extent of David's kingdom, even applying modern concepts of political control."[186]

A recent study by K. Kitchen further enhances the credibility of the biblical picture of David's empire—as defined.[187] Kitchen contends that the period of David and Solomon, although clearly a time of "Great-Power-eclipse" (i.e., some recession in the case of Egypt and Assyria and collapse in the case of Hatti), was *not* a "'dark age' throughout the ancient world," as claimed for instance by J. M. Miller.[188] Rather, the period saw the temporary flourishing of "mini-empires" comprising *heartland* along with *conquered territories* and *subject-allies*.[189] Drawing on biblical and twelfth-to-tenth-century extrabiblical evidence (especially Hittite hieroglyphic and Mesopotamian cuneiform texts), Kitchen distinguishes three such "mini-empires" in the Levant in the Late Bronze Age—namely, Tabal in southeast Anatolia; Carchemish on both sides of the west bend of the Euphrates in north Syria; and subsequently Aram-Zobah, beginning in its homeland in the Beqa' valley and extending by conquests northeastward towards the Euphrates and southward towards Maacah and Geshur and including subject allies in Aram-Damascus to the east and Hamath to the north.[190] Given the presence of these three mini-empires in the period in question, could there not have been a fourth—that is, the relatively short-lived but territorially extensive mini-empire of the Israelite United Monarchy under David and Solomon? Kitchen concludes:

> David's realm thus embraced (1) the heartlands of Judah and Israel (but not Philistia), (2) the conquered Transjordanian kingdoms of Edom, Moab, and Ammon, plus Aram-Damascus and Zobah as tributary vassals, and (3) Hamath (up to the Euphrates) as a subject-ally. This fourth mini-empire was not destined to last too long, either: a maximum of fifteen to twenty years under David (founded in his last two decades) and probably not much more than forty to fifty years at its full extent. It fell apart by the last decades of Solomon's reign (Hadad in Edom, Rezon in Damascus [cutting off access to Hamath], etc.). Thereafter, the age of mini-empires in the Levant was over. For the century ca. 950–850 BC, nobody local was supreme in the Levant, although Aram-Damascus tried its hand repeatedly; from 850 BC

onward, growing Assyrian control from Mesopotamia effectively put a practical stop to all but the most local aspirations. They and the Neo-Babylonians eventually eliminated not only the aspirations but nearly all of the local kingdoms themselves.[191]

Bearing in mind these comparisons and convergences, we may conclude that the notion of a Davidic empire, as biblically defined, is entirely plausible, and the notion of it being an anachronistic retrojection from the postexilic period can be safely laid to rest. This conclusion is not the same as claiming that the Davidic empire has been proven, but imagining what might constitute proof is difficult in any case, once the biblical narrative is set aside.

DAVID'S FAMILY AND SUCCESSOR: 2 SAMUEL 11–24

While 2 Samuel 1:1–5:5 focuses largely on David's political weal, much of the remainder of 2 Samuel focuses on his familial woes following upon his sins of adultery and murder in the Bathsheba episode of 2 Samuel 11. As intriguing, if heartbreaking, as the later chapters are, they must not be allowed to eclipse the extremely important events recounted in 2 Samuel 5:6–10:19. These chapters

> summarize the transactions, both political and theological, by which David's rule is established. Chapter 7 records the highly significant "Davidic promise," or "dynastic oracle," in which the Lord, after refusing David's offer to build him a "house" (temple), promises David that he, the Lord, will build David a "house" (dynasty) that will endure forever. This "Davidic promise" establishes, beyond all doubt, that the purposes of God for the house of David are sure. But it in no way implies that David or his descendants may not forfeit some of the temporal benefits of their privileged position if they fall into sin.[192]

Sadly, the reader of 2 Samuel does not have to wait long to begin to witness the consequences of sin—David's sin. In his book *David, the Chosen King*, R. A. Carlson divides the life of David into two parts, the period under the blessing and the period under the curse.[193] While "curse" may, in an absolute sense, be too strong a word—David is, after all, forgiven (2 Sam. 12:13)—it is nevertheless true that following his adultery with Bathsheba and his orchestrated murder of her husband, Uriah, David is left to witness his own sins of adultery and murder replicated in the lives of his children. As wretched and disturbing as is the Bathsheba episode, the one that comes after it is no better: the rape of Tamar by her half-brother Amnon, David's oldest son (2 Sam. 13). The sense of wretchedness is only exacerbated by David's inaction when he hears of it: "When King David heard of all these things, he became very angry" (13:21). That David was furious at Amnon's violation of Tamar is understandable; that he took no disciplinary action is not. The LXX and the Dead Sea Scroll (4QSam[a]), followed by NRSV, add, "but he would not hurt Amnon because he was his eldest son and he loved him." Whether or not this sentence is original, it may accurately highlight a weakness in David's handling of his sons that is seen also in 14:24 and 33 (where David seems incapable of either punishing or truly reconciling with Absalom) and in 1 Kings 1:6 (where David is reported as never crossing Adonijah). Perhaps David felt morally crippled by his own adultery and homicide, but it nevertheless remained his duty as father and as king to administer "justice and equity to all his people" (2 Sam. 8:15). His failure to do so with respect to Amnon leaves Absalom, Tamar's full brother, to fume and ultimately to take matters into his own hands. Thus, David's passivity contributes in due course to the greatest political and domestic crisis of his life, namely, Absalom's rebellion (which, notably, is fueled by Absalom's complaint that David has withheld *justice* [cf. 15:4–6]).

The tale of sin and consequence told in 2 Samuel 11–20 has a true-to-life feel about it, but is it historical? Again, we may call on McKenzie for a reading against the grain. McKenzie's reading begins with the removal of the Bathsheba episode, which he regards as having been secondarily inserted in its present context (more on this shortly). That done, McKenzie is able to postulate quite a different story in which David is depicted not so much as sinful and suffering the consequences (the biblical view) as tenderhearted to a fault. His sons get away with murder, literally, and if David is to blame at all, the fault is only that he loves too much to take action. This "stress on David's gentleness is apologetic," of course, and "a modern historian evaluating these stories will doubt that a man with David's political savvy and longevity was quite so gentle with his enemies as the writer describes."[194] In fact, "David likely was a party to Amnon's assassination,"[195] and to Absalom's death as well. "David maintained power in the same way he had attained it in the first place—by removing anyone who was in his way. This included his two oldest sons, Amnon and Absalom, both of whom came to violent ends when they stood to replace their father."[196] The linchpin of this imaginative reading is, as noted above, the removal of the Bathsheba episode. We must look more closely, therefore, at the grounds for its removal.

McKenzie's conviction that the Bathsheba episode "(2 Samuel 11–12) must have been added after Dtr had finished his history" begins with the observation that the Deuteronomist "could hardly have known the story of David's sin with Bathsheba and still held him up as a model king who always 'did what was right in Yahweh's eyes.'"[197] This observation is curious, however, since the very next phrase in the verse quoted by McKenzie (i.e., 1 Kgs. 15:5) reads, "except in the matter of Uriah the Hittite." Does this not presuppose precisely the Bathsheba episode that the Deuteronomist "could hardly have known about"? Van Seters, whom McKenzie follows in this argument, dispatches with the inconvenient reference to Uriah by simply asserting that "it is so incongruous to the praise of David that it is surely a later gloss."[198] Van Seters expunges not just this half-verse from his Deuteronomistic History, but the entire "Court History" (2 Sam. 9–20 and 1 Kgs. 1–2), on the grounds that "there is scarcely anything exemplary in David's actions in the whole of the Court History." For Van Seters, then, the whole of the "Court History is a post-Dtr addition to the history of David from the postexilic period."[199] McKenzie is apparently not willing to go this far with Van Seters, but one wonders if both are not guilty of imposing a simplistic schema on rather more sophisticated literature and then removing whatever bits do not readily fit the schema. In a telling rebuttal of Van Seters's thesis that the Court History (or Succession Narrative) "is an essay on the delegitimation of the kingship of David and his house," Gordon demonstrates how "Van Seters' approach to SN fails because contrary evidence is overlooked in his zeal to make the text conform to a particular theory."[200] The central point is as follows:

> If it is true that David is "the king after the Deuteronomist's own heart," to use Gerhard von Rad's fine coinage, then it is still necessary to inquire in what sense this applies before accepting Van Seters' judgment on the incompatibility of SN with the Deuteronomistic History (DH) in its portrayal of David. Above all, we may ask whether there is any difficulty in the standard doctrine that the Deuteronomist(s) could have regarded David as a seriously flawed individual and yet as having satisfied the basic deuteronomistic requirement of eschewal of pagan cults and loyalty to Yahweh. A distinction between David and Solomon is made on this basis in 1 Kgs 11:4–6, and the cultic criterion is, as is well known, regularly applied to the kings of Judah especially, in the books of Kings. . . . In other respects, the perspective of the Deuteronomist(s) may be "from the ground, from below Olympus, from amongst the participants," but as long as David supplies model obedience in the realm of cult he may emerge even from SN as a deuteronomistic paragon.[201]

If David were required to be without flaw or failure in order to merit the kinds of commendations he receives throughout the Deuteronomistic History, how many other episodes would have to be eliminated elsewhere in the books of Samuel? Gordon notes, for example, that "the lying schemer of 1 Samuel 21, who later confesses that he has brought about the deaths of the priests at Nob (2 Sam. 22:22), is a paler-than-usual messianic prototype."[202] In the end, McKenzie's stated reason for relegating the Bathsheba episode to secondary status is unconvincing. But later in the book he adds another.

The key verse in this instance is 2 Samuel 10:2, where David mentions the kindness that had been shown him by Nahash, king of the Ammonites. McKenzie assumes that, since "there is no other interaction between Nahash and David in the Bible that would qualify as this act of loyalty," David must be referring to the provisions with which Nahash supplied him during his flight from Absalom (2 Sam. 17:27–29). Thus, 2 Samuel 10:2 must be referring *back* to that time and to that act of kindness. Inasmuch as 10:2 is, in McKenzie's view, part of the battle account (2 Sam. 10:1–11:1a + 12:26–31) in which the Bathsheba episode is embedded, "this means that David's affair with Bathsheba probably took place after Absalom's revolt rather than before it."[203]

Does this argument fare any better than the earlier one? First of all, we are presented with an argument from silence: "there is no other interaction . . . in the Bible that would qualify as. . . ." Arguments from silence are not to be dismissed out of hand, but before their claims are granted, other possibilities must be considered. If Nahash is capable of showing David kindness on one occasion, might he not do so on more than one occasion, even if these other instances are not recorded in the Bible? Gordon postulates one such instance: "The *Nahash* whose death marked the end of friendly relations between Israel and Ammon was, presumably, the Ammonite king whom Saul defeated at Jabesh-gilead (1 Sa. 11). The cordiality between David and Nahash may, indeed, be not improbably traced to the time when David was on the run from Saul."[204] This conjecture seems perfectly reasonable, and one that effectively removes the ground from beneath McKenzie's rather larger conjecture that the Bathsheba episode followed rather than preceded Absalom's revolt.

One further argument mentioned by McKenzie[205] is that while Nathan's speech to David in 2 Samuel 12 alludes to events in chapters 13–20 ("the sword shall never depart from your house" [12:10]; "I will raise up trouble against you from within your own house" [12:11]), the reverse is not the case; "there is no allusion to David's adultery with Bathsheba in the account of Absalom's revolt." But what of 16:21–22 (also mentioned by McKenzie), which recounts Absalom's violation of David's concubines "upon the roof . . . in the sight of all Israel"? Might not these be allusions not only to Nathan's pronouncement that David's wives would be taken "in the sight of this very sun . . . before all Israel" (12:11–12) but also, not without irony, to the rooftop where it all began (11:2)? Of course, one might object that the allusion is in the other direction, but how could one know this? Furthermore, if editors at some point felt free to insert the entire Bathsheba episode into a foreign context and thereby cause the subsequent narrative to be read in an entirely different way, why would they have hesitated to insert allusions back to this (now determinative) episode, if they had felt them necessary? If, on the other hand, they did not feel the need of such back references, then why should we? In the end, the conjecture that the Bathsheba episode has been inserted secondarily must be judged not only unproven but unlikely.

At one point, at least, McKenzie himself seems unsure. He points out that "despite the general popularity of Absalom's revolt, most of David's court remained loyal to him." But there was one notable exception, "the renowned advisor Ahithophel." Why might this have been? McKenzie reasons as follows:

> The account in 2 Samuel does not explain why Ahithophel turned against David and went over to Absalom's side. He may have borne a personal grudge against David because of the Bathsheba affair. Bathsheba was the daughter of Eliam (2 Sam. 11:5), and Ahithophel had a son named Eliam, who was among David's best warriors (2 Sam. 15:12; 23:34). If these two Eliams were the same person, which is likely since both passages refer to Ahithophel as "the Gilonite," then Bathsheba was Ahithophel's granddaughter. Assuming the order of events in 2 Samuel, Ahithophel may have acted against David as revenge for Uriah's death and the humiliation of Bathsheba.[206]

But is it not precisely the order of events in 2 Samuel, particularly with respect to the Bathseba episode, that (according to the theory) we are not allowed to assume? If McKenzie's line of reasoning in the above paragraph is sound—and it appears to be, as numerous commentators will attest—then the Bathsheba episode *must have preceded* Absalom's revolt, which takes us back to the ordering of events as attested in 2 Samuel and to the more traditional understanding of David's familial struggles as finding their initial footholds in his own moral failure. If this all-too-human David seems out of keeping with the David of popular tradition, it is at least fully in keeping with the David of biblical tradition.

The final days of David's life are recorded not in 2 Samuel but in 1 Kings 1:1–2:11. Here we meet not just a human David, but a David beset with all the frailties and uncertainties of old age. This king whose blood could warm at the very sight of Bathsheba is now incapable of warming up at all, even with one of the most beautiful young virgins of the land in his arms (1:1–4). Verse 4 tells us that David did not know her (sexually), leaving us to wonder whether this situation was the result of moral strength or, as seems much more likely, physical weakness. Adonijah, next in line for the throne now that Amnon and Absalom are dead, apparently views it as the latter and seizes upon the occasion of an impotent potentate as an opportunity to launch his own bid for the throne (vv. 5–6). Several notables join him—Joab, Abiathar—but others demur—Zadok, Benaiah, Nathan, David's special guard, and so on (vv. 7–8). Why did some join and others refuse? And why, when Adonijah invited all his brothers, the king's sons, to En Rogel to sacrifice, did he not invite Solomon (vv. 9–10)? These opening verses seem almost designed to raise questions in the reader's mind, perhaps as a sort of signal to the reader that not everything will be obvious in the episodes that follow. Readers will need to attend closely to the story as it unfolds, even (perhaps especially) to those details that might seem insignificant, if they are to grasp the story's full meaning.[207]

Perhaps the biggest question of all has to do with the succession: Had David, in fact, designated Solomon to be his successor, or did Nathan and Bathsheba simply succeed in a conspiracy to convince the doddering old man that he had? Opinions among commentators vary widely, some saying one thing, some another, and perhaps we shall never know the answer for sure. Maybe that inconclusiveness is part of the point. But a few hints in the text suggest that Solomon's designation to succeed David was not simply a thought planted by others in the old king's feeble mind on the occasion of Adonijah's bid. In the immediate context is the fact that Solomon, among all the king's sons, is the only one not invited by Adonijah to En Rogel (v. 10). Why would Adonijah exclude Solomon? There is also the matter of Nathan's assumption that Adonijah's rise will immediately place Bathsheba's and Solomon's lives in danger (v. 12). Why should this be so for Solomon any more than for the other brothers? Looking ahead a bit, we have what Gordon describes as "the clearest affirmation of the legitimacy of Solomon's kingship . . . put into the mouth of Adonijah in 1 Kgs 2:15."[208] Speaking to Bathsheba, "He said, 'You know that the kingdom was mine, and that all Israel expected me to reign; however, the kingdom has turned about and become my brother's, for it was his from the LORD.'" And looking back to the notice that the Lord loved Solomon and gave him the name Jedidiah at his birth (2 Sam. 12:24–25), we have an "unambiguous statement of divine approval that puts Solomon in a unique position among David's sons as one specially favored from birth."[209]

These hints combine to suggest that Solomon gained the throne not by treachery and deceit, but by prior appointment. It will be his story that occupies our attention in the next chapter.

CONCLUSION

If, having arrived at the end of this chapter on the Early Monarchy, the biblically literate reader is left wondering about the many episodes and events recounted in 1 and 2 Samuel that have not been discussed or even mentioned, we may offer by way of explanation that our intent has not been to paraphrase the biblical material, nor even to rehearse it in full. Instead, we have thought it worthwhile to inquire if and to what degree the biblical text is deserving of credence insofar as it purports to offer a historical account of the transition from tribal league to monarchy. Even with respect to this question, much more could (and perhaps should) be said, were space not an issue. But we have tried to touch on a sampling, at least, of the main issues. In this task, we have been much helped by recent studies from McKenzie, Halpern, and others, even if our discussion, by the nature of the case, often focuses on areas in which we would approach matters differently.

What have we found? Whether it be the story of Samuel as a transitional figure on the eve of the monarchy, or the story of Saul's faltering rise to become Israel's first king, or the story of David's early achievements and his eventual replacement of Saul, or the story of David's moral failure and its consequences, we have discovered stories that not only are wonderfully told but also have a ring of truth about them. Our attempted readings have found them more coherent, more true to life, and thus more plausible historically than earlier readings have often done. This is not to deny, of course, that the books of Samuel comprise a defense, or an apology, of David. But we do not find this fact alone to be grounds for distrusting the stories. One must understand, of course, "where they are coming from"; they have a perspective, a "spin." But they are not on this account necessarily false. Nor do they necessarily present a distorted portrait, or even a whitewash. After all, "the Bible never denies or downplays David's humanity."[210]

Turning to other considerations sometimes thought to tell against the historical plausibility of the stories told in Samuel, we touched on two of the larger questions: whether Jerusalem could have been a city worth conquering in David's day, and whether David could have established an "empire" such as the Bible ascribes to him. In both cases, our investigations encouraged greater, rather than lesser, confidence in the historical plausibility of the biblical picture.

In the end we found little reason to question the value, for the historian, of the biblical testimony to Israel's transition to kingship. Both 1 and 2 Samuel and 1 and 2 Chronicles are works of historiography with their own *purposes* (which go beyond mere historical reportage) and with their own *perspectives*. Other perspectives on events are, of course, possible. David's enemies, for instance, clearly took a far more jaundiced view of his rise to power than the biblical texts do. But this fact does not discredit the biblical texts; it is, after all, precisely from the biblical texts that we are able to reconstruct the view "from the other side" in the first place. And while it makes an interesting exercise to read against the grain, to "spin" David as his enemies must have done, in the final analysis it falls to the reader to decide which spin is more believable, that of David's foes or that of his friends.

Chapter 9

The Later Monarchy: Solomon

With the death of David we pass into the period of the later monarchy—the period during which David's son Solomon ruled over Israel; during which Solomon's kingdom was split into two parts, north and south, that came to be called Israel and Judah; and during which both parts of Israel were ultimately absorbed into the great empires of the day, centered on Assyria and then on Babylon. Before we come to the description of the opening of the period itself, however, we must deal briefly with two preliminary matters: the nature of our sources and the problem of chronology.

SOURCES FOR THE LATER ISRAELITE MONARCHY

By far the greatest amount of information we possess about the period of the later Israelite monarchy comes from two biblical texts: 1–2 Kings and 1–2 Chronicles. These texts provide two particular portraits of the past painted by authors of different times and with different motivations for their work. For reasons already stated in part 1 of this book, and especially in the later part of chapter 4, we regard neither the particularity of the portraits, nor their date of composition, nor the differing motivations that evidently lie behind them, to be essentially problematic for the person interested in the history of Israel in this period. These features of our sources certainly do not cause us greater difficulty, from a historian's point of view, than the difficulty with which we are faced in the case of other sources for this period that derive from Assyria, Babylon, or Israel's nearer neighbors.[1] Our approach to the biblical texts that describe the period of the later monarchy therefore is not that of some recent historiography, which has sought (on highly questionable grounds) to predesignate as "historical" and "unhistorical" this or that aspect of the biblical stories, often with an eye to the allegedly more objective portrait of the past that extrabiblical sources of information offer. We rather take our biblical stories seriously in their entirety as artfully constructed witnesses to the past, examining and understanding their claims about that past in the context of such other evidence as genuinely bears upon the period, and coming thus to a rounded view of the period in which all the evidence, textual and otherwise, finds its proper place. The following narrative is thus not the work of "a cautious historian," inclined to ignore the biblical text altogether if only more "convincing" sources of information were available elsewhere.[2] Hopefully the narrative presents, rather, the work of a *reasonable* historian inclined to look at all the evidence and make a judgment about how it all fits together.

Both of our major sources, as well as all of our minor ones, obviously have their own particular nature, which must be taken seriously in our handling of them. First–Second Kings forms part of a long history of Israel that stretches all the way back to creation and is heavily influenced, at least from the end of Numbers onwards, by the book of Deuteronomy.[3] The focus of 1–2 Kings in particular is overall upon the failure of the Israelite monarchy to govern the people justly and in accordance with the divine will, with the ultimate consequence that Israel is absorbed into foreign empires. The account is organized via a systematically worked-out framework, already partially evident in the case of Solomon (1 Kgs. 3:2–3; 11:41–43) but certainly obvious by the point at which we begin to read of the divided kingdoms, which indeed enables the authors to achieve the difficult task of writing about two separate kingdoms while maintaining the sense that this account is the story of one people. The framework characteristically informs the reader when, in relation to the reigning king of the other kingdom (Israel or Judah), a certain monarch came to the throne, how long he reigned, and the name of his capital city. We receive information about his death/burial and his successor, and indicators of where to look for further information about him. The books offer an evaluation of him in terms of his religious policy. In the case of Judean kings, we read the name of his mother and his age at his accession to the throne. A good example of the full set of "regnal formulae" (as the various elements of the framework are often called) is to be found in 1 Kings 22:41–43, 45, 50. Aside from this framework, we also find in 1 Kings 12–2 Kings 25 various narratives concerning particular events in the reigns of the kings described, or the particular role of prophets in the flow of Israel's history; and the occasional more extended interpretive passage which seeks to draw out the significance of all that has happened from the authors' point of view.

The account of the later monarchy that is thus given us is naturally a highly selective account, and its authors never pretend otherwise. The regnal formulae continually point us to sources from which, it is implied, the material in Kings has been drawn (e.g., 1 Kgs. 11:41; 14:19, 29).[4] They thus make it quite explicit that a substantial amount of material has been omitted. The authors of Kings have selected only those incidents that serve their own purposes in narrating Israel's story. This overall purpose also influences the amount of space afforded to what is selected. A striking feature of the book is that fairly long periods of time are passed over relatively briefly, while periods of a year or less can be described at great length.[5] Some of this approach may simply be a consequence of the differing extent of the information available to the authors, but this is unlikely to be the entire explanation. What we have in Kings is a particular representation of Israel's past driven by a particular religious concern. The fact appears to be that our authors are not particularly interested in what modern readers might call "political history," if by that is meant a politics that is relatively independent of religion. Politics and religion are in this book intertwined; even where we are given information which at first sight may appear to be more "political" than "religious," closer inspection suggests that in fact this information is itself very much tied up with the religious perspective of the whole book.[6] The religious convictions of the authors dominate the telling of the history.

This perspective is equally clear in 2 Chronicles, which is based upon 1–2 Kings but strikes out in its own directions and with its own emphases.[7] Most notably, perhaps, much less interest exists in the northern kingdom in the books of Chronicles, which focus rather on Judah, the temple, and temple worship. If Chronicles omits a considerable amount of material that is found in Kings, however, and often offers its own interpretations of events mentioned in Kings in line with its overall message, we also sometimes find additional material absent from Kings. For example, we find some information here on contacts between north and south that is not found in Kings, and which helps to emphasize that, if Chronicles is not very interested in the northern kingdom as a political institution, the books are nevertheless interested in the people of the north as a continuing part of Israel.[8] These differences between Kings and Chronicles seem in large measure to be bound up with the later date of the latter (the fourth century B.C.) and the different questions being addressed at that time. The Chronicler reshapes the tradition which he inherits so that it can speak to people in his time in a way that Genesis–Kings, perhaps completed as much as two generations beforehand, can presumably do no longer.

A number of consequences arise for the historian from the fact that both Kings and Chronicles provide us with *particular* portraits of the past in this way, and from *particular* points of view. We should not, for example, make the mistake of thinking that Israel and Judah were the only kingdoms of consequence in the region at this time, simply because most of the interest of the texts falls on one or other of these kingdoms. Nor should we necessarily think that others perceived a particular king as very important, simply because the authors of Kings or Chronicles thought him, from their particular point of view, to be very important (or indeed vice versa). The same should be said, in passing, of those prophetic books that bear on this period of Israel's history and which often provide a useful cross-reference in relation to our main narrative accounts.[9] The extrabiblical texts available to the historian of the later Israelite monarchy helpfully remind us of such realities, among others, because they provide us with extrabiblical perspectives on both the ancient world in general and, sometimes, on specific events that the Bible itself describes. We encounter in their royal records, for example, the perspectives of the Assyrian and Babylonian kings who campaigned in and eventually came to dominate the region between the Euphrates and Egypt between the mid-ninth and the mid-sixth centuries B.C.[10] We encounter, too, the perspectives of those living closer to Israel, whose literary remains are available to us in the form of inscriptions from Syria-Palestine itself[11] or from immediately neighboring lands like Moab and Egypt,[12] or of early historians who wrote about the past in which ancient Israel participated.[13] All these extrabiblical sources thus play their own part in reconstructing the history of the period of the later Israelite monarchy, along with such other evidence as we also possess from disciplines like archaeology. All sources are employed in the narrative that follows.

THE CHRONOLOGY OF THE LATER ISRAELITE MONARCHY

The chronology that the book of Kings provides (upon which Chronicles also depends) is only a relative chronology. That is to say, we are only told when kings reigned in relation to other kings. We are not told (naturally enough) when they reigned in terms of our modern calendar. Our first move in providing such an "absolute" chronology for this period of Israelite history is to take into account data from Assyrian records, specifically from the *limmu*-chronicle, which lists Assyrian eponyms (officials who gave their names to successive years of the Assyrian calendar) from the middle of the ninth century B.C. to the end of the eighth, accompanied by a short notice of a particular event that happened in that year. One of these particular events, occurring in the month of Simanu in the year when a certain Bur-sagale was eponym, was an eclipse of the sun—long identified by astronomers as the one occurring on June 15, 763 B.C. in terms of our modern calendar.[14] With this information, we can work forward and backwards from 763 B.C., correlating the *limmu*-chronicle with other information from sources such as king lists and royal inscriptions that describe campaigns in terms of the king's regnal year (first, second, etc.) in order to arrive at fairly solid chronology for the Assyrian Empire, at least in that period of greatest interest to us at the moment (the period of the later Israelite monarchy). To correlate loosely the chronology of the Assyrian Empire with the major sources for our history of Israel, by noting those occasions where there is cross-referencing between them (e.g., when an Assyrian king is mentioned by the Bible, or Assyrian records mention a campaign also recorded in the Bible), is not then an overwhelmingly difficult task.

Constructing a precise chronology of Israel in the period of the later monarchy is, nevertheless, far from being a simple matter. The skeletal absolute chronology constructed by the means just described is extraordinarily helpful in providing us with a few fixed points on our chronological map from which we ourselves can work forwards and backwards within the biblical sources. Those occasions upon which Assyrian and Babylonian records intersect explicitly with the biblical texts are, however, comparatively few. Therefore, although these records certainly confirm the testimony of the book of Kings as to the order of the kings of Israel and Judah, they cannot help us very much when we ask more precise questions about the *regnal dates* of these kings. For this information, we are entirely dependent upon the biblical chronology itself, and this chronology presents us with certain difficulties if we seek precision.

We may take as an example the section of Kings that covers the period after the death of Ahab to the accession of Jehu to the throne of northern Israel (1 Kgs. 22:51–2 Kgs. 9:26). Our external sources suggest that Jehu, the assassin of Ahaziah of Judah and Jehoram of Israel, must have been on the throne of Israel by 841 B.C., in order to give tribute to the Assyrian king Shalmaneser III in that year.[15] They also suggest that a previous king of Israel, Ahab, must still have been on the throne in 853 B.C., in order to fight alongside the king of Damascus against the same Assyrian king, Shalmaneser III.[16] If Ahab later died in battle with these same Damascus Arameans, as 1 Kings 22 has it,[17] then presumably at least a few months must have passed in which Ahab turned from ally to enemy of Damascus. It is possible that these few months were also part of the year 853 B.C., and that it was in this year that Ahab died and his son Ahaziah succeeded him. However, 852 B.C. is perhaps a more likely guess. If we now do the math on these figures, subtracting 841 from 853 or 852 and counting inclusively, we arrive at a total of twelve or thirteen years for the intervening period. The authors of Kings, however, tell us that in this intervening period Ahaziah ruled for two years and his successor Jehoram for twelve (1 Kgs. 22:51 and 2 Kgs. 3:1), which provides a total of fourteen years—too many, it seems, to fit the available space. How are we to account for this figure of fourteen? Even without the dates from the Assyrian records to prompt us, we would have been led to ask questions about it on the basis of the internal evidence from 1 Kings 22:51 and 2 Kings 3:1. Here Ahaziah is said to succeed to the throne in Jehoshaphat of Judah's *seventeenth year*, while Jehoram succeeds Ahaziah in Jehoshaphat's *eighteenth* year; and eighteen minus seventeen gives us one year, not two. Apparently even the authors of Kings themselves do not intend us to understand the "two years" of Ahaziah as "two full years." With this instance and the further prompting of the tight time-scale provided by the external sources before us, we are bound then to ask if Jehoram's "twelve years" are best understood in precise terms either. This question is important, since even a slight reduction in the apparent lengths of Ahaziah's and Jehoram's reigns as "two years" and "twelve years" would bring the biblical and the external data (which are, after all, not so very greatly at variance to begin with) into entire harmony. Is it possible that periods of time which were in reality somewhat less than two and twelve years, respectively, would be indicated by an ancient chronologist using these numbers? The answer to this question is clearly in the affirmative. In part the issue is when years begin and how they are counted, and in part it is a matter of how numbers function as an intrinsic part of the literary and theological nature of a book like Kings, as well as of their historiographical nature.

Regnal years could be counted by ancient chronologists in differing ways. For example, they might count only the first whole year of a king's reign in his total number, ignoring any partial year that may have preceded the first New Year of the new king's reign. A reign described in this way (known as the post-dating or accession-year system) was almost always longer by days or months than it might appear. Another ancient way of counting involved reckoning the partial year preceding the first New Year's Day as the king's first year. This approach is known as the ante-dating or non-accession-year system. Both methods have consequences. Post-dating can make reigns appear shorter than they actually were. Ante-dating can make reigns appear longer than they actually were, since not only the part of the year preceding the New Year could be counted as one year but also the part of the second year that began with the first New Year's Day of the reign. A reign of just a few months can, therefore—if it includes within it a New Year's Day—appear as "two years," and the incomplete part of the second year can itself be included as the first year of the successor. In this way, the cumulative totals of regnal years can easily outstrip by some distance the space available for them as indicated either by synchronisms within the same texts or by evidence from outside them.

Literary and theological factors also play their part in the confusion. Tadmor has suggested that the apparent patterning of the numbers of regnal years for the Israelite kings from Jeroboam I to Jehoram (22, 2, 24, 2, 12, 22, 2, 12) has resulted from a rounding off of numbers in pursuit of easy memorization.[18] That a pattern exists is evident enough, and Tadmor may be partly correct. Generally within Kings numbers often seem to have a literary/theological rather than a strictly historiographical purpose, in line with the overall orientation of the book. A plausible argument is that at least some numbers in the chronological schema are affected by this same concern. One striking example is that the immediate successors of kings who receive news of impending judgment on their royal house characteristically reign in 1–2 Kings for "two years" (1 Kgs. 15:25; 16:8; 22:51; 2 Kgs. 21:19), including Amon son of Manasseh who falls outside the group mentioned by Tadmor. One possible conclusion is that when numbers were being "rounded off" it was more than simply a desire to aid memory that ultimately motivated the choice of some of the numbers. In this example, the chronologist may have had a desire to link these various kings together and invite reflection upon them theologically as a group.

Our discussion of the period from the death of Ahab to the accession of Jehu begins to make clear our difficulty where chronology in Kings is concerned. On the one hand, awareness of the factors that may have been involved in shaping the chronology helps to explain discrepancies which appear on the basis of straight arithmetic both within Kings and between Kings and external records. On the other hand, even in the case of two kings whose reigns fall neatly between two solid absolute dates for the history of the monarchy, calculated with the help of external records, we are unable because of the nature of the biblical text to be precise about when they reigned. We know enough to know that accommodating them both between the death of Ahab and the accession of Jehu in terms of absolute dates is not necessarily a problem. Having resolved that problem, however, we are left unable to say precisely where the boundaries lie between Ahab and Ahaziah, Ahaziah and Jehoram, and Jehoram and Jehu. We have several options, and in the absence of further external data we are not in a position to decide. The hypothesis about the likely nature of the biblical numbers, which solves our problem at the level of generality, creates a new problem at the level of specifics. If these numbers generally and for various reasons cannot necessarily be taken as precise simply as they stand, then one cannot base any precise chronology upon them.

This difficulty presents through the book of Kings as a whole. The numbers are "mysterious," to quote from a well-known book title.[19] We know enough about many of the possible reasons for their mysteriousness to know that we should not concern ourselves too much with certain things. We know about postdating and ante-dating, and we are aware of the possibility not only that one of these systems replaced the other at some point in the history of Israel, but even that the separate kingdoms of Israel and Judah may have used different systems at different times. We know that the evidence concerning the date of the New Year in Israel in general is ambiguous and that a particular question arises about whether the calendars in Judah and Israel were ever or always the same. We are aware, finally, of the possibility that some of the complications in our texts may have arisen as the result of the authors of Kings attempting to impose a uniformity on their sources in terms of a standard chronological system of their own which may not have been the same as that in some of these sources; the whole question of what the authors already found in their sources and what they did with this material in attempting to present an overall picture of the monarchy is vexed. Knowing all this, we should not be too surprised if some discrepancies of a relatively small order are present between the totals of the regnal years for kings of Judah and Israel in a given period, or between the totals implied by the synchronisms for a given period and the totals as deduced from adding up the regnal years noted alongside them, or between the lengths of the period however deduced from the strict arithmetic of the texts and the time available for it as implied by fixed points in the external records. A reasonable assumption in such cases is that some of the factors mentioned above have played their part in producing the discrepancies. To these must also be added another: in some cases the reigns being described to us likely did not in fact precede and follow on from each other in a simple manner, but to some extent overlapped. Here we must take into account the phenomenon of the "coregency"—an arrangement whereby kings, although still alive and having some kind of continuing authority, nonetheless ceded some royal powers or even effective government overall to other family members, so that a son (for example) could reign for a time as coregent along with his father.[20]

However, whether we can ever demonstrate with any certainty where precisely these factors have operated, and thus arrive at an absolute overall chronology for the reigns of the kings, is another matter. We may well be completely convinced, for example, that the difference between the totals of regnal years for kings of Israel from Jeroboam to Jehoram (ninety-eight) and kings of Judah from Rehoboam to Ahaziah (ninety-five), and the fact that the synchronisms imply a lower total number of years for the period, are most likely accounted for by some of the factors just mentioned. Whether this approach enables a precise fixing of the boundaries of royal reigns in this period is open to question, however, because we do not really know where to redistribute the "missing" or "additional" years, or whether to depend more on the regnal years or on the synchronisms. All we can say with some degree of confidence, covering all the angles, is that the schism between northern and southern kingdoms took place some time around 940–930 B.C. For the rest, moving beyond the framework of relative chronology provided by this part of Kings to any more absolute chronology is extremely difficult; similar difficulties confront us in other parts of the book.[21]

The reader should bear all this in mind. What follows is an account of the period of the later monarchy in which we seek to take the biblical tradition seriously in our overall description of the past, and try as far as possible to be precise about dates in the course of that quest. To take the biblical tradition seriously, however, is also to take seriously the nature of the chronological schema within which this description of the past is contained, and to be aware that it offers something other than a straightforward chronology. This must dictate our attitude to the numerical detail, which must not be allowed so to absorb our attention that we lose sight of the broader narrative picture.

THE REIGN OF KING SOLOMON

David's immediate successor as king of Israel was his son Solomon. We describe Solomon's reign under five headings: his early years, his rule over Israel, his relationships with the wider world, his building projects, and his religion.

Solomon: The Early Years

Our only sources of information about Solomon's early years[22] are the books of Kings and Chronicles (1 Kgs. 2–3 and 2 Chr. 1, respectively),[23] and the information with which they provide us is limited. Perhaps a hint is given as to Solomon's relative immaturity when he came to the throne in 1 Kings 3:7, not so much in his own claim to be "only a little child" (a statement about how inadequate he feels)[24] as in the Hebrew word pair "to go out/to come in," which probably has a military connotation and may imply here lack of military experience. Then again, we have an indication in the MT of 1 Kings 3:1 of an early marriage alliance with Egypt, although whether chronology or theology has dictated the position of this notice is not clear, and it is consequently unclear just how early the marriage is envisaged as being. The notice is positioned quite differently in the LXX, and possibly it was moved to its current position in MT in order to underline the point that Solomon, right at the beginning of his reign, carried with him the seeds of his own destruction.[25] We have no grounds for doubting the substance of the claim itself,[26] and indeed parallels can be adduced for the marriage of an Egyptian princess to a foreign ruler.[27] We have no further information about this marriage from the biblical texts, however, and the Egyptian records do not cast any further light on the matter.[28] Nor do we know anything further than the Kings text tells us about the various other wives Solomon is said to have had.[29]

The main concern of the authors of Kings with respect to Solomon's early years is to give us a graphic description of the realpolitik which they see as dominating them, as Solomon moved to eliminate those threats to his sovereignty which remained in the aftermath of Adonijah's attempt to seize hold of the kingship (1 Kgs. 2). First Adonijah himself is removed from the scene, then both Abiathar and Joab, and later Shimei. It seems likely from the way in which David's words are structured in 1 Kings 2:5–9 that we are intended to understand the treatment meted out to various individuals mentioned in these opening chapters as representative of Solomon's approach to the early years of his reign in general. That passage appears to present Joab as representative of those elements in the kingdom that are so enmeshed in David's Judean past that they will be unlikely to make the government of a united Israel under Solomon easy. Shimei, on the other hand, is also a partisan, though this time of the north, not the south (2 Sam. 16:5–14; 19:20). He also represents an element within the kingdom likely to be hostile to unity under a Davidic king. Between these disruptive elements from Judah and Israel (1 Kgs. 2:5–6, 8–9), hostile to harmony, stands Barzillai from Gilead in Transjordan (2:7): a model of dutiful service to his king, service that is rewarded in peaceful fellowship around the king's table. The passage is thus carefully structured so as to present Solomon with an ideal (peaceful community), and to suggest to him what kind of people from David's past have to be removed (those likely to disrupt peaceful community) if this ideal is to be attained. This passage must be understood in the light of the Judah-Israel tensions already evident in the books of Samuel (e.g., 2 Sam. 20), and soon to explode into schism again in 1 Kings 12 (compare, in particular, 2 Sam. 20:1 and 1 Kgs. 12:16). Solomon is presented in the latter part of chapter 2 as fully grasping the point—using his "wisdom" to ruthless effect in removing potential troublemakers while appearing to possess justification for doing so.

No extrabiblical evidence that bears on any of these events, nothing that might fill out the picture that the authors of Kings paint of Solomon's earliest years as king (and that the Chronicler duplicates in part). That the authors of Kings tell a plausible story of political intrigue and plotting cannot be questioned. However, that they tell a story which is particularly ideologically loaded in favor of Solomon, as some have claimed, must *certainly* be questioned. It is clear enough that the narrators of Kings do not themselves endorse Solomon's behavior, not only from the way in which chapter 2 is written, but also from the way in which chapter 3 then contrasts the "wisdom" that Solomon has already displayed with the wisdom that God gives the king to rule from this point on. This contrast is missing in 2 Chronicles 1 taken by itself, even though this chapter also contains the Solomonic prayer in a variant form. In the prayer, Solomon confesses his ignorance and his inability to rule the people justly. He asks God for wisdom, which is duly granted. The authors of Kings and Chronicles see this wisdom "from above" as the foundation of Solomonic rule. As far as the authors of Kings are concerned, such wisdom "from below" as Solomon first possessed did not promise very much.

Solomon's Rule over Israel

The authors of Chronicles are mainly interested in those aspects of Solomon's reign that concern the temple and worship. They therefore pass directly from the prayer for wisdom (2 Chr. 1:7–13) to the account of the preparations for temple building (2:1–18), pausing only briefly to describe other aspects of the Solomonic rule that are connected with the prayer (1:14–17). Of primary importance for them about Solomon's wisdom is that it led to the building of the temple. The authors of Kings, in contrast, pause at greater length early in their account to describe the Solomonic rule more generally. They present Solomon after the early years as a king unusually well-endowed by God to rule over his kingdom in justice, and provide the well-known example in 1 Kings 3:4–28 to illustrate this. The kingdom that results from God's blessing of Solomon is then described (4:1–20): it is a well-ordered kingdom—a happy, prosperous place, in which the king's subjects and the king's household have what they need to live well.

Many of the details of the Solomonic administration as described in 1 Kings 4 remain unclear, and because this chapter is all we have by way of information, the lack of clarity must remain. The first six verses provide us with a list of his chief officials,[30] from which we first deduce (vv. 2, 4) that the banishment of Abiathar (2:26–27) was at some point reversed and the promotion of Zadok which followed his deposition was nullified (2:35)—his son Azariah was now appointed in his place (v. 2). Benaiah was still in command of the army (4:4, cf. 2:35). Elihoreph and Ahijah (v. 3) held the office of secretaries, although their precise function is not known to us. Did secretaries have general managerial responsibility, or was their task a more limited one, to do with writing (annals, letters)? Jehoshaphat (v. 3) was the recorder, or "herald," or perhaps even "state prosecutor"; again, the nature of the office is unclear. Two sons of Nathan (presumably we are meant to think of the well-known prophet of 1 Kgs. 1–2) were found among Solomon's chief officials (v. 5). Azariah was in charge of the district officers of verses 7–19, and Zabud was priest and personal advisor to the king (lit. "friend of the king," cf. Hushai in 2 Sam. 15:37; 16:16; and esp. 17:5 ff.). Finally, Ahishar (v. 6) was the royal steward, in charge of the palace (cf. 1 Kgs. 16:9; 18:3; etc.), and Adoniram was in charge of forced labor (cf. 1 Kgs. 5:13–18; 9:15–22).

First Kings 4 also presents us with a picture of the manner in which Solomon governed the various regions of his kingdom. There were twelve such regions, each under a district officer whose job was to provide for the king and the royal household on an annual rota. Each district was responsible for one month in each year. It is not clear whether these officers were simply tax supervisors, ensuring that the districts paid their dues to the court, or whether they had a broader administrative role.[31] Clearly, though, this arrangement was not a tribal system of support for the royal household, although some of the tribal names known to us from elsewhere in the OT do appear here (Ephraim, v. 8; Naphtali, Asher, Issachar, Benjamin, vv. 15–18), and we are perhaps meant to think of Naphtali, Issachar, and Benjamin as districts based entirely on tribal areas. The hill country of Ephraim is not, however, to be understood as corresponding to the tribal area "Ephraim," but as including at least part of Manasseh as well (cf. Josh. 17:14 ff.); Asher is not a district by itself, but only in conjunction with the unknown Aloth. Other districts are named after towns that presumably gave their names to regions (e.g., 1 Kgs. 4:9, 12), or after regions themselves (v. 19), rather than after Israelite tribes. Here traditional tribal boundaries have had no defining impact upon the new system (e.g., v. 9, where the second district is described as comprising both Shaalbim, assigned to Dan in Josh. 19:42 and Judg. 1:34–35, and Beth Shemesh, assigned to Naphtali in Josh. 19:38 and Judg. 1:33). Solomon's arrangements thus move beyond the tribal system and have points of contact with it. They represent a new order.

In spite of the claim in verse 7 that the twelve district officers were over all Israel, a common assertion is that in fact the authors did not mean us to understand the arrangements described here as involving Judah.[32] If it appears at all, some have claimed, Judah is a thirteenth district in verse 19, where the Hebrew has "and one governor who was over the land" and the LXX explicitly provides an interpretation of this land as Judah. As a corollary to this argument, scholars usually maintain that the phrase "all Israel" does not necessarily imply "all twelve tribes" in Kings, but can refer simply to the northern tribes, "Israel." For all its popularity, however, the case is not strong. The scope of "all Israel" is sufficiently defined by the opening and closing verses of the passage: "Solomon ruled over all Israel" (v. 1) . . . "the people of Judah and Israel were happy" (v. 20). In fact, in each case in 1 Kings 1–11 the phrase can refer to the whole united kingdom of Israel (or representatives from all its tribes) that had been David's (1:20; 11:16) and is now ruled over by Solomon (3:28; 8:62, 65; 11:42). In several of these cases, moreover, that the northern tribes alone are meant (3:28; 8:65; 11:42) is simply implausible or impossible. The authors meant all Israel when they used the phrase in the Solomon story, and they meant this interpretation also in 4:7.

If readers have had difficulty with this most natural reading of 1 Kings 4, part of the reason, at least, has had to do with the perceived difficulty in finding any reference to Judean territory in the list of districts itself. The difficulty is, however, more perceived than real. Verse 10 is the crucial verse. The name "Hepher" certainly has mainly non-Judean associations in the OT (Num. 26:32–33; 27:1; Josh. 17:2–3). Hepher does appear, however, in the list of clans of Judah in 1 Chronicles 4:1–23 (v. 6). Socoh, on the other hand, is only known in the OT as the name of a Judean town (either in the Shephelah, Josh. 15:35; 1 Sam. 17:1; or in the hill-country, Josh. 15:48); no northern Socoh is known within the biblical tradition. This review leaves us with Arubboth, which is otherwise entirely unknown in the OT. We do find a town named "Arab," however, in Joshua 15:52, whose root consonants are identical with our Arubboth; this is, again, a Judean town. We thus have one clearly Judean town mentioned along with one that could be Judean, in a district whose name can plausibly be connected with a third. We can conceivably locate the third district, therefore, in Judah. The LXX interpretation of verse 19, on the other hand, is implausible, demanding that we increase the number of officials mentioned in the list covering "all Israel" to thirteen rather than twelve (and thus creating a conflict between the numbers in vv. 7 and 8–19), while also requiring that we ignore an evident distinction in the Hebrew text between the word for "governor" (v. 19, NIV) and the word for "district officer" (vv. 5, 7, and 27, NIV). The distinction implies that we are to differentiate between the one person who is "over the land" and the others who are in charge of districts. The best approach, therefore, seems to be to take the last part of verse 19 as a reference to the Azariah of verse 5: one governor over the whole land of Israel, to whom the twelve district officers just listed were responsible.

According to 1 Kings 4, then, Solomon ruled over Judah and Israel from Dan to Beersheba (4:25), and his kingdom was organized on the basis of twelve districts. If we cannot be precise about the boundaries of the kingdom for lack of sufficient information, we do not necessarily lack a fairly accurate general impression of it. If we also apparently have no nontextual evidence that can be said directly to support the text's claims, neither do we have any evidence for doubting them. The general paucity of the archaeological record with regard to the Solomonic period is, of course, well-known, and has come to have an important place in recent discussion of Israelite history that tends to ask for corroboration of the text *before* the text is taken seriously,[33] rather than asking whether evidence shows that the text should *not* be taken seriously. The extant material remains from the period in which most scholars locate Solomon have not lived up to archaeologists' expectations formed on the basis of the biblical text. Some questions are thus posed of archaeology. For example, how much may we reasonably expect of archaeology, in terms of its ability to confirm what texts in their specifics have to say? Some questions are also posed, however, of readers of the biblical texts; to this matter we turn now, as we consider Solomon's wider influence in Palestine and Syria.

Solomon and His World

The Hebrew text of Kings treats 1 Kings 4:1–20, concerning Solomon's rule over Israel, as a unit distinct from what follows it and regards all of 4:21–5:18 in our English translations as another unit, the subject matter of which is clearly "Solomon and the rest of the world." Here we read of Solomon's dominion over the kingdoms immediately surrounding Israel and of his impact on the world more generally. The area of Solomonic influence is described in 4:21 as stretching from the River (the Euphrates) to the land of the Philistines, as far as the border of Egypt. This area is further defined in 4:24 as extending from Tiphsah (on the Euphrates, east of Aleppo in Syria) to Gaza (on the western coast, in the far south of Philistia).[34] The area is relatively large, corresponding to the ideal extent of Israel's dominion as promised to Abraham in Genesis 15:18, and apparently also corresponding to a very great extent to the area of David's dominion as we may deduce it from texts such as 2 Samuel 8:1–14 and 2 Samuel 10. The countries in this region, we are told, brought tribute and served Solomon all the days of his life. They contributed to the prosperity of Israel while representing no threat to the peace of the realm. The implication of the positioning of 1 Kings 4:27–28, indeed, is that it was because of Solomon's secure position in respect of these other regions that the district officers were able to do their job effectively.

That Solomon's dominion in its extent thus corresponds to the ideal of Genesis 15:18 and in its atmosphere resembles the prophetic picture of Micah 4:1–5 is sufficient to sow the seeds of doubt in the minds of many modern readers of Kings as to the historical reliability of the text. Yet to portray an ideal is not necessarily to idealize. The fact that we are presented here with something of a "golden age" cannot be taken of itself as proving that something of a golden age did not in fact exist. Other evidence must be brought to bear. We must of course take account of the ample evidence within Kings and within the Hebrew Bible more generally that authors characteristically aim to do much more by their use of numbers than simply communicate facts; that approach is a matter of demonstrable literary convention. When we read in 1 Kings 4:26, then, of Solomon's forty thousand stalls for (perhaps teams of) chariot horses, we should take into account that equally large numbers are to be found at precisely those other points in the Solomon story where Deuteronomy 17:16–17 is most obviously the text in the background (e.g., where Solomon is accumulating gold, 1 Kgs. 10:14, or wives, 1 Kgs. 11:3). We shall probably wish to conclude that the large number in 4:26 is to be explained more in terms of what the text is trying to say about Solomon as the archetypal multiplier of horses than in terms of literal historical reference. To the extent that this kind of convention is used in the narrative about the Solomonic empire, we may be justified in speaking of "exaggeration" in the text. Literary conventions must be taken seriously;[35] perhaps some previous histories of Israel have been guilty of reading the text in too "flat" a manner, forming their impressions of Solomon's realm without giving due attention to those features of the biblical text that have more to do with literature than with history. Having taken account of these features, however, we must still ask if any hard evidence exists that the fundamental claim of this passage is false: that Solomon was the dominant ruler in Palestine and Syria during much of his reign, and that he was sufficiently renowned to attract the attention of people further afield (1 Kgs. 4:29–34; 10:1–13, 23–25).

Miller and Hayes find several problems with the claims of 1 Kings 4 in this respect, and their treatment is instructive, especially regarding their assertions about Tyre.[36] None of the information about Tyre in the Kings account, they claim, can be taken to suggest that Solomon was ever regarded as Hiram of Tyre's senior partner, or that he expanded his territorial realm at Phoenician expense. On the contrary, they say, the joint shipping venture of 1 Kings 9:26–28; 10:11–12, 22 was really a Phoenician undertaking in which Solomon was allowed to participate, and Solomon in fact ceded to *Hiram* a considerable portion of territory in the northwestern Jezreel Valley (1 Kgs. 9:10–14). In truth, however, this reading of Kings is highly curious. In 1 Kings 5, it first appears that Hiram is more an equal of Solomon than his vassal, and that his goods flow into Solomon's kingdom more as a matter of trade than of tribute. Solomon suggests to Hiram a cooperative venture (5:6), and possibly that Hiram should set the level of wages to be paid to his men. Hiram responds with proposals of his own. He suggests that his own men alone should deal with the cutting and the transporting of the wood down the coast to Israel, and that Solomon's men should only be involved after this work has been done (v. 9). The "wages," moreover, are not to be paid to his laborers, but in the form of supplies of food for his royal household. Solomon complies with this second suggestion (v. 11). He thus gets what he wanted, in the shape of the materials for the temple, but so too does Hiram. The arrangement, sealed by a treaty (v. 12), is a happy one. Thus, in respect of Hiram's *second* suggestion, Solomon apparently treats the Tyrian king not as a vassal who is required to supply goods and men to his overlord, but rather as someone who is to be worked with cooperatively and in negotiation.

Yet this relationship apparently does not hold with regard to Hiram's *first* suggestion. The narrative in 5:13–18 proceeds, in fact, as if he had not made this first suggestion about work methods at all. In spite of his attempt to avoid cooperation in the venture of the sort that Solomon had sought in verse 6, we find *exactly* such cooperation described. The cumulative picture of Solomon that is painted here, then, is of a king who is happy to negotiate with Hiram to a certain extent, but also quite prepared to ignore terms that do not suit him. Cooperation is present, but that as exists between junior and senior partners, the former of which has no ultimate ability to resist the latter's will. This arrangement is even more apparent in 1 Kings 9:10–10:29, where the real beneficiary of the "treaty" between the two kings becomes obvious. Hiram supplies Solomon with gold (9:10–14), and Solomon in turn "rewards" him with twenty towns in Galilee of dubious worth. Yet Hiram's displeasure (v. 13) does not affect his "willingness" to send men to sea to bring back more gold *for Solomon* (9:26–28; 10:11–12, 22). The Chronicles account, indeed, apparently suggests that Solomon even regained the towns themselves, if 2 Chronicles 8:2 is taken (as it plausibly may) as referring to a sequel to the events described in 1 Kings 9:10–14. In this account, Hiram's role as a vassal of Solomon rather than his equal is even more explicit throughout.[37] But this situation is already clear enough in Kings. Not the slightest hint exists in the text that Solomon is the junior partner in the joint shipping ventures, and one wonders where this claim can be grounded in evidence.[38]

If the authors of Kings represent Solomon very clearly as Hiram's superior, however, they also do not represent his domination in terms of the possession of *territory*. Miller and Hayes themselves note that we are not told that Solomon expanded his territorial realm at Phoenician expense, but they draw the strange conclusion that this undermines the authors' claim in 1 Kings 4:24 that Solomon had dominion over all the kings west of the Euphrates. A more appropriate conclusion to be drawn from the Solomon and Hiram story—and especially from 1 Kings 5, which for the authors of Kings functions as a particular example of the sort of relationship which Solomon had with other rulers in the region[39]—would be that the domination they have in mind does not necessarily involve military conquest and occupation. The assumption that it must involve such things has bedeviled more histories of Israel than that of Miller and Hayes. Yet it is only an assumption, perhaps arising from nothing more than a general connection in scholars' minds between notions of "empire" and notions of "conquest" and "occupation." We must, however, form our opinion of what the authors of Kings *meant* from what they *wrote*, not from the associations of certain words in our modern minds; and their writing implies that Solomon's dominance in the region of Syria and Palestine, while real enough, was not necessarily a result of the use of force or a matter of the possession of land. It is thus no argument against 1 Kings 4:24 that nothing suggests that David and Solomon ever subjected the Philistines, and that "one of Solomon's purposes in fortifying Gezer would have been to secure his western frontier against Philistine encroachment."[40] Rulers can "dominate" without "subjecting" (assuming that occupation is implied by the latter), and one way of doing this, of course, is to fortify cities in the proximity of those being dominated. Nor is it any argument to point out that Rezon opposed Solomon from Damascus and Hadad from Edom (suggesting a lack of Solomonic "domination" there), since the authors of Kings clearly wish to tell us (and we have no reason to doubt them) that these opponents only became a problem to Solomon in his old age (1 Kgs. 11:14–25). The marriage alliances mentioned in 1 Kings 11:1 themselves imply a state of peace for much of Solomon's reign in respect of the peoples mentioned there, including Edom.

Once the text of Kings has been taken seriously in terms of what it is and is not saying about Solomon, what remains of the case against the truthfulness of its testimony about the past? The answer, apparently, is "very little." Whitelam has recently argued,[41] for example, that research on the way in which economy and power are correlated in the rise and fall of great powers challenges the notion of a Davidic superpower in the ancient world. This research helps to explain why

Palestine has been only rarely, if ever, a regional power in its own right: a region with the infrastructural inferiority of Palestine could not compete with contemporary military powers while agricultural production and demography remained key factors in the dynamics of world power. We might respond as follows: Insights derived from the modern world may well be able to help us in our understanding of the ancient world; certainly Palestine has been rarely, if ever, a regional power in its own right. Our biblical sources, however, claim not that Solomon was any more able than other Israelite kings to compete with the great military powers of the ancient Near East but only that he had an unusual degree of dominance over Palestine for a short time. The generalities of history do not negate the specifics of the individual case, which can partly be explained precisely in terms of the apparent absence from the scene of great powers like Egypt, which was not politically or militarily dominant in the period in which historians usually set Solomon's reign.[42]

Solomon's Building Projects

Discussion of Hiram brings us naturally to a discussion of Solomon's building projects, already a major interest of the authors of Kings and an even more central interest of the authors of Chronicles. For both sets of authors, of course, the Jerusalem temple is Solomon's most important project, and both books give a considerable amount of detail concerning its construction and furnishing (1 Kgs. 6:1–38; 7:15–51; 2 Chr. 3–4). For all their detail, however, the biblical texts do not provide us with sufficient information of the kind that would enable us to make a precise reconstruction. That it had a tripartite structure is clear enough, as is the fact that it was relatively small (on one calculation, about thirty-seven by eleven by sixteen meters). The temple was apparently intended as a focal point for the worship of God rather than for use by Israelites in general as a place of worship. We have no external evidence that bears directly on the Solomonic temple, although the tripartite structure and various details are paralleled elsewhere in the ancient Near East.[43]

The Jerusalem temple was not, however, Solomon's only building project, according to the biblical sources. Both Kings and Chronicles tell us of a royal palace (1 Kgs. 7:1–8; 2 Chr. 8:1)—the authors of Kings suggest that the palace complex occupied rather more of Solomon's time and attention than the temple. First Kings 9:15–18 mentions some further building work on the walls of Jerusalem, specifically the "Millo" which had apparently been begun by David (9:24; 11:27); and at Hazor, Megiddo, Gezer, Lower Beth-horon, Baalath, and Tadmor, as well as at other unspecified sites. Second Chronicles 8:3–6 also mentions Lower Beth-horon, Baalath, and Tadmor, omitting Hazor, Megiddo, and Gezer while adding Hamath-zobah (a Solomonic conquest) and Upper Beth-horon. Hamath and Tadmor lie in the far north of the Solomonic sphere of influence, while Hazor was a strategic city in northern Palestine, situated at the juncture of the main roads to Hamath and Damascus. Megiddo guarded the pass through which the Way of the Sea crossed from the Sharon Plain into the Jezreel Valley, while Gezer and Beth-horon dominated the most direct approaches to Jerusalem from the southwest and northwest respectively. Because Baalath is associated with Beth-horon in both lists, we are perhaps to think of a Judean town (the one mentioned in Josh. 15:9–10?). The identification is uncertain, however.

One understands why Solomon should have wished to fortify those four cities in Israel whose location is fairly clear (Hazor, Megiddo, Gezer, Beth-horon). For one thing, such cities would have been important in terms of controlling the trade traffic that passed through his kingdom, notably on the Way of the Sea, which originated in Egypt and wound its way northwards and eastwards towards Damascus (cf. 1 Kgs. 10:14–15, 28–29). Nor is it strange that he might have wished to build himself a palace complex and strengthen or extend his city walls. A campaign on the northern boundaries of the area over which he claimed suzerainty is likewise comprehensible. The archaeological evidence, such as exists, creates no difficulty for the biblical testimony, even if the evidence cannot (by its very nature) prove that the story told in Kings and Chronicles is true. The evidence in question concerns Jerusalem, Hazor, Megiddo, and Gezer. The Millo of Jerusalem has often been understood to refer to a terrace system built with stone retainer walls backfilled with rubble—a structure that would have increased the building area within the old city of David on its eastern side. A structure like this has been excavated in the appropriate location, although many currently date it earlier than Solomon, leading to the suggestion that Solomon might have rebuilt the structure rather than been one of its first builders.[44] Whether it is indeed the Millo referred to in the text must remain uncertain.[45] At each of the three other sites we also find extensive building occurring in the period to which the reign of Solomon has usually been ascribed; specifically the fortification systems at each site appear similar.[46]

Building programs require labor forces, of course, and the biblical texts have quite a bit to tell us about such forces. First Kings 5:13–18 first introduces us to the task force sent to Lebanon in connection with the preparations for building the temple. This passage is often taken as implying that Solomon conscripted Israelites ("out of all Israel," v. 13) to work abroad, and 11:28 and 12:3–4, 18 are drawn into the discussion to provide support for this view. Yet 9:15–23 make a point of denying this conclusion, explicitly telling the reader that Solomon conscripted workers only from the Canaanite population of Israel. This point is exactly what the Hebrew word *mas*, "levy" (vv. 13–14), implies to the reader who knows the story of Israel up to this point (e.g., Josh. 16:10; 17:13). Two quite distinct groups are intended by the authors of Kings in 5:13–18 and 9:15–23. One comprises 30,000 Canaanites drawn from throughout Israel ("out of all Israel"), and is supervised by 550 officials (5:13–14; 9:15–23, esp. v. 23). This group works both on the temple preparations and on Solomon's other building projects (1 Kgs 9:15–19; also 2 Chr. 8:3–10, noting that the number of the supervisors differs from Kings). The other group comprises 150,000 Israelites and is supervised by 3,300 foremen (Kgs. 5:15–18). This latter group is in view in 1 Kings 11:27–28 and 12:3–4. The Chronicler, interestingly enough, makes it quite unambiguous that no Israelites were set to forced labor with regard to the temple (2 Chr. 2:17–18)—but only at the expense of obscuring the evident distinction in Kings between the two groups of workers.

It is out of the Israelite labor force at work on the Millo in Jerusalem—the northern component of the labor force of 5:15–18, kept on in Jerusalem after the temple building for further work—that Jeroboam son of Nebat emerges. An Ephraimite worker, Jeroboam was promoted by Solomon, we are told, to the position of overseer of the work on the Millo. Only the authors of Kings relate this fact, for only they describe the opposition that Solomon encounters towards the end of his reign—and Jeroboam is the most important opponent of all. To the Kings account of Solomon's last days, in fact, we must now turn, in the context of a broader consideration of the religion of Israel during the Solomonic era.

Solomon and the Religion of Israel

The authors of Kings present Solomon as a king who, in their terms, was for the most part a relatively faithful worshiper of Yahweh. That is to say, he worshiped Yahweh alone (if not offering wholehearted obedience) and did not worship other gods either alongside or instead of Yahweh. He may well have failed to build the temple quickly enough, thereby encouraging the people to continue to focus their worship on the "high places," illegitimate places of worship so far as the authors of Kings are concerned. He himself may have worshiped at such high places (1 Kgs. 3:2–15). Yet this was worship of the one God, whose house was eventually built (1 Kgs. 5–7) and dedicated (1 Kgs. 8), becoming the resting place of all the old symbols of Yahwistic faith from previous ages (8:1–9). The authors of Chronicles, likewise, represent Solomon as a faithful Yahweh worshiper, even supplying the detail that the Tabernacle was located at the high place in Gibeon (2 Chr. 1:3–6, cf. also 1 Chr. 16:39; 21:29) so as to make it quite unambiguous that Solomon's worship there was not problematic.[47] Their picture of Solomon does not even include the bulk of the material in Kings that tends to qualify Solomon's devotion to God somewhat; they prefer to stress the positives, rather than dwell on the negatives. Quite in line with this general approach, the authors of Chronicles therefore do not supply us with any equivalent to 1 Kings 11:1–8, which in the Kings account of Solomon represents the culmination of many earlier hints in the text that the king's religious devotion was not exactly as it should have been. Here we are told that after many years of relative faithfulness to Yahweh, Solomon turned away to worship other gods, under the influence of his foreign wives. He built many sanctuaries for these gods, rivals to the temple, on the Mount of Olives and elsewhere.

The evaluation of Solomonic religion offered by the authors of Kings and Chronicles is not the only possible one. To characterize Solomon as for the most part one who "loved the LORD" (1 Kgs. 3:3), but in his old age as one whose heart "was not true to the LORD his God" (11:4), is to assume a particular view of what is true and right, which need not and may not have been shared by all or many of the people of Solomon's time. Certainly our biblical sources themselves claim, and archaeological evidence also tends to suggest, that whatever many people in Israel in the later monarchic period *thought*, their religion was in practice syncretistic. If we do have a particular perspective on Solomonic religion in Kings and Chronicles, however, we have no evidence that our authors have misled us as to the facts of the matter: Solomon's religion was for the most part focused on one deity, Yahweh, and only in his later years did he become more syncretistic.[48] The authors of Kings did believe that the Solomonic temple contained certain cult items that later came to be seen as idolatrous (cf. the bronze serpent of 2 Kgs. 18:4), but that fact is not of itself a difficulty. It is also true that certain aspects of the symbolism of the Solomonic temple remind the reader of "Canaanite" religion as it is described elsewhere in our biblical texts (e.g., Deut. 12; 2 Kgs. 17:7–20). Yet the same symbol can signify differing things within differing systems of thought, and no evidence indicates that the temple symbols in question, connected as they are with fertility, were intended to do other than embody the claim that Yahweh (not other deities) was the giver of fertility, the establisher and maintainer of the cosmic order.

The authors of Kings connect Solomon's late slide into apostasy with increasing opposition to him, both within Israel proper and within his wider sphere of influence in Syria-Palestine. First Kings 11:14–25 tells us of two adversaries, Hadad and Rezon, who began to trouble him from south and north. Hadad was a victim of David's wars, according to 2 Samuel 8:3–14, and a refugee for a while in Egypt, before his return to Edom. Rezon may have been a survivor of the battle described in 2 Samuel 8:3–4 and one who was unwilling to submit in Zobah to imperial rule from Jerusalem. Rezon's private army, we are told, at some point late in Solomon's reign took control of Damascus (garrisoned by David in 2 Sam. 8:6 and clearly part of the territory dominated by Solomon in 1 Kgs. 4:24), the capital of the new Syrian state of Aram that played such an important part in Israel's subsequent history (e.g., 1 Kgs. 15:18–20). We are not told when, exactly, Hadad was allowed to leave Egypt, or when, exactly, Rezon took control of Damascus and "ruled in Aram." We may be meant to understand that both men were in fact Solomon's adversaries from early on, if "all the days of Solomon" in 1 Kings 11:25 does not simply mean "all the remaining days of his old age" (cf. 11:34). If so, only late in Solomon's reign, the authors of Kings imply, did they cause Solomon real problems and were their activities so significant that the general state of affairs could no longer be described as "rest" (5:4). A third enemy mentioned is Jeroboam, who is approached outside Jerusalem by Ahijah the prophet of Shiloh (11:29). Ahijah prophesies that a division of the kingdom will shortly take place, with all the Israelite tribes save Judah and Benjamin[49] passing under Jeroboam's control. We are not told in Kings what happened after Jeroboam had received Ahijah's message, but only that Solomon, aware of the threat, sought his death, and that Jeroboam escaped to Egypt.

No other evidence apart from the account in 1 Kings bears on the opposition that Solomon encountered at the end of his reign, and we have no reason to question this account as to its description of this opposition. The authors of Kings naturally (given their overall purpose in writing their book) emphasize divine causation in relation to the matter. If we are to probe further its other dimensions, then it is interesting that 1 Kings 12:1–4 informs us that at some point during Solomon's reign a feeling had arisen among many Israelites that life under Solomon had come to resemble the harsh labor of Egypt (cf. Exod. 1:14; 2:23). Perhaps in this context Jeroboam's opposition to Solomon was shaped. First Kings 1 reminds us that in old age kings often begin to lose their grip on power, as their own physical powers begin to fade. Perhaps Solomon's age was a factor in the increasing ability of his enemies to cause significant nuisance. Be that as it may, the account of Solomon in Kings ends by presaging not only the loss of influence of the Davidic kings outside their borders, but also the breakup of the united kingdom of Israel and Judah itself, created by David and governed with success for so much of his reign by his son.

Chapter 10

The Later Monarchy:
The Divided Kingdoms

Although the period of David and Solomon has often grasped the imagination of Bible readers down through the ages, the period during which Israel had one king who ruled over both its parts (Israel in the north and Judah in the south) was brief when compared to the following period in which Israel and Judah were each ruled by their own kings. For most of the history of the monarchy, both the Bible and our external sources inform us of the reality of separate kingdoms: a 200-year period during which the two states coexisted side by side, followed by a period of 135 years during which Judah survived alone.

THE DIVISION OF ISRAEL: REHOBOAM TO OMRI

At the beginning of the reign of Solomon's son, Rehoboam, the division of the kingdom threatened in 1 Kings 11 actually occurred, according to 1 Kings 12 and 2 Chronicles 10. Rehoboam went to Shechem so that he could be crowned king by "all Israel," but left that city—so connected with Israel's identity (Josh. 24:1–27; Judg. 8:22–23; 9)—as king over only the southern part of his father's kingdom. Thus the kingdoms of "Israel" and "Judah" (as they now come to be known) began

259

their separate existences, which continued until first Samaria (the capital of Israel for most of this period) and then Jerusalem (the capital of Judah) were conquered by invading imperial armies from Assyria and Babylon, respectively.

The Shechem assembly is often stated or implied to have been an assembly of the *northern* Israelite tribes only, Rehoboam (presumably) already having been crowned as king in Judah.[1] No narrative, however, suggests that Rehoboam had already been crowned as king in Judah, and the fact that he is called "king" in 1 Kings 12:1–20, and is evidently regarded as king by his close associates, does not prove very much.[2] Far more decisive for our understanding of the Shechem event is the fact that the phrase "all Israel" in the Solomon story in Kings (see above) cannot mean other than the whole united kingdom (or representatives from all its tribes) which had been David's and which Solomon then ruled. In view of 1 Kings 11:42 in particular, where as part of the concluding statement about the whole of Solomon's reign this phrase receives its most natural reading, "all Israel" in 12:1 must also refer to all the tribes. Rehoboam came to Shechem, we are told, to be crowned as king over the whole kingdom that his father had ruled.

Things did not go Rehoboam's way, however. Jeroboam and the tribal leaders made certain demands of the heir-designate to which he was not prepared to accede,[3] preferring to listen to the advice of younger contemporaries than to the counsel of older and wiser heads. Unwilling to be a king with the consent of all his people, he ended up as king only of a part, as "all Israel" made it clear that kingship could not simply be imposed. Two attempts at imposing his authority followed. The first involved a certain Adoram (Hadoram, in 2 Chr. 10:18), perhaps the same person mentioned in 1 Kings 4:6 and 5:14, but his mission is not made explicit. It could not have been to *reimpose* conditions of forced labor (Hebrew, *mas*) on Israel, as has sometimes been suggested, since according to the authors of the biblical texts Israel had not yet been under such conditions (see above). More likely we are to understand the sending of Adoram as the first move in the direction of trying to deal more harshly with Israel (cf. the threat of 1 Kgs. 12:13–14), whose people were to be treated under the new regime as if they were Canaanites. This move failed, and Rehoboam planned greater force, only to be persuaded by the prophet Shemaiah not to attempt a military campaign. Whether this prophetic word in itself was a sufficient reason for Rehoboam's decision, or whether other factors also came into play, we are not told. We are informed that in the meantime Jeroboam had been appointed king over "all Israel" (12:20). This puzzling claim, in the midst of a narrative that quite clearly tells us of a schism in which Rehoboam kept control of two tribes, is matched by the puzzling form of words in verse 17, which tells us that Rehoboam still ruled over all those Israelites who were living in the towns of Judah. Taking everything together, these puzzles can likely be explained in terms of the difference between the formal decision of the whole assembly of Israel, on the one hand, and the *de facto* reality on the other hand. Although the formal decision by all the tribes gathered in council was that Jeroboam should be their king, Rehoboam in fact retained control over some of the people in the kingdom. We are not told the circumstances under which this occurred;[4] we are only told of the reality of the split between north and south.[5] If no evidence exists that Judah had made Rehoboam king before the Shechem assembly, the claim of the biblical texts is certainly that they had done so by the end of the series of events described here.

It is, however, the course of the history of the majority of the tribes that is at first pursued by the authors of Kings, if only because they wish to show that Jeroboam's "exodus" out of Rehoboam's Egyptian-style hard labor leads but to another golden calf (cf. Exod. 32:1–35 and 1 Kgs. 12:25–33). Their interest lies in the religious consequences of the schism: the fact that Jeroboam, recognizing a connection between his new subjects' political and religious allegiance, initiated cultic reforms designed to exclude the possibility of any diminution or loss of power. Dan (in the far north of his new territory) and Bethel (in the far south) were made into centers of a newly reformed worship, focused on two golden calves. For the authors of Kings, this development represented an invitation to the people of Israel to worship other gods in defiance of Yahweh's words at Mount Sinai (Exod. 20:4). Jeroboam's words to them in 1 Kings 12:28 are, indeed, almost exactly the words with which the people greet the construction of the first golden calf in Exodus 32:4. Whether Jeroboam and his new subjects themselves would have viewed these reforms as a move away from Yahwism has been much debated.[6] The new worship centers certainly had deep roots in Israel's cultic past (cf., e.g., Gen. 28:18–22; Judg. 18:30). Whatever the case, Jeroboam's attempt to rival the Jerusalem cult also involved the building of a temple in Bethel (lit., "house of high places")[7] with its own altar and priesthood (1 Kgs. 12:31–32); the creation of a new central religious festival, probably intended to rival the Feast of Tabernacles (12:32–33, cf. 1 Kgs. 8:2; Lev. 23:33–43); and the extension of his new cult beyond Bethel and Dan into the rest of his kingdom (1 Kgs. 13:33). Jeroboam may also have been motivated in some of his other building work (12:25), not only by his current political and defensive needs, but also by a desire to make connections with the past. Both Penuel and Shechem are associated in biblical tradition with Israel's eponymous ancestor Jacob/Israel (Gen. 32:22–30; 33:18–34:31), and Shechem in particular with Joseph, who is essentially the link between the patriarchal period and the period of Israel's settlement in their land (Josh. 24:1–32). Be that as it may, Jeroboam at some point appears to have moved his royal residence from Shechem to Tirzah, a few miles to the northeast (1 Kgs. 14:17).[8]

The early history of the northern kingdom is portrayed in Kings as one of great political instability, which the biblical authors see as connected with the religious situation.[9] After Jeroboam's death, his son Nadab ruled only for a very short period, before being assassinated during a siege of the Philistine city of Gibbethon by Baasha from the tribe of Issachar (1 Kgs. 15:25–30). That such a siege took place at all indicates, incidentally, the way in which Israelite domination of the region, already on the wane in Solomon's later years, did not extend beyond his death.[10] No doubt this situation is partly connected with the fact that Israel and Judah, according to the authors of Kings, were in a continual state of strife throughout the period immediately after the schism (1 Kgs. 14:30; 15:32). We can imagine, however, that the internal situation in Israel also affected the climate. Baasha's dynasty did not itself long survive his death. His own son Elah was in turn assassinated by Zimri, one of his army commanders (16:8–10), who was then deposed by Omri (16:15–18). Only with the Omride dynasty, established in the wake of Omri's successful struggle with Tibni (1 Kgs. 16:21–22), did the northern kingdom apparently arrive at any measure of political stability.

Conversely, in Judah the Davidic dynasty survived the upheaval of the schism and its aftermath. Rehoboam was succeeded by two other Davidic kings in turn (Abijam and Asa). Even more clearly than they do in the case of Israel, the authors of Kings present this period as one of relative decline for Judah in relation to the Solomonic era. Rehoboam is himself presented as a king who went astray in his religious policies (1 Kgs. 14:21–24), leading all of Judah into idolatrous worship. Consequently, the writers imply, Rehoboam suffered a reverse at the hands of "Shishak king of Egypt,"[11] losing the treasure that his father had so carefully stockpiled in both temple and palace (14:26; cf. 1 Kgs. 7:51; 10:14 ff.).[12] The "golden age" of Solomon is replaced by the "bronze age" of Rehoboam (1 Kgs. 14:27–28); and the peace that Solomon had known is replaced by continual warfare (v. 30; cf. 1 Kgs. 5:4). The identity of "Shishak" is uncertain. He has often been identified with the Pharaoh Shoshenq I (c. 945–924 B.C.), the founder of the Twenty-second Dynasty in Egypt, who apparently campaigned at least once in Syria-Palestine.[13] The evidence for this identification consists of a fragment of a stela bearing his name, found at Megiddo (perhaps a victory stela), and a list of conquered cities and towns inscribed on a wall of the temple of Amon in Karnak. However, interpretive challenges regarding both the inscriptions and the biblical texts leave some room for doubt about the identification of the pharaoh and about the correlation of the biblical text with the inscriptions.[14]

Rehoboam's son Abijam is presented by the authors of Kings as a wicked king in terms of his religious policy, which is virtually all we hear about in 1 Kings 15:1–8. We are reminded, however, of the ongoing state of war between north and south (vv. 6–7); this theme is developed in 2 Chronicles 13, which unexpectedly omits all reference to the religious policy of Abijam (called Abijah in Chronicles) in general and instead recounts the story of a battle in which the king and his subjects prevailed over their northern enemies because "they relied upon Yahweh" (2 Chr. 13:18). Certain border towns and villages are said to have changed hands as a result of this battle (13:19). This state of affairs is temporary, however; Asa (who reformed worship in Judah in a way that won him qualified praise from the authors of both Kings and Chronicles: 1 Kgs. 15:9–15; 2 Chr. 14:2–5; 15:8–18) is shortly afterwards pictured in 2 Chr. 16:1–6 (cf. 1 Kgs. 15:16–22) as under great duress from Baasha, who had pushed into Benjamin and had begun to fortify Ramah, only a few miles north of Jerusalem. Faced with this threat to his capital and indeed to trade arriving from the west through the Aijalon valley, Asa sought to revive (through payment) an alliance that Abijah had had with Tabrimmon, king of Aram, now succeeded by his son Ben-Hadad I.[15] The attempt was successful, and Damascene pressure on Baasha's northern territory compelled him to abandon Ramah. Asa then in turn fortified Mizpah (just to the north of Ramah) and Geba (just to its east), securing the main roads to Jerusalem.[16] The only other military adventure of Asa's that is recorded in our biblical sources is the encounter at Mareshah, some thirty miles southwest of Jerusalem, between the Judaean army and an unidentified force from the south (2 Chr. 14:9–15; 16:8). This force may have been either Egyptian or at least sponsored by Egypt, but we have no way of knowing very much about it.[17]

Asa ruled in Judah, our biblical sources tell us, throughout a period in which the northern kingdom had five kings (1 Kgs. 15:25–16:28), before Ahab came to the throne (16:29 ff.). Both kingdoms were in a time of decline—ongoing hostility between them; political instability in the north; loss of influence over the surrounding kingdoms; and incursion by foreign powers and loss of territory.[18] Only with the arrival of the Omride dynasty in the larger, northern part of the old Solomonic empire do we apparently find this decline decelerating, as a more stable royal house arrives on the scene.

THE PERIOD OF THE OMRIDES

The Omrides (named after the first of their line, Omri) were the first northern kings to establish a dynasty successfully after the period of relative instability that ensued following the division of the kingdoms. So identified with this dynasty did the northern kingdom become, indeed, that even after the Omride period the kingdom could be referred to in Assyrian records as "the land of Omri."[19] Of Omri himself, however, we know very little, whether from biblical or other sources. Apart from the manner of his accession to the throne, we are informed in the biblical texts only about his purchase of the hill of Samaria and his building of the new northern capital there (1 Kgs. 16:23–28), in a position slightly better suited than Tirzah for international communication and the control of trade routes.[20] A commemorative stela of King Mesha of Moab (cf. 2 Kgs. 3:4) commissioned late in that king's reign looks back on a period when Omri had "humbled" Moab and had occupied some northern Moabite territory.[21] We gain the overall impression, then, of an active king who laid a solid foundation for those who followed him, and indeed was powerful enough to achieve some success beyond his borders. Yet it is also possible that Omri found himself under considerable pressure from Aram in the north. Our basis for offering this possibility lies in the fact that 1 Kings 20:34 appears to allude to Damascene victories over Omri, while the strategically important city of Ramoth Gilead in Transjordan—an Israelite city in 1 Kings 4:13—is already in the hands of the Damascus Arameans in 1 Kings 22:1–4.[22] We cannot be sure of the position, however, since 1 Kings 20:34 is not quite clear on whether in fact the Damascene campaign against *Baasha* (15:16–22) is the campaign to which allusion is being made in the first part of this verse;[23] and so quite possibly Ramoth Gilead fell to Aram earlier.

Our difficulties here, of course, lie partly in the fact that the authors of Kings are much more interested in the religious situation in Israel than in the political situation, and they often leave us to speculate about what is happening behind the scenes of their story rather than filling in all the gaps.[24] Their religious focus itself explains why we find much more material in Kings on Omri's son Ahab than we do on Omri, for Ahab is credited by them with opening the door to the worship of the god Baal in Israel through his marriage to the Sidonian princess Jezebel (1 Kgs. 16:31). Much of the material in Kings that offers us a portrait of Ahab's reign is indeed focused on the conflict at this time between Yahwism (championed predominantly by the prophet Elijah) and Baalism (championed predominantly by Jezebel, but supported by Ahab, e.g., in his building work in Samaria, 1 Kgs. 16:32–33). This conflict is itself seen as extending far beyond Ahab's reign and drawing in other members of the Omride dynasty. The battle was to be won not in Elijah's day, but in his successor Elisha's day, when a new dynasty arose under Jehu (1 Kgs. 19:15–17). The religious focus is, then, the dominant one throughout the Kings account of the Omrides, although we cannot divorce this from the associated social focus as we find it in 1 Kings 21. Here Ahab's abandonment of Yahwistic religion is portrayed as leading to his abandonment of Yahwistic laws about the possession and use of land in Israel and, indeed, laws about such subjects as false testimony, murder, and theft as well.[25]

If, according to the authors of Kings, Ahab was thus a worshiper of foreign gods and a king in whose kingdom acts of serious injustice could take place (and we have no reason to dispute these claims),[26] he was also a king who engaged to a significant extent in building projects (1 Kgs. 22:39) and was, like his father, relatively successful in military affairs. The interest in Kings lies in particular in his conflict with Aram, already a thorn in Israel's side during Baasha's reign (15:16–22) and probably also during Omri's reign (20:34). First Kings 20 tells us of further campaigns against Israel in which Aram under king Ben-Hadad II[27] headed a powerful alliance and apparently sought to reduce Israel to vassal status. Ahab was successful in two battles against the numerically superior Damascus Arameans and their allies during this campaign (near Succoth in Transjordan, perhaps, if the Hebrew behind the NIV's "tents" in verses 12 and 16 means to refer to the town of 1 Kgs. 7:46;[28] and later farther north near Aphek, 1 Kgs. 20:26; cf. Josh. 19:30 and Judg. 1:31). We are further told by Kings, however, that Ahab later lost his life in a campaign of his own designed to win back Ramoth Gilead in Transjordan, which the king of Aram had been able to retain after his initial losses (1 Kgs. 22:1–36). Our extrabiblical sources *also* know of Ahab as a king of some military capability. An inscription of the Assyrian king Shalmaneser III[29] lists Ahab of Israel among a coalition of Syrian and Palestinian kings who fought against the Assyrian army at Qarqar, on the river Orontes north of Hamath in southern Syria, in the Assyrian's sixth year (853 B.C.). On this occasion Ahab fought against a mutual foe *alongside* the king of Damascus,[30] who also appears in this text, incidentally, as superior in forces to Ahab.[31] If we are to correlate our texts, we must imagine that the Syro-Israelite alliance, if it predated the Assyrian invasion, certainly did not long survive it, and that as soon as the immediate Assyrian threat had waned,[32] conflict between Israel and Damascus was briefly renewed. Certainly no evidence exists of any Israelite presence at the subsequent battles between Shalmaneser and the Syro-Palestinian alliance in 849, 848, and 845 B.C.,[33] which is consistent with the idea of (if it cannot prove the reality of) a breakdown of relations between Israel and Damascus in the period between 853 and 849 B.C.

With Ahab's death, kingship in the northern kingdom passed in quick succession to two of his sons. Of Ahaziah we are told very little, save that he continued the religious policies of his parents and died as a result of a fall from a height (1 Kgs. 22:51–2 Kgs 1:18). Childless, he was succeeded by his brother Jehoram, of whom the authors of Kings thought a little better (2 Kgs. 3:1–3). Jehoram is presented in 2 Kings 3–8, in fact, as tolerating the Baal cult while not himself necessarily participating in it, and as having considerably better relations with Yahwistic prophets than either his father or his brother. Politically, he is described as leading an indecisive campaign against the Moabites via the desert of Edom (2 Kgs. 3:4–27), consequent upon a rebellion that is perhaps also described in the Mesha Inscription.[34] Jehoram is also presented, like his father, as being under pressure from the Damascus Arameans, even when there apparently existed an uneasy truce between Israel and Aram (2 Kgs. 5:1–8). That truce is described as breaking down into war once again in 2 Kings 6:8–7:20, where a siege of Samaria by the Damascene army is described—a siege unexpectedly lifted when the enemy troops retreated under the mistaken impression that they were under threat from a larger army approaching from both north and south (2 Kgs. 7:20). Perhaps during this war Israel recovered Ramoth Gilead, because we are later told that Jehoram was wounded at a defensive battle at this city (2 Kgs. 8:28; 9:14–15).[35]

What of the kingdom of Judah during the period of the Omrides? Here we are almost entirely dependent upon our biblical sources, since on the whole we do not even have the meager external references that we find in relation to the larger northern Israel.[36] We read in our biblical sources of three Judean kings during this period: Jehoshaphat, Jehoram, and Ahaziah. Jehoshaphat[37] is the king credited with making peace with the king of Israel (1 Kgs. 22:44), and indeed 1 Kings 22 (2 Chr. 18) records that he went with Ahab on his ill-fated Ramoth Gilead campaign. From this point onwards, the fortunes of the Omrides and Davidides were closely interconnected. Jehoshaphat also accompanied the *Israelite* (as opposed to the Judean) Jehoram in his less-than-effective campaign against the Moabites (2 Kgs. 3),[38] while his grandson Ahaziah accompanied the same Jehoram in his campaign against the new king of Aram, Hazael (2 Kgs. 8:28–29; 2 Chr. 22:5–6).[39] The two royal houses were indeed linked in this period by intermarriage, Jehoshaphat's son Jehoram being married to Ahab's daughter Athaliah (2 Kgs. 8:18, 26; 2 Chr. 21:6; 22:2–3), and over time they seemingly came to share a similar religious policy. Jehoshaphat is presented in both Kings and Chronicles as a fundamentally pious king (cf. 1 Kgs. 22:5, 43, 46; 2 Chr. 17:1–6; 18:4; 19:3–11; 20:32), though not without his faults (1 Kgs. 22:43; 2 Chr. 19:1–2; 20:33). Both his successors, however, are portrayed as idolaters under the influence of the house of Ahab (2 Kgs. 8:18, 27; 2 Chr. 21:3–6, 11–15; 22:3).

Almost all that we know about Judah's affairs apart from her involvement with Israel in this period concerns Jehoshaphat. He apparently exercised sovereignty over Edom, just as Solomon had done (1 Kgs. 22:47),[40] with the result that he was able, like Solomon, to build a fleet of ships at Ezion Geber (near Elath in Edom, v. 48; cf. 1 Kgs. 9:26–28), although not with any resultant success. The story is told in Kings in such a way as to remind us, in fact, that this period is one of decline in comparison to the period of the Solomonic empire, which is underlined when we read later of Judah's loss of Edom altogether under Jehoram (2 Kgs. 8:20–22). Chronicles likewise emphasizes the similarities and yet dissimilarities between Solomon and Jehoshaphat, recording the story of the fleet (2 Chr. 20:35–37)[41] while telling of building works and even of tribute from some Philistine cities and from the south (2 Chr. 17:1–2, 10–13), as well as of wise administrative reforms.[42] We are also told here of an Aram-inspired assault on Judah from the south (via the western coast of the Dead Sea) involving Moabites, Ammonites, and some people from the region of Mount Seir,[43] which failed when the various members of the alliance began to fight among themselves (1 Chr. 20:1–30). Both books report Jehoram's loss of Edom (2 Kgs. 8:20–22; 2 Chr. 21:8–10), and indeed the fact that even his rule in Judah was not entirely secure, since he was confronted with a revolt in the city of Libnah, a city southwest of Jerusalem, near the Philistine border. Chronicles also tells us that he had previously executed all his brothers and also certain others who, we imagine, were perceived as offering some threat to his position (2 Chr. 21:2–4).[44] Clearly the picture is of a weak king, and this picture is filled out by the Chronicler's report of attacks from the very Philistines and Arabs who had given tribute to his father (2 Chr. 21:16–17).

The period of the Omride dynasty was thus a period of relative reintegration in Israel, when the northern and southern kingdoms were once more at peace with and worked in alliance with each other. During this period, the Israelites, north and south, more or less held their own in respect of the peoples who surrounded them, now retaining territory, now losing it—although the general impression we have is of increasing weakness after the time of Ahab and Jehoshaphat. The Aramean kingdom of Damascus represented the most potent threat throughout the period, under Ben-Hadad I and Ben-Hadad II (Hadadezer), although Israel was not constantly at war with the Damascus Arameans, who had to look constantly to the Assyrian threat on their northern borders. This threat came to eclipse the entire northern kingdom in the period that followed the Omride dynasty, to which we now turn.

FROM JEHU TO THE FALL OF SAMARIA

The joint campaign conducted by Jehoram of Israel and Ahaziah of Judah against Aram provides the background against which our biblical sources describe the end of the Omrides and the near end of the Davidides.[45] As far as the authors of Kings are concerned, the catalyst was the prophet Elisha, who incited the army commander Jehu to conspire against Jehoram (2 Kgs. 9–10). Ahaziah, visiting the wounded Jehoram in Jezreel in the aftermath of their campaign, was simply caught up in his troubles. Both kings were assassinated,[46] along with Jezebel; further deaths followed, as the remaining Omrides who might challenge Jehu's grasp on power were murdered along with various relatives of Ahaziah, and the Baal-cult was removed from Samaria. Thus did Jehu succeed to the throne of Israel. In Judah, a brief period of rule by Ahaziah's mother Athaliah, who had attempted to imitate both her husband's and Jehu's ruthless tactics (2 Kgs. 11:1, cf. 2 Chr. 21:4), was itself brought to an end by the high priest Jehoiada's coup, and the young Joash succeeded to the throne under Jehoiada's regency (2 Kgs. 11–12).[47]

We know little of Jehu's reign. Our biblical sources portray a time of increased pressure from Aram (2 Kgs. 10:32–33), when the king of Damascus gained more permanent control of a greater part of Transjordan than had been the case during the Omride period. Hazael is in fact said to have conquered Transjordan as far south as the Arnon Gorge, the traditional southern limit of Israelite territory there (Josh. 12:2). At the same time we know that Syria-Palestine continued to find itself under Assyrian pressure, at least during the early periods in the reigns of Hazael and Jehu. An Assyrian annalistic fragment[48] tells us that Shalmaneser III, in the western campaign of his eighteenth year (841 B.C.), besieged Damascus, marched on to the Hauran mountains in southern Aram and thence through northern Palestine (we deduce)[49] to Ba'li-ra'si near Tyre (perhaps Mount Carmel),[50] at which time he collected tribute from "Jehu the Israelite" as well as from Tyre and Sidon.[51] During the campaign of his twenty-first year (838 B.C.), his famous Black Obelisk further tells us, Shalmaneser captured four of Hazael's cities and accepted tribute from the peoples of the Phoenician coast.[52] Only after this campaign did southern Syria and Palestine apparently gain for a brief period some respite from Assyrian military attention, a respite that lasted until the reign of Adad-nirari III.[53]

The respite to the north likely enabled the Damascus Arameans to turn their full attention on Israel and Judah and to subject these kingdoms to prolonged pressure in the last decades of the ninth century. Apart from the conquest of Transjordan, we are also informed by the biblical sources of two campaigns by the Damascus Arameans, which brought them right into the heart of Israelite territory to the west of the Jordan and threatened Jerusalem. Second Kings 12:17–18 tell us of Hazael's capture of the Philistine city of Gath (which he presumably reached by marching through Israelite territory) and of his receipt of tribute from the Judean king Joash, during a campaign that may have been designed to gain control over the western part of the incense trade, which in later times came from south Arabia via the Wadi Arabah to southern Philistia. Second Chronicles 24:23–24 further records a Damascus Aramean campaign at the end of Joash's reign that immediately preceded his death.[54] The first campaign is perhaps best located during the reign of Jehu's son Jehoahaz (c. 815–799), who in general fared even worse than his father at the hands of Aram, according to our biblical sources (2 Kgs. 13:1–7, 22–23), and thus provided absolutely no bulwark of defense (conscious or unconscious) for Judah. The second campaign must be located at the beginning of the reign of Jehoahaz's son Jehoash (2 Kgs. 13:10–13), before he began to recover territory from Hazael's successor Ben-Hadad III, as described in 2 Kings 13:24–25 (cf. 13:3, 14–19 for evidence that Aram was still dominant in the *early* part of Jehoash's reign).[55] The authors of Chronicles tell us that the conspirators who assassinated Joash of Judah did so while the king was lying wounded in the aftermath of a battle during this second Damascene campaign. From their perspective, Joash had been a good king so long as Jehoiada the priest had been alive to guide him, later falling away into apostasy (2 Chr. 24). The authors of Kings present his reign more ambiguously, although the hints are already there in 2 Kings 12 of a period late in his life when he went astray.[56]

Second Kings 13:5 already refers, in the context of Jehoahaz of Israel's reign, to a "savior" who rescued Israel from their extremity in the face of Damascene assaults, and perhaps we are meant to hear in this verse a veiled reference to the resurgence of Assyrian interest in Syria-Palestine that also resulted in a measure of relief for Israel because it began to occupy the attention of Damascus again in the north. Be that as it may, we certainly do begin to hear of renewed Assyrian military activity affecting Syria during the reign of Adad-nirari III (810–783 B.C.), both in the period in which this reign overlapped with that of Jehoahaz and in the period shortly afterwards, during the early years of Jehoash.[57] Such Assyrian campaigns provide the context in which the Israelite recovery in respect of Aram mentioned in 2 Kings 13:24–25 is comprehensible,[58] although Israel itself did not entirely escape Assyrian attention in this period.[59]

Jehoash was also apparently troubled from time to time by Moabite raiders, who waged limited warfare on Israel from the south (2 Kgs. 13:20), and on one occasion at the end of his reign by his Judean neighbors. The new Judean king Amaziah (2 Kgs. 14:1–22; 2 Chr. 25:1–28), after establishing himself on the throne in the wake of his father's assassination, gained some measure of military success against the Edomites (2 Kgs. 14:7; 2 Chr. 25:11–12). Emboldened by this success, he confronted Jehoash, for reasons that are not clear in the biblical sources, although the authors of Chronicles imply that the conflict was connected with Amaziah's discharge of some Israelite mercenaries and their subsequent assaults against Judean cities (2 Chr. 25:5–13), which were presumably designed in part compensate them for being unable to share in the spoils of the Judean Edomite campaign. The Judeans were in any case overwhelmed by the Israelites at Beth-shemesh, about twenty miles west of Jerusalem, and then the capital of Judah itself was assaulted. A section of the wall was broken down, plunder removed from the apparently refurbished temple and palace, and hostages taken away to ensure future good behavior. The way in which the story in Kings is told implies that Amaziah may himself have been kept as one of the hostages and that Judah may have been effectively governed by Israel after the battle of Beth-shemesh. We are never told in this passage that any *release* followed his capture (2 Kgs. 14:13), but we *are* informed in unusual wording that he "lived" (rather than "reigned") for fifteen years after the death of Jehoash (14:17). Just before we read of Amaziah's demise, indeed, we find the concluding regnal formulae for

Jehoash repeated (14:15–16; cf. 13:12–13), right in the midst of Amaziah's story. Then again, we must note that this *first* account in Kings of foreign capture of Jerusalem is very reminiscent of the *second from last* (2 Kgs. 24:8 ff.), where we also read of a king (Jehoiachin) taken captive with hostages, and both temple and palace being plundered. That king went on "living" (Hebrew *hyh*, as in 2 Kgs. 14:17) in Babylon for many years afterwards—still called "king" by the authors of Kings even though the king of Babylon effectively ruled over Judah (2 Kgs. 25:27–30; note the analogous use of "king of Edom" in 2 Kgs. 3:9, 26, cf. 1 Kgs. 22:47). Most significantly, precisely in that context of the deportation of Judean kings do we begin to find the regnal years of a foreign king cited (the king of Babylon: 2 Kgs. 24:12; 25:8)—the ruler who was really in control. Adding all this together, we are justified in reading 2 Kings 14:13–20 as presenting the king of Israel as the real ruler of Judah in this period,[60] both at the point of Jehoash's death and for at least fifteen years thereafter during the reign of his son Jeroboam.[61] By the end of that period, at least, Amaziah had returned to Jerusalem, for the biblical texts tell us that he fell victim to a conspiracy there and was subsequently assassinated (2 Kgs. 14:19; 2 Chr. 25:27).

We are not told in the biblical texts who conspired, but perhaps significantly we hear nothing later of any reprisals by Amaziah's son Azariah (15:1–7; contrast 14:5–6),[62] and he himself may have been implicated. We may well imagine that Amaziah would have been unpopular as the king who had led Judah to disaster and subjugation, and that many would have wished him removed. Of Azariah himself we hear almost nothing in Kings, save that he consolidated Amaziah's gains in Edom by at some point reclaiming the port of Elath (2 Kgs. 14:22; cf. 1 Kgs. 9:26). Chronicles adds to this the information that he fought successful campaigns against the Philistines and various southern enemies (2 Chr. 26:6–7), received tribute from the Ammonites (26:8, or perhaps the Meunites just mentioned in 26:7, as in the LXX), fortified Jerusalem in the aftermath of the Israelite assault on the city (26:9, 15), and initiated both agricultural and military reforms (26:10–14).[63] Whether he did all this effectively as a vassal of Jeroboam of Israel or after freeing himself from northern control is not something that our texts tell us.[64] That Judah did eventually free itself from Israelite control at some point during Azariah's long reign, and indeed gain the ascendancy over her northern neighbor, is certainly implied by an Assyrian text from the reign of Tiglath-pileser III (744–727 B.C.), which apparently knows of the Judean king as the head of an anti-Assyrian alliance in 738 B.C.[65] This event would have to be placed in the period when our biblical sources suggest that in fact Azariah's son Jotham was exercising effective governmental power in Judah as a result of his father's illness—an illness that Kings perhaps implies and Chronicles explicitly states was a result of religious shortcomings (2 Kgs. 15:5; 2 Chr. 26:16–21).[66]

The king who ruled in northern Israel during the fifteen years after the battle of Beth-shemesh and for a long time afterwards was Jehoash's son Jeroboam (usually called Jeroboam II, to distinguish him from Jeroboam son of Nebat). In a period of relative Assyrian quiescence in Syria-Palestine,[67] he carried further the

Israelite recovery begun by his father. The authors of Kings tell us that he was able to restore the boundaries of Israel from Lebo Hamath[68] to the Sea of Arabah (i.e., the Dead Sea; cf. Josh. 3:16; 12:3). This assertion represents not merely a claim that he recovered all the territory in Transjordan captured by Hazael in 2 Kings 10:32–33, but also a claim that he renewed Israel's dominion over much of southern Syria in a manner analogous to the previous Solomonic dominion. This striking achievement is reported in relatively few words in Kings, however, because the focus of interest lies instead in the religious conditions in Israel and the associated doom that the authors see as lying just ahead. The book of Amos, likewise, while both looking forward to and reflecting Israel's military successes against the Damascus Arameans,[69] is much more interested in the religious and social realities of the kingdom at this time, and in the same forthcoming disaster.[70] The recovery of Israel, while it had created wealth, had not produced social justice, and the religious piety of the people was pretense. Jeroboam and his royal house would shortly come to a violent end, and Israel would go into exile (Amos 7:10–17).

With Jeroboam's death and the assassination of his son Zechariah (2 Kgs. 15:8–12), the northern kingdom was indeed, after a brief period of recovery, on its way to destruction. The assassin Shallum held on to power for a mere month before losing both crown and life to Menachem (2 Kgs. 15:13–15), whose power base was apparently in the old Israelite capital of Tirzah (vv. 14, 16). The Hebrew text of Kings presents Menachem as making one last attempt to retain for Israel a Solomon-like empire, by engaging in a campaign that took him as far north as Tiphsah on the Euphrates River (15:16, cf. 1 Kgs. 4:24), although some textual uncertainty surrounds the identity of the city mentioned.[71] Whatever the case, during the reigns of Menachem in the northern kingdom and Azariah/Jotham in the southern kingdom, the relative lull in Assyrian military activity in Syria-Palestine came to a decisive end with the appearance in the region of the armies of Tiglath-pileser III (also know as Pulu or Pul, as in 2 Kgs. 15:19). This event began a process through which northern Israel along with most of the Syro-Hittite states to her north were within a very short period incorporated into the Assyrian empire. Menachem is described in Kings only as paying Tiglath-pileser tribute to make him a friend rather than an enemy—very likely in the aftermath of the successful Assyrian campaign of 738 B.C. against Syria and Phoenicia (2 Kgs. 15:19);[72] we know of no direct Assyrian involvement at all in Israelite affairs during the brief reign of Menachem's successor Pekahiah (2 Kgs. 15:23–26), who was, like Zechariah and Shallum, assassinated. During the reign of Pekahiah's successor Pekah, however, we read in both Kings and Chronicles of the Assyrian annexation of much of Israel's northern and eastern territory, and the deportation to Assyria of a significant percentage of her population (2 Kgs. 15:29–31; 2 Chr 5:26). This report is to be correlated with the campaigns against Philistia and Damascus noted in the *limmu*-chronicle for Tiglath-pileser's eleventh to thirteenth years (734–732 B.C.) as a result of which, Assyrian records tell us, the people of Israel overthrew Pekah and Tiglath-pileser replaced him with Hoshea.[73] Pekah's

Damascene ally Rezin also lost both his capital city Damascus and his life during this period, according to 2 Kings 16:9 (see further below on the Syro-Ephraimite war).[74] Second Kings 15:30 likewise reports the death of Pekah[75] and his replacement by Hoshea, although without mentioning Tiglath-pileser in this connection.[76] Only a few years passed, in any case, before the new Israelite king found himself imprisoned by Tiglath-pileser's successor Shalmaneser V (2 Kgs. 17:3–4) because of a failure to render tribute to Assyria and a conspiracy with Egypt,[77] a rebellion in which others may also have been involved.[78] Samaria was besieged and eventually captured around 722 B.C., and Israelites were subsequently carried off to Assyria and dispersed in various places throughout the empire.[79] In due course, Israel was transformed into the Assyrian province of Samerina.[80]

The reigning kings in Judah during this last period of the northern kingdom's existence were Jotham, Ahaz, and, in his initial years, Hezekiah. Jotham's reign is briefly described in 2 Kings 15:32–38 and in 2 Chronicles 27:1–9, where the most important detail aside from the note about victory over the Ammonites concerns the combined assault on his northern border by Rezin, king of Aram, and Pekah, son of Remaliah (2 Kgs. 15:37). This action is the beginning of the so-called Syro-Ephraimite war, which features so prominently in Isaiah 7–9 and is further described in 2 Kings 16:5–9 and 2 Chronicles 28:5–21. Ahaz in particular is described in the biblical sources as having been put under great pressure by the Syro-Ephraimite alliance, losing battles and hostages (2 Chr. 28:5–15) and being besieged in Jerusalem and deprived of Elath (2 Kgs. 16:5–6; Elath had only recently been won back for Judah by Azariah [2 Kgs. 14:22]).[81] Other parties may also have participated in the alliance, or at least they took advantage of the situation likewise to assault Judah (the Edomites [2 Chr. 28:17]; the Philistines [2 Chr. 28:18]).[82] The Judean king's response was to call on Tiglath-pileser for help, which in Kings arrives in the shape of the Assyrian campaign in Syria-Palestine of 734–732 B.C., already mentioned above (2 Kgs. 16:7–9), although Chronicles characterizes it more as affliction than as help (2 Chr. 28:20–21). Certainly as a consequence, Judah came firmly under the overlordship of Assyria; Ahaz had accepted vassal status and had offered tribute.[83] For the biblical authors, indeed, the intervention of Assyria into Judean affairs was fateful in its consequences for Judah not simply in terms of politics, but also in terms of religion. Ahaz is presented very much as a king who was open to foreign influence in his religious policy (2 Kgs. 16:2–4, 10–18; 2 Chr. 28:2–4, 22–25), even if he is not clearly (as some have argued) under foreign *control* in this policy.[84]

FROM THE FALL OF SAMARIA
TO THE SURRENDER OF JERUSALEM

With the fall of Samaria and the incorporation of much of Syria-Palestine into the Assyrian empire, only Judah was left as a relatively independent remnant of what had been Israel. On the understanding of the chronological data in Kings which is adopted in this chapter, Ahaz's son Hezekiah had become king just a few years before the end of the northern kingdom (727 B.C., following 2 Kgs. 18:9–12), although he was not yet sole ruler of the kingdom (since his fourteenth year in 2 Kgs. 18:13 is correlated with Sennacherib of Assyria's invasion of Judah in 701 B.C., implying an accession date of 714 B.C.).[85] Being certain of very much during this period of Judah's history from 727–714 B.C., or even in the period between 714 and 701 B.C., is difficult. Assyrian inscriptions touching on Judah are both sparse and ambiguous in their implications, while our biblical sources are narrowly focused, concentrating almost entirely upon the religious reforms for which Hezekiah was famous (2 Kgs. 18:3–6; 2 Chr. 29:3–31:21), on the one hand, and on Sennacherib's invasion of Judah, on the other. Second Chronicles 29:3 claims that the reform process began in Hezekiah's first year, and that at some point in this process the reforms spread outside Judah and into what had been Israel (2 Chr. 30–31). Whether this reference to "the first year" is best taken literally, or only as expressing the general conviction that Hezekiah was a king who from the beginning had reforming instincts, requires some discussion.[86]

That the Judean aspects of the reforms might have begun in 727–726 B.C. (literally in the first year in which Hezekiah exercised royal authority) is not inconceivable. A subsequent attempt at religious and perhaps political reunification of the whole people of Israel was perhaps also undertaken in the immediate aftermath of the fall of the northern kingdom, before Sargon II's control over Syria-Palestine was fully established and the situation in the new province of Samerina fully regularized after 720 B.C.[87] Although no mention is made in Sargon's annals of military action specifically against Judah in Sargon's second year (720 B.C.) when the Assyrians descended on Syria-Palestine to crush the revolt that had broken out there, another Assyrian inscription does refer to Sargon as "the subduer of the country Judah which is far away," apparently in connection with the same campaign.[88] This characterization may suggest that Judah after Hezekiah's accession did not have quite the same attitude towards Assyria as appears to have been prevalent after Ahaz's accession, and Hezekiah's interest in the old northern kingdom in particular could well be the factor that drew him into the revolt. If one then looks for a reason as to why Judah is not mentioned in other texts, we could speculate that Hezekiah perhaps retreated in the face of forthcoming military conflict with Sargon and renewed his oaths of loyalty through the payment of tribute. That the "subduing" mentioned in the Assyrian text can be understood as involving no more than the receipt of tribute from a people who had renewed oaths of loyalty is, however, the weakness of the theory that Hezekiah was involved in the revolt of 720 B.C. at all, for there is no other evidence that he was.

Similar uncertainty surrounds the Judean role in the revolt spearheaded by the Philistine city of Ashdod, which might also provide a plausible context for Hezekiah's reforms, particularly if Hezekiah's "first year" is regarded as the first year of his sole rule over Judah (714 B.C.). Assyrian records tell us of an effort by Ashdod to woo other Philistine cities along with Judah, Edom, and Moab away from Assyria, and of an attempt to gain support also from Egypt.[89] This revolt eventually led to the incorporation of the Philistine city of Ashdod into the Assyrian provincal system. However, no evidence is present in Assyrian or biblical sources either that Ashdod's attempt to win Judah over was successful or that Judah suffered any Assyrian penalties after the revolt was over.[90] If Judah was involved, we must assume once again that Hezekiah came to some arrangement with Assyria before judgment descended. The probability of Judean involvement, however, seems slight.

The first event described in Assyrian records which can thus be securely related to the statement in 2 Kings 18:7 that Hezekiah "rebelled against the king of Assyria" is the widespread revolt that broke out in Syria-Palestine, as in other parts of the empire, after Sargon's death in 705 B.C. Many of Hezekiah's activities in the old northern kingdom are perhaps best located in the years following 705 B.C., even if we allow that he was "from the beginning" a reforming king and may have instituted some religious reforms earlier in his reign. Certainly biblical tradition focuses its account of Hezekiah's reign upon events connected with the Assyrian reaction to the Syro-Palestinian revolt after 705 B.C. The new king, Sennacherib, before turning his attention to Syria-Palestine, had been involved in a campaign in southern Mesopotamia against the erstwhile king of Babylon, Marduk-apla-iddina II, who had led a revolt there in renewed pursuit of his own royal claims (703–702 B.C.). Envoys of this king (Merodach-Baladan) appear in Jerusalem in 2 Kings 20:12–19, perhaps suggesting that the anti-Assyrian resistance that arose after Sargon's death in different parts of the empire was coordinated rather than coincidental, and had its roots in long-term contacts between the different groups involved in the resistance.[91] Be that as it may, Sennacherib eventually marched into Syria-Palestine in 701 B.C., intent on reestablishing Assyrian control. Our sources indicate that Hezekiah had prepared himself well for the assault, not least in making a preemptive strike against Philistine territory associated with Gaza, whose king Sillibel (we deduce from Sennacherib's own account of the campaign) had remained loyal to Assyria, and in imprisoning the similarly loyal king Padi of Ekron.[92]

All this activity implies that Hezekiah was one of the moving forces of the revolt, which may in turn help to explain a curiosity of the Kings account of what happened next. The authors of Kings, in reporting the beginning of the Assyrian assault on Judah, indicate that when many of his cities had already fallen, Hezekiah offered Sennacherib renewed tribute if the Assyrian king would withdraw (2 Kgs. 18:13–16). This development is unsurprising, when considering that according to Sennacherib's own account the coalition had already early in the campaign collapsed. Luli, king of Sidon, had fled, and his cities had been brought to submission; others had also submitted or, in the case of Sidqia of Ashkelon, had been deported to Assyria. The striking feature about the account in 2 Kings 18, however, is that we are told that the king of Assyria did not on this occasion withdraw upon payment of tribute, choosing while Jerusalem's gates remained closed to him to continue to regard Hezekiah as a rebel. An army was thus sent from Lachish (southwest of Jerusalem) to Jerusalem, in order to persuade

Hezekiah to surrender fully (2 Kgs. 18:17 ff.).[93] Perhaps Hezekiah's prominence as a rebel explains the Assyrian reaction.

Be that as it may, the biblical accounts in 2 Kings 18:13–19:37, 2 Chronicles 32:1–22, and Isaiah 36:31–37:38 and Sennacherib's own account all agree that Jerusalem ended up being besieged by an Assyrian army because Hezekiah was perceived as not submitting to Assyrian overlordship. Kings, Isaiah, and the Assyrian records also agree that, at some point during the campaign, an Egyptian army appeared on the scene. The Assyrian text describes its appearance and the ensuing battle before it describes the siege of Jerusalem, but in so doing does not clearly intend to be strictly chronological, whereas Kings and Isaiah do clearly imply that the Egyptian advance occurred after the siege had begun. Sennacherib claims to have defeated this Egyptian force at Eltekeh, and we have no reason to disbelieve him. Perhaps it was after this Assyrian victory that Hezekiah, in an attempt to buy more time, released Padi of Ekron, whom Sennacherib claims to have "made" come from Jerusalem and to have reestablished on his throne. Whether this is the case or not, Sennacherib does not claim to have taken Jerusalem at any point, nor even to have received tribute from Hezekiah in the immediate aftermath of the siege. He tells us only that after his return to Nineveh (whose occasion he does not describe) Hezekiah sent tribute on. The silence on this matter of the conclusion of Sennacherib's assault on Hezekiah, when compared to what Sennacherib says in his inscription about other kings in the region, requires some explanation; our biblical sources give us some hints when they tell us of a mysterious reversal suffered by the Assyrians while Jerusalem lay at their mercy. The biblical authors go no further in their description of this reversal than ascribing it to "the angel of the Lord." When others have attempted an interpretation more medical than theological, they have usually wondered whether a plague of some kind might not have occasioned the Assyrian withdrawal.[94] A withdrawal there was, in any case. That Hezekiah subsequently decided to reaffirm his vassalship to Assyria by sending tribute on to Nineveh, as Sennacherib claims, is entirely plausible. Second Kings 18:13–16 suggests that he had wished to settle things in this manner in the first place; in the aftermath of Sennacherib's campaign Hezekiah was evidently isolated, with much of his territory annexed by Ashdod, Ekron, and Gaza, and significant portions of his army having deserted him.

Of Hezekiah's son Manasseh we know almost nothing apart from what our biblical sources tell us. His name occasionally appears in Assyrian records from the reigns of Esarhaddon (680–669 B.C.) and Ashurbanipal (668–c.630 B.C.), although these records are not very illuminating. He is, for example, listed in Esarhaddon's records as one of the Syro-Palestinian kings required at an uncertain date to provide forced labor for the purpose of transporting building materials to Nineveh for the construction of Esarhaddon's palace there. He was also probably involved prior to this episode in the building of the new Assyrian city of Kar-Esarhaddon on the Phoenician coast, in the aftermath of the revolt of the king of Sidon (677–676).[95] During Ashurbanipal's reign, Manasseh's Judean forces fought on the Assyrian side during the king's first campaign (in Egypt, 667

B.C.).[96] He appears for much of his reign to have been a loyal vassal to Assyria, carrying out vassal obligations of this kind in a period when Assyrian control of Palestine grew ever stronger.[97] The Assyrian records certainly do not suggest otherwise. It is all the same quite conceivable that at some point in his long reign Manasseh adopted a different course in relation to Assyria, or at least was suspected of doing so, as suggested by 2 Chronicles 33:11–13.[98] Policy changes among the rulers of Syria-Palestine with regard to Assyria were not exactly unknown throughout the period of Assyrian domination of the region, depending upon what else was happening in the empire. The most likely context for Manasseh's temporary deportation to Babylon as described in Chronicles is in fact the aftermath of the rebellion by Ashurbanipal's brother Shamash-shum-ukin, king of Babylon under Ashurbanipal's overlordship, in 652–648 B.C. During the period of Ashurbanipal's campaigning in Babylonia to quell this revolt, there was widespread disaffection in Syria-Palestine, and Manasseh could have been drawn into this sentiment, or at least have fallen under suspicion.[99] A trip to Babylon during the siege or after the fall of this city (648 B.C.) to answer charges would then be quite comprehensible. We certainly have parallels for the lenient treatment that Chronicles describes Manasseh as being afforded after his trip to Babylon, when he was restored to the Judean throne.[100] His subsequent building work and religious reforms, described in 2 Chronicles 33:14–16, imply that after his restoration he enjoyed a degree of freedom under Assyrian overlordship, perhaps because Ashurbanipal wished to have Judah as a strong buffer state between Syria-Palestine and Egypt. Egypt had itself withheld tribute a few years before Shamash-shum-ukin's rebellion, and afterwards never came under the Assyrian domination that it had experienced earlier during the reigns of both Esarhaddon and Ashurbanipal. Beginning in the period after the rebellion, indeed, with Ashurbanipal occupied with troubles elsewhere in his empire, Pharaoh Psammetichus I gradually extended Egypt's influence once again into Syria-Palestine and became more of a presence there. How far Ashurbanipal had any effective control over Manasseh in this period is uncertain.

Manasseh was succeeded on the throne of Judah by his son Amon, who reigned only briefly before being assassinated (2 Kgs. 21:19–26; 2 Chr. 33:21–25) and of whom we know virtually nothing. He was succeeded by Josiah who, in contrast to Amon, receives considerable attention in our biblical sources and is considered by the biblical authors as one of Israel's most important kings, because of his religious policy. Both Kings and Chronicles portray Josiah as one who pursued what was, from the authors' point of view, a pure form of Yahwism—a Yahwism in line with the law of Moses as contained in the Pentateuch (or more specifically in the case of Kings and perhaps also Chronicles, the book of Deuteronomy).[101] Chronicles has him beginning his reforms even before the finding of the law book in the temple, while Kings mentions reforms only afterwards. The precise connection between discovery and reform therefore remains unclear.[102]

From both accounts, however, Josiah is clearly envisaged as seeking to reform worship both in Judah and in territory that had belonged to the northern kingdom of Israel (2 Kgs. 23:4–20; 2 Chr. 34:3–7).[103] That the opportunity existed from around the time of Josiah's twelfth year onwards (2 Chr. 34:3; that is 628, B.C.) for increasing Josianic activity to the north of his capital is clear from a consideration of the political circumstances of the period. Ashurbanipal himself died around 630 B.C., plunging the Assyrian empire into an extended period of civil war and general strife from which the city of Babylon eventually emerged as the new imperial power in the east. Palestine was far from the center of events throughout the period, and whatever is true of Assyrian influence there in the period from 639 to 630 B.C., it is reasonably clear that after 630 B.C. Assyria was little interested in or capable of exercising effective control. The major power in Syria-Palestine was increasingly Egypt, reported by various ancient sources as confronting in Palestine Scythian invaders from the north during this period and as exercising some degree of suzerainty over the cities of Philistia and the Phoenician coast.[104] Egypt often appears in texts from the period of Josiah's reign as an ally of Assyria in its struggle with Babylon, sending troops to the north at least from 616 B.C. onwards to join the Assyrians in battle there.[105] At least in this *later* part of Josiah's reign, therefore, the Egyptians had effective control of the so-called "Way of the Sea," which passed from Egypt along the western coast of Palestine and then northeast via Megiddo and Damascus. They perhaps also had effective control of Judah. The situation in the *earlier* part of Josiah's reign is, however, unclear. No evidence survives from this period that the Egyptians either exercised direct control over Judah, nor that they were very interested in doing so.[106] If they did, in the midst of the many larger matters that concerned them, they presumably would not have cared very much about Josianic interest in the territory to his north that did not directly affect their interests.[107] Our sources suggest that only when Josiah, at the end of his reign, moved to confront Egypt directly in a military way, interfering with movement along the "Way of the Sea" in traditionally Israelite territory, was direct Egyptian "interest" in the Judean king kindled.

This confrontation is described in both 2 Kings 23:29–30 and in 2 Chronicles 35:20–24. Psammetichus I's successor, Neco II, marched north in 609 B.C. for what was apparently the last joint Assyrian-Egyptian engagement with the Babylonians (and their allies the Medes). After this event we no longer hear of the last Assyrian ruler, Ashur-uballit II, who had set himself up as king in Harran after the fall of Nineveh in 612 B.C.; then the struggle for supremacy in the region is directly between Egypt and Babylon. On the way to this battle, the biblical sources tell us, Neco was opposed by Josiah at Megiddo.[108] The circumstances in which this conflict was initiated are not explained in the biblical texts, and we are left to wonder whether Josiah was attempting early in the reign of the new pharaoh (who had succeeded his father in 610 B.C.) to establish his independence from an increasingly powerful Egypt, perhaps hoping to benefit from being perceived to take the Babylonians' side. If so, the attempt ended in disaster. Josiah was killed, and any limited independence that Judah might have had during the period of Assyrian decline in Syria-Palestine was entirely lost. The new king Jehoahaz (also known as Shallum, Jer. 22:11; 1 Chr. 3:15) was immediately summoned to Neco's headquarters at Riblah and removed from power; he was subsequently imprisoned in Egypt. Neco placed Jehoahaz's brother Eliakim on the throne instead, changing his name to Jehoiakim,[109] and demanded a large tribute from Judah (2 Kgs. 23:31–35; 2 Chr. 36:1–4). Syria-Palestine then becomes explicitly for the first time in one of our sources the territory that "belonged to the king of Egypt, from the wadi of Egypt to the river Euphrates" (2 Kgs. 24:7), and Jehoiakim is named a vassal king appointed by the pharaoh.[110] This situation did not, however, last for long; the same verse tells us that only shortly afterwards the king of Babylon had taken all this territory.[111] The transformation began with crushing Babylonian victories over the Egyptians in 605 B.C. at Carchemish in northern Syria (cf. Jer. 46:1–12) and then further south at Hamath. The new Babylonian king Nebuchadnezzar then marched into Syria-Palestine during his first regnal year in 604 B.C. and, among other feats, captured the Philistine city of Ashkelon. Probably around this time Jehoiakim switched his allegiance to Babylon.[112] His submission was, however, short-lived, as only a few years later he rebelled. Although in the short term this rebellion brought down upon Judah only harrying by limited Babylonian and allied forces (2 Kgs. 24:2, cf. Jer. 35:11), the end of the year 598 B.C. saw the main Babylonian army before the gates of Jerusalem and no Egyptian forces on hand to help ("the king of Egypt did not come again out of his land," 2 Kgs. 24:7). The city surrendered to the Babylonians on March 15 or 16, 597 B.C., and the new king Jehoiachin (also called Jeconiah and Coniah, Jer. 22:24–30) was deported to Babylon along with many other leading citizens and much booty.[113] The independent state of Judah had all but come to its end.

Chapter 11

Exile and After

With the surrender of Jerusalem to the Babylonians in 597 B.C. and the deportation of the king and his leading citizens, we are on the very edge of the period of Israelite history commonly known as "the exile"—although worse was yet to befall both the city and its inhabitants, as the Babylonians returned to destroy the city and further depopulate the land. We might debate the extent of the destruction and the scope of the deportation or even the degree of suffering of the people. However, the biblical texts leave the reader in no doubt about the horror that this event elicited from the people of God at the time. The theological issue was immense, and much exilic and postexilic biblical material grapples with the implications.

SOURCES FOR THE EXILIC PERIOD

Surprisingly, the Bible does not give us an extended description or narrative of the exile itself.[1] A number of texts (2 Kgs. 25:1–21; 2 Chr. 36:15–21; Jer. 39) record the fall of Jerusalem, but we only receive glimpses of the period between the fall of Jerusalem and Cyrus's decree that allowed Jews to return to Palestine to rebuild the temple (2 Chr. 36:22–23). Of such, pride of place goes to Lamentations, a poetic response to the destruction of Jerusalem. We also hear some stories set in the early exilic period about those who remain in the land, particularly events surrounding the prophet Jeremiah (Jer. 40–44). Other stories purport to describe events that take place in the land of exile in this period (Dan. 1–5), and Ezekiel prophesies to those who were carried off to the land of Babylon beginning in 597 B.C. Habakkuk has God proclaim, "I am raising up the Babylonians" (1:6). Obadiah too may find its setting in the turmoil that follows the destruction of Jerusalem. Of course, opinions vary widely about the use of these books as historical sources.

Some archaeological evidence is available for the reconstruction of this period of time. Williamson reports that the evidence shows "widespread destruction of major towns in Judah to the south of Jerusalem (e.g., Lachish, Azekah, Ramat Rahel, Arad), but of greater continuity (or reestablishment) of habitation to the north, in the territory of Benjamin (Bethel, Gibeon, Tell el-Ful, and Mizpah, the probable site of Babylonian administration)."[2] McNutt adds that the graves found in the Hinnom valley indicate that some people remained in the vicinity of Jerusalem during the exile.[3]

Extrabiblical texts pertaining to the rise and fall of the neo-Babylonian period—like the Babylonian Chronicle[4] and the Nabonidus Chronicle[5]—are relevant to our study. From these texts, we find a Mesopotamian perspective on the period.

The relative dearth of biblical and archeological, not to speak of extrabiblical textual, evidence makes reconstruction of the period difficult. As we shall see, sociological analysis has stepped into the breach and provided a number of interesting hypotheses. However, the wisdom of pitting these hypotheses against the biblical record, as is sometimes done, should be questioned, given the often-speculative nature of sociological method.

THE FALL OF JERUSALEM

Even before and certainly after his accession to the throne (605 B.C.), Nebuchadnezzar king of Babylon had had to deal with what one might call the "Jerusalem problem." His interim solution, in 597 B.C., was to cart Jehoiachin off to Babylon in chains and to place a new king—"a king of his liking" as the Babylonian Chronicle refers to him[6]—on the throne. He is identified in 2 Kings 24:17 ff. as Jehoiachin's uncle Mattaniah, who was given the new name Zedekiah (cf. also Jer. 37:1; 2 Chr. 36:10 ff.).[7] Nebuchadnezzar's strategy in thus keeping a Davidic descendant on the throne was apparently to try to control Judah through puppet kings.

However, Jeremiah 27–29 suggests that from early on in his reign (Jer. 27:1; 28:1) Zedekiah was involved in discussions with neighboring peoples about the possibility of revolt. Opinion in Judah was divided on the wisdom of such a course of action and the permanence of Babylonian dominion. No evidence exists that Judah or the neighboring peoples were involved in rebellion against Babylon in the years immediately following the surrender of Jerusalem. Jeremiah 51:59 tells us, indeed, of a journey by Zedekiah to Babylon around the same time as the above discussions, which we must surmise had something to do with renewed pledges of loyalty. At some point in the next few years, however, Judah did in fact rebel against Babylon, in circumstances that are not entirely clear, but which are no doubt connected with the machinations of Egypt under Psammetichus II (595–589).[8] Zedekiah stopped paying tribute,[9] and a new siege of Jerusalem followed (2 Kgs. 25:1 ff.; Jer. 52:4 ff.),[10] which was temporarily lifted when the new pharaoh Apries (589–570) sent an army into Palestine.[11] The siege resumed when the Egyptian army withdrew. The city eventually fell in 587 or 586 B.C.[12] after two years, with all supplies of food exhausted.

This time Nebuchadnezzar determined to exercise a more radical solution to the Jerusalem problem. Zedekiah managed to escape by night when defeat was imminent and fled in the direction of Transjordan. He was overtaken by the Babylonians near Jericho, however. His sons were executed, and he himself was blinded and deported to Babylon, never to be heard of again. Nebuchadnezzar then ordered the systematic destruction of the city that included such prominent buildings as the temple and palace (2 Kgs. 25:8–10). He also tore down the city defenses, most significantly its walls. Interestingly, the Babylonian officer named as the head of this post-victory destruction is named as a high official in Babylonian tablets.[13] Further executions occurred, and Nebuchadnezzar exiled many of Judah's leading citizens to Babylon.[14] The exact scope of this exile and its nature are debated.

THE EXTENT OF THE DESTRUCTION

The biblical record consistently records that the physical destruction of the city was massive. Houses and the king's palace were destroyed. The city's defenses were razed, but perhaps the most devastating loss to the city was the temple. The temple symbolized the presence of God to the people, even if, as Solomon's dedication speech had made clear (1 Kgs. 8), God did not really "live" in it. From Jeremiah's temple sermon, one can conclude that even those who did not consistently follow Yahweh put great pride in the temple and presumptuously believed that the presence of the temple would preserve them from defeat (Jer. 7:26). In the end, however, Ezekiel's vision describing Yahweh's abandonment of the temple on the eve of the defeat of Jerusalem was understood as representing reality more accurately (Ezek. 9–11).

That the destruction of the city had devastating consequences for the people of Judah may be seen in the book of Lamentations. Lamentations is a poem in the literary tradition of the Mesopotamian city laments, like the Lamentation over the Destruction of Sumer and Ur, that bemoaned the destruction of Ur after it was plundered by the Elamites from the east and the Amorites from the west at the turn of the third to the second millennium.[15] The biblical Lamentations was likely written in the early exilic period, though some scholars argue that the genre's *Sitz im Leben* was during the rebuilding of the temple. In any case, it paints a picture of desolation and destruction as it begins:

> How deserted lies the city,
>   once so full of people!
> How like a widow is she,
>   who once was great among the nations!
> She who was a queen among the provinces
>   has now become a slave.
>   (Lam. 1:1, NIV)

God himself had turned against his people. During their history, God had appeared many times as a warrior to help them defeat much more powerful enemies. Now, God appears as an enemy:

> Like an enemy he [God] has strung his bow;
>   his right hand is ready.
> Like a foe he has slain
>   all who were pleasing to the eye;
> he has poured out his wrath like fire
>   on the tent of the Daughter of Zion.
>   (Lam 2:4, NIV)

Although the destruction of Jerusalem and its temple was thus evidently extensive and upsetting in the extreme to the people and should not be minimized, some semblance of the old temple building may have survived or been clumsily reassembled in some fashion; for in Jeremiah 41:4–7 we hear of worshipers coming to the temple area in order to offer grain offerings and incense. That the destruction was severe is indicated by their mournful posture and attitude at the time; even with extensive destruction, though, worship continued at the temple site.

THE SCOPE OF THE DEPORTATION

Casual readers of the Bible generally assume that virtually the entire population of Judah was carried off to Babylon at this time with only the most derelict remaining behind. This picture may not be accurate. H. M. Barstad, for instance, while agreeing that Nebuchadnezzar did serious damage in the capital and crippled the national leadership, interprets the archaeological and textual evidence as indicating that the basic structure of society stayed substantially intact.[16] We must certainly acknowledge some ambiguity in the biblical testimony itself. On the one hand we have Kings and Chronicles. Kings does tell us, "Nebuzaradan the commander of the guard carried into exile the people who remained in the city, along with the rest of the populace and those who had gone over to the king of Babylon. But the commander left behind some of the poorest people of the land to work the vineyards and fields" (2 Kgs. 25:11–12, see also Jer. 39:9–10). Second Chronicles 36:21 further describes the land as desolate, enforcing the fallowing of agricultural land that should have been voluntary during sabbatical years.[17] On the other hand, however, Jeremiah gives us precise numbers that throw into question the impression given by Kings:

> This is the number of the people Nebuchadnezzar carried into exile:
>
>> in the seventh year, 3,023 Jews;
>> in Nebuchadnezzar's eighteenth year,
>>   832 people from Jerusalem;
>> in his twenty-third year,
>>   745 Jews taken into exile by Nebuzaradan
>>   the commander of the imperial guard.
>>   There were 4,600 people in all.
>>   (Jer. 52:28–30, NIV)

The destruction of Jerusalem that we are presently discussing took place in Nebuchadnezzar's eighteenth year. Thus, according to Jeremiah, we are talking about a deportation of only 832 people.[18] If one is tempted simply to say that 832 people constitutes a large group at that time and place, an additional obstacle suggests that Kings and Jeremiah are actually using numbers differently. That is, for the deportation in 597 B.C., Jeremiah records an exile of 3,023, while 2 Kings reports above 10,000 people, including the entire fighting force of 7,000 men (2 Kgs. 24:14–17), and characterizes this deportation as involving "all Jerusalem" (2 Kgs. 23:14). Attempts to harmonize by saying that Jeremiah records only the men while Kings records men, women, and children,[19] while not impossible, are certainly ad hoc and have no justification in the text itself. More likely is that the high numbers in Kings, as at other points in that book, are not intended literally.[20]

The best we can say, then, on the basis of the texts is that in 586 B.C., many were killed and others deported. The unanimous testimony of the biblical texts holds that the elite, and probably the urban elite, were carried away. Those who remained were identified as the "poor of the land" (2 Kgs. 25:12), and we return to them shortly. First, however, what was the fate of the exiles? They were compelled to leave their homes and the land that their ancestors had entered centuries before. As Klein reports, "exile meant death, deportation, destruction, and devastation."[21] They would no longer be able to serve their own interests, but would have to do the Babylonians' bidding. Berquist,[22] using hints from the biblical text as well as sociological theory, argues that they were brought to the core of Babylon in order to work in the fields as well as in administration. The expanding empire of Babylon needed more labor than the native population could supply. However, though compelled, they were not slaves. Indeed, as we think of the biblical pictures of Daniel and his three friends in Babylonia, as well as Mordecai who lived in the diaspora in Persia, we see how the exiles sometimes went beyond survival to prosperity and position within the oppressor state. Extrabiblical texts like those of the archives of the Murashu family bolster this assessment. The

Murashu family was a prominent commercial agent during the mid- to latter half of the fifth century B.C., thus overlapping with the events described in the books of Ezra and Nehemiah. Archaeologists have recovered 879 tablets belonging to this archive, which describe their financial dealings.[23] They were located in Nippur in Achaemenid (Persian) Babylonia, and their commercial dealings radiated out from there. Of interest to us is the mention of some eighty individuals with Jewish names.[24] This accounting shows that at least some of those Jews who stayed in Persia rather than returning to Palestine were integrated into the society, although these tablets make clear that at least in this case the Jews were not at the top of the social ladder. They are cited only as witnesses and as small landowners. Even the successful integration of some in any case fails to mitigate the suffering endured by many who remained behind in the diaspora.[25]

One of the most interesting extrabiblical texts that touches on the deportation is an administrative document that relates to Jehoiachin, the Judaean king deported to Babylon in the 597 B.C. siege of Jerusalem. This document lists rations for Jehoiachin and his sons, apparently in captivity in Babylon.[26] This remarkable document attests to Jehoiachin's presence in Babylon during the exile and lends credence to the reference to his release during the reign of Amel-Marduk (Evil-Merodach), Nebuchadnezzar's son and short-lived successor (2 Kgs. 25:27–30). The reference places his release in the year 561 B.C.[27]

Those Who Remained

All the sources agree that the Babylonians left some of the people in the land, typically described as the "poorest of the land" (2 Kgs. 25:12; Jer. 39:10; 52:16). To watch over these people Nebuchadnezzar placed a garrison of troops in Jerusalem and appointed a native (non-Davidic) Judaean leader named Gedaliah[28]—perhaps the same Gedaliah whose name has been discovered on two bullae.[29] Gedaliah's capital was moved from the destroyed Jerusalem to the city of Mizpeh, which had been identified with Tell en-Nasbeh about six miles from the former capital. Our information about what happened next derives mainly from Jeremiah 40–43—the lengthiest account of Judah in the immediate postexilic period, albeit with a focus on the fate of Jeremiah himself. That prophet, who had at God's direction consistently encouraged Judah to submit to Babylon, had been given a choice about his fate by Nebuchadnezzar. Rather than accompany the exiles to Babylon, he opted to stay behind and live in Palestine, where he was witness to the attempts of Gedaliah to bring the different elements of the remnant of Judaeans back to the land where they would help plant and harvest the crops. Apparently, Judaeans had scattered to the surrounding countries of Moab, Ammon, and Edom in the face of the Babylonian threat.

Among these people was a man named Ishmael who was of royal blood (Jer. 41:1) and for that reason may have had aspirations towards resisting the Babylonians and leading a restoration. Whatever his motives, he plotted against and assassinated Gedaliah and massacred the Babylonian troops who were stationed in Judah. This action, of course, could mean only one thing. Nebuchadnezzar would have to take vengeance and restore order. Ishmael, who was under the employ of the king of Ammon, committed further atrocities not only against the Babylonians but also against his own people. Another Judaean leader, Jonathan of Kareah, resisted him, but eventually felt that leaving Palestine would be safer, considering that Nebuchadnezzar was on his way. So he and his group grabbed Jeremiah against his will and left for Egypt. We never hear directly of this group again, but this episode may explain at least partially the later large Jewish community in Egypt known from the Elephantine Papyri as well as from the production of the Septuagint, an early Greek translation of the Old Testament.

Even after the depopulation of the land, many remained. A natural conclusion would be that these people moved to take over some of the vacated land, and if so, their joy at the later return from exile by those who had left, if present at all (see below), would not be unalloyed. As Williamson indicates, later evidence also suggests that some foreign people, like the Edomites, took advantage of the situation and moved into Judaean territory,[30] a move perhaps attested to by Obadiah.

Questioning the Exile

In keeping with a general skepticism concerning the history of ancient Israel, some recent discussions concerning the exile have taken place. Virtually every scholar is willing to agree that some traumatic event happened to the inhabitants of Jerusalem in the sixth century, but they not only question the extent of the trauma, as alluded to in the paragraphs above, but also whether exile rather than deportation is the right understanding of the text. An exile supposes a return, it is said, and also a privileging of those who did return to the promised land even over against those who remained in the land as well as those who remained in the dispersion. An exile, as opposed to a deportation, also presupposes an ethnic continuity between those who were exiled and those who returned, something that not all scholars are willing to grant.

This question is an important one because the exile, like the exodus, is an important transition point in Israelite and later Jewish history. The exile has left a huge impression on the minds of the descendants of the Israelites. Modern scholarship too treats the exile as an important moment, since the latter part of the history of Israel is commonly divided into pre- and postexilic. Those contemporary scholars who question the status of the exile look back to C. C. Torrey as a father figure. Torrey had questioned the exile, but his views were overwhelmed by the wave of historical optimism that W. F. Albright and his followers represented.[31] Torrey is getting his say again now that a form of historical skepticism is coming into prominence as represented in this issue by P. R. Davies and R. P. Carroll.[32] Much of this debate depends on issues of historical methodology described and debated in the first chapters of this book. For one thing, the ideological tendencies of the biblical report of the exile and return discourage Davies, Carroll, and others from treating them as talking about actual events.

Other scholars of the exile, however, have pointed out that the ideological bias of other ancient historical reports have not led us to discard them as sources of actual history.[33] Furthermore, as B. Becking argues, the fact that some evidence exists outside the Bible for the exile (see discussion of the Jehoiachin ration text above) should lead one to give the presumption of veracity to other aspects of the biblical record that are not yet directly supported.[34]

THE FALL OF BABYLON

Babylon under Nabopolassar (626–605) and his son Nebuchadnezzar (605–552) was a formidable empire. After the latter's death, however, he was succeeded in relatively quick succession by his son Amel-Marduk, his son-in-law Neriglissar, and his grandson Labashi-Marduk. We are not certain what brought to the throne the final king of Babylon, Nabonidus (555–539), but his idiosyncrasies help explain what led to the final demise of an independent Babylonian empire. Nabonidus was from Harran, which was the worship center for Sin, the moon god. We know from a quasi-autobiographical account of his mother that his devotion to the lunar deity was a family matter.[35] In any case, his privileging of the cult of the moon god led to the alienation of the powerful Marduk priesthood and eventually the loss of the people's affection. Indeed, though we are uncertain of his motives,[36] Nabonidus moved to Tema in what is today Saudi Arabia and left his son and coregent, Bel-shar-usur (Belshazzar) on the throne in Babylon.[37] Sources indicate that he returned to Babylon in 543 B.C. in the light of threats from over the Zagros mountains.

In the meantime, on the other side of those mountains, Cyrus was on the rise. He was the son of a Persian king (Cambyses I) who had married a daughter of the Median king Astyages. Astyages himself was Cyrus's first conquest (550 B.C.); with his defeat of his grandfather, Cyrus united the Persians and Medes. Next, Cyrus defeated Lydia under Croesus, after a brief siege of his capital city Sardis; then he turned his attention to the neo-Babylonian empire. Daniel 5 reflects the eve of the empire, with Belshazzar throwing a banquet where the writing on the wall indicated his almost immediate defeat. Before reaching the city of Babylon, Cyrus had defeated a major Babylonian army at Opis. Ancient tradition explains that alienated elements within Babylon assisted Cyrus so that he did not have to shed blood as he entered the city.[38] The year was 539 B.C.—a date that marks the transition, because of what followed Cyrus's victory, to the postexilic period.

SOURCES FOR THE POSTEXILIC PERIOD

The biblical evidence for the postexilic period is more extensive than for the exile. The decree of Cyrus and the initial return of exiles to Judah are narrated briefly at the end of Chronicles (2 Chr. 36:23–24). The most extensive witness to the period is Ezra-Nehemiah, in reality a single book.[39] However, a close look at its contents shows that it presents a somewhat restricted view. Ezra 1–6 is a historical record largely of the events of the early postexilic period, namely, from the decree of Cyrus until the rebuilding of the temple, thus 539–515 B.C. The Ezra and Nehemiah memoirs, discussed below, describe what takes place during the first year of Ezra's return (458 B.C.) and for the twelve years in which Nehemiah served as governor of the Persian province of Yehud (445–433 B.C.). The book of Esther purports to narrate a crisis in the Jewish community in Persia that takes place during the reign of Xerxes/Artaxerxes (between 486 and 465 B.C.). The postexilic prophets Haggai, Zechariah, and Malachi also provide some insight into this time period.

Extrabiblical sources that are relevant to our study are numerous. Among the most helpful are the Cyrus cylinder, the Behistun inscription, the inscription of Udjahorresnet, as well as the Aramaic Elephantine papyrus. These and other texts come into play as we try to fill out the picture of the period. Interestingly, we also have the testimony of early Greek historians like Herodotus, Xenophon, and Ctesias, all contemporaneous with the Persian Empire. Traditionally, Herodotus has been considered basically reliable because he researched his study and showed himself critical of his sources at points, but Xenophon and particularly Ctesias have never met with the same level of confidence. However, in the present skeptical climate, no ancient historian escapes suspicion, including Josephus, the first-century-A.D. Jewish historian, particularly since he wrote long after the events of this period and often simply paraphrased the biblical story line.

According to the experts, the Persian period (often called Iron III in archaeologists' terminology) is difficult to distinguish in the archaeological record of Palestine.[40] McNutt also acknowledges this limitation but cautiously suggests that "the archaeological data we do have do seem to be consistent with some elements in the biblical record."[41]

THE EARLY POSTEXILIC PERIOD

The Cyrus Decree

In three places, we hear that Cyrus issued a decree that the exiles from Judah be allowed to return to Jerusalem and rebuild the temple that had been destroyed by Nebuchadnezzar. We quote the version found in Ezra 1:2–4 (see also 2 Chr. 36:23 and, in Aramaic, Ezra 6:3–5):

> "This is what Cyrus king of Persia says:
> "'The LORD, the God of heaven, has given me all the kingdoms of the earth and he has appointed me to build a temple for him at Jerusalem in Judah. Anyone of his people among you—may his God be with him, and let him go up to Jerusalem in Judah and build the temple of the LORD, the God of Israel, the God who is in Jerusalem. And the people of any place

where survivors may now be living are to provide him with silver and gold, with goods and livestock, and with freewill offerings for the temple of God in Jerusalem.'" (NIV)

This decree triggered a return to Judah that probably took place in waves, most of which we do not hear about. The text is selective, and we only read about those groups that returned under the leadership of Sheshbazzar and Zerubbabel with the intention of rebuilding the temple. On the surface, this gesture seems remarkably magnanimous on the Persian monarch's part, and certainly the returnees saw the hand of God in it and expressed gratitude toward Cyrus.

Additional information concerning Cyrus and his foreign policy, however, calls into question any idea that Cyrus was acting with entirely selfless motivation or with any special interest in Judah or its God. In 1879, Rassam uncovered a barrel-shaped cuneiform document that is now in the British Museum and is commonly referred to as the Cyrus Cylinder. In this document, which is focused in particular on a Babylon that is now a vassal of Cyrus, the king reveals that his policy of restoring foreign cults goes well beyond Judah to encompass many nations. The relevant lines read:

> All the kings of the entire world from the Upper to the Lower Sea, those who are seated in throne rooms, (those who) live in other [types of buildings as well as] all the kings of the West land living in tents, brought their heavy tributes and kissed my feet in Babylon. (As to the region) from . . . as far as Ashur and Susa, Agade, Eshnunna, the towns of Zamban, Me-Turnu, Der as well as the region of the Gutians, I returned to (these) sacred cities on the other side of the Tigris, the sanctuaries of which have been ruins for a long time, the images which (used) to live therein and established for them permanent sanctuaries. I (also) gathered all their (former) inhabitants and returned (to them) their habitations. Furthermore, I resettled upon the command of Marduk, the great lord, all the gods of Sumer and Akkad whom Nabonidus has brought into Babylon to the anger of the lord of the gods, unharmed, in their (former) chapels, the places which make them happy.[42]

Unsurprisingly in a document with a focus on Babylon, no mention of Yahweh or Judah is made here. However, this text confirms what looks like a widespread Persian foreign policy of allowing at least certain people who had been subjugated by the Babylonians to return to their homelands and rebuild their cults. Because of the idiosyncratic religious views of Nabonidus described above, the Babylonian people, including the powerful Marduk priesthood, also benefited from Cyrus's policy of restoring certain native cults. The Persians desired satisfied vassals, particularly those on the fringes of the empire like Judah, who could serve as a buffer toward their true enemies, whether Egypt or Greece or both.

Observers have long commented that the Cyrus edict in Chronicles and Ezra seems to reflect a Jewish perspective, which has raised doubts in some minds about its authenticity. Note, however, that the Cyrus Cylinder itself has a Babylonian perspective.[43] Perhaps Cyrus commissioned native scribes to compose these decrees in a language that their recipients could understand and appreciate.

Alternatively, what we may have in Ezra 1:2–4 (as Halpern suggests) is a paraphrase and selective rendition of the original Cyrus decree.[44] No matter what the Persian motivation or the scope of its restoration, the Jewish community living in exile saw the hand of God in this decree.

The Identity and Function of Sheshbazzar and Zerubbabel

Sheshbazzar and Zerubbabel are two names associated with the early postexilic period. They are both described as leaders of the community, and they both have connections with the rebuilding of the temple. However, some ambiguity surrounds their identity, and not surprisingly, scholarly controversy has arisen concerning their role and their relationship.

Sheshbazzar is only mentioned in the book of Ezra (1:8, 11; 5:14, 16).[45] He is called "the prince of Judah" (1:8), not necessarily indicating a connection to the royal (Davidic) family (see further below), but certainly pointing to the fact that he was a recognized and important leader. He is associated with the first return after the decree of Cyrus and is charged with the return of the temple vessels that had been taken by Nebuchadnezzar and placed in his temple in Babylon. In Ezra 5, Sheshbazzar is again mentioned, this time in the context of a letter written during the reign of Darius (522–486 B.C.) about his earlier activities. We here learn that Cyrus had appointed Sheshbazzar as governor of Yehud (the name the Persians gave the province that occupied the area formerly known as Judah) and that he laid the foundation to the temple.

Zerubbabel, who is more extensively mentioned in Ezra-Nehemiah as well as in Haggai and Zechariah,[46] is also mentioned in conjunction with an early return to Yehud soon after the Cyrus decree, but likely this wave is later than the one that brought Sheshbazzar back. Most likely this wave of exiles returned in the late 520s. Zerubbabel is associated with Jeshua/Joshua, the high priest, in Ezra 2, and the two are also related in Zechariah. According to Ezra 3, Zerubbabel and Jeshua rebuilt the altar and started official sacrifices again; strikingly, in light of what was attributed to Sheshbazzar above, they are also said to have laid the foundation of the temple itself (Ezra 3:10). However, the text informs us that Zerubbabel, Jeshua, and the others were approached by "the enemies of Judah and Benjamin" (see further below) who volunteered their services in the rebuilding. After they were rebuffed, the "enemies" succeeded in shutting down their efforts, and the construction project languished for some time. At this moment, the text abruptly narrates later opposition to the resettlement of the people of God (4:6–23) before picking up the story of the rebuilding of the temple. Ezra 4:24–5:1 describes how the prophets Haggai and Zechariah started exhorting the people of God to complete the job of rebuilding the temple. This took place in the second year of Darius (520 B.C.), and again there was opposition, this time associated with Tattenai the governor of the province of Trans-Euphrates (see below). However, after Darius checked the official records from the time of Cyrus, he determined that this project should be completed, and so it was.

The first chapter of Haggai describes God's message to Zerubbabel to return to the task of rebuilding the temple. Haggai also records Zerubbabel's obedient response to God's demand, which takes place in Darius's second year, namely 520 B.C. In this chapter, we learn that Zerubbabel is governor of Yehud. The book of Haggai's tantalizing conclusion is a divine oracle to Zerubbabel that, though circumstances are dubious at present, the people of God have a momentous future. Indeed, the book concludes with a strong affirmation of the governor: "I will take you, my servant Zerubbabel son of Shealtiel, and I will make you like my signet ring, for I have chosen you" (Hag. 2:23). Zechariah, a prophet who also encouraged the rebuilding of the temple at this time, has an oracle that not only prods Zerubbabel, Jeshua, and the people to the task at hand but also positively appraises the governor. His importance is associated with the rebuilding of the temple according to Zechariah 4:7–8. He and Jeshua are the two olive branches beside the two gold pipes that pour oil into the gold lampstand. They are those who are "anointed to serve the Lord of all the earth" (4:14).

The above is a straightforward reading of the biblical text concerning these two important biblical personages. Scholars, though, have recognized some problems with the biblical picture presented. One of the most important has to do with the relationship between Sheshbazzar and Zerubbabel in connection with the temple: they are both said to have laid the foundation of the temple. This confusion has led some to raise the possibility that there is really only one individual here and that this one individual has two names.[47] We only have to look at the book of Daniel to see that an individual can have two names (Daniel/Belteshazzar), and Daniel is not the only place in which such a phenomenon occurs. We see name changes throughout the Bible, including Abram/Abraham, Jacob/Israel; Ruth/Naomi; Tiglath-pileser/Pul. However, as we observe below, the text is amenable to a quite reasonable harmonization without recourse to the theory of two names for one individual.

More interesting is the possible connection between both these men and the line of David. David had been promised a son on the throne forever (2 Sam. 7), and the exile had thrown that promise into doubt. Earlier in the previous century, many scholars thought that Sheshbazzar was a descendant of David. In the first place, we have seen that Ezra calls him a "prince of Judah." Close study of the word often translated "prince" (nasi?), however, indicates that this usage does not necessarily point to royal lineage, since the word can mean only "leader" in certain contexts.[48] Some have further pointed to 1 Chronicles 3:18, which mentions a Davidic descendant from around this time with the name Shenazzar, close enough to invite speculation that this person is really our Sheshbazzar. Recent studies, though, have thrown serious doubt on the connection.[49] On the other hand, the biblical text is united in its support of a Davidic ancestry to Zerubbabel. First Chronicles 3:19 is unambiguous in placing Zerubbabel in the line of David.[50] On the basis of the oracle found in Zechariah 4:6–10, Zerubbabel, the Davidic descendant, was argued to be "a royal actor in the temple rebuilding ceremony."[51] One can only imagine the messianic expectation that was likely kindled when

Zerubbabel became governor. We add to that the expectation signaled in Haggai's concluding oracle, and we can be sure that many people thought that the restoration of the Davidic throne was imminent.

Zerubbabel accomplished the task with which he was charged, the reconstruction of the temple. Of that much, we are sure. However, he then disappears, textually speaking, without a trace. What happened? Was he removed by the Persians precisely for the expectations that he aroused? That is one theory, but the most truthful answer is that we do not know. In any case, we know he was not the final answer for the people of God.

In conclusion, Sheshbazzar and Zerubbabel were Babylonian-appointed governors of a small part of the Persian Empire. They were commissioned to return with other exiles and begin the process of restoring the community in Jerusalem and specifically the reconstruction of the temple. The work began during Cyrus's reign, but was halted for a while because of opposition from the "enemies of Judah and Benjamin." The work on the temple was then completed during Darius's reign in 515 B.C. The broader historical context indicates that the Persians had their own self-interest in mind. The Persian government was interested in having loyal vassals in their native lands who could support the expansionist and defensive strategies of the core of the empire. Attention has been drawn to an Egyptian analogy to Sheshbazzar and Zerubbabel, not to speak of the later Ezra and Nehemiah, and that is Udjahorresnet of Egypt. Udjahorresnet was an admiral in the Egyptian navy under Amasis and then Psammetichus III until the Persian defeat of Egypt in 525 B.C. under the rulership of Cambyses. Indeed, Cambyses had convinced Udjahorresnet to join his cause. He served the cause of Persia, while Cambyses reciprocated by restoring the Egyptian cult. After Cambyses's untimely death, Udjahorresnet served Darius in Egyptian matters, and Darius supported the latter in further restoration of certain Egyptian institutions including the "codification and enforcement of local lawcodes."[52] Sheshbazzar, Zerubbabel, Ezra, Nehemiah, and Udjahorresnet thus all fit into a pattern that shows an intentional strategy on the part of their Persian overlords. The biblical perspective, though, is that God was working behind the scenes using Persia to restore Judah just as he earlier used Nebuchadnezzar to judge Israel (Dan. 1:1–3).

The Postexilic Governors of Yehud and Its Neighbors

The Bible describes the following individuals as holding the position of "governor" in Persian-controlled Yehud in the period after the conquest.[53] Sheshbazzar is first (Ezra 5:14), appointed by Cyrus and commissioned to begin the return of the exiles to Yehud. Next was Zerubbabel, probably governor during the revived period of rebuilding the temple, perhaps from 520 to 510 B.C. He is named governor in Haggai 1:1, 4. After a period of time (see below for reasons for our dating), Nehemiah was governor from 445 to 433 B.C. (Neh. 5:14; 12:26).

Earlier in the previous century, A. Alt maintained that Ezra was Yehud's first provincial governor, and that before that time the governor ruled from Samaria.[54]

In this way, Alt and his followers attempted to explain the tensions that arose between Nehemiah and people like Sanballat. However, his viewpoint completely ignored the biblical evidence that Sheshbazzar and Zerubbabel were also called governors. Some modified Alt's view by saying that Zerubbabel so aroused Davidic-messianic expectations that he was deposed, an act mentioned nowhere but supposedly implied, and that the governorship of Yehud was revitalized with Nehemiah.

More information about Yehud's postexilic governors has undermined this theory. Our information has been expanded by inscribed coins, seals, and pottery.[55] From a bulla and a seal, we learn about Elnathan, who was married to a woman named Shelomith. Elnathan was likely governor of Yehud after Zerubbabel, since evidence (1 Chr. 3:19) indicates that Shelomith was the daughter of Zerubbabel.[56] Shelomith's Davidic ancestry likely enhanced Elnathan's attractiveness for the governorship.[57] From a jar impression we learn about a governor[58] named Yeho'ezer who is thought to have ruled from about 490 to 470 B.C. We know the name of yet one more governor in the period before Nehemiah and that is Ahzai, also known through a jar impression. Nehemiah was clearly not the first governor of Yehud as Alt thought. We also have information from yet other sources of governors in the period after Nehemiah, most notably Bagohi, who is mentioned in the Elephantine papyrus. His significance for the dating of Nehemiah is treated below.

A Citizen-Temple Community?

Brief mention needs to be made of an often-discussed but frequently rejected theory concerning social-political relationships during the period of the return. This theory presents a model of postexilic Yehud that goes by the name "citizen-temple community" and was offered by J. P. Weinberg.[59] Weinberg argues for a difference between the Persian province of Yehud and the Jewish community that returned from the exile. The latter was given special considerations by the Persian community as they returned, which brought them into tension with the province. According to Weinberg, the Jewish community was a minority in the early days as they rebuilt the temple, but a majority at the time of Ezra and Nehemiah. Thus, leaders like Sheshbazzar and Zerubbabel were not rulers of the province but of a minority Jewish community that had Persian support. The temple was the center of this Jewish community. In this way, Weinberg and his followers understand the conflict that met the returnees as they tried to build the temple and later the wall.

Weinberg's theory has attracted quite a bit of attention, but also its critics, and the latter are persuasive. Among other problems, Weinberg continues to follow Alt's faulty position concerning the province of Samaria mentioned above. He also misuses Ezra 2/Nehemiah 7 in order to determine the population of Yehud at the time of Nehemiah. Recent population estimates based on firmer methods have shown that he has grossly overestimated the population at the time of the return from the exile.[60] With Williamson, one of his most effective critics, we conclude "that there was a considerably closer overlap between the Jewish community and the Persian province of Judah in terms of both population and administration than the citizen-temple community model suggests, and nowhere is there evidence that the Jewish community was treated differently from others who may have lived within the province."[61]

The Building of the Temple

The "Cyrus Decree" focuses on the temple. According to Cyrus, God had appointed him to rebuild the temple destroyed by the Babylonians. This commission leads him to allow the return right after he took control of Babylon and its vassals. According to Berquist, Cyrus was motivated less by his stated theological reasons and more by military-economic goals.[62] Yehud was on the border of the Persian Empire and for purposes of future expansion and/or defense of its boundaries having a content and relatively strong vassal on the periphery of the empire was helpful. In particular, Persian interests in Egypt necessitated safe roads with available provisions for its armies through Yehud.

With that in mind, Cyrus not only gave permission for the rebuilding of the destroyed temple but also provided the resources to accomplish the task. In the first place, he returned the temple vessels (Ezra 1:7–11) to Jerusalem. These dishes, bowls and other utensils were taken from Jerusalem by Nebuchadnezzar (Dan. 1:1–2) and kept in the temple of his god, presumably Marduk, in Babylon. This act was symbolic of Judah's subservience to Babylon, and the return of these objects would have been of significant encouragement to the people of God. In a scene reminiscent of the exodus, and perhaps intentionally so,[63] the neighbors of the returning Yehudites gave them precious metals and other gifts, among which were items that could be used in the rebuilding process.

Some ambiguity surrounds the question of what condition the temple area was in during the exilic period. Our postexilic descriptions certainly suggest that the whole area was in need of repair. Jeremiah 41, however, mentions a group of worshipers who come to Jerusalem from surrounding areas apparently soon after 586 B.C. to offer sacrifices at "the house of God" (v. 4). In the minds of many, this phrase suggests that the altar was still standing at that time.[64] Conceivably, though, these worshipers would have been content to go to the place of the destroyed temple and perform a makeshift sacrifice without an altar; we really have no idea what was in their minds. Alternatively, perhaps the altar was destroyed when Nebuchadnezzar returned in 582 B.C. for yet another punitive assault of Jerusalem and a further deportation. We might even more simply imagine that the years of neglect between the time period of Jeremiah 41 and the return to Jerusalem after 539 B.C. would have required extensive repair or even a rebuilding of the altar.

In any case, Ezra tells us that the altar was the first part of the structure that was repaired, and relatively early—during Cyrus's reign. In addition, the foundations were also repaired in this early period. But who was responsible for this early work on the temple? At first glance, a contradiction is apparent. In some texts, Zerubbabel is said to be the initiator of the temple reconstruction and to him is ascribed the rebuilding of the temple and the laying of the foundation (Ezra 3:8; Zech. 4:6–10; Haggai), while others say it was Sheshbazzar (Ezra 5:14–16). Perhaps, though, both men were involved in various phases of temple reconstruction in some way and in some relationship to one another,[65] and the biblical text is simply not interested in smoothing out the details of how this worked. Williamson offers an alternative possible understanding of the different statements about temple rebuilding in the early postexilic period.[66] He follows Talmon in arguing that the relevant section of the book of Ezra is not chronologically sequential, but that Ezra 4:4–5 is a type of summary statement.[67] Thus, the "fear" of 3:3 is the same as that cited in 4:4. The bottom line is that 3:1–6 refers to a dedication of the altar during the time of Cyrus, while the action of 3:7–4:3 takes place during Darius's time period, after 520 B.C.[68]

In any case, this work was just the beginning of what turned out to be a very long process. Opposition soon rose to the rebuilding of the temple, and our sources suggest that this opposition along with perhaps financial struggles and even the people's lack of interest led to a cessation of building activity during the remainder of Cyrus's reign. Ezra 4:1–5 narrates the early opposition to the rebuilding.

Not until the reign of Darius did temple building begin again. After Cyrus's death, his son Cambyses came to the throne and ruled from 530 until 522 B.C. Cambyses is best known for his defeat of Egypt. He died as he was returning to Persia after this campaign to deal with a revolt in the capital Persepolis, led by his (supposedly deceased) brother Baridya (Smerdis). His death initiated some ambiguity in the succession. After a struggle with a pretender named Gaumata, Darius, a usurper, took the throne. He proved to be an extremely able ruler over the Persian Empire (522–486 B.C.). At this time Haggai and Zechariah preached that it was God's will that the temple now be completed. Thus, under the leadership of Zerubbabel, the temple was finished in 515 B.C. The temple and its associated priesthood would continue to grow in its importance in postexilic religion up until its destruction in A.D. 70.

Who Were the "Enemies of Yehud" in the Early Postexilic Period?

As we observed in the previous section, the early returnees ran into opposition as they set about the task of reconstructing and in particular rebuilding the temple. Ezra 4:1–5 narrates the conflict, when a group identified as "the enemies of Judah and Benjamin" approach Zerubbabel and the other leaders and asks if they might join in the rebuilding. The leaders spare no time in rebuffing their invitation to help, and then the "enemies" set about trying to stop the rebuilding. The identity of this group is obscure to modern readers, and their closer identification has been the subject of much debate. They further describe themselves as people who worship the same God. They have done so, they say, since they came to the land at the time of Esarhaddon, the king of Assyria. In addition, the narrator refers to them as "people of the land" in Ezra 4:4. To many, these signals seem to be conflicting.

Some recent scholars have suggested that the returnees came into conflict with the vast majority of people who had stayed in the land and were not exiled.[69] Above, we recognized that only a minority of people, probably a majority of the leadership only, had actually been removed from the land. Thus, as the exiles returned, they came into conflict with the ones who remained. This tension was exacerbated by the fact that the exiles, descended from the upper crust of pre-exilic society, may have been condescending toward those who remained. Indeed, as the exiles returned, so this theory goes, they would have pushed those who remained out of the prime real estate.[70]

While this theory is interesting, it is not rooted in actual evidence—at least not the evidence that has accumulated that plenty of land was available to go around when the returnees entered the land after the Cyrus decree.[71] The theory specifically ignores the evidence of the biblical texts that draw attention to the distinct identity of the opponents. These people have their origins in the land as far back only as the Assyrian king Esarhaddon—the end of the eighth or the first couple of decades of the seventh century B.C.[72] They were probably descendants of foreign peoples exiled into the northern kingdom who had adopted the worship of the local god and probably also married the remnants of the northern tribes who remained in the land after the 722 B.C. deportation of Israelites by the Assyrians. Perhaps after 586 B.C. they married into southern families that stayed in the land as well.

That is to say, Zerubbabel came into conflict only with an ethnically mixed and religiously syncretistic element among those who remained in the land—not with "the masses." He saw the inappropriateness of these people in particular participating in the rebuilding of the temple, and he rejected their offer. Later, we see that Nehemiah and Ezra ran into similar problems as they tried to reconstruct Yehudite society and the walls of Jerusalem.[73]

Two of the opponents to the temple building are named—Tattenai and Sether-Bozenai—and are identified as officials of Trans-Euphrates. As Yamauchi points out:

> Tattenai was at first mistakenly identified by scholars with Ushtannu, the satrap over Babylon and Trans-Euphrates, until Olmstead pointed out the correct identification in 1944. In a document dated June 5, 502, we have attested a Ta-at-tan-ni the *pahat* or governor subordinate to the satrap. Sethar-Bozenai may have functioned as a Persian official known as the *pat-ifrasa* or *frasaka* (inquisitor or investigator).[74]

THE MIDDLE POSTEXILIC PERIOD:
THE BOOK OF ESTHER

We have little information about the period between the first waves of return under Sheshbazzar and Zerubbabel and the later restoration accomplished under the leadership of Ezra and Nehemiah. The first half of the fifth century B.C. was a time of significant turmoil after the original stability following the establishment of the Persian Empire. During the first half of the fifth century, Persia now had to contend with Greece and Egypt, and things did not always go in the favor of the Persians.

While C. L. and E. M. Meyers's case for an early fifth-century date for the oracles of Zechariah 9–14 is possible, it is not certain. We turn instead to the book of Esther, itself highly debated as a historical source, to fill out at least one aspect of Jewish existence during this period.

Ezra and Nehemiah give us information about two discrete periods: the early postexilic period from the first return to the rebuilding of the temple (ca. 539–515 B.C.), and the period from the return of Ezra down to the rebuilding of the wall of Jerusalem under Nehemiah (see below). The story of Esther begins in the third year of the reign of Ahasuerus, a Persian king who is also known by his Greek name Xerxes (486–465 B.C.), and thus between the two time periods described in Ezra-Nehemiah. In addition, Ezra and Nehemiah follow the story of those people who return from their captivity to the land of promise. There they meet up again with the descendants of those who had remained in the land. The book of Esther gives us a window on yet a third community of the people of God, those who chose to stay in foreign lands. They are part of the Diaspora, or scattering of the people of God, that continues down to the present day.

The book of Esther does not tell us why Esther and Mordecai or the others decided to stay. The reasons were probably varied. Some probably could not return, though they wanted to. Others had reached some measure of success and happiness in the land of their captivity and did not want the rough life of a returnee. Perhaps Mordecai and Esther were among this latter group. After all, we know Mordecai and Esther by their Persian names,[75] which perhaps suggests that they had assimilated well; certainly Mordecai was a very important person in the Persian bureaucracy.

We know something about this time period from outside the Bible, primarily from Greek and Persian sources. Indeed, one of the greatest of all Greek historians, Herodotus (490–425 B.C.), lived during the events of Xerxes' reign. In the present skeptical age, doubt exists about how far the Greek historians can be trusted.[76] We can certainly, however, be confident that we can trace the history of the Persian Empire in general terms from where we left it in 515 B.C. down through the early reign of Xerxes. The big problem that developed for Persia during the end of the sixth and first part of the fifth centuries was Greece. Persia had hoped to expand the empire and its revenues by pushing into Greece, but Darius was stopped at the Battle of Marathon in 490 B.C. Xerxes early in his reign defeated Athens and set it on fire; however, Greek resistance merely hardened. Xerxes moved again on Greece from Sardis in 481 B.C. and won a significant victory at Thermopylae before losing a major conflict in 480 B.C. at Salamis. The Delian League was a Greek tool to band together against Persia, and they increasingly troubled Persia, indeed all the way down to 333 B.C. when Alexander finally defeated Persia once and for all.

With his eyes focused on Greece in this way, Xerxes did not support Yehud in the manner of Darius. The financial needs of the empire had increased, and evidence indicates that taxes increased, but support for internal projects in Yehud decreased. As a matter of fact, the only biblical mention of Xerxes outside of Esther is found in Ezra 4 (see v. 6) in the list of times when Yehudites ran into opposition in building the temple.

Esther lived in this context—if indeed we allow that the book of Esther provides, or even intends to present, historical information about this person and her times. Certainly the history of interpretation confirms that Esther was usually taken as a historical narrative. Indeed, the book is grouped with other historical books in the Septuagintal order of the biblical books that modern Christian translations follow.[77] However, this genre identification is out of favor among most scholars today and certainly needs to be nuanced. Most scholars understand Esther as a kind of historical romance or novella. S. Talmon, for instance, argues that the book is permeated with wisdom issues and themes, which are in tension with a historical presentation.[78] Berg has drawn attention to a number of parallels between the Joseph story and Esther,[79] and Gerleman has done the same with the exodus story.[80] By drawing attention to such parallels, the intention is to minimize the historical and maximize the literary and theological intention in writing the Esther story. On the other hand, Dillard and Longman have criticized both these approaches and have insisted on the inappropriateness of pitting historical concerns against literary artifice and specifically wisdom themes.[81] Esther indeed is a literary tour de force, masterfully using irony, satire, and repetitive themes and motifs,[82] but all history has a self-conscious presentation.[83] Genre signals within the book, they maintain, communicate a historical concern (Esth. 2:23; 10:1–3).

Even those scholars most skeptical of the historical quality of the book of Esther recognize that the author knew Persian institutions, customs, and events well. Levenson, who has no belief in the historicity of the text and identifies it as a novella, acknowledges that the author is well aware of details of the Persian Empire. He states that "the author knows, for example, its size, its postal system, and a considerable number of details about its court life (3:13; 8:10) and employs a number of words and a few names of indisputable Persian origins."[84] Many scholars are content in the same way to affirm the accurate reflection of social and historical background in the book yet to deny its historicity on the ground that (as A. Berlin states it so well) ". . . to judge a story's historicity by its degree of realism is to mistake verisimilitude for historicity."[85]

To one group of scholars, then, the book is a story with a historylike quality. To others, it is history with a storylike quality. In such a case, the disagreement is not over the facts of the case. Both groups readily acknowledge the dramatic and highly literary quality of the account, while also affirming the veracity of the general historical background. The details are such that they would not likely be independently confirmed in any case. Therefore, one's approach to the ultimate historical trustworthiness of the story depends on one's starting point: Will the reader embrace the apparently historical testimony of the book of Esther unless (s)he finds compelling reasons not to do so, or will (s)he adopt a more skeptical stance, insisting that the story in the book must be proven to be historically true before embracing it as such?

The whole question of "proof" at the level of the detail of the book is itself, of course, a complicated one. According to the biblical account, for example, Esther was Xerxes' queen from his seventh to his twelfth year. According to the Greek sources, however, Amestris was his queen during this time. Attempts have been made to identify Amestris with either Vashti or Esther,[86] but this issue has not reached a resolution. Is this "proof" that the book of Esther is mistaken? Or is it merely that we do not yet possess enough information to come to a final judgment? Again, Persian queens, according to Herodotus (3:84), had to be chosen from one of seven Persian families, a fact that would rule out the king's choice of a Jewish woman. However, we know that Amestris herself was not from one of the seven families, and therefore Herodotus's principle does not seem to be absolute. What does this say about Herodotus's own testimony, and how it should be handled in relation to the Bible's testimony? The duty of historians is to handle all sources, and not merely some of them, with intelligence.

THE LATE POSTEXILIC PERIOD

The primary textual resource for the late postexilic period is the book of Ezra-Nehemiah. In particular, Ezra 7 through Nehemiah 13 is relevant for the period of time presently under consideration. Within these chapters scholars commonly recognize two memoirs, one by Ezra (Ezra 7–10; Neh. 8) and one by Nehemiah (1–7; 12:27–43; 13:4–31). We must understand the nature of these two "memoirs" before utilizing them in our historical reconstruction.

In the first place, the genre of the Ezra and Nehemiah texts is indeed "memoir." Most biblical historiographical texts are presented in third-person omniscient narration. This form, conversely, claims direct eyewitness testimony, and some have gained confidence from this in forming a very positive opinion of the text's historicity. If someone was *there*, how can we gainsay their account? Nonetheless, we must remember that eyewitnesses can skew the data as much as a later account. This charge has, in particular, been leveled against the Nehemiah memoir.[87] Furthermore, an eyewitness may have more personally at stake than a later nonparticipant in the events that are being described. One need only consult Nehemiah 13 to see that Nehemiah is deeply and personally invested in the events he narrates. On the other hand, a first-person account is not inherently problematic in terms of gaining access to the "actual events" either, and if Nehemiah is defending himself to contemporaries, then he would have to take into account the possibility of counterclaims, which explains the posture that he strikes. In addition, Williamson has shown that Nehemiah's first-person account is generally supported by third-person reports within the book of Nehemiah,[88] which "serves both to support the general historical drift of the narrative and to underscore Nehemiah's own bias from a different direction."[89] The criticism of Ezra's memoir is even more fundamental on the part of some scholars, going beyond the charge that first-person speech is often ideologically colored and extending even to the claim that Ezra never existed.[90] However, we believe that again Williamson has provided a credible defense of the usefulness of this material in historical reconstruction, and because the arguments are far too complex to present here, we simply reference his careful work.[91]

A second aspect of the texts under consideration of which we need to be aware is that Ezra 7–Nehemiah 13 covers only a limited number of years in the second half of the fifth century. In the first place, the transition from Ezra 6 to 7, though marked by a simple and vague "after these things," is actually a period of a number of decades.[92] Second, the time covered in the two memoirs is episodic and of disputed chronological order and placement (see below on the "Order of the Missions of Ezra and Nehemiah"). Williamson summarizes the episodic nature of the material:

> . . . it is impressed upon us yet again to what an extent we are dependent upon the somewhat spasmodic light which our sources shed upon this period. Well illuminated are the building of the second temple, the twelve months of Ezra's work, the building of the wall under Nehemiah and its immediate sequel (say 12 months), and an unchronological account of various reforms some twelve or fifteen years later.[93]

The nature of our material now being more fully understood, our view is that Ezra-Nehemiah is an important source to the history of the time surrounding the work of Ezra and Nehemiah. Other textual resources occasionally throw light on this period of time, and we point these out as they become relevant.

The Order of the Missions of Ezra and Nehemiah

Ezra-Nehemiah provides data relevant to the date of the missions of the two men at the center of its narrative. Ezra 7 clearly names Artaxerxes as the Persian king at the time of Ezra's return to the province of Yehud, and more specifically says that he "arrived in Jerusalem in the fifth month of the seventh year of the king" (7:8). On the surface, this seems an easy equation since we know that Artaxerxes I began his reign in 465 B.C., thus making his seventh year 458 B.C. Equally clearly, the book of Nehemiah begins "in the month of Kislev in the twentieth year" (of Artaxerxes), apparently placing the beginning of his work in Yehud in the year 445 B.C.

However, the matter is not quite as clear as it appears on the surface, and scholars have been quick to point out some problems. Some of these are easily seen and others are subtle. In the former category, according to some readings of the text,[94] is the fact that Ezra and Nehemiah never overlap as one might expect of two great men with a common desire to serve God in a relatively small city. Ezra is not there to receive Nehemiah with open arms, and nowhere do they work in tandem. On a more subtle level, we might note that the figure of Meremoth son of Uriah, who appears to be a vigorous wall builder with Nehemiah (Neh. 3:4, 21), is a mature priestly leader with Ezra in Ezra 8:33–34, which is strange if Ezra is to be placed before Nehemiah chronologically. Ezra also mentions a wall that is in Jerusalem at the time he arrives (Ezra 9:9), which seems odd if Nehemiah's activity is still in the future. One last example shall suffice. In Ezra 10:6, Ezra goes to the room of a man named Jehohanan, the son of Eliashib, and the question arises whether the latter, Eliashib, is the same person mentioned in an Elephantine papyrus (AramP 30:18). If so, the latter—we know—lived in 408 B.C., which would make a meeting with an Ezra dated to an earlier period difficult if not impossible.

For these reasons, some scholars propose different dates for Ezra. The leading alternative dates are after Nehemiah. One proposal, fast on the wane, is the idea that the text that reports Ezra's work as beginning in the seventh year of Artaxerxes' reign has a textual corruption and should read the "twenty-seventh" (thus 438 B.C.) or thirty-seventh (thus 428 B.C.) year of Artaxerxes. However, this solution has absolutely no textual support and should be abandoned.[95] Another alternative reading suggests that it is the seventh year of Artaxerxes, but of Artaxerxes II, not Artaxerxes I, which would date the beginning of Ezra's work to 398 B.C.

However, the problems that led to the alternative hypotheses are not real problems. Close reading of the Ezra narrative indicates that it only covers a year's time,[96] suggesting a possible reason that the two do not overlap (i.e., Ezra was there for a very short period of time). In any case, the two need not be mentioned together even if they did overlap. Yamauchi refers to other famous contemporaries who are not mentioned together, like Jeremiah and Ezekiel, or Zechariah and Haggai.[97] In terms of the other, more subtle or detailed issues, we note that the reference to the wall in Ezra 9:9 could be, and evidence indicates probably is, a metaphorical reference to the protection provided by the Persian kings, not a reference to a literal wall.[98] Williamson also reminds us that the names Jehohanan and Eliashib are very common names,[99] as are Meremoth and Uriah.[100] In any case, we stand with the vast majority of scholars today who prefer the traditional order of events, with Ezra arriving in 458 B.C. and Nehemiah in 445 B.C.[101]

Ezra and Nehemiah in the Context of Persian Politics

The biblical text takes a decidedly Yehudite viewpoint when presenting the missions of Ezra and Nehemiah. From the perspective of the author of Ezra-Nehemiah, no further explanation was needed than that God had "put it into the king's heart to bring honor to the house of the LORD in Jerusalem" (Ezra 7:27, NIV) by allowing Ezra and then Nehemiah to return to the land of their forefathers. Artaxerxes I did more than allow them to go; he equipped them for their journey with the authority of a governorship and money in order to restore Yehudite society and, under Nehemiah, to rebuild the defensive structures of the city.

Furthermore, Ezra and Nehemiah were charged with reasserting the authority of the law of God, reaffirming the divine covenant.

Recent research into this time period suggests that the king's desire to praise God might have been bolstered by concerns of a more earthly type. K. Hoglund set the stage for the most recent understanding of the Persian motivation for the work of Ezra and Nehemiah when he placed their work within the broader framework of the military-political events of their day.[102] His reading of the biblical text was informed by the archaeological discovery of a distinctive type of fortress in Yehud built during the middle of the fifth century. In addition, Greek sources told of events in the area as well. What emerges from his study is the idea that Artaxerxes bolstered Yehud in order to have a friendly and reasonably strong ally to protect the border of his empire against the growing threat from Greece and Egypt.

Other scholars have followed and developed his ideas further,[103] and the following picture is most directly gleaned from the research of J. Berquist.[104] Like Hoglund, Berquist understands Artaxerxes' desire to help Yehud to lie in the fact that the western border of his empire was threatened by Egypt and Greece. The leaders of Egypt, Inarus, and of Greece, Pericles, allied with one another to take on Persia.[105] Artaxerxes' chief general, Megabyzus, joined with Sparta against Athens and was victorious against them. However, Artaxerxes granted the Greek leaders their freedom in 454 B.C., and then Sparta allied itself with Athens. However, they too were defeated by Megabyzus and signed a peace treaty ("The Peace of Callias") in 449 B.C. The next problem for Artaxerxes was the rebellion of his general, who was in Syria at the time; this problem was only temporary, with Megabyzus returning to the Persian cause.

The research of Hoglund, Berquist, and others make clear that Yehud enjoyed Persian patronage for self-serving motivations at least during the early part of Artaxerxes' reign,[106] which would include the Persian support for Ezra's codification and reaffirmation of native Israelite law.[107] Berquist suggests that once the threat from the west subsided, at least temporarily, the Persians did not any longer extend such generous privileges to Yehud.[108]

Who Were the "Enemies of Yehud" in the Later Exilic Period?

We earlier noted the opposition that arose against the early returnees when they rebuilt the temple. According to Ezra-Nehemiah, opposition continued in the later period when the next step of reconstruction of the city continued. Two such cases appear in Ezra 4:6–23.[109] These took the form of neighbors who contacted Persian authorities to request the prohibition of rebuilding. First, Ezra 4:6 briefly and vaguely refers to a letter of accusation written during the reign of Xerxes (486–465 B.C.). A lengthier narrative that follows this verse recounts another anti-Yehudite effort during the reign of Artaxerxes. This episode is not more specifically dated during the reign of Artaxerxes, but must have been relatively early, certainly predating Nehemiah's royally commissioned, successfully completed effort. The text informs the reader of the successful attempt by officials of the Persian province of "Beyond the River" to shut down the efforts to rebuild the walls on the grounds that wall building signifies the potential of rebellion. To bolster their accusation, they further cited a previous history of rebellion against other overlords. Three names are given for the accusers: Bishlam, Mithredath, and Tabeel. They further identify themselves as people who were deported into Samaria by the Assyrian king Ashurbanipal.[110]

According to Nehemiah 2, Artaxerxes changed his mind in the twentieth year of his reign when he agreed to support Nehemiah in his request to rebuild the walls and other structures in Jerusalem. Above, we examined the likely motivations in terms of a possible threat from Greece and Egypt. Indeed, the king wrote a letter informing the officials of the province Beyond the River to provide Nehemiah with the materials necessary to accomplish his task. However, Nehemiah 2:10 concludes this episode with a foreboding note: "When Sanballat the Horonite and Tobiah the Ammonite official heard about this, they were very much disturbed that someone had come to promote the welfare of the Israelites" (NIV).

When Nehemiah and the Yehudites actually started working on the walls, these two were joined by a third, Geshem the Arab, who began to threaten and complain to the king. Though the king had granted permission, this group could conceivably have caused trouble by spreading the rumor that instead of supporting the Persian king in his plans they actually were part of the rebellion. Nehemiah stood firm, though, and would not yield to their protests or allow them a part of it (2:20). Apparently, they, like the protestors at the time of Zerubbabel, felt that they had a kinship and claim in the work being done in Jerusalem. Nehemiah 4 describes the dramatic conditions accompanying the restoration efforts. Death threats from Sanballat, Tobiah, and Geshem reached their ears, so they had to post guards while they built.

Who were these men and why were they so opposed to what Nehemiah was doing? While we can make out some of the details of the answers to these questions, the text is not interested in telling us about motivations. Sanballat was the governor of Samaria,[111] and he and his family are attested outside of the Bible. The Elephantine Papyri had already shown that Sanballat's son Delaiah followed him as governor of Samaria. A papyrus discovered at Wadi ed-Daliyeh in 1962 indicates that he had a grandson whose name was also Sanballat and who was also governor. This relationship suggests a dynastic approach to the office, as well as providing a good example of the practice of papponymy (the naming of a grandson after his grandfather).[112] In any case, Sanballat's animosity against the Yehudite restoration and Nehemiah may have been out of jealousy and anger that he and others were not allowed to participate. Tobiah's name indicates that he too may have thought himself a co-religionist with Nehemiah.[113] According to Mazar, he was the governor of Ammon. A high priest named Eliashib was closely aligned with both of these men (Tobiah and Sanballat). He rented storerooms to Tobiah in the temple (Neh. 13:4–5), and one of his grandsons married into Sanballat's family (Neh. 13:28). For that reason, Nehemiah drove that high priest away from him. These two close neighbors were joined by Geshem the Arab. We now have a reference to Geshem, king of Qedar, on a silver container that was found at Tell el-Maskhuta in Egypt.[114] Dumbrell's study of the Qedarites discovers that "her confederate or allied peoples were distributed from the Syrian desert to North Arabia and were found in the Persian period to the south of Palestine and in the Delta region."[115] The connection with Palestine might explain why Geshem would have been concerned about the work of Nehemiah, though he was not as tied to the region as Sanballat and Tobiah, who are mentioned more often.

Transitions to the Intertestamental Period

Eshkenazi does a masterful job of delineating three major themes in the book of Ezra-Nehemiah and then shows how they reverberate through the whole.[116] These themes indicate that the time period of Ezra and Nehemiah witnessed a transformation from a time of elite leaders, narrow holiness, and oral authority to a time of community, spreading holiness, and the authority of written documents. Adopting the language of the nineteenth-century German philosopher Hegel, she notes a move from a poetic age to a prosaic one. She admirably does not denigrate this transition but rather speaks of the sanctification of the prosaic.

First, we see a shift from leaders to community. The Old Testament specializes in charismatic individuals: Abraham, Moses, Samuel, David, and Daniel are just a handful of examples. Indeed Ezra and Nehemiah are striking characters, but Eskenazi charts how these men are absorbed, Ezra willingly and Nehemiah reluctantly, into the community. The community accomplishes the task of rebuilding the temple and wall of Jerusalem. The people turn to the Lord in corporate allegiance at the end.

Second, holiness is no longer restricted to certain special places. This theme is especially clear when the temple is rebuilt. This rebuilding is the goal of the return, and when the structure is finished and consecrated, we almost expect the book to end. However, the house of God is not built once the temple is finished (Ezra 6:15); it continues, and more of Jerusalem is built. When the walls are finished, they too are consecrated (not "dedicated," so NIV, see Neh. 3:1), indicating that they were considered a part of a rebuilt "Holy City" (Neh. 11:1). Once temple, city, and walls are rebuilt, then come the "grand opening" ceremonies (Neh. 8–13).

The third major theme of the book, according to Eskenazi's analysis, is the shift from oral to written authority. The role of written documents in the book is amazing to see. Letters from kings initiate and stop action on both the level of actual events and the story. The most important written document, however, does not have human origin but is the Torah of Yahweh. The people rededicate themselves to this divinely given book at a great covenant renewal ceremony at the end of the book (Neh. 8–10).

While Eskenazi's analysis is compelling and rich, it does not exhaust the theological message of this profound book. D. Green notes that Ezra-Nehemiah is a book about the building of "two walls."[117] Most obviously, we recognize "Nehemiah's wall," a wall that physically separates the people of God from their enemies, the unclean "Gentiles." On the other hand, "Ezra's wall," the law of God that it was his mission to teach, erected a spiritual boundary between Israel and all other people. In essence, Ezra's law, which included a strong emphasis on the prohibition of intermarriage, constituted a people fit to live within Nehemiah's walls. At the end of the book of Ezra-Nehemiah, we have a holy people living in a holy city.

CONCLUSION

With Ezra and Nehemiah, we bring our biblical history of Israel to its conclusion. These books provide the latest narrative treatment of Israel's past from within the confines of the canon. True, some of the prophecies and wisdom books may be products of a later period, but this assertion is a matter of speculation. Also some of the visions and dreams of a prophet like Daniel look forward to the next few centuries. Narrative history as such, however, has come to an end, and with its end comes the end of our extended reflection on it. The biblical history of Israel is over, even though its history carries on down through the Intertestamental Period, into New Testament times, and beyond.

Notes

Chapter 1: The Death of Biblical History?

1. K. W. Whitelam, *The Invention of Ancient Israel: The Silencing of Palestinian History* (London: Routledge, 1996), 35, 69.
2. Ibid., 51, 68–69.
3. Ibid, 161. The sentiments are specifically attributed here to Garbini, but they appear clearly to parallel Whitelam's own.
4. The abbreviated review that follows is based on the much fuller discussion in I. W. Provan, "The End of (Israel's) History? A Review Article on K. W. Whitelam's *The Invention of Ancient Israel*," *JSS* 42 (1997): 283–300.
5. Whitelam, *Invention*, 23.
6. Ibid., 33.
7. See further I. W. Provan, "Ideologies, Literary and Critical: Reflections on Recent Writing on the History of Israel," *JBL* 114 (1995): 585–606.
8. T. L. Thompson, *Early History of the Israelite People from the Written and Archaeological Sources*, SHANE 4 (Leiden: Brill, 1992), 13, 81.
9. Apart from the writings of Whitelam and Thompson, we may note here such books as N. P. Lemche, *Ancient Israel: A New History of Israelite Society*, BSem 5 (Sheffield: JSOT, 1988); G. Garbini, *History and Ideology in Ancient Israel* (New York: Crossroad, 1988); P. R. Davies, *In Search of "Ancient Israel,"* JSOTS 148 (Sheffield: JSOT, 1992); and G. W. Ahlström, *The History of Ancient Palestine from the Palaeolithic Period to Alexander's Conquest*, ed. D. V. Edelman, JSOTS 146 (Sheffield: JSOT, 1993).
10. Davies, *Search*.
11. Whitelam, *Invention*, 177, reporting on views in recent scholarly writings among which he numbers his own; and more explicitly, 204–5.
12. Ibid., 119; compare the comment on Gottwald towards the end of 118.
13. Ibid., 181–83.
14. A particularly striking example is provided in this respect by his treatment of the so-called Merneptah Stela (ibid., 206–10).
15. Ibid., 183.
16. Ibid., 23.
17. Ibid., 34–35.
18. J. A. Soggin, *History of Israel: From the Beginnings to the Bar Kochba Revolt, AD 135* (London: SCM, 1984); J. M. Miller and J. Hayes, *A History of Ancient Israel and Judah* (Philadelphia: Westminster, 1986).
19. Soggin, *History*, 18–40.
20. That is, they were first collected in such sources as the Pentateuchal J and E, and later in such texts as the Pentateuch.

21. We may note as a particular example his suggestion that the first part of the book of Joshua describes the past as a period in which Israel "accepted humbly and passively what God them offered in his mercy" (Soggin, *History*, 30).
22. Miller and Hayes, *History*, 54–79.
23. Ibid., 58.
24. Ibid., 74.
25. Ibid., 78.
26. Ibid., 80–119.
27. Ibid., 87, 90 (quote on 90).
28. Note, e.g., ibid., 65–67.
29. Ibid., 129.
30. Note the extended discussion in ibid., 132–48.
31. Ibid., 159.
32. Note the description of the nature of the David material in ibid., 152–56, as well as their comments about extrabiblical documents and archaeological information in ibid. 159–60.
33. Ibid., 193.
34. So Whitelam, *Invention*, chap. 4
35. For an excellent and full account of the history of historiography, see E. Breisach, *Historiography: Ancient, Medieval, and Modern* (Chicago: University of Chicago Press, 1983), to which the following summary is heavily indebted.
36. The term "positivism" itself has recently come to be used somewhat loosely in discussion about the nature of science to refer simply to the modern critical/empirical scientific approach to reality in general, whether or not any all-encompassing claims about the nature of valid knowledge are made. H. M. Barstad, "History and the Hebrew Bible," in L. L. Grabbe (ed.), *Can a 'History of Israel' be Written?*, JSOTS 245/ESHM 1 (Sheffield: Sheffield Academic Press, 1997), 37–64, thus suggests (on 51, n. 35) that a useful definition of positivism in the context of a discussion about history would be "belief in scientific history"—a suggestion with which we have considerable sympathy, in that it highlights the truth that all avowedly scientific history, whether fully positivistic or not, inevitably contains positivistic elements within it.
37. J. Huizinga, *Geschichte und Kultur* (Stuttgart: Kröner, 1954), 13, cited in translation from R. Smend, "Tradition and History: A Complex Relation," in D. A. Knight (ed.), *Tradition and Theology in the Old Testament* (Philadelphia: Fortress, 1977), 49–68, on 66.
38. H. G. A. Ewald, *The History of Israel*, ET of the 2d ed.; 6 vols. (London: Longmans, Green and Co., 1869), 1.13. The German volumes were first published in 1843–1855.
39. See Ewald, *History*, vol. 1, *passim*, but especially 13–45 (on tradition); 45–62 (on writing and historical composition); and 288–362 (on the patriarchs), noting the consideration of agnosticism on 305.
40. Thus, e.g., "Archeological and inscriptional data have *established the historicity* [our emphasis] of innumerable passages and statements of the Old Testament": W. F. Albright, "Archaeology Confronts Biblical Criticism," *American Scholar* 7 (1938): 176–88, on 181.
41. T. L. Thompson, *The Historicity of the Patriarchal Narratives*, BZAW 133 (Berlin: De Gruyter, 1974), 328.
42. Thus, e.g., J. Van Seters, *Abraham in History and Tradition* (New Haven, Conn.: Yale University Press, 1975), who agrees with Wellhausen that the stories of the patriarchs do not afford us historical knowledge of the patriarchs but only of the period in which the stories about them arose, thinks that this period is the exilic rather than the late preexilic period. Garbini, *History and Ideology*, 81, asserts on

the other hand that the patriarchal stories are fictions that inform us about Israel's postexilic national ideology.

43. Such questions were already asked in the nineteenth century by scholars like R. Kittel, *A History of the Hebrews*, 2 vols. (London: Williams and Norgate, 1895), who believed that historians like Wellhausen were unduly negative in their assessment of the patriarchal traditions and argued that saga and oral tradition could reflect past happenings accurately.

44. As G. E. Wright, "What Archaeology Can and Cannot Do," *BA* 34 (1971): 70–76, reminds us, how the process of "proving" is supposed to work is by no means clear: "The skeptic always has the advantage because archaeology speaks only in response to our questions and one can call any tradition not provable" (75). He goes on to suggest the following in relation to debates about whether archaeology has "proved" things to be the case: "Both sides of the controversy use the term 'proof' in ways inadmissible, even absurd, with regard to any past cultural, political, socio-economic history" (75).

45. We should emphasize that at least the question of what archaeology could or could not verify had already been raised, for example, by M. Noth, e.g., in his *History of Israel*, ET of the 2d ed. (London/New York: Black/Harper and Row, 1960), 45–46. Since Noth did, however, share the general view of tradition that we are outlining here, his doubts on this specific point did not make him an exception with regard to beginning a history of Israel with the patriarchs (see further below).

46. The major exception is J. Bright, *A History of Israel*, 2d ed. (Philadelphia: Westminster, 1972), which does in fact offer a much more nuanced discussion of tradition and history in relation to the patriarchs than is commonplace (68–85). Here no presumption is made against tradition in terms of historicity, and although archaeology may provide us with a plausible backdrop against which to read the tradition, it cannot in the nature of the case prove that the stories of the patriarchs happened just as the Bible tells them. Nor, on the other hand (Bright reminds us), has archaeology contradicted anything in the tradition. Such a defense of tradition runs against the grain of recent biblical historiography, and some scholars were always likely to be suspicious of a closet "fundamentalism" in someone who said that "to scout the traditions, or to select from them only what appeals to one as reasonable, represent no scholarly defensible procedure" (74). On "fundamentalism," "naiveté," and "critical scholarship," however, see further below. What is clear is that Bright's position is certainly not vulnerable to attacks of a positivist kind, grounded in the absence of archaeological "proof" for the claims of tradition. See further his *Early Israel in Recent History Writing: A Study in Method*, SBT 19 (London: SCM, 1956).

47. There is, for example, no independent attestation of the Exodus, and for some scholars the very nature of the narrative describing it appears to give rise, in principle, to verification problems (thus G. W. Ahlström, *Who Were the Israelites?* [Winona Lake, Ind.: Eisenbrauns, 1986], 46: "Since the biblical text is concerned primarily with divine actions, which are not verifiable, it is impossible to use the exodus story as a source to reconstruct the history of the Late Bronze and Early Iron I periods"). The question of whether archaeology "proves" that an Israelite conquest of Canaan did or did not take place has likewise been a matter of extended discussions over many decades.

48. J. Wellhausen, *Prolegomena to the History of Israel* (Atlanta: Scholars Press, 1994)—a reprint of the 1885 edition, which contained as an appendix Wellhausen's article "Israel," *Encyclopaedia Britannica*, 9th ed. (1881), 13:396–431.

49. Wellhausen, *Prolegomena*, 318–27, 342, 464–65. Abraham is in all likelihood, e.g., "a free creation of unconscious art" (320), and the patriarchal tradition is "legend" (335).

50. Ibid., 464–65.

51. Ibid., 360.

52. We might also add that his starting point with regard to literary activity is far from securely grounded in argument either. If Wellhausen's claim is that "the question why it was that Elijah and Elisha committed nothing to writing, while Amos a hundred years later is an author, hardly admits of any other answer than that in the interval a non-literary had developed into a literary age" (465); then the obvious response is that we in fact know neither that Elijah and Elisha committed nothing to writing, nor that Amos was an author. We know only that we do not possess a "book of Elijah" or a "book of Elisha," whereas we do possess a book of Amos. We can deduce nothing about Israel's cultural history from these facts.

53. For this point and the description of Noth's views that follows, see esp. Noth, *History*, 1–7, 42–84, 121–27.

54. Ibid., 85–97.

55. Ibid., 86–87.

56. Ibid., 88.

57. Thus ibid., 42: "History can only be described on the basis of literary traditions, which record events and specify persons and places. Even archaeological discoveries can only be understood and appreciated in relation to information from literary sources"; 46–47: "What knowledge of any real accuracy and historical substance of the ancient Orient should we possess if we had all the material remains excepting the literary relics in the widest sense of the word?"; 48: "In general, it [Palestinian archaeology] must not be expected to yield positive evidence concerning particular historical events and processes, except when it leads to the fortunate discovery of written documents. . . . [I]n the nature of things it is only rarely that archaeological evidence is forthcoming to prove that a particular event actually took place and that it happened as described in the written records. . . . [T]he archaeological illumination of the general situation in any particular period does not in any way enable us to dispense with the study of the nature of the traditions enshrined in the records which have been handed down." For similar views, see further R. de Vaux, "On Right and Wrong Uses of Archaeology," in J. A. Sanders (ed.), *Near Eastern Archaeology in the Twentieth Century* (Garden City, N.Y.: Doubleday, 1970), 64–80; and Wright, "Archaeology."

58. Noth, *History*, 48. Cf. similarly Wellhausen, *Prolegomena*, 46: "What *must* have happened is of less consequence to know than what actually took place."

59. Some scholars have indeed drawn attention to possible ancient Near Eastern (rather than Greek) parallels to the kind of tribal organization that may be implied in the book of Judges. Note, e.g., W. W. Hallo, "Biblical History in Its Near Eastern Setting: The Contextual Approach," in V. P. Long (ed.), *Israel's Past in Present Research: Essays on Ancient Israelite Historiography*, SBTS 7 (Winona Lake, Minn.: Eisenbrauns, 1999), 77–97 (orig. 1980).

60. It should perhaps be said in Noth's defense, however, that at least he was seeking to verify a *tradition* (however misguided such an attempt might have been) that he held in high regard. Some later uses of sociological "parallels" in respect of the premonarchic period have had few noticeable points of contact with the tradition at all and, lacking such, are open to the question as to whether they have much connection with historical reality either (as opposed to a connection only with the fertile scholarly imagination). For example, G. Mendenhall's reconstruction of "what actually happened" in the creation of Israel ("The Hebrew Conquest of Palestine," *BA* 25 [1962], 66–87), with its focus on an Israelite revolt against dominant Canaanite urban culture, is simply a reading into the past of modern socioeconomic and religio-ethical principles with little serious connection to biblical tradition (see the critique of A. J. Hauser *JSOT* 7 [1978], 35–36).

N.K. Gottwald, *The Tribes of Yahweh: A Sociology of the Religion of Liberated Israel, 1250–1000 B.C.E.* (Maryknoll, N.Y.: Orbis, 1979), offers a similar theory, dismissing nonsociological notions such as "chosen people" out of hand along with the traditions that use such language. He is quite unperturbed by the absence of even the slightest hint of a revolution in the biblical text. Mendenhall later attacked Gottwald, ironically, for reading into biblical history the program of a nineteenth-century ideology. The same move away from verification into fantasy can be seen in still more recent writings from a similar standpoint. In this respect, although M. Weber, *Ancient Judaism* (New York: The Free Press, 1952) is often cited near the beginning of the list of scholars who have brought sociological insights to bear on the history of Israel (since he is by common consent the father of modern sociological study of religion), associating him with his alleged successors is unfair, for Weber, too, took the biblical tradition seriously. It was to the tradition that he turned when he was looking for societies that had, like Protestant European society, a religious-ethical base to their economic system. He found such a base in the covenant theology that underlay the organization of tribal Israelite society and its prophetic religion.

61. Noth, *History*, 90–91: "one must be careful how one uses this material, since it derives from a relatively remote area, from a comparable, but different, historical setting."

62. See the excellent discussion by A. D. H. Mayes, "The Period of the Judges and the Rise of the Monarchy," in J. H. Hayes and J. M. Miller (eds.), *Israelite and Judaean History* (London: SCM, 1977), 285–331, on 299–308.

63. Noth, *History*, 91.

64. Ibid., 91–97.

65. Ibid., 42–43.

66. Ibid., 72.

67. B. O. Long, in his review of T. L. Thompson's *The Origin Tradition of Ancient Israel, 1: The Literary Formation of Genesis and Exodus 1–23*, JSOTS 55 (Sheffield: JSOT Press, 1987), makes the following cogent point in reference to this kind of assumption: "Literary analyses . . . are theoretical explanations for discontinuities which we observe in our reading of the canonical text. I am not sure that they contribute much, if anything, to the question of what . . . might be directly historical. That judgment must rest on other grounds" (*JBL* 108 [1989]: 327–30, on 330).

68. A. Kuenen, *De godsdienst van Israël tot den ondergang van den joodschen staat*, 2 vols. (Haarlem: Kruseman, 1869, 1870), 1:32–35.

69. Davies, *Search*, 32–33.

70. Ibid., 84–87.

71. Ibid., 86

72. J. H. Hayes, "The History of the Study of Israelite and Judean History," in Hayes and Miller, *Israelite and Judean History*, 1–69, on 3.

73. Ibid., 61.

74. Soggin, *History*, 387 n.13.

75. N. T. Wright, *The New Testament and the People of God* (London: SPCK, 1992), 105, in relation to historical study of the NT.

76. Thus, e.g., when Soggin (*History*, 32) claims that "the critical discipline of writing the history of Israel has now existed for more than a century," listing Kuenen and Stade as his starting points; and when he claims that before this time "the tendency was to accept the texts in a basically uncritical way, paraphrasing them or at best only criticizing them superficially," then all he really appears to be doing is using the label "critical" as a means of blessing predecessors whose starting points in the tradition are the same as (Stade) or slightly later (Kuenen) than his own, and of cursing everyone else.

Chapter 2: Knowing and Believing: Faith in the Past

1. T. L. Thompson, "A Neo-Albrightean School in History and Biblical Scholarship?" *JBL* 114 (1995): 683–98, on 697. The article is a response to I. W. Provan, "Ideologies, Literary and Critical: Reflections on Recent Writing on the History of Israel," *JBL* 114 (1995): 585–606, and itself finds an answer throughout I. W. Provan, "In the Stable with the Dwarves: Testimony, Interpretation, Faith and the History of Israel," in A. Lemaire and M. Sæbø (eds.), *Congress Volume: Oslo 1998*, Papers of the 16th Congress of the International Organisation of the Societies for Old Testament Study (Leiden: Brill, 2000), 281–319. Readers especially interested in the exchange are directed to this latter essay, upon which the present and the following chapter are partially based.

2. E.g., J. Habermas, *Knowledge and Human Interests*, trans. J. J. Shapiro (London: Heinemann, 1972); M. Hesse, *Revolutions and Reconstructions in the Philosophy of Science* (Brighton: Harvester, 1980).

3. E. Breisach, *Historiography: Ancient, Medieval and Modern* (Chicago: University of Chicago Press, 1983), 239. The following summary of "dissenting" historians is heavily indebted to Breisach.

4. Ibid., 279.

5. Ibid., 281.

6. A. J. Ayer, *Philosophical Essays* (Westport, Conn.: Greenwood Press, 1980), 167–90, on 168. The discussion that follows this comment illustrates well the difficulties of responding to such philosophers if one grants their basic premises.

7. Breisach, *Historiography*, 332.

8. J. Appleby, L. Hunt, and M. Jacob, *Telling the Truth about History* (New York: Norton, 1994), 194.

9. C. Watkins Smith, *Carl Becker: On History and the Climate of Opinion* (Carbondale, Ill.: Southern Illinois University Press, 1956), 103.

10. These "great stories" are commonly referred to as metanarratives—overarching accounts of reality that claim to make sense of it and to allow coherent explanation of its various aspects (e.g., the idea of history as humankind's upward progress).

11. However, the postmodern response to modernity is in this respect, as in others, not a new phenomenon. Skepticism about the acquisition of objective knowledge in the modern world is as old as the Pyrrhonism of the seventeenth century, and is to be found among thinkers throughout the succeeding centuries. Among those skeptical of our human ability to gain objective historical knowledge per se may be numbered T. Lessing, who opposed the idea that history was a science with the notion that history was a creative act that gave meaning to meaningless life: all historiography is myth created by those who wish to engender faith and hope in the future.

12. T. Reid, *Essays on the Intellectual Powers of Man*, in R. Beanblossom and K. Lehrer (eds.), *Thomas Reid's Inquiry and Essays* (Indianapolis: Hackett, 1983), 6/5:281–82.

13. R. G. Collingwood, *The Idea of History* (Oxford: Oxford University Press, 1970), 234–35.

14. The complexity of the decision-making processes in this regard is nicely illustrated by Aharoni's discussion of the date of stratum II at Beersheba: see Y. Aharoni, "The Stratification of the Site," in Y. Aharoni (ed.), *Beer-Sheba I: Excavations at Tel Beer-Sheba, 1969–1971 Seasons* (Tel Aviv: Tel Aviv University Institute of Archaeology, 1973), 4–8, on 5–7. On the general topic, see E. Yamauchi, "The Current State of Old Testament Historiography," in A. R. Millard, J. K. Hoffmeier, and D. W. Baker (eds.), *Faith, Tradition and History: Old Testament Historiography in its Near Eastern Context* (Winona Lake, Ind.: Eisenbrauns, 1994), 1–36, on 32–36.

15. The correlation of sites on the ground with places mentioned in texts is by no means as straightforward as it is sometimes made to appear by those who are keen

to "prove" or "disprove" the truthfulness of texts. To take one example: is Tell ed-duweir really the ancient city of Lachish? It probably is, but see G. W. Ahlström, "Tell ed-duweir: Lachish or Libnah?" *PEQ* 115 (1983): 103–4, and the further reading cited there. For a different example, see B. M. Bennett Jr., "The Search for Israelite Gilgal," *PEQ* 104 (1972): 111–22.

16. Egyptian records imply, for example, a siege of Megiddo lasting several months at some point during the first campaign in Palestine of Pharaoh Thutmose III (1479–1425 B.C.). This in turn implies a fortified lower terrace in the city during the Late Bronze Age I archaeological period, for in the absence of such a terrace, Thutmose would have enjoyed unrestricted access to the upper town. The archaeological evidence in itself, however, would not lead to the supposition that the lower terrace was necessarily fortified at that time: the fortifications that have survived are apparently significantly earlier. See B. Halpern, "Centre and Sentry: Megiddo's Role in Transit, Administration and Trade," in I. Finkelstein et al. (eds.), *Megiddo III: The 1992–1996 Seasons*, SMNIA 18, 2 vols. (Tel Aviv: Emery and Claire Yass Publications in Archaeology, 2000), 535–75, esp. 539–42. It is above all because Halpern takes the Egyptian *testimony* about the siege of Megiddo seriously that he nonetheless argues that a fortification existed in the Late Bronze I period, arguing (plausibly) that the Middle Bronze fortification on the lower tell "remained in use through the first part of the 15th century" (540).

17. C. Schäfer-Lichtenberger, "Sociological and Biblical Views of the Early State," in V. Fritz and P. R. Davies (eds.), *The Origins of the Ancient Israelite States*, JSOTS 228 (Sheffield: Sheffield Academic Press, 1996), 78–105, on 79–80.

18. G. E. Wright, "What Archaeology Can and Cannot Do," *BA* 34 (1971): 76.

19. P. R. Ackroyd, "Historians and Prophets," *SEÅ* 33 (1968): 18–54, on 20–21.

20. The approach is discussed in C. A. J. Coady, *Testimony: A Philosophical Study* (Oxford: Clarendon, 1992), 199–223. This excellent philosophical study of the dependence of human knowledge on testimony undergirds the present chapter in numerous ways, and repays careful study. E. Shils, *Tradition* (Chicago: University of Chicago Press, 1981) is another general study worthy of note in this context.

21. These and other historians are discussed entertainingly and illuminatingly by J. Clive, *Not By Fact Alone: Essays on the Writing and Reading of History* (London: Collins Harvill, 1990). Clive is himself a historian who understands very clearly the extent to which written history is "knowledge of the past filtered through mind and art" (cf. his Preface). A. Rigney, *The Rhetoric of Historical Representation: Three Narrative Histories of the French Revolution* (Cambridge: Cambridge University Press, 1990), further compares and contrasts Michelet with both Lamartine and Blanc. Each of these wrote histories some sixty years after the French Revolution which they describe; each of them deployed his own particular discursive and narrative strategies to represent and give meaning to events; and each of them revealed, in so doing, his particular ideology.

22. On the contrary, we encounter a real concern for accuracy and truthfulness, whether we read ancient authors like Tacitus (*Annals* 1.1), Cicero (*De Oratore*, 2. ii. 6–9), or the biblical writer Luke (Luke 1:1–4); early medieval authors like Wipo or John of Salisbury (see E. Breisach, *Historiography: Ancient, Medieval and Modern* ([Chicago: University of Chicago Press, 1983], 124–25, 144); or any number of historians from the thirteenth through to the eighteenth centuries. Modern prejudice rather than acquaintance with the past characterizes the past as otherwise.

Chapter 3: Knowing about the History of Israel

1. B. Halpern, "Text and Artifact: Two Monologues?" in N. A. Silberman and D. Small (eds.), *The Archaeology of Israel: Constructing the Past, Interpreting the Present*, JSOTS 237 (Sheffield: Sheffield Academic Press, 1997), 311–41, on 337.

2. Theologians, at the same time, have conceded that "real" history resides elsewhere than in biblical testimony, while basing their theology on the testimony: note, e.g., G. von Rad's concession to positivism in his *Old Testament Theology*, trans. D. M. G. Stalker, 2 vols. (Edinburgh and London: Oliver and Boyd, 1962), 1:105–28.

3. M. Sternberg, *The Poetics of Biblical Narrative: Ideological Literature and the Drama of Reading* (Bloomington: Indiana University Press, 1985), 31, depending partially on H. Butterfield, *The Origins of History* (New York: Basic Books, 1981), 80–95.

4. J. M. Miller and J. Hayes, *A History of Ancient Israel and Judah* (Philadelphia: Westminster, 1986), 74, 129, 159.

5. For the crucial nature of verification in the view of these authors, cf. Miller and Hayes, *History*, 78. For examples of virtual apology, note, e.g., 129, 159–60.

6. J. A. Soggin, *History of Israel: From the Beginnings to the Bar Kochba Revolts, AD 135* (London: SCM, 1984), e.g., 98 on the patriarchal narratives; 110 on the exodus.

7. E.g., P. R. Davies, "Whose History? Whose Israel? Whose Bible? Biblical Histories, Ancient and Modern," in L. L. Grabbe (ed.), *Can a "History of Israel" Be Written?*, JSOTS 245/ESHM 1 (Sheffield: Sheffield Academic Press, 1997), 104–22, on 105, asserts that "the use of biblical historiographical narrative for critical reconstruction of periods that it describes (rather than periods in which it was written) is precarious and only possible where there is (*sic*) adequate independent data." We can see nothing in his preceding discussion, however, that justifies this conclusion, and indeed, we find his earlier assertion itself ungrounded and out of step with both logic and experience, that "the historical testimony of any work will be relevant in the first instance to the time in which it was written" (104). For ungrounded assertion of the same kind cf. T. L. Thompson, "Defining History and Ethnicity in the South Levant," in Grabbe (ed.), *History*, 166–87, on 180: "We all know that the real world which such so-called [ancient] 'historiographies' reflect is that of their author's; and they are never any better than that."

8. On the complexity of the interpretative task facing the archaeologist, see F. Brandfon, "The Limits of Evidence: Archaeology and Objectivity," *Maarav* 4 (1987): 5–43.

9. The complexity of the notion of verification is well illustrated by the scholarly debate that followed the discovery of the Tel Dan inscription. For a convenient summary of the debate, see F. C. Cryer, "Of Epistemology, Northwest-Semitic Epigraphy and Irony: The '*BYTDWD*/House of David' Inscription Revisited," *JSOT* 69 (1996): 3–17; and for an assessment, K. A. Kitchen, "A Possible Mention of David in the Late Tenth Century BCE, and Deity *DOD as Dead as the Dodo?" *JSOT* 76 (1997): 29–44.

10. Note in this regard the debate concerning material culture and ethnicity between W. G. Dever, "The Identity of Early Israel: A Rejoinder to Keith W. Whitelam," *JSOT* 72 (1996): 3–24, and K. W. Whitelam, "Prophetic Conflict in Israelite History: Taking Sides with William G. Dever," *JSOT* 72 (1996): 25–44. The debate is ostensibly about what the archaeological data reveal to be true about the inhabitants of the central highlands of Palestine during the late 13th and early 12th centuries B.C. Decisive for the positions ultimately adopted in each case, however, is the attitude of each scholar to the biblical traditions, in terms of their usefulness to the historian as interpretative keys for the archaeological data. It would greatly help such scholarly debate about what it is that *particular* archaeological data "suggest" or "prove" if scholars were able to articulate more clearly their views on what it is that such data are *generally* able to "suggest" or "prove," and on what part their own interpretative theory plays in producing "suggestion" or "proof."

11. Thus the "knowledgeable" T. L. Thompson of our opening quotation now has this to say, in his "Historiography of Ancient Palestine and Early Jewish Historiography: W. G. Dever and the Not So New Biblical Archaeology," in V. Fritz and P. R. Davies (eds.), *The Origins of the Ancient Israelite States*, JSOTS 228 (Sheffield: Sheffield Academic Press, 1996), 26–43, on 32: "It may well be ironic that it is this recognition of our ignorance of this period's history—indeed that the recognition of such ignorance is the hallmark of our field's cutting edge—that marks the most conclusive results of this generation's historical research!" That ignorance would be the inevitable end-point of the "method" employed could safely have been predicted some time ago.

12. G. E. Wright, "What Archaeology Can and Cannot Do," *BA* 34 (1971): 76.

13. A. Richardson, *History Sacred and Profane* (London: SCM Press, 1964), 251.

14. Thus, e.g., E. A. Knauf, "From History to Interpretation," in D. V. Edelman (ed.), *The Fabric of History: Text, Artifact and Israel's Past*, JSOTS 127 (Sheffield: JSOT Press, 1991), 26–64, on 45–47, accepts that the historian should first and foremost be concerned with primary sources, produced in the course of the events as they were happening, rather than with sources produced after the events. The latter he (tendentiously) describes as designed "to clarify for future generations how things were *thought* [our emphasis] to have happened" (46).

15. Thus, e.g., G. W. Ahlström, "The Role of Archaeological and Literary Remains in Reconstructing Israel's History," in Edelman (ed.), *Fabric*, 116–41.

16. Thus, e.g., P. R. Davies, *In Search of "Ancient Israel,"* JSOTS 148 (Sheffield: JSOT, 1992), 32–36.

17. The phrase is C. A. J. Coady's (*Testimony: A Philosophical Study* [Oxford: Clarendon, 1992], 201). His entire chapter on "the disappearance of history," which combats skepticism about the transmission of tradition, should be consulted. Note also the following studies that are relevant to the argument that follows here, while by no means exhausting all that might be said about the possibility of the preservation of accurate historical memories in biblical texts—even in texts that describe a very early period: W. W. Hallo, "Biblical History in its Near Eastern Setting: The Contextual Approach," in V. P. Long (ed.), *Israel's Past in Present Research: Essays on Ancient Israelite Historiography*, SBTS 7 (Winona Lake, Ind.: Eisenbrauns, 1999); B. Halpern, "Erasing History: The Minimalist Assault on Ancient Israel," in Long (ed.), *Israel's Past*, 415–26; A. Lemaire, "Writing and Writing Materials," in *ABD*, 6:999–1008, which has a voluminous bibliography attached; A. Millard, "The Knowledge of Writing in Iron Age Palestine," *TynBul* 46 (1995): 207–17; K. A. Kitchen, "The Patriarchal Age: Myth or History," *BARev* 21, no. 2 (1995): 48–57, 88, 90, 92, 94–95; R. S. Hendel, "Finding Historical Memories in the Patriarchal Narratives," *BARev* 21, no. 4 (1995): 52–59, 70–71.

18. The quote is from R. S. Hess, "Literacy in Iron Age Israel," in V. P. Long, G. J. Wenham, and D. W. Baker (eds.), *Windows into Old Testament History: Evidence, Argument, and the Crisis of "Biblical Israel"* (Grand Rapids: Eerdmans, 2002), 82–102, on 84, whose argument forms the basis of our whole paragraph. Hess takes as his starting point two recent articles by I. M. Young, "The Question of Israelite Literacy: Interpreting the Evidence, Parts I–II," *VT* 48 (1998): 239–53, 408–22, in which Young argues, first, that mass literacy could not have been a feature of Iron Age Israel and, second, that reading and writing must have been limited to scribes, priests, and administrators. Hess notes also the role of D. W. Jamieson-Drake's *Scribes and Schools in Monarchic Judah: A Socio-Archeological Approach*, JSOTS 109/SWBA 9 (Sheffield: Almond, 1991), in reawakening interest in the general issue of literacy in ancient Israel. Jamieson-Drake contended that writing was largely absent in Iron Age Israel until after the eighth century B.C. This has become a popular if erroneous scholarly view in

recent times. Hess in fact shows that "all assumptions about illiteracy throughout Palestine for the thirteenth century as well as the early Iron Age (1200–1000 BC) must be questioned and re-examined" (85).

19. The extrabiblical evidence thus bears out the impression created by the biblical texts, which assume without qualification that not only leaders such as Joshua could read and write (Josh. 8:32, 34; 24:26; cf. 18:4–9), but also simple citizens such as the young man of Succoth in Judg. 8:14.

20. Hess, "Literacy," 95. Hess is not alone in his positive assessment of widespread (and early) Israelite literacy. B. S. J. Isserlin, *The Israelites* (New York: Thames and Hudson, 1998), for instance, resists the view that literacy was "essentially confined to a scribal class" and cites graffiti evidence of literacy in "possibly Israelite" settlements already in the thirteenth to eleventh centuries (20, 220–21). W. G. Dever argues for functional literacy in Israel as early as Iron I (*What Did the Biblical Writers Know and When Did They Know It? What Archaeology Can Tell Us about the Reality of Ancient Israel* [Grand Rapids: Eerdmans, 2001], 114) or at least by the tenth century (ibid., 143, 202–3, 209, 211), and for a vital oral tradition before that (ibid., 279–80; citing approvingly S. Niditch, *Oral World and Written Word: Orality and Literacy in Ancient Israel*, LAI [London: SPCK, 1997]). J. K. Hoffmeier, *Israel in Egypt: The Evidence for the Authenticity of the Exodus Tradition* (Oxford: Oxford University Press, 1997), 16, maintains that "there is no reason to deny the ability to write and record information prior to the Iron Age." A. R. Millard makes the case for early Israelite literacy most strongly in a number of studies additional to the one mentioned above (in chronological order): "The Question of Israelite Literacy," *Bible Review* 3 (1987): 22–31; "Books in the Late Bronze Age in the Levant," in S. Izre'el, I. Singer, and R. Zadok (eds.), *Past Links: Studies in the Languages and Cultures of the Ancient Near East*, Israel Oriental Studies XVIII (Winona Lake, Ind.: Eisenbrauns, 1998), 171–81. On the possible reasons that not more extrabiblical written evidence of Israel's early history has survived, see also the following studies by Millard: "Evidence and Argument," *Buried History* 32 (1996): 71–73; "Observations from Eponym Lists," in S. Parpola and R. M. Whiting (eds.), *Assyria 1995* (Helsinki: 1997), 207–11.

21. See R. T. Beckwith, *The Old Testament Canon of the New Testament Church, and Its Background in Early Judaism* (Grand Rapids: Eerdmans, 1985), 80–86.

22. See, e.g., J. K. Hoffmeier, "The Structure of Joshua 1–11 and the Annals of Thutmose III," in A. R. Millard, J. K. Hoffmeier, and D. W. Baker (eds.), *Faith, Tradition, and History: Old Testament Historiography in its Near Eastern Context* (Winona Lake, Ind.: Eisenbrauns, 1994), 165–79, who demonstrates that Joshua 1–11 exhibits formal parallels to the campaign descriptions in Thutmose III's annals. He writes (176): "Both employ long narratives to describe the most important campaigns and short, terse reports of less-significant actions using repetitive, stereotyped language. The summary statement is attested in both, as well as references to the booty taken (Josh 8:27, 11:14)." As an explanation for the similarities, Hoffmeier proposes that "the parallels shown here . . . may be attributed to the Hebrews' borrowing of the Egyptian daybook scribal tradition for recording military actions." Egyptian daybooks "are more like the log of a ship than a flowing narrative, recording day-to-day accounts, comprised of repetitive entries and little variation" (169–70). Daybook style (*Tagebuchstil*) may be detected, according to Hoffmeier, in sections of Joshua such as 10:28–42 and 11:10–14. These brief stereotypical reports contrast with the fuller treatment given other events in Josh. 1–11, such as the crossing into Canaan and the taking of Jericho (chapters 1–6), the eventual taking of Ai (7:1–8:28), and the covenant with and defense of the Gibeonites (9:1–10:14).

While some have argued that this "combination of long and short reports" is "an idiosyncrasy characteristic of the first millennium because this kind of mixing is found in Assyrian military texts" (173, referring to J. Van Seters's contention in "Joshua's Campaign of Canaan and Near Eastern Historiography," *SJOT* 2 [1990]: 1–12; esp. 7), Hoffmeier points out that the same phenomenon is present in the Egyptian annals—the pharaoh's first campaign (against Megiddo) taking 110 lines to report, while some of the other reports get only 10 lines (171). Furthermore, the annals' report of events surrounding the battle of Megiddo and the book of Joshua's report of events surrounding the battle of Jericho show similar structure (divine commission, intelligence gathering, march through difficult terrain, setting up of camp, siege of the city, victory [174]). These and other factors lead Hoffmeier to conclude that "minimally, the similarities illustrate that the Joshua narrative is no orphan when compared to a piece of Egyptian military writing and that whatever ideological concerns may have shaped the Joshua narratives, they remain comparable to their counterparts elsewhere in the second-millennium Near East" (173). He believes that "the New Kingdom period, when Israel would most likely have departed from Egypt and entered Canaan, is the most likely time for the Egyptian daybook tribal traditions to have been embraced by Israelite scribes and thus to leave its mark on the composition of Joshua 1–11" (179).

23. For example, J. G. McConville, *Grace in the End: A Study of Deuteronomistic Theology* (Grand Rapids: Zondervan, 1993), draws attention to the episode in Josh. 22:9–34 of the altar constructed by the Transjordanian tribes. With the territorial allotments for the Cisjordanian tribes completed (see the summary in 21:43–45), Joshua blesses the two and a half tribes from Transjordan and sends them back to their inheritances (22:1–8). The episode's complicating action occurs when, at the Jordan crossing, the Transjordanian tribes pause to build an imposing altar (22:10). This action (100) "provoked the ire of their fellow-Israelites because it implicitly challenged the centrality and supremacy of Shiloh as the place of worship for all Israel, as well as the rights of Yahweh among his people (vv. 16–20). The 'Deuteronomic' character of the issues here is beyond dispute. However, the fact that the 'altar of the LORD' is at Shiloh, not Jerusalem, is hard to square with a definition of 'Deuteronomic' in terms of the Josianic reforms that promoted worship in Jerusalem and aimed to suppress it elsewhere, especially in the northern territory. For this reason, it is hard to avoid the conclusion that at least a core of the present narrative belongs to a time before the period of the monarchy, when the centrality of Shiloh in Israel was in fact being asserted (cf. Jdg 21:21 [*sic*; read 21:12?]; 1Sa 1–3)." Biblical references supporting the notion that Shiloh served as a central sanctuary include Judg. 18:31; Ps. 78:60; Jer. 7:12.

24. The captivity of the land mentioned in Judg. 18:30 is assumed by many commentators to be the Assyrian captivity of the northern kingdom that culminated c. 722 B.C.. If this association were correct, then a *terminus a quo* for this section of Judges could be set at that date. McConville (*Grace in the End,* 110) contests this interpretation, however, arguing that nothing in the text would indicate this specific association. On the contrary, the reference in the immediately following verse to "as long as the house of God was at Shiloh" (18:31) suggests that "'the captivity of the land' referred to in v. 30 is most naturally understood in relation to its [Shiloh's] fall, the historical context of this event being the Philistine ascendancy prior to the time of Saul." This would suggest a *terminus a quo* for (at least this section of) the book of Judges sometime after the middle of the eleventh century.

25. See, e.g., V. P. Long, *The Reign and Rejection of King Saul: A Case for Literary and Theological Coherence,* SBLDS 118 (Atlanta: Scholars Press, 1989), 183–90. For further discussion of ways in which the biblical corpus, although strictly speaking without peer in antiquity, does bear traits of literary genres for which ancient Near

Eastern parallels can be cited, see, e.g., H. Cazelles, "Biblical and Prebiblical Historiography," in Long (ed.), *Israel's Past*, 98–128 (Fr. original 1991); *idem*, "Die biblische Geschichtsschreibung im Licht der altorientalischen Geschichtsschreibung," in E. von Schuler (ed.), *XXIII. Deutscher Orientalistentag vom 16. bis 20. September 1985 in Würzburg: Ausgewählte Vorträge*, ZDMG Supplement 7 (Stuttgart: Franz Steiner Verlag Wiesbaden GMBH, 1989), 38–49; Hallo, "Biblical History"; A. Malamat, "Doctrines of Causality in Hittite and Biblical Historiography: A Parallel," *VT* 5 (1955): 1–12; J. R. Porter, "Old Testament Historiography," in G. W. Anderson (ed.), *Tradition and Interpretation: Essays by Members of the Society for Old Testament Study* (Oxford: Clarendon Press, 1979), 125–62; J. H. Walton, "Cultural Background of the Old Testament," in D. S. Dockery et al. (eds.), *Foundations for Biblical Interpretation* (Nashville: Broadman & Holman, 1994), 255–73.

26. The data is drawn from a paper delivered by B. Halpern at the AAR/SBL congress in San Francisco in 1997, which to our knowledge remains unpublished. It is by no means an exhaustive account containing all that might be said. For example, W. G. Dever notes that 1 Sam. 13:19–21 knows of the ancient *pym* weight, which appears to have been in use only in the ninth to seventh centuries B.C.: see H. Shanks, "Is This Man a Biblical Archaeologist? *BAR* Interviews William Dever, Part Two," *BARev* 22, no. 5, (1996): 30–37, 74–77, on 35–36.

27. The absurdity, itself articulated by Hume, is the subject of analysis in G. E. M. Anscombe, "Hume and Julius Caesar," *The Collected Philosophical Papers of G. E. M. Anscombe, 1: From Parmenides to Wittgenstein* (Oxford: Blackwell, 1981), 86–92, who reminds us (89): "Belief in recorded history is on the whole a belief *that there has been* a chain of tradition of reports and records going back to contemporary knowledge; it is not a belief in the historical facts by an inference that passes through the links of such a chain."

28. The folly of making such deductions has been illustrated time and again as data have been produced that support testimony that hitherto had stood alone: see briefly on this E. Yamauchi, "The Current State of Old Testament Historiography," in Millard et al. (eds.), *Faith, Tradition, and History*, 26–27. We may add to Yamauchi's list the following: that until the recent discovery of the Tel Dan inscription, we did not possess independent extrabiblical attestation of a Davidic dynasty as early as the ninth century B.C. That should not have been a compelling reason for disbelieving in such a dynasty; and it is surprising that those who felt the said compulsion are so immune to the opposite compulsion now that the inscription *has* been found.

29. L. L. Grabbe, "Are Historians of Ancient Palestine Fellow Creatures—or Different Animals?" in Grabbe (ed.), *History*, 19–36, on 21 n. 6.

30. G. W. Ahlström, "Role," 118, 134; Ahlström, *History*, 50.

31. Note H. M. Barstad, "History and the Hebrew Bible," in Grabbe (ed.), *Can a "History of Israel" be Written?* 45–46 n. 25, on the curiosity of taking this "appearance" of innocence seriously.

32. Ahlström, *History*, 28–29, 44.

33. Ahlström, "Role," 117.

34. See, e.g., other comments in Ahlström, *History*, 22–23, 31, which recognize the creative, constructive aspects of archaeology and leave us wondering where "neutral history" is to be found.

35. C. Schäfer-Lichtenberger, "Sociological and Biblical Views of the Early State," in Fritz and. Davies (eds.), *The Origins of the Ancient Israelite States*, 82; cf. 79–82 overall. Note further G. N. Knoppers, "The Vanishing Solomon: The Disappearance of the United Monarchy from Recent Histories of Israel," *JBL* 116 (1997): 19–44, on 44: "Comparing literary texts with material evidence is highly

fraught, but concentration on material remains is no guarantee of objectivity. Interpreting material artifacts themselves is a profoundly subjective enterprise. The significance of material remains, no less than literary remains, is not self-evident. . . . New archaeological and epigraphic data are welcome, but just as likely to complicate the interpretation of old evidence as they are to clarify it."

36. H. Shanks, "Is This Man a Biblical Archaeologist? *BAR* Interviews William Dever, Part One," *BARev* 22, no. 4 (1996): 30–39, 62–63, on 35

37. Grabbe, "Creatures," 24–26.

38. For a rebuttal of Grabbe's second conclusion, see V. P. Long, "How Reliable Are Biblical Reports? Repeating Lester Grabbe's Comparative Experiment," *VT* 52 (2002): 367–84.

39. H. Niehr, "Some Aspects of Working with the Textual Sources," in Grabbe (ed.), *History*, 156–65, on 157–58.

40. A voluminous bibliography is available which addresses, in some way or another, the selective and highly ideological nature of Assyrian scribal compositions. A good place to begin is with the brief summary discussion in M. Brettler, *The Creation of History in Ancient Israel* (London: Routledge, 1995), 94–97, and the helpful footnote references there; or with M. Liverani, "The Deeds of Ancient Mesopotamian Kings," in J. M. Sasson (ed.), *Civilizations of the Ancient Near East*, 4 vols. (Peabody, Mass.: Hendrickson, 1995), 4:2353–66. We may note here further only two of the many resources: F. M. Fales (ed.), *Assyrian Royal Inscriptions: New Horizons in Literary, Ideological and Historical Analysis* (Rome: Instituto per L'Oriente, 1981); and K. L. Younger Jr., *Ancient Conquest Accounts: A Study in Ancient Near Eastern and Biblical History Writing*, JSOTS 98 (Sheffield: JSOT Press, 1990), 61–124. It is the easy availability of such resources that makes so puzzling the manner in which Assyrian texts have been employed in some recent studies of the history of Israel.

41. The point is well made in respect of ancient Near Eastern texts generally by A. R. Millard, "Story, History and Theology," in Millard et al. (eds.), *Faith, Tradition and History*, 37–64, who proceeds to use mainly Assyrian examples.

42. A. Kuhrt, *The Ancient Near East C.3000–330 B.C.*, 2 vols. (London: Routledge, 1995), 2:459.

43. For a brief and good recent discussion of these and other sources for the neo-Assyrian empire, see ibid., 473–78, 501–5, 540–43.

44. Not only the Assyrian annals are selective. The same is true of the Assyrian King List, which is influenced by such things as which kings the authors of the list recognized or knew about, or wished to tell others about; and of the *limmu*-chronicle, which lists Assyrian eponyms (officials who gave their names to successive years of the Assyrian calendar) from the middle of the ninth century B.C. to the end of the eighth, accompanied by a short notice of a particular event that happened in that year. A particular event is of necessity an event that has been selected from among many; and the chronicle does not in fact always identify the same significant event as the corresponding annals for a certain year. The brevity of the entries themselves produces certain challenges in interpreting them, not least in terms of deducing where the military campaigns that they often mention might actually have taken place. The correlation of Assyrian textual toponyms with ancient regions or cities is often fraught with difficulty. As S. Parpola, *Neo-Assyrian Toponyms*, AOAT 6 (Neukirchen-Vluyn: Neukirchener Verlag, 1970), says, "Especially the location of peoples and countries presents difficulties, for many peoples did not stay permanently in one place . . . and the ancients themselves were apparently not always well informed about the exact borders of foreign countries" (xv). We are not dealing here, any more than in any other area of historical endeavor, with an exact science.

45. The Babylonian Chronicle is an important source for ancient Near Eastern history from 744 B.C. to 668 B.C.: a year-by-year account of political events as they affected the region of Babylonia, which also provides useful cross-references for the claims of Assyrian texts.

46. For the relevant texts and some comment, see D. D. Luckenbill, *The Annals of Sennacherib*, UCOIP 2 (Chicago: University of Chicago Press, 1924), 14, 23–47 (esp. the transition from fifth to sixth campaigns on 38), 61–63.

47. Even the *limmu*-chronicle, to which we refer as a "chronicle," is far from "objective" in this narrow sense. It presents a particular point of view. For example, the chronicle knows of a certain Shamshi-ilu as both eponym for 752 B.C. and also the holder of the important state and military office of *turtanu* (commander-in-chief). We do not know when he became *turtanu*, although he must have ceased holding this office before 742 B.C., when another man is thus named. In any case, that is the chronicle's perspective on Shamshi-ilu. The reality was probably a good deal more complex, however. His own inscriptions from his provincial residence of Til-Barsip describe him as, among other things, "governor of the land of Hatti"—effectively the Assyrian ruler of the west. His claimed victory over Argishti of Urartu is plausibly identified by many with the Urartian campaigns recorded in the chronicle for the period 781–774 B.C., although the list itself would lead us to think of Shalmaneser IV as the prime mover. The Pazarcik Stela suggests that it is in fact Shamshi-ilu's campaign against Damascus that appears in the chronicle for 773 B.C. Here is an important "semi-royal" figure, then; and the case of Shamshi-ilu is not the only example of apparently differing perspectives in our Assyrian records of this kind. We may note also, e.g., Nergal-erish (eponym for 803 and 775), who was governor of Rasappa according to the chronicle, but ruler of much else besides according to various inscriptions, and who took a prominent role in various western campaigns.

Such examples raise interesting questions about the precise relationship between what is claimed in our various texts about the wielders of power in the Assyrian Empire at any given point and the realities of power on the ground. We are reminded of the inevitable reality that even "chronicles" always describe the past selectively and from a particular point of view, with the intention to persuade the reader of some truth. As Kuhrt says of Shamshi-ilu in particular (*Ancient Near East*, 2:493): "In the Assyrian perspective, he and his predecessors were provincial governors, servants of the Assyrian king; but within their area of authority and in relation to neighbours they could present themselves . . . as local dynasts."

48. For example, the uninitiated reader of the version of Sennacherib's annals that appears on the Oriental Institute Prism Inscription might imagine that (s)he had found there a straightforward record of Sennacherib's eight military campaigns. Yet we know of other campaigns not recorded there, and whether the "eight" campaigns of which we read were in fact of similar nature and importance is questionable. In Luckenbill's view (*Annals*, 14; see further above), the omitted Que campaign was a far more serious military undertaking than the so-called "fifth" campaign of 699 B.C. that preceded it and which was merely a raid carried out on some villages because "royal vanity demanded royal campaigns to be recorded in high-sounding phrases on dedicatory cylinders and prisms or on the walls of the steadily growing palace at Nineveh." For further commentary on Sennacherib's inscriptions, see A. Laato, "Assyrian Propaganda and the Falsification of History in the Royal Inscriptions of Sennacherib," *VT* 45 (1995): 198–226. The movement of the reader from text to historical event plainly requires some caution. Nor is Sennacherib an isolated case; note, for example, the discussion in A. T. Olmstead, *Assyrian Historiography: A Source Study* (Columbia: University of

Missouri Press, 1916), 53–59, of the various ways in which "campaigns" of Ashurbanipal's reign are treated in the records of that reign.

49. Kuhrt, *Ancient Near East*, 475.

50. The fixed point from which Egyptian chronology is retrojected is the relatively late sacking of Thebes by the Assyrian emperor Ashurbanipal in 664 B.C. Since this was also the last year of the rule of Pharaoh Taharka, in Thebes, we can then work back from Taharka using Manetho's history of Egypt as it is partially preserved in Josephus, along with the accounts of Herodotus and Diodorus Siculus (a Greek historian living in Sicily who wrote a partial history of Egypt in the first century B.C.). Adjustments may then be made where possible in reference to archaeological finds (e.g., inscriptional evidence). Ancient Egyptian chronology, just as much as ancient Israelite history, obviously depends heavily upon testimony, interpretation, and faith; and archaeological finds suggest, in fact, that Manetho's dates should not in any case be added together cumulatively to produce a history of Egypt, but that there must have been some coterminous dynasties in Egypt (as in Assyria). The number of such coterminous dynasties is still an uncertain matter. For a good brief discussion of Egyptian chronology, see Kuhrt, *Ancient Near East*, 2:623–26, whose comment on the period of interest to us here (the "third intermediate period," 1069–664 B.C.) reminds us of how carefully we must tread as historians of Israel in using Egyptian sources: "It is quite impossible to write a narrative history [of Egypt in this period], as there are so many gaps" (626).

51. N. P. Lemche, *Ancient Israel: A New History of Israelite Society*, BSem 5 (Sheffield: JSOT, 1988), 52–54.

52. W. Abraham, *Divine Revelation and the Limits of Historical Criticism* (Oxford: Oxford University Press, 1982), 105.

53. W. Pannenberg, *Basic Questions in Theology*, ET, vol. 1 (Philadelphia: Fortress, 1970), 39–50.

54. Coady, *Testimony*, 198.

55. B. Halpern, *The First Historians: The Hebrew Bible and History* (San Francisco: Harper and Row, 1988), 28.

56. Davies, "Whose History?," 105.

57. J. M. Robinson, *A New Quest of the Historical Jesus*, SBT 25 (Chicago: Allenson, 1959), 77. The book provides numerous interesting reflections on historiography and historical method in relation to the New Testament.

Chapter 4: Narrative and History: Stories About the Past

1. This is not to deny the historiographical impulse of other genres. One thinks, e.g., of "historical psalms," or of the numerous poetic compositions sprinkled throughout the narrative histories, or of the historical settings and import of much of the prophetic corpus.

2. See, e.g., L. Gossman, "History and Literature: Reproduction or Signification," in R. H. Canary and H. Kozicki (eds.), *The Writing of History: Literary Form and Historical Understanding* (Madison: University of Wisconsin Press, 1978), 3–39.

3. So C. B. McCullagh, *Justifying Historical Descriptions* (Cambridge: Cambridge University Press, 1984), 129, summarizing Wilhelm Windelband's introduction of the terminology in his 1894 inaugural address as rector of the University of Strassburg, entitled "History and Natural Science."

4. L. Stone, "The Revival of Narrative: Reflections on a New Old History," *Past and Present* 85 (1979): 3–24.

5. Stone, "Revival," 5.

6. Stone highlights three such attempts: "the Marxist economic model, the French ecological/demographic model, and the American 'cliometric' methodology" (ibid., 5).
7. Ibid., 7.
8. Ibid.
9. Ibid., 8.
10. Further justification for dismissing the biblical texts is sometimes sought in assumed late datings for many (or all) biblical books and supposed disconfirmation by archaeological research; see, e.g., N. P. Lemche, "On the Problem of Studying Israelite History: Apropos Abraham Malamat's View of Historical Research," *BN* 24 (1984): 94–124, on 122; T. L. Thompson, *The Historicity of the Patriarchal Narratives*, BZAW 133 (Berlin: De Gruyter, 1974), 327–28. In addition, Thompson would apparently have us believe that the character of biblical texts as theologically shaped narratives precludes any intention on the part of their authors to refer to a real past and thus any access for us via the texts to such a past (T. L. Thompson, "Historiography of Ancient Palestine and Early Jewish Historiography: W. G. Dever and the Not So New Biblical Archaeology," in V. Fritz and P. R. Davies [eds.], *The Origins of the Ancient Israelite States*, JSOTS 228 [Sheffield: Sheffield Academic Press, 1996], esp. 38–43).
11. N. P. Lemche, *The Israelites in History and Tradition,* LAI (Louisville, Ky.: Westminster John Knox Press, 1998), 166.
12. P. R. Davies, *In Search of "Ancient Israel,"* JSOTS 148 (Sheffield: JSOT, 1992).
13. Lemche, *The Israelites*, 166.
14. See, e.g., Brandfon, "Limits."
15. See V. P. Long, "The Future of Israel's Past: Personal Reflections," in V. P. Long (ed.), *Israel's Past in Present Research: Essays on Ancient Israelite Historiography*, SBTS 7 (Winona Lake, Ind.: Eisenbrauns, 1999), 586–87.
16. Lemche, *The Israelites*, 29.
17. Contrast W. G. Dever's very candid description of his own spiritual journey in the foreword to his recent *What Did the Biblical Writers Know and When Did They Know It?: What Archaeology Can Tell Us about the Reality of Ancient Israel* (Grand Rapids: Eerdmans, 2001), ix–x.
18. See, e.g., Lemche's discussion of the Tel Dan stela (*The Israelites*, 38–43), his early assertion that the Ekron inscription may have been a fake (ibid., 182 n.38), etc. Dever cites other examples of scholars dismissing inconvenient evidence by alleging fakery and asks simply, "What can one say when scholars resort to such desperate measures to deny or to suppress evidence that may threaten their cherished theories?" (*Biblical Writers*, 208–9).
19. Stone, "Revival," 8–9.
20. Ibid., 13.
21. See J. M. Miller, "Reflections on the Study of Israelite History," in J. H. Charlesworth and W. P. Weaver (eds.), *What Has Archaeology to Do with Faith?* (Philadelphia: Trinity Press International, 1992), 72, who offers a critique of this reductionistic position.
22. See, e.g., H. G. M. Williamson, "The Origins of Israel: Can We Safely Ignore the Bible?," in S. Ahituv and E. D. Oren (eds.), *The Origin of Early Israel—Current Debate: Biblical, Historical and Archaeological Perspectives*, Beer-Sheva 12 (Jerusalem: Ben-Gurion University of the Negeb Press, 1998), 141–51.
23. For a helpful discussion of the historical impulse in the OT, see especially chap. 1 of Y. Amit, *History and Ideology: An Introduction to Historiography in the Hebrew Bible*, trans. Y. Lotan, BSem 60 (Sheffield: Sheffield Academic Press, 1999).
24. See, e.g., D. M. Gunn, "New Directions in the Study of Biblical Hebrew Narrative," *JSOT* 39 (1987): 65–75.

25. P. R. Davies, "The History of Ancient Israel and Judah," *JSOT* 39 (1987): 3–4; on 4.
26. J. Barton, *Reading the Old Testament: Method in Biblical Study* (London: Darton, Longman and Todd, 1984), 191.
27. P. Barry, "Exegesis and Literary Criticism," *ScrB* 20, no. 2 (1990): 28–33; on 33.
28. See Dever's trenchant critique of antihistorical tendencies in the "Bible as Literature" movement in chap. 1 of *Biblical Writers*.
29. G. A. Yee, "Introduction: Why Judges?" in G. A. Yee (ed.), *Judges and Method: New Approaches in Biblical Studies* (Minneapolis: Fortress Press, 1995), 1–16; on 11–12.
30. So D. Robertson, *The Old Testament and the Literary Critic* (Philadelphia: Fortress Press, 1977); for discussion, see V. P. Long, *The Reign and Rejection of King Saul: A Case for Literary and Theological Coherence*, SBLDS 118 (Atlanta: Scholars Press, 1989), 13–14.
31. As reported in C. Baldick, *The Concise Oxford Dictionary of Literary Terms* (Oxford/New York: Oxford University Press, 1990), 19. Marc Brettler's hesitancy to speak of biblical narrative as "literature" may stem from his functional, as opposed to structural, definition of "literature," which tends to push the concept in the direction of pure, autotelic literature; citing John Ellis, Brettler contends that "literary texts are defined as those that are used by a society in such a way that *the text is not taken as specifically relevant to the immediate context of its origin*" (*The Creation of History in Ancient Israel* [London: Routledge, 1995], 16).
32. See especially I. W. Provan, "Ideologies, Literary and Critical: Reflections on Recent Writing on the History of Israel," *JBL* 114 (1995): 585–606.
33. So Gossman, "History and Literature," 39.
34. H. White, "The Historical Text as Literary Artifact," in Canary and Kozicki (eds.), *Writing of History*, 41–62, on 62.
35. U. Cassuto, "The Beginning of Historiography among the Israelites," in U. Cassuto, *Biblical and Oriental Studies. Vol. 1: Bible* (Jerusalem: The Magnes Press, 1973 [essay first published in 1951]), 7–16.
36. For a more thorough discussion of the relationship of history and literature, see V. P. Long, *The Art of Biblical History*, ed. Moisés Silva, FCI 5 (Grand Rapids: Zondervan, 1994), 149–54.
37. "Introduction to the Old Testament," in R. Alter and F. Kermode (eds.), *The Literary Guide to the Bible* (Cambridge, Mass.: The Belknap Press of Harvard University, 1987), 17.
38. Ibid., 21.
39. W. H. Dray, R. G. Ely, and R. Gruner, "Mandelbaum on History as Narrative: A Discussion," *HTh* 8 (1969): 275–94; on 286.
40. Ibid., 289.
41. H. White, *The Content of the Form: Narrative Discourse and Historical Representation* (Baltimore and London: Johns Hopkins University Press, 1987).
42. In *HTh* 27 (1988), 282–87.
43. Ibid., 286–87.
44. Long, *Art of Biblical History*, esp. 106–7.
45. S. G. Crowell, e.g., writes, "The linguistic approaches of Ankersmit, Lyotard, White, and Kermode all deny to the past any narrative structure" ("Mixed Messages: The Heterogeneity of Historical Discourse," *HTh* 37 [1998]: 220–44, on 237).
46. F. Kermode, "Introduction to the New Testament," in Alter and Kermode (eds.), *Literary Guide to the Bible*, 380.
47. P. Ricoeur, *Time and Narrative*, 3 vols. (Chicago: University of Chicago Press, 1984–88; French original: 1983–85). For analysis, see K. J. Vanhoozer, *Biblical*

Narrative in the Philosophy of Paul Ricoeur: A Study in Hermeneutics and Theology (Cambridge: Cambridge University Press, 1990).

48. P. Ricoeur, "Life: A Story in Search of a Narrator," in M. C. Doeser and J. N. Kraay (eds.), *Facts and Values: Philosophical Reflections from Western and Non-Western Perspectives* (Dordrecht/Boston/Lancaster: Martinus Nijhoff Publishers, 1986), 130.

49. D. Carr, *Time, Narrative, and History* (Bloomington: Indiana University Press, 1986); Carr, "Narrative and the Real World: An Argument for Continuity," *HTh* 25 (1986): 117–31.

50. Idem, "Narrative," 117.

51. A. Rigney, "Narrativity and Historical Representation," *Poetics Today* 12 (1991): 591–601; under review is Hayden White's *The Content of the Form*. The essay concludes with a useful select bibliography on matters pertaining to narrativity, historiography, and literary theory.

52. Ibid., 594–95.

53. Ibid., 595. Probably what those who make the latter assertion are expressing is their (mistaken) belief that it is *only* the first- and second-tier factors—i.e., large-scale environmental and societal features—that are the actual causes of historical change (the "why"), and not third-tier individual actors and actions, which merely explain how in fact the inevitable historical change took place.

54. Ibid., 591.

55. F. E. Deist, "Contingency, Continuity and Integrity in Historical Understanding: An Old Testament Perspective," *Scriptura* 11 (1993): 99–115, on 106.

56. H. M. Barstad, "History and the Hebrew Bible," in L. L. Grabbe (ed.), *Can a "History of Israel" be Written?*, JSOTS 245/ESHM 1 (Sheffield: Sheffield Academic Press, 1997),

57. Ibid., 62–63. See supporting literature cited by Barstad, ad loc.

58. Ibid., 64.

59. Ibid.

60. For discussion, see Long, *Art of Biblical History*, 60–63.

61. Brettler, *Creation of History*, 139.

62. "Revival," p. 17.

63. Stone characterizes Brown's portrait as "postimpressionist" and, in his subsequent discussion, as *pointilliste*, but he still regards it as a work of history. Not all painters are postimpressionists, of course, and portraits may be rendered in a range of styles from highly realistic (almost photographic) to very impressionistic. To extend the analogy, other kinds of visual representation beyond portraits are also available now in our technological age: not only photographs, but X rays, CAT scans, and the like. If asked which type of visual representation is most *accurate*, the answer one would give would very much depend on the *kind* of information being sought. For medical purposes, the X rays and CAT scans will be preferred; a police detective might prefer a photograph; but a family wishing to hang above the mantel a reminder of the appearance and personality of a loved one can do no better than a well-rendered portrait.

64. This "pictorial approach" is not to be confused with the early Wittgenstein's "picture theory" of language: "Wittgenstein's explanation consists in the striking idea that a sentence is a *picture*. He meant that it is *literally* a picture, not merely *like* a picture in certain respects" (so N. Malcolm, "Wittgenstein, Ludwig Josef Johann," in P. Edwards (ed.), *The Encyclopedia of Philosophy*, 8 vols. [New York: Macmillan, 1967], 8:327–40, on 330). Wittgenstein's later philosophy implicitly rejects his former "picture theory" (ibid., 336).

65. In addition to the works of White already cited, the following offers a short sampling of relevant titles, in ascending chronological order: *Metahistory: The His-*

torical Imagination in Nineteenth-Century Europe (Baltimore and London: Johns Hopkins University Press, 1973); "Historicism, History, and the Figurative Imagination," *HTh* 14 (1975): 48–67; "The Fictions of Factual Representation," in A. Fletcher (ed.), *The Literature of Fact: Selected Papers from the English Institute* (New York: Columbia University Press, 1976), 21–44; *Tropics of Discourse: Essays in Cultural Criticism* (Baltimore and London: Johns Hopkins University Press, 1978); "The Value of Narrativity in the Representation of Reality," *Critical Inquiry* 7 (1980): 5–27; "The Question of Narrative in Contemporary Historical Theory," *HTh* 23 (1984): 1–33.

66. See, e.g., F. R. Ankersmit, "Historical Representation," *HTh* 27 (1988): 205–28; "Historiography and Postmodernism," *HTh* 28 (1989): 137–53; "Statements, Texts and Pictures," in F. Ankersmit and H. Kellner (eds.), *A New Philosophy of History* (Chicago: Universtiy of Chicago Press, 1995), 212–40; "Hayden White's Appeal to the Historians," *HTh* 37 (1998): 182–93; "Danto on Representation, Identity, and Indiscernibles," *HTh* 37 (1998): 44–70.

67. H. Kellner, "Introduction: Describing Redescriptions," in Ankersmit and Kellner (eds.), *A New Philosophy of History*, 1–18, on 8.

68. Ankersmit, "Statements, Texts and Pictures," 238.

69. We noted already William Dray's criticisms of White in the section entitled "Narrativity: Reality or Illusion?"

70. So C. Lorenz, "Can Histories Be True? Narrativism, Positivism, and the 'Metaphorical Turn,'" *HTh* 37 (1998): 309–29, on 323.

71. Ibid., 327.

72. Ibid., 324–25.

73. H. Kellner, "Introduction," 4.

74. Ibid., 5.

75. Ankersmit, "Danto," 67–68.

76. Kellner, "Introduction," 2.

77. Ibid., 18.

78. D. Levin, *In Defense of Historical Literature: Essays on American History, Autobiography, Drama, and Fiction* (New York: Hill and Wang, 1967).

79. Ibid., 3.

80. Ibid. Biblical scholars often make the point that something is always lost when a poem (e.g., a psalm) is reduced to a mere paraphrase of its content. Few scholars would dispute this basic point, that a biblical poem's value and essence comprise more than its paraphrasable content. That the same is true of prose narratives is, however, frequently overlooked.

81. Ibid., 23.

82. While not entirely irrelevant to the first- and second-tier (nomothetic) concerns that characterized the *Annales* school and that continue to characterize some current OT scholarship, the biblical narratives focus chiefly on third-tier (idiographic) concerns involving individuals and groups and their discrete actions.

83. Levin, *Defense*, 31.

84. Ibid., 31–32.

85. J. P. Fokkelman, *Vertelkunst in de bijbel: Een handleiding bij literair lezen* (Zoetermeer: Boekencentrum, 1995); now available in English: J. P. Fokkelman, *Reading Biblical Narrative: An Introductory Guide*, trans. I. Smit (Louisville, Ky.: Westminster John Knox Press, 1999).

86. I would like to thank Peter Williams and my longtime friends Kees and Doris Minnaar for checking my translation of the Dutch. Any remaining infelicities are, of course, my own responsibility. (The reader may now wish to compare Smit's translation in ibid., 208–9.)

87. Fokkelman, *Vertelkunst*, 214–15.

88. The following discussion is adapted in part from 105–9 of V. P. Long, "Reading the Old Testament as Literature," in C. C. Broyles (ed.), *Interpreting the Old Testament: A Guide for Exegesis* (Grand Rapids: Baker, 2001), 85–123.

89. R. Alter, *The Art of Biblical Narrative* (New York: Basic Books, 1981); other useful treatments include S. Bar-Efrat, *Narrative Art in the Bible*, trans. D. Shefer-Vanson (Sheffield: Almond Press, 1989); A. Berlin, *Poetics and Interpretation of Biblical Narrative* (Sheffield: Almond Press, 1983); D. M. Gunn and D. N. Fewell, *Narrative in the Hebrew Bible*, OBS (Oxford: Oxford University Press, 1993); T. Longman, *Literary Approaches to Biblical Interpretation*, FCI 3 (Grand Rapids: Zondervan, 1987); J. L. Ska, S.J., *"Our Fathers Have Told Us": Introduction to the Analysis of Hebrew Narratives*, SBib 13 (Rome: Editrice Pontificio Istituto Biblico, 1990).

90. *The Poetics of Biblical Narrative: Ideological Literature and the Drama of Reading* (Bloomington: Indiana University Press, 1985).

91. The following is but a small sampling: R. Alter, "How Convention Helps Us Read: The Case of the Bible's Annunciation Type-Scene," *Prooftexts* 3 (1983): 115–30; C. E. Armerding, "Faith and Method in Old Testament Study: Story Exegesis," in P. E. Satterthwaite and D. F. Wright (eds.), *A Pathway into the Holy Scripture* (Grand Rapids: Eerdmans, 1994), 31–49; R. P. Gordon, "Simplicity of the Highest Cunning: Narrative Art in the Old Testament," *SBET* 6 (1988): 69–80; V. P. Long, "Recent Advances in Literary Method as Applied to Biblical Narrative," chap. 1 in *Reign and Rejection*; R. E. Longacre, "Genesis as Soap Opera: Some Observations about Storytelling in the Hebrew Bible," *JTT* 7, no. 1 (1995): 1–8; S. Prickett, "The Status of Biblical Narrative," *Pacifica* 2 (1989): 26–46; P. E. Satterthwaite, "Narrative Criticism: The Theological Implications of Narrative Techniques," in W. VanGemeren (ed.), *The New International Dictionary of Old Testament Theology and Exegesis,* 5 vols. (Grand Rapids: Zondervan), 1:125–33.

92. In *What Is Narrative Criticism?* (Minneapolis: Fortress, 1990), M. A. Powell distinguishes two aspects of narratives: story and discourse: "*Story* refers to the content of the narrative, what it is about. A story consists of such elements as events, characters, and settings, and the interaction of these elements comprises what we call the plot. *Discourse* refers to the rhetoric of the narrative, how the story is told. Stories concerning the same basic events, characters, and settings can be told in ways that produce very different effects" (23).

93. Alter, "Convention," 117–18.

94. I. W. Provan, *1 and 2 Kings*, NIBC (Peabody, Mass: Hendrickson, 1995), 40.

95. See discussion in ibid., 47–48.

96. A further irony is that Hadad was released to attack Solomon "by an old enemy of Israel [Pharaoh] whom he [Solomon] had unwisely treated as a friend (1 Kgs. 3:1)" (ibid., 95).

97. E. L. Greenstein, "Biblical Narratology," *Prooftexts* 1 (1981): 201–8, on 202.

98. See V. P. Long, "First and Second Samuel," in L. Ryken and T. Longman III (eds.), *A Complete Literary Guide to the Bible* (Grand Rapids: Zondervan, 1993), 165–81; esp. 170–72, where this and other examples of key-word style and also wordplays are described.

99. See, e.g., R. K. Gnuse, "Holy History in the Hebrew Scriptures and the Ancient World: Beyond the Present Debate," *BTB* 17 (1987): 127–36; A. R. Millard, "Israelite and Aramean History in the Light of Inscriptions," *TynBul* 41 (1990): 261–75 (esp. 267–69); J. H. Walton, "Cultural Background of the Old Testament," in D. S. Dockery et al. (eds.), *Foundations for Biblical Interpretation* (Nashville: Broadman and Holman, 1994), 266–67.

100. S. B. Parker argues, e.g., that in the royal inscriptions from Zinjirli containing such references we have stories possessing neither a greater nor a lesser corre-

spondence to "history" than the biblical accounts of Asa and Ahaz ("Appeals for Military Intervention: Stories from Zinjirli and the Bible," *BA* 59 [1996]: 213–24).

101. J. M. Miller and J. Hayes, *A History of Ancient Israel and Judah* (Philadelphia: Westminster Press, 1986),

102. In addition to our comments already, see the discussion of 1 Kings 1–11 in Provan, *Kings*, 23–90, especially his comments on 1 Kgs. 3:1–3; 4:26, 28; 5:14; 6:38–7:1.

103. Cf. Long, *Art of Biblical History*, 82: "the Chronicler presents a *second* painting of Israel's monarchical history, not an *over*painting of Samuel-Kings. It is now widely acknowledged that both the Chronicler and his audience were well familiar with the Samuel-Kings material, and that the Chronicler's aim was to recast and supplement, not repress or supplant, the earlier history."

104. See Miller, "Reflections," 72.

Chapter 5: A Biblical History of Israel

1. K. W. Whitelam, *The Invention of Ancient Israel: The Silencing of Palestinian History* (London: Routledge, 1996), 161.

2. One might argue the point as to how far we might *deduce* aspects of the still-later history of Israel from certain texts. For example, the later chapters of the book of Daniel arguably have something to say about the period of Greek imperial rule over the ancient Near East (and do so whether they are considered to be prophecy or an after-the-fact account). We have chosen, however, not to become involved in the challenging business of extracting history from such veiled and difficult texts. Apocalyptic language is notoriously imprecise.

3. For a recent apology for this approach, see Dever's discussion of "convergences" between textual and artifactual evidence (*What Did the Biblical Writers Know and When Did They Know It?: What Archaeology Can Tell Us about the Reality of Ancient Israel* (Grand Rapids: Eerdmans, 2001), 91, 106, and *passim*). Dever cites scores of examples of such convergences in his chapters 4 and 5 (97–243). From such convergences, he concludes, *inter alia*, that "the biblical notion of a United Monarchy—or at least an early 'state'—ca. 1020–925 B.C. is not a figment of the biblical writers' imaginations, but is based on a fundamental reality" (159). This amassing of pertinent convergences is highly instructive.

4. If it is true, therefore, that it is now widely conceded "that the study of history should not be restricted to the analysis of differences, the novel or the unique" (K. W. Whitelam, "Recreating the History of Israel," *JSOT* 35 [1986]: 45–70, on 56), it is equally true that historical method must be deficient that fails to analyze "differences, the novel or the unique" along with everything else. Yet this manner of "method" finds its advocates among historians of Israel. Note, for example, the view of R. B. Coote that we should set aside "notions of the unique or sublime ethnic, national, religious, moral, or social character of Israel . . . and instead examine the sparse evidence with an eye for what is usual, normal and expected in the history of Palestine" (*Early Israel: A New Horizon* [Minneapolis: Fortress, 1990], viii). We insist, on the contrary, that history is no more about generalities than about specifics, although we are interested in what can be said about generalities as the background against which to read the specifics.

5. It may be particularly helpful where it is genuinely based on evidence from the past rather than simply speculation bound up with the present. A perennial problem, of course, with nomothetic analysis of Israel's past is how to justify conclusions about what is "usual, normal and expected in the history of Palestine" from the usually somewhat "sparse evidence" available to us. Yet conclusions drawn

from evidence are still vastly preferable to conclusions already contained in the governing assumptions of the enquirer—an all-too-present feature of recent work on the history of Israel that seeks to employ a nomothetic approach. Scholars have sometimes perceived the problem in the work of others while paradoxically failing to perceive it in their own. Thus N. P. Lemche, for example, in his review in *Bib* 69 (1988): 581–84, of R. B. Coote and K. W. Whitelam's *The Emergence of Early Israel in Historical Perspective*, SWBA 5 (Sheffield: Almond Press, 1987), chides the latter for their inattention to the Amarna Letters and wonders whether it is because the Letters do not support the theory that Coote and Whitelam are advancing. He notes that "it will always be difficult to limit the possibilities of the human race to act against the presuppositions of a fixed model for its behaviour" (583). Yet the same Lemche thinks nothing of dismissing biblical traditions out of hand and adopting "a broader socio-cultural approach" to Israel's history (*Ancient Israel: A New History of Israelite Society*, BSem 5 [Sheffield: JSOT, 1988], 7), which depends among other things upon "experience of the relationships which have obtained in traditional peasant societies and pre-industrial urban societies in the Third World in recent times" (ibid., 101).

6. We do so in consistency with our earlier discussions about how far human knowledge comes from specific testimony and how far it derives from models of general behavior (offered, e.g., by sociology and anthropology), from the generalities of events (as assumed by those advocating the principle of analogy), or from straightforward empiricism (as some imagine in the case of archaeology). The reader is referred to the preceding chapters for the detail of this discussion.

7. For example, the reader will not find in this volume the kind of argument offered by I. Finkelstein, *The Archaeology of the Israelite Settlement* (Jerusalem: Israel Exploration Society, 1988), 302, who considers the general lack of a parallel for nomadic invasion of settled lands decisive in resolving the question of whether the Israelites were responsible for the archaeologically indicated destruction of Canaanite cities in Palestine around the presumed time of Israelite settlement in the land.

8. We are not even sure whether those who say they believe them really mean it. It certainly appears to be extraordinarily difficult to live consistently and successfully as a human being with such a set of basic assumptions.

9. See, e.g., J. M. Miller, "Reading the Bible Historically: The Historian's Approach," in S. R. Haynes and S. L. McKenzie (eds.), *To Each Its Own Meaning: An Introduction to Biblical Criticisms and Their Application* (Louisville, Ky.: Westminster/John Knox Press, 1993), 11–26, esp. 12–13. A reverse variety of this hybrid class (metaphysical nontheists and methodological theists) is also alleged to exist by P. R. Davies, "Whose History? Whose Israel? Whose Bible? Biblical Histories, Ancient and Modern," in L. L. Grabbe (ed.), *Can a "History of Israel" Be Written?*, JSOTS 245/ESHM 1 (Sheffield: Sheffield Academic Press, 1997), who faults W. G. Dever and B. Halpern—both agnostics or atheists by Davies's account—for nevertheless espousing a "view of history that is theistic" (117, n.19).

10. Ibid., 116–17.

11. Ibid., 116.

12. The quoted phrase is from H. White, "The Value of Narrativity in the Representation of Reality," *Critical Inquiry* 7 (1980): 5–27, and is worth viewing in its broader context:

> Now, the capacity to envision a set of events as belonging to the same order of meaning requires a metaphysical principle by which to translate difference into similarity. In other words, it requires a "subject" common to all of the *referents* of

the various sentences that register events as having occurred. If such a subject exists, it is the "Lord" whose "years" are treated as manifestations of His power to cause the events which occur in them. The subject of the account, then, does not exist *in time* and could not therefore function as the subject of a narrative. Does it follow that in order for there to be a narrative, there must be some equivalent of the Lord, some sacral being endowed with the authority and power of the Lord, existing in time? If so, what could such an equivalent be? (19).

13. For discussion of the antitheological tendencies in some historical-critical approaches, see the section by that name in V. P. Long, *The Art of Biblical History*, ed. Moisés Silva, FCI 5 (Grand Rapids: Zondervan, 1994), 123–35.

14. It is never wise to operate for very long with a severely truncated view of reality. In particular, we agree with H. W. Wolff that worldviews that are "founded in only a *portion* of reality" inevitably limit "the freedom of research into the *total* of actual events" ("The Understanding of History in the Old Testament Prophets," in Long [ed.], *Israel's Past in Present Research: Essays on Ancient Israelite Historiography*, SBTS 7 [Winona Lake, Ind.: Eisenbrauns, 1999], 535–51, on 548). See further Long, *Art of Biblical History*, 132–35.

15. It has unsurprisingly and typically been the case that modern historians have viewed disparagingly the pedagogic aspect of premodern historiography and have regarded it as one of its regrettable deficiencies that necessitates beginning "scientific" historiography from the ground up. Note, e.g., Soggin (*History of Israel: From the Beginnings to the Bar Kochba Revolt, AD 135* [London: SCM, 1984], 20–21) on the history of early Rome. Soggin is dismissive of historians like Livy or Tacitus because of their tendency to provide their readers with models for behavior that might be embraced or avoided. He writes, for instance, that "to argue as a historian that the gesture of Mucius Scaevola persuaded Porsena to return to his own territory is no more than congenial naivety, congenial because it is prompted by memories of school-days." Our own view is that it is simply an error to think that the presence of pedagogic purpose in historical literature is necessarily problematic for the historian.

16. The quotation comes from Cobban via A. Richardson, *History Sacred and Profane* (London: SCM Press, 1964), 92–93, and derives originally from Voltaire's *Dictionnaire philosophique*, art. *Histoire*. See further Richardson himself (256): "The unpardonable crime in the exposition of the history of ideas is dullness, the failure to recognize and communicate the existential challenge of the past to the present. It can be avoided only by those who are vitally concerned with history because they are alive to the urgent questions of their own day."

Chapter 6: Before the Land

1. See A. Kuhrt, *The Ancient Near East C. 3000–330 B.C.*, 2 vols. (London: Routledge, 1995), 1:74–117, for a helpful introduction to the history of Mesopotamia in this period, and 332–81 for the remainder of the second millennium and beyond.

2. Ibid., 1:118–224.

3. Ibid., 1:225–82 on the Hittites; 283–331 on the Hurrians (specifically the Hurrian kingdom of Mitanni), and also on other aspects of the situation in Syria and the Levant in the second millennium, especially the Egyptian domination of the city-states of Syria-Palestine c. 1550–1150 B.C., which provides the context for the Amarna letters mentioned below.

4. Debate ensues over the status of Gen. 38 (the account of Judah and Tamar) within the Joseph story; however, J. Goldingay, "The Patriarchs in Scripture and

History," in A. R. Millard and D. J. Wiseman (eds.), *Essays on the Patriarchal Narratives* (Winona Lake, Ind.: Inter-Varsity Press, 1983), 1–34, on 11–12, has made a strong case that it should be considered part of the Joseph story, or better stated the "Jacob story," since Gen. 37–50 treats the sons of Jacob.

5. Study of the patriarchal promises has been at the heart of the work of C. Westermann on Genesis. Cf. his *Genesis: A Commentary*, trans. J. J. Scullian (Minneapolis: Augsburg, 1984–86); idem, *The Promise to the Fathers: Studies on the Patriarchal Narratives* (Philadelphia: Fortress Press, 1980). The most accessible treatment of this theme is D. J. A. Clines, *The Theme of the Pentateuch*, JSOTS 10 (Sheffield: JSOT Press, 1978).

6. W. Brueggemann, *Genesis*, Interpretation (Atlanta: John Knox, 1982), 204–87.

7. Cf. G. W. Coats, *Genesis with an Introduction to Narrative Literature*, FOTL 1 (Grand Rapids: Eerdmans, 1983), 102.

8. B. Halpern, *The First Historians: The Hebrew Bible and History* (San Francisco: Harper and Row, 1988), 8.

9. J. Van Seters, *Prologue to History: The Yahwist as Historian in Genesis* (Louisville, Ky.: Westminster/John Knox Press, 1992), 1–2, 213; quote on 1.

10. G. Wenham, "Pentateuchal Studies Today," *Themelios* 22 (1996), 3–13, on 3, expresses (though I do not believe he shares this view) conservative anxiety over the distance between event and text by this question: "If it was written so long after the events it describes, how can we be sure that they actually happened, let alone that they are reported accurately?"

11. We must recognize that Mosaic authorship of the Pentateuch is a strong ancient tradition; see R. B. Dillard and T. Longman III, *An Introduction to the Old Testament* (Grand Rapids: Zondervan, 1994), 39–40. This tradition, however, is not firmly rooted in the Pentateuch or in the Bible. Technically, the book of Genesis is anonymous (so G. C. Aalders, *Genesis*, Bible Student's Commentary [Grand Rapids: Zondervan, 1981], 5). In terms of strictly *biblical* tradition, the most that might be claimed, on the basis of later references to the "law" or "book of Moses," is that some of the material in the Torah extends back at least to the time of Moses (Josh. 1:7, 8; 2 Chr. 25:4; Ezra 6:18; Neh. 13:1; cf. also New Testament passages that associate the Torah with Moses—Matt. 19:7; 22:24; Mark 7:10; 12:26; John 1:17; 5:46; 7:23). Indeed, no good reasons exist to reject this tradition.

12. R. Smend, "Tradition and History: A Complex Relation," in D. A. Knight (ed.), *Tradition and Theology in the Old Testament* (Philadelphia: Fortress Press, 1977), 49–68, struggles with precisely this issue: "The historian's main points of orientation—the objective fact, the eyewitness account, the presumed completeness of the data—have been called the 'three vague concepts,' and if there is any field in which the historian can lose his faith in this triad then it is the Old Testament" (53).

13. So, rightly, R. Hess, "Early Israel in Canaan: A Survey of Recent Evidence and Interpretations," *PEQ* 125 (1993): 125–42, on 139, ". . . if one could date a particular text early or late, this in itself would say nothing about its historical worth."

14. Cf. Gen. 11:31; 14:14; 32:32, etc.

15. Cf. G. A. Rendsburg, "Biblical Literature as Politics: The Case of Genesis," in A. Berlin (ed.), *Religion and Politics in the Ancient Near East* (Bethesda: University Press of Maryland, 1996), 50.

16. See Van Seters, *Prologue to History*, who argues for an exilic date for the book of Genesis.

17. See Dillard and Longman, *Introduction*, 39–48.

18. For an excellent survey of recent approaches to the question of composition, see T. D. Alexander, *Abraham in the Negev: A Source-Critical Investigation of Genesis 20:1–22:19* (Carlisle, England: Paternoster, 1997), 1–31.

19. So for example R. Alter, *The Art of Biblical Narrative* (New York: Basic Books, 1981).

20. Perhaps all three factors require to be considered, as D. Carr, *Reading the Fractures of Genesis* (Louisville, Ky.: Westminster John Knox Press, 1996) suggests.

21. E. R. Thiele, *The Mysterious Numbers of the Hebrew Kings: A Reconstruction of the Chronology of the Kingdoms of Israel and Judah*, rev. ed. (Grand Rapids: Eerdmans, 1965), 28.

22. The approximate length of time suggested by Exod. 12:40 seems to be supported by Gen. 15:13, which says that Abraham's descendants will be in Egypt for four hundred years.

23. See, e.g., E. H. Merrill, *Kingdom of Priests: A History of Old Testament Israel* (Grand Rapids: Baker, 1987); W. C. Kaiser, *A History of Israel: From the Bronze Age through the Jewish Wars* (Nashville: Broadman and Holman, 1998), 55.

24. These and other ambiguities are presented in J. Bright, *A History of Israel*, 2d ed. (Philadelphia: Westminster Press, 1972), 120–121.

25. For a good survey of the discussion, consult either M. J. Selman, "Comparative Customs and the Patriarchal Age," in Millard and Wiseman (eds.), *Essays on the Patriarchal Narratives*, 91–140, or B. L. Eichler, "Nuzi and the Bible: A Retrospective," in H. Behrens et al. (eds.), *DUMU-E₂-DUB-BA-A: Studies in Honor of Ake W. Sjoberg* (Philadelphia: Samuel Noah Kramer Fund, 1989), 107–19.

26. C. J. Gadd, "Tablets from Kirkuk," *RA* 23 (1926): 49–161.

27. Eichler, "Nuzi and the Bible," 108–9. A sample of some of the early studies drawing these connections includes S. Smith, "What Were the Teraphim?" *JTS* 33 (1932): 33–36; M. Burrows, "The Story of Jacob and Laban in the Light of the Nuzi Tablets," *BASOR* 163 (1961): 36–54.

28. W. F. Albright, "Abram the Hebrew: A New Archaeological Interpretation," *BASOR* 163 (1961): 36–54.

29. C. Gordon, "Biblical Customs and the Nuzi Tablets," *BA* 3 (1940): 1–12.

30. E. A. Speiser, *Genesis*, AB (Garden City, N.Y.: Doubleday, 1964).

31. See Speiser, "The Wife-Sister Motif in the Patriarchal Narratives," in J. J. Finkelstein and M. Greenburg (eds.), *Oriental and Biblical Studies* (Philadelphia: University of Pennsylvania Press, 1967), 62–82.

32. Bright, *History*, 2d ed., 79. Later editions are more careful in their assertions.

33. One of the first was M. Greenberg, "Another Look at Rachel's Theft of the Teraphim," *JBL* 81 (1962), 239–48.

34. J. M. Weir, "The Alleged Hurrian Wife-Sister Motif in Genesis," *Transactions of the Glasgow University Oriental Society* 22 (1967/68): 14–25. See also D. Freedman, "A New Approach to the Nuzi Sisterhood Contract," *JANES* 2 (1970): 77–85, and S. Greengus, "Sisterhood Adoption at Nuzi and the 'Wife-Sister' in Genesis," *HUCA* 46 (1975): 5–31.

35. Eichler, "Nuzi and the Bible," 113.

36. T. L. Thompson, *The Historicity of the Patriarchal Narratives*, BZAW 133 (Berlin: De Gruyter, 1974); J. Van Seters, *Abraham in History and Tradition* (New Haven, Conn.: Yale University Press, 1975).

37. J. Van Seters, "The Problem of Childlessness in Near Eastern Law and the Patriarchs of Israel," *JBL* 87 (1968): 401–8.

38. While they agree in their criticisms of the biblical portrait of the patriarchs, they disagree in their positive assessment of the material. Van Seters believes they reflect the conditions of the late monarchical period and stem from the exilic and postexilic periods and dates the material to this time. Thompson rejects this view and argues that the text is the product of a postexilic perspective.

39. In *Genesis 16–50*, WBC (Dallas: Word Publishing, 1994), xx–xxv, xxx–xxxv.

40. Ibid., xxxiv.

41. I am grateful to Graham Davies for a stimulating lecture and discussion of this feature of the text of the patriarchal narratives ("Genesis and the Early History of

Israel," delivered at the Colloquium Biblicum Lovaniense XLVIII). I strongly suspect that he would not extend his conclusions as far as I have, however.

42. Of course, careful attention has to be devoted to the development of a reasonable method of comparison. I have considered this question in regard to another issue of biblical-Near Eastern comparison in T. Longman III, *Fictional Akkadian Autobiography* (Winona Lake, Ind.: Eisenbrauns, 1991), 23–38.

43. Eichler, "Nuzi and the Bible," 119. See further, by way of example, the interesting study of T. Frymer-Kensky ("Patriarchal Family Relationships and Near Eastern Law," *BA* 44 [1981]: 209–14), who argues in respect of Abraham's adoption of his household servant and then later his taking of Hagar as a concubine (Gen. 15 and 17) that these customs are attested in the first half of the second millennium. This leads her to conclude that "it is the cuneiform evidence that elucidates and illuminates the patriarchal material, indicating its historical authenticity by demonstrating its fidelity to the cultural mores of the ancient Near East" (209).

44. K. A. Kitchen, "The Patriarchal Age: Myth or History?" *BARev* 21, no. 2 (1995): 48–57, 88, 90, 92, 94–95. Again, these arguments do not "prove" the historical veracity of the patriarchal narratives, but they are certainly consistent with their historicity. We find the criticisms of Kitchen's approach offered by R. S. Hendel, "Finding Historical Memories in the Patriarchal Narratives," *BARev* 21, no. 4 (1995), unpersuasive in the main; Kitchen himself deals with them in his "Egyptians and Hebrews, from Ra'amses to Jericho," in S. Aḥituv and E. D. Oren (eds.), *The Origin of Early Israel—Current Debate: Biblical, Historical and Archaeological Perspectives*, Beer-Sheva 12 (Jerusalem: Ben-Gurion University of the Negeb Press, 1998), 65–134. Hendel himself offers an interesting argument on the antiquity of the patriarchal traditions when he cites a tenth-century Egyptian reference to Arad as "Fort Abram."

45. J. K. Hoffmeier, *Israel in Egypt: The Evidence for the Authenticity of the Exodus Tradition* (Oxford: Oxford University Press, 1997), 33. He cites the Medinet Habu relief that reports a conflict between the Philistines and Rameses III in 1177 B.C.

46. Ibid., 202. See the similar argument by A. R. Millard (quoting K. Kitchen) in "Methods of Studying the Patriarchal Narratives as Ancient Texts," in Millard and Wiseman (eds.), *Essays on the Patriarchal Narratives*, 35–54, on 44.

47. J. Walton and V. Matthews, *The IVP Bible Background Commentary: Genesis-Deuteronomy* (Downers Grove, Ill.: InterVarsity Press, 1997), 48.

48. Note the reference to an Old Babylonian tablet by Speiser, *Genesis*, 179, and Millard, "Methods," 49–50.

49. D. J. Wiseman, "Abraham Reassessed," in Millard and Wiseman (eds.), *Essays on the Patriarchal Narratives*, 144–49.

50. Y. Muffs, "Abraham the Noble Warrior: Patriarchal Politics and Laws of War in Ancient Israel," *JSS* 33 (1982): 81–107, on 106.

51. A. H. Konkel, "*gwr*," *NIDOTTE*, 1:837.

52. W. G. Dever, "Palestine in the Second Millennium BCE: The Archaeological Picture," in J. H. Hayes and J. M. Miller (eds.), *Israelite and Judaean History* (London: SCM, 1977), 70–120; V. H. Matthews, "Pastoralists and Patriarchs," *BA* 44 (1981): 215–18; idem, "The Wells of Gerar," *BA* 49 (1986): 118–26; I. Cornelius, "Genesis xxvi and Mari: The Dispute over Water and the Socio-economic Way of Life of the Patriarchs," *JNSL* 12 (1984): 53–61. This approach has been criticized, but unpersuasively, by T. L. Thompson, "The Background of the Patriarchs: A Reply to William Dever and Malcolm Clark," *JSOT* 9 (1978): 2–43.

53. Cornelius, "Genesis xxvi and Mari," 56.

54. The text (Gen. 14:4) specifically mentions twelve years, but the verse with its reference to the rebellion in the thirteenth year may be playing with an "x, x+1" numerical parallelism, so the number may not be intended literally.

55. Source critics in particular often claim that the text does not fit with any of the other sources and consider it an addition to these sources. Among these scholars, whether the idiosyncratic nature points to an early date or a late date for the book is subject to debate.

56. So Muffs, "Abraham the Noble Warrior," who also shows that each element of Gen. 14 has its exact counterpart in the laws of war and in the etiquette of booty restoration found sporadically in the international treaties of Boghazköy and Ugarit.

57. V. Hamilton, *Genesis*, 2 vols., NICOT (Grand Rapids: Eerdmans, 1990), 1:410, points out that this name does not match the name of any known single deity in the Canaanite pantheon.

58. J. G. Gammie, "Loci of the Melchizedek Tradition of Genesis 14:18–20," *JBL* 90 (1971): 385–96.

59. Rendsburg, "Biblical Literature as Politics," 55–56. J. A. Soggin, "Prolegomena on the Approach to Historical Texts in the Hebrew Bible and the Ancient Near East," *Eretz Israel* 24 (1993): 212–15, argues that the text points to the Persian period when the area east of the Tigris dominated Mesopotamia proper.

60. Two of the most interesting discussants of these issues are M. Astour and J. A. Emerton. Astour ("Political and Cosmic Symbolism in Genesis 14 and Its Babylonian Sources," in A. Altmann and J. A. Emerton (eds.), *Biblical Motifs: Origins and Transformations* [Cambridge, Mass.: Harvard University Press, 1966], 65–112) argues that Gen. 14 was a product of the Deuteronomic school from the late sixth century B.C. and reflects political realities of that time period. He believed that the four kings represent Babylon, Assyria (Ellasar), Elam, and Hatti, the four corners of the world. Furthermore, he believes that the Deuteronomic historian found a kindred spirit in, and thus was inspired by, the so-called Spartoli texts. Emerton provides an effective refutation of Astour's thesis, however ("Some False Clues in the Study of Genesis xiv," *VT* 21 [1971]: 24–47), showing how much speculation is involved in it. In a second article ("The Riddle of Genesis xiv," *VT* 21 [1971]: 403–39), he presents a very complex five-stage redactional history of the passage.

61. We do have a list of Elamite kings from 2100 to 1100 B.C. Albright first identified Chedorlaomer with an unknown king named Kudur-Lagamar, but later argued that it is Kudur-Nahuti, who was an aggressive military presence in the ancient Near East from 1625 to 1610 B.C.

62. Hamilton, *Genesis*, 1:402, also points out that the itinerary of the four kings is given with "geographical exactness."

63. K. Kitchen, *Ancient Orient and Old Testament* (Chicago: InterVarsity Press, 1966), 45.

64. Note the recent article by O. Margalith, "The Riddle of Genesis 14 and Melchizedek," *ZAW* 112 (2000): 501–8, who argues that the text is a *para-mythe* that fits in with the events of the thirteenth century B.C.

65. Coats, *Genesis*, 265–66.

66. G. W. Coats, "Joseph, Son of Jacob," in *ABD*, 3:979.

67. E. Fry, "How Was Joseph Taken to Egypt? (Genesis 37:12–36)," *The Bible Translator* 46 (1995): 445–48.

68. J. Vergote, *Joseph en Egypte: Geneses chap. 37–50 à la lumière des études égyptologiques récentes* (Louvain: Publications Universitaires, 1959).

69. Kitchen has contributed to our understanding in a number of studies, particularly "Joseph," in *NBD*, 617–20; "Genesis 12–50 in the Near Eastern World," in R. S. Hess et. al. (eds.), *He Swore an Oath: Biblical Themes from Genesis 12–50* (Cambridge, England: Tyndale House, 1993), 77–92.

70. Hoffmeier, *Israel in Egypt*. I am greatly indebted to Hoffmeier's work in this section.

71. The major dissent, however, comes from an Egyptologist, D. Redford, *A Study of the Biblical Story of Joseph*, VTS 20 (Leiden: Brill, 1970), whose interpretations (which tend to denigrate the historical authenticity of the Joseph narrative) are disputed by Kitchen and Hoffmeier even while they have acknowledged his positive contributions.

72. Hoffmeier, *Israel in Egypt*, 97.

73. Ibid.

74. Kitchen, "Genesis 12–50 in the Near Eastern World," 79–80.

75. Hoffmeier, *Israel in Egypt*, 84–88; J. Currid, *Ancient Egypt and the Old Testament* (Grand Rapids: Baker, 1997), 74–82.

76. Kitchen, "Genesis 12–50 in the Near Eastern World," 90.

77. Walton and Matthews, *Bible Background Commentary*, 75.

78. Hoffmeier, *Israel in Egypt*, 87–88. Cf. also K. Kitchen, "Egyptians and Hebrews, from Ra'amses to Jericho," in Aḥituv and Oren, *Origin of Early Israel*, 105–6): ". . . a biblical writer or writers might well have known the king's name, but in everyday intercourse and documentation (outside of official datelines, which the biblical writers had no need of), people in the Ramesside period customarily spoke of their ruler as 'Pharaoh' or 'Pharaoh our good lord, LPH', and the like— *not* by name! . . . Again, Egyptian and biblical usage marched together through changing times."

79. Hoffmeier, *Israel in Egypt*, 94–95.

80. Contra Kitchen's numerous (but rather naive) pleas that he is simply being "factual."

81. For instance, the "land of Rameses" (Gen. 47:11) may be seen as an anachronism that reflects the time of the narrator or later; see Walton and Matthews, *Bible Background Commentary*, 79.

82. See *ANEP*, 35. Disagreements among Egyptologists about the interpretation of astronomical data, the length of some reigns, and the extent of overlapping dynasties in Egypt have resulted in competing chronological schemes existing for ancient Egyptian history. The dates for individual pharaohs should only be regarded as approximate, therefore. Even if we leave aside radical chronological theories that would result in the substantial lowering of many dates, dates for the pharaohs can still vary on differing schema by as much as twenty to thirty years. See further Kuhrt, *Ancient Near East*, 1:11–12 and *passim*.

83. Hoffmeier, *Israel in Egypt*, 112–14.

84. See *ANET*, 119, and the discussion in B. Lewis, *The Sargon Legend: A Study of the Akkadian Text and the Tale of the Hero Who Was Exposed at Birth*, ASOR Dissertation Series 4 (Cambridge, Mass.: American Schools of Oriental Research, 1980), and Longman, *Fictional Akkadian Autobiography*.

85. Hoffmeier, *Israel in Egypt*, 138–40.

86. As a nomadic tribe, Midian did not possess land as such, and the reference to "the land of Midian" is therefore at first sight curious. Presumably, though, the reference is to the place where their wanderings were focused: in north Arabia on the east side of Aqaba (Hoffmeier, *Israel in Egypt*, 143).

87. For the text, see *ANET*, 18–22; and W. W. Hallo and K. L. Younger (eds.), *The Context of Scripture*, vol. 1 (Leiden: Brill, 1997), 77–82.

88. G. W. Coats, *Exodus 1–18*, FOTL IIA (Grand Rapids: Eerdmans, 1999), 39.

89. G. Hort, "The Plagues of Egypt," *ZAW* 69 (1957): 84–103, and *ZAW* 70 (1958): 48–59.

90. The exact translation of the Hebrew word for this plague is a matter of debate.

91. See below for these and other geographical locations that are noted in the itinerary of Israel's wilderness journey.

92. Compare, for instance, 1 Kgs. 9:26 and Jer. 49:21 (in reference with what today we would call the Gulf of Aqabah) with Num. 33:10–11 (connected to the Gulf of Suez).

93. Hoffmeier, *Israel in Egypt*, 209.

94. B. F. Batto, "The Reed Sea: Requiescat in Pace," *JBL* 102 (1983): 27–35.

95. C. J. Humphreys, "The Number of People in the Exodus from Egypt: Decoding Mathematically the Very Large Numbers in Numbers 1 and 26," *VT* 48 (1998): 196–213. Criticisms may be found in J. Milgrom, "On Decoding Very Large Numbers," *VT* 49 (1999): 131–32; and R. Heinzerling, "On the Interpretation of the Census Lists by C. J. Humphreys and G. E. Mendenhall," *VT* 50 (2000): 250–52; and Humphrey's response in "The Numbers in the Exodus from Egypt: A Further Appraisal," *VT* 50 (2000): 322–28. The debate continues at the time of writing.

96. Since the number in Num. 1:46 counts only males twenty years old and up, the figure is better understood as a military registration than as a population census.

97. Hoffmeier, *Israel in Egypt*, 109, 110–11, suggests that this approach is in keeping with Egyptian practice of never naming an enemy, while R. Hendel, who believes that later Israel is formed from a variety of different experiences rather than a single Exodus experience, says that it allows people with different experiences of Egyptian oppression through the ages to identify with the tradition ("The Exodus in Biblical Memory," *JBL* 120 [2001]: 607–8). See n. 78 above.

98. If, on the other hand, we follow the alternative chronology in the Septuagint, which suggests that we add only 440 years to the figure of 966, we arrive at a very *late* fifteenth-century Exodus.

99. *ABD*, 2:702.

100. *ABD*, 2:703.

101. The Merneptah Stela confirms only that Israel existed in some form by the late thirteenth century. It does not help us discover whether the Israelites left Egypt only shortly before that time, or substantially so.

102. B. Waltke, "The Date of the Conquest," *WTJ* 52 (1990): 181–200, on 200.

103. See *ANET*, 230–34.

104. This site is to be identified with the site known as Tjeku in Egyptian literature. Generally, Succoth/Tjeku is associated with Tell el-Maskhouta. Tjeku was a military area, so we imagine that the Israelites may have had to pass through quickly.

105. Etham is related to an Egyptian word for "fort."

106. Though a Semitic term meaning "fort," the location is known as "the Migdol of Seti" in Egyptian as well. At the time of the writing, exciting excavations are proceeding at Tell el-Borg under the leadership of James Hoffmeier (North Sinai Archaeological Project). This site was clearly occupied between 1450 and 1200 B.C., and Hoffmeier's working hypothesis is that it is biblical Migdol.

107. Recent work by Stephen O. Moshier of Wheaton College and the North Sinai Archaeological Project has gone far, however, in reconstructing the geography of the area presumed to be the arena for the crossing of the sea and Israel's early wanderings.

108. Kitchen, "Egyptians and Hebrews," 65–131, on 92.

109. Other itineraries are related in the Pentateuch, and also in Josh. 3–4, and they all have a similar pattern. They provide the structural glue for this section of the Bible, binding the different stories together. See G. W. Coats, "The Wilderness Itinerary," *CBQ* 34 (1972): 135–52.

110. G. I. Davies, "The Wilderness Itineraries: A Comparative Study," *TynBul* 25 (1974): 46–81.

111. W. W. Hallo, "The Road to Emar," *JCS* 18 (1964): 57–88.

112. C. Krahmalkov, "Exodus Itinerary Confirmed by Egyptian Evidence," *BARev* 20 (1994): 54–62, on 56. The Egyptian evidence that he cites relates directly to the

wilderness wanderings, however, only in their last phase. Z. Kallai, "The Wandering-Traditions from Kadesh-Barnea to Canaan: A Study in Biblical Historiography," *JJS* 33 (1982): 175–84, on 178, adds that "not only is Num. 33 consistent in its literary form, but the sequence of the stations, as far as can be ascertained, is geographically sound," although he quickly adds that the same cannot be said for all the itinerary traditions in the Pentateuch.

113. As Kitchen ("Egyptians and Hebrews," 78) reminds us, it is "an area still far too little explored in terms of modern archaeology."

114. The earliest tradition is from Eusebius of Caesurea. By this time, a monastery at Jebel Musa commemorating the events at Sinai was already present.

115. It is likely the presupposed framework for the promises in Gen. 12.

116. For details, see J. G. McConville, "*berit*," in *NIDOTTE*, 1:746–55; M. G. Kline, *Treaty of the Great King* (Grand Rapids: Eerdmans, 1963).

117. Many, like Wellhausen himself, have thought that some of the laws were introduced as separate collections. He felt the oldest law code was "the book of the Covenant" (Exod. 20:22–23:19), followed by the Deuteronomic law associated with the reform of Josiah in the seventh century B.C.

118. See J. J. Finkelstein, "The Laws of Ur-Nammu," *JCS* 22 (1969): 66–82.

119. R. W. Klein, "Back to the Future: The Tabernacle in the Book of Exodus," *Interp* 50 (1996): 264–76, on 264. Some scholars go so far as to question whether any actual object lies behind the description of the tabernacle.

120. K. Kitchen, "The Tabernacle—A Bronze Age Artefact," *Eretz Israel* 24 (1993): 119*–29* as well as idem, "The Desert Tabernacle: Pure Fiction or Plausible Account?" *BR* 16 (2000): 14–21.

121. While Moses' faith also did not waver, according to the biblical text, he was not permitted to enter the promised land because of a later act of faithlessness (Num. 20:1–13).

122. This structure is seen most vividly in the two census accounts in Num. 1 and 26. See D. Olson, *The Death of the Old and the Birth of the New: The Framework of the Book of Numbers and the Pentateuch*, BJS 71 (Chico, Calif.: Scholars Press, 1985).

123. See *The Holman Bible Atlas* (Nashville: Broadman and Holman, 1998), 71; J. M. Miller, "The Israelite Journey through (around) Moab and Moabite Toponymy," *JBL* 108 (1989): 577–95; and Kallai, "Wandering-traditions."

124. See *ABD*, 4:48–49.

125. As we follow the story through Numbers, we see that Moab and Midian are used almost interchangeably. The account begins with Balak hiring Balaam, the prophet, to curse Israel, but he is unable to do so (Num. 22–24). After this fails, we hear of a plot that is initially successful to lure Israel into false worship through the seduction of "Moabite women" (Num. 25:1), but later we hear of a "Midianite woman" named Cozbi (Num. 25:14–15). Finally, in Num. 31, retribution is said to come against the Midianites. T. R. Ashby (*Numbers*, NICOT [Grand Rapids: Eerdmans], 589) suggests that we have here a "Moabite contingent of Midianites," the latter of which ally themselves with a host of different groups.

126. *ABD*, 6:643.

127. D. J. A. Clines, *The Theme of the Pentateuch* (Sheffield: Sheffield Academic Press, 1999).

Chapter 7: The Settlement in the Land

1. So E. D. Oren on page 1 of his "Opening remarks" to S. Ahituv and E. D. Oren (eds.), *The Origin of Early Israel—Current Debate: Biblical, Historical and Archaeological Perspectives*, Beer-Sheva 12 (Jerusalem: Ben-Gurion University of the Negeb Press, 1998).

2. Cf., e.g., W. G. Dever, "Is There Any Archaeological Evidence for the Exodus?," in E. S. Frerichs and L. H. Lesko (eds.), *Exodus, the Egyptian Evidence* (Winona Lake, Ind.: Eisenbrauns, 1997), 67–86. For a strong rebuttal, see K. A. Kitchen, "Egyptians and Hebrews, from Ra'amses to Jericho," in Ahituv and Oren (eds.), *Origin of Early Israel*, 65–131.

3. Oren, "Opening Remarks," 2.

4. On the general approach that seeks, as far as possible, to take a fresh look at each body of evidence on its own before attempting a synthesis, see W. G. Dever, *What Did the Biblical Writers Know, and When Did They Know It?: What Archaeology Can Tell Us about the Reality of Ancient Israel* (Grand Rapids: Eerdmans, 2001), especially his discussion of the "convergence" method in his chap. 4. Cf. also idem, "Archaeological Data on the Israelite Settlement: A Review of Two Recent Works," *BASOR* 284 (1992): 88.

5. Z. Kallai, "Biblical Historiography and Literary History: A Programmatic Survey," *VT* 49 (1999): 338–50, on 338.

6. Virtually all histories of Israel and Joshua commentaries contain some treatment of the dominant theories; for a recent, succinct summary in a commentary, see D. M. Howard Jr., *Joshua*, NAC 5 (Nashville: Broadman and Holman, 1998), 36–40. The following is a sampling of pertinent essays: R. Gnuse, "BTB Review of Current Scholarship: Israelite Settlement of Canaan: A Peaceful Internal Process—Part 2," *BTB* 21 (1991): 109–17; R. S. Hess, "Early Israel in Canaan: A Survey of Recent Evidence and Interpretations," *PEQ* 125 (1993): 125–42; B. S. Isserlin, "The Israelite Conquest of Canaan: A Comparative Review of the Arguments Applicable," *PEQ* 115 (1983): 85–94; J. M. Miller, "Israelite History," in D. A. Knight and G. M. Tucker (eds.), *The Hebrew Bible and Its Modern Interpreters* (Philadelphia: Fortress Press; Chico, Calif.: Scholars Press, 1985), 10–12; B. K. Waltke, "The Date of the Conquest," *WTJ* 52 (1990): 181–200; M. and H. Weippert, "Die vorgeschichte Israels in neuem Licht," *TRu* 56 (1991): 341–90; E. Yamauchi, "The Current State of Old Testament Historiography," in A. R. Millard, J. K. Hoffmeier, and D. W. Baker (eds.), *Faith, Tradition, and History: Old Testament Historiography in its Near Eastern Context* (Winona Lake, Ind.: Eisenbrauns, 1994), 1–36; K. L. Younger Jr., "Early Israel in Recent Biblical Scholarship," in D. W. Baker and B. T. Arnold (eds.), *The Face of Old Testament Studies: A Survey of Contemporary Approaches* (Grand Rapids: Baker, 1999), 176–206; see esp. 178–91.

7. W. F. Albright, "The Israelite Conquest of Canaan in the Light of Archaeology," *BASOR* 74 (1939): 11–23.

8. Y. Yadin, "Is the Biblical Account of the Israelite Conquest of Canaan Historically Reliable?" *BARev* 8, no. 2 (1982): 16–23.

9. G. E. Wright, *Biblical Archaeology*, new and rev. ed. (Philadelphia: Westminster Press, 1962), 84.

10. Beginning with the fixed date of Solomon's accession, c. 970 B.C., and working backward, David's reign would have commenced c. 1010, and Saul's c. 1030 (on an approximately twenty-year reign for Saul—see chap. 8 on the early Israelite monarchy). Samuel followed Eli, and Eli is said to have judged Israel forty years (1 Sam. 4:18; possibly a round number), so even assuming some overlapping with the later judgeships (e.g., Samson), we arrive at a likely date for Jephthah not later than the early eleventh century. See also K. A. Kitchen and T. C. Mitchell, "Chronology of the Old Testament," *NBD*, 186–93.

11. Wright, *Biblical Archaeology*, 84.

12. J. J. Bimson, *Redating the Exodus and Conquest*, JSOTS 5 (Sheffield: JSOT, 1978), chap. 1. Cf. also W. G. Dever, "Israel, History of (Archaeology and the 'Conquest')," in *ABD*, 3:545–58; esp. the chart on 548.

13. "Early Israel," 179.
14. The burning of Jericho is mentioned in Josh. 6:24, of Ai in 8:28, and of Hazor in 11:11, 13.
15. So B. S. J. Isserlin, *The Israelites* (New York: Thames and Hudson, 1998), 57. The point is well demonstrated by Isserlin in an earlier study in which he asks "to what extent the destruction of settlements can serve as an indicator of conquest"; after examining three well-documented invasions—the Norman conquest of England in A.D. 1066, the Muslim Arab conquest of the Levant in the seventh century A.D., and the Anglo-Saxon occupation of England in the fifth—Isserlin concludes that "in none of the three cases referred to for comparison is the destruction of settlements an archaeologically significant feature, even though textual references would lead one to expect this" ("The Israelite Conquest of Canaan," 87). Coming to the same conclusion but on the basis of a closer analogy is A. R. Millard's "Amorites and Israelites: Invisible Invaders—Modern Expectation and Ancient Reality" (a paper read at The Future of Biblical Archaeology: Reassessing Methodologies and Assumptions, a consultation held in Deerfield, Illinois, August 12–14, 2001). Cf. also D. Merling, *The Book of Joshua: Its Theme and Role in Archaeological Discussions*, AUSDDS 23 (Andrews University Press, 1997), 270; E. Yamauchi, "The Current State of Old Testament Historiography," 36.
16. A. Alt, "Die Landnahme der Israeliten in Palästina," *Reformationsprogramm der Universität Leipzig* (1925); available in English translation as "The Settlement of the Israelites in Palestine," in idem, *Essays on Old Testament History and Religion* (Sheffield: Sheffield Academic Press, 1989 reprint), 133–69.
17. In a larger sense, Noth seems to have warmed gradually to the significance of archaeological evidences in questions of historical probability; see R. de Vaux, "The Hebrew Patriarchs in History," reprinted in V. P. Long (ed.), *Israel's Past in Present Research: Essays on Ancient Israelite Historiography*, SBTS 7 (Winona Lake, Ind.: Eisenbrauns, 1999), 470–79; esp. 475–77 (French orig. 1962–63; English trans. 1972).
18. For a brief summary of criticisms, with reference to their chief advancers, see Younger, "Early Israel," 180–81.
19. See, e.g., V. Fritz, "Conquest or Settlement? The Early Iron Age in Palestine," *BA* 50 (1987): 84–100. While incorporating insights from the infiltration hypothesis, Fritz in fact understands his approach as an alternative to all the reigning hypotheses—the so-called invasion hypothesis, the infiltration hypothesis, and the revolution hypothesis (84). He argues largely on the basis of archaeological evidence for a "symbiosis hypothesis" (98–99). As for the textual evidence, he states bluntly, "Joshua is of no historical value" (98).
20. G. Mendenhall, "The Hebrew Conquest of Palestine," *BA* 25, no. 3 (1962), 66–87.
21. *The Tenth Generation: The Origins of the Biblical Tradition* (Baltimore and London: Johns Hopkins University Press, 1973).
22. Mendenhall, "Hebrew Conquest," 73–74.
23. Ibid., 81.
24. Ibid., 85.
25. Ibid., 66.
26. G. E. Mendenhall, "Ancient Israel's Hyphenated History," in D. N. Freedman and D. Frank Graf (eds.), *Palestine in Transition: The Emergence of Ancient Israel* (Sheffield: Almond Press, 1983), 91–103, on 99.
27. N. K. Gottwald, *The Tribes of Yahweh: A Sociology of the Religion of Liberated Israel, 1250–1000 B.C.E.* (Maryknoll, N.Y.: Orbis Books, 1979).
28. Mendenhall, "Ancient Israel's Hyphenated History," 91.

29. See chap. 4 of the present work.
30. On all these criticisms, see Younger ("Early Israel," 181–82), who credits N. P. Lemche (*Early Israel: Anthropological and Historical Studies on the Israelite Society before the Monarchy*, VTS 37 [Leiden: E. J. Brill, 1985]) with the first three. Cf. also Hess, "Early Israel," 130–31, for further critical analysis.
31. Mendenhall, *Tenth Generation*, 226.
32. Hess, "Early Israel," 127.
33. Younger, "Early Israel," 182–91.
34. W. G. Dever, *What Did the Biblical Writers Know;* I. Finkelstein and N. A. Silberman, *The Bible Unearthed: Archaeology's New Vision of Ancient Israel and the Origin of Its Sacred Texts* (New York: The Free Press, 2001).
35. So Younger, "Early Israel," 184.
36. Dever, *What Did the Biblical Writers Know*, 110.
37. Ibid., 119.
38. Ibid., 113.
39. Ibid., 116.
40. Ibid., 108–24.
41. Ibid., 121. Dever illustrates his point by citing the tendency of Americans on Thanksgiving Day to "patriotically identify with those Pilgrims who came over on the *Mayflower* (as though we were all card-carrying members of the Daughters of the American Revolution)."
42. Two of his most recent treatises are Finkelstein and Silberman, *The Bible Unearthed* (mentioned above), and Finkelstein, "The Rise of Early Israel: Archaeology and Long-Term History," in Ahituv and Oren (eds.), *Origin of Early Israel*, 7–39.
43. "The Rise of Early Israel," 10.
44. See, e.g., I. Finkelstein, *The Archaeology of the Israelite Settlement* (Jerusalem: Israel Exploration Society, 1988); idem and N. Na'aman (eds.), *From Nomadism to Monarchy: Archaeological and Historical Aspects of Early Israel* (Washington, D.C.: Biblical Archaeology Society, 1994).
45. "The Rise of Early Israel," 24–25.
46. Ibid., 8.
47. Ibid., 26.
48. Ibid., 25.
49. Hess, "Early Israel," 129.
50. Ibid., 130.
51. Finkelstein, "The Rise of Early Israel," 16.
52. L. E. Stager, *Ashkelon Discovered* (Washington, D.C.: Biblical Archaeology Society, 1991), 9, 19, 31.
53. Note Younger's cautionary remarks, "Early Israel," 196.
54. For summaries of each, see ibid., 187–91.
55. "The Rise of Early Israel," 9–10.
56. See P. R. Davies, *In Search of "Ancient Israel*," JSOTS 148 (Sheffield: JSOT, 1992), 11, where he distinguishes "three Israels: one is literary (the biblical), one is historical (the inhabitants of the northern Palestinian highlands during part of the Iron Age) and the third, 'ancient Israel', is what scholars have constructed out of an amalgam of the two others." Chaps. 2, 3, and 4 of Davies's book are dedicated to ancient, biblical, and historical Israel respectively. In a sense, of course, this tripartite distinction is correct and helpful, but Davies surely goes too far in the size of the wedge that he drives between the three.
57. See our discussion in chap. 3, sect. 2 above.
58. Younger, "Early Israel," 206.
59. See J. M. Miller, "Is It Possible to Write a History of Israel without Relying on the Hebrew Bible?" in D. V. Edelman (ed.), *The Fabric of History: Text, Artifact,*

and Israel's Past, JSOTS 127 (Sheffield: Sheffield Academic Press, 1991), 93–102; especially 100 (cited by Younger, "Early Israel," 193).

60. For an insightful discussion of these matters, see R. S. Hess, "Early Israel," esp. 138–39.

61. R. Polzin, *Moses and the Deuteronomist: A Literary Study of the Deuteronomistic History* (New York: Seabury, 1980).

62. D. M. Gunn, "Joshua and Judges," in R. Alter and F. Kermode (eds.), *The Literary Guide to the Bible* (Cambridge, Mass.: The Belknap Press of Harvard University, 1987), 102–21.

63. L. Alonso Schökel, "Narrative Art in Joshua-Judges-Samuel-Kings," in Long (ed.), *Israel's Past*, 255–78 (originally in Spanish: "Arte narrativa en Josué-Jueces-Samuel-Reyes," *Estudios Bíblicos* 48 [1990], 145–69).

64. K. L. Younger Jr., "The Configuring of Judicial Preliminaries: Judges 1.1–2.5 and Its Dependence on the Book of Joshua," *JSOT* 68 (1995): 75–92.

65. K. R. R. Gros Louis and W. Van Antwerpen Jr., "Joshua and Judges," in L. Ryken and T. Longman III (eds.), *A Complete Literary Guide to the Bible* (Grand Rapids: Zondervan, 1993), 137–50.

66. H. J. Koorevaar, "De Opbouw van het Boek Jozua" (Diss. Theol., Leuven, University of Brussels, 1990).

67. N. Winther-Nielsen, *A Functional Discourse Grammar of Joshua: A Computer-Assisted Rhetorical Structure Analysis*, ConBOT 40 (Stockholm: Almqvist & Wiksell, 1990); see also idem, "The Miraculous Grammar of Joshua 3–4: Computer-Aided Analysis of the Rhetorical and Syntactic Structure," in R. D. Bergen (ed.), *Biblical Hebrew and Discourse Linguistics* (Dallas: Summer Institute of Linguistics, 1994), 300–319.

68. K. L. Younger Jr., *Ancient Conquest Accounts: A Study in Ancient Near Eastern and Biblical History Writing*, JSOTS 98 (Sheffield: JSOT, 1990).

69. L. D. Hawk, *Every Promise Fulfilled: Contesting Plots in Joshua* (Louisville, Ky.: Westminster/John Knox Press, 1991).

70. D. W. Gooding, "The Composition of the Book of Judges," *Eretz-Israel* 16 (1982): 70–79.

71. B. G. Webb, *The Book of the Judges: An Integrated Reading*, JSOTS 46 (Sheffield: JSOT, 1987).

72. L. R. Klein, *The Triumph of Irony in the Book of Judges*, JSOTS 68 (Sheffield: Almond Press, 1988).

73. M. Brettler, "The Book of Judges: Literature as Politics," *JBL* 108 (1989): 395–418.

74. D. I. Block, "Echo Narrative Technique in Hebrew Literature: A Study in Judges 19," *WTJ* 52, no. 2 (1990): 325–41; idem, "Will the Real Gideon Please Stand Up? Narrative Style and Intention in Judges 6–9," *JETS* 40/3 (1997): 353–66; idem, *Judges, Ruth*, NAC 6 (Nashville: Broadman and Holman, 1999).

75. R. G. Bowman, "Narrative Criticism: Human Purpose in Conflict with Divine Presence," in G. A. Yee (ed.), *Judges and Method: New Approaches in Biblical Studies* (Minneapolis: Fortress, 1995), 17–44.

76. R. H. O'Connell, *The Rhetoric of the Book of Judges*, VTS 63 (Leiden: Brill, 1996).

77. Y. Amit, *The Book of Judges: The Art of Editing* (Leiden: E. J. Brill, 1999).

78. Cf. J. Barton, "Historical Criticism and Literary Interpretation: Is There Any Common Ground?" in S. E. Porter, P. Joyce, and D. E. Orton (eds.), *Crossing the Boundaries: Essays in Biblical Interpretation in Honour of Michael D. Goulder* (Leiden: E. J. Brill, 1994), 3–15; H. H. Klement, "Modern Literary-Critical Methods and the Historicity of the Old Testament," in Long (ed.), *Israel's Past*, 439–59 (originally in German: "Die neueren literaturwissenschaftlichen Methoden und die Historizität des Alten Testaments," in G. Maier [ed.], *Israel in Geschichte und*

Gegenwart [Wuppertal/Giessen und Basel: R. Brockhaus Verlag/Brunnen Verlag, 1996], 81–101).

79. Polzin, *Moses and the Deuteronomist*, 13.

80. Ibid., 14.

81. "Narrative Art in Joshua-Judges-Samuel-Kings," 257.

82. *Ancient Conquest Accounts*, 265.

83. It is worth noting in passing that the book of Judges will open with the words "After the death of Joshua."

84. So R. S. Hess, *Joshua: An Introduction and Commentary*, ed. D. J. Wiseman, TOTC (Downers Grove, Ill.: InterVarsity Press, 1996), 307.

85. Cited earlier, n. 66.

86. See R. D. Nelson, *Joshua: A Commentary*, OTL (Louisville, Ky.: Westminster John Knox Press, 1997), 116.

87. Howard, *Joshua*, 213.

88. Ibid., 213 n.130, which see for bibliography and further discussion of this issue.

89. Whether the stones that were plastered and inscribed are the same as the stones of the altar is not entirely clear either in Josh. 8 or in Deut. 27. In Deut. 27, Moses gives instructions to set up large stones, coat them with plaster, and write upon them (vv. 2–4). In v. 5 he orders the building of an altar, and in v. 6 he describes the kind of stones to be used, which would suggest a second set of stones. In v. 8, however, Moses returns to the issue of writing "all the words of this law" on "the(se) stones."

90. The appositional phrase "blessings and curses" in v. 34 seems to delimit what is meant by "all the words" (cf. Exod. 20:1), but v. 35 may suggest a more exhaustive reading.

91. Younger, *Ancient Conquest Accounts*, 241–47.

92. See L. E. Stager, "Forging an Identity: The Emergence of Ancient Israel," in M. D. Coogan (ed.), *The Oxford History of the Biblical World* (New York/Oxford: Oxford University Press, 1998), 171.

93. For a nuanced discussion of the different ways in which terms like "conquer" and "conquest" are used not just in the Bible but in ancient Near Eastern and more modern conquest accounts, see Younger, *Ancient Conquest Accounts*, 243–44.

94. For discussion of details, see Hess, *Joshua*, 216–17.

95. The Anakim are elsewhere in the OT associated with the Nephilim (Num. 13:33) and the Rephaim (Deut. 2:11) and are presented as a race of "giants" (see R. S. Hess, "Nephilim," *ABD*, 4:1072–73). An intriguing extrabiblical reference is the thirteenth-century Egyptian Papyrus Anastasi I, which "describes bedouin in Canaan, 'some of whom are of four cubits or five cubits (from) their nose to foot and have fierce faces'" (so Hess, *Joshua*, 218 n.3; citing E. Wente, *Letters from Ancient Egypt*, SBLWAW [Atlanta: Scholars Press, 1990], 108). Hess explains that "five Egyptian cubits would be 2.7 metres" (or almost 9 feet!).

96. Judg. 1:9–15 covers essentially the same ground as Josh. 15:13–19, "generalizing to Judah the actions that Josh. 15:13–14 had attributed to Caleb" (Block, *Judges*, 92). The passage functions (along with Judg. 1:8) as a "flashback" in its context of Judg. 1 (see E. H. Merrill, *Kingdom of Priests: A History of Old Testament Israel* [Grand Rapids: Baker, 1987], 143–44).

97. Note the reference in both v. 16 and v. 23 to Joshua taking the whole land.

98. Of some thirty occurrences in Josh., five are in chap. 1 and twenty-one are in chaps. 13–24. Otherwise, the verb occurs only in 3:10 (twice; with "God" as subject), 8:7 (in the context of "seizing" Ai), and 12:1 (with reference to the territories "occupied beyond the Jordan toward the east").

99. The verb here rendered "subdued" occurs but once in Joshua. Prior to Joshua, the verb occurs only in Gen. 1:28 of subduing the earth (bringing it under control)

and in Moses' instructions to the two and a half Transjordanian tribes, instructing them that they must accompany Israel into Canaan until the land should be
subdued (Num. 32:22, 29).

100. Hess, *Joshua*, 229–86. See also his "A Typology of West Semitic Place Name Lists
with Special Reference to Joshua 13–21," *BA* 59, no. 3 (1996): 160–70.

101. Hess, *Joshua*, 248–49. Some such notion may help to explain why the numbers
do not seem to add up in 15:32 (which gives the total of Judah's southernmost
towns as twenty-nine, while the actual count in vv. 21–32 seems to be thirty-six);
could the larger number attest to the addition of new towns as they emerged, while
the original sum was left unchanged? (For other possibilities, see Howard, *Joshua*,
341.) Alternatively, could some of the names be appositional (variant names of the
same site), as may be the case with Gederah and Gederothaim in 15:36? If the second name in this case is treated as appositional to the first, the site total of fourteen towns in 15:36 is maintained. Another possible example of an apposition
joined by *waw* is 19:2 "Beersheba, (Sheba)"; again the sum comes out correctly
when the second name is treated as appositional. Alternate names are sometimes
explicitly introduced using the Hebrew pronoun *hîʾ*, as in 15:49, 54, 60, but this
may not always have been the case. If the rendering of Josh. 16:2 as "Bethel (that
is, Luz)" (NIV) is correct, then this would be an example of asyndectic appositional
juxtaposition (cf. also 19:8, Baalath-beer, Ramah of the Negeb).

102. Hess, *Joshua*, 249.

103. Webb, *Book of the Judges*, 28.

104. Klein, *Triumph of Irony*, 193.

105. So, e.g., Merrill, *Kingdom of Priests*, 143–44. Cf. Polzin's observation that "The
Book of Judges, like Joshua, briefly recapitulates the previous book before interpreting it further" (*Moses and the Deuteronomist*, 148). For an attempt to explain
the attack on Jerusalem (v. 8) as following the defeat of Bezek (vv. 4–7), see Block,
Judges, 91–92 (though Block concedes that the "chronological relation between
vv. 5–7 and 8 is not clear").

106. So Webb, *Book of the Judges*, 115. Our analysis of the book of Judges owes much
to studies by Webb, Gooding, and others, but in the interest of economy of presentation, we shall limit footnoting to the most essential points of contact or to
direct quotations.

107. The book of Joshua records compromises made with Rahab and with the
Gibeonites, but not by Israel's instigation.

108. See Webb's chart, *Book of the Judges*, 99.

109. While it seems appropriate to divide the overture into the sections described
above, it is also worth observing that the sections are linked together in a sophisticated fashion. The concluding verses of the first movement (2:1–5) provide a
rationale for what has gone before and also anticipate further elaboration in the
verses that constitute the second movement. In other words, they serve a transitional function. Similarly, the last section of the second movement (2:16–3:6)
serves as a transition between what has preceded and what will receive further
elaboration in the "variations" section.

110. *Book of the Judges*, 30.

111. For discussion of this surprise revelation, see Block, *Judges*, 511–12.

112. *Eretz-Israel* 16 (1982): 70–79.

113. Based on Gooding's discussion and Webb's summary (*Book of the Judges*, esp. 35).

114. So Webb, *Book of the Judges*, 177.

115. Ibid., 35.

116. Ibid., 179.

117. Ibid., 172.

118. Ibid., 178.

119. Ibid., 175–76.
120. *The Bible Unearthed*, 120.
121. J. M. Miller and J. Hayes, *A History of Ancient Israel and Judah* (Philadelphia: Westminster Press, 1986),
122. Ibid., 89.
123. Ibid.
124. See V. P. Long, *The Art of Biblical History*, ed. Moisés Silva, FCI 5 (Grand Rapids: Zondervan, 1994), 71–73 and *passim*.
125. *History*, 91.
126. J. Bright, *A History of Israel*, 4th ed. (Louisville, Ky.: Westminster John Knox Press, 2000), 178.
127. Calculated on the basis of Caleb's statement in Josh. 14:7 that he was forty years old when first sent to explore the land (Num. 13:6) and eighty-five years old when he received Hebron as his inheritance (Josh. 14:10). If thirty-eight years of wandering elapsed between Caleb's initial exploration and the beginning of the conquest (cf. Deut. 2:14), then a simple calculation indicates that some seven years must have elapsed between the beginning of the conquest under Joshua and the allocations of the conquered territories.
128. While the Bible offers no information on the length of Samuel's tenure between the death of Eli and the anointing of Saul, Joshephus writes, "He was ruler and leader of the people after the death of the high priest Eli, for twelve years alone, and together with King Saul for eighteen more. Such then was the end of Samuel" (*Ant.* 6.294). This and subsequent citations of Josephus are from The Loeb Classical Library (London: Heinemann, 1930–1965).
129. Representing, e.g., one generation, two generations, or a long time, a very long time, or something along these lines.
130. For a summary of the regional pressure points, see the chart in Block, *Judges*, 62.
131. We note, for instance, that no years are given for Shamgar (Judg. 3:31).
132. For more detailed discussions attempting somewhat greater precision, see Block, *Judges*, 59–63; and especially Merrill, *Kingdom of Priests*, 146–51.
133. G. W. Ramsey, *The Quest for the Historical Israel: Reconstructing Israel's Early History* (Atlanta: John Knox Press, 1982), 101.
134. W. G. Dever, *What Did the Biblical Writers Know*, 121–22.
135. A. Ben-Tor and M. T. Rubiato, "Excavating Hazor, Part II: Did the Israelites Destroy the Canaanite City?" *BARev* 25, no. 3 (1999): 22–39, on 24. Whether Ben-Tor and Rubiato regard these as two pictures as mutually exclusive or as simply stressing different aspect of Israel's emergence in Canaan is not clear.
136. Bright, *History*, 129.
137. Ibid., 130.
138. J. R. Spencer, "Whither the Bible and Archaeology," *Proceedings, Eastern Great Lakes and Midwest Biblical Societies* 9 (1989): 14.
139. "The Literary and Historical Problem of Joshua 10 and Judges 1," *JNES* 5 (1946): 105–14.
140. *The Biblical Account of the Conquest of Palestine* (Jerusalem: Magnes, 1953; reissued by the same publisher in 1985 as *The Biblical Account of the Conquest of Canaan*, with a preface to the reissue by M. Greenberg), cited by B. K. Waltke ("The Date of the Conquest," *WTJ* 52, no. 2 [1990]: 189) as having "convincingly harmonized the differences between Joshua and Judges 1."
141. For an insightful, recent discussion of the basic issues (with helpful bibliographic notations), see D. R. Ulrich, "Does the Bible Sufficiently Describe the Conquest?" *Trinity Journal* 20, no. 1 (1999): 53–68. On the dependence of Judg. 1:1–2:5 on structures and trajectories introduced already in Josh. 13–19, see K. L. Younger Jr., "The Configuring of Judicial Preliminaries." Specifically,

Younger argues that this section of Judges makes explicit what Joshua had already implied: namely, that Judah was generally more successful than other tribes, especially Dan, in occupying its allotted territory.

142. See K. A. Kitchen, *The Bible in Its World: The Bible and Archaeology Today* (Exeter: Paternoster, 1977), 90–91.

143. Ibid., 90.

144. *Ancient Conquest Accounts*, 246.

145. It is in this sense that "The non-fulfilment of the [patriarchal] promise [of full possession of the land] is acknowledged but Yahweh is vindicated" (Webb, *Book of the Judges*, 122).

146. See Long, *Art of Biblical History*, 186–89.

147. For the full text, with introduction and bibliography, see *ANET*, 376–78; see also *ANEP*, 115, 148. A fragmentary duplicate of the inscription exists also in the Temple at Karnak.

148. According to K. Kitchen, "Egyptians and Hebrews, from Ra'amses to Jericho," in S. Aḥituv and E. D. Oren (eds.), *The Origin of Early Israel—Current Debate: Biblical, Historical and Archaeological Perspectives*, Beer-Sheva 12 (Jerusalem: Ben-Gurion University of the Negeb Press, 1998), 100.

149. For specifics on the Egyptian determinatives in this stela, see Kitchen, "Egyptians and Hebrews," 101.

150. *What Did the Biblical Writers Know*, 118.

151. G. W. Ahlström and D. Edelman, "Merneptah's Israel," *JNES* 44, no. 1 (1985): 59–61. Similarly, see D. V. Edelman, "Who or What Was Israel?" *BARev* 18, no. 2 (1992): 21, 72–73. In response to Edelman and Ahlström's reading of the Merneptah Stela, Rainey ("Anson F. Rainey Replies," *BARev*, 18, no. 2 (1992): 73–74) prefers the interpretation originally suggested by F. Yurco, which sees Canaan and Kharu as parallel elements. Rainey argues that Kharu is an Egyptian designation for the territory of Canaan, based perhaps on Hurrian (biblical Horite?) elements who lived in the region. Rainey takes very seriously the determinative on Israel and believes that Israel is distinguished in the inscription as an ethnic group, though he admits that Egyptian scribes of the period did have "some leeway in representing the various foreign entities, especially mobile groups" (74).

152. Kitchen, "Egyptians and Hebrews," 102.

153. Dever, *What Did the Biblical Writers Know?*, 119.

154. Isserlin, *The Israelites*, 56.

155. So B. Halpern, "Settlement of Canaan," *ABD*, 5:1130, basing his view on Israel's depiction as "Shasu" (i.e., "pastoralists of the Transjordan"). For a different argument coming to similar conclusions, see A. F. Rainey, "Rainey's Challenge," *BARev* 17, no. 6 (1991): 56–60, 93. For an opposing view that would see "at least *some* of the Israelites" as coalescing "out of Canaanite society," see F. J. Yurco, "Yurco's Response," *BARev*, 17, no. 6 (1991): 61; cf. also Yurco's earlier groundbreaking study, "3,200-Year-Old Picture of Israelites Found in Egypt," *BARev* 16, no. 5 (1990): 20–38.

156. J. Bimson, "Exodus and Conquest: Myth or Reality?" *Journal of the Ancient Chronology Forum* 2 (1988), writes, "Fritz has argued that the settlements mark the sedentarization of semi-nomads who had entered the land long before 1200 BC: 'Their "migration" into the land must therefore have occurred in the 14th century or already in the 15th' [1981:71]" (at the time of writing, Bimson's essay is available on-line at *http://www.nunki.net/isis/jacf2article1.htm*).

157. Noteworthy also is the possibility that "Qazardi the chief of Aser" mentioned in Papyrus Anastasi I (see *ANET*, 475–79, section xxiii), a satirical letter dated near the end of the thirteenth century B.C., may offer an extrabiblical reference to the

tribe of Asher known from the OT (for discussion of this and other Egyptian evidences, see J. M. Miller, "The Israelite Occupation of Canaan," in J. H. Hayes and J. M. Miller (eds.), *Israelite and Judaean History* (London: SCM, 1977), 245–52.

158. B. Halpern, "Text and Artifact: Two Monologues?" in N. A. Silberman and D. Small (eds.), *The Archaeology of Israel: Constructing the Past, Interpreting the Present*, JSOTS 237 (Sheffield: Sheffield Academic Press, 1997), 335.

159. J. Bimson, "Old Testament History and Sociology," in Craig C. Broyles (ed.), *Interpreting the Old Testament: A Guide for Exegesis* (Grand Rapids: Baker, 2001), 141.

160. For the history of the discovery, see N. Na'aman, "Amarna Letters," *ABD*, 1:174–81. The best English edition of the letters is W. L. Moran, *The Amarna Letters* (Baltimore and London: Johns Hopkins University Press, 1992; French original 1987). A selection of letters is also available in *ANET*, 483–90.

161. Na'aman, "Amarna Letters," 174.

162. I.e., EA (=El-Amarna) 243, EA 246, EA 254, EA 271, EA 273–74, EA 286–90, EA 298–99, EA 305, EA 318, and AO 7096 (for a convenient listing and summary of contents, see Merrill, *Kingdom of Priests*, 105).

163. Merrill, *Kingdom of Priests*, 100.

164. N. Na'aman, "Habiru and Hebrews: The Transfer of a Social Term to the Literary Sphere," *JNES* 45, no. 4 (1986): 271–88.

165. Ibid., 271. For the history of this attempted equation, see M. Greenberg, *The Hab/piru* (New Haven, Conn.: American Oriental Society, 1955), 3–12.

166. For a convenient listing, see Bright, *History*, 4th ed., 94–95. Bright concludes that the *'apiru* are "a people found all over western Asia from the end of the third millennium to about the eleventh century" (95).

167. For discussion of the etymology of the Sumerian term as "murder(er)" and its possible sense in Akkadian as "robber" or "displaced person," see Merrill, *Kingdom of Priests*, 100.

168. N. P. Lemche, "Habiru, Hapiru," *ABD*, 3:7.

169. Na'aman, "Habiru and Hebrews," 272. So also A. Kuhrt, *The Ancient Near East C. 3000–330 B.C.*, 2 vols. (London: Routledge, 1995), 1:320: "It is unlikely that they were a culturally and linguistically coherent group. Intensive studies of contexts in which the term appears suggest that it was applied to a range of people: runaway slaves, political exiles, brigands and landless peasants, i.e. people on the margins of society. . . ."

170. Na'aman, "Habiru and Hebrews," 275.

171. Ibid., 271.

172. Ibid., 285.

173. For discussion, see Merrill, *Kingdom of Priests*, 101.

174. D. Fleming, "Refining the Etymology for 'Hebrew': Mari's *'IBRUM*,'" unpublished paper delivered at the SBL Annual Meeting in Denver, November 2001. We here express appreciation to Fleming for making his paper available to us.

175. Ibid., 8–9.

176. Cf. ibid.

177. Or one must attempt, as T. J. Meek did, to reverse the biblical order and place the conquest under Joshua before the exodus under Moses (see Merrill, *Kingdom of Priests*, 102).

178. M. W. Chavalas and M. R. Adamthwaite, "Archaeological Light on the Old Testament," in Baker and Arnold (eds.), *The Face of Old Testament Studies*, 59–96, on 90. Merrill (*Kingdom of Priests*, 102–8) argues forcefully that the Amarna Letters provide a backdrop to the period *following* the initial conquest under Joshua.

179. "The Rise of Early Israel," 31.

180. M. R. Adamthwaite, "Lab'aya's Connection with Shechem Reassessed," *Abr-Nahrain* 30 (1992): 1–19, esp. 8–12. See Chavalas and Adamthwaite, "Archaeological Light," 90 n.138, for further support.
181. Isserlin, *The Israelites*, 55.
182. "Archaeological Light," 90.
183. Cf. J. J. Bimson, "Merenptah's Israel and Recent Theories of Israelite Origins," *JSOT* 49 (1991): 3–29.
184. E. Noort observes that, geographically speaking, an east-west conquest in the southern Jordan Valley could not have proceeded any other way: "An Jericho ging wörtlich kein Weg vorbei" ("Klio und die Welt des Alten Testaments: Überlegungen zur Benutzung literarischer und feldarchäologischer Quellen bei der Darstellung einer Geschichte Israels," in D. R. Daniels et al. [eds.], *Ernten was man sät: Festschrift für Klaus Koch zu seinem 65. Geburtstag* [Neukirchen-Vluyn: Neukirchener Verlag, 1991], 553).
185. For details on all these, see B. G. Wood, "Did the Israelites Conquer Jericho? A New Look at the Archaeological Evidence," *BARev* 16, no. 2 (1990): 44–58.
186. Wood (ibid., 54) quotes geophysicist Amos Nur of Stanford University as follows: "Today Adam is Damiya, the site of the 1927 mud slides that cut off the flow of the Jordan. Such cutoffs, typically lasting one to two days, have also been recorded in A.D. 1906, 1834, 1546, 1267, and 1160."
187. For fuller discussion and the pertinent literature, see ibid., esp. 47–49.
188. Wood wrote a Ph.D. dissertation on the topic: B. G. Wood, "Palestinian Pottery of the Late Bronze Age: An Investigation of the Terminal LB IIB Phase" (Ph.D. dissertation, University of Toronto, 1985). An expanded version of one part of Wood's dissertation is available as B. G. Wood, *The Sociology of Pottery in Ancient Palestine: The Ceramic Industry and the Diffusion of Ceramic Style in the Bronze and Iron Ages*, JSOTS 103; JSOT/ASOR Monographs 4 (Sheffield: JSOT, 1990).
189. K. M. Kenyon and T. A. Holland, *Excavations at Jericho*, vols. 3–5 (London: British School of Archaeology in Jerusalem, 1981–83).
190. Wood, "Did the Israelites Conquer Jericho," 50.
191. K. M. Kenyon, "Jericho," in D. Winton Thomas (ed.), *Archaeology and Old Testament Study* (Oxford: Clarendon Press, 1967), 271.
192. See Wood's discussion, "Did the Israelites Conquer Jericho," 52.
193. Information based on a personal conversation with Wood.
194. A point made by Wood in response to P. Bienkowski, "Jericho Was Destroyed in the Middle Bronze Age, Not the Late Bronze Age," *BARev,* 16 no. 5 (1990): 45–69; see B. G. Wood, "Dating Jericho's Destruction: Bienkowski Is Wrong on All Counts," *BARev* 16, no. 5 (1990): 45–69, on 47.
195. See the preceding note.
196. "Dating Jericho's Destruction," 47–48.
197. See Wood, "Did the Israelites Conquer Jericho," 52–53; and Wood's further discussion in "Dating Jericho's Destruction," 49.
198. Wood, "Dating Jericho's Destruction," 47.
199. E.g., J. K. Hoffmeier, *Israel in Egypt: The Evidence for the Authenticity of the Exodus Tradition* (Oxford: Oxford University Press, 1997), 7; Howard, *Joshua*, 178; Waltke, "The Date of the Conquest," 192; J. L. Sheler, *Is the Bible True? How Modern Debates and Discoveries Affirm the Essence of the Scriptures* (New York: HarperSanFrancisco, 1999), 90–91.
200. We have noted already Bienkowski's challenge and Wood's response, and in our opinion Wood makes the better case.
201. A. Mazar, *Archaeology of the Land of the Bible: 10,000–586 B.C.E.* (New York: Doubleday, 1990), 331.
202. Isserlin, *The Israelites*, 57.

203. J. A. Callaway, "Ai (Place)," *ABD*, 1:125–30; excavation results displayed in chart form on 127.

204. W. F. Albright, "The Kyle Memorial Excavation at Bethel," *BASOR* 56 (1936): 2–15. Cf. Wright, *Biblical Archaeology*, 80–81.

205. So Hoffmeier, *Israel in Egypt*, 7.

206. For a site plan of excavations at et-Tell, see Callaway, "Ai (Place)," 128.

207. J. A. Callaway, "Ai (et-Tell): Problem Site for Biblical Archaeologists," in L. G. Perdue, L. E. Toombs, and G. L. Johnson (eds.), *Archaeology and Biblical Interpretation: Essays in Memory of D. Glenn Rose* (Atlanta: John Knox Press, 1987), 97.

208. See Howard, *Joshua*, 179.

209. J. M. Grintz, "'Ai Which Is Beside Beth Aven: A Reexamination of the Identity of 'Ai," *Bib* 42 (1961): 201–16; K. A. Kitchen, *Ancient Orient and Old Testament* (Chicago: InterVarsity Press, 1966), 63–64; B. Z. Luria, "The Location of Ai [Hebrew]," *Beth Mikra* 35 (1989–90): 197–201; D. Livingston, "Further Consideration on the Location of Bethel at el-Bireh," *PEQ* 126 (1994): 154–59; Bimson, "Old Testament History and Sociology," 139.

210. For bibliography of the debate, see Howard, *Joshua*, 180, n.40.

211. Livingston has directed excavations at Khirbet Nisya, and more recently Wood has been excavating at Khirbet el-Maqatir; for bibliography, again see Howard, *Joshua*, 180, nn.38–39.

212. J. M. Miller, "Old Testament History and Archaeology," *BA* 50 (1987): 55–63, on 60.

213. Ibid., 59.

214. See W. G. Dever, "Qedah, Tell el-," *ABD*, 5: 578–81.

215. Ibid., 578–79.

216. Hazor is mentioned, e.g., in the Egyptian Execration Texts of the nineteenth century, the Mari letters of the eighteenth, the Amarna letters of the fourteenth, and so forth.

217. "Excavating Hazor: Part II," 22.

218. Ibid., 36.

219. Ibid., 38.

220. Ibid., 38–39.

221. Block, *Judges*, 189.

222. Hess, *Joshua*, 214, n.1.

223. *Redating*, 188–89.

224. Ibid., 189.

225. While worthy of serious consideration, Bimson's thesis has not succeeded in gaining much of a following in print. Perhaps sympathetic scholars are reticent to find themselves on the receiving end of a verbal caning such as B. Halpern dishes out in "Radical Exodus Redating Fatally Flawed," *BARev* 13, no. 6 (1987): 56–61.

226. *Redating*, 194.

227. Y. Yadin, "Further Light on Biblical Hazor," *BA* 20 (1957): 34–47, on 44.

228. Y. Yadin, "The Third Season of Excavating at Hazor," *BA* 21 (1958): 30–47, on 31.

229. *Redating*, 193.

230. Ibid., 200.

231. Ibid., 199.

232. Precision in such matters is difficult. Codirector of the Megiddo excavation B. Halpern, for instance, observes that for sites like Megiddo and Hazor, "only the last layers' destroyers can be fixed; they were the Assyrians of the late 8th century. . . . " (B. Halpern, *David's Secret Demons: Messiah, Murderer, Traitor, King* [Grand Rapids: Eerdmans, 2001], 473).

233. So A. F. Rainey, "Hazor," in G. W. Bromiley (ed.), *The International Standard Bible Encyclopedia* (Grand Rapids: Eerdmans, 1982), 2:637.

234. A succinct description of the archaeology of Laish/Dan is provided by the site's longtime excavator in A. Biran, "Dan (Place)," *ABD*, 2:12–17; cf. also D. W. Manor, "Laish (Place)," *ABD*, 4:130–31.

235. A. Biran, "To the God Who Is in Dan," in A. Biran (ed.), *Temples and High Places in Biblical Times* (Jerusalem: The Nelson Glueck School of Biblical Archaeology of Hebrew Union College-Jewish Institute of Religion [Hebrew], 1981), 142–51.

236. Manor, "Laish," 130.

237. A. Malamat, "Syro-Palestinian Destinations in a Mari Tin Inventory," *IEJ* 21 (1971): 31–38.

238. See *ANET*, 242

239. A. Biran, "Dan," in Perdue, Toombs, and Johnson (eds.), *Archaeology and Biblical Interpretation*, 101–111, on 105.

240. Ibid.

241. Manor, "Laish," 131.

242. "Dan," 106.

243. Ibid., 101 and 105–6, respectively.

244. "Forging an Identity," 167. Stager's comment about the Sea Peoples expresses his skepticism regarding the common scholarly suggestion that "the Danites were not a part of Israel, but rather a member of the Sea Peoples' confederation, to be identified with the Danaans of Homer and the Denyen in Rameses III's inscription" (ibid.).

245. "Dan," 104.

246. J. G. McConville (*Grace in the End: A Study of Deuteronomistic Theology* [Grand Rapids: Zondervan, 1993], 110) points out that nothing in the text in fact would indicate this specific association: "the 'captivity of the land' referred to in v. 30 is most naturally understood in relation to its [i.e., Shiloh's] fall, the historical context of this event being the Philistine ascendancy prior to the time of Saul."

247. See our discussion of Shiloh below.

248. "Dan," 106.

249. Quite likely the Gibeonites, and their associated cities (see Josh. 9:17), were non-indigenous Canaanites, having migrated from the north after the collapse of the Hittite empire (for a summary of onomastic and archaeological evidence, see Hess, "Early Israel," 127). On the possible identification of the Hivites (the designation used for the Gibeonites in Josh. 9:7) with non-Semitic Hurrians, see D. W. Baker, "Hivites," *ABD*, 3:233–34. Outside the Bible, Gibeon is first mentioned by Pharaoh Shoshenq I (*ANET*, 242).

250. P. M. Arnold, "Gibeon," *ABD*, 2:1010.

251. *History*, 72.

252. See Chavalas and Adamthwaite, "Archaeological Light," 83; cf. Kitchen, "Egyptians and Hebrews," 108.

253. E.g. Y. Aharoni, *The Land of the Bible: A Historical Geography*, trans. A. F. Rainey, rev. and enlarged ed. (Philadelphia: Westminster Press, 1979), 215–16.

254. For sample photographs and drawings, see J. B. Pritchard, *Gibeon, Where the Sun Stood Still: The Discovery of a Biblical City* (Princeton, N.J.: Princeton University Press, 1962), 73.

255. Ibid., 156.

256. Ibid.; for text, see *ANET*, 247.

257. *ANET*, 235.

258. Pritchard, *Gibeon*, 157.

259. Ibid., 157–58.

260. I. Finkelstein, "Seilun, Khirbet," *ABD*, 5:1069–72, on 1069.

261. For a brief history of excavation, see ibid., 1069.

262. "The Rise of Early Israel," 23.

263. Ibid.
264. Finkelstein, "Seilun," 1071.
265. Ibid., 1072.
266. Ibid.
267. Ibid.
268. Ibid.
269. "Forging an Identity," 170.
270. Ibid., 150.
271. R. S. Hess, "Shechem," *NIDOTTE*, 4:1214.
272. A. Zertal, "Has Joshua's Altar Been Found on Mt. Ebal?" *BARev* 11, no. 1 (1985): 26–43.
273. Ibid., 31.
274. Ibid., 35.
275. A. Kempinski, "Joshua's Altar—An Iron Age I Watchtower," *BARev* 12, no. 1 (1986): 42, 44–49.
276. A. Zertal, "How Can Kempinski Be So Wrong!" *BARev* 12, no. 1 (1986): 43, 47, 49–53.
277. *Archaeology of the Land of the Bible*, 350.
278. Ibid. Cf. the cautious optimism of Isserlin, *The Israelites*, 242. For a more complete summary of evidence and discussion, see Hess, "Early Israel," 135–37.
279. "Has Joshua's Altar Been Found on Mt. Ebal?" 43.
280. Ibid., 31.
281. Ibid., 32.
282. Ibid., 34.
283. See ibid., 42.
284. Hess, *Joshua*, 174.
285. So Finkelstein, "The Rise of Early Israel," 10.
286. *Israel in Egypt*, 32.
287. "The Rise of Early Israel," 20. The works to which Finkelstein refers are B. Hesse and P. Wapnish, "Can Pig Remains Be Used for Ethnic Diagnosis in the Ancient Near East?" in N. A. Silberman and D. Small (eds.), *The Archaeology of Israel: Constructing the Past, Interpreting the Present*, JSOTS 237 (Sheffield: Sheffield Academic Press, 1997), 238–70; and L. E. Stager, *Ashkelon Discovered*.
288. Halpern, *David's Secret Demons*, 457 (and n.59 for more complete bibliography).
289. *The Israelites*, 62. Finkelstein also recognizes an east-to-west trend in hill-country demographic expansion, which he links to "ecological and socio-economic" factors ("The Rise of Early Israel," 27).
290. *Israel in Egypt*, 32. Bimson contends that "Israel existed *before* the shift to new settlement patterns that supposedly brought Israel into being" ("Old Testament History and Sociology," 140; see nn.66 and 68 for a brief summary of the debate that this contention has sparked).
291. N. A. Silberman ("Who Were the Israelites?" *Archaeology* 45, no. 2 [1992]: 22–30) maintains that formerly settled populations, later to be identified as Israelites, led a pastoralist existence for several centuries in Canaan before beginning to settle again in newly founded hill-country villages toward the end of the thirteenth century (29–30). In support of the notion that an Israelite conquest may have been followed by a period of pastoralism before the conquered sites were reoccupied, E. Yamauchi notes that "in the Aegean world, after the destruction of numerous Mycenaean settlements ascribed by Greek traditions to the Dorians, who were pastoralist Greeks from the north, there is also a considerable gap in reoccupied settlements" ("The Current State of Old Testament Historiography," 34).
292. Dever agrees, at least with respect to the book of Judges: "While modern archaeology may call into question the historicity of Joshua, it provides rather dramatic

corroboration of the account in Judges, even in obscure details" ("Israel, History of," *ABD*, 3:555). Dever's less favorable verdict regarding the book of Joshua results largely from his Albrightian misreading of the nature of the conquest described by the book.

293. Finkelstein, "The Rise of Early Israel," 7.
294. Cf. Hess, "Early Israel," 139.

Chapter 8: The Early Monarchy

1. R. P. Gordon, *1 & 2 Samuel*, ed. R. N. Whybray, OTG (Sheffield: JSOT Press, 1984), 9; hereafter *1 & 2 Samuel* (OTG) to distinguish it from R. P. Gordon, *I & II Samuel: A Commentary*, LBI (Grand Rapids: Regency Reference Library, Zondervan, 1986), hereafter simply *I & II Samuel*.
2. According to Eusebius and Jerome, 1 and 2 Samuel were originally one book. The division into two books appears to follow the practice of the Septuagint (hereafter LXX). For discussion, see B. S. Childs, *Introduction to the Old Testament as Scripture* (Philadelphia: Fortress, 1979), 266–67. Where the context makes the sense unambiguous, we shall sometimes refer to 1 and 2 Samuel simply as Samuel or the book of Samuel.
3. Both quotes are from excerpts in A. Preminger and E. L. Greenstein (eds.), *The Hebrew Bible in Literary Criticism* (New York: Ungar, 1986), 556–57. Cf. also Long, "First and Second Samuel," L. Ryken and T. Longman III (eds.), *A Complete Literary Guide to the Bible* (Grand Rapids: Zondervan, 1993), 165–181.
4. See the section in this chapter, "David's Rise and Saul's Demise," 215–27.
5. R. Dillard, "The Reign of Asa (2 Chronicles 14–16): An Example of the Chronicler's Theological Method," *JETS* 23 (1980): 207–18, on 214.
6. Childs, *Introduction to the Old Testament as Scripture*, 646–47.
7. To imagine, as some have argued, that "the diverse poems, traditions, literary complexes, and books that make up the Old Testament" could have all been composed in the exilic or postexilic period is highly dubious: "the various biblical writings may have achieved their final and definitive form in the post-exilic period, but it seems implausible that the Persian age witnessed the very composition of all these books" (G. N. Knoppers, "The Historical Study of the Monarchy: Developments and Detours," in Baker and Arnold [eds.], *The Face of Old Testament Studies*, 207–35; quotes from 212). With respect to the issue of "definitive form," the theory of a Deuteronomistic History stretching from Deut. to 2 Kgs. has dominated scholarship since Martin Noth, although some now prefer to speak of a "Primary History" comprising Genesis–2 Kings and to distinguish this from a "Secondary History" comprising the Chronicler's work and Ezra-Nehemiah. See, e.g., D. N. Freedman, "The Earliest Bible," in M. P. O'Connor and D. N. Freedman (eds.), *Backgrounds for the Bible* (Winona Lake, Ind.: Eisenbrauns, 1987), 29–37; idem, "The Nine Commandments: The Secret Progress of Israel's Sins," *Bible Review* 5, no. 6 (1989): 28–37, 42; P. J. Kissling, *Reliable Characters in the Primary History: Profiles of Moses, Joshua, Elijah, and Elisha*, JSOTS 224 (Sheffield: Sheffield Academic Press, 1996).
8. Cf. R. Dillard, "David's Census: Perspectives on 2 Samuel 24 and 1 Chronicles 21," in W. R. Godfrey and J. L. Boyd (eds.), *Through Christ's Word: A Festschrift for Dr. Philip E. Hughes* (Phillipsburg, N.J.: Presbyterian and Reformed, 1985), 94–107; esp. 99–101.
9. For broader, more nuanced discussion of all these matters, see V. P. Long, *The Art of Biblical History*, ed. Moisés Silva, FCI 5 (Grand Rapids: Zondervan, 1994), 76–86.
10. B. Halpern, *David's Secret Demons: Messiah, Murderer, Traitor, King* (Grand Rapids: Eerdmans, 2001), 75.

11. Ibid., 99, 101.
12. E.g., on the "History of Saul's Rise," see M. White, "Searching for Saul: What We Really Know about Israel's First King," *Bible Review* 17, no. 2 (2001): 22–29, 52–53.
13. J. M. Miller and J. Hayes, *A History of Ancient Israel and Judah* (Philadelphia: Westminster Press, 1986), 126.
14. Ibid., 126–28.
15. R. P. Gordon, *1 & 2 Samuel* (OTG), 12.
16. Ibid.
17. Ibid.
18. For a critical analysis of the source-critical and redaction-critical theories as they relate to the Deuteronomistic History, and particularly to the books of Samuel, see R. P. Gordon, *1 & 2 Samuel* (OTG), esp. 14–20.
19. Ironically, "enhanced appreciation of the literary quality" of biblical narratives has not always led to enhanced appreciation of the testimonial value in matters historical. As R. Gordon remarks with respect to the so-called Succession Narrative, the biblical writer's "vivid portrayal of persons and events, once explained by the writer's proximity to what he was recounting," are now cited by some as evidence simply of "his imaginative and descriptive powers of writing" (R. P. Gordon, "In Search of David: The David Tradition in Recent Study," in A. R. Millard, J. K. Hoffmeier, and D. W. Baker (eds.), *Faith, Tradition, and History: Old Testament Historiography in its Near Eastern Context* (Winona Lake, Ind.: Eisenbrauns, 1994), 285–86).
20. Works by seminal thinkers such as Alter, Polzin, and Sternberg need not be reiterated here (they are widely known and, in any case, have been mentioned earlier in this volume). For specific discussion of selected features of Hebrew narrative style as these pertain to the texts of Samuel, see V. P. Long, *The Reign and Rejection of King Saul: A Case for Literary and Theological Coherence*, SBLDS 118 (Atlanta: Scholars Press, 1989), 21–42.
21. A. Lemaire, "The Tel Dan Stela as a Piece of Royal Historiography," *JSOT* 81 (1998): 3–14, on 10.
22. Ibid., 11.
23. The chronological issue is discussed more fully in our treatment of the Divided Monarchy.
24. Though estimates of even this date vary slightly from scholar to scholar: Cogan places it at 928 B.C.; Finegan at 931; Hayes and Hooker at 926; and Thiele at 930. See M. Cogan, "Chronology," in *ABD*, 1:1002–11 (chart on 1010); J. Finegan, *Handbook of Biblical Chronology: Principles of Time Reckoning in the Ancient World and Problems of Chronology in the Bible*, rev. ed. (Peabody, Mass: Hendrickson, 1998) (chart on 261); J. H. Hayes and P. K. Hooker, *A New Chronology for the Kings of Israel and Judah and Its Implications for Biblical History and Literature* (Atlanta: John Knox Press, 1988); Thiele, *Mysterious Numbers*, new rev. ed. (Grand Rapids: Academic Books, 1983) (chart on 10).
25. For a survey and analysis of the various theories, see Long, *Reign and Rejection*, 71–75.
26. M. Noth, *Überlieferungsgeschichtliche Studien: Die sammelnden undbearbeiteten Geschichtswerke im Alten Testament* (Tübingen: Max Niemeyer, 1957), 24; idem, *Geschichte Israels*, 2d ed. (Göttingen: Vandenhoeck & Ruprecht, 1969), 163; K. A. D. Smelik, *Saul, de voorstelling van Israels eerste Konig in de Masoretische tekst van het Oude Testament* (Amsterdam: Drukkerij en Uitgeverij P. E. T., 1977), 71.
27. Long, *Reign and Rejection*, 72.
28. These include some witnesses to the so-called Lucianic recension—i.e., MSS oe$_2$; other witnesses to the Lucianic recension reflect MT; LXX[B.] omits 13:1 entirely.

29. A similar solution to the problem of Saul's regnal formula was offered already by medieval Jewish commentator Isaac Abrabanel, who suggested that Saul's yearling status refers to the time that elapsed between his secret anointing in 1 Sam. 10 and the "renewal" of the kingdom in 11:14–15, and that the two-year reign refers to the time between Saul's official inauguration in 13:1 and the anointing of David in 1 Sam. 16 (for bibliography and further discussion, see Long, *Reign and Rejection*, 75).

30. For a brief discussion, see F. F. Bruce, *The Acts of the Apostles: The Greek Text with Introduction and Commentary* (Grand Rapids: Eerdmans, 1951), 264–65, who cites J. A. Bengal's view that "Here the years of Samuel the prophet and Saul the king are brought into one sum."

31. On the text-critical question, both the Latin Vulgate and early Jewish tradition support the reading "two," not "twenty-two"; for further discussion, see note f. in the Loeb edition of Josephus, *ad loc.* As to logic, 1 Sam. 25:1 seems to indicate that Samuel's death took place during the period of David's flight from Saul. Already at this point David is a capable warrior with hundreds of men under his command. But if it were the case that Saul reigned twenty-two years after Samuel's death, then David (who was approximately thirty at Saul's death) could have been no older than eight! If Saul continued on the throne for only about two years after Samuel's death, then David would have been about twenty-eight when Samuel died, which fits the biblical picture much better.

32. Some may object to the idea that Saul must have been forty years old (or more) at the time of his anointing, grounding their objection in the belief that he was but a youth when he appears in 1 Sam. 9. For a corrective to this common misunderstanding, see Long, *Reign and Rejection*, 204–05.

33. Further uncertainties are introduced by the possibility that a brief coregency of David and Solomon may have taken place.

34. We take up the issue of Samuel's multiple roles below.

35. F. M. Cross, *Canaanite Myth and Hebrew Epic* (Cambridge, Mass.: Harvard University Press, 1973), 223. So also C. Westermann, *Grundformen prophetischer Rede, Beiträge zur evangelischen Theologie* (München: Christian Kaiser Verlag, 1960), 70: "die Epoche der Prophetie mit der Epoche des Königtums in Israel zusammen fällt"; the latest English translation is C. Westermann, *Basic Forms of Prophetic Speech*, trans. H. C. White, foreword by G. M. Tucker (Louisville, Ky.: Westminster/John Knox Press, 1991).

36. For a rebuttal of the common theory that Samuel's birth narrative is a reworking of an old birth narrative of Saul, see R. P. Gordon, "Who Made the Kingmaker? Reflections on Samuel and the Institution of the Monarchy," in Millard et al. (eds.), *Faith, Tradition and History*, 263–66.

37. For fuller discussion, see Long, "First and Second Samuel," 171.

38. So Gordon, *1 & 2 Samuel* (OTG), 35.

39. Cf. ibid.

40. Gordon, *I & II Samuel*, 108.

41. Ibid.

42. L. Rost, *The Succession to the Throne of David*, HTIBS (Sheffield: Almond Press, 1982; Germ. orig. 1926), 6–34.

43. Rost deemed it a cult myth (*hieros logos*) for the temple in Jerusalem, probably composed already in David's reign or early in Solomon's (see Gordon, *1 & 2 Samuel* [OTG], 30–31).

44. Major studies include (in order of their appearance): F. Schicklberger, *Die Ladeerzählungen des ersten Samuel-Buches: Eine literaturwissenschaftliche und theologiegeschichtliche Untersuchung*, FB 7 (Würzburg: Echter Verlag, 1973); A. F. Campbell, *The Ark Narrative (1 Sam. 4–6; 2 Sam. 6): A Form-critical and*

Traditio-historical Study, SBLDS 16 (Missoula, Mont.: SBL and Scholars Press, 1975); P. D. Miller Jr. and J. J. M. Roberts, *The Hand of the Lord: A Reassessment of the "Ark Narrative" of 1 Samuel* (Baltimore: Johns Hopkins University Press, 1977).

45. This fact alone would not be determinative, as it is certainly possible that some characters could have been well enough known to have required no introduction; possible examples would include the first mention of Jonathan, without introduction or even epithet, in 1 Sam. 13:2, the first mention of Joshua in Exod. 17:9, and even the first mention of Eli in 1 Sam. 1:3. For full discussion of this issue with respect to 1 Sam. 13:2, see Long, *Reign and Rejection*, 75–77, where it is argued that the suppression of Jonathan's relationship to Saul just at this point in the narrative may have served the negative characterization of the latter.

46. For concise discussion and evaluation of this and other issues surrounding the theory of an Ark Narrative, see Gordon, *1 & 2 Samuel* (OTG), 30–34.

47. Miller and Roberts, *Hand of the Lord*, 19.

48. J. T. Willis, "An Anti-Elide Narrative Tradition from a Prophetic Circle at the Ramah Sanctuary," *JBL* 90 (1971): 288–308; idem, "Cultic Elements in the Story of Samuel's Birth and Dedication," *ST* 26 (1972): 33–61; idem, "Samuel versus Eli: 1 Sam. 1–7," *TZ* 35 (1979), 201–12.

49. E.g., the fact that Samuel is not mentioned in chaps. 4:1b–7:1 and the fact that chaps. 1:1–4:1a describe a time of peace, in contrast to the section that follows ("An Anti-Elide Narrative Tradition," 298).

50. Ibid.

51. For specifics, see ibid., 298–99, and particularly Chart II on 299.

52. Cf., e.g., K. A. D. Smelik, "The Ark Narrative Reconsidered," in A. S. Van der Woude (ed.), *New Avenues in the Study of the Old Testament*, OTS 25 (Leiden: E. J. Brill, 1989), 128–44; N. Na'aman, "The Pre-Deuteronomistic Story of King Saul and Its Historical Significance," *CBQ* 54 (1992): 638–58.

53. Gordon, *1 & 2 Samuel* (OTG), 33–34.

54. N. Na'aman, "The Pre-Deuteronomistic Story," 654.

55. Our own approach, following Willis ("Samuel versus Eli," 207), is not to deny that the materials incorporated in 1 Sam. 1–7 may have "passed through earlier oral or written stages" but, rather, to "emphasize the *coherence* of the material as it was used by a redactor, collector, or author to apply to his audience for the purpose of communicating a theological truth." Further, it seems reasonable to assume, again with Willis (ibid., 208), that "the theology of the redactor or tradent was largely shaped by the traditions which he inherited, rather than that he imposed his theology on those traditions, else he would not have preserved the traditions which he did."

56. Cf. Miller and Hayes, *History*, 134–35.

57. On this view that "the historical role of Samuel has been considerably exaggerated in the tradition," see Mayes, "The Period of the Judges," in J. H. Hayes and J. M. Miller (eds.), *Israelite and Judaean History* (London: SCM, 1977), 324–25 (quote from 330).

58. H. Gressmann, *Die älteste Geschichtsschreibung und Prophetie Israels*, Die Schriften des Alten Testaments II, 1 (Göttingen: Vandenhoeck & Ruprecht, 1910), 27.

59. M. J. Buss, "Prophecy in Ancient Israel," in K. Crim et al. (eds.), *The Interpreter's Dictionary of the Bible: Supplementary Volume* (Nashville: Abingdon, 1976), 694–97, on 694.

60. J. H. Grønbæk, *Die Geschichte vom Aufstieg Davids (1. Sam. 15–2. Sam. 5): Tradition und Komposition*, ATDan 10 (Copenhagen: Munksgaard, 1971), 68.

61. J. Blenkinsopp, *A History of Prophecy in Israel: From the Settlement in the Land to the Hellenistic Period* (Philadelphia: Westminster Press, 1983), 67.

62. R. P. Gordon, "Who Made the Kingmaker?" 262.
63. Gordon, *1 & 2 Samuel* (OTG), 27. For further discussion, see Long, *Reign and Rejection*, 58–60.
64. On this narrative technique generally, cf. J. T. Willis, "The Function of Comprehensive Redactional Joints in 1 Sam 16–18," *ZAW* 85 (1973): 294–314.
65. It might even be argued that the passage of twenty years, mentioned just prior to Samuel's next appearance (see 7:2–3), would have allowed Samuel time to grow up and grow into the leadership position he evidently holds in 1 Sam. 7 and after.
66. R. A. Carlson, *David, the Chosen King: A Traditio-Historical Approach to the Second Book of Samuel* (Stockholm: Almqvist och Wiksell, 1964).
67. See Long, "First and Second Samuel," 167–68.
68. Cf. Gordon, *1 & 2 Samuel* (OTG), 42.
69. That many of the kings referred to are associated with cities does not preclude the possibility that some of them ruled over wider territories (see, e.g., Josh. 13:20–21).
70. For a corrective to the common assumption that Samuel's warnings in 1 Sam. 8:11–17 reflect abuses during the reign of Solomon, see I. Mendelsohn, "Samuel's Denunciation of the Kingship in the Light of Akkadian Documents from Ugarit," *BASOR* 143 (1956): 17–32, who argues on the basis of Ugaritic parallels that they reflect, rather, the practices common among Canaanite kings of Samuel's day. Further, see Gordon, *1 & 2 Samuel* (OTG), 42–43.
71. See, e.g., H. Donner, "Basic Elements of Old Testament Historiography Illustrated by the Saul Traditions," *Die Ou-Testamentiese Werkgemeenskap in Suid-Afrika* 24 (1981): 40–54; G. von Rad, "The Beginnings of Historical Writing in Ancient Israel," *The Problem of the Hexateuch and Other Essays*, trans. E. W. Trueman Dicken (Edinburgh: Oliver & Boyd, 1966), 166–204; Van Seters, *In Search of History: Historiography in the Ancient World and the Origin of Biblical History* (New Haven, Conn.: Yale University Press, 1983), 247.
72. Miller and Hayes, *History*, 129. Cf. A. Mazar, *Archaeology of the Land of the Bible: 10,000–586 B.C.E.* (New York: Doubleday, 1990), 371: "the archaeological evidence for the period of the United Monarchy is sparse" and "often controversial." Moreover, "the time of Saul hardly finds any expression in the archaeological record" (ibid.). Even the long-standing assumption, first made by Albright, that the remains of an Iron I tower at Tell el-Ful is architectural evidence of Saul's building activity at Gibeah, his capital (perhaps cf. 1 Sam. 22:6; 23:19; 26:1), is now widely disputed; see P. M. Arnold, *Gibeah: The Search for a Biblical City*, JSOTS 79 (Sheffield: JSOT, 1990), 51–53.
73. See J. Licht, *Storytelling in the Bible* (Jerusalem: Magnes, 1978).
74. J. Licht, "Biblical Historicism," in H. Tadmor and M. Weinfeld (eds.), *History, Historiography and Interpretation: Historiography in the Ancient World and the Origins of Biblical History* (New Haven and London: Yale University Press, 1983), 107–8.
75. *The Royal Dynasties in Ancient Israel: A Study on the Formation and Development of Royal-Dynastic Ideology* (Berlin: Walter de Gruyter, 1977), 42.
76. Bright, *History*, 188.
77. W. W. Cannon, "The Reign of Saul," *Theology* 25 (1932): 326–35, on 326.
78. Esp. V. P. Long, *Reign and Rejection*; idem, *Art of Biblical History*, chap. 6; idem, "How Did Saul Become King? Literary Reading and Historical Reconstruction," in Millard et al. (eds.), *Faith, Tradition and History*, 271–84. Other studies attempting more integrated readings of the Saul narratives include U. Berges, *Die Verwerfung Sauls: Eine thematische Untersuchung*, Forschung zur Bibel, 61 (Würzburg: Echter Verlag, 1989); D. V. Edelman, *King Saul in the Historiography of Judah* (Sheffield: JSOT Press, 1991); R. Polzin, *Samuel and the Deuteron-*

omist: A Literary Study of the Deuteronomic History. Part 2: 1 Samuel (San Francisco: Harper & Row, 1989).

79. Bright, *History*, 187–88.

80. L. Eslinger, "Viewpoints and Point of View in 1 Samuel 8–12," *JSOT* 26 (1983): 61–76.

81. Ibid., 65.

82. M. Tsevat, "The Biblical Account of the Foundation of the Monarchy in Israel," in *The Meaning of the Book of Job and Other Biblical Studies: Essays on the Literature and Religion of the Hebrew Bible* (New York: KTAV, 1980), 77–99, esp. 83–84; D. J. McCarthy, "The Inauguration of Monarchy in Israel: A Form-Critical Study of I Samuel 8–12," *Interpretation* 27 (1973): 401–12, esp. 403; B. S. Childs, *Introduction to the Old Testament as Scripture*, 277–78.

83. Eslinger, "Viewpoints," 66.

84. For much fuller discussion, including a rebuttal of the tendency since Wellhausen to date pro-monarchical sentiments early and antimonarchical sentiments late, see Long, *Reign and Rejection*, 173–83.

85. W. A. Irwin, "Samuel and the Rise of the Monarchy," *AJSL* 58 (1941): 113–34, quote from 117.

86. Donner, "Basic Elements," 43.

87. *The Constitution of the Monarchy in Israel*, HSM 25 (Chico, Calif.: Scholars, 1981); "The Uneasy Compromise: Israel between League and Monarchy," B. Halpern and J. D. Levenson (eds.), *Traditions in Transformation: Turning Points in Biblical Faith* (Winona Lake, Ind.: Eisenbrauns, 1981), 59–96.

88. "Saul's Rescue of Jabesh-Gilead (1 Sam 11 1–11): Sorting Story from History," *ZAW* 96 (1984): 195–209.

89. On the validity of distinguishing these three stages, see Edelman, "Saul's Rescue," 198 n.9.

90. "Uneasy Compromise," 63.

91. Ibid., 70; more recently Halpern has attempted to chart the A and B source all the way from 1 Sam. 8 to 2 Sam. 1 (*David's Secret Demons*, 277–79). For a critical evaluation of Halpern's two-source theory, see Long, *Reign and Rejection*, 191–93.

92. "Saul's Rescue," 197–99.

93. Edelman (ibid., 200–202) notes only that this episode "appears to augment the discussion of the first stage of the process of installing a king" and to look forward to the public coronation that eventually occurs in 11:14–15.

94. Ibid., 200. Others who seek to explain the apparent relationship between chaps. 10 and 13 in traditio-historical terms include H. J. Stoebe, "Zur Topographie und Überlieferung der Schlact von Mikmas, 1 Sam 13 und 14," *TZ* 21 (1965): 277–80; J. M. Miller, "Saul's Rise to Power: Some Observations concerning 1 Sam 9:1–10:16; 10:26–11:15 and 13:2–14:46," *CBQ* 36 (1974): 162; T. N. D. Mettinger, *King and Messiah: The Civil and Sacral Legitimation of the Israelite Kings*, ConBOT 8 (Lund: CWK Gleerup, 1976), 97; and most recently Arnold, *Gibeah*, 89–90.

95. My translation. Many modern translations read "do whatever . . . ," though this wording is indicated neither by the Hebrew text nor by the context, when rightly understood.

96. Cf. also the focus on the Philistines early in the narrative (9:16).

97. Because Saul would surely have needed no geography lesson in this particular region, some commentators are troubled by Samuel's mentioning the Philistine garrison: P. K. McCarter Jr. (*I Samuel*, AB [Garden City, N.Y.: Doubleday, 1980], 182), for instance, opines that "this notice is immaterial at this point and probably secondary." Our own view is that, despite Saul's knowledge of the area,

Samuel's reference to the Philistine presence did indeed have a point (as we shall attempt to show).

98. This understanding of the significance of 1 Sam. 10:5 in context is anticipated already in the writings of David Kimchi (1160–1235), who sees in Samuel's reference to the Philistine presence a hint that Saul "should remove them from there and save Israel out of their hands" (my translation of Kimchi's commentary to 1 Sam. 10:5 found in standard editions of the rabbinic Hebrew Bible). Other commentators who have sensed something of the significance of 10:5 include R. Kittel, *Geschichte des Volkes Israel*, 7th ed., 3 vols. (Gotha: Leopold Klotz, 1925), 2:82; A. Lods, *Israel from its Beginnings to the Middle of the Eighth Century*, trans. S. H. Hooke (London: Kegan Paul, Trench, Trubner, 1932), 353; C. J. Goslinga, *Het eerste boek Samuël*, Commentaar op het Oude Testament (Kampen: J. H. Kok, 1968), 223; Smelik, *Saul*, 107.

99. Sternberg (*The Poetics of Biblical Narrative: Ideological Literature and the Drama of Reading* [Bloomington: Indiana University Press, 1985], 186) explains this technique as follows:

> From the viewpoint of what is directly given in the language, the literary work consists of bits and fragments to be linked and pieced together in the process of reading: it establishes a system of gaps that must be filled in. This gap-filling ranges from simple linkages of elements, which the reader performs automatically, to intricate networks that are figured out consciously, laboriously, hesitantly, and with constant modifications in the light of the additional information disclosed in later stages of reading. Even genres considered far from sophisticated . . . demand such gap-filling.

"In works of greater complexity, the filling-in of gaps becomes much more difficult and therefore more conscious and anything but automatic." To achieve preferred status, an interpretive hypothesis involving the filling of gaps must create "maximal relevance among the diverse features and levels [of the text]" and bring together "more elements than the alternative hypothesis" (ibid., 187).

100. For a defense of this view, see Long, *Reign and Rejection*, 227–28.

101. For further explanation of the above sequence, see Long, *Art of Biblical History*, 216–18; and for a full treatment, including interaction with diachronic theories, see Long, *Reign and Rejection*, chap. 7, "Toward an Integrated Reading of Saul's Rise, with Special Attention to the Portrayal of Saul."

102. W. Brueggemann, *First and Second Samuel*, Interpretation (Louisville, Ky.: John Knox Press, 1990), 99, 101.

103. Ibid., 100.

104. For a defense of "charge" as the better rendering in this context, see Long, *Reign and Rejection*, 87 n.95.

105. Ibid., 173.

106. So A. Cooper, "The Act of Reading the Bible," in *Proceedings of the Eighth World Congress of Jewish Studies (1981)* (Jerusalem: Magnes, 1983), 61–68, on 68.

107. A. D. H. Mayes, *The Story of Israel between Settlement and Exile: A Redactional Study of the Deuteronomistic History* (London: SCM, 1983), 9.

108. T. Ishida, *The Royal Dynasties in Ancient Israel: A Study on the Formation and Development of Royal-Dynastic Ideology* (Berlin: Walter de Gruyter, 1977), 26.

109. And if our reading of the Saul narratives is basically correct, it is no longer possible simply to peel away supposed later additions to reveal "a complete pro-Saul, admittedly apologetic, history" (so M. White, "Searching for Saul," 24).

110. *The Succession to the Throne of David*, esp. 109–12; anticipated by J. Wellhausen, *Prolegomena to the History of Israel* (Atlanta: Scholars Press, 1994; German 3rd

ed., 1886) (so Gordon, *1 & 2 Samuel* [OTG], 61–63, q.v. for a convenient survey and evaluation of studies of HDR).

111. For Rost, HDR "comprised only pieces and fragments from 1 Samuel 23:1 through to 2 Samuel 5:10" (so Gordon, ibid., 62), while according to the most generous theories it begins at 1 Sam. 15:1 and ends with 2 Sam. 7 (so, e.g., Mettinger, anticipated by Grønbæk for the former limit and by Weiser for the latter; for bibliography and discussion, see Gordon, ibid., 62–63).

112. Ibid., 63.

113. Whether David was the youngest of seven brothers (cf. 1 Chr. 2:13–15) or of eight (as suggested by 1 Sam. 16:6–10; 17:12–15) is much debated. One possibility is that he was number eight and that the Chronicler abbreviated the list of David's brothers to allow him to occupy the favored seventh position.

114. As S. L. McKenzie points out, the Bible devotes more space to David than to any other character, including even Moses and Jesus, if the Psalms be taken into account (*King David: A Biography* [Oxford: Oxford University Press, 2000], 2).

115. *King David*, 45.

116. *David's Secret Demons*, xv.

117. P. R. Davies, "'House of David' Built on Sand," *BARev* 20, no. 4 (1994): 54–55, on 55. Cf. also idem, *Search*, 16–48, 69. Similar views are also expressed in various places by N. P. Lemche (e.g., "Is It Still Possible to Write a History of Ancient Israel?" *SJOT* 8, no. 2 [1994]: 165–90; esp. 183–89); T. L. Thompson (e.g., *Early History*, 306–7, 415–23), and others. For a popular overview of the debate, and a taste of its acrimony, see C. Shea, "Debunking Ancient Israel: Erasing History or Facing the Truth," *The Chronicle of Higher Education*, 21 November 1997, A12–A14; cited also by McKenzie, *King David*, 9. For a thorough summary and balanced critical appraisal of the controversy over the United Monarchy, see G. N. Knoppers, "The Vanishing Solomon: The Disappearance of the United Monarchy from Recent Histories of Israel," *JBL* 116 (1997): 19–44; and more briefly, idem, "The Historical Study of the Monarchy: Developments and Detours," in Baker and Arnold (eds.), *The Face of Old Testament Studies*, esp. 215–21.

118. J. A. Soggin, *An Introduction to the History of Israel and Judah* (Valley Forge, Pa.: Trinity Press International, 1993), 32.

119. For the initial reports on the discoveries, see A. Biran and J. Naveh, "An Aramaic Stela Fragment from Tel Dan," *IEJ* 43 (1993): 81–98; idem, "The Tel Dan Inscription: A New Fragment," *IEJ* 45 (1995): 1–18.

120. A. Lemaire, "'House of David' Restored in Moabite Inscription," *BARev* 20, no. 3 (1994): 30–37.

121. K. A. Kitchen, "A Possible Mention of David in the Late Tenth Century BCE, and Deity *DOD as Dead as the Dodo?" *JSOT* 76 (1997): 29–44.

122. The following is a modest sampling of essays not already mentioned (in ascending chronological order): B. Halpern, "The Stela from Dan: Epigraphic and Historical Considerations," *BASOR* 296 (1994): 63–80; E. A. Knauf, A. de Pury, and T. Römer, "*BethDawid* ou *BaytDod*? Une relecture de la nouvelle inscription de Tel Dan," *BN* 72 (1994): 60–69; A. Rainey, "The 'House of David' and the House of the Deconstructionists," *BARev*, 20, no. 6 (1994): 47; D. N. Freedman and J. C. Geoghegan, "'House of David' Is There!" *BARev*, 21, no. 2 (1995): 78–79; T. Muraoka, "Linguistic Notes on the Aramaic Inscription from Tel Dan," *IEJ* 45 (1995): 19–25; W. M. Schniedewind, "Tel Dan Stela: New Light on Aramaic and Jehu's Revolt," *BASOR* 302 (1996): 75–90; A. Lemaire, "The Tel Dan Stela as a Piece of Royal Historiography," *JSOT* 81 (1998): 3–14; B. Becking, "Did Jehu Write the Tel Dan Inscription?" *SJOT*, 13, no. 2 (1999): 187–201; J.-W. Wesselius, "The First Royal Inscription from Ancient Israel: The Tel Dan Inscription Reconsidered," *SJOT*, 13, no. 2 (1999): 163–86.

123. Quoted in Shea, "Debunking Ancient Israel," A13.
124. *King David*, 15; see 11–16 for fuller discussion of the three inscriptions. McKenzie is far from convinced by Kitchen's attempt to find a reference to the "highland/heights of David," which in the context of Shoshenq's inscription must be set, according to Kitchen, in southern Judah and the Negev. Specifically, McKenzie finds it "highly unlikely that the highlands of southern Judah and the Negev bore David's name simply because he spent some time there" (ibid., 15–16). But is it not the case that whenever particularly important individuals (or those who go on to become important) are known to have had an association with a particular place, that association is long-remembered and even celebrated? On my ancestral family farm in West Virginia, set on the bank of the Kanawa River, one can still view a massive poplar stump at the edge of the river that is to this day known as Washington's tree, simply because George Washington once visited the farm (some two and a half centuries ago) and tied his boat to that particular tree.
125. The summary statement of 1 Kgs. 15:5 that "David did what was right in the sight of the LORD, and did not turn aside from anything that he commanded him all the days of his life, except in the matter of Uriah the Hittite" should not be made to say more than it does; it appears to be stressing David's cultic fidelity, rather than asserting moral or ethical perfection, save in one instance.
126. *David's Secret Demons*, 5, 6, and 53, respectively. It is difficult to see how these three statements, especially the last, can be squared with Halpern's comment elsewhere that "the biblical version, in the books of Samuel, presents a man who never did exist, a ruler altogether too good to be true" (ibid., xvi). Is Halpern perhaps confusing the David of the biblical narratives with the David of popular imagination?
127. Ibid., 72.
128. *King David*, 44; cf. 35.
129. On the genre of royal apology, see H. A. Hoffner Jr., "Propaganda and Political Justification in Hittite Historiography," in H. Goedicke and J. J. M. Roberts (eds.), *Unity and Diversity: Essays in the History, Literature, and Religion of the Ancient Near East* (Baltimore: Johns Hopkins University Press, 1975), 49–62; T. Ishida, "The Succession Narrative and Esarhaddon's Apology: A Comparison," in M. Cogan and I. Eph'al, *Ah, Assyria: Studies in Assyrian History and Ancient Near Eastern Historiography Presented to Hayim Tadmor*, ScrHier 33 (Jerusalem: Magnes Press, 1991), 166–73; P. K. McCarter Jr., "The Apology of David," *JBL* 99 (1980): 489–504; H. Tadmor, "Autobiographical Apology in the Royal Assyrian Literature," in H. Tadmor and M. Weinfeld (eds.), *History, Historiography and Interpretation* (Jerusalem: Magnes, 1984), 36–57. For more literature, see McKenzie, *King David*, 196–97 n.12.
130. See Halpern's discussion of David's "ten little indians"—i.e., Nabal, Saul and his sons at Gilboa, Ishbaal, Abner, Saul's other descendants, Amnon, Absalom, Amasa, and Uriah—in his chap. 4 entitled "King David, Serial Killer" (*David's Secret Demons*, 73–103). Cf. McKenzie's listing of ten charges that must have been aimed at David and which his "apology" attempts to answer (*King David*, 32–34).
131. Gordon, *1 & 2 Samuel* (OTG), 65–66.
132. See ibid., 66.
133. McKenzie, *King David*, 5.
134. Ibid., 5–6.
135. Ibid., 44.
136. Ibid., 84–85.
137. I had a friend who, after working for two full years as a junior partner creating a corporate insurance policy, suddenly became a multi-millionaire when the senior

partner unexpectedly died of a heart attack just as the purchase was going through. No charges were brought against my friend.

138. McKenzie, *King David*, 44.

139. D. Barthélemy et al., *The Story of David and Goliath: Textual and Literary Criticism. Papers of a Joint Research Venture*, OBO 73 (Fribourg, Suisse: Éditions Universitaires; Göttingen: Vandenhoeck and Ruprecht, 1986). See also E. Tov's more popular treatment, which appeared in the same year: "The David and Goliath Saga: How a Biblical Editor Combined Two Versions," *Bible Review* 2, no. 4 (1986): 34–41.

140. We may note, e.g., that McKenzie (*King David*, 71) believes that "the Septuagint (LXX) preserves the original version of the story," while Halpern (*David's Secret Demons*, 7) observes that "it looks as though the [shorter] Greek text was harmonizing apparent contradictions."

141. Barthélemy et al., *The Story of David and Goliath*, 105. For a concise summary of results in which Gooding broadens the scope of his investigation to set the Goliath episode in the context of the sweep of 1 Sam., see ibid., 145–54.

142. Gooding (ibid., 83) sees three possibilities for when the truncation may have taken place: "(i) at the level of the transmission of the Hebrew text; (ii) at the level of the translators into Greek; (iii) at the level of some reviser of the Greek." On what may have led to the shortening, he writes (ibid., 103):

> To me it is instructive to find modern scholars, on the ground of the supposed difficulties discussed above, deciding that the MT's account contains serious discrepancies. It strengthens me in my view that in Hellenistic times similar unfamiliarity with the conventions of ancient heroic single-combat led other learned scholars to feel similar difficulties and to attempt to eliminate them by excision.

143. Halpern, *David's Secret Demons*, 7.

144. Gooding, in Barthélemy et al., *The Story of David and Goliath*, 60.

145. Ibid., 79–80.

146. Ibid., 101.

147. Halpern, *David's Secret Demons*, 7.

148. Ibid., 8.

149. Ibid. Cf. also McKenzie, *King David*, 76.

150. It is worth noting that following the descriptions of how four descendants of Rapha were killed by different Israelite heroes (21:15–21), the summary in 21:22 credits David in a general sense, along with his men, for the victories.

151. There was a time when this was the majority view among scholars; see C. F. Keil and F. Delitzsch, *Commentary on the Old Testament* (Grand Rapids: Eerdmans, n.d.), 2:465–66.

152. Indeed, it is "considered one of the most disturbed in the Hebrew Bible" (W. Brueggemann, "Samuel, Book of 1–2," in *ABD* 5:957).

153. For ancient audiences, a particularly entertaining moment must have been when Achish of Gath offered in 1 Sam. 28:2 to make David his bodyguard (lit. "keeper of my head") for life. Having already collected one Gittite head (i.e., Golaith's; cf. 1 Sam. 17:51, 54, 57), the irony of David's being put in charge of another is palpable.

154. Even against "unprotected" individuals David is sometimes prevented from shedding blood (cf. 1 Sam. 25). On the function of 1 Sam. 25 as part of David's training in nonretaliation and on its relationship to the two sparings of Saul in chaps. 24 and 26, see R. P. Gordon, "David's Rise and Saul's Demise: Narrative Analogy in 1 Samuel 24–26," *TynBul* 31 (1980): 37–64.

155. McKenzie, *King David*, chap. 4.

156. Ibid., 85.

157. Ibid., 80, 84–85, respectively.
158. Ibid., 86.
159. Ibid., 87.
160. More on this below.
161. *King David*, 186.
162. Some may object that 1 Sam. 15 must be left out of consideration on the grounds that it is "Deuteronomistic" in character and therefore late. As J. G. McConville, *Grace in the End: A Study of Deuteronomistic Theology* (Grand Rapids: Zondervan, 1993), 56–57, has argued, however, "the tendency to date Deuteronomy in the seventh century owes much to habit; the data themselves are capable of quite other constructions." Ironically, "the close connection once supposed between Deuteronomy and the reform of King Josiah is no longer taken for granted; yet the connection with the seventh century has largely been retained" (ibid., 45–46).
163. Long (*Reign and Rejection*, 168) describes 1 Sam. 15 as pivotal or transitional: "From the ideological perspective characteristic of the narrative, 1 Sam 15 marks the effective end of Saul's reign. *De facto* Saul will continue to occupy the throne for some time to come, but *de jure* his rejection is an accomplished fact. Having rejected Yahweh's word, he will no longer receive it (cf. 28:15). The vital link with Israel's Great King has been severed, and henceforth Yahweh's attention will fall upon another. In this sense, then, the chapter also serves as an introduction to the 'Rise of David'. After ch. 15, David will be the protagonist and Saul the antagonist."
164. David's description of Jonathan's love as "passing the love of women" has occasionally been cited as suggesting a homosexual relationship between the two. For a well-grounded rebuttal of this view, see McKenzie, *King David*, 85, and also McKenzie's discussion of "love" as "political loyalty" (84).
165. Cf., e.g., the strong cautionary remarks in G. Barkay, "What's an Egyptian Temple Doing in Jerusalem?" *BARev*, 26, no. 3 (2000): 48–57, 67.
166. M. Steiner, "David's Jerusalem, It's Not There: Archaeology Proves a Negative," *BARev* 24, no. 4 (1998): 26–33, 62–63.
167. Ibid., 62, 33, and 26, respectively.
168. J. Cahill, "David's Jerusalem, It Is There: The Archaeological Evidence Proves It," *BARev* 24, no. 4 (1998): 34–41, 63.
169. Ibid., 34–35.
170. N. Na'aman, "David's Jerusalem, It Is There: Ancient Texts Prove It," *BARev* 24, no. 4 (1998): 42–44. See Na'aman's notes 1 and 2 for references to published reports in which Kenyon and Shiloh cite Late Bronze Age remains structures, pottery, and strata.
171. EA 285–90.
172. Na'aman, "David's Jerusalem," 42–43. See also, on the Amarna evidence, N. Na'aman, "Cow Town or Royal Capital? Evidence for Iron Age Jerusalem," *BARev* 23, no. 4 (1997): 43–47, 67.
173. EA 290.
174. Na'aman, "David's Jerusalem," 44.
175. See, e.g., the brief summary, with references, in H. Shanks, "The Missing Millennium in Jerusalem's Archaeology," *BARev* 26, no. 5 (2000): 34–37. More fully, see Cahill, "David's Jerusalem," and even Steiner, "David's Jerusalem," who admits that Late Bronze Age material has been found in tombs on the Mount of Olives, that there may be evidence of an Egyptian temple north of the Old City from that period, and that at least one Iron Age I structure and several hundred Iron Age I potsherds have been found (27 and 29).
176. Shanks, "Missing Millennium," 36.
177. Na'aman, "Cow Town or Royal Capital?" 44.

178. Barkay, "What's an Egyptian Temple Doing in Jerusalem?" 50.
179. Halpern, *David's Secret Demons*, 428.
180. Dever, *What Did the Biblical Writers Know*, 131.
181. Shanks, "Missing Millennium," 34–35.
182. Those taking a dim view of the possibility of a Davidic empire include G. Garbini, *History and Ideology in Ancient Israel* (New York: Crossroad, 1988), 21–32; P. R. Davies, *In Search of "Ancient Israel,"* JSOTS 148 (Sheffield: JSOT, 1992), 69; T. L. Thompson, *Early History of the Israelite People from the Written and Archaeological Sources*, SHANE 4 (Leiden: Brill, 1992), 331–34. For further bibliography, see Na'aman, "Cow Town or Royal Capital?" 67 n.24.
183. On all these, see Gordon, *I & II Samuel*, 242–45. In 1 Chr. 18:10 Joram ("Yahweh is exalted") is listed as Hadoram ("Hadad is exalted"), prompting Gordon (ibid., 244–45) to remark that "it is possible that Hadoram, on his accession to the throne, had his name changed by either David or Solomon in token of his vassal status."
184. Merrill (*Kingdom of Priests*, 300–302), for instance, differentiates "the various spheres over which David and Solomon exercised political influence" as follows: *homeland* ("geographically co-extensive with the older tribal territories"); *the provinces* ("kingdoms and states immediately contiguous to Israel" including "Damascus, Ammon, Moab, Edom and several smaller principalities"); *vassal states* ("client nations—including Zobah, Hamath, Arabia, and possibly Philistia—[which] were brought under Israelite control by military or diplomatic means, but were allowed to retain a certain measure of autonomy"); and, under Solomon, *allied states* (Tyre, Phoenicia, Egypt?). Cf. also Kitchen's analysis discussed below.
185. M. Liverani, *Prestige and Interest: International Relations in the Near East ca. 1600–1100 B.C.* (Padova, Italy: Sargon, 1990), 59; quoted by Na'aman, "Cow Town or Royal Capital?" 67.
186. Ibid.
187. K. Kitchen, "The Controlling Role of External Evidence in Assessing the Historical Status of the Israelite United Monarchy," in V. P. Long, G. J. Wenham, and D. W. Baker (eds.), *Windows into Old Testament History: Evidence, Argument, and the Crisis of "Biblical Israel"* (Grand Rapids: Eerdmans, 2002), 111–30.
188. Ibid., 126, citing J. M. Miller, "Separating the Solomon of History from the Solomon of Legend," in L. K. Handy, ed., *The Age of Solomon: Scholarship at the Turn of the Millenium*, SHCANE 11 (Leiden: Brill, 1997), 13–14.
189. Cf. the four-part breakdown by Merrill described in n. 184 above.
190. For descriptions of all these, with accompanying maps, see Kitchen, "Controlling Role," 116–23.
191. Ibid., 125.
192. Long, "First and Second Samuel," 169. On the "Davidic Covenant (2 Samuel 7)," see the chapter by that name (chap. 7) in Gordon, *1 & 2 Samuel* (OTG), 71–80.
193. Cf. J. A. Soggin, *Introduction to the Old Testament: From Its Origins to the Closing of the Alexandrian Canon*, trans. J. Bowden, 3d ed., OTL (Louisville, Ky.: Westminster/John Knox Press, 1989), 222.
194. McKenzie, *King David*, 165.
195. Ibid., 166.
196. Ibid., 188.
197. Ibid., 34–35.
198. *In Search of History*, 290.
199. Ibid.
200. Gordon, "In Search of David," 291 and 294–95, respectively.

201. Ibid., 289.
202. Ibid., 290.
203. McKenzie, *King David*, 155–56.
204. Gordon, *I & II Samuel*, 250.
205. *King David*, 160.
206. Ibid., 167–68.
207. For an example of such a reading, see I. W. Provan, *1 and 2 Kings*, NIBC (Peabody, Mass: Hendrickson, 1995).
208. "In Search of David," 295.
209. Ibid.
210. McKenzie, *King David*, 189.

Chapter 9: The Later Monarchy: Solomon

1. These sentiments go against the grain of much recent writing on the later monarchy, which has only been willing at best to concede that there is material useful for historical reconstruction within 1–2 Kgs. (even if the selectivity of the information provided, the theological and sometimes propagandistic intentions of the authors, and indeed sometimes their mistakes in identifying kings and locating events in the reigns of kings make life difficult for the historian); so J. M. Miller and J. Hayes, *A History of Ancient Israel and Judah* (Philadelphia: Westminster Press, 1986), 218–23, on the separated kingdoms. First–Second Chronicles has been widely dismissed as derivative of and more tendentious than Kings. Even the additional material we find therein has been viewed with suspicion, especially where it is suspected of being there because it promotes the political or theological case that the authors are presenting (ibid., 223–24). A more recent trend has been the virtual or complete dismissal of 1–2 Kgs. itself as a primary source for the history of Israel or Palestine because of its selectivity and its ideology.
2. The allusion is to the comments of ibid., 193, about the Genesis–Kings material about Solomon in particular.
3. For further information on the nature of 1–2 Kgs., see I. W. Provan, *1 and 2 Kings*, NIBC (Peabody, Mass: Hendrickson, 1995), 1–21.
4. They thus suggest a practice within Israel that was common throughout the rest of the ancient Near East: the retention of contemporary records, especially at the royal court or in temples, and the compilation of later documents on their basis. One thinks most of all of the annals of the Assyrian kings when reading in 1–2 Kgs. of the chronicles of the kings of Judah and Israel. We know that Jerusalem was already fully capable of producing documents back in the Late Bronze Age—the El Amarna letters testify to that: see further G. N. Knoppers, "The Vanishing Solomon: The Disappearance of the United Monarchy from Recent Histories of Israel," *JBL* 116 (1997): 40–42, and *ANET*, 483–90.
5. We may note, for example, that whereas the account of Manasseh's reign of fifty-five years occupies only eighteen verses (2 Kgs. 21:1–18), the account of the religious reform in Josiah's eighteenth year takes up forty-one (2 Kgs. 22:3–23:23). Zimri, who ruled for seven days (1 Kgs. 16:15–20), gets almost as much space as Omri (1 Kgs. 16:21–28), who ruled for twelve years, and Azariah (2 Kgs. 15:1–7), who ruled for fifty-two.
6. Thus we are sometimes told, for example, of various achievements or failures of Judean kings in language that appears "neutral," as if the authors had suddenly come across something in their sources that they thought interesting, but of no particular religious significance. We are told of Asa's war with Baasha, for example (1 Kgs. 15:16–22); this kind of information has often been regarded as more "secular" than much of what we find elsewhere in the book. The fact is, however,

that Asa's reign (like those of other Judaean kings) is patterned on the earlier reign of Solomon and is meant to be read in that context. The point being made is that faithfulness like Solomon's no longer brings Solomon's glory in its wake. These are different times—times of humbling for David's descendants (11:39). See further Provan, *Kings*, 124–27.

7. For further information on the nature of 1–2 Chr., see H. G. M. Williamson, *1 and 2 Chronicles*, NCB (London: Marshall, Morgan and Scott, 1982), 1–33.

8. See ibid., 24–26, 237.

9. We may note here the prophetic books of Isaiah, Hosea, Amos, and Micah, which help us in relation to the eighth century (the reigns of Jeroboam II in Israel and Uzziah/Azariah, Jotham, Ahaz, and Hezekiah in Judah); and Jeremiah, Ezekiel, Daniel, Nahum, Habakkuk, and Zephaniah, which help us in relation to the later seventh and very early sixth century—from Josiah to the end of the kingdom of Judah.

10. For a description of the Assyrian and Babylonian sources, see chap. 3.

11. Note, e.g., the Samaria, Arad, and Lachish ostraca (i.e., inscribed potsherds), some of which are translated in *ANET*, 321–22 (for a photograph of an ostracon from Lachish, see *ANEP*, 86); or the Zakkur (Zakir) inscription, *ANET*, 655–56.

12. Note, e.g., the Mesha inscription (the "Moabite Stone," *ANET*, 320–21; photograph in *ANEP*, 85); and the Shoshenq inscription, the best access to which is via the photographs, charts, and discussion in D. M. Rohl, *A Test of Time, 1: The Bible—From Myth to History* (London: Century, 1995), 120–27, although his understanding of the chronology is unusual (see also the photograph in *ANEP*, 118).

13. Note, e.g., the extended histories of the fifth-century B.C. Greek historian Herodotus and the first-century A.D. Jewish historian Josephus (who preserves parts of the *Babyloniaca* of Berossus written in Greek in the early Seleucid period).

14. See M. Kudlek and E. Mickler, *Solar and Lunar Eclipses in the Near East*, AOATS 1 (1971).

15. The "Black Obelisk" of Shalmaneser III has Jehu paying tribute to him in Shalmaneser's eighteenth year (841 B.C.): see *ANET*, 280, and the photographs in *ANEP*, 120–22.

16. A "Monolith Inscription" of Shalmaneser III from Kurkh has Ahab at the battle of Qarqar in Shalmaneser's sixth year (853 B.C.): see *ANET*, 278–79.

17. The Hebrew word *ʿaram*, which often appears in 1–2 Kgs., is sometimes translated into English as "Syria" (e.g., RSV) and sometimes as "Aram" (as NIV). The former is best avoided, since Syria is commonly used in different contexts for the much larger region north of Palestine of which the Aramean kingdom of Damascus only ever formed a southern part. We shall in fact follow the NIV in using Aram as a synonym for southern Syria, reserving the term "Syria" for the whole region that includes southern and northern Syria (known as "Hatti" in the earlier Assyrian sources). A consequential problem arises, however, when the *people* of Aram are referred to, since Arameans did not only inhabit Damascus and its territory. We shall therefore use words or phrases like "Damascene" or "Damascus Arameans" when referring to the people of the kingdom of Aram, in order to avoid confusion.

18. H. Tadmor, "The Chronology of the First Temple Period: A Presentation and Evaluation of the Sources," in Soggin, *History*, 368–83, on 374–76.

19. E. R. Thiele, *The Mysterious Numbers of the Hebrew Kings: A Reconstruction of the Chronology of the Kingdoms of Israel and Judah*, rev. ed. (Grand Rapids: Eerdmans, 1965). This book makes a number of interesting and plausible suggestions in both general and specific terms. It does not take sufficient account, however, of the likely literary and theological function of some of the numbers, and in striving too much for an impossible precision tends towards unwieldy and not quite plausible solutions.

20. Coregency creates the possibility that particular periods of time are being described and counted in the text from rather different points of view, depending upon whether the focus of attention is on the ruler who has ceded power or the ruler who is effectively exercising it, and depending on whether the beginning date of a king's reign is being given in terms of his accession as coregent or his accession as sole king in his own right (or indeed the date of his *designation* as future king). The excessive employment of coregencies to resolve even the smallest discrepancy in the chronology of Kings has rightly been criticized, and arises from a belief that the chronological schema provides or ought to provide more numerical precision than in fact is the case. There is solid evidence in Kings, however, that coregencies occurred in Israel; we may note by way of example the case of Azariah of Judah, who is said to have been struck by an illness that resulted in his son Jotham's taking over effective control of the government (2 Kgs. 15:5). Therefore, although the idea of coregency should not be pressed to an implausible extent, it should certainly be considered in cases where the evidence is capable of that explanation.

21. For example, although the chronological data for the period from the fall of Samaria until the destruction of the temple in Jerusalem seem generally transparent because we can work backwards from the various synchronisms that exist between kings Jehoiakim and Zedekiah of Judah and king Nebuchadrezzar of Babylon, if we do work back from the beginning of Josiah's reign (c. 640 B.C.), adding the total regnal figures for Amon, Manasseh, and Hezekiah together (eighty-six years), then we have Hezekiah coming to the throne in 726 B.C. The fall of Samaria in 722 B.C. apparently occurred in Hezekiah's sixth year, however (2 Kgs. 18:10), which implies an accession date around 727 B.C. It is probable in this case that we have lost a certain number of months from some of the reigns of these kings which add up to the "missing" year—various figures have been rounded off. Where precisely these months are to be located, however, and in which years the beginnings and ends of the various royal reigns are to be placed, is unclear, and would only be clarified by further extrabiblical discoveries.

22. The precise date of Solomon's accession to the throne of Israel is impossible to establish. If the division of the kingdom of Israel took place at some point around 930 B.C., and this is also the assumed year of Solomon's death, then a forty-year reign (1 Kgs. 11:42) would place his accession around 970 B.C. "Forty years" is likely not meant literally, however; forty is a round figure that is often used in the Old Testament. Further, the date of 930 B.C. depends on a correlation of a campaign in Palestine of the Egyptian ruler Shoshenq I around 925 B.C. with the campaign mentioned in 1 Kgs. 14:25 as occurring in Rehoboam of Judah's fifth year; and this correlation is uncertain (see further below).

23. For the interpretation of the texts that lies behind the way in which they are used in the historical narrative that follows, readers should consult above all Provan, *Kings,* and Williamson, *Chronicles.*

24. That he could not have been very young seems clear from the fact that his son Rehoboam must have been born right at the very beginning or shortly before the beginning of his reign (cf. 1 Kgs. 11:42 with 1 Kgs. 14:21).

25. That is, he married a non-Israelite in contravention of Deut. 7:3–4, and was insufficiently concerned in general about appropriate worship of God (cf. Deut. 12 and 1 Kgs. 3:2–3).

26. Soggin, *History,* 80–81, appears to consider implausible that a Pharaoh could both make a marriage alliance with Solomon *and* provide refuge for his enemies (1 Kgs. 11:14–22). He has evidently neglected to reflect both on the complex nature of politics and on the important question as to whether the Pharaoh giving his daughter in marriage was in any case the same Pharaoh who sheltered

Solomon's "enemies." Hadad was in fact sheltered by an unnamed Pharaoh of David's time (perhaps Amenemope, 993–984 B.C.), while Jeroboam was sheltered by "Shishak" (perhaps Shoshenq I or Osorkon I; see further below). Between Amenemope and Shoshenq ruled Siamun (978–959 B.C.) and Psusennes II (959–945 B.C.). K. A. Kitchen, *The Third Intermediate Period in Egypt (1100–650 B.C.)* (Warminster: Aris and Phillips, 1973), 279–83, regards Siamun as the Pharaoh who conquered Gezer (1 Kgs. 9:16) and gave it to Solomon as a dowry along with his daughter. See further A. Malamat, "A Political Look at the Kingdom of David and Solomon and Its Relations with Egypt," in T. Ishida (ed.), *Studies in the Period of David and Solomon and Other Essays* (Winona Lake, Ind.: Eisenbrauns, 1982), 189–204.

27. Kitchen, *Third Intermediate Period*, 282–83. Parallels do not prove anything, of course, any more than the absence thereof. They are simply interesting.

28. K. W. Whitelam, *The Invention of Ancient Israel: The Silencing of Palestinian History* (London: Routledge, 1996), 163, appears to find it highly significant that no extant Egyptian record of the marriage exists. Given the nature and extent of the documentary evidence that gives us those glimpses of the ancient past upon which we base our stories about it, however, this is not significant at all.

29. First Kings 11:1–3 tells us of seven hundred wives and three hundred concubines, which is presumably an exaggeration. Song 6:8 speaks of sixty queens and eighty concubines, and even these figures must be understood in their poetic context.

30. For a more extended discussion of the precise nature of the tasks of Solomon's officials, see G. H. Jones, *1 and 2 Kings*, NCB, 2 vols. (London: Marshall, Morgan and Scott, 1984), 1:134–38.

31. See T. N. D. Mettinger, *Solomonic State Officials: A Study of the Civil Government Officials of the Israelite Monarchy*, ConB (Lund: Gleerup, 1971), 111–27. An interesting Egyptian parallel is noted by D. B. Redford, "Studies in Relations between Palestine and Egypt during the First Millennium B.C., 1: The Taxation System of Solomon," in J. W. Wevers and D. B. Redford (eds.), *Studies on the Ancient Palestinian World: FS Winnett*, TSTT 2 (Toronto: University of Toronto Press, 1972), 141–56.

32. Note, for example, Soggin, *History*, 82–83.

33. So, e.g., Whitelam, *Invention*, 160–73.

34. Note also 1 Kgs. 8:65, which mentions that people from all over the region of Syria-Palestine celebrated the dedication of Solomon's temple, including people from the far north (the Hamath region) and from the far south (the Wadi of Egypt).

35. On the importance of taking the literary conventions of a text seriously, in respect of numbers and other features of the text, see K. L. Younger Jr., "The Figurative Aspect and the Contextual Method in the Evaluation of the Solomonic Empire," in *The Bible in Three Dimensions: Essays in Celebration of Forty Years of Biblical Studies in the University of Sheffield*, ed. D. J. A. Clines et al., JSOTS 98 (Sheffield: JSOT Press, 1990), 157–75.

36. Miller and Hayes, *History*, 214–16.

37. Williamson, *Chronicles*, 197–202.

38. E. A. Knauf, "King Solomon's Copper Supply," in E. Lipinski (ed.), *Phoenicia and the Bible*, StudP 11 (Leuven: Peeters, 1991), 167–86, on 168–69, appears to ground the claim in the general observation that the trade between Israel and Tyre involved the passage of subsistence goods from the former to the latter and luxury goods from the latter to the former, which is "typical for the exchange between first world countries and third world countries, between developed and developing nations" (168). To this we must respond that it is entirely unclear of what relevance to ancient Syria-Palestine are observations drawn from the way in which

the modern capitalist world economy functions, and ask further how the mere observation of trade patterns in any case infallibly informs the observer as to the character of the power relations bound up with the exchange. The status of Knauf's counter-reading of the biblical texts is itself unclear, however; having offered it, he proceeds to develop a quite different (although equally imaginative) scenario, that "the historical Solomon was an Egyptian satellite, not a Phoenician dependent" (186). Solomon, it seems, must have been in any event *somebody's* dependent, rather than the dominant king of the biblical text.

39. The events concerning the preparations for the building of the Temple form in Kings part of the discourse about Solomon and the nations, and the Hiram story must be read in that context. The connection between the general case of the nations and the particular case of Hiram naturally does not come to expression in Chronicles, where the context of the story of the preparations for the building of the temple is somewhat different.

40. Miller and Hayes, *History*, 214.

41. Whitelam, *Invention*, 169–73, depending on P. Kennedy, *The Rise and Fall of the Great Powers: Economic Change and Military Conflict from 1500 to 2000* (London: Fontana, 1988).

42. See Kitchen, *Third Intermediate Period*, 272–86, on the later pharaohs of the twenty-first dynasty.

43. For a recent summary (with extensive bibliographical footnotes) of the archaeological evidence of relevance to the Solomonic area, including the evidence of relevance to our thinking about the Jerusalem temple, see Knoppers, "The Vanishing Solomon," *passim*. A recent book that deals particularly with the relationship of our biblical narrative to other temple-building narratives from the ancient Near East, and has much of interest in it, is V. A. Hurowitz, *I Have Built You An Exalted House: Temple Building in the Bible in Light of Mesopotamian and Northwest Semitic Writings*, JSOTS 115 (Sheffield: JSOT Press, 1992), which makes the point that our Solomon temple narrative is stylized in terms of the normal literary pattern in Mesopotamia.

44. See Knoppers, "The Vanishing Solomon," 29–30.

45. See Jones, *Kings*, 1:214–15, for a discussion of the various structures to which the term "Millo" might refer.

46. See Knoppers, "The Vanishing Solomon," 22, though noting the complexity involved in interpreting the data, 27–29. The whole article illustrates clearly just how imprecise a science of archaeology often is, and why it is so foolish to give up our primary reliance on written texts in favor of versions of the past constructed solely on archaeology's "sure results." What he says in respect of certain sites in the Negev in particular can be generalized (31): "Scholars can agree on the importance of certain sites, but come to diametrically opposed conclusions about what this means for historical reconstruction."

47. First Kings 1:39 and 2:28–30 might be taken by themselves to imply that the tent pitched by David for the ark in 2 Sam. 6:17 is the Tabernacle itself (cf. 2 Sam. 7:2, 6). The Chronicler, however, is at great pains to stress that David's tent in Jerusalem (the location of the ark) is not the Tabernacle, and to place the Tabernacle (the location of the altar, cf. 1 Kgs. 3:4) at Gibeon.

48. For the opposing view that preexilic Israelite worship centered on the temple was not so very different from the kind of worship that various OT authors condemn as "Canaanite," see M. Barker, *The Older Testament: The Survival of Themes from the Ancient Royal Cult in Sectarian Judaism and Early Christianity* (London: SPCK, 1987); M. J. Mulder, "Solomon's Temple and YHWH's Exclusivity," *OTS* 25 (1989): 49–62.

49. Benjamin is for some reason not highlighted in 11:30–39, but simply presupposed in the numbers (twelve minus ten leaves two, cf. 12:21). The reason that the authors felt that Davidic rule over Benjamin could be presupposed and not explicitly referred to is difficult to know. One possibility is that they regarded Benjamin simply as Jerusalem's own territory, on the analogy of the Canaanite city-state. This territory came with the city, as it were, and needed no special mention. Certainly Jerusalem is regarded as belonging to Benjamin in Josh. 18:21–28, and Rehoboam has control over Benjamin in 1 Kgs. 12:21.

Chapter 10: The Later Monarchy: The Divided Kingdoms

1. So, e.g., J. A. Soggin, *History of Israel: From the Beginnings to the Bar Kochba Revolt, AD 135* (London: SCM, 1984), 190–93.
2. It may well be that his close associates and perhaps even Judaeans generally did indeed regard him as king, but that point does not prove that his kingship did not have to be confirmed by an Israelite assembly which included Judah. Nor does the fact that authors call someone "king" necessarily mean that at that particular point in the narrative that person was in fact king. Authors can and do refer to such persons anachronistically.
3. Although we are told in general that the people of Israel had found Solomon's regime, in part or as a whole, unduly harsh, the biblical texts do not make clear the substance of the people's complaint. A natural presumption, given Jeroboam's involvement in the events, would be to think that the complaint centered on Solomon's manpower requirements in relation to his building program, notwithstanding the authors' views that the forced labor to which the Canaanite population was subjected was not of the same order as the labor that the Israelites performed. It is possible, although this suggestion inevitably is speculation, that other aspects of Solomonic rule were also not appreciated by his subjects (see Miller and Hayes, *History*, 230–31).
4. Second Chronicles 11:5–12, 23, can perhaps be taken to imply, however, that by no means all the people in the southern part of Solomon's kingdom were wholehearted supporters of the Davidic king in Jerusalem, since the "cities of defense" mentioned there seem to have been positioned more with internal than external threats in mind.
5. The fact that the biblical sources speak in this way, however, does help to remind us that northern Israel remained the larger and more powerful segment of the old United Kingdom, and that from a northern Israelite and political point of view Judah would have been the smaller, breakaway territory from "Israel," not themselves. The authors of Kings themselves remind us of the political reality (even while deploring the religious consequences of the schism in respect of the northern Israelites in particular) by their continued use of the phrase "all Israel" of the northern tribes alone in 1 Kgs. 15:27, 33; 16:16–17—a phrase that reminds the reader of Judah's current position outside the tribal confederation. For some helpful comments on the relative size and strength of Israel and Judah, see Miller and Hayes, *History*, 233–34.
6. It has been argued both that Jeroboam in effect only substituted calves for ark and cherubim, in a slightly different version of the worship of the Lord in Jerusalem (so Miller and Hayes, *History*, 242: "The difference between the Ark-cherubim and the bull images was primarily one of religious iconography rather than theology"), and that Jeroboam deliberately set out to lead his people (back) into Canaanite worship, and chose his symbols carefully with that end in mind (so N. Wyatt, "Of Calves and Kings: The Canaanite Dimension in the Religion

of Israel," *SJOT* 6 (1992): 68–91). We do not have access to the thoughts of Jeroboam and his subjects, of course, so saying what their intentions were is impossible. The authors of Kings certainly associate the newly reformed worship with the worship of Canaanite deities as early as 1 Kgs. 14:15.

7. See I. W. Provan, *1 and 2 Kings*, NIBC (Peabody, Mass: Hendrickson, 1995), 110.

8. Tirzah is probably to be identified with modern Tell el-Far'ah (North), a site commanding the principal route from the hill country to the Jordan Valley and also routes to north and south. The desire for control of the roads of Palestine, especially by establishing settlement at major highway junctions, helps to explain the rise of important cities at sites such as Shechem, Tirzah, and (later) Samaria. See Y. Aharoni, *The Land of the Bible: A Historical Geography*, trans. A. F. Rainey (Philadelphia: Westminster Press, 1962), 53–57, esp. 55–56.

9. Idolatry is regarded as the fundamental reason that the early Israelite dynasties did not survive, and prophetic intervention as one of the catalysts that brought about their ends (1 Kgs. 13:1–10; 14:7–11; 16:1–4). Personal or group motives that are not explicitly described in Kings would obviously have been involved in the individual coups, and there were doubtless other factors about which we may speculate that led to their success. We speculate without evidence, however. Miller and Hayes, for example (*History*, 234–37), wonder whether the north (in contrast to the south) had no generally accepted royal theology that could help sustain a dynasty on the throne in difficult times. This factor may have contributed to the northern instability, for all we know, although we do later find periods of relative stability in the north (e.g., under the Omride dynasty).

10. See Aharoni, *Land*, 281: "The recurrent notices about siege operations . . . against 'Gibbethon, which belongs to the Philistines' . . . apparently Tell Melat west of Gezer, prove that the boundaries of Israel, Philistia and Judah met in that vicinity during this period." Israelite decline is also indicated, of course, by what we read of relations with Aram in 1 Kgs. 15:18–20, where it becomes clear that Aram is an independent power that at different points is found in alliance with Israel and with Judah.

11. The authors of Chronicles also record Rehoboam's apostasy and Shishak's invasion, linking the two quite explicitly as cause and effect (2 Chr. 12), although they preface their account with another which suggests that Rehoboam, in his initial period of rule, was rather more like his father Solomon in his early years (2 Chr. 11:5–23). Here we read of the building program and administrative innovations in Judah and Benjamin that were apparently designed to strengthen Rehoboam's hold over this territory (11:5–12, 23).

12. First Kings 14:26 represents the first of a series of notices in Kings about the loss of treasure from the temple and the palace (15:18; 2 Kgs. 14:14; 16:8; 18:15–16; 24:13), the culmination of which will come in 2 Kgs. 25. The "all" of our text, as the comparison of all the texts concerned reveals, is not to be taken literally. The Hebrew word *kol*, "all, everything," is often used hyperbolically in the OT, in the same way as numbers are (cf., for example, Josh. 10:40–42; 2 Kgs. 11:1–2). See further M. Brettler, "2 Kings 24:13–14 as History," *CBQ* 53 (1991): 541–52.

13. The date of the campaign, if it took place at all, is entirely uncertain, given that the list itself is not dated. The campaign is often described as the campaign of his twentieth year (c. 925 B.C.) on the dubious premise that it occurred in the year prior to the instructions given by the Pharaoh to erect a court and gateway at the temple of Karnak. These instructions are dated, to his twenty-first year (see further D. M. Rohl, *A Test of Time, 1: The Bible—From Myth to History* [London: Century, 1995], 414, n. 2 for chap. 5).

14. The surface similarity between "Shishak" and "Shoshenq" in terms of sound is, of course, inviting. Yet the stela fragment tells us nothing of specific usefulness

for a history of Israel; and much discussion has taken place about the significance of the sequence of names in the Karnak inscription and about whether it refers to an actual campaign or represents merely a generalized Egyptian boast that might relate to various campaigns or indeed to none (following in an Egyptian literary tradition that began with Thutmose III, of listing places over which dominion was claimed; see *ANET*, 242–43). If the Karnak inscription *were* to be read as offering a campaign itinerary, then a particular difficulty from the point of view of the biblical texts would be that the inscription appears to paint a picture of an army that only passed through Judah on its western side on its way to fight a campaign in northern Israel. We do not know, however, whether the conventions governing this kind of text (if it *is* this kind of text) were such that accounts were required to be entirely comprehensive. Perhaps we possess a selective text that does not mention every Judean city that was taken in the campaign. Perhaps, on the other hand, Shoshenq did not attack Jerusalem on his way north precisely because Rehoboam bought him off with treasure (we note that the biblical texts do not imply that Jerusalem fell to an army), and/or he truly was not very interested in Jerusalem in the first place, while the interest in Kings and Chronicles at this point in their stories is in Jerusalem and the temple; the way they tell the story reflects the fact that they see the (potential) Egyptian threat only from this point of view. Perhaps Shoshenq was more interested in Jeroboam, so recently a refugee at his court (1 Kgs. 11:40), because (we might speculate) promises about his future loyalties had been extracted from Jeroboam before his departure from Egypt, and these promises had not been fulfilled. A conclusion is impossible given the current state of our knowledge. The biblical text itself may in fact refer to a quite different campaign of Shoshenq, of which we have no other record, or to a quite different pharaoh (Shoshenq's successor Osorkon I). Our sources for Egyptian history are limited in terms of its detail. Readers interested in pursuing the matter further may read initially K. A. Kitchen, *The Third Intermediate Period in Egypt (1100–650 B. C.)* (Warminster: Aris and Phillips, 1973), 293–302, 432–47; Aharoni, *Land*, 283–90; and Rohl, *Test of Time*, 120–127, whose discussion reflects his unusual view of Egyptian chronology and of the name "Shishak," which he thinks has its origins in a shortened form of the name "Ramesses."

15. The name "Ben-Hadad" appears in reference to kings of Aram at various points throughout the narrative in Kings: here in 1 Kgs. 15:18–20, of a king contemporary with Asa and Baasha and later with Omri (deduced from 1 Kgs. 20:34); in 1 Kgs. 20, of a later contemporary of Ahab (the reference back to Ben-Hadad's father trading in Samaria in 20:34 demonstrates that the two Ben-Hadads are to be differentiated); and in 2 Kgs. 13:3–5, 14–25, of the usurper Hazael's son. These kings are commonly referred to, therefore, as Ben-Hadad I, II, and III. Two points must be kept in mind, however. First, the name Ben-Hadad (or more accurately its Aramaic equivalent "Bar-Hadad") is in all likelihood not the only name by which these kings were known. Assyrian inscriptions certainly appear to know of at least two of them by different names: the Ben-Hadad (II) who in 2 Kgs. 8:7–15 is assassinated by Hazael is known to the Assyrians as Adad-idri (= Hb./Aram. "Hadadezer"), while the Ben-Hadad (III) who ruled after Hazael may well have been the king known to the Assyrians as Khadianu (= Hb./Aram. "Hezion") or Mari'. The possibility arises, therefore, that "Ben-Hadad" was only one of the personal names of some of the kings of Aram, or indeed a throne name adopted upon the accession of some or all of them, or simply a title held by some or all (as the "Mari'" mentioned above is probably itself a *title* given to Khadianu). An analogy is offered by the "Bar-Gush" who is mentioned alongside Ben-Hadad in the stela of Zakkur king of Hamath (*ANET*, 655–56). He is probably

to be identified with a king of Bit-Agusi (lit., "house of Gusi," perhaps a famous ancestor) who is known in other sources by another name entirely: see further A. Kuhrt, *The Ancient Near East C. 3000–330 B.C.*, 2 vols. (London: Routledge, 1995), 2:394–95, for a brief discussion of the naming of ancient Aramean states.

Second and consequently, we cannot be sure whether our biblical Ben-Hadads are really Ben-Hadad I, II, and III, because other kings of Damascus known to us may also (for all we know) have possessed such a name or title, and indeed we certainly cannot be at all sure that we yet know of all the kings of Damascus who ruled during our period. Our sources are very patchy in this regard. To name and number our kings thus is therefore to do no more than adopt a useful convention for the sake of clarity. (Another aid to clarity: the chapter in fact assumes a sequence of Damascus kings during the period of the divided monarchy in Israel as follows: Rezon, Tabrimmon, Ben-Hadad I, Ben-Hadad II [Adad-idri], Hazael, Ben-Hadad III [Mari', Khadianu], Rezin [Rakhianu in the Assyrian texts]. The list can only be regarded as highly provisional, however, in view of the current state of our knowledge.)

16. See Aharoni, *Land*, 282–83, for further discussion.
17. For a discussion, see H. G. M. Williamson, *1 and 2 Chronicles* NCB (London: Marshall, Morgan and Scott, 1982), 263–65.
18. Although the biblical texts are not always clear about whether loss of territory, where described, is thought of as anything more than temporary, we may perhaps be safe in thinking that some Israelite territory remained in Damascene hands by the close of the period we have been describing, and that some of Judah's southernmost territories were not effectively under Jerusalem's control. The locations of Rehoboam's cities of defense (2 Chr. 11:5–12) may themselves indicate what the effective range of his control was: as far south as Adoraim and Ziph and as far west as Lachish, Azekah, and Aijalon (see Aharoni, *Land*, 290–94).
19. See, e.g., the excerpts from the annals of Tiglath-pileser III and Sargon II in *ANET*, 283–85, where the phrase has its Assyrian form *Bit-Huumria*.
20. Samaria lies in a valley opening to the west of Tirzah, and retains most of the advantages of that site while allowing easier access to the Way of the Sea (a major international highway—Aharoni, *Land*, 41–49) and the coastal plain. The first two building phases that archaeologists at Samaria have identified may plausibly be taken as the work of Omri and Ahab, respectively.
21. The Mesha Inscription or Moabite Stone was discovered near the ruins of ancient Dibon, which lay a short distance north of the river Arnon (see *ANET*, 320–21; photograph in *ANEP*, 85).
22. We see no justification at all for regarding 1 Kgs. 20 and 22:1–38, along with the Elisha stories in 2 Kgs. 2; 4:1–8:15, as pertaining to the period of the Jehu dynasty rather than the period of the Omri dynasty (so, e.g., Miller and Hayes, *History*, 259–64). The argument that they do seems to arise out of an expectation that neither texts nor the reality to which they refer can be complex—that periods in the past are not and cannot be represented as periods of ebb and flow and of complicated personal relationships and commitments. One could certainly write a story of the past that is simpler than the one we find in Kings, and such a simple story we sometimes find in histories of Israel. Whether that story is more accurately an account of Israel's past, however, is another matter. We can imagine a neatly compartmentalized history, for example, in which sharp conflict exists between prophets and kings in the Omride period and a "close supportive relationship" between them in the period of Jehu's dynasty (Miller and Hayes, *History*, 262). The Hebrew narrative as a whole does not present us with such a neatly compartmentalized history, however, and even the Elisha narratives taken alone (which Miller and Hayes cite in particular) do not suggest it. Jehoram of Israel,

for example, reveals himself throughout his story as someone who is happy to treat prophets in the proper way when things are going well, but not quite so content to do so when things are going badly (e.g., 2 Kgs. 6:8–33, which is far from suggesting a close relationship overall). Prophetic help can be offered to kings in the book of Kings, on the other hand, without much "support" being implied (e.g., 2 Kgs. 3:4–27). It is certainly true that the relationship between Jehoram and Elisha is presented as complex, but then many relationships are complex. See further Provan, *Kings*, 181–203.

23. Ahab's "father" was not strictly Baasha, of course, but words like "father" and "mother" are often used somewhat vaguely in Hebrew narrative to include other relationships. Ben-Hadad here is possibly alluding to interaction between his father Ben-Hadad I (cf. 1 Kgs. 15:16 ff.) and two different precedessors of Ahab, namely Baasha and Omri (who evidently allowed Aram some trading rights in his new capital of Samaria). Still, a much more probable reading is that the father of Ahab in the first part of the verse is the same as the king in view in the second, and that Omri had suffered defeats which themselves led on to trading concessions.

24. Miller and Hayes, *History*, 251–52, take the more cynical view that the authors of Kings have omitted material that would suggest (in conflict with their theology) that the wicked Omrides were successful monarchs. No evidence, however, supports the view that the authors of Kings held the kind of simplistic theology here ascribed to them, and Miller and Hayes's own observations on Jehoshaphat bear this out. Jehoshaphat was for the authors of Kings a relatively righteous king, yet "one would conclude from their summation of Jehoshaphat's reign that he too was a second-rate ruler with no successes worthy of mention" (252).

25. Provan, *Kings*, 157–60.

26. Miller and Hayes, *History*, 253–55, suggest that the events behind the Naboth story occurred much later than Ahab's reign, but their arguments are exceedingly weak. In particular, one cannot fix the timing of a prophetic oracle on the basis of a time reference in past reported speech (255).

27. In view of 1 Kgs. 20:34, which speaks of Ben-Hadad's father as a contemporary of Omri, the Damascus kings of 1 Kgs. 15 and 1 Kgs. 20 must clearly be differentiated as Ben-Hadad I and II.

28. Difficulty arises with the usual translation of 1 Kgs. 20:1 in terms of a "siege" of Samaria, for the remainder of the narrative in 20:1–21 clearlys shows that Ben-Hadad is some way from the city. Messengers travel back and forwards from the Aramean camp to Samaria (vv. 2 ff.), which is accessible to the "elders of the land" (v. 7), and can be left by an army (vv. 15–17) that is only confronted after Ben-Hadad receives reports of their movements. The "siege" is evidently from a distance, the "attack" more generalized (on Samaria's territory) than specific (on Samaria itself). A more general translation of the Hebrew seems appropriate in the circumstances (e.g., "brought pressure to bear" on Samaria).

29. The "Monolith Inscription" of Shalmaneser III from Kurkh: see *ANET*, 278–79. Shalmaneser is the first Assyrian king whose campaigns are known to have affected Israel directly, although his father Ashurnasirpal II (883–859 B.C.) reached northern Syria and Phoenicia during his campaigns and received tribute from such coastal cities as Tyre and Sidon.

30. The name of the king is given in the Assyrian inscription as Adad-idri (= Hb./Aram. Hadadezer), while Ahab's opponent (and his sons' contemporary) in Kings is called Ben-Hadad (1 Kgs. 20; 2 Kgs. 8:7–15). We often find the same individual carrying more than one name in ancient sources (see above), which includes the OT itself (e.g., the same person is called Jehoahaz and Ahaziah in 2 Chr. 21:17; 22:1). Such variation cannot count as evidence in favor of the kind of thoroughgoing revision of history offered by Miller and Hayes for the period

of the Omride and Jehu dynasties, when they seek to identify the biblical Ben-Hadad of 1 Kgs. 20, not with Adad-idri, but with the later Ben-Hadad of 2 Kgs. 13:3–5, 14–25 and of the stela of Zakkur (see further below). Miller and Hayes argue that some of the biblical texts that in reality pertain to Jehu's dynasty are now found in Kings describing Omri's dynasty.

31. The overall impression of the inscription in this respect may no doubt be taken seriously, even if the individual numbers of such texts should be subjected to the same scrutiny as numbers in Hebrew narrative. It seems unlikely in particular that Ahab should have deployed more chariots at Qarqar than all his allies put together, and more than Shalmaneser himself.

32. Shalmaneser claims to have defeated his enemies at Qarqar, which may be true, although such claims cannot necessarily be taken at face value. Even if victorious, the fact remains that the Assyrians apparently did not return to the region until 849 B.C., and when they did return they once again had to fight. Opinions about the result of the battle among historians differ: see M. Elat, "The Campaigns of Shalmaneser III against Aram and Israel," *IEJ* 25 (1975): 25–35 for a discussion. For a detailed account of Assyrian history from the ninth to the seventh centuries B.C. overall, and of the Babylonian empire that followed in the late seventh and early to mid-sixth centuries B.C., see *CAH,* vol. 3, part 1 (2d ed., 1982), 238–81, and vol. 3, part 2 (2d ed., 1991), 1–321.

33. These are the campaigns of Shalmaneser's tenth, eleventh, and fourteenth years (see *ANET,* 279–80 for sections of the relevant texts and *ANEP,* 120–22 for photographs). It is sometimes said (e.g., Soggin, *History,* 209) that Shalmaneser III claims to have fought against the same alliance in these campaigns as in 853 B.C., but this claim cannot be deduced from the evidence, which refers to the alliance rather vaguely in various ways and using various numbers, chief among which is the evidently symbolic number "twelve" which often appears in Assyrian sources in relation to Syro-Palestinian kings (see, for example, the much later Prism B text [lines v 54 to vi 1] from Esarhaddon's reign that is translated in *ANET,* 291).

34. The inscription (*ANET,* 320–21) might actually be taken to suggest that Mesha's military actions against Israel began during Ahab's reign (the literal "son" of Omri). Ahab is not mentioned by name in the inscription, on the other hand, and the numbering of Omri's reign and half of his "son's" reign as "forty years" is certainly very far from the biblical figure (twenty-three, 1 Kgs. 16:23, 29), even as a round number. At the same time, the claim that "Israel has perished forever" is clearly an exaggeration, whatever military success Mesha might have had. Various possibilities present themselves as we attempt to put the inscription and the biblical text together. Perhaps Mesha is exaggerating not just the length of time northern Moab was occupied and the extent of his victories, but also the extent to which his whole reign was one of military action against Israel. That is, he is perhaps keen to stress his accession to the throne as the turning point in Moab's fortunes, when in fact his rebellion did not begin until much later (after Ahab's death). Perhaps, on the other hand, he is using the word "son" loosely of a king of Omri's house, rather than of Ahab, and does not even mean to tell us that his rebellion began during Ahab's reign (note the analogies of Ben-Hadad and Bar-Gush above). Finally, Mesha did perhaps oppose Ahab with some measure of success, and the inscription may not be correlated with our Kings texts at all, which then refers to a later rebellion, perhaps after a reestablishment of Israelite control. We must always remember that the gaps in our knowledge are enormous.

35. No convincing evidence exists that this Jehoram is the same person as Jehoram of Judah, ascending first to the Judean throne and then to the united throne of both kingdoms (*contra* Miller and Hayes, *History,* 280–82; cf. J. Strange, "Joram, King of Israel and Judah," *VT* 25 [1975]: 191–201). The name itself cannot be

taken as indicating this connection, especially in a situation where two royal families are so closely associated (cf. the name "Ahaziah" that is used of both Israelite and Judean kings in this period). Nor do the variants in 2 Kgs. 1:17 suggest it; the addition of "brother" there only makes unambiguously clear what is later clear from 2 Kgs. 8:16 (where Joram is described as a son of Ahab). Finally, one cannot deduce very much from the absence of synchronisms in the LXX, nor from the elements of the regnal formulae for individual kings (especially since formulae are in any case not consistently given throughout Kings).

36. The Tel Dan inscription provides a notable if disputed exception: see further below.

37. Unclarity is evident in the textual tradition regarding the precise point of transition between the reigns of Jehoshaphat and his father Asa. The MT tradition has Asa overlapping slightly with Ahab, while the LXX tradition has Jehoshaphat coming to the throne slightly earlier in relation to the Israelite kings and overlapping slightly with Omri. The significance of all this is not clear. One factor that makes assessment difficult is the disagreement among textual experts as to whether the slightly different chronological data sometimes found in the LXX when compared to the MT result in general from anything other than the fact that the translators themselves struggled (as many generations of exegetes have done since) to make sense of the difficulties found in the chronology of their Hebrew text. One possible explanation, however, is that Jehoshaphat ruled jointly with his father for a couple of years in a coregency. If this joint rule is the case, then perhaps both LXX and MT reflect this reality while referring to only one aspect of the overlap involved. MT stresses the connection between Asa and Ahab and LXX the link between Jehoshaphat and Omri. Some support for the idea of a brief coregency between Asa and Jehoshaphat is found in 2 Chr. 17:7, where Jehoshaphat's religious reforms are said to have begun in his third year. This report may indicate that, for the authors of Chronicles, this time was the beginning of his effective rule, since they characteristically emphasize that good rulers displayed reforming zeal from the beginning of their reigns (Williamson, *Chronicles*, 282–83, noting also the examples of Hezekiah in 2 Chr. 29:3 and Josiah in 2 Chr. 34:3).

38. This campaign evidently took place during the period of Jehoshaphat's coregency with his son, who was also named Jehoram (cf. 2 Kgs. 1:17; 3:1; 8:16).

39. The seizure of the throne of Aram from Ben-Hadad II or Adad-idri (Hadadezer) by Hazael is recorded not only in 2 Kgs. 8:7–15 but also in a fragmentary Assyrian text (*ANET*, 280, second column, "on a basalt statue"). Both texts stress that Hazael came, as it were, from nowhere. Second Kings 8:13 has Hazael refer to himself as a "mere dog," while the Assyrian text refers to him as the "son of nobody." He clearly came to power at some point between Shalmaneser's campaign in the west in his fourteenth year (845 B.C.), when Adad-idri/Hadadezer was still on the Syrian throne (see *ANET*, 280, "according to the Bull Inscription"), and the campaign of Shalmaneser's eighteenth year (841 B.C.), by which point Hazael had taken over as king (see *ANET*, 280, "according to the Black Obelisk"). The fragmentary text may perhaps imply that the coup occurred nearer the latter date than the former, although events are perhaps being telescoped as they are being summarized.

40. When we are told in 1 Kgs. 22:47 that a "deputy" ruled in Edom, we are essentially being told that Jehoshaphat controlled Edom as Solomon had controlled his various districts (cf. the same Hebrew word used of Solomon's various officials in 1 Kgs. 4:5, 7, 27; 5:16; 9:23). For that reason, the "king" of Edom who turns up in alliance with Judah in 2 Kgs. 3 is noticeably in a supporting role. Miller and Hayes (*History*, 279–80) argue that this deputy was in fact an Omride

appointee, but this argument depends on their view that Israel dominated Judah during Ahab's reign (278–79), and no convincing evidence exists to support the claim. Occasional Judean support for Israel's military campaigns implies no more than an alliance of equals, and the nonmention of Judah in nonbiblical records can imply perceived insignificance on the part of the authors, or even nonparticipation in the events described there, without implying anything about Judah's relationship with Israel. That the alliance of Phoenicia, Israel, and Judah implied by the marriages of Ahab to Jezebel and Jehoram to Athaliah had something to do with trade (*History*, 279) seems, on the other hand, highly likely.

41. The story is rather different in each book. The emphasis in Kings falls on the wrecking of the fleet and on Jehoshaphat's unwillingness to take Israelites with him; the intention seems to be to contrast this unwillingness with Solomon's willingness to take Sidonians on board his ships (1 Kgs. 9:27). Jehoshaphat did not have Solomon's success. Moreover, the peace between north and south was sometimes simply the absence of hostility between two rival kingdoms rather than the real unity of the Solomonic empire. The emphasis of Chronicles, on the other hand, falls on the reality of Jehoshaphat's cooperation with Ahaziah (leaving the question of the willingness to include Israelite sailors aside), and finds in this a *reason* that Jehoshaphat did not have Solomon's success.

42. See Williamson, *Chronicles*, 287–91, on 2 Chr. 19:4–11.

43. Ibid., 293–95.

44. These "princes of Israel" are not to be seen as *northern* princes (Miller and Hayes, *History*, 281–82), but simply as Israelite princes in the same sense that Jehoshaphat is an Israelite king in the MT of 2 Chr. 21:2 (see Williamson, *Chronicles*, 247, 304).

45. Probably to these same events the fragmentary Tel Dan inscription also alludes, although we cannot be certain. The inscription appears to commemorate a victory by an Aramean king over kings of both Israel and Judah: for the stela fragment pertaining to this, see A. Biran and J. Naveh, "An Aramaic Stele Fragment from Tel Dan," *IEJ* 43 (1993): 81–98. If two further fragments have been correctly joined together and correctly associated with the first fragment, then the Aramean king is likely claiming responsibility for the deaths of the other two, Ahaziah of Judah and Jehoram of Israel: for the fragments pertaining to this, see A. Biran and J. Naveh, "The Tel Dan Inscription: A New Fragment," *IEJ* 45 (1995): 1–18. If so, then we may assume that the Aramean king is Hazael, and that he is engaging in the oversimplification and hyperbole typical of victory stelae; although the deaths of Ahaziah of Judah and Jehoram of Israel certainly followed their war with Hazael, the biblical testimony suggests that the events surrounding them were more complex than the stela implies. For easy access to the heated debate about the Tel Dan stela, see in the first instance G. N. Knoppers, "The Vanishing Solomon: The Disappearance of the United Monarchy from Recent Histories of Israel," *JBL* 116 (1997): 36–40.

46. The death of Ahaziah is recorded differently in Kings and Chronicles, and indeed in different ancient versions of these books. Second Kings 9:27–28 tells us that Jehu pursued Ahaziah from Jezreel in the direction of Beth-haggan. The MT then has Jehu instructing his men to ambush Ahaziah at some point on the road ahead, without telling us whether this ambush was at least partially successful. We are told only that Ahaziah fled to Megiddo and died there. Other versions tell us that Ahaziah was in fact wounded in the ambush, and imply thereby that he died from his wounds in Megiddo. Second Chronicles 22:9 tells us of a search for Ahaziah, who is found hiding (or recovering from his wounds, as the LXX apparently has it) in Samaria. He is brought to Jehu and put to death. The circumstances of Ahaziah's death are thus clouded in uncertainty, although a plausible conclusion

is that even if he was wounded during his flight, he was later executed by Jehu in Megiddo, and that the Chronicler's "Samaria" is to be understood as "territory of which Samaria is the capital" rather than as the capital—the territory just searched by Jehu in his pursuit of the Judean king.

47. Miller and Hayes, *History*, 303–4, are skeptical about the biblical accounts here, wondering why Athaliah would kill her own grandchildren, and whether anyone with a remote claim to the throne could have survived the purges of Jehoram and Athaliah and the events of 2 Chr. 21:16–17. Even if we could be sure that Athaliah's position would indeed have been stronger rather than weaker with her grandchildren alive, however (and we do not know enough about Judean rules of succession and customs of government to be sure), one must ask whether those who are keen to wield power always act in ways that seem rational to others. History would tend to suggest that such people sometimes seem far from rational. We must note on the other hand that the biblical sources themselves do not consider it "likely" that anyone with a remote claim to the throne could have survived to replace Athaliah; they present the Davidic dynasty as all but finished. They tell us, however, that against all "likelihood" one child did in fact survive, and we have no good reason to question this information.

48. See *ANET*, 280, foot of first column.

49. Shalmaneser's most likely route, in view of what his records tell us, would have taken him through Gilead, to the south of the Sea of Galilee, and via Jezreel to the coast. Hosea 10:14 may preserve a memory of this march through northern Palestine, since "Shalman" is probably an abbreviated form of the king's name and "Beth-Arbel" may plausibly be identified with Irbid in Gilead, about thirty kilometers southeast of the Sea of Galilee.

50. See Aharoni, *Land*, 310.

51. For a photograph of the pictorial representation of Jehu's submission to Shalmaneser on the Black Obelisk, see *ANEP*, 122.

52. See *ANET*, 280, second column.

53. The campaign of Shalmaneser III's twenty-first year was, so far as we know, the last of his campaigns directly affecting southern Syria and Palestine. We do not hear from Assyrian sources of another such campaign until the fifth year of Adadnirari (810–783)—that is, 806 B.C.—when this king reports that tribute paying by the kings in the region had ceased during the reign of his father Shamshi-Adad V (see *ANET*, 282, "Saba'a Stela"). In all likelihood, paying of tributes had ceased (if it ever truly began) even before this time, during the upheaval and revolt of Shalmaneser's last years on the Assyrian throne. Both Adad-idri (Hadadezer) and Hazael appear in the OT as successful and powerful monarchs unshaken by Assyrian aggression; consonant with this presentation, no evidence exists that Damascus ever fell to Shalmaneser III. We must doubt how effective Shalmaneser ever was in southern Syria. Shamshi-Adad himself (823–811 B.C.), preoccupied with troubles nearer home, appears never to have crossed the Euphrates, maintaining a quieter Assyrian presence in the west through his control of Til-Barsip, a strategically important city that secured passage across the river when it was required.

54. On this occasion we clearly do not have two different accounts of the same campaign (see Williamson, *Chronicles*, 325–26).

55. That Ben-Hadad III was not as successful in his military ventures as his father Hazael had been is also suggested by the Aramaic stela of Zakkur, king of Hamath, which celebrates this king's successful resistance to Ben-Hadad and a coalition of several northern Syrian rulers (see *ANET*, 655–56). It is unclear, on the other hand, whether the Melqart stela (*ANET*, 655, beginning at the foot of column 1) has anything to do with Ben-Hadad III at all and, if it does, whether it implies anything about his control of northern Syria (cf. Miller and Hayes, *History*, 293–94).

56. Ambiguity surrounds 2 Kgs. 12:2, part of which could be read either as "all the years Jehoiada the priest instructed him" (cf. 2 Chr. 24:2) or as "all his days, because Jehoiada the priest instructed him." In favor of the former is the striking fact that, while the reader of Kings has by this point become accustomed to the idea of northern kings meeting a violent end, the only Judean king so to die thus far has been the wicked Ahaziah. Just a suggestion appears in Kings, therefore (as there may be also in the case of Asa in 1 Kgs. 15:18–24), that Joash went astray later in his reign, and the authors of Chronicles make this explicit. Even the temple restoration, however, does not reflect quite so well on Joash in Kings as it does in Chronicles (see Provan, *Kings*, 223–24).

57. For example, the Saba'a inscription (*ANET*, 282, top of first column) describes the Assyrians besieging Damascus and exacting tribute in Adad-nirari's fifth year, which appears to have been one of several campaigns west of the Euphrates during the first half of Adad-nirari's reign, although several of these military expeditions seem to have been organized by provincial governors rather than by the king himself (see Kuhrt, *Ancient Near East*, 2:491–93, for a brief description of the period, and Miller and Hayes, *History*, 299, for another of Adad-nirari's inscriptions [the Rimah stela] which on this occasion mentions Jehoash of Israel as a tribute-payer). The paucity of the records for Adad-nirari's reign makes it difficult to be certain about their exact number and date. See further A. Millard, "Adad-nirari III, Aram and Arpad," *PEQ* 105 (1973): 161–64.

58. Miller and Hayes, *History*, 298–302, offer a highly speculative and unconvincing reconstruction of Jehoahaz's reign, using material about the Omrides abstracted from an earlier part of Kings, in which Jehoahaz rather than Jehoash emerges as the king who deserves primary credit for successfully challenging the Arameans. If it is not clear that the "problems" which they find in reading Kings justify the excision of this material in the first place, neither is it clear that their relocation of it makes things any easier.

59. Note that both the Calah and the Rimah inscriptions (*ANET*, 281–82; Miller and Hayes, *History*, 299) claim that tribute passed from Israel to Assyria in this period.

60. A reasonable reading would be—as the cases of Zedekiah (discussed below) and the king of Edom (discussed above) demonstrate—that Amaziah's infant son Azariah was also already regarded as "king" of Judah at this time. Certainly we may suspect that the large total of Azariah's regnal years as given in 2 Kgs. 15:2 (fifty-two) includes the sixteen years from the battle of Beth-shemesh to the death of his father—i.e. that Azariah was regarded as having begun his rule at the time when his father went into Israelite "captivity." Kings, when noting that Azariah himself in the later period of his reign was relieved of responsibility for government even though still alive, speaks of this event in a manner which may imply that he was regarded as already effectively dead (2 Kgs. 15:5; see Provan, *Kings*, 240). "Dead" men do not, strictly speaking, occupy regnal years.

61. This interpretation in turn helps to explain the curious wording of 2 Kgs. 14:22 (see ibid., 237), where Amaziah's son Azariah is reported as consolidating Amaziah's gains in Edom by claiming the port of Elath (cf. 1 Kgs. 9:26) at some point after Jehoash's death (as it seems from the Hebrew).

62. Azariah is also known in the biblical texts as Uzziah, e.g., 2 Kgs. 15:13, 30, 32, 34.

63. On the archaeological evidence, see Williamson, *Chronicles*, 336–37; and Aharoni, *Land*, 313–14, along with map 28.

64. That a Judean king could have conducted campaigns in the east as well as the south during the period of Jeroboam II's strength in the north and could have

initiated various reforms in his kingdom, whether as a vassal or as a free agent, is clear enough (*contra* Miller and Hayes, *History*, 311). To what extent Judah remained under Israel's shadow after the death of Amaziah is, however, unclear. The intriguing phrase "Judah in Israel" in the MT of 2 Kgs. 14:28 ("he restored Damascus and Hamath to Judah in Israel") could be taken as implying a continuing Israelite claim over Judah during Jeroboam's reign, and even as a description from a northern point of view of the whole of Israel-Judah in this period (see Provan, *Kings*, 240). Even if so, however, we have no way of measuring how the claim and the reality match up. The "rogue" chronological notice in 2 Kgs. 15:1, on the other hand—which does not fit easily into any plausible chronological schema that we might devise for the period of the kings—could be taken as implying that Azariah did attain a measure of independence from Jeroboam around the latter's twenty-seventh year, i.e., around twelve years after the death of Amaziah. We simply do not have enough information to decide such a question. Whatever is the case, we have some evidence that Judah and Israel were still closely associated after Jeroboam's death during the early period of Menachem's reign—by which time Judah, however, was temporarily the senior partner in the relationship (see further below).

65. See *ANET*, 282–83, "slabs found in Calah." Some uncertainty accompanies the text, however, which has led scholars to question whether the "Azriau" mentioned in it is really Azariah of Judah, or perhaps someone of the same name who governed a quite different state further to the north (perhaps "Yaudi" [Sam'al], a small independent kingdom known from the Aramaic inscriptions from Zenjirli). See further N. Na'aman, "Sennacherib's 'Letter to God' on His Campaign to Judah," *BASOR* 214 (1974): 25–39, esp. 36–39. Yet to correlate the two names is at least to identify Azriau with a known king of the period rather than with an entirely unknown one; the arguments deployed against the identification are not compelling. See further the reading noted in B. Becking, *The Fall of Samaria: An Historical and Archaeological Study*, SHANE 2 (Leiden: Brill, 1992), 3 n.9.

66. Second Chronicles 26:23 further implies that, as a result of the illness, Azariah was buried in a place different from the burial place of other Judean kings, which is interesting in view of the Uzziah inscription dating from the Second Temple period which records the place where Uzziah's bones were brought and enjoins the reader not to move them. See Miller and Hayes, *History*, 310; and J. A. Fitzmeyer and D. J. Harrington, *A Manual of Palestinian Aramaic Texts*, BibOr 34 (Rome: Biblical Institute Press, 1978), 168–69, 223–24.

67. Assyria did not apparently trouble Syria-Palestine very much in the period between Adad-nirari III and Tiglath-pileser III. Her kings were beset by other troubles and only infrequently ventured out on military campaigns in the west.

68. Lebo Hamath is commonly supposed to be located to the southwest of Hamath itself. The difficulty with this view, however, is that in 1 Kgs. 8:65 the phrase "from Lebo Hamath to the Wadi of Egypt" seems to be intended as a designation of the whole Solomonic empire, analogous to the phrases "from the River to the land of Philistines, as far as the border of Egypt" and "from Tiphsah to Gaza" in 1 Kgs. 4:21, 24 (contrast the designation of Israel proper in 4:25—"from Dan to Beesheba"). In 2 Kgs. 14:28, indeed, Hamath (along with Damascus) is itself mentioned as part of the area over which Jeroboam exercised dominion; and 15:16 MT implies that Tiphsah, well to the northeast of Hamath, was also within reach of Israelite troops at this time. It seems evident from these texts that the authors of Kings thought of Lebo Hamath as lying to the north of Hamath.

69. We may note Amos 1:3–5, which looks forward to Aram's defeat, and Amos 6:13–14, which presupposes the recovery of Transjordan, although Amos predicts a future reversal of the situation in which Israel will again be oppressed from Lebo

Hamath to the Wadi of the Arabah. The heading to the book of Hosea likewise places the first phase of this prophet's activity in the period of the rule of Jeroboam and Azariah.

70. Note, e.g., Amos 6:1–7, with its opaque reference, in the midst of a judgment oracle, to reverses suffered by Calneh, Hamath, and Gath (v. 2). The nature of the reference makes it difficult to know whether Israelite (and Judean) victories are also in view here, although the last two cities mentioned appear also in 2 Kgs. 14:28 and 2 Chr. 26:6.

71. The Old Greek translation has an entirely implausible "Tirzah" while the Lucianic recension of the LXX has "Tappuah," about twenty-four kilometers southwest of Tirzah. Yet that Menachem might have wished to fight a campaign to the northeast of Hamath in order to reassert an Israelite claim to the territory there is comprehensible, and that he did so early in his reign is entirely possible, either before the Assyrian campaigns of 743–740 B.C. began or during these years as part of the anti-Assyrian struggle in the region. Whether Judah was involved in this struggle throughout this entire period (if we take the "Azriau of Judah" text in *ANET*, 282–83, to imply that it was involved for *some* of the time) is an interesting question. Certainly no reference to Judah in the Assyrian records would imply this. Both these records and the biblical texts in fact imply that Aram under Rezin was the driving force in the anti-Assyrian alliance by around 735 B.C., and the biblical texts portray Aram as Judah's enemy in this period. We are entitled to believe, therefore, that if Judah was early involved in anti-Assyrian resistance, then after the defeat mentioned in the "Azriau of Judah" text, Judah did not involve itself further in anti-Assyrian activity. It may be no coincidence that Ahaz, who later called for Assyrian help against Aram and Israel, evidently attained some kind of royal status around 742 B.C., which must coincide fairly closely with the date of the (presumed) Judean defeat. Perhaps his influence led to a change in Judean policy, which in turn may later have led to the Syro-Ephraimite attack on Judah—erstwhile allies now disgruntled by a lack of Judean cooperation.

72. The Assyrian records also record Menachem as a tribute payer to Tiglath-pileser: see *ANET*, 283, first column. For a summary of the course of events from 738 to 732 B.C. and exhaustive reference to the relevant texts, see Becking, *The Fall of Samaria*, 1–20.

73. See the fragmentary text translated in *ANET*, 283–84.

74. A reasonable deduction can be made from the fact that his name always appears first in connection with Pekah in biblical texts (2 Kgs. 15:37; 16:5; Isa. 7:1–8; 8:6) that Rezin was the dominant partner in their relationship, as Aramean kings had before often been dominant. Whether Rezin headed anything that can be described as an anti-Assyrian coalition in this period must be open to more question, although support for the idea can be found in 2 Kgs. 16:6 taken with 2 Chr. 28:17–18, and in the Assyrian descriptions of Tiglath-pileser's campaigns in 734–732 overall, which perhaps imply concerted opposition to Assyria (*ANET*, 282–84). On both points, see further below.

75. The math clearly shows that Pekah could not have reigned for twenty years over Israel (2 Kgs. 15:27), if what is meant is that twenty years elapsed between taking over from Pekahiah and giving way to Hoshea. Working backwards from the fall of Samaria at the juncture of the reigns of the Assyrian kings Shalmaneser V and Sargon II (722 B.C.), we would arrive at a starting date for Pekah's reign (if we were simply to add together the figures for Hoshea, 2 Kgs. 17:1, Pekahiah, 2 Kgs. 15:23, and Pekah) of around 753 B.C.—well before the accession of Tiglath-pileser III in 744 B.C., whom we know overlapped with Pekah's predecessor Menachem. Miller and Hayes, *History*, 324, plausibly suggest that Pekah

already ruled the portion of Israelite territory mentioned in 2 Kgs. 15:29 before succeeding Pekahiah in Samaria, arguing that this territory was already under Aramean control and that Pekah was effectively Rezin's delegate there. His "twenty years" include this earlier period. Possibly some of this territory was already under Aramean control by the time of Rezin's defeat at the hands of Tiglath-pileser. Assyrian sources themselves suggest that by this time the southernmost limits of the Aramean kingdom extended into Gilead. However, 2 Kgs. 15:25 clearly knows of Pekah as one of Pekahiah's high officials rather than as a separate ruler. Although the Arameans may have had something to do with Pekah's decision to rebel, therefore (note that his power base is indeed in Gilead [2 Kgs. 15:25])—which in turn explains the close association thereafter between Rezin and Pekah—no evidence shows that Pekah was in reality a "king" before he was king in Samaria. He may nevertheless—as a way of claiming legitimacy, perhaps as the "true" successor to Jeroboam II—have counted his regnal years from an earlier period when he was not really a king.

76. Whether Tiglath-pileser really appointed Hoshea or simply accepted the situation while continuing to claim overlordship over the new king is difficult to know in the circumstances.

77. The Egyptian ruler is apparently named in 2 Kgs. 17:4, although it is not certain that "So" is intended as a personal name rather than a place-name (perhaps "Sais"). The pharaoh in question might have been Osorkon IV of the Twenty-second Dynasty (730–715 B.C.; "So" might be an abbreviation of Osorkon) or Tefnakht, founder of the overlapping Twenty-fourth Dynasty (727–720 B.C.), which was based in Sais. For a chronological table see Kuhrt, *Ancient Near East*, 2:624; and for a good discussion of the issues, see further J. Day, "The Problem of 'So, King of Egypt' in 2 Kings 17:4," *VT* 42 (1992): 289–301.

78. Josephus (*Ant.* 9.283–87) relates that Shalmaneser waged war against Phoenicia during the reign of Luli king of Tyre. He cites Menander, whose work is based on fragments of the Tyre archive.

79. The biblical sources (2 Kgs. 17:3–6; 18:9–11) testify to only one siege and conquest of Samaria—the one by Shalmaneser V, also referred to in the Babylonian Chronicle—and they identify these events as the crucial ones in bringing an end to Israel as a separate state. This account may represent a simplification of a more complex state of affairs, however. Shalmaneser's successor, Sargon II, also describes himself as besieger and conqueror of the city, and as the deporter of Israelites; in fact, Samaria was still causing Sargon difficulty in his second year (720 B.C.). Uncertainty remains about how to interpret this evidence. Did Sargon absorb Shalmaneser's conquest of Samaria into his own record in order to claim more success for himself than he actually achieved and perhaps also to give himself legitimacy (as a usurper of the throne) by connecting himself with the previous reign? Alternatively (or in addition), did his own armies indeed subsequently besiege and capture Samaria for a second time early in his reign? Or is there some other solution to this puzzle? Whatever the case, Sargon and not Shalmaneser apparently brought a final end to Israelite independence, following up the successes of his precedessor in Syro-Palestine and consolidating them. For the extrabiblical texts and a comprehensive discussion see Becking, *Fall of Samaria*, 21–60; cf. also *ANET*, 284–85.

80. How far the Assyrian treatment of Israel overall may be described as part of a "pattern" of political dominance which operated under Tiglath-pileser III and his successors (Miller and Hayes, *History*, 320–22) must be questioned, because it seems clear that Assyrian treatment of the different states that they confronted is far from revealing consistency of thought or action. We are not so confident that any general policy other than "what might be thought to work at the moment" can

be detected in the way that some territories were allowed a relative degree of autonomy in relation to the empire while some were annexed into the Assyrian provincial system and sections of their populations (especially the leading members of communities) relocated. On the other hand, a reasonable assumption is that the point of such a relocation, along with the associated introduction of foreign populations into the new province (as in 2 Kgs. 17:24–41), was to reduce the chance of future trouble by dispelling any strong sense of community and leadership. Another reasonable assumption is that the Assyrians would have been content not to go to the trouble of absorption of territory where they did not think it necessary for their ends, especially when having a "buffer-zone" of semi-independent peoples between the borders of their empire and the borders of Egypt would have no doubt been useful.

81. A further indication that Rezin was the senior partner in the Syro-Ephraimite alliance, and particularly that he effectively controlled Transjordan, is that he rather than Pekah is said to have taken Elath. That he apparently gave it to Edom is perhaps a further indication of wider primacy within a more general anti-Assyrian alliance.

82. Williamson, *Chronicles*, 348.

83. The building inscription translated in *ANET*, 282 (foot of column one) also mentions Ahaz, who is here given his fuller name of Jehoahaz, as a tribute payer in the context of the Assyrian campaigns without being explicit about the circumstances. The biblical sources suggest that, whatever happened after the campaign was over, Ahaz certainly sent a gift to the Assyrian king beforehand, along with his plea for help (cf. 2 Kgs. 16:8; 2 Chr. 28:21).

84. No firm evidence exists that Tiglath-pileser would have imposed Assyrian religion on vassal states as an aspect of political control: see J. W. McKay, *Religion in Judah under the Assyrians 732–609 BC*, SBT 26 (London: SCM Press, 1973).

85. If Hezekiah's fourteenth year were calculated from Hezekiah's accession in the sixth year before the fall of Samaria (727 B.C., 2 Kgs. 18:10), we would have a date of 714 B.C., when Sennacherib (704–681 B.C.) was not even on the throne of Assyria. By far the best solution is to imagine that Hezekiah ruled jointly with his father Ahaz from 727 to 714, and that 2 Kgs. 18:13 reflects a sole accession date in 714. An argument sometimes made is that Isa. 14:28–31 implies the death of Ahaz in 727 in the same year as the death of Tiglath-pileser III, who is plausibly regarded as the "rod" that struck Philistia (referring to his campaign of 734 B.C.). We are not required by the text, however, to correlate the death dates of the two kings, and indeed a date of 714 B.C. makes perfectly good sense for the oracle, which then becomes a warning to the cities of Philistia of what faces them if they underestimate Tiglath-pileser III's successor and pursue plans for revolt.

86. Williamson, *Chronicles*, notes a tendency in Chronicles to place the beginning of the reforming activities of good kings at the earliest point in their reigns, and suggests that these chronological notices have the purpose more of characterizing a reign than of giving precise dates (see, e.g., 282, 352, 397–98). The question of precise dating, if of interest to the enquirer, therefore requires careful handling in each case.

87. For a full and helpful discussion of 2 Chr. 30–31, see ibid., 360–78.

88. See *ANET*, 285 ("second year," beginning at the foot of the first column) and 287 ("Nimrud inscription," first column).

89. See *ANET*, 287 ("Prism A," top of first column).

90. For a biblical perspective on the revolt, see Isa. 20:1–6. We do not count 2 Kgs. 18:13–16 as evidence. The reading of 2 Kgs. 18–19 offered in this chapter rather assumes that we take seriously the apparent intention of the authors that we are to read their narrative in 2 Kgs. 18:13–19:37 consecutively—something that

other histories of Israel have been most reluctant to do. For the detailed exegesis, see Provan, *Kings*, 252–62. In particular, we do not find at all plausible the suggestion that a "second campaign" of Sennacherib is embedded in the biblical narrative, which must be distinguished from the campaign of 701 B.C. Such a campaign is implied neither by the biblical texts nor by the Assyrian records, and the theory that proposes it is unnecessary.

91. We take 2 Kgs. 20:1–19 to be a "flashback" to the period before the death of Sargon II in 705 B.C. (*contra* Provan, *Kings*, 263)—to the period around 713/712 B.C., in fact (taking our lead from the implication in 2 Kgs. 20:6 that Hezekiah's illness occurred fifteen years before his death, and that the Babylonian visit occurred around the same time), when Marduk-apla-iddina II was still enjoying his first spell of kingship in Babylon (721–710 B.C.). Sargon II reconquered Babylonia after 710 B.C. and drove him into exile in Elam, but he remained a thorn in Assyria's side throughout the succeeding years (see Kuhrt, *Ancient Near East*, 2:578–86).

92. See 2 Kgs. 18:8; 20:20; 2 Chr. 32:3–6, 28–29; Isa. 22:8–11; and the relevant section of the annals of Sennacherib as translated in *ANET*, 287–88.

93. For an analogy to the practice of besieging a major city while continuing operations elsewhere in the surrounding region, we may compare Tiglath-pileser's campaigns in Syria in 743–740 B.C. The appearance of the *turtanu* (RSV "Tartan") before the gates of Jerusalem is no surprise. Lachish was itself soon overwhelmed by Sennacherib, as implied by 2 Kgs. 19:8 and confirmed by the Assyrian reliefs and associated text which portray the siege and conquest of the city (see *ANET*, 288, "epigraph from a relief"; and *ANEP*, 129–32).

94. Herodotus 2.41 tells of a story he learned in Egypt involving a horde of field mice that invaded the Assyrian camp, which some scholars take as an indication of plague.

95. See *ANET*, 291 ("Prism B," v 54 to vi 1, foot of first column).

96. See *ANET*, 294 ("Cylinder C," foot of first column).

97. Esarhaddon not only dominated Syria-Palestine, but in 671 B.C. succeeded in taking Memphis in Egypt and gaining a measure of control over Lower Egypt (see, e.g., the section of the Zenjirli stela, a victory stela set up in northern Syria, which is translated in *ANET*, 293, first column). Ashurbanipal was likewise able in 664 B.C. to take Thebes (see *ANET*, 294–96, "Cylinder C"; for a biblical text that looks back on this event, see Nah. 3:8–10).

98. The fact that 2 Kgs. does not imply that any major changes took place during Manasseh's reign (Miller and Hayes, *History*, 375–76) is an insufficient ground upon which to rest a claim that no major changes did in fact take place. To argue in such a way is to forget that history in Kings, as in Chronicles, is theologically shaped, and that the fact that Chronicles is theologically shaped does not mean that the events it describes cannot have happened. On both the theological shaping and the history of 2 Chr. 33, see Williamson, *Chronicles*, 388–95.

99. McKay, *Religion in Judah*, 25–26.

100. B. Oded, "Judah and the Exile," in J. H. Hayes and J. M. Miller (eds.), *Israelite and Judaean History* (London: SCM, 1977), 435–88, on 455–56.

101. The phrase "book of the law" which is found in the accounts of the finding of the book in 2 Kgs. 22 and 2 Chr. 34 is only used in the Pentateuch of Deuteronomy, e.g., Deut. 28:61; 29:21.

102. As already noted above, however, the Chronicler's chronology of reform during the reigns of good kings may best be taken not so much as a literal claim about timing as a statement about the king's overall character.

103. Miller and Hayes (*History*, 401) are skeptical about 2 Chr. 34:6–7, with its reference to Josianic activity in Manasseh, Ephraim, Simeon, and Naphtali, but

without justification. "Highly general, sweeping statements" can nonetheless accurately reflect past reality (albeit in a highly general and sweeping way), and the nature of the later Persian provincial system implies only that Josiah's attempt to reclaim northern Israel was largely unsuccessful in the end, not that the attempt was never made.

104. On the Scythians (perhaps the "foe from the north" of Jer. 4:5–6:30), see, e.g., Herodotus 1.105. On Egyptian suzerainty over Philistia and Phoenicia, see Herodotus 2.157 (which reports Pharaoh Psammetichus I's capture of Ashdod).

105. Psammetichus (664–610 B.C.) began his reign as a client-king of the Assyrians, who had just brought the Twenty-fifth Dynasty in Egypt to an end; although in the course of his reign he was able once again to achieve independence from Assyria and indeed unite Egypt under one ruler, relations between the two empires appear to have remained mainly friendly throughout this period. Certainly the Egyptians did not hesitate to provide support for the Assyrians when the latter were confronted by the Babylonians.

106. Miller and Hayes (*History*, 383–85, 388–90) hypothesize that Judah was already under Egyptian dominance and indeed an Egyptian vassal early in the reign of Josiah, but their conclusion is not entailed by the evidence that they cite. Jeremiah 2 does not clearly date from shortly after 627 B.C., nor imply Judah's submission to Egypt. There is moreover no evidence that Egyptian campaigns in the north in support of Assyria preceded 616 B.C., nor even that they had effective control of the main highways of the eastern Mediterranean seaboard much before this date—we simply do not know, for example, precisely when the Scythians ceased being a threat to Egypt in Palestine. Finally, we have no evidence that Judean soldiers were fighting as vassals under Egyptian auspices early in Josiah's reign (although clearly the Egyptian army was indeed swelled in this period by foreign immigrants and mercenaries, including Judeans: see Kuhrt, *Ancient Near East*, 2:636–46, esp. 640). In fact, little evidence exists that Egypt's interest in Palestine even in the later period of Josiah's reign was connected with anything other than commerce and trade—albeit that they expected to be able to move troops through Palestine when they wished to do so.

107. To conduct religious reforms in Bethel and generally in cities of Manasseh, Ephraim, and as far north as Naphtali is naturally to lay renewed claim to this territory as Israelite, but not necessarily to do so in a way that would disturb a more powerful neighbor who cared more about passage through Syria-Palestine than about possession of Syro-Palestinian territory as such. One can imagine, indeed, that Egypt might have been quite content to see direct Assyrian control of Palestine eroded to this extent, because it could only have been in Egypt's long-term interests.

108. B. Halpern, "Centre and Sentry: Megiddo's Role in Transit, Administration and Trade," in I. Finkelstein et al. (eds.), *Megiddo III: The 1992–1996 Seasons*, SMNIA 18, 2 vols. (Tel Aviv: Emery and Claire Yass Publications in Archaeology, 2000), 569, plausibly suggests that Josiah may have captured Megiddo from either the Egyptians or the Assyrians prior to the battle.

109. To give someone a new name is to make clear that one has power over that person. In both 2 Kgs. 23:34 and 24:18, loss of name symbolizes loss of power. Judah no longer controls her own destiny.

110. We gain from the book of Jeremiah invaluable insight into the period from the beginning of the reign of Jehoiakim until just after the fall of Jerusalem in 586 B.C. The intense period of this prophet's activity appears to have begun early in the reign of Jehoiakim (Jer. 26:1; cf. 1:1–3). Jeremiah saw Babylon as Yahweh's instrument in bringing judgment upon Judah and regarded Babylonian domination for an extended period as divinely ordained. He spoke out strongly

throughout the reigns of Jehoiakim and Jehoiachin about the judgment to fall on Judah at the hands of the Babylonians (e.g., in the oracles against Jehoiakim and Jehoiachin in 22:13–30), and after the surrender of Jerusalem in 598 B.C. he counseled Zedekiah and the Judeans to remain in submission to Babylon (Jer. 27–29). During the subsequent advance of the Babylonians and the siege of Jerusalem, he urged the city's surrender and foretold of imminent catastrophe (e.g., Jer. 37–38).

111. Habakkuk 1–2 appears to reflect this period in which the Babylonian threat to Syria-Palestine was growing.

112. Second Kings 23:36–24:6 tells us that at some point after his appointment as king by the Egyptians in 609 B.C., and in the context of a Babylonian invasion, Jehoiakim changed his allegiance to Nebuchadrezzar, only to rebel against him again after "three years." This rebellion, the text implies, led to the siege of Jerusalem in 598 B.C. (2 Kgs. 24:8–17). If so, then the rebellion is best dated to 601 B.C., and set in the context of Nebuchadrezzar's failed attempt to invade Egypt and his withdrawal to Babylon to refit his army, whence he returned once again in the years following 600 B.C. to tighten his grip on the Levant. The "invasion" that first won Jehoiakim's allegiance then correlates with Nebuchadnezzar's campaign of 604 B.C.—the first of eight campaigns during the next ten years directed at establishing Babylonian control over Syria-Palestine—although the Babylonian Chronicle for 604 B.C. does not explicitly mention Judah in the context of that campaign. Where 2 Chr. 36:6–7 and Dan. 1:1–7 fit into such a scenario is not entirely clear, with their implication (taken together) that Jehoiakim, in his third year, had already suffered siege in Jerusalem and had experienced at least the threat (and probably the reality) of personal deportation to Babylon along with other leading citizens. Very likely, however, this "third year" is not to be understood in respect of 609 B.C. (his Egyptian appointment), or even 604 B.C. (his Babylonian vassalship), but in respect of his (apparent) assertion of independent rule in 601 B.C. The "siege" of Dan. 1:1 is the same as the one we read about in 2 Kgs. 24:10.

113. For a summary of Nebuchadnezzar's movements in 601–597 B.C., see *ANET*, 563–64, comparing with 2 Kgs. 24:8–16. Among the exiles—although Kings does not tell us this—was the prophet Ezekiel, whose prophetic ministry begins a few years later in Babylon (Ezek. 1:2–3). What exactly happened to Jehoiakim, Jehoiachin's father, is uncertain. He was still apparently alive when Jerusalem surrendered, even though Jehoiachin was king (and co-ruler?); 2 Chr. 36:6–7 and Dan. 1:1–7 imply as much, and this is also Josephus's understanding (*Ant.* 10.96). However, whether he was then killed or deported is not clear. Josephus stands in favor of the former, and the Kings account is consistent with this claim in that it says that Jehoiakim rested with his fathers (2 Kgs. 24:6, sc. in Jerusalem) and does not mention him in the list of deportees. Second Chronicles and Daniel, on the other hand, could be read as saying that Jehoiakim was deported (Williamson, *Chronicles*, 412–14).

Chapter 11: Exile and After

1. This point is also made by J. G. McConville, "Faces of Exile in Old Testament Historiography," in V. P. Long (ed.), *Israel's Past in Present Research: Essays on Ancient Israelite Historiography*, SBTS 7 (Winona Lake, Ind.: Eisenbrauns, 1999), 527.

2. H. G. M. Williamson, "Exile and After: Historical Study," in D. Baker and B. Arnold (eds.), *The Face of Old Testament Studies* (Grand Rapids: Baker Book House, 1999), 252.

3. P. M. McNutt, *Reconstructing the Society of Ancient Israel* (London/Louisville, Ky.: SPCK/Westminster John Knox Press, 1999), 184.
4. W. W. Hallo and K. L. Younger (eds.), *The Context of Scripture*, vol. 1 (Leiden: Brill, 1997), 1:467–68.
5. *ANET*, 305–7.
6. See ibid., 564, under "year 7."
7. Second Chronicles 36:10 identifies Zedekiah, however, as the *brother* of Jehoiachin. First Chronicles 3:15–16 reports that Jehoiachin had both a brother and an uncle named Zedekiah, and it has been suggested that the two have simply become confused here, which seems unlikely, however, when both are obviously known to the authors and one is so clearly indicated in source texts that they knew (Kings and Jeremiah). Another possibility is simply that "brother" is being used somewhat loosely here in the sense of "relative."
8. For biblical evidence of Judean reliance on Egypt at this time, see, e.g., Ezek. 17:11–21, which attacks Zedekiah for breaking covenant with Nebuchadnezzar. For extrabiblical evidence, see the Lachish ostracon III in *ANET*, 322, which appears to describe the passage through Lachish of a Judean delegation on the way to Egypt. Ammon and Tyre were apparently also involved in the rebellion (Ezek. 21:18–23; 26–28).
9. According to Josephus (*Ant.* 10.108–115), King Zedekiah began to favor the Egyptians in his ninth year. According to E. von Voigtlander, "A Survey of Neo-Babylonian History" (Ph.D. dissertation; University of Michigan, 1963), 112, Zedekiah "yielding to foolish counsels, decided to break his agreement with Babylon and to omit, or perhaps reduce, the amount of the yearly tribute."
10. That Nebuchadnezzar also assaulted other Judean cities is to be expected, and is indicated by Jer. 34:6–7. The Lachish ostraca (*ANET*, 321–22) apparently illustrate what life was like in one of the cities mentioned in this passage prior to the Babylonian assault. Some of the Arad ostraca (*ANET*, 568–69) may also date from this time, but the dating and interpretation of these ostraca is less certain than that of their Lachish counterparts.
11. See Jer. 37:1–10; also Herodotus 2.161 and Diodorus Siculus 1.68.1.
12. Debate exists over whether 587 or 586 was the year in which Jerusalem fell. For a recent survey and interesting solution, see O. Edwards, "The Year of Jerusalem's Destruction," *ZAW* 104 (1992): 101–6. We shall refer to the date in what follows as 586 B.C.
13. For Nabuzaradan (Jer. 52:12) equals Nabu-zer-iddinam, see von Voigtlander, "A Survey," 133.
14. The distress of this period appears to be reflected in the prophecy of Obadiah, which suggests in particular (along with other biblical texts) that Edom was able to exploit the situation to its own gain.
15. W. W. Hallo and W. K. Simpson, *The Ancient Near East: A History*, 2d ed. (Fort Worth, Tex.: Harcourt Brace College Publishers, 1998), 71–72, 83.
16. H. M. Barstad, *The Myth of the Empty Land: A Study in the History and Archaeology of Judah during the "Exilic" Period* (Olso: Scandanavian University Press, 1996).
17. See R. B. Dillard, *2 Chronicles*, WBC (Waco, Tex.: Word Publishing Company, 1987), 302, for the view that the numbers and language here are symbolic.
18. Gauging what proportion of the population we are speaking about is difficult. Population estimates are a difficult matter. D. L. Smith-Christopher, "Reassessing the Historical and Sociological Impact of the Babylonian Exile (597/587–539 BCE)," in J. M. Scott (ed.), *Exile: Old Testament, Jewish, and Christian Conceptions* (Leiden: Brill, 1997), 17, notes that estimates for the population of Jerusalem at this time vary from 24,000 to 250,000.

19. For instance, F. B. Huey Jr., *Jeremiah; Lamentations*, New American Commentary (Nashville: Broadman, 1993), 438.

20. "All" is often used very loosely in the OT (cf., for example, Josh. 10:40–42; 2 Kgs. 11:1–2), and numbers frequently seek to do more than straightforwardly reflect historical reality. In this context both the numbers "ten thousand" (2 Kgs. 24:14) and "seven thousand" (2 Kgs. 24:16) occur earlier in Kings in relation to "remnants" of Israel which survive in difficult times (cf. 2 Kgs. 13:1–7, of the number of foot soldiers left to Jehoahaz of Israel in the desperate days of Aramean oppression; and 1 Kgs. 19:18, of the number of the remnant in Elijah's days). Therefore, the authors of Kings may be making a theological point here: that those days when significant remnants were left in Israel are now past. If precision about numbers is impossible under these circumstances, clearly, at least, sizeable deportations of people important for the independent rule and prosperity of Judah took place, which would have had a detrimental effect on the ability of the Judeans in the future to organize and manufacture for rebellion.

21. R. W. Klein, *Israel in Exile: A Theological Interpretation* (Philadelphia: Fortress Press, 1979), 2.

22. J. Berquist, *Judaism in Persia's Shadow: A Social and Historical Approach* (Minneapolis: Fortress Press, 1995), 15–17.

23. See M. W. Stolper, *Entrepeneurs and Empire: The Murashu Archive, the Murashu Firm, and Persian Rule in Babylonia*, Uitgaven van het Nederlands Historisch-Archaeologisch Instituut te Istanbul 54 (Leiden: Brill, 1985).

24. R. Zadok, *The Jews in Babylonia during the Chaldean and Achaemenian Period*, SHJPLI 3 (Haifa: University of Haifa, 1979), and M. D. Coogan, *West Semitic Personal Names in the Murasu Documents*, HSM 7 (Atlanta: Scholars Press, 1976).

25. This point is well stated and defended by Smith-Christopher in "Reassessing the Historical and Sociological Impact."

26. *ANET*, 308.

27. A debate has existed since the time of Noth and von Rad as to whether this release ends the book of Kings on a positive note or not. See most recently D. F. Murray, "Of All the Years of Hopes—or Fears?: Jehoiachin in Babylon (2 Kings 25:27–30)," *JBL* 120 (2001): 245–65.

28. Gedaliah was apparently the grandson of King Josiah's secretary Shaphan (2 Kgs. 22:3–14). Precisely what position he held under the watchful eye of the Babylonian officials is unclear, since the word "governor" that appears in many translations of 2 Kgs. 25:22–24 in association with his name is not found in the Hebrew texts; quite possibly the Babylonians (if not the biblical authors) regarded him as a king.

29. N. Avigad, *Bullae and Seals from a Post-Exilic Judean Archive*, Qedem 4 (Jerusalem: Institute of Archaeology, Hebrew University, 1976), 25, questions the identification of the Gedaliah of the bullae with the Gedaliah of Jer. 36, but see, more to the point, J. A. Dearman, "My Servants the Scribes: Composition and Context in Jeremiah 36," *JBL* 109 (1990): 412–13.

30. Williamson, "Exile and After," 253.

31. See his "The Exile and the Restoration," in *Ezra Studies* (New York: STAV, 1920/1970), 285–340.

32. See their respective chapters in L. L. Grabbe (ed.), *Leading Captivity Captive: "The Exile" as History and Ideology*, JSOTS 278 (Sheffield: Sheffield Academic Press, 1998).

33. See R. Albertz, "The Exile as an Urgent Case for Historical Reconstruction without Biblical Texts: The Neo-Babylonian Royal Inscriptions as 'Primary Sources,'" in Grabbe (ed.), *Leading Captivity Captive*, who argues that the explicit ideology of the Babylonian documents of the day have not led to their rejection as historical sources.

34. We should be clear, however, that Becking is not supporting the idea that the biblical texts are entirely accurate; see his "Ezra's Re-Enactment of the Exile," in Grabbe (ed.), *Leading Captivity Captive.* This view is supported by Barstad in his essay in the same volume, "The Strange Fear of the Bible: Some Reflections on the 'Bibliophobia' in Recent Ancient Israelite Historiography," 120–27, on 126.

35. See T. Longman III, *Fictional Akkadian Autobiography* (Winona Lake, Ind.: Eisenbrauns, 1991), 97–103.

36. Perhaps Tema was built as a shrine to the moon god and/or as a way to develop commercial and military connections. More likely, however, is the explanation that Nabonidus moved there in the light of a developing power struggle with the Marduk priesthood.

37. For Nabonidus and Belshazzar, see P.-A. Beaulieu, *The Reign of Nabonidus King of Babylon (556–539 B.C.),* Yale Near Eastern Researches 10 (New Haven/London: Yale University Press, 1989).

38. Herodotus provides an alternative tradition where Cyrus stopped the flow of water through a city river gate, allowing him to forcibly breach the city.

39. So H. G. M. Williamson, *Ezra, Nehemiah,* WBC (Waco, Tex.: Word Publishing, 1985), xxxiii–xxxv, and many others; but the view that Ezra and Nehemiah are separate books is enjoying a resurgence in some recent writing. See B. Becking, "Ezra's Re-Enactment," 47–48.

40. E. Meyers, *Second Temple Studies, II. Temple Community in the Persian Period,* JSOTS 175 (Sheffield: Sheffield Academic Press, 1994), 26.

41. McNutt, *Reconstructing the Society,* 185.

42. The translation is from *ANET,* 316.

43. A. Kuhrt, "The Cyrus Cylinder and Achaemenid Imperial Policy," *JSOT* 25 (1983): 83–97, refers to the "Babylo-centricity of the text."

44. B. Halpern, "A Historiographic Commentary on Ezra 1–6: Achronological Narrative and Dual Chronology in Israelite Historiography," in W. H. Propp, B. Halpern, and D. N. Freedman (eds.), *The Hebrew Bible and Its Interpreters,* Biblical and Judaic Studies 1 (Winona Lake, Ind.: Eisenbrauns, 1990), 93.

45. We should also mention that Sheshbazzar is mentioned in 1 Esd. (2:12, 15; 6:18, 20).

46. Zerubbabel is also mentioned in 1 Esdras and Ecclesiasticus.

47. A recent advocate of this view is J. Lust, "The Identification of Zerubbabel with Sheshbazzar," *ETL* 63 (1987): 90–95.

48. So the article on *nasi'* in NIDOTTE, 3:171–72.

49. Most notably, P.-R. Berger, "Zu den Namen *ššbṣr* und *šn'ṣr*," *ZAW* 83 (1971): 98–100.

50. However, 1 Chr. 3:19 presents Zerubbabel as the son of Pedaiah, whereas Haggai and Zechariah regard him as the son of Shealtiel. S. Japhet, "Sheshbazzar and Zerubbabel—Against the Background of the Historical and Religious Tendencies of Ezra-Nehemiah," *ZAW* 94 (1982): 66–68, 71, 72, discusses this problem and concludes that "in spite of these difficulties, there is no doubt . . . that Zerubbabel son of Shealtiel is of Davidic lineage" (72).

51. D. L. Petersen, "Zerubbabel and Jerusalem Temple Reconstruction," *CBQ* 36 (1974): 366–72, on 372.

52. The quote is from J. Blenkinsopp, "The Mission of Udjahorresnet and Those of Ezra and Nehemiah," *JBL* 106 (1987): 409–21, which informed the discussion in this section (quote from 413).

53. H. G. M. Williamson, "The Governors of Judah under the Persians," *TynBul* 39 (1988): 59–82.

54. A. Alt, "Die Rolle Samarias bei der Entstehung des Judentums," in *Festschrift Otto Procksch zum 60. Geburtstag* (Leipzig: A. Deichert and J. C. Hinrichs, 1934), 5–28.

55. An important publication supplying the information concerning the bullae and the seals is Avigad, *Bullae and Seals*.

56. See E. M. Meyers, "The Shelomith Seal and the Judean Restoration: Some Additional Considerations," *Eretz Israel* 18 (1985): 33*–38*.

57. If so, it casts doubt on the theory that Zerubbabel was deposed because of his Davidic ancestry.

58. For a discussion of the jar and seal impressions from this period as well as the controversy over the reading and interpretation of the Hebrew word that is often translated "the governor" (*hphh*), see L. L. Grabbe, *Judaism from Cyrus to Hadrian*, vol. 1 (Minneapolis: Fortress, 1992), 68–69.

59. See his *The Citizen-Temple Community*, trans. D. L. Smith-Christopher, JSOTS 151 (Sheffield: Sheffield Academic Press, 1992), though this is based on much earlier work.

60. C. E. Carter, "Opening Windows onto Biblical Worlds: Applying the Social Sciences to Hebrew Scripture," in Baker and Arnold (eds.), *The Face of Old Testament Studies*, 439, who also indicates how closely Weinberg's model is dependent on his large population estimate.

61. Williamson, "Exile and After," 251–52. See also his fuller study "The Governors of Judah under the Persians," *TynBul* 39 (1988): 59–82.

62. Berquist, *Judaism in Persia's Shadow*, 62–63.

63. This view is supported by Williamson in his publications on this period.

64. See G. N. Knoppers, "The Historical Study of the Monarchy: Developments and Detours," in Baker and Arnold (eds.), *The Face of Old Testament Studies*, 232, and references there to the work of P. R. Ackroyd.

65. See T. C. Eskenazi, "Sheshbazzar," in *ABD*, 5:1207–8, who cites M. B. Yashar, "On the Problem of Sheshbazzar and Zerubbabel," *Beth Mikra* 27 (1981): 46–56 (in Hebrew).

66. See Williamson, *Ezra, Nehemiah*, 40–51.

67. In Talmon, "Ezra and Nehemiah," in *The Interpreter's Dictionary of the Bible, Supplementary Volume* (Abingdon: Nashville, 1976), 322.

68. The reference to the "second year after their arrival at the house of God in Jerusalem" (3:8) is accordingly understood to refer not to the second year after 539 B.C., but rather to two years after they start getting serious about rebuilding the site (thus, Williamson, *Ezra, Nehemiah*, 47). I find this a weakness in Williamson's argument in that 3:1, the immediately preceding chronological notice, refers to seven months after the initial return and, as we have seen in reference to Jer. 41, even the destroyed temple was considered the "house of God."

69. J. Berquist, *Judaism in Persia's Shadow*, 26, actually distinguishes three competing groups at this time: those who remained and two parties among the returnees—those who had been urban exiles and those who had been rural exiles. He suggests that the urban exiles would have been the most interested in furthering Persian imperial policy, which would have included rebuilding the temple.

70. McNutt, *Reconstructing the Society*, 183, 199, reflects this theory as well.

71. Note the revised and radically lower population estimates for the Persian period as described by C. Carter, "Opening Windows onto Biblical Worlds," 421–51, on 440.

72. O. Margalith, "The Political Background of Zerubbabel's Mission and the Samaritan Schism," *VT* 41 (1991): 312–23, on 316.

73. Part of the problem is that *ʿam haʾareṣ* is used elsewhere in the Bible to refer to the upper crust of society among the people of God. We simply have to understand that the phrase here is being used more generally of people who live in the land.

74. E. Yamauchi, *Persia and the Bible* (Grand Rapids: Baker, 1992), 156.

75. Mordecai means "man of Marduk," while one hypothesis is that Esther's name is related to the goddess Ishtar. We do know that Esther had a Hebrew name as well, Hadassah (Esth. 2:6).

76. See H. Sancisi-Weerdenburg and A. Kuhrt (eds.), *Achaemenid History II: The Greek Sources* (Leiden: Nederlands Instituut Voor Het Nabije Oosten, 1987). For an English translation of Herodotus, see the translation by A. D. Godley in the Loeb Classical Library (New York: G. P. Putnam's Sons, 1922).

77. Esther follows Ezra-Nehemiah. In Jewish tradition, Esther is found in the Writings, a rather miscellaneous collection of what appear to be late compositions. In particular, Esther is within the Megillot, the five scrolls, books that are connected to important Jewish festivals. Esther is connected with the Feast of Purim.

78. S. Talmon, "'Wisdom' in the Book of Esther," *VT* 13 (1963): 419–55. But see the telling critique of this thesis by M. V. Fox, *Character and Ideology in the Book of Esther* (Columbia: University of South Carolina Press, 1991), 142–44. E. Bickerman, *Four Strange Books of the Bible* (New York: Schocken, 1967), 171–240, drew attention to parallels with *Arabian Nights* and concluded that the book is a folktale.

79. S. B. Berg, *The Book of Esther: Motifs, Themes, and Structure*, SBLDS 44 (Missoula, Mont.: Scholars Press, 1979), 123–42.

80. G. Gerleman, *Studien zu Esther*, BibS[N] 48 (Neukirchener-Vluyn: Neukirchener Verlag, 1966); idem, *Esther*, BKAT 21 (Neukirchen-Vluyn: Neukirchener Verlag, 1970–73).

81. R. B. Dillard and T. Longman III, *An Introduction to the Old Testament* (Grand Rapids: Zondervan, 1994), 193–94.

82. See W. McClarty, "Esther," in *A Complete Literary Guide to the Bible* (Grand Rapids: Zondervan, 1993), 216–29.

83. So V. P. Long, *The Art of Biblical History*, ed. Moisés Silva, FCI 5 (Grand Rapids: Zondervan, 1994).

84. J. D. Levenson, *Esther*, OTL (Louisville, Ky.: Westminster John Knox Press, 1997), 23.

85. A. Berlin, *Esther* (Philadelphia: JPS Publishing Company, 2001), 10. A similar conclusion is reached by L. M. Wills, *The Jewish Novel in the Ancient World* (Ithaca, N.Y.: Cornell University Press, 1995), 7: "But alas, the perception of historiography, like the perception of reality, is an illusion. The author of Esther was not writing history; he was imitating the writing of history even making a burlesque of it. Historiography is not a comic genre, and Esther is very comic. . . ."

86. J. S. Wright, "The Historicity of the Book of Esther," in J. B. Payne (ed.), *New Perspectives on the Old Testament* (Waco, Tex.: Word, 1970), 37–47; and W. H. Shea, "Esther and History," *AUSS* 14 (1976): 227–46.

87. D. J. A. Clines, "The Nehemiah Memoir: The Perils of Autobiography," in *What Does Eve Do to Help? And Other Readerly Questions to the Old Testament*, JSOTS 94 (Sheffield: Sheffield Academic Press, 1990), 124–64. Grabbe, *Judaism from Cyrus to Hadrian*, 1:30, would agree.

88. H. G. M. Williamson, "Post-Exilic Historiography," in R. E. Friedman and H. G. M. Williamson (eds.), *The Future of Biblical Studies: The Hebrew Scriptures* (Atlanta: Scholars Press, 1987), 189–207.

89. Williamson, "Exile and After," 257.

90. This is the view of G. Garbini, *History and Ideology in Ancient Israel* (New York: Crossroad, 1988), 151–69.

91. Williamson, *Ezra, Nehemiah* xxviii–xxxii; idem, "Exile and After," 258.

92. Below we argue that the gap is the period between 515 and 458 B.C.

93. Williamson, "Post-Exilic Historiography," 198.

94. Indeed, the two men are said to be together during the reading of the law in Neh. 8, but these scholars believe that Nehemiah was a late addition to this narrative. See J. Blenkinsopp, *Ezra-Nehemiah*, OTL (Philadelphia: Westminster Press, 1988), 288–89.

95. See the comments by E. Yamauchi, "The Reverse Order of Ezra/Nehemiah Reconsidered," *Themelios* 5 (1980): 12–13.

96. This is the view of Grabbe, *Judaism from Cyrus to Hadrian*, 1:89–90.

97. Yamauchi, "The Reverse Order," 9.

98. Williamson, *Ezra, Nehemiah*, 136.

99. Ibid., 151.

100. Ibid., 121–22.

101. See the most recent conclusion of Williamson, "Exile and After," 256.

102. K. Hoglund, *Achaemenid Imperial Administration in Syria-Palestine and the Missions of Ezra and Nehemiah*, SBLDS 125 (Atlanta: Scholars Press, 1992).

103. See McNutt, *Reconstructing the Society*, 182; O. Margalith, "The Political Role of Ezra as Persian Governor," ZAW 98 (1986): 110–12; C. L. Meyers and E. M. Meyers, *Zechariah 9–14*, AB 25c (Garden City, N.Y.: Doubleday, 1993), 20–21; Meyers in *Second Temple Studies*, 27–30; and T. C. Eskenazi, "Current Perspectives on Ezra-Nehemiah and the Persian Period," *Currents in Research: Biblical Studies* 1 (1993): 71–72.

104. J. Berquist, *Judaism in Persia's Shadow*, 105–20.

105. See *CAH*, vol. 4, 2d edition, ed. D. M. Lewis, et al. (Cambridge: Cambridge University Press, 1992), 144, 266, 276.

106. Again, the analogy of the relationship between Udjahorresnet and Darius as well as Sheshbazzar and Zerubbabel is clear: see our earlier comments above, as well as Blenkinsopp, "The Mission of Udjahorresnet."

107. R. Steiner, "The *mbqr* at Qumran, the *epikopos* in the Athenian Empire, and the Meaning of *lbqr'* in Ezra 7:14: On the Relation of Ezra's Mission to the Persian Legal Project," *JBL* 120 (2001): 623–46, has again shown how Persian support for Ezra's legal reform has analogies elsewhere in the empire, particularly in Egypt. He provides possible reasons that Palestinian reform took longer to implement than Egyptian reform.

108. D. Janzen, "The 'Mission' of Ezra and the Persian-Period Temple Community," *JBL* 119 (2000): 619–43, argues that the letter of Artaxerxes to Ezra (Ezra 7:12–26) that commissions Ezra is at odds with Ezra's actual actions as described in the narrative. He argues that narrative is more historically reliable than the letter on the basis of the fact that Ezra acts like a known type of temple official (the Babylonian *satammu*) in the narrative. However, that he has established an irresolvable tension between the letter and the narrative is not clear. Recently, Janzen's argument has been devastated by the critique offered by R. Steiner, "The *mbqr* at Qumran," 638–43.

109. The literary structure of Ezra 4 is confusing at first. It begins by describing the opposition that arose during the rebuilding of the temple, then interrupts that to report the accusations at the time of Xerxes and Artaxerxes. Finally, in the last verse of the chapter it returns to the issue of rebuilding the temple during the earlier reign of Darius. Williamson, *Ezra, Nehemiah*, 57, helpfully introduces the notion of a "repetitive resumption" to explain the contours of the chapter.

110. Although we have no external attestation to such a deportation at the time of Ashurbanipal, the mention of Elam in v. 9 is interesting since Ashurbanipal was the only neo-Assyrian king to defeat Susa. Indeed, he had numerous campaigns in that area.

111. Sanballat was called "the Horonite," which may be a reference to Beth-horon in the lower part of Samaria.

112. Thus F. M. Cross, "A Reconstruction of the Judean Restoration," *JBL* 94 (1975): 4–18.
113. His name ends with a Yah element. See B. Mazar, "The Tobiads," *IEJ* 7 (1957): 17–45.
114. See the discussion in Williamson, *Ezra, Nehemiah*, 192.
115. W. Dumbrell, "The Tell el-Maskhuta Bowls and the Kingdom of Qedar," *BASOR* 203 (1971): 33–44, 44; quoted from Williamson, *Ezra, Nehemiah*, 192.
116. T. C. Eskenazi, *In an Age of Prose: A Literary Approach to Ezra-Nehemiah* (Atlanta: Scholars, 1988).
117. D. Green, "Ezra-Nehemiah," in Ryken and Longman (eds.), *Literary Guide*, 206–15.

Index of Biblical Passages

Where not otherwise apparent, main discussions are marked with bold numerals.

Index of Scholars Cited

While authors or titles may be referenced many times in the body of our work, this index lists only substantive discussions and at least one reference to provide full bibliographic details.

Index of Select Topics

Where not otherwise apparent, main discussions are marked with bold numerals.